In Dreams Begin Responsibilities

by Jonathan Rosenbaum

HAT & BEARD PRESS | LOS ANGELES

Table of Contents

Reading, Hearing, Watching:

Introduction

"So complex is reality, and so fragmentary and simplified is history, that an omniscient observer could write an indefinite, almost infinite, number of biographies of a man, each emphasizing different facts; we would have to read many of them before we realized that the protagonist was the same."

—Jorge Luis Borges, 1943

"I get a great laugh from artists who ridicule the critics as parasites and artists manqués—such a horrible joke. I can't imagine a more perfect art form, a more perfect career than criticism. I can't imagine anything more valuable to do, and I've always felt that way."

—Manny Farber, 1977

First, a few ground rules.

Because most of us live in a culture where our marketers also tend to be our preferred editors, epistemologists, and censors, I want to override their usual restrictions that govern collections of this kind by drawing upon my literary criticism and my music criticism (mostly of jazz) as well as the film criticism that I'm usually known for, meanwhile charting some of the potential and actual interactivity between these arts (and, in passing, some others, e.g., theater, dance, painting, sculpture, architecture, criticism) in order to define some of the attributes of my own particular niche-market, at least as I'm defining and addressing it here. And because appreciation is what's being foregrounded here, I've mostly avoided negative and mixed reviews and made room for capsule reviews as well as longer pieces.

Wanting my different kinds of criticism to commingle in this book as they have in my life, I've ordered the pieces chronologically (apart from linking two Sonny Rollins documentaries in reviews written four decades apart). Sometimes the dates are only approximate when I can't pinpoint them. This allows readers to trace the persistence and/or development of certain ideas and preoccupations over the book's span. Reconfiguring them in this context, by foregrounding certain undercurrents in my arguments, may also alter the ways that they're read and perceived. Although the selection of one-hundred pieces encompasses almost six decades, the second half of these texts comes disproportionately from only the past 15 years, after I retired from my twenty-year stint at the *Chicago Reader* and returned to freelancing. Obviously some of my tastes and opinions have shifted between 1964 and 2023, but I've tried to respect a certain continuity of subjects, concerns, and works here regarding film, music, literature—and even dreams, for that matter. I can't pretend that my choices here encompass all I've had to say about these subjects and continuities, so I refer to previously collected pieces of mine that deal with related issues in some of the introductory notes. Furthermore, I should admit that my jazz criticism tends to be far less "professional" than my film and literary criticism, due to my amateur status as a jazz buff, which is why my choices in this case have been more selective (omitting, for instance, most of my reviews of jazz films for *Monthly Film Bulletin*, although a couple are included). And the absence of any essays here on movie musicals can be explained by my having already collected those on *Gentlemen Prefer Blondes* in my book *Placing Movies*, *Latcho Drom* in *Movies as Politics*, and, among others in *Essential Cinema*, *The Umbrellas of Cherbourg*, *Nashville*, *Up Down Fragile*, *The Young Girls of Rochefort*, and *Distant Voices, Still Lives*. (My reflections on Bernard Herrmann's score for *Taxi Driver* can also be found in the latter volume.)

As a child, my love for storytelling (in books, movies, and radio) and for music all developed concurrently, and sometimes even interactively. I suspect my first love was for music—I'm told that one of the first words I uttered was "rec" for "record"—but my favorite 78s (e.g., *Tubby the Tuba*, *Peter and the Wolf*, *Alice in Wonderland*) had music that told stories. I remember fondly a 78 I had of "Button Up Your Overcoat" or something similar with a color picture superimposed over its grooves, designed like a Norman Rockwell cover for the

Saturday Evening Post—a fleeting artefact of the late 1940s or early fifties known to me as a "picture record". And the interactive glories of radio captivated me long before my family acquired a black and white TV.

In retrospect, I'm sure that part of why William Faulkner's *Light in August* and John Updike's *Rabbit, Run* both made such lasting impressions on me as a teenager were their movie-like uses of the present tense, and the musicality of the narrative structures of *Citizen Kane* and *Sunrise* during the same period (such as the shifting tempi of the former and the three-movement construction of the latter) were comparable revelations.

Around the same time that I was discovering these masterpieces, André Hodeir—one of the guiding lights of this book, along with the better-known Borges and Farber—published a lengthy, enthusiastic review of *Hiroshima mon amour* praising its innovative uses of both musical and literary forms in the March-April 1960 *Evergreen Review*—an essay I discovered only years later in *Evergreen Review Reader 1957-1961*. And the marginality assigned to cross-cultural analysts and artists such as Hodeir persists. The common practice in publishing of targeting and thus isolating separate markets has led to an unnatural segregation of these interests into strictly mercenary and automatic reflexes that this book is designed to challenge, or at least circumvent. For the record, editors at two leading academic presses expressed enthusiasm for the concept behind this book before their marketing experts vetoed it. The facts that publicists can have more say in such matters than editors and that they tend to follow the Reaganite principle of exploiting and exhausting old markets rather than creating new ones are part of the gloomy prospects of contemporary academic publishing in the U.S. And even the *Chicago Reader*—which, apart from the *Soho News*, afforded me more freedom than any other publication I've written for on a regular basis—discouraged me from writing book reviews for them.

My personal investments in literature, music, and film have gone beyond my interests as a fan and consumer. I wrote fiction and some poetry in my teens and twenties, including three novels and a good many stories, although only one of the earliest (and shortest) of these stories was published in a mainstream venue ("Now and Then," written when I was thirteen and published over a year later in the November 1957 issue of *The Magazine of Fantasy and Science Fiction*). I played clarinet in my high school band in Alabama and in a few domestic jam sessions, and also became an amateur jazz pianist in my teens. Both these activities (literary and musical) have continued more sporadically ever since. My filmmaking activities have also been both limited and scattered: writing a commissioned, unrealized screenplay in Paris, subtitling a couple of features, serving as consultant on the posthumous re-editing of two Orson Welles features (*Touch of Evil* and *The Other Side of the Wind*), mentoring filmmakers at Béla Tarr's wonderful FilmFactory in Sarajevo (2013-2015), and working as a camera assistant, consultant, and interviewee on Mehrnaz Saeed-Vafa's *A House is Not a Home: Wright or Wrong* (2020). Even so, all these experiences played roles in exercising, as well as shaping, some of my critical reflexes.

Paradoxically, although film has commonly been regarded as the art absorbing all the other arts, the relationships between these arts based on influence and common ground have often been neglected. But I hasten to add that a few sympathetic readers of my writing have already called attention to its literary and musical attributes. James Naremore wrote of my first book, "It can be appreciated both for its literary values and for what it tells us about watching movies," and Tami Williams' blurb for my most recent book, *Cinematic Encounters 2: Portraits and Polemics* (2019), compares it to "a well-composed musical score, [with] energetic rhythmic effects."

I also believe nowadays in niche-markets as opposed to the more marketable mainstream channels because they tend to be more focused and generative. If we consider Italian Neo-Realism and the French New Wave in cinema, bebop in jazz, The Beatles in rock, and the Beat writers in literature, new movements in art tend to be launched by small, interactive groups of friends and associates. To address the mainstream usually means to exchange one's own brand for the aura of whatever mainstream venue one has acquired. One reason among others why I haven't included my dissenting piece on Ingmar Bergman, commissioned by the *New York Times* for its Op Ed page on August 4, 2007, is that my editor there asked me to rewrite it several times with his own specifications, so that it belongs to him and the *Times* more than it belongs to me. I prefer to brand myself, whereas attaching myself to a mainstream venue usually means accepting a view of criticism whereby critics tend to become essentially parasites guiding consumer choices rather than participants in a community discussion that begins before a review is printed or posted and continues long afterwards. And communal niche-markets are often less predictable than one might assume. I count Farber as a major influence on my grasp of criticism as a form of art, yet our respective political orientations were different, and some of our Hollywood preferences were the opposites of those orientations. Despite his eclectic conservatism, Farber and his moviegoing family favored Warners among the major studios, whereas my liberal family paradoxically preferred the most conservative and upper-crust studio, MGM.

I've deliberately thwarted the assumptions underlying such otherwise irre-placeable collections as the Library of America's *Farber on Film: The Complete Film Writings of Manny Farber* (2009) and two Viking collections of Jorge Luis Borges, *Collected Fictions* (1998) and *Selected Non-Fictions* (1999). The Library of America volume omits all of Farber's other critical writing (mostly about art) as well as the entirety of the extended 1977 interview he carried out near the end of his writing career (included in the expanded 1988 edition of *Negative Space*), which concluded with the quotation cited above.

The Viking collections of Borges's fiction and non-fiction segregate the most radical and interactive aspects of his art into mutually exclusive volumes. The quote from Borges comes from "On William Beckford's *Vathek*" in the latter of these. (This was published the year I was born; Farber's interview was published the year that I moved back to the U.S. from Europe.)

I should add that the performative possibilities of critical writing have been vividly realized in some of the lectures of both Borges and Farber as well as by Jean-Pierre Gorin, and these are especially relevant in today's era of podcasts and audiovisual forms of criticism. This is why I've made room here for Ehsan Khoshbakht's conversational interview with me about jazz and cinema. Allowing literature and film to coexist in these pages seems especially fitting during an era when it has finally become possible to handle movies like books via such perks as browsing, reseeing, perusing them in broadcasted or impromptu install-ments, watching them at home and sometimes keeping them—and even adding English subtitles to English-language films, as I often like to do, combining the pleasures of watching, listening, and reading in one go and also making it easier to follow whenever I can't quite catch a line of dialogue.

In his teens, Farber was a jazz devotee who played a saxophone (he especially cherished Lester Young), and this influence carried over into his semi-impro-visational lecturing style, full of breezy bluster and abrupt, unforeseeable turns, at the University of California, San Diego, a style that Jean-Pierre Gorin embraced and developed for his own purposes at the same venue. (My inability to match their skills, especially back then, prevented me from getting rehired at the same university—fortunately, as it turned out, because it enabled me to start writing *Moving Places*, my first published book as an author, with its own quirky forms of performative flight and bluster.) I'm sorry that these Farber and Gorin lectures aren't available on DVD or Blu-Ray, but Gorin's *"Pierrot"* Primer, a thirty-six-minute audiovisual analysis of Jean-Luc Godard's *Pierrot le fou* on the 2007 Criterion release, offers a reasonable facsimile. The witty inflections and riffs of Gorin's delivery lurch forward in an off-the-cuff manner suggesting some of the swerves and detours of the film he's discussing, and when he briefly bows out to let Godard's soundtrack take over, replacing his voice and words with Jean-Paul Belmondo's voice and Godard's chosen words, it's rather like he's "trading fours"—exchanging four-measure improvs—with his master's movie.

It's still criticism, even mimetic criticism, though not necessarily the same kind that can be appraised in textual form. I'm also not sure how helpful it might be to cross-reference Farber's painting with action-painting, even if the two developed concurrently. But I'm fairly certain that his criticism should be experienced as an outgrowth of action-painting—a spontaneous form of action-criticism in which thought becomes translated into physicality and existential presence, and one that Farber's prose on the page also suggests whereby the twist of a thought can become a dance step or a bleat, sometimes even both when a tenor player like Young performs it. The near-equivalence of playing a musical instrument and dancing is especially evident in vibraharp soloists such as Lionel Hampton and Milt Jackson, and in the frenetic, twisted gestures of Keith Jarrett attacking or caressing piano keys. Furthermore, as Cate Blanchett shows in *Tár*, there are also certain forms of upper-torso dance inherent in conducting.

This imposes a different set of criteria in judging criticism as an act or activity and not merely as a market-driven form of advertising—a performative act with unpredictable slides, leaps, cascades, somersaults, and muttering or mumbling asides that evolves over time, just like a jazz solo.

"You cannot hang an event on the wall, only a picture," Mary McCarthy famously cautioned in her review of Harold Rosenberg's seminal *The Tradition of the New*—a review aptly titled "An Academy of Risk" and found in *On the Contrary* (though not, alas, in the McCarthy collection *A Bolt from the Blue and Other Essays*, presumably because it was edited with a literary bias that short-changes her range in the same way that Borges and Farber have been). No, you can't hang an event on a wall, but you can watch it on a DVD and then place that disk on a shelf, like a book. So action can still be preserved in an object, and in an era when we can finally access films the same way we can access books—thus altering the nature of their social reception—the value of also viewing them as literary and musical events invites our exploration. This is something new and potentially exciting that Farber, Gorin, and others have brought to criticism: Kevin Lee and Chloé Galibert-Laîné, online, on Radu Jude, Georges Franju, and Serge Daney; Yuri Tsivian and Joan Neuberger, discussing and illustrating Eisenstein's *Ivan the Terrible* on the Criterion DVD, quite apart from their valuable books on the same topic. And there are many others—so many, in fact, of varying range and quality, that the task of discovering the most useful and pleasurable becomes as daunting as carving out one's personal niche-market of what films to access (rather than sliding passively into the more predictable realms of the mainstream's manufactured hits, where the choices are already made for us by ads and Oscars). For that matter, one of the perks for me in compiling this collection was discovering continuities in my writing that certain ingrained forms of capitalist self-censorship had hidden from my awareness.

The recurrence over separate texts of certain key artists including Chantal Akerman, Roland Barthes, Charles Burnett, John Coltrane, Miles Davis, Manny Farber, William Faulkner, André Hodeir, Ahmad Jamal, Keith Jarrett, James Joyce, Abbas Kiarostami, Stanley Kubrick, Spike Lee, Charles Mingus, Marcel Proust, Thomas Pynchon, Susan Sontag, Jacques Tati, and Orson Welles—testifies to a continuity and evolution of my concerns over the past half-century, so that my decisions to link Howard Hawks to Duke Ellington, Roland Barthes to Art Tatum, and Dreyer to Faulkner all came long before I thought about this collection. These aren't merely favorite artists; they also have served as guides to my critical methodologies and even at times to my sense of ethics.

Ground Rules 2, 3, and 4: All the selected pieces here are previously uncollected, at least in my own books, and are arranged in (loose) chronological order, giving them an autobiographical aspect shared by my first book (*Moving Places: A Life at the Movies*, 1980 & 1995) as well as one of my recent ones (*Cinematic Encounters: Interviews and Dialogues*, 2019). Like those two books, it allows for different voices apart from mine, but in this case—as in *Placing Movies, Greed, Movies as Politics, Essential Cinema, Movie Wars, Goodbye Cinema, Hello Cinephilia*, and *The Unquiet American*—the voices don't belong to others except incidentally.

"In dreams begin responsibilities," however, is a line I've cribbed from William Butler Yeats, and Delmore Schwartz cribbed it long before me for the title of his memorable 1937 story in the first issue of *Partisan Review*, recounting the dream of a twenty-one-year-old male in which he goes to the movies and encounters onscreen his parents having their first date. I've clung to these four words for most of my adult life as a kind of motto, and it figures in a couple of the texts collected here. I suspect its pertinence stems from the mixed blessing of growing up inside a work of art—a Frank Lloyd Wright house built for my parents, owned today by the town of Florence, Alabama as a tourist attraction. (This mixed blessing is a subject explored in depth by Mehrnaz Saeed-Vafa in her 2020 film *A House is Not a Home: Wright or Wrong*.) It also came from experiencing the dreams provided by the stories read by my father to me and my brothers two nights a week and, even more, by the movies being shown locally by him and my grandfather at the latter's theaters (a topic explored in my first book, *Moving Places: A Life at the Movies* [1980 & 1995]). Does this mean that responsibilities can persist after waking from dreams? I like to think so, especially because that's when all the material in this book was written, however many nudges or "first drafts" my dreams may have contributed.

I often regard movies as literature by another means, and in different ways, movies and music—and music and literature—can also be regarded as alternate versions of one another. "There's much more story in a piece of music by John Coltrane or Patti Smith than in most films now," Godard once said to me, interrelating all three arts in a 1980 interview where he also expressed some of my own intentions as a critic when he remarked, "I like to think of myself as an airplane, not an airport." My own airplane (not my airport) is a website archiving most of my writing—jonathanrosenbaum.net, originally launched as jonathanrosenbaum.com in 2008—which usually attracts between 750 to 1500 visitors per day from over 120 countries. I find this audience to be far more focused (and interactive, partly via social media) than my much larger audience in Chicago was during my two decades of reviewing films at the *Reader*.

My fifth and final ground rule: This book is warmly dedicated to that audience—and to the memory of my brother Alvin (1945-2022), who died happily while this introduction was being written and taught me something very precious by doing so.

Chicago, December 2023

"Doctor Kubrick": or How I Stopped Worrying and Learned to Love the Movie

From the Bard Observer, *March 30, 1964, bylined "Jon Rosenbaum". I've done a light edit on this review and made a few cosmetic trims. I had recently turned twenty-one, and as I wrote in my book* Placing Movies, *"The review prompted an unsolicited favorable comment from the best teacher I ever had—Heinrich Blücher, the husband of Hannah Arendt and Bard's presiding philosophical guru—and its dialectical play undoubtedly bore the mark of his Hegelian influence."*

Another reason why I'm resurrecting this early review is to point to a concrete example of how the cast of a particular period can inflect and even determine a movie's meaning. When I'd gone to see the movie near Times Square with some of my best friends, one of them Kathy Stein—who sixteen years later became my editor at Omni—*emerged from the shock of that experience devastated and in tears. For her, seeing the end of the world as comic was not only frightening but morally hateful, and her passionate response made a permanent impression on me. The unlikelihood of anyone of college age having that sort of reaction to* Dr. Strangelove *today tells us something important, I suspect, about what's happened to our sensibilities since then—not only in relation to the idea of nuclear holocaust, but also in relation to comedy. I think it's possible that we've lost something.*

Somehow, the idea has gotten around that *Dr. Strangelove* is a comedy. Stanley Kubrick, the film's director, has made a few statements to advance this belief; the press has conscientiously showered us with reassuring testimonies to the fact; and, indeed, after having seen the film, I find it difficult to conceive of anyone sitting through it without laughing. Nevertheless, I feel that the term "comedy"—used nowadays to identify everything from *Twelfth Night* to the Three Stooges—has become so bereft of meaning that it seems an injustice to shuffle Kubrick's work in with all the others that have ever begged that label. Whatever one could call the film, it is not another "lafforama"—one of those Billy Wilder express trains like *One, Two, Three*, which encourages us to dismiss our anxieties by laughing about them. Kubrick lets us have our cake, all right, but whoever tries to eat it too will likely wind up choking.

A number of reviews have spoken about *Strangelove* as if it were a congenial exercise in audience therapy. ("All kidding aside, movie fans, it's a very funny film that squeezes plenty of chuckles out of what is basically a serious matter, i.e., nuclear destruction. If the real thing happened, it wouldn't be much of a laughing matter, but as long as the idea remains conjectural, there's still room enough for man to keep his Innate Sense of Humor—which is, after all, what makes him Human—and Laugh at his own Petty Foibles.")

If this quality—this bland assumption that Kubrick is gently poking us in the ribs—was anywhere evident in *Dr. Strangelove*, it would probably be a very satisfying movie. As it stands, it is something much less than that, and much more: it comes close to obliterating our sense of humor in the process of exploiting it. If we are still laughing at the end of the movie, this is not, I think, because we are still amused; rather it is because Kubrick has convinced us of the impossibility of any other reaction. For *Strangelove* is more than a dissertation on the absurdity of the arms race, more than a political club designed to bludgeon us out of our complacency; it is a film not about the Bomb but about men. The Bomb itself is relatively harmless: when it makes its eventual appearance near the film's close and sprouts a graceful mushroom, the effect is somewhat superfluous, for the point has already been made.

To anyone familiar with Kubrick's previous films (which include *The Killing*, *Paths of Glory*, and *Lolita*, as well as *Spartacus*, which he disowns as a strictly commercial project), his career exhibits the sustained energies of a misanthrope, tempered always with the most brutal kind of humor. He is the only director I can think of who would have tried to make the hero of *Lolita* more comically pathetic than he already was in the book. This film was at best a collection of unconnected pieces, but Kubrick was able to infuse parts of it with a fresh, anxiety-ridden brand of comedy which Peter Sellers beautifully implemented, and which is brought to fruition in *Strangelove*. It is a comic technique which produces anxiety in the audience as well as in the actors, and it finds no fuller or more frightening image than in the figure of Dr. Strangelove, who is brought into full play only at the film's conclusion.

The character of Strangelove is central to the film's theme and final impact, but this is mainly due to the proliferation of scenes and characters that precede his appearance...Men are shown as victims of their own bureaucracy and incompetence, and the imminence of the Bomb increases as the camera continually crosscuts from crazy general to War Room to bomber and back again. As the pace accelerates, the film moves toward a vision of total madness, but it is not until the actual dropping of the bomb that it completely realizes the ultimate target of its satire. It is not the Bomb, the bureaucracy, the incompetence nor the insanity. It is the source from which all these aberrations sprang: mankind itself.

The bomb is released, and the commander of the plane, Major Kong (a Texan, played by Slim Pickens), wearing a cowboy hat and yelling ecstatically, rides the bomb like a stallion. The camera takes a sudden downward plunge to dash after him, rushes towards the ground, and for a split-second, the screen turns completely white: there is a breath-stopping pause and then the scene switches back to the War Room, where Dr. Strangelove makes his final speech.

The doctor (played by Sellers, who also handles two other roles) is a German scientist, presumably the consummate bomb-expert, strapped into a wheelchair and sporting a nervous smile; physically, he is little more than an accumulation of twitches. As he begins to tell the President his plans for creating an underground society, nervous laughs constantly interrupt his voice as often as his twitches, and his artificial hand begins to spring up involuntarily to make a Nazi salute. At this point it becomes clear that competence (or "expertise") is as much an evil of Man as his lack of it. The view of Man that is concentrated in *Strangelove* is horrifying enough to make the Bomb look like a blessing rather than a threat. As he continues to talk, his hand keeps springing up until he is forced to direct all of his attention to keeping it down. Eventually it moves towards his throat and begins to strangle him; like mankind, he is a machine that has gone berserk. When, shortly afterwards, he springs out of his wheelchair with a cry of exaltation ("Mein Fuhrer! I can walk!"), we are offered some horrible insight into the only kind of victory that Kubrick believes man can achieve.

An argument can be made—and indeed, *has* been made in several reviews— that a comedy of this sort is sick and tasteless. This seems a confusion of disease with diagnosis; we do not call a doctor "sick" or "tasteless" if he makes out a report that his patient has syphilis. It can also be argued that the film fails because it lacks an alternative to the madness it portrays (i.e., even Swift and Rabelais maintained some concept of the ideal). Since *Dr. Strangelove* is miles away from suggesting any ideals, I find this unanswerable, although it can be stated that it asks a sane mind to recognize madness. Basically, I believe that the movie is hateful as far as it is successful, and unsuccessful insofar as it is likable; for its success depends on the strength of its vision and its ability to convince us, and I doubt seriously whether any of us is un-man enough to take it. As an experience, however, none of us is likely to forget it.

A Home Movie of Homelessness:
Review of *Reminiscences of a Journey to Lithuania*

This appeared in the November 2, 1972 issue of The Village Voice *and was commissioned by Andrew Sarris, bless him. I've always been grateful for this opportunity to write about a film that I love, and one that I continue to cherish.*

Jonas Mekas's *Reminiscences of a Journey to Lithuania*, a film dedicated "to all the displaced people in the world," has itself become the object of some displacement. Screened jointly with Adolfas Mekas and Pola Chapelle's *Going Home* at the New York Film Festival, defined in the program as a non-narrative film and by its author as a home movie, it has become a casual victim of "convenient" programing and somewhat deceptive labels. Whatever "non-narrative" and "home movie" mean—and I think the latter describes *Going Home* pretty accurately—they are less than helpful in describing the achievement of what must be called Jonas Mekas's testament. If they must be used, let it be understood that *Reminiscences* is a home movie about homelessness, a non-narrative film with one of the most beautifully constructed and articulated narrative lines in autobiographical cinema.

Going Home, a rambling collection of travel photos and family poses, resembles the jazzy surfaces of *Hallelujah the Hills*, joke titles and all, and registers not unlike a boastful list of possessions (the secret metaphysic behind every family album): this is my garden, my Moscow, my family, my Lithuania. A Gene Autry tune accompanies shots of Adolfas wrestling a calf, and a great point is made about the size of noses in the Mekas household. It all comes across somewhat like Gogol without the madness—that is to say, a lot like William Saroyan: much nostalgia, and tears jerked perhaps a little too freely, for the moisture quickly evaporates.

Reminiscences, on the contrary, exhibits a continual fight against nostalgia, despite an underlining effort to reconcile years and distances, and addresses the state of displacement and dispossession through the disciplines of its structure. It is frequently said that whatever happens in a movie occurs in the present tense; but unless the film is silent or shot with direct, synchronized sound, the "present moments" it records are different slices of time overlapped—generally the sights of one present, the sounds of another.

Reminiscences, juxtaposing past footage with spoken reflections from a later date, is a film of many presents and many pasts, and much of its moving resonance comes from the ways in which different times complement, evoke, explain, define, and reinforce one another.

Each of the three sections defines a different definition of "home". The first shows Jonas's early years in America, mainly 1950 to 1953 in the sorrowful streets of Brooklyn, shot with his first Bolex. ("We loved you, New World... but you did...lousy...things to us," he says on the soundtrack, and the everyday street images seep into the ellipses and pauses, telling us more than streets or words could say alone.) "One Hundred Glimpses of Lithuania, August 1971," a journey back to his family and native village, comprises the second and longest part, and here we feel even more the desperate pull between sound and image: an unleashed camera rushing about to take everything in as though to repossess it, a continual movement of pans, exposure changes, and cuts; against this a somber narration conveying loss, distance, stasis: "You led sad and hard lives, the women of my childhood." Part three, shot later the same month, details a visit to a Hamburg suburb—the site of a slave camp where he and Adolfas spent a year during the war ("When we asked around, nobody knew that a labor camp was there—only the grass remembered")—and then a trip to Vienna, where he once planned to attend school (a dream shattered by the war) and where he now luxuriates in the company of friends, the richness of Vienna's past. But even the temporary comfort of Vienna is disrupted by change: the film ends with the burning of a fruit market, perhaps destroyed (the narration speculates) to make way for a modern replacement.

Clearly the protagonist of *Reminiscences* is not the Jonas Mekas whom we see on the screen. Nor is it quite the Jonas Mekas that readers of the *Voice* have come to know—the Pied Piper of avant-garde cinema with the profile of Pan and the charming intimidation of a poet-salesman. No, it is the accented voice with its imperfect English, its deliberate pauses, its tragic seriousness and depth which is coming to terms with the rest of what we see and hear; a disembodied consciousness seeking to fix it all at last, spurred by necessity into an unnatural eloquence. This Mekas can be glimpsed intermittently in the notebook format of *Diaries, Notes, and Sketches,* in the attempt to find Walden pond in Central Park, peace at a friend's wedding, a lost childhood in the glories of a circus. But the "diaries" only show blossoms that have sprung from displacement—still blossoming, still very much "work-in-progress." *Reminiscences,* a finished work, gives us blossoms too, but it also gives us more of what the earlier work—and what the "American experience"—seems to suppress and inhibit: it gives us roots.

One Man's Meat is Another Man's Poisson

Written in Paris for the Village Voice, *who ran it in their March 29, 1973 issue. The clever title is theirs. This is by far the most challenging book review I've ever had to write. I recall showing a draft of it to Paul Auster for his comments, and I luckily and coincidentally around the same time became friends with a former young pal and neighbor of Pynchon's while he was writing this novel in Manhattan Beach. I'm sorry that I've lost track of her after we met a few more times in the States.*

GRAVITY'S RAINBOW
A novel by Thomas Pynchon.
Viking Press, $15 and $4.95.

"He who leaps into the void owes no explanation to those who watch."

—Jean-Luc Godard, 1958

There's a creepy little story called "Don't Look Behind You," a paranoid classic of sorts, that scared the wits out of me as a kid. It was the final story in a collection by Fredric Brown, *Mostly Murder,* and it assured me at the outset that it would be the last story I'd ever read. The narrator is a printer who becomes an accomplished counterfeiter, goes mad, and develops a taste for murdering people at random, always with a knife. He's decided that he's become so adept at killing that he can even warn his victims in advance; the story, in fact, is his warning. He's carefully printed up this story and with his elaborate skills has bound it into only one copy of the book, the one you're reading; for obvious reasons he's chosen a collection whose last story is called "Don't Look Behind You," and wherever you happen to be, he's somewhere nearby, waiting for you to finish it.

Pynchon's third novel, set in western Europe 1944-45, ends in a movie theater where all of us—"old fans who've always been at the movies (haven't we?)"—are about to be obliterated by a V-2 rocket traveling faster than the speed of sound, and God help me, I believe that too; it's two decades since I first encountered that Brown story, and reading Pynchon makes me even more scared.

Paranoia, logically extended, eventually produces genuine agents of destruction, and the horror of Pynchon's vision is not merely that we're all victims of obsessive plots, but that we're all obsessive builders of them. Insofar as we participate in the plot-making of *Gravity's Rainbow*—and the multiple ambiguities, confusions, and intrigues essentially oblige us to, along with the essentially helpless characters—we're helping to prepare our own annihilation, and worse yet, We're Getting a Big Bang Out of It. Although this mad and maddening present-tense novel charts the assembly of a rocket immediately before and after the bombing of Hiroshima, we gradually realize that it's a missile aimed at us, now, inside that movie theatre, appearing overhead like the first evening star. Shall we make a wish? "The screen is a dim page spread before us, white and silent," and we're clapping loudly for the show to start.

The appalling whiteness that shines on the next blank page is many things. It is the mixture of all colors, flashing like a rainbow from the rocket's tail. It is the essence of Weissmann, mastermind of the rocket—a character exported from Pynchon's first novel, *V.*, re-christened Captain Blicero (his SS code name), and a fair stand-in for the Faustian White Man currently bent on controlling/destroying the planet, with all the ceremonial aplomb of a Dr. Mabuse, or a Cecil B. De Mille. It is the whiteness of semen, coming from the phallus that is the rocket's human counterpart, orgasm equaling obliteration (le petit mort, goes the French phrase). But above all, it is the whiteness of a nihilist void that envelops us all, which the rocket obligingly fills.

If I insist on using the present tense and first person plural, this is not only because *Gravity's Rainbow* concludes with the phrase, "Now everybody—". In a sense the entire book is phrased as a dialogue between then/there/them and now/here/us, a fusion of dialectics between Europe and America, history and news, "movies" and "reality," idea and experience, Frontierland and Tomorrowland.

A friend of Pynchon's has told me that he has never been to Europe, and biographical blurbs state that he was born in 1937. Like Brown's narrator, he is an expert counterfeiter, and quite apart from all his loving pastiches—from Raymond Chandler to William Burroughs, *Superman* to Robert Crumb, and encompassing quite a few of the best and worst "trash" movies of all time—he counterfeits history, geography, science, and countless other disciplines. Thus the extraordinarily realized image of wartime London and environs over the first 100-odd pages is a likely product of long hours at the library, late movies on TV, and a prodigious imagination. But as we read on, the gravitational influence of future events speeds the narrative, like the ultimate rocket, toward the target of our contemporary experience, and we increasingly find ourselves caught in an on-flight movie, anachronistically confusing, where today is seen as yesterday, yesterday as today. Like many transatlantic passengers, we are subject to fits of jet lag.

The commanding symbol and structural outline of *V.* was that initial letter itself, an elusive, multi-faceted expression of a Great Female Principle—relentlessly and fruitlessly pursued by one Herbert Stencil, in search of his identity; blissfully ignored by one Benny Profane; who settles for "yo-yoing" and other local comforts; both of these lines intersecting to form the cusp of the *V. Gravity's Rainbow*, a V-2 in more ways than one, inverts the V and rounds it out to form a rocket/phallus/parabola, a Great Male Principle, combining the Stencil and Profane impulses into a single character's trajectory—a pathway approximating the movement from erection to ejaculation.

Early in the novel we discover that Tyrone Slothrop, an American lieutenant in London, is getting erections in relation to the V-2 bombings; these rockets are falling in a "Poisson distribution," and an Allied group known as PISCES (Psychological Intelligence Schemes for Expediting Surrender: "whose surrender is not made clear") enlists him in a series of Pavlovian experiments without letting him know about his unusual talent for duplicating and predicting—or is it provoking?—these hits on a map of his sexual adventures. Duped into a love affair on the Riviera, and slowly discovering that he is being manipulated, he splits for an incognito jaunt across sections of Switzerland and Germany, in search of the truth about his past and penis.

But halfway through the novel, he starts to relent—gradually moves from being a narrative thread (a cog in the plot) to a scattered set of random impulses. We learn that "Personal density is directly proportional to temporal bandwidth'... 'Temporal bandwidth' is the width of your present, your now...(and) the narrower your sense of now, the more tenuous you are. It may even get to where you're having trouble remembering what you were doing five minutes ago, or even—as Slothrop now—what you're doing *here*, at the base of this colossal embankment..."

Thus Slothrop, down the other side of the parabola, is gradually phased out of the novel as a visible presence—undergoing a fragmented sort of "Poisson distribution" of his own, fading away into disembodied legend (a trace of grafitti: "Rocketman Was Here"), and opting out of all the Faustian power trips and Oedipal searches that constitute most of Pynchon's world. Turning away from the King Kong metaphysics of knowledge and power, truth and illusion, sadism and masochism, he follows the yellow brick road toward entropy and dissolution, and when last seen as an integral whole, "after a heavy rain he doesn't recall," is watching "a very thick rainbow...a stout rainbow cock driven out of pubic clouds into earth, green wet valleyed Earth, and his chest fills and he stands crying, not a thing in his head, just feeling natural...."

There is no question that once Slothrop starts to disappear, the book becomes harder and harder to read. Jokes tend to stop being funny, the musical-comedy routines (a Pynchon specialty) grow tiresome, habitual flights of invention begin to seem more like compulsive word-chewing, and the twitching of the narrative from one apparently arbitrary center to another often appears itself like dispersions of random energy. Meanwhile, most of the quasi-naturalistic premises that have helped to sustain our interest have all but evaporated, to be replaced by myth and ritualistic mumbo-jumbo, Tarot cards and magic, Germanic science-fiction crossed with homespun visions of hell: hysterical virtuosity becoming virtually hysteria. "If there is something comforting—religious, if you want—about paranoia, there is still also anti-paranoia, where nothing is connected to anything, a condition not many of us can bear for long."

Yet it seems likely that these exasperations are intentional and even organic to Pynchon's purposes, for they create a gaping void of chaos and incoherence that only the rocket can fill. And the only ones free from the conversion of confusion into lethal energy are those, like Slothrop, who step out of the narrative line—including those readers who fall by the wayside and don't finish the book. Everyone else becomes fuel or target for the rocket, which is readied for launching. Like one of Mussolini's trains, it takes off precisely according to schedule.

But it lands in silence, destroying us faster than its sound can travel, and just as the whiteness of the final empty page is a blend of all colors, the silence is an amalgamation of every sound. One recalls how all the tortured aspirations and cruelty jokes of Nathanael West's *The Day of the Locust* become fused into the wail of the hero, imitating a police siren as loudly as he can. *Gravity's Rainbow*, which begins with a scream, marshals together every subsequent vibration into a deafening silence, a soundtrack to accompany the blinding whiteness of the movie screen. No warning, and little time for any anticipatory response, save for the "What?" of Richard M. Nixon that heads the novel's final section, or the cryptically beautiful hymn by Slothrop's ancestor that all but concludes it.

Pynchon's theme, style, and vision do not exactly develop from book to book, or even from sentence to sentence: they expand, usually in all directions at once, like an exploding galaxy. Conspiracies become vaster and more intricate, circles expanding inside of expanding circles inside a head, which means the head must grow larger. On my second trip through *Gravity's Rainbow*, I made an index to keep up with all the minor characters (they number over 150), bought a German dictionary, read Rilke and Henry Adams, bugged friends for information about calculus and English history, poked around Shirer and Speer, consulted *TV Movies* (sorry, Tom, *The Return of Jack Slade* was released in 1955; Blodgett Waxwing couldn't have seen it twenty-seven times during World War II), and skimmed through a book on the Tarot. All these things were provisionally useful, and I may have advanced my liberal education a decimal point or two, but I still don't know who the Kenosha Kid is, and perhaps I never will. No matter: I doubt that anyone could account for everything going on in *Gravity's Rainbow*, even Pynchon himself, although I suppose he has an edge on the rest of us.

But despite the bigger canvas of this novel, the greater wealth of detail and complexity, the palette of colors and level of draftsmanship remain essentially the same. A continual war between random and compulsive energies is waged through *V.*, *The Crying of Lot 49*, and *Gravity's Rainbow*, preventing all three from being either completely formed or completely formless, and although the last succeeds somewhat in plotting these impulses on a single parabolic curve, the achievement is never more than partial: much of Slothrop's "systematic" quest for his identity seems aimless, and a lot of his subsequent scattering seems "systematically" random.

Put another way, *Gravity's Rainbow* is at once Pynchon's most structured book and his most digressive. Beneath the intimidating edifice of his grand design creeps the same fungus of local and momentary amusements that ran through the first two novels, and if the 760 pages of this novel were laid end to end, one might well discover that whole yards of it were devoted to marginalia. Some of this is wonderful: the name of a law firm ("Saliteri, Poore, Nash, De Brutus, and Short"), Proverbs for Paranoids sprinkled into the storyline like raisins, a dozen limericks devoted to rocket-sex metaphors, an airborne barrage of custard pies (thrown from balloon to plane by Slothrop at the face of a favorite villain), a riotous improvisation on pinball machines. Other readers may wince at these examples and laugh at the ones I consider sophomoric; the point is that, as Marx remarked, quantity changes quality, and there are times when one longs for the relative compactness of *The Crying of Lot 49*, where the central metaphors had more of the hard precision of poetry, less of the soft meanderings of run-on prose.

But this is quibbling. Set against the lax spots of *Gravity's Rainbow*—bar-room brawls and sailor shenanigans that seem to keep running variations on *Mr. Roberts*, for better and for worse—are sequences that redeem everything. No room to discuss properly a nine-page passage (pages 127 to 136) that may be the most beautiful stretch of sustained lyricism Pynchon has ever given us, with cadenzas like jazz solos based on chord changes by Dickens, a grand rhythmic sweep worthy of Faulkner in his prime, and an emotional rawness that is wholly Pynchon's own. Nor could I do proper justice here to the magical-surreal appearances of Malcolm X and Mickey Rooney (among others), the death of Webern, the description of a German Disneyland called Zwolfkinder, the tear-jerking romance between Roger and Jessica (in the purest '40s style of Hollywood heartbreak), the comic extravagance of characters like Frau Gnahb ("the terror of the high seas") and the black-market vessel she steers along the Baltic coast, a page of conversation about the eroticism of suicide, or a mystic Western staged in central Asia. The book is a treasure-chest, and a world is still waiting to be found in it.

Predictions are foolish and comparisons risky, yet I can't help but wonder whether *Gravity's Rainbow* will seem as dated in forty years as Dos Passos's *U.S.A.* appears today. Will it be as remote to current preoccupations, but as significant as a time capsule, an accurate rendering of precisely how everyone was freaking out in the late '60s and early '70s? A curious accomplishment to suggest for a novel that purports to be set in the mid-'40s, but I think it might. If we are around for another forty years, I suppose it will have to age: each generation, after all, at least during this century, tends to selfishly regard itself as the last. There have been many dreams of apocalypse before this one, and many others—let us hope—that will follow. But let those living or not living in 2013 worry or not worry about this problem. For now, it is enough to dive into *Gravity's Rainbow* and experience the most gifted American novelist under forty, writing at his peak.

Sonny Rollins Live at Laren

From Monthly Film Bulletin, *Vol. 43, No. 509, June 1976.*

Sonny Rollins Live at Laren
Netherlands, 1973
Director: Frans Boelen

The essential value of this film made for Dutch TV—a no-nonsense recording of the Sonny Rollins Quintet performing four numbers at the "International Jazzfestival" at Laren in August 1973—is the music itself, and the unusual courtesy with which it is treated by the filmmakers. Apart from a few brief pans across enthusiastic members of the audience, all the action is centered on stage, and the various angles caught by the two cameramen—each of whom is occasionally glimpsed in footage shot by the other—are all admirably related to a direct appreciation of the music, with none of the attempts to pump up excitement artificially that infect most jazz films. [...] Rollins, playing very close to the top of his form, begins "There Is No Greater Love" with one of his imaginative a capella intros before launching into the theme in medium tempo; serviceable solos follow from [Yoshiaki] Matsuo [guitar], [Walter] Davis [Jr.] [piano] and [David] Lee [drums], and then a rousing return by the leader, improvising with unflagging energy before resuming the theme and ending with one of his Byzantine free-form cadenzas. Briefly introducing the band members, he continues with an infectious calypso, "Don't Stop the Carnival"—developing a riff by ending each phrase with a sustained note while exploring an anthology of ways of leading up to it—which unravels as a continuous solo. Then come two of his best compositions—his memorable theme from the less memora-ble *Alfie*—with solos by Rollins, Matsuo and Davis, and four-bar exchanges between Rollins and Lee in which the former characteristically usurps some of the latter's space in an overflow of asymmetrical invention; and his 'West Indian' classic "St. Thomas," performed as an encore, an all-Rollins number shot with a barrage of his inimitable tonguing attacks—sardonic, percussive volleys of notes springing forth like pellets—and generally featuring his most swinging playing in a very spirited set, with creative punctuations from Davis. The group plays quite cohesively throughout, with Matsuo providing unobtru-sive support, [Bob] Cranshaw's Fender bass standing in without difficulty for his usual double bass, Davis tight and crystal-clear on a well-tuned Steinway Grand, and Lee playing with a low-flame intensity that carries Rollins like a thin layer of grease in a simmering skillet; the film ends unceremoniously on his abandoned drum set.

Recommended Viewing (and Listening): *Saxophone Colossus* on Blu-Ray

Blog post, August 5, 2017 (excerpted).

Most of what makes this 1986 Robert Mugge documentary, named after Rollins' best early album and produced by his late wife Lucille, so special is Sonny Rollins himself—currently approaching his eighty-seventh birthday—as a performer and improviser and his irrepressible stamina and power, combined with his choreographic skill in standing, walking, leaping, and tilting every which way while he plays his tenor sax and pours out his endless inventions. I've often thought in the past that jazz vibes players are the most cinematic of performers, because they can only play vibes by dancing, but Rollins has the rare and paradoxical capacity of doing the same thing while looming before us like a veritable mountain. At one point we even see him breaking his heel after leaping from the stage but continuing to play while lying on his back.

Black and Tan (1929)

From Monthly Film Bulletin, *vol. 43, no. 510, July 1976. For the precisions here about Miley and Whetsol, I'm indebted to jazz and film scholar, David Meeker.*

Duke Ellington rehearses his "Black and Tan Fantasy" for a club date in his flat with trumpet Arthur Whetsol until interrupted by two men from the piano company, sent to remove the instrument because he has fallen behind in the payments. Dancer Fredi Washington bribes the movers with a bottle of gin into telling their boss that no one was home. Duke tells Fredi that they can't take the job at the club because of her heart condition, but despite her faintness, which causes her to see multiple images, she insists on performing her dance and collapses at the end of her number. A chorus of other dancers is brought on, but Duke stops their band in the middle of their tune so that he and his men can stand by Fredi on her deathbed. There, at her request, they play the "Black and Tan Fantasy" as she loses consciousness.

Dramatic films which use jazz organically (*To Have and Have Not* is a supreme example) are few and far between, while jazz films which feature the music dramatically are perhaps even rarer. The singularity of *Black and Tan*, which comprises the first appearance of Duke Ellington on film, is that it fuses both categories—developing a sort of poetic synthesis in less than twenty minutes that, while clearly awkward and dated in many of its ingredients, nevertheless demonstrates, at the very onset of the sound period, that the two new art forms of this century don't necessarily have to trample on one another. Written and directed by Dudley Murphy, who made a short with Bessie Smith (*St. Louis Blues*) earlier the same year—apparently with some of the same sets and uncredited bit players—and previously executed Fernand Léger's ideas

29

in *Ballet mécanique*, *Black and Tan* uses arty trappings and a creaky plot, but has a sharp enough sense of form to turn both of these liabilities into assets. After the title tune is presented embryonically in rehearsal—unfortunately without the participation of Bubber Miley, the remarkable trumpeter who played a substantial role in Ellington's early conceptions, but well-performed by Arthur Whetsol in the Miley manner—the action is temporarily pre-empted by some low comedy involving the piano movers, racist stereotypes with a surreal, inventive use of language ("Bro-ther, re-move yuh anatomy from that mahogany," one announces to Ellington, remarking that he hasn't paid anything on it since last "Octuary;" his jockey-sized sidekick is variously called "Action," "Sarasparilla," and "Eczema"). But this is quickly bypassed when the scene shifts to the club, where two eerie dances are performed by five men of ascending height in tuxedos, making strict linear formations on a mirror-like floor while the Ellington band plays behind them. Even more strangely, when the point of view shifts to Fredi Washington, the first number is repeated precisely, immediately upsetting one's sense of linear time, while one's visual bearings are confused by the splitting up of the musicians and already duplicated dancers into a myriad mosaic. By the time Washington has made her own entrance and gone into her wild shimmying number, the mood and music have both turned fairly demonic, and a sudden shot of her gyrations from beneath the glass floor, echoing [René Clair's] *L'entr'acte*, increases the dislocation. Soon afterwards, the scene shifts once again to her death chamber, where the chiaroscuro effects, compression of space (the entire Ellington band and Hall Johnson Choir appears to be crowded around her bed and silhouetted on the far wall), and powerful, relentless thumping of Wellman Brand's bass heard against the ensemble on "Same Train" are so extreme that the effect is truly unsettling. When the assemblage goes into a "full-dress" version of the title tune at her dying request—complete with solos on trumpet, trombone, and [Barney] Bigard's piercing clarinet—the spare, growling blues with which the film began, which literally quotes the famous "Funeral March" from a Chopin piano sonata in the fifth and sixth bars, and again the eleventh and twelfth, has grown into a Dionysian lament. Assuming once again Washington's viewpoint, the camera focuses on Ellington in an image that gradually blurs, like a guttering candle. Then she dies, and the camera cuts to the last and most disturbing image—another blurred shot of Ellington that is no longer justified by Washington's viewpoint, thereby collapsing the film's coordinates of space as well as time into the realm of pure idea, or pure music; and both slowly fade away in the same flickering breath.

On Alfred Hitchcock, Michael Snow, and André Hodeir

From the New York portion of my "London and New York Journal," in Film Comment, *July-August 1976.*

April 9: *Family Plot.* Hitchcock has made a movie about his own sexy forms of duplicity and deception, which include sound and image, sumptuous musical scores and cuddly Hollywood types...what better subject for him? But to judge from a lot of local remarks, this gem is apparently one of the Master's lightweights because it doesn't contain any guilt (unless one discounts the wealthy dowager's regrets about the past which set the double-plot in motion) or murders or contemporary gloss. Apparently death, sex, and money aren't as significant as New York City or Watergate unless they're seen through a stained glass, darkly. *[2023 note: This entry followed a discussion of* Taxi Driver.*]*

Three separate friends have complained that the sequence with Barbara Harris and Bruce Dern in the brakeless car is "embarrassing": I'm not sure whether this means corny or old-fashioned or something else, although this clearly wasn't the experience of the three audiences I saw it with during the first eight days of its run. If by "embarrassing" they mean that it makes its own strategies evident and obvious, I can only concur. In a rare burst of candor, Hitchcock finally places the transcendental where it belongs—in a crystal ball—and devotes his energy to showing us how a thriller works. That the film's visual structure is witty enough to rhyme its crystal ball with a religious amulet and symbol of wealth (the giant diamond), and to suggest elsewhere that both are like TV screens—so that Hitchcock's own appearance consists of his video silhouette, behind glass—only helps to show that *Family Plot*'s true lucidity (like Lang's in *Spies* or *The 1000 Eyes of Dr. Mabuse*) is its manner of equating its own narrative devices with its characters' actions, creating a mirror-surface which lets an audience watch its own responses rather than get lost in them. All mirrors, to be sure, are potentially "embarrassing."

And if the devices in question are old-hat or corny, a thin coating of contemporary gloss is all that conceals the same qualities in *Taxi Driver* or *All the President's Men* behind their "significant" subject matter. From this standpoint, it's the latter films which are really escapist, not *Family Plot*, because the experiences they offer contain practically no self-reflecting mechanisms—merely "food for thought" in the grand old Sunday supplement tradition of Stanley Kramer.

April 12: I purchase a copy of Michael Snow's *Cover to Cover*, which, along with the Hitchcock, is the most interesting filmic experience America has afforded me so far this trip. It costs a hefty $12.50 in soft cover, $20.00 in cloth (co-published by the presses of the Nova Scotia College of Art and Design and New York University), but unlike filmic experiences which cost a fraction as much, you can take it home with you. As with *Family Plot*, it is essentially concerned with its own manipulations, but on the other hand it isn't a movie but a book.

Or is it? A lot of the fascination inherent in this singular object of 320 pages is its curious hybrid nature, halfway between book and film in the experience it offers. Rumor has it that Snow himself regards it exclusively as a "bookish" book, but part of its value as an open work is that it imposes no precise itinerary in how one "reads" it. One can flip through the photographs/pages on either the right or left, forward or backward, or take them more slowly and consecutively—in which case it becomes apparent that the reverse side of each page is a reverse-angle, with the frequent visibility of each camera only foregrounding the processes that much further.

Rather than attempt to spell out the book's narrative and continuity (which Regina Cornwell has already helpfully done, despite a faulty page count, in the March-April *Studio International*), I'd rather draw attention here to its playful dialectic between "reading" and "watching," which includes such "bookish" traits as the upside-down flip-overs on pages 163 and 171, and such pure "movie" tricks as the disappearance of the stray male onlooker between pages 189 and 191. (The pages are unnumbered, alas, so one must count from the cover to reach these examples, as I did.) The ambiguities of such transitions bring to mind another unique hybrid: André Hodeir's extraordinary jazz composition based on a James Joyce text, *Anna Livia Plurabelle* (available on the French Epic label, EPC 64695), which explores the differences and relationships between musical and literary logic through an intricate series of jazz pastiches and verbal puns, developed simultaneously. *Cover to Cover* embarks on an analogous adventure, with pages serving as the equivalent of film frames, in an exhilarating exploration into the nature of narrative continuity in both media.

Hollywood's Jazz

From the March 1978 American Film. *This was my first contribution to that late but unlamented magazine, and its inaccurate title wasn't mine. The American Film Institute needlessly and provincially tends to restrict itself to national and industrial product (i.e., Hollywood), unlike the British Film Institute,* Cinémathèque Française, *and most comparable international organizations.*

American Film *was a rather dull mainstream monthly mostly supporting the AFI's slant whose fees were largely supporting me and paying my rent while I was writing my first (and, to date, least mainstream) book to be published,* Moving Places: A Life at the Movies. *Some of the magazine's obligatory blandness undoubtedly found its way into this article.*

Cuing the audience into the threat of impending violence in *Blackboard Jungle* (1955) and *Looking for Mr. Goodbar* (1977), director Richard Brooks has very different aces up his sleeve. In the earlier film, he uses jazz—a blaring, evil-sounding Stan Kenton record. It's played on a jukebox by Josh (Richard Kiley), a mild-mannered jazz buff and schoolteacher, who is mugged by a gang in an alley while the song is still playing. In the more recent film—where, incidentally, Richard Kiley plays the heroine's bombastic father—Brooks uses disco singles blasting away in bars, and a strategically placed strobe light. The latter is conveniently given to the Diane Keaton heroine as a Christmas gift, so that we can see her stabbed to death in her flat under its mocking staccato rhythms.

In both cases, the cuing device works as a kind of symbol for the lower depths of dread and paranoia—predicting disaster before it comes, then hyping it full throttle when it arrives. And the fact that Brooks no longer uses jazz to attain this effect may say something about the changing status of jazz in movies since the fifties. It has gone from *Blackboard Jungle*, *The Man with the Golden Arm*, and *Touch of Evil* to simply another set of colors within the musical spectrum. Indeed, now that jazz in one form or another can be found in elevators and dentists' waiting rooms as often as in bars, its implicit meaning in films is hardly the same as it once was.

In *Blackboard Jungle*, Josh's taste for jazz makes him a sacrificial lamb, as his rare set of 78s is smashed to bits by his class after he tries to lull them with

Bix Beiderbecke's "Jazz Me Blues." Five years later, in Brooks' *Elmer Gantry*, the public exposure of the hero as a charlatan is momentarily turned into an expressionist witches' sabbath when a demonic jazz trumpeter appears and bleats his "blue" notes straight into Gantry's face.

Why does this conceit appear somewhat quaint today? Having been partially reabsorbed in the pop mainstream, jazz is no longer assumed to be automatically synonymous with decadence and the forces of darkness. It can finally be experienced and evaluated on its own terms—just as we may have to wait for the 1990s before we can respond objectively to strobe lights and disco hits.

With this newly acquired freedom, there's a lot we can do. For one thing, we can begin to look back on the sixty-year partnership of jazz and film with a certain objectivity and we can try to determine why they've often behaved together like spiteful siblings. (Both are roughly contemporaneous with the twentieth century, having grown out of socially disreputable origins and having fought for serious recognition.) We're helped in this task by the publication of a big new reference work on the subject—David Meeker's *Jazz in the Movies: A Guide to Jazz Musicians 1917-1977*. If we survey the 2,239 films that are described in this catalog (out of which, I should confess, I've seen little more than a fifth), we encounter a range of collaborations in shorts and features, fiction films and documentaries which throws a much richer and broader world into relief.

Part of this world, to be sure, is composed of the "jazz film," a subgenre basically devoted to the recording of performances. But of more interest are the successful collaborations between the expressive possibilities of both jazz and film. And of special interest is the fact that the ways in which jazz has been used in movies invariably tells us a great deal about the social, ethnic, aesthetic, and cultural biases of diverse societies and periods. An interesting study, for instance, could be devoted to charting the various responses of film producers to integrated jazz groups in the thirties, forties, and fifties, which would provide a kind of thumbnail social history. Sometimes black musicians were forced to play off-screen while white stand-ins mimed their solos.

If memory serves, the first jazz film I ever saw was a ten-cent "soundie" in an arcade in 1953. Soundies were pint-sized, three-minute movies shown inside the glass bubbles of jukeboxes known as Mills Panoram Machines. According to Meeker, "The films were produced at a rate of five or six per week and featured most of the popular entertainers of the time, usually performing their current record hits." Among the best are a few jam-packed numbers by Fats Waller, Duke Ellington, Nat "King" Cole (when he was a pianist as well as a singer), and Meade Lux Lewis.

The advantages and drawbacks of such productions roughly match those found in *Jivin in Be-bop*, a 1947 short feature made for black audiences. It presents Dizzy Gillespie's big band (including the two main soloists of the future Modern Jazz Quartet, Milt Jackson and John Lewis) with singer Helen Humes interlaced with belly dancers and dull comedians. The sloppy synchronization of music with musicians is often aggravating, yet the pasteboard décor and the drive of some of the tunes make it a fascinating record of the period.

If we want to be scholarly about it, we can say that the first known conjunction of jazz and the fiction film took place in 1917 in *The Good for Nothing*, a silent comedy which showed the Original Dixieland Band. Rumor has it that Charlie Chaplin, a fan of the group, made a brief and uncredited appearance in this lost film.

Leaping ahead to the sound film, we come upon two remarkable shorts made in 1929 by Dudley Murphy. *St. Louis Blues* remains our only film record of the magisterial Bessie Smith. For this reason alone, its hackneyed and rather condescending plot is not so much transcended as obliterated the moment the great singer launches into the title tune. The other short is *Black and Tan*, which marks the first film appearance of Duke Ellington. It also starts with a comparably dated plot and then works wonders with it. Fredi Washington, a pretty dancer with a heart condition, bribes two piano movers with a bottle of gin so that Duke can continue to rehearse his "Black and Tan Fantasy". Cut to a nightclub engagement where she insists on dancing a wild, demonic number until she collapses. Dissolve to her deathbed, where Duke's band and the Hall Johnson Choir—all crowded around her and silhouetted on a far wall—play "Black and Tan" once again at her request.

James Agee refers to a jam session in *Phantom Lady* "used as a metaphor for orgasm and death—which in turn become metaphors for the jam session." I can't vouch for the accuracy of that, but unquestionably *Black and Tan* equates death and orgasm with its music in an obsessively eerie way. [...]. Compressing vaudeville, "atmosphere," diverse avant-garde tropes of the twenties, and wonderful music into nineteen minutes, this unlikely gem has seldom been surpassed for making jazz and film do things together that neither could achieve separately.

Thirty years later, Ellington's score for and brief appearance in *Anatomy of a Murder* present an equally successful (if much more laid-back) use of jazz as a dramatic device. James Stewart's hero, a small-town lawyer in Michigan, is a jazz buff who plays a little piano, and the music becomes an extension of his personality as it pervades the film. A similar equation is used in an earlier Otto Preminger film, *The Man with the Golden Arm*, with Frank Sinatra as an aspiring drummer addicted to heroin and wedded to a bombastic Elmer Bernstein score.

Keeping jazz off-camera often permits its impact to register more subliminally. How many critics have remarked on Martial Solal's effective score for Jean-Luc Godard's *Breathless*, which alternates an elliptical jazz-piano motif for Jean-Paul Belmondo with a lush, parodic chorus of strings for Jean Seberg? The sharp division of the sexes that one invariably finds in Godard is neatly summarized by this musical contrast, and comparable directorial aids can be found in the music of such films as *Alfie*, *Mickey One*, *No Sun in Venice*, and *Elevator to the Gallows*.

§

Some directors are more adept at using jazz than others, and it's worth considering some of the reasons why. Improvisation is at the root of jazz, and directors who like to improvise on occasion, such as Robert Altman, seem to have a special feeling for the music. They can be as different as John Cassavetes (in his first two features, *Shadows* and *Too Late Blues*) and Howard Hawks. In the movies of Hawks, musical get-togethers between allies always have strong communal functions, and even the nicknames of characters seem to belong to the world of jazz. Only *Ball of Fire* (1941) and its remake, *A Song is Born* (1948), use unadulterated jazz explicitly to advance the mood of fellowship in the plot, but the principle is the same in the songfests of *Only Angels Have Wings*, *To Have and Have Not*, *Gentlemen Prefer Blondes*, and *Rio Bravo*.

The use of a single number in *Ball of Fire* could serve as a model for how jazz can extend the range of a film. This occurs after a reel of exposition showing Gary Cooper and six other meek bachelors in a Victorian house at work on an encyclopedia. After Cooper resolves to go out into the world to bolster his impoverished grasp of current slang, we hear big band music over a "montage" sequence showing him collecting phrases all over the city. Then we cut to him in a nightclub, where a slow pan to the right reveals the Gene Krupa orchestra. Barbara Stanwyck (as "Sugarpuss" O'Shea) makes a grand entrance and proceeds to sing "Drum Boogie," a swinging romp whose infectious beat quickly takes over the place.

Cut off from his scholarly friends, Cooper's initial response to this collective feeling is embarrassment; yet by the end, he's moving his hands—discreetly but nimbly—to the music. For an encore, "Sugarpuss" and Krupa plant themselves at a nearby table, and Krupa offers a reprise of his drumming with wooden matches on a matchbox while a group of spectators huddles around them. From Victorian parlor to lively club, the transition from one form of coziness to another is remarkably fluid. Spatially as well as rhythmically, the spirited music is permitted to call all the shots.

In contrast, the uses of jazz by several other filmmakers turn the music into a solitary, almost solipsistic kind of pleasure. Altman's *The Long Goodbye* begins with Elliott Gould humming and singing snatches of the title tune while Dave Grusin's off-screen piano trio improvises on the melody in a different key; the overall effect is at once plaintive and unsettling. Two very different—and unjustly neglected—films expand on this notion. In Norman McLaren's delightful abstract short *Begone Dull Care*, the lively improvisation of Oscar Peterson's piano is matched perfectly by McLaren's improvised doodles, drawn directly onto the film negative. The hero of James B. Harris's live-action *Some Call it Loving* is a wealthy baritone sax player who inhabits a strange world where everyone caters to his secret wishes. The music played by his group magically captures the disturbing perfection of his self-contained dreamworld, feeding on its own fantasies.

One category, the musical biography, has generally produced mixed results, perhaps because the plots of such movies are usually restricted to sentimental formulas. For some reason, the heyday of this subgenre was the fifties, when *Young Man with a Horn*, *The Glenn Miller Story*, *The Benny Goodman Story*, *The Five Pennies* and *The Gene Krupa Story* all appeared. The most that can be said for these movies is that they occasionally offer worthwhile music *[2022: Louis Armstrong and Danny Kaye's vocal duet on "Saints" in* The Five Pennies, *available on YouTube, is a particular delight]* along with their saccharine stories, even if the famous "lives" in question are often mangled beyond recognition.

The most recent and notable encounter of jazz and Hollywood is *New York, New York*, and if certain details in this film are uncomfortably reminiscent of ones found in musical biographies, it must be quickly added that the movie rises well above them in other respects. The problem here is principally the music rather than the characters—sax player Jimmy Doyle, played by Robert De Niro, and singer Francine Evans, played by Liza Minnelli.

The main difficulty with Doyle's music in dramatic terms is that it simply isn't good enough. During both his auditions in the film—at a Brooklyn dive and in a Virginia dance hall—he delivers little more than a string of warmed-over clichés. When we discover much later that his combo's version of the title tune has hit the top of the charts in *Down Beat*—right above Charlie Parker's "Mohawk"!—the required suspension of disbelief is more than any self-respecting jazz fan can manage.

This is not to fault the capabilities of either director Martin Scorsese (whose uses of music elsewhere, in *Mean Streets*, *Alice Doesn't Live Here Anymore*, and *Taxi Driver*, is often brilliant) or swing tenor Georgie Auld, who ghosted all of Doyle's solos. The important point here is that whatever else the film has to offer, most of the jazz elements have been needlessly glossed over. The tension generated between the two leads in non-musical scenes gets thrown off-balance, because only Francine's music gets the film's full attention: (Compare her version of the theme song with Doyle's.)

Consequently, it is Liza Minnelli and Diahnne Abbott who convey most of the jazz feeling in the movie. Through a curious alchemy, the jazz becomes Hollywoodized while some of the "Hollywood" numbers are allowed to swing.

Any lessons to be learned from this? Mainly an obvious one—that if *New York, New York* had better jazz it would have been a better movie. But also a more general one: that the way jazz is used in any film winds up telling us a lot about the people who made it. We discover something about their eyes, their ears, their sense of rhythm and pacing, and their storytelling abilities, not to mention their cultural attitudes. To regard jazz as an expendable or neutral element is to turn one's back on all the cinematic and dramatic possibilities it has to offer.

Take Two: *The 5,000 Fingers of Dr. T.*

The principal source of this article in the October 1978 American Film *was a lengthy phone conversation I had with Theodor Seuss Geisel (1904-1991), better known as Dr. Seuss. This happened while I was teaching in the Visual Arts Department at the University of California, San Diego, and booked* The 5,000 Fingers of Dr. T. *for one of my film classes. I believe this was for one of Raymond Durgnat's classes that I took over for him after he unexpectedly and rather mysteriously returned to London in the middle of a quarter. (He was also a big fan of the film.)*

Geisel, the main auteur of the film (at least as I saw it), also lived in San Diego, and hoping that he could come to the class as a guest lecturer, I managed to get ahold of his address and wrote him a letter. By way of replying with a friendly refusal, Geisel called me one day at the house in a Del Mar canyon that I was subletting and politely begged off, explaining that his relation to this movie was rather traumatic. To explain himself, he gave me a lengthy account of his friendship in the U.S. Army with Carl Foreman and Stanley Kramer, their joint project to make a fantasy film, and various disastrous occurrences that interfered with the original plans. I also recall asking him if I could write about this and he said sure, as long as I didn't quote him—which is why I refrained from mentioning our phone conversation in the article but feel that I can acknowledge it now. (Another thing I refrained from mentioning, at his request, was the fact that Kramer wound up directing a good deal of the film after Roy Rowland suffered some sort of breakdown during the film's production.)

I've tweaked the editing of this piece in a few spots, but some of the prescribed and expected blandness remains—as it does in the movie I'm writing about.

Neglected films come in various shapes and sizes. There are movies whose aesthetic importance is overlooked or whose social impact has been forgotten simply because prints are scarce or unavailable. There are movies nurtured by nostalgia, touchstones or tombstones of former feelings, that are more prone to reappear like phantoms on television.

Then there is a third category: the unclassifiable oddity. Without a comfortable pigeonhole to encapsulate its essential qualities—a familiar genre, star, or auteur—it is doomed to walk the night as an isolated freak, excluded from most textbooks and popular histories because it doesn't "fit" any ordinary survey standards.

The 5,000 Fingers of Dr. T. is one such outcast, although for me it also has distinctly nostalgic overtones. I first saw it when I was ten years old, on a family trip to New York in June 1953, shortly after it opened. I liked it so much that I returned to it twice when it eventually reached my hometown in Alabama later in the year.

Bart Collins (Tommy Rettig), the movie's hero, was also ten, which obviously helped to bolster my attachment to this weird musical fantasy. But that wasn't the whole story. I could sense that this movie postulated—and was postulated on—a certain form of rebellion against the adult world. Aside from short episodes at the beginning and the end, the film is offered as Bart's nightmare, a pure distillation a ten-year-old boy's grasp of his world and his sense of the degree to which adults occupy and control it.

The film was written by Alan Scott and Dr. Seuss. The latter's name, of course, was no less familiar to us. I knew that his real name was Theodor Seuss Geisel. I had checked out from the library several of his illustrated children's books, including *The Cat in the Hat* and *Horton Hatches the Egg*. I also knew that he'd created the title character of *Gerald McBoing-Boing*, the cartoon that had won an Academy Award for 1950.

What I hadn't realized then was that Geisel had already been associated with two previous Oscar winners. While he was attached to Frank Capra's filmmaking unit during World War II, he wrote an indoctrination film, *Your Job in Germany*, which was later released by Warner Bros. under the title *Hitler Lives*, and won the 1945 Academy Award as the best documentary short. The following year, as a civilian, in collaboration with his wife, Helen Marion Palmer, he wrote *Design for Death*—described in the press as "a history of the Japanese people"—which was released by RKO and won the Academy Award for best documentary feature.

It was during the war that Giesel, Kramer, and Carl Foreman, all serving together in Capra's film unit, first hit on the idea of some day concocting a lavish film fantasy. After the war, Kramer went on to become a producer, and Foreman worked with him as scriptwriter on *Home of the Brave, Champion, The Men*, and *Cyrano de Bergerac*.

But during the production of *High Noon*, Foreman was summoned to testify before the House Committee on Un-American Activities. Unlike Kramer, he refused to cooperate and immediately was blacklisted. Foreman severed his association with Kramer and moved to England, and the director's post on Kramer and Geisel's project—now an expensive production to be distributed by Columbia Pictures—went to Roy Rowland, a former assistant to W.S. Van Dyke on *Tarzan* films.

Geisel's idea for the film stemmed from piano lessons he'd had as a boy "from a man who rapped my knuckles with a pencil whenever I made a mistake....I made up my mind I would get even with that man. It took me forty-three years to catch up with him." Thus was born the ferocious Dr. Terwilliker (Hans Conreid), Bart's authoritarian piano teacher whose institute serves as the sole location of Bart's feature-length dream.

Certain changes in Geisel's conception were made for commercial reasons. In the "real-life" episodes, Bart befriends a plumber named Zabladowski working in his house who turns up later in Bart's dream, where he functions as an alternate father figure. Geisel wrote the part for Karl Malden, but it was decided, instead, to use Peter Lind Hayes, a popular radio star who formed a singing team with Mary Healy. Healy herself was given the role of Bart's mother. This led to an injection of "romantic" interest between Bart's mother and Zabladowski.

Various difficulties beset the shooting. Probably the most spectacular of these involved the climactic title sequence, when Dr. T. marshals 500 boys to play his own composition, "Ten Happy Fingers," on two gigantic keyboards—a notion of Busby Berkeley at his wildest. The scene required the film's most spacious set, designed by Rudolph Sternad and built on RKO's largest sound stage.

The problems started when three days of rain began to flood the set. Only about 400 boys were eventually used in this sequence. Between takes, all of them gorged themselves on hot dogs in the studio commissary. One boy became ill on the set and threw up—setting off a violent chain reaction. The resulting surrealism must have been more unsettling than anything Salvador Dali might have imagined.

As a paranoid fantasy, the film is quite straightforward. Falling asleep after a piano lesson with Dr. T., Bart finds himself in the dream institute as the first recruit for the 5000-fingered recital, forced to wear an official Terwilliker beanie. Soon the boy is in flight from legions of guards, the most bizarre of which are Judson and Whitney (John and Robert Heasley), Siamese twins connected by a single gray beard who pursue Bart on roller skates. After attempting to enlist the aid of a reluctant Zabladowski—who is installing sinks to prepare for the influx of 499 other boys—Bart discovers that Dr. T. has issued an order to have the plumber disintegrated at dawn.

Continuing his flight, Bart comes across a dungeon in which are kept all the musicians who play instruments other than the piano. The real Dr. T. had described them as "scratchy violins, screechy piccolos, nauseating trumpets, et cetera, et cetera." This occasions the film's most remarkable sequence—a ballet choreographed by Eugene Loring and featuring an assembly of green-skinned prisoners performing on outlandish instruments.

One xylophone is a radiator, and another is played by several men with brightly colored, crisscrossing mittens. Dress dummies serve as bass fiddles, and violinists and tuba players carry wraparound instruments encasing their entire bodies. Other parts of the orchestra suggest torture instruments (an enormous harp strummed by prisoners' heads), surreal objects (a man dancing on a drum with abnormally long mallets) and circus props (a man on a high wire sailing across the set to strike a small cymbal).

Bart carries the execution order to Zabladownski and engages him in a blood pact, joining together their pricked thumbs and getting him to assent to the Boy Scouts' pledge. But Terwilliker's guards turn up, and Bart and Zabladowski are imprisoned in a dungeon. There they concoct a magic potion designed to sabotage the grand recital by swallowing up noise, through Zabladowski warns that it may be "atomic."

The formula works, and the 500 little boys, led by Bart, celebrate their palace revolution and defeat of Dr. T. by pounding out a discordant version of "Chopsticks" with their hands and feet. (The only exception—an indelible passing detail—is a tearful boy who still wants to play "Ten Happy Fingers.") The portion proves to be atomic after all, sending up smoke, crackling sparks, and finally explosions.

Bart awakes in terror beside his piano, and in a hasty conclusion, it is implied that maybe the preceding wasn't only a dream. He and Zabladowski still have bandages on their thumbs from their blood pact. The movie ends with Bart playing outside with a baseball and mitt, accompanied by his dog, an image of Middle American normality that evokes Norman Rockwell.

§

Why was the film such a resounding flop at the box office, reportedly losing more than a million dollars? Acknowledging certain lapses—mainly a few descents into tacky sentimentality or awkward pictorial whimsy—I would still guess that its commercial failure stemmed from its strangeness and originality, which gave audiences more than they could handle.

Like the contents of Bart's pockets that go into the "Music-Fix" magic potion—an endless assortment of objects that is beautifully "rhymed" with the confiscated possessions of the 499 other boys—the movie remains a rather awesome hodgepodge. The steps of different shapes and sizes leading up to Dr. T.'s headquarters, and the Flash Gordon-like paraphernalia found inside, suggest the "mental projections" of German expressionist films from *The Cabinet of Dr. Caligari* to *Metropolis*. But the tunes of Frederick Höllander (alternately chipper and saccherine) and the extravagant use of '50s Technicolor interact with this tradition in a decidedly peculiar way, as if Dr. Mabuse and Esther Williams were suddenly to find themselves in the same movie.

Seen today, the film has an additional layer of interest as a complex reflection of American attitudes and feelings during that period. For one thing, the popular applications of Freud are everywhere apparent, as in the dreamlike equation made by Bart after his blood pact with Zabladowski. He accepts the plumber as a father figure and, consequently, as a husband for his widowed mother (in striking contrast to Dr. T., who holds his mother under a sinister hypnotic trance).

If we pick up some clues from the sociological approach of Raymond Durgnat—one of the few critics to have acknowledged the film's special interest—the kinship of this oddity with other movies of the period becomes much more apparent. Far from being a "pure" fantasy, its nightmarish landscapes and details evoke Cold War anxieties linked in the public's mind with Russia, Korea, and the atomic bomb, as well as memories of World War II. Such diverse details as the electrified barbed wire and searchlights surrounding the Terwilliker institute and the grotesque goose steps performed by Dr. T.—after being dressed in his elaborate "Do-Mi-Do Duds" for the recital—hark back to related fears.

The anti-egghead bias of the early '50s is clearly bound up within the portrayal of Dr. T. As embodied in Hans Conreid's brilliant performance, the character is a veritable anthology of negative responses to Europeanized and "feminized" notions of high culture. From his pink powder-puff slippers and his vaguely continental accent to his stern disciplinary manner, he makes a striking contrast to the "manly" working-class virtues of an all-American Zabladowski.

None of this is meant to suggest that the film can't—or shouldn't—be enjoyed by children and adults today. On the contrary, when it was revived at a children's show at Filmex in Los Angeles last spring, the response was overwhelmingly warm and enthusiastic. I'm sure that many of the ten-year-old boys must have identified with Bart as strongly as I did twenty-five years ago. And the movie's cockeyed inventions still shine with a singularity that places this film in a class by itself.

Remember My Name

This review appeared in the Spring 1979 issue of Film Quarterly. *I consider it Part 1 of a two-part consideration of Alan Rudolph, carried out over a span of a dozen years, to be followed by my much more ambivalent take on* Mortal Thoughts *for the April 26, 1991* Chicago Reader, *which deals with some of the same issues involving both class and music.*

Alan Rudolph's film was financed by Columbia, then written off as a disaster before it was released, but it has been running successfully in Paris for months and opens shortly in New York. It strikes me as the most exciting Hollywood fantasy to come along in quite some time. Admittedly, I'm a Rivette enthusiast; I'm fascinated by narrative suspension and indeterminacy, and tend to lose interest when a plot is laid out in full view, because I've usually seen it before. *Remember My Name* deliberately suspends narrative clarity for the better part of its running time, and never entirely eliminates the ambiguities that keep it alive and unpredictable—even though its themes, thanks to Alberta Hunter's offscreen blues songs, are never really in question. It will only confound spectators and critics who perceive movies chiefly through their plots.

A simple look at Rudolph's plot shows it to be as sketchy, in narrative terms, as the blues written and sung by Hunter—and no less expedient and suggestive for his own purpose, which is to offer a concerto for Geraldine Chaplin. Rudolph has said that he wanted to do "an update on the themes of the classic women's melodramas of the Bette Davis, Barbara Stanwyck, Joan Crawford era;" one could also cite the Warner Brothers social protest films of the thirties as a useful reference point. Either way, the aim clearly isn't to imitate the models or criticize them à la *Movie Movie*, but to use them the way a jazz musician uses chord changes—as a launching pad, not a destination.

Newly emerged from twelve years in prison, Emily (Chaplin) drives into a town where Neil (Anthony Perkins) works as a hardhat, and starts bugging both him and his wife Barbara (Barry Berenson) for mysterious reasons: calling their home and then hanging up, driving past Neil on a construction job, yanking flowers out of their garden, and entering the house when Neil's away to explore the rooms and confront Barbara in the kitchen (asking her, "Are you a good fuck?" and remarking that she met Neil "in the back of a crowded car" when he was twenty years old).

Meanwhile, Emily starts sleeping with her black landlord, Pike (Moses Gunn), in exchange for some domestic furnishings. Alone in her room, she rehearses a speech to Neil ("I didn't cry when you disappeared...") She argues her way into a job in Thrifty Mart, incurs the enmity of Rita (Alfre Woodard), a black coworker, assaults her, and stabs Rita's boyfriend with a pencil when he comes on to her. Barbara, who witnesses this event by chance, has Emily arrested for smashing her window, forcing a confrontation between Neil and the two women in turn. Emily sees Neil at the police station and finally delivers her speech about her emotional and sexual obsession with him "over the past 4,380 days." Neil convinces Barbara to drop charges, then confesses that he was once married to Emily, who went to prison for running over a woman he was having an affair with.

Appalled by this information, Barbara leaves him. Neil gets fired, phones Emily, meets her in a bar, gets drunk, and lets her make love to him. In the morning, Emily swipes his credit card to buy a new wardrobe before driving away, leaving Neil to face a resentful Pike.

The flimsiness and banality of such a fictional world—which asks us to accept Perkins as a shifty, no-account hardhat, and Chaplin as a rough equivalent to Toshiro Mifune in *Yojimbo*—is readily apparent. Rudolph uses a form of narrative striptease to keep his plot suspenseful, but this turns out to be partially a ruse; a fully legible and comprehensive fictional world isn't what he's after, as we see, for example, from the fact that he never definitively clarifies whether or not Emily steals money from the Thrifty Mart cash register.

Indeed, Emily's "sincerity" is an ambiguous issue on one level or another in virtually every scene. No less duplicitous, ambivalent, and opaque than Ophüls' *Madame de...*, she literally makes herself up as she goes, and the only proper way to respond to this challenge is to improvise along with her, assigning her a set of ephemeral, almost discontinuous identities while being strung along on Rudolph's narrative and stylistic continuities. Thus, while narrative exposition (including Emily's separate actions), matching camera movements and repeated blues motifs, both singly and in concert, imply an unwavering singleness of purpose, the actual performance of Emily (and of Chaplin) proceeds like a series of bold experimental forays and flourishes around this obsession, a virtuoso "solo" that swirls through diverse possibilities while hitting all the octaves.

If one could take Emily apart the way Bulle Ogier takes apart the Russian doll in *L'amour fou*, one might find only a succession of deceptive layers stripped away to reveal a void—an empty center that the rest of the film defines. But in fact, the rest of the film asks us to put her together, out of the same fragments of her past that she is struggling to free herself from, so that we "fully" grasp her social identity at the same point that she puts it behind her—abandoning us along with Neil and Pike to make a fresh start.

Before this happens, she's an outcast shopping for an identity, trying on everything that could conceivably fit. Her first and last stop in town in this very symmetrically designed movie is significantly at a clothes store, where she stakes out a wardrobe like a samurai choosing weapons. (This proves to be all that she needs; driving past a familiar poster—"Use a gun/Go to prison/ That's the law"—she can only smile.) Sufficiently armed, she stalks through the remainder of the film with as much pizzazz as any Norman Mailer hero, using her eccentricities largely as diversions to throw her victims off balance.

Consider her approach to a recalcitrant Pike when she wants window drapes and clean sheets for her room. "I know what you want, you want me to beg for favors—okay, I'll beg." She gets down on her knees in an abject parody of begging, hands outstretched: "Clean sheets? Clean sheets? Gimme clean sheets—drapes for my window..." Then she suddenly, violently leaps to her feet and cries, "Don't you dare kiss me!", slaps him, and falls into his arms, disarming him completely. "Takes a woman to take a man outa himself," he mutters bemusedly—incidentally suggesting why *Remember My Name* qualifies as a male fantasy more than feminist tract. Then, to save himself a bit of honor, he adds: "But to do that she's gotta be better than him."

And she is: not only with Pike, but with every other man (and woman) she encounters, each of whom is gradually dismantled by her arsenal of discontinuous, seemingly contradictory moves. The psychological logic of this strategy is that her past and her obsession are wholly matters of monotony and stasis—as fixed and rigid, in a way, as the traditional blues forms used by Hunter. And the only way that she (or we) can work though this limitation is to improvise on the given chords—assuming diverse roles and stances in relation to the action while forging ahead in the existential present.

This is the first time I've ever wholly accepted Geraldine Chaplin in an American film—perhaps because it's the first American film that's been built around her unusual and inventive mannerist talents. Her role as Opal, the obnoxious groupie in *Nashville*, was obviously central to Altman's conception, and was reportedly conceived of as a parody of his own role as director; yet his failure to develop this role beyond satirical platitudes while continuing to use her as an identification point for the spectator eventually revealed a certain hollowness at the center of that conception. (The part was distorted, too, in the final editing, leaving one with the impression that Opal was really supposed to be a BBC correspondent, not just a pathetic fraud pretending to be one.)

Annie Oakley in *Buffalo Bill and the Indians* offered Chaplin a more nuanced role and yielded a much subtler performance, but this wound up getting buried under the braggadocio of the male hamming that ultimately swamped the film. And as the reception co-ordinator in *A Wedding*, she was handed another satirical cutout like Opal to mimic.

It was Rudolph's first (and previous) feature, *Welcome to L.A.*, that probably gave Chaplin her first real chance to show her wares in an American context. (I'm unfamiliar with most of her work for her husband Carlos Saura, and have only the dimmest recollection of *Dr. Zhivago*; but in Rivette's still unreleased *Noroît*, where she plays a solitary avenging pirate—clearly anticipating her avenging ex-con in *Remember My Name*—her capacities as a mime, often evocative of her father's, are allowed to function powerfully in a completely nonrealistic mode.) What she lacked was a strong enough conception to "place" her eccentric character and performance in a particular context. Richard Baskin's narcissistically self-pitying and droning songs—establishing a thematic center that her secondary role was supposed to help illustrate – projected a charming (if unlikely) sort of self-conviction, but not enough to support and enhance a major performance. This is what the firmer and tighter strategies of *Remember My Name* generously provide.

Some residue of Robert Altman's influence in a few off-center gags and motifs—a loony customer at the Thrifty Mart; several TV news reports about a catastrophic earthquake in Budapest (which everyone ignores); a thematic preoccupation with dwelling units and locks—shouldn't disguise the fact that Rudolph develops a much stronger independence from his producer's style here than in *Welcome*. The audacity of teaming Chaplin with a black octogenarian blues singer in an audiovisual "duet" implies a stylistic discipline and concentration that is not apparent in Altman's other recent productions, where notational gags and details claim most of the space—crowding out the possibility of the kind of "star" performance that Chaplin gives here. Settling on a tight yet relaxed framework where the anger and passion of a wounded outsider can define its own awesome limits, Rudolph allows both women to wail, and the results are spellbinding.

The True Auteur: *Richard Pryor Live in Concert*

*This was written for the May 1979 issue of the long-defunct Canadian film maga-
zine* Take One *during the same time I was writing my first book,* Moving Places.
*Pryor's passionate form of self-examination and autocritique obviously struck a
very personal chord for me—and a musical metaphor seems appropriate for Pryor's
performative literature.*

*To contextualize this review a little further, I had recently written an angry
attack on* The Deer Hunter *for the March issue of the same magazine, soon after
a reviewer in the* Soho News *had compared it favorably to Tolstoy. For more on
Pryor, see "Pryor Commitments" on my website.*

Richard Pryor Live in Concert has nothing in particular to do with the art
of cinema; it merely happens to be the densest, wisest, and most generous
response to life that I've found this year inside a first-run movie theater. A
theatrical event recorded by Bill Sargeant, the entrepreneur who similarly
packaged Richard Burton's Broadway production of *Hamlet* and a celebrated
rock concert (*The T.A.M.I. Show*) fifteen years ago, and more recently filmed
James Whitmore's impersonation of Harry Truman (*Give 'Em Hell, Harry!*),
it is nothing more nor less than a Pryor stand-up routine given last December
28th at the Terrace Theater in Long Beach, California, lasting about an hour
and a quarter. (Patti LaBelle, the singer who preceded Pryor, is omitted from
the film but gracefully acknowledged in the credits.)

Now that officially recognized "cinema art" in the U.S. mainly consists of
narcissistic, masculine self-pity (Allen, Coppola), xenophobic self-righteousness
(Lucas, Schrader), or steamrolling combinations of the two (*Midnight Express,
The Deer Hunter*), it's perhaps only natural to find an artist like Pryor confidently working the other side of the street. As fine as he's often been inside the
schemes of others—from the broken bum in James B. Harris's neglected and
beautiful *Some Call it Loving* to the triumphant Daddy Rich in *Car Wash*—he's
clearly never had a filmic opportunity before this one to let his imagination
flourish at full stretch. Working entirely without props, gimmicks, or excuses,
he creates a world so intensely realized and richly detailed that it puts most
million-dollar blockbusters to shame.

Most of this world, one quickly discovers, is autobiographical, although no less fanciful for being so. In swift succession, Pryor can use his voice and body to impersonate members of his family (from his grandmother to his own children), a horn player in Patti LaBelle's band, the tires and motor of a car he "killed" with a Magnum (to stop his wife from leaving him in it), numerous animals (including deer, horses, monkeys, and an especially diversified range of Tex Avery-like dogs), John Wayne, a heart attack he recently underwent, a Chinese waiter, a couple of black prizefighters, a host of silly white folks, and even himself, in interaction with all the preceding.

It's the interaction, in fact, that pushes Pryor's gifts to the forefront of his art—the fact that he takes on none of his subjects from a safe, voyeuristic distance, but is constantly implicating himself in whatever he's dealing with. In the course of sympathetic reviews, both Andrew Sarris and Vincent Canby have objected to what they regard as Pryor's reverse racism at the beginning of his performance; for me, these gags were only further evidence of Pryor's boundless empathy. The first time I saw this movie, in a midtown Manhattan theater where the audience was predominantly black, his intuitions about my own insecurities were so acute that I was immediately won over. In point of fact, his impersonations of whites are probably more hilarious and more accurate than any "equivalents" offered in white minstrel shows. It was refreshing to learn, contrary to the incessantly hammered-in xenophobia of so many recent Hollywood packages—from *Sorcerer* and *Star Wars* to *Midnight Deer Hunter Express*—that political ties can still be found, renewed and/or tested among diverse groups inside an auditorium, not broken up and subdivided on the way in by diverse forms of racism and class distinction.

The political issue is basic: Are commercial movies today public forums and community meeting-places, or private sites of narcissistic pleasure, figurative or literal porn images to masturbate to? (A tasty bit of aggressive agit-prop like *The China Syndrome* falls neatly between these categories.) There's no question that Pryor belongs to the first camp, because his comedy is a matter of recognition, not confirmation. He lets it all hang out, including how he works. When he falls to the floor in his heart-attack routine, or impersonates his grandmother beating himself as a child—one word per stroke as he sculpts a staccato, crablike chain of blows given and received across the stage, oppressor and victim maniacally encased inside the same voice and body—it seems to be his body thinking, remembering, and speaking as much as his mind. But of course, as Yvonne Rainer reminds us, the mind is a muscle—a lesson demonstrated constantly by Pryor, along with Jacques Tati and Jerry Lewis (in contrast to, say, Lenny Bruce and Woody Allen).

It's revealing to compare Pryor's deer hunt with Michael Cimino's. The latter is so concerned with filling out his pre-set mythical honcho diagram (a bit like painting with numbers) that it would never occur to him to wonder how a deer drinks water when he/she is afraid. Pryor not only wonders; he becomes a frightened deer drinking water—along with himself as a kid and his father watching—in order to find out. Yet who gets praised for "novelistic" depth? A Cimino, who'll always have to rent his deer from central casting and then ignore it, in order to keep his vision "pure" and calcified; not a Pryor who, wanting to keep his vision alive and impure, will have to look for it in his guts, not send out for it like a cheese Danish. It's Pryor becoming a whole movie in himself through sheer force and determination who deserves the auteur status. (By contrast, how much of Cimino's authorship can be attributed to the $13 million that financed it?)

There's something about the way that Pryor copes with life (at least on a stage) that is positively liberating. What some people have termed obscenity—which has helped to keep the bulk of his work away from the audience who could most appreciate it – is miles away from the violation of taboo pursued by, say, Norman Mailer; Pryor uses language and gesture as a complex means of expression, not a mere act of rebellion. At his most beautiful and poetic, he is actually capable of celebrating the death of his father—at age fifty-seven while making love to an eighteen-year-old woman—comically exploring the ramifications of all this from her viewpoint as well as from his, and encapsulating the event in a heroic line that seems worthy of a John Donne: "He came and went at the same time."

The Greening of Switzerland

This was the first thing I ever wrote for The Soho News *(May 14, 1980), a small-time weekly competitor of* The Village Voice *that I wrote for every week for about a year and a half (1980-81), reviewing books as well as movies on a fairly regular basis. I did sixty-eight pieces for them in all, and this first effort, as I recall, was a kind of trial balloon.*

Doctor Fischer of Geneva or the Bomb Party
By Graham Greene
Simon and Schuster, $9.95

"The meat is excellent, but I have no appetite," remarks the noble, grief-stricken narrator of Graham Greene's opulent twenty-first novel—plain old Alfred Jones, a middle-class voyeur like us—at the climactic title party, in response to a query from the wealthy title host and villain. Then he adds more confidentially, to the reader, "I helped myself to another glass of Mouton Rothschild; it wasn't for the flavor of the wine that I drank it, for my palate seemed dead, it was for the distant promise of a sort of oblivion." The same sort of delicious oblivion, one might add, that we normally expect from a new Greene novel—which is the sort that the latest one amply supplies.

Nobody but nobody offers sexier, more glamorous Catholic guilt than Greene at his best. Thirty years back, George Orwell was already noting that Greene seemed to share the Baudelaire-derived notion that "there is something rather distingué in being damned" whereby "Hell is a sort of high-class nightclub..." That was around the same time that Greene was scripting *The Third Man*, a thriller whose charismatic, amoral villain, Harry Lime (Orson Welles), was a postwar profiteer trafficking in diluted penicillin in Vienna's black market. The leering Mr. Lime had a neat way of summing up Switzerland—the ostensibly "neutral" setting of Greene's latest version of *Faust*. It occurred in a speech reportedly furnished by Welles himself, who claimed to have copied it from an old Hungarian play. "In Italy for thirty years under the Borgias they had warfare, terror, murder, bloodshed—they produced Michelangelo, Leonardo da Vinci and the Renaissance. In Switzerland they had brotherly love. 500 years of democracy and peace, and what did that produce? The cuckoo clock."

Graham Greene, on the other hand, produces metaphysical fairy-tale thrillers about innocence and damnation—which might be described roughly as flirtation contests between the two. And the uncommon pleasure of *Doctor Fischer of Geneva or the Bomb Party* (only 156 pages long, and I defy you to read them in more than one sitting; lots of snowy landscapes, perfectly timed for hot summer reading) is that it knows exactly what buttons to push to get its sleek effects.

§

Like certain other septuagenarian craftsmen—the Hitchcock of *Family Plot*, the Bresson of *Lancelot of the Lake*, or even the Matisse who devoted himself to paper cutouts—Greene is smart enough to realize that all he has to do to is reduce his gestures to irreducible signs, nothing more, and everyone will catch the signals. He can tenderly give his hero an artificial hand to replace the one he lost in the London blitz, bestow his heroine (and her late mother) with a passionate love of Mozart, and virtually the rest of their trembling vulnerability can be sketched in by us, who naturally want to protect them.

Alfred Jones, fiftyish translator for a chocolate factory in Vevey (the fashionable resort of Daisy Miller in the James novella), meets Anna-Luise, twentyish daughter of evil millionaire Dr. Fischer, mysterious inventor of Dentophil Bouquet toothpaste. The rest is artful plotting, casting, and set decoration. And because it's Greene who's delicately pulling all the strings, we can be made to believe that it's genuinely love at first sight—with Alfred becoming the kindly father that Anna-Luise never had, and she becoming both the wife and daughter that he lost in childbirth twenty years before.

Dr. Fischer—playing a sort of elusive giant lemon here in relation to *The Third Man*'s Lime (another "natural" cameo part for Welles when the inevitable movie adaptation gets made)—is variously identified with God Almighty and Satan, even by the secular romantic couple, and provides as much gratuitous nastiness as any fairy-tale bogeyman. An embittered sadist who spends most of his visible time humiliating a circle of rich acquaintances at specially planned parties—concocting diverse endurance tests for them to undergo in exchange for lavish presents, in order to demonstrate their unlimited greed and hypocrisy—he registers with a compositional purity rarely found in mortals. A sour version of the artist as frustrated tycoon, he hovers over the action like a malignant presence even when he isn't around physically, through the cruelty of his deeds.

Greene's shapely plot is a delight to experience, and none of the game should be given away here. For Greene, plot is character, and the brief portraits sketched above are scarcely more than his narrative starting points. (I've omitted the court of grotesques surrounding Fischer at his fancy bashes: already a veritable cast of character actors—including an American widow with blue hair, an alcoholic movie actor, and an international lawyer shaped like the number seven—they line up rather symmetrically in dramaturgical terms, like *Twelve Angry Men* or the *Boys in the Band*.)

If, dramatically speaking, the book peaks a few pages before it ends—arguably, a serious flaw in a miniature—this might be due to an odd surfeit of liberal sanity that unexpectedly overtakes Greene's apocalyptic fantasy at the last minute. Mutatis mutandis, it's a little bit like calling in Kurt Vonnegut Jr. to write an epilogue to *Sophie's Choice*. But Greene can be forgiven for diluting his splendid nonsense with sense and trafficking in bromides, for he wants to let us off easy. How can we find it in our hearts to refuse him?

Dr. Percy to the Rescue
[on Walker Percy's *The Second Coming*]

From The Soho News, *July 9, 1980.*

The Second Coming
By Walker Percy
Farrar, Straus & Giroux, $12.95

If reading Faulkner is sometimes like going on a desperate and delicious three-day bender, perusing the clear-headed work of old Doc Percy—a practical-minded (if nonpracticing) Southern M.D., now in his mid-'60s—is usually more like taking a healthy antidote the next morning, and recovering one's senses with dry irony and mordant wit. At least it has seemed that way up until now, to a Southern expatriate like myself who cherishes both writers (and a fellow moviegoer who appreciates what these very different noble Southern novelists have learned to steal from movies).

But *The Second Coming*—Percy's fifth novel, after *The Moviegoer, The Last Gentleman, Love in the Ruins*, and *Lancelot*—happily makes hash of this conceit by offering both pleasures in succession, the night before and the morning after, without so much as a hangover. How does Percy do it? Partially, I think, by splitting himself in two, like any self-respecting Gemini, and then making music out of his intertwining, alternating voices that ultimately merge: an old-fashioned love story, and one with a happy ending. Plotting out his narrative trajectory by crosscutting between Will Barrett and Allie Huger, who eventually compose his couple, he shrewdly fuses his existential and semiotic concerns with his style and story, to the point where you can't even tell them apart.

Faulkner worked with narrative counterpoint, too, but differently—in *Light in August* (split between Lena Grove and Joe Christmas) and *The Wild Palms* (split between two separate, nonconverging narratives about love). Cinematic crosscutting principles are already quite evident—*The Wild Palms* even contains a passing reference to Eisenstein—but the calculated avoidance of any synthesis of these parallel lines is clearly a romantic's solution.

Walker Percy, a classicist and a Catholic, obviously has different fish to fry, and a different range to fry them on. His meanest small-town targets, like Flannery O'Connor's, are always genuine Dixie mediocrities (check out Ewell McBee here, with his "Jarmar Sansabelt slacks and shirt-sleeve white shirt," or Barrett's born-again daughter Leslie, or all his characters who say "There you go"), while Faulkner's Snopses are mainly too mythic or awful to qualify. As far as existential dread, metaphysical décor and class behavior are concerned, *The Second Coming* is actually closer to Sontag's *Death Kit* than to anything by the author of *As I Lay Dying*. (If Percy were less modest, he could have called this book *Life Kit*.)

Like Faulkner, though, he's smart enough to realize that what we bring to movies may turn out to be even more complex than what movies bring to us. "Who is he," he asks in his beautiful 1956 essay "The Man on the Train" (included in *The Message in the Bottle*), "this Gary Cooper person who manages so well to betray nothing of himself whatsoever, who is he but I myself, the locus of pure possibility?"

Will Barrett—a fiftyish, multimillionaire widower and golfer in Linwood, North Carolina, roughly twice as old as we were when we last encountered him, as the title hero of *The Last Gentleman* (Percy's remake of *The Idiot*)—gradually loses his mind, and escapes from home and country club. Meanwhile, Allison Huger—troubled daughter of Barrett's onetime girlfriend Kitty Vaught, in her late teens or early twenties—escapes from Valleyhead Sanitarium, sets up house in an abandoned greenhouse she has inherited, and gradually schools herself in sanity.

The alternation of chapters between these characters is a kind of conceptual counterpoint, and the formal symmetries that they make together are intricately worked out. Will gets blackouts and keeps falling down, Allie brightly keeps hoisting him (and other things) up. Her greenhouse, into which he literally falls from a cave, is a fairy-tale cottage; his cave—where he goes in search of a sign from God—summons up Plato's parable.

Following both of these klutzy, lovable eccentrics, Percy's temperate style passes repeatedly over the same incidents and ideas in their heads like an endlessly rotating, scanning searchlight, each time teasing out and illuminating fresh aspects of their minds. And the most film-derived part of this method is to juxtapose their complementary natures via crosscutting long before they compose an actual couple. There's even what filmmakers call a "match cut" between the end of Chapter 3 ("He remembered everything") and the beginning of Chapter 4 ("She remembered nothing").

What he remembers includes his father's first attempt at violent suicide, while what she forgets includes recent electroshock at the hospital. Both of these facts gradually expand, like film sequences in repeated Proustian playback, as concepts that are central in molding the identity of each. To engineer her escape from Valleyhead before she knows she's getting electroshock, she writes herself a letter to read afterward—"Instructions from Myself to Myself"—splitting herself in two. To engineer his own retreat into a cave, he writes two letters, one to an uncle of Allie's named Sutter Vaught—something of a straw man, as it turns out, for the character never gets the outrageous letter or puts in a single appearance.

Part of Percy's devious strategy has always been to scatter red herrings like daisies wherever he goes. In *The Last Gentleman*, Sutter was the book's Seymour Glass/Mr. Natural figure, both guru and spokesman; intriguing as he was, waiting for his next journal entry to appear was a little bit like getting ready for another Chinese fortune cookie. Here he's half-promised and never delivered, and his failure to show up unexpectedly proves to be very satisfying. It's nice to discover that Percy and Barrett no longer need him.

While the identity of Will appears to be dissolving like an Alka-Seltzer, the identity of Allie—who has to put together a workable self in order to live in the world—is going through a process of accumulation and growth.

Much of the deepest pleasure afforded by *The Second Coming* is the pleasure of watching this slow accretion of existential anchors—spelled out by Percy in wise and generous detail that charmingly evokes *Robinson Crusoe*. While Will becomes increasingly convinced that the world is coming to an end because all the Jews in North Carolina are fleeing for Israel, Allie doggedly and patiently figures out what she needs to transport a stove into her greenhouse (rope, blocks and creepers), what they're called, and how to get them.

"Imagine being born with gold-tinted corneas," Allie thinks at one point, "and undertaking a lifelong search for gold. You'd never find it." But silvery

Will and golden Allie find one another because language-happy Percy lets them. There has often been a certain tension in his writing between his poetic instincts and the relative inelegance of philosophy and language theory, which commonly aims at correctness rather than grace. This may help to account for the rhythmic quirkiness of his prose, which genuinely appears to be composed sentence by sentence rather than paragraph by paragraph.

What makes *The Second Coming* seem like a decisive step forward is the degree to which questions about style and language become indistinguishable from questions about the characters and their spiritual health. Everything gets worked into the act of storytelling, coming out as naturally as breath. If the novel, as stated above, curiously combines the benefits of the night before and the morning after, this isn't because either of Percy's romantic leads "cures" the other. More precisely, it's because Allie/Will does the job on Will/Allie, and vice versa.

Compare the fancy Faulknerian prose that is uncharacteristically occasioned at separate junctures by each character. Then notice how, in the scenes between them, Percy lets their verbal mannerisms—his recitation of dry bone facts, her taste for puns and rhymes—cross over and intertwine in tuneful duets.

Here's Barrett recalling his father's final attempt at suicide: "And what samurai self-love of death, let alone the death of everyday fuck-you love, can match the double Winchester come of taking oneself into oneself, the cold-steel extension of oneself into mouth, yes, for you, for me, for us, the logical and ultimate act of fuck-you love and fuck-off world, the penetration and union of perfect cold gunmetal into warm quailing mortal flesh, the coming to end all coming, brain cells which together faltered and fell short, now flowered and flew apart, flung like stars around the whole dark world."

And here's Huger settling down in her greenhouse: "One way to escape the longeurs of clock time marching out into the future ahead of her was to curl away from it, going round and down into her dog-star Sirius self so there she was curled up under, not on, the potting table...She lit a candle and the soft yellow light made a room in the dark and time went singing along with cicada music and not even the screech owl was sad except that just at dusk there rose in her throat not quite panic but something rising nevertheless. She's swallowed it, all but the aftertaste of wondering: tomorrow will it be worse, even a curse?"

§

Even the proverbial end of the world and the death of the soul can be fun if it's Walker Percy who comes to the last-minute rescue. Appearing in the midst of a cinematically barren summer, it is no great shakes to say that *The Second Coming* tops every new movie in sight. Perhaps it's more to the point to say that, unlike most movies, Percy doesn't leave us alienated afterward. Writing further about Gary Cooper in "The Man on the Train," he notes that "Everything depends on his gestural perfection—an aesthetic standard which is appropriated by the moviegoer at a terrific cost in anxiety." *The Second Coming* gives not a hoot for anybody's gestural perfection. It is only concerned with mundane Southern matters—how to live, act, and write, gracefully, responsibly, and well.

A Fond *Madness*

If I'd had to depend entirely on the quality and interest of the films released in any given week, I probably wouldn't have remained a movie reviewer for several decades. Luckily, I often found ways of writing about other topics, using the film or films being released as excuses. An obvious example of this freedom at The Soho News *was the following piece about* Mad *that I did in 1980, for the July 16 issue, occasioned by a very forgettable comedy released that week.*

Though the ads for the crude, uneven *Up the Academy* are at some pains to link the movie to *Mad*—a publication (first a comic book, then a magazine)—now in its twenty-eighth year, the connection clearly has more to do with packaging than with contents. Like the *Star Trek* "meals" you could purchase at McDonald's last winter, or the entrepreneurial spirit that continues to invent such anomalous items as Donald Duck grapefruit juice, it bears all the earmarks of a promotion gimmick that plays merry havoc with existential and ontological identities. The apparent logic is to duplicate at least the packaging principles of *Animal House*, which had its own dubious linkups with *National Lampoon*. But even the preteens who read *Mad* will know they've been tricked.

A half-human piece of pasteboard usually designated as Alfred E. Neuman—and labeled Alfred E. Weinberg, founder of Weinberg Military Academy, in the ads—is trotted out at the beginning and end, furnished with a comic-strip bubble that says, "What, me worry?" and afforded a couple of stiff marionette gestures. This more or less exhausts the producers' responsibility to *Mad* readers, past and present; yet even as a substitute for nothing, it's pretty bogus. This is particularly true for an old fan of the comic book like myself, who wasn't introduced to Alfred E. Neuman until the mid-'50s—around the same time that the comic book became a magazine, and the first *Mad* paperbacks started appearing—and who considers him a symbol of *Mad*'s decline rather than its essence.

§

The old *Mad* was a central reference point in my preteen environment, but it didn't spring full-blown from a void. By the time I was first exposed to it at a Jewish camp in Maine, during the summer of '53 when I was ten, I'd already discovered Jerry Lewis in *My Friend Irma* in 1949, attended a live concert of Spike Jones in '51, thrilled to a brutally hilarious Western takeoff called *Skipalong Rosenbloom* the same year, and first encountered *Son of Paleface* in '52—to mention just a few related enterprises.

The aesthetic impression made on me by *Mad* in '53 could be called deceptively auteurist. I was acutely aware of the styles of individual artists who drew (and, I assumed, wrote) the stories, but only dimly conscious of the role played by Harvey Kurtzman—who, along with publisher William Gaines, invented *Mad* the year before. According to Roger Price's preface to *The Mad Reader*, Jack Davis, Wallace Wood, and Bill Elder (my favorite) were essentially gifted *metteurs en scène* who executed Kurtzman's designs, but that wasn't the way I understood it at the time.

Less ambiguous was *Mad*'s overall ethnic thrust—explicitly New York working-class-Jewish in nearly all its comic pet phrases and emblems (like furshlugginer, Potzrebie, chicken fat, and halavah), ferociously aggressive in its sex, its violence, its hyperventilated maverick goofiness, and its virtual lust for defying every taboo in sight. As Donald Phelps was later to observe of the magazine, "Both the humor and the sheer awfulness of *Mad*—which are inseparable—depend on the intimate response of the New Yorker to the wastefulness with which he comes in direct or indirect contact every day: the scraps of discarded food which adorn the street—New York's insignia ought to be a half-eaten pizza lying on the sidewalk..." An aesthetic, in short, of garbage, which Phelps called "The Muck School." More honest about its own obscenity than, say, Scrooge McDuck diving through his mountains of coin, *Mad*'s perverse humor was like a weekend with Henry Miller after a year with Ronald Reagan.

Alfred E. Neuman was never a true emblem of this irreverence because he was finally too respectable and domesticated a representative of that world: a harmless, ugly bar mitzvah boy with a shit-eating grin and potato-chip ears—not a disgruntled adult howling for blood, which is what the raunchy comic book more often reflected.

Up the Academy is no *Zéro de conduite*, but some of the anarchic impulse of the old *Mad* is at least fitfully suggested. One can't, however, really compare the social impacts of the old *Mad* and the new movie, because the contexts are much too different. The homophobic gags with the dance instructor can't be said to violate a taboo in the same way that a parody of Archie and Jughead as repulsive creeps with switchblades functioned in the '50s. Even if the gags had been progay, they still couldn't function as a transgression in the way that *Mad* once could (and did).

§

In June 1954, Robert Warshow's "Paul, the Horror Comics, and Dr. Wertham" appeared in *Commentary*—a very thoughtful consideration of E.C. Comics (which included *Tales from the Crypt*, *Shock SuspenStories*, and *Panic*, as well as *Mad*), specifically in relation to Warshow's ten-year-old son, Paul, and himself, and to the controversy stirred up by Dr. Fredric Wertham's lurid polemic against comics, *Seduction of the Innocent* (a perfect Cold War title, evoking Whittaker Chambers and J. Edgar Hoover). My father read the Warshow essay and, precocious little twerp that I was, I read it too—even though it was written for my father just as unequivocally as *Mad* was produced for me. Warshow was right to call the Wertham book "a kind of crime comic book for parents": on a trip to Birmingham [Alabama], my father and I came across a copy in a bookstore and we both looked at the frightening illustrations of comic book violence with the same sort of seedy fascination we might have had for pornography.

No question about it: E.C. Comics were grizzly and kinky (which eventually led to the comic-book equivalent of a Hays Office, issuing seals of approval to practically everyone except E.C.) That's what made them so exciting and attractive—and what makes a sodden lump like Neuman, and the more sober, glib, and formula-ridden magazine that this character-emblem ushered in, cold potatoes by comparison.

"What, me worry?" indeed! In the final analysis, Neuman insulted and circumscribed the disaffected, alienated *Mad* audience simply by defining it in market terms and then exploiting it like a tobacco company, which enabled *Mad* to become big business. (Present circulation is 1.8 million, over five dozen paperback collections are in print, and Parker Brothers sold a million *Mad* board games last year.)

§

An interesting enigma: Why did many adults have so much contempt for Jerry Lewis and *Mad* in the '50s? How much of that tension was generational? Could it be that, even before rock 'n' roll, a certain kind of humor was already declaring the independence of one generation and culture from another? It's easy to forget that in the early '50s, the form of this humor could be avant-garde. The Spike Jones concert I'd attended was a mixed-media happening avant la lettre, and for an exciting period, *Mad Comics* came out with a completely different cover every issue, so different that one had trouble finding it on the racks. (Each cover would mock a new adult totem: Picasso, *The Saturday Evening Post*, racing forms, the Mona Lisa—or even the ugly school notebooks that grownups would force on helpless kids.)

Warshow, who was already hip to the relationship of *Mad* to Jerry Lewis and Spike Jones (as well as the Marx Brothers and the Three Stooges), aptly noted that "The tendency of the humor, in its insistent violence, is to reduce all culture to indiscriminate anarchy." (On '50s TV, Sid Caesar and Ernie Kovacs were the main exponents of this principle.) The final page of "Famous Family Album Rejects," a feature in the current July issue of the magazine, gives us would-be childhood snapshots of Terry Savalas, Julia Child, Albert Einstein, Bert Lance, Ralph Nader, and Henry Kissinger—a typical instance of the process whereby every disparate cultural icon becomes equal under the democratic, jeering gaze of "Muck School" humor.

Mad Comics did this too, and so does the recent movie *1941*—which can largely be read as an homage to the spirit of *Mad*, above all in its fixed, sneering stance in relation to the action. (In relation to parody, too, the movie has the same dogged one-upmanship—the kind which says, "I can do a period dance hall sequence better than *New York, New York*, a more slam-bang special effects space chase than the one near the end of *Star Wars*, a snazzier opening than *Jaws*, etc.)

While the politics of *Mad* has always been more or less defeatist, the last two issues of the magazine virtually institutionalize this position in separate features. "Election Year Jabberwocky" (July) and the "Vote Mad/Alfred E. Neuman for President" cover of the September issue both line up all the obvious candidates—with the curious absence of John Anderson in each case—and treat them to the same homogenizing process undergone by Savalas, Einstein & Co. in "Fabulous Family Album Rejects."

§

A further example of *Mad*'s avant-gardism, and one still clinging like barnacles to the magazine, is its frequent references to its own formal properties (and those of the media it parodies), a technique identified by Russian formalist critic Viktor Shklovsky as "baring the device." Countless examples from the comic could be cited: in "*Starchie*," attention is directed to the fact that the faces of both heroines, Biddy and Salonica, are drawn identically. In a *Robinson Crusoe* takeoff, the title hero tears off part of the frame of the comic book square he's inside when he needs a straight line for a ruler. "*Dragged Net*," a very funny analysis of the old TV show, concentrates on the dramatic use of its booming theme song and other structural devices.

The same general tendency is evident in recent issues of the magazine. "*Star Bleech—The (Gacck!) Motion Picture*" (July) features such exchanges as, "She's— she's some kind of ROBOT!!" "At least SHE has an EXCUSE for her acting! What's YOURS?" Better yet, James Garner's father in "*The Crockford Files*" (September) remarks at one point that "It's this INFLATION, Sonny! Why, this crummy magazine WE'RE in costs 75¢!" Unfortunately, the artwork is much less dynamic or interesting than that in any of my '50s examples.

§

Robert Warshow was about thirty-seven when he wrote about *Mad*, the same age I am now. Unlike Warshow, I have no kids, so if I take a parental position about preteens reading *Mad*, this has to be toward myself in the early '50s. What kinds of residue did the original *Mad* leave? Some traces of adolescent whimsy that tend to juice up my writing like chicken fat (with comparable caloric excess); a hatred for the corporate languages of mass media; a certain taste for the giddy sensation of sudden distance from an artwork created by "baring the device"; and a hysterical, puritanical relationship to sex, money, and violence that mixes love and hatred for all three so intricately—as in the movies of Tex Avery, Samuel Fuller, Jerry Lewis, Otto Preminger, Jerzy Skolimowski, and Frank Tashlin—that a volatile, smoky cocktail emerges from the conflict.

Reactionary Humor and Southern Comfort
(Review of *A Confederacy of Dunces*)

From the August 27, 1980 issue of The Soho News.

A Confederacy of Dunces
By John Kennedy Toole
Foreword by Walker Percy
Louisiana State University Press, $12.95

Is it by mere chance, or through some form of subtly earned tragic irony, that this brilliantly funny, reactionary novel is being published during a reactionary period, apparently about a decade and a half after it was written? God knows what it might have been like to read this in the mid-'60s. I suspect it would have been less warmly received—one reason, perhaps, why it wasn't published way back then.

What I mean by Reactionary Humor is the boring literary schemes of Tom Sawyer, not the expedient escape tactics of Huck Finn. Broadly speaking, it's what we learn to expect from the perennial antics of Blondie and Dagwood, Amos and Andy, Franny and Zooey, Laurel and Hardy (and Marie and Bruce, in Wallace Shawn's recent play), not to mention W.C. Fields, Rainer Werner Fassbinder, Archie Bunker, and Woody Allen.

One can even say that Reactionary Humor is what we get from Don Quixote—a figure mentioned twice by Walker Percy (along with Oliver Hardy and Thomas Aquinas) in the foreword to this remarkable, posthumous New Orleans novel, whose author killed himself at the age of thirty-two. Or at least we get it until that terrible moment at the end of Cervantes' novel, when the dying Don suddenly repudiates his delusions and finds himself sane again.

The heroes and victims of Reactionary Satire are usually the same people. They live according to an improbable cosmic law that declares human personality to be an unalterable given, incapable of undergoing any development or improvement. Following this narrow philosophy—a familiar form of Southern comfort—one quickly arrives at the conclusion that one's character, idiosyncratic warts and all, is as inescapable as one's skeleton.

There's an explicit economic reason for most Reactionary Humor. If neurosis (Woody Allen), corpulence (Oliver Hardy) and stupidity (Krazy Kat) continue to attract paying customers, who wants to see an Allen with his problems licked, a Hardy signed up with Weight Watchers, or a Krazy Kat enrolled in college? So, at the worst, one domesticates one's problems by proxy, resigns oneself to their status as spoiled pets, and chuckles at their semi-permanence, rather than make any effort to solve them.

All of John Kennedy Toole's preposterous characters seem mired in this condition—to the profit of nothing but the author's despairing, affectionate scorn and slapstick. The diverse New Orleans inhabitants of a sleazy nightclub, city street, police station, factory office, and classy gay party vibrate with the same celestial ineptitude: a mainly unemployed fat slob with an MA who's never gotten further away from home than Baton Rouge (the hero); his dimwitted mother and her dimwitted friends, including a pathetic cop named Patrolman Mancuso and an elderly suitor called Claude Robichaux who blames everything on "the comuniss"; and an assortment of other grotesques that what the hero calls Fortune keeps throwing in his bumbling path.

§

Learn how to think progressively in relation to a Fassbinder weepie or an Allen comedy—that is, speculate on what might happen if the characters could behave differently, were able to change and grow—and these artful entertainments no longer dispense their customary solace. Yet put the bars back on the cages surrounding these maladjusted freaks, and they regain their fascination, seem to become "fully rounded" figures again—possibly because they represent the sluggish, defeatist sides of ourselves.

It's hard to imagine anyone more fully rounded than Toole's monstrous hero, Ignatius J. Reilly—a gargantuan, balloon-shaped medievalist and virgin who consumes many hot dogs, pastries, Dr. Nuts, and Doris Day movies. He has acute digestive problems involving his pyloric valve, wears absurd clothes (a green hunting cap, later a pirate suit), berates his arthritic and alcoholic mother (with whom he lives), writes in Big Chief tablets, and rails continuously against the modern world for its lack of "theology and geometry." In other respects, Reilly is no more than a plump octave—the top and bottom notes in a silly scale of human frailty and disaster-prone pathos, conveyed through intricate plotting by all the other characters in Toole's confederacy of dunces.

The novel's title comes from Swift—"When a true genius appears in the world, you may know him by this sign, that the dunces are all in confederacy against him"—but the measured loftiness of both the prose style and the elaborate plot construction intermittently suggests some of the finer tuning of an Alexander Pope. (A Dunciad of Confederates almost works as an alternate title.) The fact that Ignatius Reilly is a "true genius" and an obnoxious asshole at the same time, and to roughly equal degrees (with the asshole, however, having the upper edge), is an essential part of the overall comic vision.

§

It probably runs against the grain of the book's calculated neoclassical "timelessness" to insist that the author has discernible political biases of his own. But run and insist we must, for the temporal setting of the novel—like the fact of Toole's suicide in 1969—becomes an unavoidable aspect of its meaning in 1980. Based on some scant internal evidence—mainly the descriptions of a few movies seen by Ignatius—the action seems set around 1962, when the civil rights movement was already in full swing, but other fringe causes (like war resistance, feminism, and Gay Lib) had yet to receive much mass attention. It seems typical of the book's defeatism, though, that all political activity in it is regarded as equally hopeless and misguided.

A fair amount of the author's ridicule and venom is reserved for female liberals and liberationists—notably the horrendous wife of a jeans manufacturer, who insists on "rehabilitating" a senile office employee in order to torment her cynical husband, and Ignatius' Bronx-based girlfriend and correspondent, Myra Minkoff (mainly a Woody Allen nightmare), whose Reichian projects seem similarly designed to provoke and infuriate the slob hero. Coincidentally or not, both these women are Jewish.

By contrast, Mancuso and Robichaux, the ostensible right-wingers in the book, are depicted as lovably harmless and ineffectual creatures—sweety-pie stooges. In separate episodes, Ignatius (another Catholic) improbably organizes black workers at the jeans factory and homosexuals in the French Quarter, for improbable anarchist reasons of his own; both schemes, partially designed to provoke Myna Minkoff in turn, predictably end in madcap disasters.

In his Forward, Percy inadvertently comes on like an old-style Southerner when he celebrates a young porter named Burma Jones, a "black in whom Toole has achieved the near-impossible, a superb comic character of immense wit and resourcefulness without the least trace of Rastus minstrelsy." Read that phrase in reverse, and you'll see that Percy is implying that it's nearly impossible to imagine "a superb comic (black) character of immense wit and resourcefulness" without some traces of Ole Rastus—a reactionary Southern bias that the funny but two-dimensional Jones partially reflects. Then there are the gay characters, whom Toole seems to fear even more than his female leftists—beer-can-crushing lesbians who threaten to beat Ignatius to a pulp, males who emit an "emasculated version of an Apache war cry" when he unplugs a phonograph playing Lena Horne.

I realize that I've been using "reactionary" here mainly as a dirty word. Yet perhaps because Toole committed suicide at some point after completing this novel, and because it's virtually impossible to imagine an Ignatius free of his hangups, and because I'm writing this during an insufferable heat wave lacking both theology and geometry, when flesh seems heavier and weaker than ever, I can't help but wonder if the unexpected triumph of liberalism at the novel's conclusion is the right ending for this book to have. I can't quite believe it.

The dreaded Myrna arrives in the nick of time to shuttle Ignatius out of the state in her car. The end that I'd anticipated was much more quixotic and bleak: Ignatius undergoing shock treatments (which is literally the fate that Myrna saves him from, after his mother, now engaged to Robichaux, is persuaded by a friend to phone the hospital). This would have been decidedly less Yankee-contemporary and more Southern-medieval in flavor, like submitting Quixote to the Spanish Inquisition. But *A Confederacy of Dunces* was written in more hopeful times than these. And Toole was moved to give Ignatius another improbable chance—a gesture he regrettably failed to make on his own behalf.

Barthes of My Heart

This appeared in the September 10, 1980 issue of The Soho News. *Maybe it qualifies less as a book review than as a short polemic, but if I recall this assignment—my first review of a book by Barthes—accurately, I had some space limitations. (My "Barthes & Film: 12 Suggestions" can be found in* Placing Movies *and on my website.)*

New Critical Essays
By Roland Barthes
Translated by Richard Howard
Hill & Wang, $10.95

It's reported that when a celebrated American film critic *[2023: this was Pauline Kael]* was asked what she thought of French theory, she replied that the trouble with folks like film theorists is that they forget movies are supposed to be fun. When this response was quoted to me, my heart sank. It made me feel as if all the fun I'd had reading Roland Barthes over the years was no longer legal—that it wasn't even supposed to exist.

I'm not trying to pretend here that all of Barthes goes down easily: I still haven't gotten all the way through *S/Z*, a favorite among some American lit-crit academics. And I'll grant you that he may be an acquired taste for puritanical empiricists who mistrust too much sensual, imaginative, and poetic play in their literary puddings—particularly when these occur outside of fiction, and under the auspices of social and aesthetic analysis.

But next time you're in a decent bookstore, sneak a look at the opening paragraph of the first essay in *New Critical Essays*, on the epigrams ("reflections or sentences and maxims") of La Rochefoucauld. And tell me who else among contemporary intellectuals since Eisenstein has exhibited such a rollicking, euphoric style, phrase by phrase, thought by thought.

One shouldn't be put off by the occasional obscurity and/or campiness of Barthes' reference points and apparent subjects. The concept of the critic as some enlightened Buddha of the marketplace, affixing all the proper price tags to consumer items, seems entirely foreign to his talents and temperament. Apart from his early (and now, perhaps, rather dated) defenses of Robbe-Grillet in *Critical Essays*, I can think of few occasions when he's made me want to read or reread other writers, at least right away. Even here, when he deals with the traumas of Flaubert while writing sentences and the names used by Proust, he makes me want to rethink these authors more than reread them.

Somewhat like the late virtuoso jazz pianist Art Tatum, who swamped and devoured any musician he tried to accompany, Barthes' voice is sufficiently mellifluous to crowd out other voices—even the ones he is occasionally called upon to sponsor or introduce. That's why an essay such as "Pierre Loti: *Aziyadé*," the last in this collection—about a writer and book I doubt I'll ever encounter firsthand—comes across not as a gangplank leading to something else, but as a flamboyant, extended circus act in its own right. Consider the opening sentence. which amply explains how film critic Gilbert Adair could once describe Barthes' style to me as creamy:

> In the name Aziyadé, this is what I read and what I hear: first of all the gradual explosion (like a bouquet of fireworks) of the three brightest vowels in the French alphabet (the opening of the vowels = the opening of the lips, of the senses); the caress of the z, the sensuous, plump palitalization of the y, this entire sonorous series sliding and spreading, subtle and rich; next a constellation of islands, stars, peoples, Asia, Georgia, Greece; and then a whole literature: Hugo who in his *Orientales* uses the name Albaydé, and behind Hugo all of philhellene romanticism; Loti, a traveler specializing in the East, the bard of Istanbul; the vague notion of a feminine character (some *Désenchantée*); finally the prejudice of dealing with an insipid, sweetish, old-fashioned novel: in short, from the (sumptuous) signifier to the (paltry) signified, utter disappointment.

If the concluding phrase suggests the circus equivalent of being shot from a cannon onto a tightrope and then leaping from three successive trapezes, only to land in a five-gallon can of Mello Yello, the reader should bear in mind that Barthes intends to build on precisely such an effect. One sentence later, he's suggesting that, "Perhaps we, too, can learn to disappoint the name Aziyadé in the right way and, having slipped from the precious name to the pathetic image of an outdated novel, work our way back to the idea of a text: fragments of the infinite language which tells nothing but in which occurs `something unheard-of and shadowy.'"

Readers who find the above sentence pretentious are cordially invited to check out the essays here on the plates of the *Encyclopedia* and the mythology of Jules Verne, which cheerfully demonstrate just how pretentious *we* can be—and pretentiously misguided—when we think that we're doing simple, mundane things (like having fun). For playful, adventurous readers who like to scavenge as well as savor what they read, *New Critical Essays* is like a small bouquet of eight flowers from the late master, fresh and ready to be mixed into a hardy and heady salad.

Cliff Notes from Mt. Olympus:
Nabokov's *Lectures on Literature*

From the November 26, 1980 Soho News. *For my younger readers, and even for some of my older ones, it might be helpful to add that the "snake oil salesman" alluded to in my final sentence is (or, rather, was) Ronald Reagan. My follow-up review of Nabokov's* Lectures on Russian Literature *(Nov. 17, 1981) can be found on my website.*

Lectures on Literature
By Vladimir Nabokov
Harcourt Brace Jovanovich

"Let us not kid ourselves," intones the tall athletic Russian professor to his students at Cornell. "Let us remember that literature is of no practical value whatsoever, except in the very special case of somebody's wishing to become, of all things, a professor of literature. The girl Emma Bovary never existed; the book *Madame Bovary* shall exist forever and ever. A book lives longer than a girl."

No doubt. And even at the price of four first-run movies, this long-awaited volume of aristocratic riches has got to be the publishing bargain of the year. Comfortably oversized, decked out with plentiful reproductions of the Great Man's notes, annotated teaching copies, diagrams, and sketches, it might be the best analysis of fiction by a practitioner to have come along since *The Lonely Voice*, Frank O'Connor's masterly study of the short story.

Never mind that this is only Part I, with a companion volume on Russian writers still on the way. *[2022: a third volume in the same series on* Don Quixote *was also published.]* These Wellesley and Cornell lectures, delivered between 1941 and 1958 (until the runaway success of *Lolita* finally enabled Nabokov to retire from teaching)—splendidly edited by Fredson Bowers, warmly introduced by

John Updike—offer as good a do-it-yourself course in nineteenth and twentieth century European fiction as a student is likely to find, inside or outside a university.

A control freak who wrote out every lecture word for word, in advance—the same method he employed with interviews (explicated at some length in his collection *Strong Opinions*)—Nabokov was no less exacting in spelling out the precise details of an imaginary location or object. These included the physical layouts of Mansfield Park, Dr. Jekyll's house, the Samsa flat in Kafka's "The Metamorphosis," a Proustian orchard and the "pathetic and tasteless" cap worn by Charles Bovary on his first day of school. Like the diverse routes traced through Dublin and *Ulysses*, these descriptions—careful enough to be drawn in careful sketches—are regarded virtually as prerequisites to serious participation in a fictive space. It's no wonder, then, that Nabokov has so many wisecracks reserved for Freud and Freudians. ("I am interested here in bugs," he says in his Kafka lecture, which decisively proves that Gregor is a beetle and not a cockroach, "not in humbugs.") As a concrete recounter and recaster of dreams himself, he knew his competition when he saw it.

By the same token, he knew quite well who his competition wasn't: "I differ from Joseph Conradically," he asserted in one interview, and equally disassociated himself from "Faulkner's corncobby chronicles," "Mann's asinine *Death in Venice*," and "*Finnegans Wake*, that petrified superpun."

§

Much of the time, as Updike points out, we are simply being read to—but read to by someone whose selections and commentary constitute a very personalized reading. Nabokov's *Bleak House* is a Dickens quite deliberately shorn of social significance, through a series of quick, snooty exclusions that often register like an emigré crank's major defense against the vicissitudes of troublesome history. Satire is meaningful only insofar as it transcends and outlasts its objects, while "study of the sociological or political impact of literature has to be devised mainly for those who are by temperament or education immune to the aesthetic vibrancy of authentic literature."

One suspects that Nabokov, who had the politics (or nonpolitics, depending on the church of your choice) of an upper-class snob, would have felt little kinship with the Russian Formalists. Yet the whimsical accuracy of his formal observations is often no less apt and eclectic than theirs. Charles' cap and the Bovary house in Yonville are described in the form of a layer cake; to trace the movement of Fanny's emotions in *Mansfield Park*, Jane Austen "uses a device that I call the knight's move, a term from chess."

No less acute are discussions of Flaubert's uses of counterpoint, structural transitions, an "unfolding method of description" (a bit like the layer cake), the French imperfect tense, and "the word *and* preceded by a semicolon"— potentially difficult or elusive aspects of form or style that the Master makes easy through the tempered grace of his exposition.

§

Not all these lectures are equally inspired. (The one on Proust—limited by the fact that the accompanying class assignment was to read only the first of the novel's seven volumes—is a distinct disappointment.) None was prepared for publication by Nabokov himself, and a certain lack of satisfying completion seems to hover over a few, including those on Dickens and Stevenson.

My own favorites are the extraordinary examinations of *Madame Bovary* and "The Metamorphosis," which seem to engage the greatest number of Nabokov's talents and emotions. Both emerge as occasions for the lecturer's deeply felt hatred for mediocrity on all levels. In the case of the Kafka tale, the reading is built as methodically as a legal brief. "Let us first of all study every detail in this story; the general idea will come of itself later when we have all the data we need." By the time Nabokov arrives at his critical epiphany, the preparatory work makes it shine with absolute conviction: "Here is a point to be observed with care and love. Gregor is a human being in an insect's disguise; his family are insects disguised as people."

His patient, chapter-by-chapter appreciation of *Ulysses*—first in his personal pantheon of twentieth century prose masterpieces (followed by "The Metamorphosis," Bely's *Petersburg*, and "the first half of Proust's fairy tale")— runs a close third to his empathetic treatments of Flaubert and Kafka. Here his discourse is enlivened by the most commonsensical caveats and objections.

Part 2, Chapter 4, of *Ulysses*, set in newspaper offices, "seems to me to be poorly balanced, and Stephen's contribution to it is not especially witty. You may peruse it with a skimming eye." And the mixing and intertwining of "the theme of sex" and "the theme of the latrine" in *Ulysses*—which, in my own college days, once made Ted Weiss refer to readers of that book as "conno-sewers"—is criticized not for its frankness but for its lack of verisimilitude, assuming that Leopold Bloom "is supposed to be a rather ordinary citizen".

If there's a more reasonable way of dealing with the literal overflow of Joyce, I don't know what it is. In fact, if one were trying to define what a cultivated sense of civilization consists of—a utopian task, perhaps, in a country poised on the brink of investing its future in a snake oil salesman—one could conceivably do worse than cite such a distinction.

Reading about Looking and Looking at Reading: Review of *Camera Lucida* and *If on a Winter's Night a Traveler*

From The Soho News, *August 18, 1981 issue. I was pleased to hear from Susan Sontag that this was one of my pieces that she clipped.*

Camera Lucida: Reflections on Photography
By Roland Barthes
Translated by Richard Howard
Hill and Wang, $10.95.

If on a Winter's Night a Traveler
By Italo Calvino
Translated by William Weaver
Harcourt Brace Jovanovich, $12.95

In most bookstores, the new Barthes and Calvino books stare at one another like mutually envious friends in their separate ghettos, eyeing one another across a great divide and empty space: the social space separating essay from fiction.

Barthes' grief-stricken gaze at photography sees beyond it to his own desire, then sees beyond that desire to the hypothetical Proustian (or Jamesian) novel he will never write—a nervous gaze that leaps like a butterfly across a crowded garden, never lingering with any simple petal-like photo for long, frustrated and impatient at the uselessness of this activity in summoning back his beloved mother. Calvino's chipper, common-sensical look at the erotics of reading—the same subject addressed in Barthes' *The Pleasure of the Text*, but approached here in the form of a love story—is more steady and measured and continuous, seeing only one brightly suspended plot after another, each one pulled out like colored scarves from a magician's hat—each another sign that you can always shake away the blues if only you can convince yourself that there's always another scarf to pull.

Calvino, with all his unfinished miniplots, never quite gets around to starting the essay about fiction and narrative he wants to write. Barthes, with all his unfinished miniessays (a crystalline form developed in the aphoristic formats of all his late books, where characteristically each paragraph—rather than, say, each sentence or page—offers a fresh beginning), never quite manages to start the novel about his own life that his writing has been flirting with for years. ("It must all be considered as if spoken by a character in a novel," reads the handwritten inscription that opens the *mise en scène* and *mise en page* of *Roland Barthes by Roland Barthes*, only four pages away from Barthes at age ten clinging to his mother, in a photograph captioned, "The demand for love.")

If on a Winter's Night a Traveler is an interesting title for what Calvino's novel keeps shrouded in darkness, an ellipsis with seemingly infinite tacked-on extensions, a way to begin all over again. *Camera Lucida: Reflections on Photography* (or *La Chambre Claire: Note sur la photographie*, in the original), on the contrary, promises the closure of light and clarity, the framing of an end that encloses the bright self like a coffin.

"You are about to begin Italo Calvino's new novel, If on a winter's night a traveler," starts you-know-who at the beginning of you-know-what. "Relax. Concentrate. Dispel every other thought. Let the world around you fade." Just like a movie, whose nonstop pacing Calvino at every point seems to be emulating. "Such are the two ways of the Photograph," concludes Barthes at the end of his last (nonposthumous) book. "The choice is mine: to subject its spectacle to the civilized code of perfect illusions, or to confront in it the wakening of intractable reality."

Criticizing "A Sign in Space" in Calvino's *Cosmicomics* because it "comes perilously close to being altogether too reverent an obeisance to semiology," Gore Vidal signals the influence of later Barthes that imposes itself no less insistently on *If on a Winter's Night a Traveler*. Barthes, returning the regard, refers to Calvino near the end of *Camera Lucida*—specifically "what Calvino calls `the true, total photograph,'" which, Barthes explains, identifies reality with truth, "becomes at once evidential and exclamative" and "bears the effigy to that crazy point where affect (love, compassion, grief, enthusiasm, desire) is a guarantee of Being. It then approaches, to all intents, madness; it joins what Kristeva calls "la vérité folle." Some fun, this "true, total photograph," which

Barthes makes sound like a snake consuming its own tail—which may actually describe his own giddy practice in *Camera Lucida* better than Calvino's.

Each section of *Camera Lucida* (half as long a book as Calvino's novel, though it has twice as many chapters, four dozen in all) begins with the drama of Barthes "happening upon" a photograph—a narrative event that gives us all the roomy lassitude of an event in a novel by James or Proust. In Part I, this is a picture of Napoleon's youngest brother, Jerome, which makes Barthes reflect with amazement that he is looking at eyes that looked at the Emperor. Part II, "Chapter" 25, makes a quantum leap to Barthes' alienated responses to pictures of his mother shortly after her death, his consternation that these photographs refused (objectively speaking) to speak. Neither Jerome nor Mme. Barthes appear photographically in *Camera Lucida* (although the latter, as noted above, figures at the beginning of *Roland Barthes by Roland Barthes*), and, like much of *A Lover's Discourse*, the form of personal disclosure employed has a lot to do with indirection.

Studium and *punctum* are the key Latin terms in Barthes' phenomenological musings about his own experiences of certain photographs (most of which are reproduced)—the first comprising "application to a thing...a kind of general, enthusiastic commitment," the second consisting of "that accident" in a photograph "which pricks me (but also bruises me, is poignant to me)." Not so much an erotics of seeing, exactly, as a dynamics of sight that includes the studying gaze as well as the piercing revelation.

Barthes uses the terms to stand for the dialectical registers of the spectatorial consciousness—much as *plaisir* (pleasure) and *jouissance* (bliss or coming) are used in *The Pleasure of the Text* to stand for dialectical registers of reading consciousness. Here, however, the notions of *plaisir* and *jouissance* play a more problematical role. There's less of the kind of play that's reflected in Calvino's sexy narrative glosses on earlier Barthes, where he appears to be representing via his characters the "readerly text" (as two readers who are lovers) and the "writerly text" (as a reader and writer who are potential lovers):

> Lovers, reading of each other's bodies (of that concentrate of mind and body which lovers use to go to bed together) differs from the reading of written pages in that it is not linear. It starts at any point, skips, repeats itself, goes backward, insists, ramifies in simultaneous and divergent messages, converges again, has moments of irritation, turns the page, finds its place, gets lost. A direction can be recognized in it, route to an end, since it tends toward a climax, and with this end

in view it arranges rhythmic phrases, metrical scansions, recurrence of motives....

...What makes lovemaking and reading resemble each other most is that within both of them times and spaces open, different from measurable time and space.

At times I am gripped by an absurd desire: that the sentence I am about to write be the one the woman is reading at the same moment. The idea mesmerizes me so much that I convince myself it is true: I write the sentence hastily, get up, go to the window, train my spyglass to check the effect of my sentence in her gaze, in the curl of her lips, in the cigarette she lights, in the shifts of her body in the deck chair, in her legs, which she crosses or extends.

Wasn't it Barthes himself who compared narrative to both striptease and the Oedipal search, suggesting that all three activities were closely related? But words are infinitely extendable, like sections on a train or strips of film, while still photographic images are closed and final—one thing accounting for the different tempers of these beautiful, related, and irreconcilable books.

Excremental Visionary [on John Waters' *Shock Value*]

From The Soho News *(September 22, 1981).*

Shock Value: A Tasteful Book about Bad Taste
By John Waters
Delta

If conventional means wedded to conventions, then John Waters, amiable sleaze director of *Pink Flamingos*, *Female Trouble*, and *Polyester*, is as conventional as you or I, maybe even more so. The not-so-surprising thing about *Shock Value*, a "tasteful" (meaning cautious) memoir about his special brand of bad taste, is that it proves him to be literary, too—at least in a minor Mark Twain vein. Pithy aphorisms rub shoulders with sly asides and wry homilies. Here are a few jewels among gritty jewels:

All people look better under arrest.

I never watch television because it's an ugly piece of furniture, gives off a hideous light, and, besides, I'm against free entertainment.

Since the character [in *Female Trouble*] turns from teenage delinquent to mugger, prostitute, unwed mother, child abuser, fashion model, nightclub entertainer, murderess, and jailbird, I felt at last Divine had a role she could sink her teeth into.

Sometimes I just sit on the street and wait for something awful to happen.

The more obscure a town I visit, the greater appeal it has for me, since I figure there's an audience for anything in New York, but if you can get a following in, say, Mobile, Alabama, you really must be doing something right.

Since [the Hanafi Muslim sect] had given the ultimate bad movie reviews by killing people to protest the showing of *Mohammad, Messenger of God*, one could only tremble at the thought of what they might have pulled had they seen, say, *The Deep*.

I think it's healthy to see your parents often (sort of a tune-up), but I think it's neurotic to actually hang around with them.

A Grove Press freak around the same time that he was getting expelled from NYU for a pot bust, Waters has a flaky imagination that is often furnished by the conceits of Genet and Burroughs. The former is undoubtedly responsible for both the moniker of Divine (his principal star, a larger-than-life drag queen—described as a she or he according to context) and the equally passionate "crime is beauty" poetics of Waters' masterpiece and concerto for Divine, *Female Trouble*. It was Genet, after all, who once defined art as the capacity to make you eat shit and like it—which is just what Divine visibly does with dog crap in the celebrated and climactic showstopper of *Pink Flamingos*. William S. Burroughs, on the other hand, who offers a blurb on the back of *Shock Value*, can easily be detected in a passage like the following, which describes a Baltimore dusk-to-dawn kung-fu grindhouse so scuzzy and violent that even Waters stays away:

I've always imagined huge crowds inside, some shooting up, others guzzling from brown paper bags. Hopped-up ushers patrol with nightsticks instead of flashlights and break up popcorn-snatchings, switchblade fights, and gang bangs. The audience pelts the screen with leftovers from the day's robberies and breaks into karate fights whenever Bruce Lee appears on the screen. Driven to hysteria by all the gore, they take audience participation to new heights by stabbing and shooting one another, all in the name of entertainment.

Unlike Genet or Burroughs, Waters can't really be considered a tough customer. There is nothing at all in *Shock Value* about his sex life and sexual preferences, for instance, or the charming ten-minute exploitation spin-off he shot in 1970 called *The Diane Linklater Story*. But you can learn all you want to about how the uglier shock effects in his low-budget movies are achieved.

As it happens, the shit-eating in *Pink Flamingos* is real, while the shit-stain on Divine's underpants when (through the miracle of the medium) he fucks himself in *Female Trouble* is fake. Yet one suspects that if the reverse were true, no essential facet of Waters' aesthetics would be violated. Regarding vomit, he freely admits that after prolonged efforts to get Divine to barf for real in his movies, he finally had to simulate the desired act with a can of creamed corn, some catsup, and a little water. (Can we possibly find it in our hearts to forgive him?) After commenting rather eruditely on the importance of vomit in Swedish films of the '60s, he roundly condemns "films such as *An Unmarried Woman* for including vomit scenes that are patently unauthentic."

Despite these and other fixations, it's pretty evident throughout that Waters cares more about people than he does about either puke or pimples. And, grotesque as it may seem, the other film director's autobiography that *Shock Value* most reminds me of is Jean Renoir's *My Life and My Films*—in part because of its rich and diverse enjoyment of human nature. Renoir often appreciates friends for their animal natures; Waters is thrilled by a mean, toothless hillbilly woman glaring at Perrier bottles in a supermarket, "unable to contain her rage that somebody was stupid enough to buy water." "Look at those disgusting trees stealing my oxygen!" shrieks Mink Stole as she speeds down the highway in *Desperate Living*—the only major Waters movie without Divine, hence missing what F.R. Leavis would call a moral center. But look at all the other Waters regulars congregating around the edges—from the hideously made-up Susan Lowe to the batty and babbly Edith Massey to the 400-pound Jean Hill—and they embody a moral universe of some ferocity, one that Waters ultimately backs to the hilt.

A line from the synopsis of *Female Trouble* oddly evokes the tortured world of *A Confederacy of Dunces*: "Taffy grows into a severely maladjusted young lady, tracks down her father and kills him, and in one final act of rebellion turns Hare Krishna to get on her mother's nerves." Perhaps more significant is the fact that for Waters, "the most chic and glamorous" opening of the film was in the Baltimore City Hall Jail, which had previously allowed him to shoot on the premises, and that the response of the prisoners to the movie "would mean a lot more to me than the *New York Times* review." "*Multiple Maniacs* really helped me to flush Catholicism out of my system, but I don't think you ever can lose it completely," begins one paragraph, which ends, "Being Catholic always makes you more theatrical." In a way, Waters seems about as socially well-adjusted as Salvador Dali and the late Flannery O'Connor, two other excremental Catholic visionaries and gifted, gabby self-publicists with a taste for violent splash. He almost gives the whole game away when he describes shooting a scene in

Female Trouble in which Divine, Cookie Mueller, and Susan Walsh cut their fingers with a razor to pledge their "sisterhood". One of the actresses, he reports, got too carried away, cut too deeply, and passed out as soon as the take was over; but this scene was cut out of the final film because the shadow of the mic was visible. In other words, blood runs deep, but illusionism in a Waters movie runs still deeper. He's still assuring readers in the last paragraph of the book that he only thinks terrible thoughts, he doesn't live them—an American transcendentalist through and through.

In spite of the author's cheerful morbidity about following and aesthetically relishing trials and violent crimes (he boasts ordering tapes of the mass suicides in Guyana through a *New York Times* ad, and playing them at his parties when he wants his guests to leave), he turns out to be an old-fashioned humanist, too. Significantly, in my favorite chapter, "Baltimore, Maryland—Hairdo Capital of the World," which clarifies his vision of the world as much as anything does, he allots roughly equal space to Mrs. Mac, the Rat Lady—a black woman who goes out every day in her Ratmobile to hunt down and exterminate slum rodents—and William Donald Schaeffer, the mayor, both of whom he clearly reveres. He's never more American—at least in the home-grown, naïve sense—than when he claims to be apolitical. At the Berlin Film Festival, he tells us, the "buffs are unbelievably serious and went crazy when I told them my films aren't political. 'Yes they ARE!!' they screamed, and I backed off a little; I guess you can read anything you want into a screenplay."

Nonsense. The anarchist delirium of *Pink Flamingos* and *Female Trouble*— more relevant to life, I would think, than to art—is as wide as Waters' aesthetic range as a filmmaker is narrow. As a writer, though, he belongs strictly to the mainstream. The truth of the matter is that Waters is a fellow who picks up the same sort of maladjusted strays that a Reaganite would quickly consign to the incinerator—a moralist with some wit who not only protects and nurtures these strays but also organizes them (see *Desperate Living*), respects them, and trains them, allows them to grow teeth, and enables them to fight back. John Waters not political? Give me a break.

Michael Snow

From Omni *(September 1983). An oversight prevented me from including this in a previous collection of mine,* Cinematic Encounters: Interviews and Dialogues. *Like most of my other pieces for* Omni, *it charts my efforts to introduce experimental work to a mainstream audience.*

For a conceptual artist who's more often concerned with representation than with straight entertainment, Canadian filmmaker Michael Snow can be a pretty jokey fellow. In fact, of all the avant-garde artists I know, he may well be the one who laughs the most and the hardest. His longest and craziest movie—the 260-minute, encyclopedic *"Rameau's Nephew"* by *Diderot (Thanx to Dennis Young) by Wilma Schoen*—contains a grab bag of assorted puns, puzzles, and adages, from lines like "eating is believing" and "hearing is deceiving" to a mad tea party where words and sentences recited backward are then reversed to sound vaguely intelligible. Even "Wilma Schoen" in the title is an anagram for Snow's name. One of his shortest works, the eight-minute *Two Sides to Every Story*, is projected on two back-to-back screens, simultaneously showing the same events in the same room from opposite angles.

Just as typical, in the living room of Snow's house in Toronto, where I recently interviewed him, is a front door that isn't in use—or rather is in use, but not as a front door. Over the side facing inside the room is a life-size color photograph of a painting of the same door. A concept of a front door in place of a real one? A statement about representation instead of a portal to walk through? Perhaps a bit of both. But there's another detail in the photograph that makes the whole thing funnier and stranger: a gigantic hand in the foreground holding a lit match. This image is many times larger than life, totally contradicting the supposed equivalence between the real door and the represented door.

Perceptual and conceptual gags of this kind abound in Snow's work. Sometimes they're amazingly literal: After making an epic film trilogy in the late Sixties and early Seventies about possible ways of moving the camera—zooming, panning back and forth, and rotating every which way—he built a set on rollers for a section of another film (*Presents*, 1981). Then he used a couple of forklifts to jerk the whole flimsy construction to and fro so that the camera wouldn't have to budge an inch. In the ensuing slapstick mayhem (a needle on a Bach record skips wildly, walls and furniture shake, objects crash to the floor, actors are buffeted about), something about the perception of movement—as well as the intimate relationship between creation and destruction—is being explored.

Just a few short subway stops away from Snow's house is the best known and most popular of all his works, *Flight Stop*. It isn't a movie, but it makes many people think of one. Located in the largest enclosed shopping mall on the continent, Eaton Center, which reportedly attracts more visitors annually than Niagara Falls, this photographic sculpture consists of sixty fiberglass geese, each suspended from three wires and glued to a contoured photograph of a real goose. Extended over about six stories, the geese seem to be landing in formation, and there's something eerily cinematic about the overall spread, as if each bird were a separate stop-frame in a dispersed simulation of animated flight.

For epic visual breadth, perhaps the only Snow creation to rival *Flight Stop* is the three-hour film, *La Région Centrale* (*The Central Region*, 1971), in which a computer-operated camera spins in endlessly changing configurations around an uninhabited mountain landscape in northern Quebec. It probably wouldn't be an exaggeration to call this film one of Snow's least popular works—it certainly has the fewest laughs. But that's largely because it's so scary. There's a direct assault on the senses, including one's center of gravity, as the flip-flopping camera makes circular patterns at variable speeds that no human being could possibly duplicate, producing an experience roughly akin to riding a demonic ferris wheel. "I wanted to make the film a condensed day," Snow explained. "It isn't, really, but it does start in daylight, and then there's sunset and sunrise, and it's over at something like eleven."

In order to make the film, Snow enlisted the help of Montreal technician Pierre Abeloos, who designed a machine that used audio tapes to program the camera's 360-degree movements without any direct human contact. Then Snow went out looking for a wild location, where nothing man-made was visible, finally settling on an area near Sept-Iles, on the Gulf of St. Lawrence. Renting a helicopter, he flew there with three crew members, installed Abeloos's machine on a remote mountain plateau, and hid from camera range with the others for five cold days in September while the film was being shot.

Why was it so vital to have nothing human either in front of the camera or behind it? "On the one hand, I wanted to have the machine make the film," Snow told me. "But on the other hand, I wanted to make what you see more yours than the cameraman's or the director's, in a way. Even though the height of the camera is the usual human standing height, five feet or so, it makes for a kind of experience that's not anthropomorphic; it's an experience that comes explicitly from the machinery."

"Ultimately," Snow went on, "the director or the artist is removed just one step in this particular case. Because it *is* directed. And it *is* controlled. But the control is not that control of directing your heartstrings. It makes the wilderness yours in one sense, because there's such a distance between the means of recording it and the kind of thing that the wilderness is. And it also brings into question the whole process of the perception of nature."

Forever resourceful in reusing material, Snow later remounted Abeloos's machine in a video-installation piece with four monitors. "The camera goes in the center and you can set it for different patterns. It's really nice; the National Gallery of Canada bought it. It's called *De là* [*From There*]. Obviously it's a completely different thing from the film, because you get involved in watching the machine move and seeing the kind of drawing that it makes on the monitors, relating the movement to the kinds of images that are produced."

Something of a prankster and philosopher at the same time, Snow, in his mid-fifties, has a flair for starting off with an unlikely or outrageous idea and somehow making it work. In his first major film (*Wavelength*, 1967), forty-odd minutes long, he begins with a stuttering camera zoom across an eighty-foot Manhattan loft: not much action, as most movies go, but he uses this central concept like a clothesline on which to hang abstract notions about space, time, color, waves, death, storytelling, and representation. (Characteristically, the shooting took him a week and the editing, a couple of weeks, "but I did spend a lot of time musing—a year.") In Snow's most recent film (*So Is This*, 1982), with roughly the same running time, he has the brass to fill his silent screen with nothing but one printed word after another; his imagination and resources keep audiences amused and involved all the way through.

How does he pack so much into so little? In *Wavelength*, the zoom's journey across the loft—joined on the soundtrack by a sine wave gradually moving from its lowest note to its highest—starts uneventfully. But as the camera approaches the four double windows and intervening wall space of the other side of the loft, a man is heard breaking into the building and walking upstairs. He staggers into the frame and drops dead on the floor—just before the zoom blithely lurches past him. Still later, a woman enters, discovers the moribund body, and phones her boyfriend while the camera steadily approaches one of the photographs posted on the central wall space. The photo proves to be a picture of sea waves. The sound of an approaching police siren merges with the sine wave, which by now has risen from 50 to 12,000 cycles per second.

As prosaic as all this sounds, Snow has been passing his painterly image through many changes along the way. He uses a variety of color filters, film stocks, superimposed flashbacks of earlier stages in the zoom, and qualities and degrees of processing and light exposure to keep the film moving like a kaleidoscope; yet it seems to be practically standing still. (Many of the same technical variations in *Wavelength* are used to comparably fluid effect on the single words in *So Is This*.) In Snow's elegant description of the movie's progress, "The space starts at the camera's—spectator's—eye, is in the air, then is on the screen, then is within the screen—the mind." He has also described the film as a "pun on the room-length zoom to the photo of sea waves, through the light waves, and on the sound waves."

A simpler and wittier forward camera movement defines a 1976 Snow short called either *Breakfast* or *Table Top Dolly*. In this case, a camera fronted by a sheet of see-through plastic slowly creeps across a table, converting an artistic still-life of groceries—eggs, orange juice, sugar, Dixie cup, plates, and fruit—into a sticky, gooey mass of garbage while the sounds of dishwashing are heard offscreen. A movie about consumption? If eating is believing and hearing is deceiving, you'd better believe it.

Program Notes for the North American Theatrical Premiere of
The Tiger of Eschnapur & The Indian Tomb (Sept. 14, 1983)

On January 3, 1978, during my first visit back to London after moving from there to San Diego in early 1977, I attended a private screening at the British Film Institute of glorious new prints of Fritz Lang's Indian films. Three years later, when I was invited to program "Buried Treasures" at the Toronto Festival of Festivals, I was delighted to be able to book these prints and thus hold what I believe was the North American premiere of Fritz Lang's penultimate films in their original versions, uncut and subtitled in English rather than dubbed. Luckily, Film Forum's Karen Cooper attended this screening, and two years later, when she booked these prints for a theatrical run, she commissioned me to write this.

First of all, three very dissimilar quotes:

1) "Every filmmaker, in a sense, defines the essence of cinema, but is there another for whom it is so nakedly, and so unequivocally, as with Lang, the ultimate metaphor?...With Lang, what else can one speak about but a vision of a vision? This does not imply a pointless duplication in which Lang's art fritters itself away, enmeshed in its own rhythm; on the contrary, it broadens the horizon in all directions, and validates Lang's answer to the question, 'What is the most indispensable quality for a filmmaker?': 'He must know life.' Life, here, should be understood as the locus within which vision is exercised. There remains the question of what lies behind this word 'vision', exactly what power Lang invests it with, and in what form it appears, tangibly or intangibly.

"Herein lies the explanation for the enthusiasm, inexplicable to some, of certain Lang admirers for his last three films. Filmed in Germany, using a theme and stories from his early period, by a man made master of fiction in all its guises by his American experience, *The Tiger of Eschnapur*, *The Indian Tomb*, and *The 1000 Eyes of Dr. Mabuse* present the paradox of being at once remarkably veiled and disconcertingly open. Seemingly naive, almost puerile—particularly in the case of the Indian diptych, since a certain grave urgency of theme may be glimpsed beneath the serial conventions and inconsequence of the last Mabuse film—these films, theoretical in the extreme, discard the reassuring alibi of the American tradition while simultaneously transposing the tradition's basic artificiality to a Germany where nothing has survived: they repudiate the positive aspects of the myths underlying Lang's German period, reducing them to their own level within a dual adventure, individual and collective, involving the cinema and historical awareness. With exceptional integrity, this destructive-reflective irony of Lang's toys with the hackneyed stories placed at his disposal, seemingly in derisory fidelity to himself...As for the two Indian films, dazzling moments flitting through precariousness, they tell only of a fine and judicious persistence in which despair surfaces, in which the mise en scène, and even the very idea of mise en scène, looms, as Blanchot said of writing, in the silence that envelops it, a sundering of the elements which compose it, an inability to lie carried to the point of tragedy."

—Raymond Bellour, 1966

2) "Fritz Lang has a morality of iron, one feels that in each of his shots and his camera placements, but one also feels that in his relations with his producers; he's the only one who succeeds in making a super-production that isn't a super-product. *Der Tiger von Eschnapur* and *Das Indische Grabnal* are the only films that are super-productions without being super-products, which are made with all the money that he had at his disposal without creating a smokescreen. And which nevertheless are not made against money; because now, that's easier to do: Godard, in his evolution, has discovered that it is necessary to make oppositional films. But for a man of Fritz Lang's generation, this wasn't possible, an idea like that. And yet he succeeded in making these two films, where he really gave something to the Germans who had been dying of hunger for so many years—since '33 and even before '33, up to the Wahrungs-Reform for which the leftist intellectuals had so much contempt, until the moment when the people would begin again to be able to know a little what it meant to live: this is what has been called the German economic miracle. For a good many people, this was the first time that they finally revived, that they were eating normally—of course there was the speculation and all the rest, okay. (The arrival of the consumer society, that's the negative aspect of it.) But Fritz Lang, at this moment, made something for the people that

was a gift, let's say, of gold. Without it being a golden calf. That's the important thing. Anyone else would have made a golden calf. The producer was really eager to make a golden calf. Fritz Lang made a film."

—Jean-Marie Straub, 1970

3) "If you respect the Fritz Lang who made *M* and *You Only Live Once*, if you enjoy the excesses of style and the magnificent absurdities of a film like *Metropolis*, then it is only good sense to reject the ugly stupidity of *Journey to the Lost City*. It is an insult to an artist to praise his bad work along with his good; it indicates that you are incapable of judging either."

—Pauline Kael, 1963

Why has it taken almost a quarter of a century for Fritz Lang's penultimate films to open in the U.S. in their original form? A key work (albeit an off-key one) by a great director, Lang's Indian diptych confounds most critical categories by playing both ends against the middle—yielding a deliberately "unsophisticated" film by one of the most sophisticated of all filmmakers, and one made without the slightest trace of condescension for its audience. Created for children and undiscriminating adults, *Der Tiger von Eschnapur* and *Das Indische Grabnal* has succeeded in Europe with both popular audiences and an intellectual minority—and languished in obscurity, to the best of my knowledge, everywhere else. (In the U.S. and England, it has previously shown only in a dubbed, mutilated and re-edited version known respectively as *Journey to the Lost City* and *Tiger of Bengal*, 95 minutes long—which is less than half the length of the 198 minute original.) In the distances formed between the three critical statements cited above, particularly between the first two and the third, a cultural gap of a good deal more than just twenty-odd years and the Atlantic Ocean can be felt. If we are to understand the passion for conceptualism and abstraction in Bellour's appreciation, the moral and national-historical fervor of Straub's testimony, and the no less characteristic mistrust of or disinterest in these qualities in Kael's curt dismissal—it becomes necessary to see these films in all their contradictory uniqueness and paradoxical magnificence, without oversimplifying the case made by any of these three positions.

In support of Kael's verdict, it might be noted that Lang himself expressed ambivalence towards his Indian films. *[2012 postscript: The late David Overbey, a friend of Lang's in his late years, told me that Lang would routinely refer to these films as "that Indian shit."]* And we must acknowledge that the films abound with the sort of unpolished artifice that we associate with Grade-Z serials: an Indian princess (Debra Paget) dressed in snazzy Folies-Bergères outfits; a fake cobra moved about with less-than-invisible wires; a glimpsed human frame operating a tiger suit; lepers who come straight from central casting; an implausible plot kept moving by divine intervention and obscure psychological motivations. On the other hand, it should be stressed that (a) despite Kael's qualms about insulting artists, she is all too willing to settle here for a grotesque travesty version of the film that Lang himself categorically disowned, and (b) whatever the amusement potential of Lang's pasteboard melodramatics, the films do not qualify as camp in the manner of, say, *Cobra Woman* or *Glen or Glenda?*, where the sheer unshakable conviction of Maria Montez in the former and Edward D. Wood Jr. in the latter becomes the source of hilarity. On the contrary, apart from the crudeness of a few special effects, the Indian films project a naïveté that is anything but inadvertent—a *knowing* naïveté that needs to be recognized and discussed as such, on its own terms.

A few words about the films' origins: After shooting his last American film, *Beyond a Reasonable Doubt*, in 1956, Lang travelled to India with the hopes of making a film called *Taj-Mahal*, which foundered over casting problems (spurred, according to Lang, by the different ideals of beauty in the West and the East). A couple of years later, he received an offer from a German producer to remake a film which he and Thea von Harbou had scripted and prepared in 1920 for producer-director Joe May—a film which Lang had intended to direct himself, but which was directed instead by May. Agreeing to adapt his original script, Lang returned to Germany and worked on what was almost certainly his most lavish production since the 1927 *Metropolis*—shot over 89 days, 27 of them in India (modest next to the 310 days and 60 nights of shooting on *Metropolis*, but unquestionably a luxury after his two decades in Hollywood).

Committed to sensual pleasure in a way that *Beyond a Reasonable Doubt* and *The 1000 Eyes of Dr. Mabuse* clearly are not, *The Tiger of Eschnapur* and *The Indian Tomb* thus hark back to the origins of Lang's career—or at least the earliest part of that career that we still have access to [in 1983], the 1919-20 two-part *Die Spinnen* (*The Spiders*), shown at Film Forum four years ago. In order to pursue this pleasure, we and Lang alike have to submit to a willful second childhood, a reinvention of the magic of the "fever dream" and the endless serial. And if Lang's subsequent *1000 Eyes* is morosely post-TV, his Indian films are triumphant pre-TV in form as well as substance. The difference between *Raiders of the Lost Ark* and the Indian films is the difference between engineering and architecture (and it is important to recall that Lang, the only son of an architect, originally planned to follow in his father's footsteps).

Spielberg/Lucas construct an engine to get us as efficiently as possible, in bite-size TV units, to nowhere in particular, shedding images like petals en route. Lang, more interested (like his villains) in foundations that last—images and ideas alike—builds a temple (or tomb) around these ancient supports. Working in a genre that he all but invented himself half a century earlier, he allows his taste for design to fester in every shot—whether it's getting his hero to smash together two red-turbaned heads, comic-book style, in the opening sequence, dressing his heroine in polka dots, or filling his geometrical décors with other obsessively repetitive patterns. The result is a kind of dream architecture, a pulp India where all the characters become lost in one another's obsessions.

Lang's last German films are obsessed with representation (reflections in pools, one-way mirrors, TV monitors) and the communication and non-communication existing between cells in a vast human beehive, comprising the outer limits of a bleak moral universe. (Even the spider's web in *The Indian Tomb*, an instance of divine intervention, seems to reproduce this pattern in miniature.) In *The 1000 Eyes*, this universe becomes a nightmare organization of total surveillance. In the sunnier Indian films, it is mainly split between fairy-tale simplicities above ground and social/aesthetic abstractions underground (a tribe of repressed lepers, printed arrows, and a labyrinth of crumbling narrative and architectural foundations which become atomized and disassociated from one another, without the unifying gaze of a Mabuse)—an odd truce between innocence and apocalypse, between the birth and death of storytelling. Spectators who can't respond comfortably to the more contemporary cardboard décors of *Hammett* and *Querelle*—perhaps because they need to be anchored by pseudo-realistic settings—aren't likely to feel any better inside Fritz Lang's head twenty-odd years ago. But those who choose to linger for awhile ("What is an hour in the history of the universe? We have plenty of time...") and listen to Lang's *1001 Nights* may possibly wind up suspecting that his subterranean caverns comprise the only cave in movies worthy of Plato's.

Olaf Stapledon: The Father of Modern Science Fiction

Published under a pseudonym in the August 1985 issue of High Times. *The reason for the pseudonym was my unhappiness with the editor's thoughtless editing; I've tried to repair some of the damage here, and have added a few tweaks and updates.*

Stapledon's work has garnered much more attention since 1985, including a book by Leslie Fiedler, and all the fiction discussed here is currently in print. Dover has excellent editions pairing Last and First Men *with* Star Maker *and* Odd John *with* Sirius, *and* An Olaf Stapledon Reader *(1997) includes all of* The Flames *and samplings from the others. I don't have much to say here about* Odd John *(celebrated elsewhere, in my coedited* Movie Mutations*), but this novel may serve as the best single introduction to Stapledon's work. However, having recently seen the late Jóhann Jóhannsson's experimental feature loosely based on* Last and First Men *(2020), I wonder if that might serve the same function. On the other hand (reflecting now with some light skepticism in 2022), I suspect that Stapledon's reduced literary status largely stems from his pedestrian prose style. If only he could have written like Ray Bradbury, we'd have something much easier to cherish.*

Without Olaf Stapledon (1886-1950), science fiction classics as diverse as *Childhood's End, Dune,* the *Foundation* trilogy, *Methuselah's Children, More Than Human, The Sirens of Titan, Solaris,* and *2001: A Space Odyssey* might never have existed. No one in the whole field of science fiction has worked on as broad a canvas—the remaining history of mankind (*Last and First Men*), the birth and death of the cosmos (*Star Maker*)—or delved into such mystical, arcane matters as the psychology and aesthetics of stars in their dancing orbits, or plant men who function as vegetables by day and as animals by night.

More ambitious, far-reaching and mind-boggling than any other SF practitioner, this English philosophy teacher and leftist who died thirty-five years ago is still far from becoming a household name, either in the U.S. or England. But there are plenty of signs that an awakened interest is finally beginning to take hold. Two excellent book-length studies have appeared in this country over the past three years, and about ten years ago, one English enthusiast, Harvey Satty, announced the formation of an Olaf Stapledon Society. One also finds the author's name cropping up in unexpected places—from the Phil Kaufman remake of *Invasion of the Body*

Snatchers, where Veronica Cartwright recommends *Star Maker* to a Bellicec Mud Bath customer as "must reading" to Saul Bellow's *Mr. Sammler's Planet,* whose eponymous hero discusses and claims to have known Stapledon.

Over half a century ago, when Stapledon's first novel was published in 1930—a "history" of the remaining two billion years of mankind entitled *Last and First Men*—he certainly had more clout in the higher literary circles. Arnold Bennett, Winston Churchill, Alfred Kazin, J.B. Priestly, V.S. Pritchett, Hugh Walpole, and H.G. Wells all expressed admiration for this strange fruit from a late-blooming author, who was already well into his mid-forties when he started writing fiction. "No other book had a greater influence on my life," Arthur C. Clarke would say later—an admission borne out in his most ambitious fictions, *Childhood's End* and *The City and the Stars,* as well as *2001: A Space Odyssey;* and Stapledon's subsequent *Star Maker* would draw a fan letter from no less than Virginia Woolf.

In its totality, *Last and First Men* tells a story, and a sadly elegaic one, about "this brief music that was man"—but it is a story in which whole eons of individual generations often take on the qualities of single characters. And the plot takes many unexpected turns: the Second Men, for example, emerge about 98,000 years in the future, after a global holocaust reduces the world population to thirty-five people who happened to be around the North Pole at the time.

Stapledon followed up *Last and First Men* with an inferior sequel, *Last Men in London* (1932), in which the same Neptunian narrator takes up temporary mental residence in an individual in present-day England. Then came a more conventionally plotted science fiction novel on the superman theme, *Odd John: A Story Between Jest and Earnest* (1935), which remains possibly his best-known work. His greatest work, *Star Maker* (1937), came next—a book conceived on so grand a scale that the entire "action" of *Last and First Men* is summarized in less than a single paragraph, a passing detail in a monumental tapestry. (In the first of three "time scales" included as appendices, the beginning and end of Homo Sapiens covers only the tiniest of blips.)

Even more difficult to synopsize than either of the *Last Men* books, *Star Maker,* described by Brian Aldiss as "the one great grey holy book of science fiction," begins and ends with a conventional Englishman in a small town, retreating to a hillside in the midst of a quarrel with his wife to contemplate the stars. There he experiences a vision which allows him to travel across the universe in a disembodied state, visiting first inhabited worlds in other solar systems whose spiritual evolutions parallel that of man. Gaining telepathic communication with representatives from these other planets, he joins a community of symbiotic spirits who travel across the universe to learn about life on worlds more and more remote from their own. The gradual expansion of this "we" to include the consciousness of the entire cosmos—which eventually includes even the alien psychology of stars and their own interactions—ultimately brings this collective mind face to face with the *Star Maker* itself, and a climactic recognition of the nature of the creation of the cosmos—not to mention a series of other cosmoses which preceded and will follow this one.

Conceptualizing and visualizing this staggering immensity is no easy matter, yet Stapledon's low-key, even somewhat stodgy manner makes it seem lucid, imaginable, and anything but abstract. An agnostic throughout his life, he remains a rarity among writers by being a rational mystic with a sense of the concrete, a humanist visionary with a profound—and profoundly English—sense of the everyday. His mainly humdrum, unpretentious, even mundane prose—which has partially served to prevent him from acquiring either the reputation of a modernist or the popularity of a yarn-spinner—is actually a crucial part of his equipment, and a central aspect of his strength. Paradoxically, without his banality, we would never believe in the splendor of his designs. This suggests that a full yet unexceptional sense of the ordinary is needed as a ground bass or as a backdrop on which to compose a melody or construct a vision of the extraordinary.

Following *Star Maker*, Stapledon published six more novels between 1942 and 1950, the year of his death, at least two of which—*Sirius: A Fantasy of Love and Discord* (1944) and *The Flames: A Fantasy* (1947)—deserve to be regarded as classics. The first of these is the most powerful of Stapledon's "intimate" novels (*Odd John* is a close runner-up) and by all counts one of the strangest love stories ever written, chronicling the relationship between a dog who develops a human brain capacity and a girl (and, eventually, woman) who grows up with him. The latter, a novella, is a tale recounted from a madhouse by a narrator who believes he's in telepathic communication with a sentient flame that can still remember the solar explosion that produced the planets.

Significantly, Stapledon didn't consider himself a science fiction writer. Although he admitted in a 1937 interview that he had read Verne, Wells, and Edgar Rice Burroughs, he added that he had come across his first SF magazine only the previous year, and was anything but impressed. As the great Argentinian writer Jorge Luis Borges once noted, introducing his 1965 edition of *Star Maker* (*Hacedor de estrellas*), Stapledon's style "suggests that before writing he had read a great deal of philosophy and not many novels or poems." Attending a public discussion with Borges in Santa Barbara in 1986, shortly before his death, I asked him to comment on this book, and he replied that he hadn't reread it since the '60s, "but of course, once you've read it, you can never forget it."

In his introduction, Borges also drew attention to the author's honesty and paradoxical lack of hubris: "Stapledon doesn't shore up inventions to distract or stupefy the reader; with an honest rigor, he pursues and retraces the complex and obscure vicissitudes of his coherent dream....From our contemporary vantage point, *Star Maker* is more than a prodigious novel, it is a possible and plausible representation of the plurality of worlds and their dramatic history." In short, it is almost as if Stapledon were dutifully furnishing a mundane road map which allows the reader to stroll at leisure through infinity and eternity, seeing and marveling at whatever there is to see.

An American in Paris [*Round Midnight*]

In part because I had unkind things to say about his first feature in 1974, writing at the time from Paris, my relations with Bertrand Tavernier (1941-2021) tended to be strained, even though both of us periodically tried to overcome this rift. To his credit, he was the one who made the first gesture, inviting me to join him for a meal in Chicago many years later.

Part of my audition for the job of the Chicago Reader'*s film critic in Spring 1987 was writing three sample long reviews, only one of which they published, on* Radio Days, *although they paid me for all three. The other two were on* Platoon *and* Round Midnight, *and I've abridged the latter somewhat to avoid repeating myself. Following the* Reader'*s star rating system, I gave* Radio Days *one star,* Platoon *two, and* Round Midnight *three.*

For more about Charlie Parker, see my essay about Clint Eastwood's Bird *in* Placing Movies.

I just can't take that bullshit, you dig? They want everybody who's a Negro to be an Uncle Tom, or Uncle Remus, or Uncle Sam, and I can't make it. It's the same all over, you fight for your life—until death do you part, and then you got it made.

—Lester Young in Paris, 1959

There are plenty of cases to make against *Round Midnight*: sentimentality, French chauvinism, an unmistakable vagueness and softness of conception around the edges. But it would be a pity to let these shortcomings allow one to overlook the fact that someone has finally made a fiction feature about jazz with love and respect for and some modicum of understanding about its subject. That it has taken the sound cinema well over half a century to accomplish this is less a mystery than a scandal. That the one to accomplish this should be a *petit-maître* of French middle-class cinema might in some ways be an even harder pill to swallow. But accomplish it Tavernier has, and before all else, this modest if unprecedented achievement deserves to be acknowledged and applauded.

Considering the nearly parallel developments of film and jazz as the new art forms of this century, it is disheartening to consider how seldom they've been able to work together interactively without some fatal compromise on either side (which usually means one serving as ballast for the other). The documentaries have been hampered by a nervous reluctance to let the music speak for itself, characteristically interrupting numbers with distracting cutaways and voiceovers (which often perversely tell us how great the music we're no longer hearing is supposed to be), while the fiction films have been undone both by ignorance about the music and by an uncertainty about how to integrate it into a dramatic context. For examples of the latter, one could cite otherwise sympathetic fiction films like *Too Late Blues* and *New York, New York*, as well as otherwise unsympathetic ones like *Paris Blues* and *The Cotton Club*; from this standpoint, Martin Scorsese's cameo in *Round Midnight* can be viewed as a form of penance for his indifference to jazz history in *New York, New York*.

Significantly, all these problems were admirably faced and solved by a single filmmaker in 1929, the first year of talkies. In two low-budget shorts made respectively with Bessie Smith and Duke Ellington, *St. Louis Blues* and *Black and Tan*, filmmaker Dudley Murphy set precedents that in some respects no subsequent jazz films have lived up to, *Round Midnight* included.

Acutely aware of this neglect, Tavernier sets out to rectify the balance. Some of the results of this scrupulous integrity may be apparent only to jazz aficionados, but they are there all the same, and virtually for the first time. Nearly all of the music is recorded live, and we're usually allowed to listen to it without impediments, as an extension of the characters and narrative rather than as some discontinuous interlude leading away from them. If Tavernier cuts away from the bandstand for a flashback or flash-forward over the continuing music, this usually serves only to increase the dramatic impact of coming back later— accepting and even exploiting the mental drift that often accompanies listening to music without ever using this as a pretext for letting us forget that the music is there. Furthermore, the lengthy takes and contemplative camera movements allow one to linger over the music and crawl into its textures: there is none of the pile-driving or force-feeding that one comes to expect from rock videos.

The musicians hired are among the best now playing, and if the film never goads them into the brilliance that they've shown on other occasions, the overall level of performance is still high. (Regrettably, the most exciting number— Sandra Reaves-Phillips' exuberant version of a Bessie Smith blues at a party jam session—is missing from the soundtrack album.) The most conspicuous case of a musician playing below his best is also probably the most justifiable in terms of plot: Dexter Gordon, who suffered from health problems during the shooting, plays a character who is so clearly past his peak that references to his former brilliance partially have to be accepted on faith. Fortunately, Gordon's extraordinary qualities as an actor make this faith pretty easy to come by. Insofar as the script is virtually sculpted around his particular place in jazz history, the part of Dale Turner is tailor-made for him—even though it must be emphasized that it is a real part and not a transparent cover for Gordon himself.

As a crucial figure linking swing and bebop who spent many years as an expatriate himself (mainly in Copenhagen), Gordon conveys a cool demeanor within a hard bop context, and ranges across the spectrum of jazz like few of his contemporaries. Given this spread, there is a certain logic in basing his character on both Lester Young and Bud Powell (with embellishments from his own career as well as Ben Webster's), even though this produces a rather blurry collage at times. From Young comes Dale Turner's personalized slang, drinking problem, a singer (Lonette McKee) meant to remind us of Billie Holiday, and a recounted traumatic experience in the army. From Powell comes the long Paris exile, the French jazz buff named Francis who takes care of his idol, and the black woman who takes care of him before Francis comes along (named Buttercup, after Powell's wife). Mainly omitted from Turner's background, except by the barest suggestion, is the long history of Powell's mental illness and electroshock treatments—as well as the frenetic, driven quality of Powell's playing.

A key musician for Jack Kerouac and some of the other Beat writers, Gordon all but minted certain hipster gestures and stances—such as holding up his tenor sax horizontally after a number to greet applause, and reciting the lyrics to certain ballads before performing them—many decades ago, and it is not surprising to hear that he has acted before. His earliest film performances are with Louis Armstrong's band in *Atlantic City* and *Pillow to Post*, two minor musicals of the mid-'40s. While doing time in Chino (a California prison without bars) on a narcotics charge in the mid-'50s, he did his first real acting in *Unchained*, a low-budget feature shot there (his best line: "They can't write it the way we play it, man; just forget the music and follow us"). In 1960 he acted on stage in the first Los Angeles production of *The Connection*; since then he has done the same play in Denmark and a couple of bit parts in Swedish films.

Towering at a gangling 6'5" over his French admirers, Gordon has an otherworldly comic air evocative of Tati's Monsieur Hulot, and his singular acting style demands to be read and appreciated in jazz terms. Like most of the patron saints of this movie—Count Basie, Miles Davis, Thelonious Monk, Lester Young—Gordon builds his best dramatic effects on ellipsis and short-hand, knowing just when to lay out or hold back with a pregnant pause, playing a teasing guessing-game with his audience about when he'll come up with his next phrase. A master of witty delivery, Gordon has an uncanny knack for taking humdrum lines—"you know, it just occurs to me that bebop was invented by the cats who *did* get out of the army"—and turning them into profundities with his gravel-heavy voice. Part of this is a consequence of who Gordon is as well as what he says; insofar as *Round Midnight* contrives to combine some measure of documentary with its very romantic fiction, he figures as a witness as much as a participant, and from this standpoint, few living musicians are better qualified. (Significantly, he and the other musicians in the cast collaborated on their own dialogue.) A veritable monument in ruins, Gordon can charge the movie with unusual power through his presence alone.

And what has all this, one might ask, to do with Bertrand Tavernier? As a director whose well-crafted, middle-class/middle-brow forays have often suggested a passionate defense of mediocrity—his Oscar-winning *Sunday in the Country* comprising in this respect a veritable Oatmeal Manifesto—he has not so much abandoned his customary muse here as obliged some of us to reconsider it. Dale Turner is presented to us throughout from the vantage point of Francis Borier (François Cluzet), an adoring French fan with cocker spaniel eyes who is as mediocre a personality as one could hope to find in any Tavernier film. Like the characters most often played by Philippe Noiret in other Tavernier features, he functions partially as the director's surrogate and partially as his model of exemplary mediocrity. Based on the real-life Francis Paudras, who cared for Bud Powell during his years in Paris, this divorced commercial artist with a young, neglected daughter is presented to us without a shred of irony. ("You know, you changed my life," he says to Turner at one point. "Without you, I never would have read Rimbaud.") Yet as drippy as he is, he serves as an ideal narrative device for honestly conveying Tavernier's own distance from his subject. All proportions guarded, his role resembles that of the narrators Lockwood and Nelly Dean in *Wuthering Heights*—the square, humane witness of a Heathcliffian legend who can offer us only a partial portrait, compelling us to imagine the rest.

Before he was a film director, Tavernier worked as a film critic specializing in American cinema, and *Round Midnight*, set in the Paris of 1959, can also be regarded as an elegy to the widescreen Hollywood movies of his youth, and a tribute to the jazz of that period as well. The plaintive wail of Miles Davis is often recalled (most often when Gordon switches to soprano sax), and no less nostalgic a spell is conjured up by Alexandre Trauner's beautiful period sets—loving recreations of Paris's Blue Note and New York's Birdland (both made to glow like pirates' lairs), and a couple of Paris exteriors—the outside of the Blue Note and a Left Bank Hotel habituated by black musicians—which blend the real with the dreamlike in a poetic manner recalling Trauner's nineteenth century Paris in *Children of Paradise*. It is easy to forgive some of the cornball pretexts from a director so bent on recapturing the visceral pleasures of jazz and movies alike: reconstructing an old-fashioned montage sequence out of something like *The Hustler* (1961); cutting in mid-flight from a posthumous big-band rendition of Turner's ode to his lost daughter to Turner's first performance of the same melody in Birdland some years earlier.

What rankles about Tavernier's customary embrace of a realist aesthetic is its flattery of middle-class taste, confirming what an audience already thinks it knows. Without actively denying this aesthetic (apart from Trauner's non-realistic exteriors), *Round Midnight* complicates it by maintaining such a shy, reverential distance from Turner—a character about whom we know surprisingly little, for all his impact and resonance—that we're allowed some complacency only about what we feel; what we know remains altogether less certain.

French idolatry for some kinds of art clearly has its excesses, and one wishes that Tavernier had a bit more sense of the potential foolishness of the humorless Francis, gazing endlessly at silent home movies of his blitzed-out hero. At the same time, putting these and related excesses alongside the puritanical refusals of our usual Anglo-American indifference, it theoretically becomes possible to prefer them, at least as a guide to seeing how we could savor our lives a bit more than we do. *Round Midnight* implies at the very least that France has offered a warmer haven to some black American musicians than their own country has. Obviously this idea isn't restricted to the French—the bitter poetry of Lester Young's statement at the head of this review suggests a similar notion—and Tavernier's plot is sufficiently close to what actually happened to Bud Powell when he returned to the states to give this sentiment some added weight. Yet even if we accept this as self-righteous chauvinism, *Round Midnight* justifies its own claims simply by existing. (If an American director had made a fiction feature about jazz as serious, we might have cause for complaint. Made as a French-American co-production, the film apparently owes the participation of Warners to producer Irwin Winkler, as well as Clint Eastwood's enthusiasm for the project as a jazz buff.)

Getting back to a lesson provided by Dudley Murphy's early jazz shorts, the greatest affinity between film and jazz as art forms may be the degree to which they remain collective enterprises, depending on accommodation, coordination, and shared feelings: Bessie Smith singing out her sorrow in a crowded bar, Duke Ellington performing his "fantasy" with his band huddled around the death bed of a cherished friend. From this standpoint, it may be misleading to regard *Round Midnight* as an auteurist film in relation to either Tavernier or Gordon. Better to see it as a complex three-way transaction between them and us, with lots of others helping. Within such exchanges, Francis's love for Dale and Tavernier's love for the music become two parts of the same process which we're invited to share—for better and for worse.

Full Metal Jacket

This capsule review was the first thing I wrote for Chicago Reader *(for their August 1, 1987 issue) after I was hired as their main reviewer.*

Stanley Kubrick shares with Orson Welles and Carl Dreyer the role of the Great Confounder—remaining supremely himself while frustrating every attempt to anticipate his next move or to categorize it once it registers. This odd 1987 adaptation of Gustav Hasford's *The Short-Timers*, with script-writing assistance from Michael Herr as well as Hasford, has more to do with the general theme of colonization (of individuals and countries alike) and the suppression by male soldiers of their female traits than with the specifics of Vietnam or the Tet offensive. Elliptical, full of subtle inner rhymes (for instance, the sound cues equating a psychopathic marine in the first part with a dying female sniper in the second), and profoundly moving, this is the most tightly crafted Kubrick film since *Dr. Strangelove*, as well as the most horrific; the first section alone accomplishes most of what *The Shining* failed to do. With Matthew Modine, Adam Baldwin, Vincent D'Onofrio, and R. Lee Ermey.

Our Man in Nicaragua [on *Walker*]

From the Chicago Reader *(December 4, 1987).*

What is it about the American mind that insists on regarding itself as apolitical? It would be easier to understand such an attitude in a country with less political freedom than this one; here it seems willfully self-denying, like ordering a hamburger in a Chinese restaurant. From a Marxist and existential standpoint, being "apolitical" means accepting, hence supporting, the status quo—a political position like any other, acknowledged or not. Yet there is something in the national consciousness that resists such acknowledgment.

Reagan's appeal has always rested in part on this form of self-deception, which can be traced back to most of his movie roles—the assumption that anyone as bland and as familiar as a favorite uncle can't be sullied by anything as dirty as politics or ideology. The belated discovery that Reagan's "apoliticism," so closely linked with his triumph as Pure Image, chiefly consists of his capacity to do nothing at all, hasn't eliminated the desire to fill the void with another static, charismatic presence—another movie, in short, to tide us over the many crises to come. And it seems likely that any candidate who is tactless enough to broach politics too overtly will be about as popular as someone who turns on the house lights in the middle of a feature.

It shouldn't be surprising that our taste in movies tends to run the same way. Insofar as overt politics of any kind in a movie are deemed suspect, *Red Dawn* gets knocked along with *Born in Flames*. But in a conservative era like this one, right-wing movies ranging from *The Deer Hunter* to *Top Gun* to *Fatal Attraction* are widely perceived as apolitical, while left-wing movies like *Matewan* and even liberal ones like *Cry Freedom* are often chided for "preaching to the converted."

Even some of our more sophisticated writers succumb to some version of this doublethink. In Pauline Kael's review of *Uncommon Valor* several seasons back, one read that, "*In Raiders of the Lost Ark*, Arabs are casually dispatched—it's as if the hero were skeet shooting—but the tone is clearly a parody of old-movie conventions, and I wouldn't call the picture racist. Thoughtless, maybe, but not racist." What are the implications of this? That racist movies are thoughtful, and that unthinking pictures—the thoughtless variety—have no ideology at all: just like Reagan.

Given such a context, Alex Cox's *Walker*, a bracing throwback to the "irresponsible" radically minded commercial movies of the late '60s and early '70s—a movie that wears its politics on its sleeve, and overtly addresses the present—hasn't got much of a prayer. It turns on the house lights, which is bound to make many of our reviewers livid. But if it weren't for the (unacknowledged) fact that political films of any kind are now regarded as unseemly in the world of entertainment, it wouldn't carry half the corrosive charge that it has.

A period movie that was mainly filmed on location in Nicaragua, *Walker* can be described as a delirious fantasy and black comedy inspired by the real-life exploits of William Walker, an American from Nashville who served as the self-appointed president of Nicaragua from 1855 to 1857. Insisting on an unbroken continuity between past and present and reveling in deliberate anachronisms, the movie presents Walker as a full-scale lunatic—a Nero or Caligula ruled by Manifest Destiny whose delusions and excesses are not at all irrelevant to those of our country in Nicaragua today. In overall thrust, this has no more subtlety than a political cartoon; stylistically, it abounds in explicit echoes of Sam Peckinpah, Sergio Leone, Robert Altman, and *Apocalypse Now*.

There are plenty of bones that one can pick with this position. Aiming for something visionary rather than reasoned, the film plays fast and loose with some of the historical facts, although it must be admitted that some of the most extreme details—such as Walker, a onetime abolitionist, altering the Nicaraguan constitution to reinstitute slavery in 1856—are solidly based on actuality. More generally, depicting Walker as mad is effective as a rhetorical strategy but something of a cop-out as an analytical tool. To the degree that insanity is a social rather than a medical concept, it makes perfect sense to say that this country is capable of committing insane acts in relation to the world community. But calling Walker crazy impedes rather than sharpens under-standing, just as calling Reagan or Oliver North or even Hitler crazy does; apart from expressing the intensity of one's horror, it explains next to nothing. If we grant the term poetic legitimacy, then at the very least the film should start rather than end with this insight, if it wants to teach us anything new.

Furthermore, as Cox and scriptwriter Rudy Wurlitzer freely admit, they are impressed as well as appalled by the figure of Walker. As with Kurtz in the heart of darkness, or Aguirre, or one of the mad Roman emperors, his obsti-nate fanaticism is too theatrical not to be compelling in some way; and like Wrong Way Corrigan he is too much of a loser not to command some tokens of our sympathy. It might be added, though, that what makes him sympathetic or compelling doesn't necessarily make him any more comprehensible, apart from luring us into a movie about him. The movie-made charisma of a Walker, North, or Reagan is precisely what leads us to divorce them from a political context, and if charisma were all that *Walker* had in mind, it wouldn't be taking us anywhere.

Fortunately, the film has a lot more on its mind than that. A consideration of how and why it got made in the first place is important in understanding its overall meaning. The movie was provoked by a dare made to Cox by two Nicaraguan soldiers wounded by the contras whom he met in a bar in Leon in 1984; they asked him why he didn't make a film in Nicaragua, and scoffed at his excuses about the complications that would be involved. Later, after Cox came across a reference to Walker in a magazine article and began researching the subject, he enlisted the novelist Rudy Wurlitzer to help him draw up an outline. On a return trip to Nicaragua in late 1985, Cox and producer Lorenzo O'Brien met with the Nicaraguan film commission and Roman Catholic Church, both of whom provided locations in Managua and Granada, and nine months later they acquired financing from executive producer Edward R. Pressman.

Although the original plan was to shoot half the film in Mexico, the full cooperation of the Sandinista government—which was in no way contingent on any veto power to censor or alter the film, unlike the situation the filmmakers would have encountered in Mexico—convinced them to remain in Nicaragua. The shooting all took place far away from the war against the Contras in the north, but some Sandinista troops under their regular officers served as extras, playing Walker's local opponents. All the materials needed for the production had to be shipped from countries other than the U.S., and the fact that an American-financed film could be made opposing an American-supported war in the same country where the war was being fought undoubtedly brought an idealistic fervor to the production that infected the crew. The additional fact that Cox was the same age as Walker, 32, when he arrived in Nicaragua with a team about the same size as Walker's "58 Immortals" in 1855, certainly wasn't lost on him or Wurlitzer, and the film's anarchic spirit complicates its explicit anger to make room for such ambiguities and overtones.

Even without the unusual production difficulties of *Walker*, Alex Cox's talent is passionately anarchic, for better and for worse. In each of his films to date, a plethora of good ideas are dropped and either kicked out of sight or trampled underfoot by excess energy. His short *Sleep Is for Sissies* was nothing but scattershot ideas competing with one another for prominence; *Repo Man* began as a tug-of-war between a well-delineated view of a particular underside of LA and a paranoid sci-fi fantasy, with the former eventually (and regrettably) giving way to the latter; and even the relatively contained *Sid & Nancy* was all over the place with runaway diversions. In *Walker*, the various elements tend to get plastered over one another, as in a palimpsest, so that few of them are allowed to build or accumulate—except for the fascination with the title character, the intensity of the nonstop violence, and the fiery beauty of David Bridges's cinematography, which probably makes this the most attractively shot Cox movie to date.

In the case of the witty script, many of the secondary meanings and ironies are concerned with language. Wurlitzer's novels (*Nog*, *Flats*, *Quake*, and *Slow Fade*) and previous scripts (including *Two-Lane Blacktop*, *Pat Garrett and Billy the Kid*) are partially grounded in existential notions about language, and much of this sensibility is brought to bear in his handling of Walker's lunatic myopia. Before he went to Nicaragua, Walker was devoted to his deaf-mute fiancée, Ellen Martin, and mastered sign language in order to communicate with her; for Walker's biographer Albert Z. Carr, her death in a cholera epidemic in 1848 was a major turning point in his life.

Played by real-life deaf mute Marlee Matlin, who won an Oscar for her role in last year's *Children of a Lesser God*, Ellen Martin is depicted as a clear-sighted radical who sees through the dangerous nonsense of Walker's obsession with Manifest Destiny, and Wurlitzer gets some high comedy out of Walker censoring her brutal remarks to others (conveyed through subtitles such as "Go fuck a pig") while translating them into euphemisms. Much later, Walker's relationship with the comparably lucid Dona Yrena (Blanca Guerra), a highly placed Nicaraguan woman in Granada, abounds in similar discrepancies between two language systems out of joint. Even Walker's own offscreen narration, which eerily alternates between first and third person—it was inspired by Walker's book *The War in Nicaragua*, which has the same peculiarity—displays a related linguistic derangement. One only regrets that Ed Harris plays Walker without a southern accent, which surely would have given the latter's rhetoric more regional flavor; dressed like a country deacon, the character registers in other respects as gentrified Bible Belt.

For Wurlitzer, Walker's inability to see what is under his nose, which makes his bloody exploits and arbitrary decisions—and the U.S.'s current ones against the Sandinistas—possible, is largely a matter of being trapped inside rhetoric. In a book just issued by Harper & Row also called *Walker*—containing an introduction by Wurlitzer (with extracts from the screenplay, Ed Harris's journal, and Walker's writings), an abridged version of Carr's 1963 biography, and a lengthy conversation between director and screenwriter—Wurlitzer clarifies this point in terms of current politics: "We don't have the right to interpret Nicaragua for Nicaraguans. . . . It's not our business with left governments, right governments, any governments, you know? And we must defend our right to be innocent that way. Our fight not to be sophisticated. We must defend our right not to join that language, to be innocent and to refuse that dialogue."

"Clearly this is no ordinary asshole," remarks Dona Yrena in Spanish when she first hears Walker spouting his exalted babble. A well-educated southerner who entered the University of Nashville at twelve and graduated with honors at fourteen, went on to study medicine in Edinburgh and Paris, abandoned promising careers in journalism and law, and became an American hero for launching a stupid and unsuccessful campaign in Sonora, Mexico that violated treaty agreements, all before he went to Nicaragua, Walker was a bundle of so many contradictions that the movie has had to scale him down a bit in order to make him graspable at all. Interestingly enough, Ed Harris's portrayal of him more or less starts where his version of John Glenn in *The Right Stuff* left off—as flamboyant rigidity, with thoughts so pressing that they seem ready to burst out of his head.

Where the movie cheats a little in relation to the real Walker is in the degree to which it makes him out to be a simpleton. (If only our misguided figureheads were so legible, we might know what to do with them.) When Cornelius Vanderbilt (Peter Boyle) asks him, "Does Nicaragua mean anything to you?" he replies, "Nothing at all," whereas the real Walker—who may never have actually met Vanderbilt before the latter sent him to Central America to protect his trade interests—had already written enthusiastically about Vanderbilt's involvement in Nicaragua for the *San Francisco Herald*. Similarly, while the real Walker invited his two brothers to join him in Granada, the movie Walker is embarrassed and aloof when they turn up on their own initiative, looking for money and glory.

In many other respects, however, the movie stays chillingly close to the record. Most of Walker's speeches come straight out of the history books, and the treatment of him as an idealist who betrayed nearly all of his own principles—he started out as an opponent of slavery and supporter of women's rights—is no less authentic. Yet on the other hand, because the movie is ultimately—and for good reason—more interested in the present than the past, its fidelity to history is in some respects beside the point. If the real Walker was so popular in his day that a Broadway show was written about him, it's logical enough that the movie makes him *Time*'s "Man of the Year" in 1857, and puts him on the covers of *People* and *Newsweek* as well. The mocking use of contemporary Latin pop music and other anachronistic details makes perfect sense in this context, because Walker's grim sincerity is every bit as up-to-date as Ollie North's.

After a long period of political quietism and cowardice in American cinema, compounded by the half-truths of movies like *Platoon* and the quarter-truths of movies like *The Color Purple*, it is a pleasure to find that three first-rate features have been released this year about the idiocy of the U.S. in the third world, each of them completely different from the other two. *Ishtar*, the first of these to emerge, hasn't even been perceived as political; critics who have derided it for not being more like the old Hope and Crosby Road pictures seem to have unconsciously regretted the absence of any accompanying old-fashioned imperialism in Elaine May's world view. The political orientation of *Full Metal Jacket*, reflecting Stanley Kubrick's expatriate status, has confused some commentators as well; but surely no one can have any doubts about where *Walker* stands. While the standard view of its *Ubu Roi* extremism would be to call it excessive, it might be worth considering whether what it describes is any less so. And excessive or not, the exhilaration and lyricism of its furious anger and wit are such that they could enlighten us all.

Wise Blood

From the Chicago Reader, *February 1, 1988.*

Along with *The Man Who Would Be King* and *The Dead*, this is John Huston's best literary adaptation, and perhaps his very best film—a very close rendering of Flannery O'Connor's remarkable first novel about a crazed southern cracker (a perfectly cast Brad Dourif) who sets out to preach a church without Christ, and winds up suffering a true Christian martyrdom in spite of himself. The period, local ambience, and deadly gallows humor are all perfectly caught, and apart from the subtle if pertinent fact that this is an unbeliever's version of a believer's novel, it's about as faithful a version of O'Connor's grotesque world as one could ever hope to get on film, hilarious and frightening in equal measure. O'Connor conceived her novel as a parody of existentialism, and Huston's own links with existentialism—as the director of the first U.S. stage production of *No Exit*, as well as Sartre's *Freud* script—make him an able interpreter. With Harry Dean Stanton, Amy Wright, Daniel Shor, Ned Beatty, and Huston himself as the hero's fire-and-brimstone grandfather. The producer is Michael Fitzgerald, whose family's friendship with O'Connor guaranteed the fidelity and seriousness of the undertaking (1979).

Tough Guys Don't Dance

I don't recall when I reviewed this for the Chicago Reader, *but I first saw the film at the Toronto Film Festival in September 1987, where I met Mailer at his press conference. For a much lengthier discussion of this film, see my 2014 dialogue with Justin Bozung on my website.*

Norman Mailer's best film, adapted from his worst novel, shows a surprising amount of cinematic savvy and style from a writer whose previous film efforts (*Wild 90, Beyond the Law, Maidstone*) were mainly unvarnished recordings of his own improvised performances. Working for the first time with a mainstream crew and budget and without himself as an actor, he translates his high rhetoric and macho preoccupations (existential tests of bravado, good orgasms, murderous women, metaphysical cops) into an odd, campy, raunchy comedy thriller that remains consistently watchable and unpredictable—as goofy in a way as *Beyond the Valley of the Dolls.* Where Russ Meyer featured women with oversize breasts, Mailer features male characters with oversize egos (although the women here also do pretty well in that department), and thanks to the juicy writing, hallucinatory lines such as "Your knife is in my dog" and "I just deep-sixed two heads" bounce off his cartoonish actors like comic-strip bubbles; even his sexism is somewhat objectified in the process. Indeed, it isn't clear why Mailer doesn't regard this as a comedy. Coaxing good performances out of his male actors (Ryan O'Neal, Lawrence Tierney, Wings Hauser) and mannerist displays from his actresses (including Isabella Rossellini and Debra Sandlund), he is certainly capable of broad strokes—the southern accents are laid on with a trowel—but his framing, editing, and uses of sound and music are often fresh and tangy. Whatever has induced Mailer to clean up his act, he has introduced an effective (if convoluted) flashback structure, trimmed the fat off his prose, eliminated digressions, and shown some genuine flair with his Provincetown locations, including his own home. The results are giddy and singular—100 percent Mailer, and one of those rare occasions when a novelist's obsessions and vision have been brought to the screen intact.

Privileged Moments [*Rembrandt Laughing*]

From the Chicago Reader *(September 29, 1989). For the record, Jon Jost has been a friend since 1977.*

"The essence of Jean-Luc Godard's *La femme mariée*," John Bragin wrote in the mid-'60s, "is the transmutation of the dramatic into the graphic." While this formula doesn't account for everything in *Rembrandt Laughing*, Jon Jost's ninth feature, I think it provides a helpful clue to the overall direction taken by this masterful, elliptical account of a little over a year in the lives of a few friends in San Francisco.

For all his mastery and originality as a maverick independent, Jost has often alienated audiences with the harshness of his themes and the apparent distance from which he views his subjects and his characters. A '60s radical who spent over two years in federal prison for draft resistance, he has lived without a fixed address for most of his twenty-six-year career as a filmmaker, and the alienation as well as the clarity stemming from his wanderlust has seeped into many of his fiction features. These have often centered on isolated individuals: a private detective in *Angel City* (1977), a drifter out of work in *Last Chants for a Slow Dance* (1977), a drug dealer in *Chameleon* (1978), a Vietnam vet in *Bell Diamond* (1987). Even the two people who form the focus of the 1983 *Slow Moves* register more as lonely individuals than as a couple.

Rembrandt Laughing, however, was made during one of the longest stationary periods in Jost's adult life, when he was living in San Francisco, and the difference in the film's overall ambience is striking. (It was shot, fairly casually and intermittently, over the first two months of 1988, usually an hour or two at a time.) For once all of the characters are physically and spiritually grounded in a specific community and milieu, which means that the silences that exist between them are more often shared moments than gaping disjunctures or tortured absences in communication. In many respects it was made collectively with Jost's friends—one of the lead actors (Jon A. English) composed the music, another (Nathaniel Dorsky) contributed a small section of footage, and most of the plot and (largely improvised) dialogue were worked out with the cast. It is nonetheless very much a Jost film, but with a warmth, philosophical depth, and overall sense of relaxation that are relatively new to his work.

Although the first and last scenes in *Rembrandt Laughing* are symmetrically structured and juxtaposed—both depict early morning visits of Martin (English) to Claire (Barbara Hammes), a woman he used to live with—there's a random drift to many of the intervening sequences; they tend to focus more on everyday activities of various characters than on dramatic events. A few significant incidents do occur in these sequences—Martin's friend Daniel (Dorsky), who is also a former lover of Claire's, asks Martin to be the executor of his will; another character suddenly breaks into tears while looking at the San Francisco Bay with Claire, because her husband left her—but most of the time the characters are simply working or spending time together: telling stories, serving and eating food, sharing memories.

It is also worth pointing out that insofar as *Rembrandt* has a story, it is not always an easy one to follow, and if I give away much of the plot here, I don't think that I'll be spoiling the experience the film has to offer, which has more to do with the telling of the story than with any conventional narrative suspense. (I should give fair warning, however, that my synopsis will include a couple of delayed revelations in the story line, so some readers may prefer to skip what follows until after they've seen the film.) Martin's first visit to Claire is occasioned by the fifth anniversary of their breakup, which he still regrets. He presents her with a photocopy of a Rembrandt etching, a self-portrait that shows the artist uncharacteristically laughing (which is subsequently used in the film to mark divisions between days). The two characters are mainly isolated from one another in separate shots—Claire still in bed or in the bathroom, Martin fixing her breakfast in the kitchen—and there's a certain pathos in the way that Martin keeps hoping she'll guess the reason for his surprise visit. The disjointedness of their responses to one another recalls earlier Jost films, but Claire gives Martin an affectionate hug before he leaves, and the scene concludes with a feeling of tenderness that somewhat mollifies Martin's petulance about Claire not remembering their relationship as fondly as he does.

Later we see Claire and Martin at their jobs—Claire at an architect's office, Martin doing woodwork at a picture framer's—followed by another long scene when Martin visits Daniel, an old friend who collects sand from various countries around the world and keeps it in bottles, the scene in which Martin agrees to be the executor of Daniel's will. (It's only much later, in the final scene, that the film obliquely reveals that Daniel also used to live with Claire.) It is here that the film's transmutation of the dramatic into the graphic first becomes fully apparent: the scene opens with an extreme close-up of miso soup being stirred while the two friends chat offscreen; somewhat later there's a comparable close-up of some pebbles in a dish, and still later the camera focuses on some sand from Crete that Martin has brought for Daniel. (It's worth noting that none of the extreme, extended close-ups of objects here and elsewhere in the film are static shots: the grains of sand, for instance, are lightly stirred by air currents.) The close-up of the pebbles is overlaid and eventually overtaken by rapidly dancing flashes of light (the footage contributed by Dorsky) that create a ravishingly beautiful kind of abstract scherzo over the easygoing offscreen conversation, which is accompanied by a strange rattling sound that seems connected with the pebbles (thematically if not in terms of the story). In contrast with the intensity of these three extended close-ups, Martin and Daniel are shown rather obliquely, and rarely within the same frame. The overall effect of this unorthodox sequence is to elevate the cosmic subtext of the conversation—the sense of infinity and mortality that hovers around the edges of the talk before Daniel brings up the matter of his will—so that it proceeds simultaneously with the more mundane everyday chitchat.

A week later we see Claire at work again, and Martin trying out for a job as an "explainer" to kids on tours at a San Francisco science museum called the Exploratorium. After running through his carefully prepared spiel, which ends with the line "I can explain everything," Martin expresses concern to his potential employer about the implied hubris of that claim. The next day Martin prepares to compose some music on his synthesizer; he listens to Beethoven's *15th Quartet in A Minor* on earphones—a piece that is often heard again, becoming a motif rather like the Rembrandt etching and lending a sense of gravity to other events.

The next evening we see Martin talking to a bail bondsman (Jerry Barrish) about Daniel, who was arrested for possessing some grass and who turns out to have run up a $3,000 debt in unpaid parking tickets. This is the least successful scene in the picture, made especially unfortunate by the melodramatic appearance of two very unconvincing fake-Hollywood gangsters who wind up shooting the bondsman for a purely gratuitous reason. Just as the earlier sequences can be partially traced to some of the best work of Godard (the bowl of miso soup, for instance, springs directly from a similarly framed cup of black coffee in *2 or 3 Things I Know About Her*), this sequence seems derived from the absurdist bursts of violence in some of Godard's lazier work—with the difference that Godard at least knows the Hollywood crime movies that he's spoofing, while Jost, it seems, can only grope after an imitation of a spoof. This sequence ends more agreeably with a 360-degree tracking shot around a sushi bar where Claire is eating with a new boyfriend, Jim (Jim Nisbet); Jost himself can be glimpsed sitting at the bar, and since he credits himself with photographing the entire film, one can only wonder what technical stunt was needed to pull this remarkable shot off.

The film fully regains its stride in the two closing sequences. The first of these is set a month later, and shows virtually all the characters in various everyday activities; the overall ambience is relaxed and lyrical, recalling some of the interludes in Alain Resnais' *Muriel*. Claire is in bed with Jim, Martin is watering his lawn, the bail bondsman (surprisingly still alive) gazes at the ocean, and Daniel is ice-skating—the latter occasioning another bit of virtuoso camera work.

In the final sequence, set a year later, Martin again appears at Claire's apartment, this time carrying a heavy box. It emerges that Daniel has died and left his sand collection to Claire, and Martin is delivering it; Jim is still around, and this time it is he who fixes breakfast. Here again, the leisurely life-style of the characters is depicted at some length, although by now the characters have grown in density (English's performance in particular has become increasingly convincing and lifelike over the course of the film). Jim reads the paper while Claire and Martin arrange the bottles of sand on her windowsill. At one point there's another extended extreme close-up: this time it's of what appears to be unusually dark sand. Later in the scene we discover that these are Daniel's ashes, which he has bequeathed to Claire so that he can "keep on living with her," as he explains in an accompanying letter. Claire doesn't know whether to laugh or cry about this, and winds up doing something in between; Martin embraces her, comforting her in much the same way that she comforted him toward the end of the first sequence.

The above synopsis is far from complete; it omits, for example, that on various occasions different sorts of printed texts crawl across the screen, at odd moments and usually at odd angles. More important, it omits the very pleasurable opening sequence, before the credits, of Martin bicycling over to Claire's—the whirring sound of the pedals and the oblique images of a foot, a turning wheel, moving pavement, and occasional shadows. They add up to a sensual blend that is every bit as exciting as Daniel's ice-skating—not to mention the extended close-ups on various textures, including a beautiful shot of the rippling water of the San Francisco Bay. The elemental power of these privileged, electric moments in the film are in a sense what the whole story is "about," to the same degree that both the image of Rembrandt, the painter of gloom, laughing and the sound of Beethoven's *15th Quartet* (identified by the composer on the manuscript as a "song of thanksgiving to the Deity on recovery from an illness, written in the Lydian mode") are variations of the same basic feelings and ideas.

What may seem initially off-putting about the film is the degree to which portions of the story appear to be self-consciously "thought up" rather than discovered. As a storyteller, Jost has often shown a certain awkwardness in ordering events and controlling exposition—in striking contrast to his consummate command and skills as a cinematographer and sound recorder. But as *Rembrandt Laughing* suggests, the usual motives and satisfactions of storytelling don't interest him very much; he uses plot, well or badly, as a vehicle for arriving at something else—in this case the poetry and textures of everyday life. Implicit in the film's moving final synthesis, and much closer to metaphor and poetry than to story and prose, is the realization that water, sand, ashes, pebbles, people, bicycling, ice-skating, and even fixing breakfast are much closer to being the same things than we ordinarily choose to suppose. I realize that this concept, as it's baldly and awkwardly expressed here, may not make too much sense as prose; but go and see what Jost does with it cinematographically and you'll get a much better idea of what I mean.

Disjointed [on *Mo' Better Blues*]

From the Chicago Reader, *August 10, 1990.*

First the good news: strictly as an *exercise de style*, Spike Lee's fourth joint is in certain respects the liveliest and jazziest piece of filmmaking he's turned out yet. From the arty close-ups behind the opening credits of—and liquid pans past, and dissolves between—trumpet, lips, and lovers' grasping hands in blue, yellow, amber, and green to the matching semicircular crane shots that frame the story, this is a movie cooking with ideas about filmmaking. Bringing back a good many of the featured players in *Do the Right Thing*, and introducing to the Spike Lee stable the highly talented Denzel Washington, Cynda Williams, Wesley Snipes, and Dick Anthony Williams (among others), it's a movie bursting with personality and actorly energy as well.

Unfortunately, when it comes to characters, story, music, and the relationships between the three, *Mo' Better Blues* is both confused and unconvincing—a lot of loose ideas and platitudes rattling around in search of a movie. If I hadn't expected more from Lee than simple diversion, the fair-to-middling music and the razzmatazz visuals might have sufficed. It all depends on what you're looking for; personally, I was hoping for a jazz movie and a love story.

On the basis of his previous movies—particularly the last two, *School Daze* and *Do the Right Thing*—it was easy to predict that Lee would have trouble with a movie about a jazz musician. Both of those movies have unnecessarily cluttered scores that seem to imply, as a matter of general principle, that any music at all is better than none—which means that at times the music competes with dialogue, distracts from the actors and mise en scène, and assigns anomalous moods and meanings to scenes that would work perfectly well without them. Insofar as such tactics tend to camouflage dead moments in the script or direction—at the same time they banish silence and its virtues from the soundtrack—one could make the ungenerous assumption that Lee is using them cynically, to hide his own weak spots, but I don't think this is his main motivation. Since I believe that Lee is serious, personal, and complex as a filmmaker, I think the problem runs much deeper.

Without delving too deeply, questions about Lee's family dynamics seem unavoidable considering the peculiar stresses in his work. The scores for all of his features, written by his father, jazz bassist and composer Bill Lee, are invariably cluttered orchestral works that function less as film scores than as rather pretentious autonomous compositions. (One can find a related if usually less severe problem in Francis Coppola's occasional use of music by his father, Carmine.) The fact that Lee comes, as he puts it, from a "jazz household" was part of his stated motivation for making the film, and while it may give *Mo' Better Blues* a bit more backstage authenticity than either *Round Midnight* or *Bird*, Lee's movie has a considerably less developed feeling for the music.

Whatever the specific motivations, the music seems to provoke—or at least become the occasion for—a lack of certainty in Lee's directing and editing that usually takes the form of scattershot restlessness. (I'm not speaking so much of his admirable eclecticism as of the impression that he's floundering when he has to work directly in relation to music.) Skittishly leaping from one shot to the next or between a stationary and a moving camera, and (to an even greater extent) relying too heavily and frequently on close-ups, Lee gratuitously hypes up his shots—much the way a beginning writer might overuse italics or exclamation points. It's as if he felt obliged to simultaneously adhere to his father's hectoring structures and break free of them, without a battle plan for how to proceed on either front.

The anxious moves that ensue point to Lee's succumbing to the music-video syndrome: they generally have nothing to do with building a structure and everything to do with reaching for immediate effects that often make larger structures impossible, which actively works against many of Lee's larger dramatic aims. The results are an overloaded soundtrack and an overloaded direction that often barely seem to be on speaking terms, although they're both churning away at full blast. And as mistrustful as I generally am of vulgar Freudianism, it's hard to overlook the oedipal conflicts that crop up in the plots of *School Daze* and *Do the Right Thing*, made especially complex in the latter case because the father figure, Danny Aiello, is white. In *Mo' Better Blues*, father and son are complicitous buddies, but the implied inevitability of the son replicating the attitudes of the father produces a number of ambiguities and ironies, not all of them hopeful.

The basic plot of *Mo' Better Blues* is so hackneyed that it could be described this way: Gifted Jazz Trumpeter Bleek Gilliam (Washington) Is Too Obsessed With His Art to Care for Feelings of Others or to Realize That His Best Friend Giant (Lee), a Compulsive Gambler, Does a Lousy Job of Managing His Quintet and Keeping White Club Owners (John and Nicholas Turturro, a Tweedledum and Tweedledee Act) From Exploiting Them. Selfish Bleek Romances Two Women at Once, Indigo (Joie Lee) and Clarke (Cynda Williams), and Is Indifferent to the Musical Ambitions of Both Clarke and His Sax Player Shadow (Wesley Snipes). When Both Ladies and the Gangsters Who Back Giant's Bookie Converge at the Club, Giant Is Seriously Beaten; Bleek, Coming to His Defense, Gets His Chops Busted, Ending His Career as a Musician, Then Falls From Sight...

I'm not claiming that such a plot is unserviceable, only that Lee conceives of it in more or less these simplistic terms, without much shading or nuance. (And with a few changes, Bleek, his loft, and his two girlfriends become in many ways a replay of the heroine, her loft, and her boyfriends in *She's Gotta Have It*, Lee's first feature.) He clearly wants to use this plot much the same way that a jazz musician uses a popular standard, as a basis for riffs and improvisations—beginning and ending his movie with virtually identical sequences the way a jazz musician begins and ends a number with a given theme. It's a legitimate enough approach, and, up to a point, Lee manages to justify it with his ideas and his energy. But it's a concept that ultimately gets him into trouble.

A good jazz musician will use a familiar theme not merely as a point of departure but as a site for rediscovery. But Lee's use of familiar themes remains perfunctory. Bleek's obsession with his music is a given, but nothing that we see or hear fleshes out this concept in a persuasive or compelling way, and Washington himself is much too poised and self-contained to suggest Bleek's obsessiveness. (His trumpet playing, dubbed by Terence Blanchard, is basically Miles Davis twice removed—and subdued—by way of Wynton Marsalis, Freddie Hubbard, and other postmodernist Miles imitators: obsessive is the last thing that anyone would call it. And an extended rap piece that Bleek writes and performs with his group, called "Pop Top 40," is arguably not even very musical, whatever its other virtues.)

When Bleek disappears for a year, we have no idea where he goes or what he does, or even whether his family knows of his whereabouts, and significantly we don't much care. We accept the vagueness—if we accept it—like so much else in the film, as a mere trope filling out a design, similar to the long stretches of background music that we aren't supposed to hear so much as overhear (a curious attitude to take toward the music that the movie's romantic hero is supposed to be obsessed with). And when we hear Clarke sing for the first time, toward the end of the film soon after Bleek's return from the netherworld, it isn't clear whether he's hearing her sing for the first time as well—which would be important if the characters had any depth. Similarly, Bleek's friendship with Giant and his relationships with both Indigo and Clarke are never distinctive enough to convey any sense of urgency or uniqueness. Regrettably, the only motifs in the story that seem to energize Lee's writing are Bleek's relationship to his father and the familiar theme of competition—whether it's between Bleek and Shadow or between Indigo and Clarke—and even here, the plot points occasionally seem forced. (Though both Giant and Bleek complain about Shadow's solos being too long, for instance, we never hear anything to substantiate this charge.)

I'm not claiming that Lee doesn't have any ideas about how to use and integrate music in his film; the problem, rather, is that he doesn't know how to sustain them. Two of his best ideas are "improvisations" of mise en scène based on particular well-known jazz pieces—Miles Davis's first recording of *All Blues* (from the classic *Kind of Blue* album) and *Acknowledgement*, the opening movement of John Coltrane's *A Love Supreme*. *All Blues* is a moody Davis composition written in 6/8 time, with a pronounced sense of three beats (a mournful unison background riff) against four (a wailing trumpet solo). Lee uses it to accompany a lovemaking scene between Bleek and Clarke, and he lyrically translates this notion of three against four, and riff against melodic line, by making Bleek's loft appear to spin in a dreamy circle around the couple (corresponding to the riff) while they (corresponding to the trumpet solo) remain fixed in the foreground. It's a lovely idea, but Lee doesn't seem to know how to follow it up; other shots that are stylistically unconnected follow as the song continues, with the consequence that the music becomes less and less important, eventually serving as mere background bustle. This means that what starts out as a tribute to the music winds up as a minor insult to it.

In the case of *A Love Supreme*—which Lee planned to name his film after, until Coltrane's widow denied him permission, reportedly because of the film's use of profanity—Lee again starts off with a powerful idea that he quickly dissipates. *Acknowledgement* begins magisterially with an almost out-of-tempo tenor sax cadenza accompanied by impressionistic cymbal work (by Elvin Jones) that suggests the pulse of crashing waves—something closer to a pure, burnished sound than a steady succession of beats or notes. Lee uses the piece just after Bleek's climactic reunion with Indigo, accompanied by a gorgeous long shot of the Statue of Liberty and the Staten Island ferry under a blood red sky. It's a lovely epiphany that, like the earlier one, becomes more and more diluted by further shots detailing their reunion and other subsequent events, all of which eventually grinds the music underfoot—and literally buries it under other sounds—instead of illustrating or enhancing it, as it was apparently meant to do.

To my mind, the only time that Lee succeeds in integrating jazz dramatically for anything longer than a single shot is toward the end of the film when Clarke sings "Harlem Blues" with Shadow and Bleek's former rhythm section. The cutting here is almost as nervous as it is during the other musical numbers, but because this is the first and the only time that we hear her sing—and a moment that coincides with the return of Bleek to the jazz world—the scene carries a punch that not even Lee's directorial uncertainties can undermine. (By contrast, the nadir of his editing to music is his ludicrously cornball cross-cutting between Giant getting beaten on the street and aggressive shots of the musicians playing inside the club—a concept, linking jazz to violence and back alleys, that was cheap and old hat even back when Richard Brooks used it to juice up an alley bashing in *Blackboard Jungle* in 1955.)

An entertaining failure packed with incidental pleasures, *Mo' Better Blues* is no less personal and independent a work than Lee's other features, and in some ways it's even more experimental. It gives us our last opportunity to savor the comic gifts of the late Robin Harris (one of the sidewalk kibitzers in *Do the Right Thing*, who here plays a nightclub comic very much like himself), a highly stylized view of New York that is quite different from the New Yorks of *She's Gotta Have It* and *Do the Right Thing*, some hip nods to jazz history (in the names of clubs and in the musical montage heard over the final credits), and lots of lively wit in the dialogue.

Furthermore, one can only applaud the overall spirit of experimentation, especially in the editing, that leads to highly unconventional sequences reflecting the characters' particular states of mind: Bleek's literal confusion between Indigo and Clarke is effectively illustrated by a series of graceful matching cuts (evocative of Buñuel's *That Obscure Object of Desire*) that have him making love to and arguing with both of them at the same time; later, Lee charts the mutual uncertainties of Bleek and Indigo, when they meet after a year apart, with highly disconcerting mismatches in the editing. For all the confusion and inadequacy on view here, Lee can't be accused of either backing away from the promise of *Do the Right Thing* or following the abject practice of attempting a sequel or remake. For better and for worse, you might just say that like his dimly imagined hero, he's simply trying a few things out.

Sex and Drugs and Death and Writing [on *Naked Lunch*]

From the Chicago Reader *(January 17, 1992). For other detailed considerations of film adaptations of novels, see my review of Bill Forsyth's* Housekeeping *adapted from the Marilynne Robinson novel in the January 22, 1988 issue of the* Chicago Reader, *also available on my website, as well as my treatments of* The Big Sleep, Greed, Indignation, *and* Other Voices, Other Rooms *in this book.*

And some of us are on Different Kicks and that's a thing out in the open the way I like to see what I eat and vice versa mutatis mutandis as the case may be. Bill's Naked Lunch Room . . . Step right up. Good for young and old, man and bestial. Nothing like a little snake oil to grease the wheels and get a show on the track Jack. Which side are you on? Fro-Zen Hydraulic? Or you want to take a look around with Honest Bill?"

—William S. Burroughs, introduction to *Naked Lunch* (1962)

The first time I read William S. Burroughs's *Naked Lunch*—or at least large portions of it—was in 1959, a few months after its first printing, in a smuggled copy of the seedy Olympia Press edition fresh from Paris. As I recall it was missing most or all of the accompanying matter—the introduction ("Deposition: Testimony Concerning a Sickness"), "Atrophied Preface" ("Wouldn't You?"), and appendix ("Letter From a Master Addict to Dangerous Drugs")—that gave so much body, flavor, shape, and outright usefulness to the Grove Press edition published in the United States three years later. Without this fancy dressing it read like a simple parade of fantasy horrors laced with gallows humor and separated by ellipses, and to my sixteen-year-old mind it was interesting only for its wild and extravagant obscenities—precisely what had caused it to be banned in the first place.

When I later came to read and reread the American edition the work no longer seemed quite so formless. The introduction provided biographical, moral, and metaphysical focus—the story of Burroughs' fifteen-year heroin addiction, and what he called the pyramid of junk and the algebra of need—while the "preface" at the end was full of lovely formal and thematic clues about what Burroughs was up to. Moreover, both sections were written in a powerfully condensed, poetically precise American vernacular that arguably surpassed everything else in the book—in fact they were so pungently written that they placed the entire work in a fresh perspective. (The prosaic appendix, by contrast, was useful mainly in my early experiments with peyote and marijuana, and Burroughs as a reference point on this subject was secondary to the lyrical effusions of other Beat writers, namely Jack Green and Jack Kerouac.)

This second helping of *Naked Lunch* had such an impact on me that on my first trip to Paris a few years later I snatched up any other Burroughs books I could find, *The Ticket That Exploded* and *Dead Fingers Talk* (the second was confiscated by British customs—in those days such a book could be deemed illegal in England before it was published there). During the remainder of the '60s I continued to keep up with Burroughs: *Nova Express*, *The Soft Machine*, the American edition of *The Ticket That Exploded* (also superior to its Olympia forerunner), and many pamphlet-size publications from obscure smaller presses.

But even then my enthusiasm for Burroughs was waning. By the '60s Burroughs had come under the influence of painter Brion Gysin and was fully committed to cut-ups—a technique of arbitrarily folding texts by himself and others and grafting the halves together to see what unexpected meanings flashed out of the jumble. To me this sort of Dada throwback, which usually produced meager results, was only a mechanical means of effecting sudden changes of syntax in mid-sentence, a sort of druggy turnaround that Burroughs had already achieved much more forcefully by instinct in his earlier writing.

These "natural" cut-ups allowed some passages to undergo mysterious sea changes of emphasis and focus in the midst of a monotone patter, and permitted certain similes and metaphors to sprout independent lives and narratives of their own in the course of seemingly logical arguments. Two examples from *Naked Lunch*, both from the "Atrophied Preface":

> Sooner or later The Vigilante, The Rube, Lee the Agent, A.J., Clem
> and Jody the Ergot Twins, Hassan O'Leary the After Birth Tycoon,
> The Sailor, The Exterminator, Andrew Keif, 'Fats' Terminal, Doc
> Benway, 'Fingers' Schafer are subject to say the same thing in the

same words to occupy, at that intersection point, the same position in space-time. Using a common vocal apparatus complete with all metabolic appliances that is to be the same person—a most inaccurate way of expressing Recognition: The junky naked in sunlight . . .

You can cut into *Naked Lunch* at any intersection point. . . . I have written many prefaces. They atrophy and amputate spontaneous like the little toe amputates in a West African disease confined to the Negro race and the passing blonde shows her brass ankle as a manicured toe bounces across the club terrace, retrieved and laid at her feet by her Afghan Hound . . .

What seemed natural and funny in *Naked Lunch* began to seem forced and abstruse in some of the later books. Furthermore, the relentless misogyny of Burroughs's writing, coupled with the eventual knowledge that he had killed his own wife, finally got to me, and my ardor for his work went through a distinct cooling-off phase.

Still, I yield to no one in my admiration for the second edition of *Naked Lunch*. It may not be politically correct, but neither is *War and Peace* (as Tolstoy, in his subsequent born-again decrepitude, was the first to admit). Neither, for that matter, is David Cronenberg's highly transgressive and subjective film adaptation of *Naked Lunch*, which may well be the most troubling and ravishing head movie since *Eraserhead*. It is also fundamentally a film about writing—even *the* film about writing, the same one that filmmakers as diverse as Wim Wenders (in *Hammett*), Philip Kaufman (in *Henry & June*), and the Coen brothers (in *Barton Fink*) have been trying with less success to make. Part of what makes it politically incorrect is that it posits an intimate interdependence between the act of creation and the act of murder.

Heads explode. Parasites fly at people's faces. Television sets breathe. A woman grows a spike in her armpit and unleashes a cataclysm on the world. These are the startling images David Cronenberg uses to shock and disturb us as his films travel through a nightmare world where the grotesque and the bizarre make our flesh creep.

—Jacket copy, *The Shape of Rage: The Films of David Cronenberg* (1983)

My acquaintance with Cronenberg is much spottier than my acquaintance with Burroughs, and it was made at a relatively late stage in his career. I was impressed but repelled by *Scanners* when it came out in 1981, but I walked out of a revival of *They Came from Within* (1975) a few years later, more repulsed than enlightened, and felt pretty neutral about *The Dead Zone* (1983) and *The Fly* (1986). It was only three or four years ago, when I caught up with *Videodrome* (1982) on video (I've seen it again at least twice), that I realized just how brilliant Cronenberg is. I didn't exactly warm to *Dead Ringers* (1988), but it was such a tour de force that I couldn't help but think Cronenberg's craft was growing by leaps and bounds. A subsequent look at *The Brood* (1979) further persuaded me that his oeuvre has an overall coherence and complexity unmatched by any other contemporary horror director, including David Lynch and George Romero.

All of Cronenberg's recent works are linked by a style and vision that belong to a particular annex of contemporary art, an annex that might be called biological expressionism. Burroughs is a longtime resident of this annex, and so is his disciple J.G. Ballard; Lynch is the most obvious example of another filmmaker of this persuasion. What all these biological expressionists have in common is a certain deadpan morbidity about the body that borders on comedy—and a tendency to depict paranoia, helplessness, and insect horror in such a way that "inside" and "outside" become indistinguishable.

Dipping into *The Shape of Rage* (a critical collection published in Canada, unfortunately no longer in print), I discovered that several other critics had arrived at some of these connections before I did. I learned from a lengthy interview in the same book that Cronenberg, born in 1943 in Toronto, grew up hoping to become a writer, and that Burroughs was a seminal influence, along with Henry Miller, Vladimir Nabokov, and Samuel Beckett. The fact that Cronenberg is Canadian also seems to have shaped his work. Piers Handling, the editor of the collection, speculates that Cronenberg's "benign but misguided" father figures, who are usually scientists—Dr. Benway (Roy Scheider) in *Naked Lunch* is a near facsimile—point to a specifically Canadian sensibility, an alienated consciousness that incorporates repression, puritanism, a sense of marginality and victimization, a feeling of entrapment, and perhaps even "a colonized mentality." ("The land has been exploited but not for the profit of the people who live there.") Moreover, Handling argues that the fear of external horrors in the first films has been replaced by the fear of internal horrors in all the films subsequent to *The Brood*, and that the "internalization of this dread achieves its apotheosis in *Videodrome*." It's back again with a vengeance in *Naked Lunch*.

I was forced to the appalling conclusion that I would never have become a writer but for Joan's death, and to a realization of the extent to which this event has motivated and formulated my writing. I live with the constant threat of possession, and a constant need to escape from possession, from Control. So the death of Joan brought me in contact with the invader, the Ugly Spirit, and maneuvered me into a lifelong struggle, in which I have no choice except to write my way out.

—Burroughs, introduction to *Queer* (1985)

Perhaps the most transgressive aspect of Cronenberg's adaptation is that it follows the general approach of some of the very worst movie versions of literary classics—for example, *Hemingway's Adventures of a Young Man* and *Mishima*—by turning what was once fiction into ersatz biography of the author. The vulgar presumption of this approach is that the artist's life counts for more than the art itself, which is regarded as little more than a symptom. In effect, whatever the artist has done to transform and transcend the banality of his or her own experience is undone by the filmmakers, who turn it back into raw material; by assuming that biography and art are coextensive and virtually interchangeable, they produce works that lack the integrity of either. (The loud, expressionist décor of *Mishima* with its Las Vegas glitz confirms Dave Kehr's judgment: "The point of all this mad organization—which is like a term paper outline prepared by a Dexedrine addict—is to hide an almost complete lack of content.")

On the face of it, this brand of biographical psychobabble is what Cronenberg has done. He reduces the many protagonists of the book to one, William Lee (Peter Weller), who is clearly meant to be Burroughs himself; indeed, Weller's fine performance is often little more than an uncanny impersonation. The film opens in New York in 1953, where Lee is working as an exterminator who hangs out with two writers easily recognizable as Allen Ginsberg and Jack Kerouac (Michael Zelniker and Nicholas Campbell), neither of whom appears in recognizable form in the narrative sections of Burroughs's book. Cronenberg also supplies a drug-addicted wife, Joan (Judy Davis), plainly modeled after Burroughs's wife Joan Vollmer, who also isn't in the book. There's even a fanciful restaging of Burroughs shooting his wife by playing a game of William Tell with her, getting her to balance a drinking glass on her head, firing at it, and missing.

In fact, Burroughs shot his wife in Mexico City in 1951. In 1953 he wasn't even in New York but traveling about South America looking for the hallucinogenic drug yage; his only stint as an exterminator was in Chicago in 1942, a year or so before he first met Ginsberg and Kerouac in New York. In other words, while the movie is full of references to Burroughs's life it isn't really biography at all, and in fairness to Cronenberg it should be added that this is perfectly evident almost from the start—when a gigantic insect starts talking to Lee, enlisting him as an "agent" and giving him orders. It's rather as if Cronenberg has taken snippets from *Naked Lunch*, various Burroughs autobiographical texts (chiefly "Exterminator!" and the 1985 introduction to *Queer*), a few details of Burroughs's biography, and assorted Burroughs-inspired fancies of his own and placed them all inside a kaleidoscope—or, to switch metaphors, performed an elaborate cut-up with them. Even the film's haunting and lovely score, which juxtaposes classical themes by Howard Shore with wailing free-form alto-sax solos by Ornette Coleman backed by Coleman's trio, creates an ambience that is not so much Burroughs as commentary on Burroughs.

What emerges is recognizable but fully transformed Burroughs material. In the film, Lee gets into trouble when he discovers that someone has been stealing his roach powder. His boss, A.J. Cohen, is livid: "You vant I should spit right in your face!? You vant!? You vant!?" This line and Cohen both appear in "Exterminator!" but the missing bug powder is Cronenberg's addition. When Lee applies to a Chinaman in the office for more powder he gets a curt reply: "No glot. . . . C'lom Fliday." This line comes from the final words of *Naked Lunch*, a passage that's glossed ninety pages earlier: "In 1920s a lot of Chinese pushers around found The West so unreliable, dishonest and wrong, they all packed in, so when an Occidental junky came to score, they say: 'No glot. . . . C'lom Fliday.'"

Shortly after Lee discovers that his wife has been shooting the missing bug powder and is now addicted, two cops arrest him, take him to a decaying office with vomit-green walls, and leave him alone with a gigantic bug who actually gets off on the very substance that is supposed to exterminate it ("Say Bill," it says, "do you think you could rub some of this powder on my lips?"). The bug orders him to kill his wife, insisting that she's an "Interzone" agent and not even human. Later, after Joan asks Lee to rub some bug powder on her own lips and they make love, he procures another drug called "black meat" from the sinister Dr. Benway—a drug made from dried "aquatic Brazilian centipedes" that is supposed to get Joan off her habit. But at this point Lee winds up "accidentally" killing her.

Significantly, Lee trades his gun for a portable typewriter at a pawnshop; he then travels to Interzone, a North African city like Tangier where most of the remainder of the film is set. Lee's "ticket" to Interzone, however, which he shows to one of his writer friends, is the drug-filled syringe procured from Benway, so it's highly questionable whether Lee or the film ever really leaves New York. (Enslaved by his addiction, he may not even leave his flat.) If one looks closely at certain scenes in Interzone, fragments of New York are plainly visible—a patch of Central Park seen from a window, even an Eighth Avenue subway entrance seen from a car—and at one point Lee remarks that a certain living room reminds him of a New York restaurant. Lee's flats in New York and Interzone are nearly identical, and he even encounters Kiki (Joseph Scorsiani), who becomes his lover in Interzone, initially in a New York waterfront bar.

Bearing all this in mind, the extreme distortions of Paul and Jane Bowles, fictionalized as Tom and Joan Frost (Ian Holm and Judy Davis) in the Interzone sections, have to be seen as projections of Lee—and beyond that, projections of Cronenberg—rather than as tenable figures having anything to do with literary history or with Burroughs himself. Tom Frost is an older and more overt Lee who acts openly on his desires; Joan is an alternate version of his wife, "addicted" to lesbianism as the other Joan was addicted to bug powder. These characters, as well as Yves Cloquet (Julian Sands), Hans (Robert A. Silverman), and Kiki, show that Cronenberg has taken considerable license in fashioning this world, which clearly has more relationship to his own universe than to Burroughs's.

Cronenberg's method for "adapting" *Naked Lunch* is roughly analogous to Burroughs's device of "natural" cut-ups, a process of hallucinatory transformation: roach powder becomes hallucinogenic drug, drug taking becomes sex, roach becomes paranoiac operative, wife becomes insect, and Interzone becomes New York experienced in a drugged state. Later, when Lee becomes a writer in Interzone, the transformations become even more dense and metaphorical: typewriters, for example, become talking cockroaches or Mugwumps (a Burroughs beastie that the film works wonders with, in New York and Interzone alike), functioning variously as Ugly Spirits, muses, prophets, psychiatrists, lovers, friends, bosses, and drug dispensers, so that writing, sex, and drugs become virtually interchangeable. The moment of each transformation, moreover, becomes impossible to pinpoint, because the identities do not strictly mutate but overlap or interface—rather like the colored geometric shapes that traverse the screen in the film's beautiful opening credits.

Some of these principles of transformation operate formally in a series of short experimental films made in England in the '60s by the late Antony Balch, now available on video, all of them involving Burroughs as writer or actor/performer. (The best are *Towers Open Fire* and *The Cut-Ups*.) The transformations here often involve one character assuming the identity of another. A more mainstream, thematic approach to such transformations can be found in two later shorts by Gus Van Sant that are fairly literal adaptations of Burroughs texts: *The Discipline of DE* (1978) develops from a how-to essay with Zen-like behavioral tips (mainly on housework shortcuts) into a specific fictional illustration, a shoot-out between a Wyatt Earp protege and Two Gun McGee; *Thanksgiving Prayer* (1991) quickly turns from a counting of American blessings into a parade of all-American horrors.

Cronenberg's approach is neither a strict application of Burroughs's cut-up principles (as in Balch) nor a straightforward adaptation of his texts (as in Van Sant) but an absorption of certain principles and texts from Burroughs into the filmmaker's particular cosmology and style. The resulting portrait—and it should be stressed that Cronenberg's *Naked Lunch*, unlike Burroughs', is a portrait of a single character—is not of Burroughs or Cronenberg but of some mysterious composite, an overlap and/or interface of these two personalities.

> [The biographer did not] share Burroughs' misogyny, which at the bottom was probably an attempt to smother his own contemptible femininity. Born in his hatred of the secret, covered-up part of himself that was maudlin and sentimental and womanly, misogyny was his form of self-loathing.."
>
> —Ted Morgan,
> *Literary Outlaw: The Life and Times of William S. Burroughs* (1988)

The philosophical parallels between Lynch's *Eraserhead* and this film are striking. Both movies are often creepy comedies generated by lurid puritanical imaginations infected by guilt and a will toward censorship, echo chambers of projections and disavowals. When William Lee is "enlisted" as an agent in Interzone, the reports he types up turn out to be *Naked Lunch* itself, a book he has no recollection of writing. (In his introduction Burroughs said, "I have no precise memory of writing the notes which have now been published under the title *Naked Lunch*.") Lee's homosexuality and his drug taking provoke comparable disavowals, as he projects his desires onto others. Whether he's engaged in sex, drugs, or writing, Lee can be seen simultaneously as a voyeur and as an active participant in the diverse intrigues and activities of Interzone, which corresponds to the inner zone of his head. Like "innocent" Henry in *Eraserhead*, he ultimately figures as both progenitor and victim of the diverse horrors surrounding him.

But a key difference between Lynch and Cronenberg corresponds to an equally key difference between Cronenberg and Burroughs. Though Lynch's vision depends on darkness and cruelty and Burroughs's more pessimistic and mature vision is tinged with feelings of great loss and sorrow, neither artist can be said to have a tragic vision—as Ballard does, at least in *Empire of the Sun*. Cronenberg has such a vision, and his *Naked Lunch*, like *Dead Ringers*, is suffused with it.

The central tenet in *Naked Lunch* is that Lee needs his wife in order to live and needs to kill her in order to write, and all the film's transactions and transformations derive from this appalling fact. He literally has to kill his wife again and again in order to keep on writing, and this condemns him to perpetual psychic imprisonment. (It's no wonder that by the end of the film Benway, Lee's bisexual father figure, has enlisted him in the CIA as a secret agent posing as an American journalist, and sent him off to an old-style totalitarian state: Annexia, a Cronenberg invention.) Given Lee's tragic dilemma, the matching aphorisms that appear at the beginning of the movie resound with irrevocable finality. The first comes from Hassan I Sabbah, an 11th-century Persian religious agitator much admired by Burroughs: "Nothing is true, everything is permitted." And the second comes from Burroughs himself: "Hustlers of the world, there is one Mark you cannot beat. The Mark inside . . . "

Rivette's Rupture (*Duelle* and *Noroît*)

From the Chicago Reader *(February 28, 1992). My writing about most of Rivette's other features and further commentary about these two can be found on my website and in my previous collections, especially* Placing Movies, Movies as Politics, Essential Cinema, *and both volumes of* Cinematic Encounters.

Dagger in hand, I scaled the heights of raw power, thanks to the male role that Rivette gave me. . . . This kind of sexual metamorphosis, this strange androgyny, never appeared in the French cinema before Rivette. After I performed the role of Giulia in *Noroît* I felt that I was capable of anything. Rivette changed my ideas about acting; for me, he is a kind of Mao and his films are a Cultural Revolution.

—Bernadette Lafont in an interview, 1977

Though no one would ever think to call Jacques Rivette a realist, the fact remains that all of his first six features take place in a sharply perceived environment that can arguably be called the "real world." An acute sense of place and period brought into focus largely by means of "documentary" techniques informs these haunting movies, giving them all a pungent flavor that can only be described as the taste of a particular time, milieu, and culture. But because they're quintessentially French—Gilles Deleuze has aptly written that Rivette is the most French of the New Wave directors who came to prominence in the '60s—fantasy might be said to form an essential part of the texture of this real world.

In *Paris Belongs to Us* (1960), *L'amour fou* (1968), and the separate four- and twelve-hour versions of *Out 1* (1971 and 1972), the fantasies tend to be paranoid, having to do with conspiracy and betrayals, concealed plots and machinations. In

The Nun (1966), an adaptation of a Diderot novel set in the eighteenth century, these fantasies all evoke freedom, chiefly through the film's sound track—the "outside" as experienced by a nun confined to her cell. And in *Celine and Julie Go Boating* (1974), in which the heroines' word-spinning fantasies eventually give birth to an alternative plot that the two periodically enter, the world they inhabit at the outset is firmly anchored in a vivid sense of Montmartre during a lazy summer. In effect this initial setting corresponds to the first two paragraphs of *Alice in Wonderland*—that drowsy, necessary moment on a riverbank before Alice notices that the rabbit rushing past her is actually speaking.

Twhylight and *Nor'wester*, the two features Rivette made in 1976, break profoundly with this tradition, and the six features he's made since, including the recent *La belle noiseuse*, have been different as a consequence. (These are the designated English titles of the 1976 features, though they're better known as *Duelle* and *Noroît* respectively. Significantly, both the English and French titles of both films are invented words: "duelle," for instance, is the feminized form of "duel," which has the same meaning in French as in English.) Though Rivette's last eight films, including *Twhylight* and *Nor'wester*, make use of the "documentary" techniques (such as direct sound recording) that characterize his first period, one's sense of a real and recognizable world in them is much more attenuated. Some might even argue that Rivette's work has never fully recovered from the profound rupture created by these two films. Both represent violent rejections of the contemporary world, including a retreat from politics—a position that has to be seen in relation to the failed French revolution of May 1968, the implicit subject of *Out 1*—though both can be read as psychodramas full of political implications. It may be significant that *Cahiers du cinéma*, the magazine that has been most supportive of Rivette's work and that was for sixteen years the principal outlet for his own criticism, has never dared to run a review of either movie. (They were originally meant to be parts two and three of a quartet of features to be called *Scènes de la vie parallèle*—"Scenes of Parallel Life." It was never completed.)

Rivette once remarked that Griffith's *Intolerance* has more to say about the year in which it was made, 1916, than about any of the historical periods it covers. In the same way, sixty years later, *Twhylight* and *Nor'wester* undoubtedly have a lot to say about 1976, but these films confound any ordinary definitions of period by deliberately making all their temporal references inconsistent: in fact they could be called transitional works between the modernism of Rivette's first six features and the postmodernism of his last six.

His original intention was to shoot all four films of the quartet in swift succession, then edit them in the order of their releases. But after suffering a nervous collapse a few days into the shooting of the third feature—intended to be part one of the series, starring Albert Finney and Leslie Caron—Rivette decided to edit each of the two films he had already shot and canceled the other two. *Duelle*, the first edited, had a very brief run in Paris; *Noroît* has never opened in France at all. Tonight these rarely seen movies are starting their first run in Chicago at Facets Multimedia, where they will play for a week.

All four films were to take place within a partially invented mythological framework corresponding to the forty days of the traditional carnival cycle, a period that includes three lunar phases when rival goddesses of the moon and sun come to earth and mingle with mortals. All the films were to feature on-location and on-screen musicians improvising live accompaniment to the action without functioning as characters themselves, and each film would employ a different kind of music. The first film would be a love story, the second a film noir thriller, the third a pirate adventure, and the fourth a musical featuring Carolyn Carlson's modern dance company; Rivette intended to increase the amount of music from one feature to the next.

The proposal Rivette drafted to acquire a state subsidy for this mad, ambitious project included the following passages:

> The ambition of these films is to discover a new approach to acting in the cinema, where speech, reduced to essential phrases, to precise formulas, would play a role of "poetic' punctuation. Not a return to silent cinema, neither pantomime nor choreography: something else, where the movement of bodies, their counterpoint, their inscription within the screen space, would be the basis of the mise en scène. . . .

> To create one's own space through the movements of one's body, to occupy and traverse the spaces imposed by the décors and the camera's field, to move and act within (and in relation to) the simultaneous musical space: these are the three parameters on which our actors are going to attempt to base their work.

In contrast to the films that immediately preceded and followed this project —*Out 1* and *Celine and Julie Go Boating* before, *Merry-Go-Round* and *La pont du nord* after—the actors did not improvise any of their lines or collaborate on the scripts; their creative contributions were strictly a matter of facial expressions, poses, and gestures. By design, however, the scripts were merely sketched out before the films went into production, and the dialogue was usually written each day only a few hours before shooting. The general idea was to arrive at the unexpected through the chance encounters between particular actors, locations, and dramatic situations, inflected in diverse and unforeseeable ways by the music.

I had the opportunity to watch parts of the shooting of both films—three full days on *Twhylight*, five on *Nor'wester*—and they were drastically different from any other shootings I've ever witnessed, and considerably more exciting. Most shootings are dull because of the technical delays and programmatic approaches toward creativity, usually intended to realize an idea thought up long before. Rivette's suspenseful shootings were full of surprises as the moods of various scenes shifted and developed. Much of this was the result of the musicians' improvisation during and between takes, and much of it came from Rivette's own desire to be surprised by what he saw.

I was also present at the world premiere of *Nor'wester* at the London Film Festival. Rivette introduced it by cheerfully announcing that the main reason he'd wanted to become a film director was to meet his favorite actresses. I pass on this disconcerting comment because it points to an aspect of both films that has made them difficult to deal with critically. While neither contains any significant nudity (in contrast to *La belle noiseuse*), both have an essentially worshipful relation to their actresses that has very different ideological implications in each film—and ambiguous implications in both. While experimental filmmaker Yvonne Rainer and critic Annette Michelson both indignantly walked out after only ten minutes of one of the first screenings of *Twhylight* because of what they perceived as its sexism, Bernadette Lafont, who played the dictatorial head of a band of pirates in *Nor'wester*, subsequently praised Rivette as a sexual revolutionary (in the interview quoted above). Curiously, all three women may have been right.

The mythological framework of both films reflects Rivette's compulsive cinephilia—in particular, a simultaneously serious and ironic view of movie actresses as goddesses. It's worth adding that goddesses and mortal females are the prime movers in both movies, although only in *Nor'wester* do they assume the positions of power usually accorded to men. (In both films the male characters are secondary. The two who are most prominent—Pierrot [Jean Babilée] in *Twhylight*, Ludovico [Larrio Ekson] in *Nor'wester*—are played by very graceful dancers, and the others, all in *Nor'wester*, are treated chiefly as love objects by the female pirates.) There's also a significant class difference between the goddesses and the mortals, although this is much more apparent in *Twhylight* than in *Nor'wester*.

In both films the identities of the sun and moon goddesses are clarified only belatedly—the revelations come especially late in *Nor'wester*—and both plots eventually hinge on the possession of a precious magical jewel that will allow the goddesses to remain on earth past their allotted forty days and thereby become mortal. It also destroys mortals, bringing on madness and death, in the process of converting them into immortal deities. In both films the intense desire to possess this jewel might be likened to the kind of desire set in motion by film narrative itself: "mortal" viewers wish to become "immortal" through their emotional investments in movie stars, and "immortal" movie stars wish to become "mortal"—ordinary folks like you and me—through their emotional identification with viewers.

The mythological framework of the sun and moon also influences the visual design of both films, affecting costumes, makeup, and the lighting of certain scenes. The various phases of the moon are motifs in both, and in the climactic sequence of *Nor'wester* the unmasking of the characters is echoed by the "unmasking" of the full moon as clouds drift past it.

Rivette drew on specific sources for the style and much of the dialogue in these films. Before each was shot, he screened a different Hollywood movie for the cast and crew. Mark Robson's *The Seventh Victim* (1943), probably the best of all the masterful black-and-white horror quickies produced by Val Lewton, was the stylistic reference point for *Twhylight*, and Fritz Lang's lyrical and evocative color period adventure *Moonfleet* (1955) served the same function for *Nor'wester*.

Both films also incorporate many lines of dialogue from particular plays—Jean Cocteau's *Chevaliers de la table ronde* (1937) in *Twhylight*, and Cyril Tourneur's *The Revenger's Tragedy* (1607 or 1608) in *Nor'wester*. These lines are often wrenched out of context, though. In *Nor'wester*, the Tourneur lines are all recited in English by Geraldine Chaplin and Kika Markham, the two English-speaking actresses in the cast. The role played by the Jacobean tragedy is more substantial in *Nor'wester* than that of the Cocteau play in the earlier film: printed titles indicating the act and scene numbers of the Tourneur play appear throughout, and I'm told that the film's main inspiration was screenwriter Eduardo de Gregorio's description to Rivette of an Italian production of the play in which the sexes were reversed. The weird English spellings that crop up in the subtitles during *Nor'wester*'s final sequence—a "masquerade ball" that concludes with all the remaining characters killing each other off—are deliberate efforts to evoke Tourneur's archaic English, and were done in consultation with Rivette himself.

In *Twhylight*, the film noir references go far beyond allusions to *The Seventh Victim*. Many of the settings are prompted by other noir classics—an aquarium from *The Lady From Shanghai*, a greenhouse from *The Big Sleep*, a row of lockers from *Kiss Me, Deadly* (whose "Great Whatsit"—a Pandora's box containing nuclear energy—bears more than a passing resemblance to this film's deadly but sought-after jewel). The Cocteau references also go much further than the quotations from *Chevaliers de la table ronde*: I'm thinking especially of the uses of mirrors, the casting of Jean Babilée (who performed Cocteau's ballet *Le jeune homme et la mort* in the '40s), and a setting and crucial line ("Je me revengerai") that both derive from Robert Bresson's rather noir-ish *Les dames du bois de Boulogne*, which Cocteau wrote the dialogue for.

When *Twhylight* and *Nor'wester* were screened one after the other at the London Film Festival in 1976, Rivette mentioned to me afterward that it probably wasn't a good idea to see them both together. I've just watched them back to back a second time—as well as separately many other times—and I tend to agree. Each movie is a full meal in itself, and despite their interesting similarities, they are still too different to establish a context together that's mutually enhancing. It's probably better, however—though not strictly necessary—to see them in the order in which they were made.

If I had to recommend one film over the other, it would be hard to know which one to choose. *Twhylight* has a much more difficult plot but is perhaps the more conventionally beautiful: its reinvented, somewhat campy Paris of plush casinos and archaic dance halls alludes to many periods at once but can still be loosely located within a tradition of nostalgic French fantasy shared by such filmmakers as Cocteau and Georges Franju. Its live music is performed almost exclusively by pianist Jean Wiener, a veteran composer who scored many films for Jean Renoir, and consists mainly of antiquated-sounding ditties and tangos. (As in *Nor'wester*, the live music crops up in plausible or semiplausible settings—a hotel lobby, casino, dance hall, and dance studio—as well as completely implausible ones, such as a hotel room and aquarium. The means by which the camera discovers or doesn't discover Wiener in these settings, and the ways in which the actors respond to or ignore his music, are both fascinating and unsettling.)

Nor'wester is easier to follow, more spectacular in terms of its locations (a 12th-century fortress on the Brittany coast and a reconstructed 17th-century chateau), and considerably more outlandish—and therefore more difficult—in its emotional tone and affect. Properly speaking, it belongs to no recognizable era or film genre; the female pirates could be seventeenh-, eighteenth-, or nineteenth-century characters, although they use a telegraph and radio in an early scene and at least one ship is motorized. At different junctures *Nor'wester* suggests a western, a pirate film, a violent Jacobean tragedy, a 19th-century romantic melodrama complete with incest, a demonic (or klutzy) black comedy, a radical lesbian science fiction war film, a musical, and an experimental dance pageant. The music—played by a gifted trio, Jean Cohen-Solal, Robert Cohen-Solal, and Daniel Ponsard, who also contributed a few eerie sound elements to *Twhylight*—runs the gamut from modernist free jazz to neoprimitive folk, employing everything from flutes and traditional European stringed instruments to African and South American percussion.

Both movies suddenly cut to black and white in climactic sequences. Both explore uncanny acting registers that veer unexpectedly from frivolous to fiendish, from passionate to parodic; and both occasionally abandon dialogue altogether and express the drama in terms of pantomime or dance. (Interestingly enough, some of Chaplin's aggressive gestures and abrupt, angular movements can also be found in her subsequent performance in Alan Rudolph's *Remember My Name*.) Both are structured around the successive elimination of all the characters, and both are remarkable and eclectic constructions of mise en scène, with elaborately plotted camera movements and many unconventional cuts. And both, in the final analysis, do so many things to unhinge our notions of what movies are that we may remember them afterward like shards of unfathomable dreams—beautifully textured and intensely realized reveries that obstinately evade all our usual methods of understanding and appropriation.

War Fever [on *Matinee*]

This review appeared in the Chicago Reader *on February 5, 1993.*

I suggested a few new promotional gimmicks for the play—a closed black coffin outside the theater and Oriental incense to get the audiences in the mood. The stage manager agreed to try another of my ideas—Count Dracula would vanish on stage in a cloud of smoke, then suddenly reappear in the audience. Snarling at the frightened spectators, he would again vanish and appear back on stage. I began to learn firsthand the value of good publicity and showmanship.

Adolf Hitler was unwittingly to teach me the lesson again nine years later. Hitler was indirectly responsible for opening the doors of Hollywood for me.

—William Castle, *Step Right Up! I'm Gonna Scare the Pants Off America: Memoirs of a B-Movie Mogul*

It's not the Russians — it's Rumble-Rama.

—Lawrence Woolsey (John Goodman) in *Matinee*

As luck would have it, I saw Joe Dante's ferocious yet lighthearted new comedy, *Matinee*—about John F. Kennedy "standing up to" Nikita Khrushchev while the world held its breath—barely an hour after reading in the paper that the world was holding its breath to see if Bill Clinton, in his first days of office, would "stand up to" Saddam Hussein. Despite the intriguing coincidence I doubt that many of my colleagues will jump to the conclusion that Dante has made a movie with anything at all to say about the way we live and think today. (Remember *Deep Cover*: just another cop thriller, most said or implied, with no relevance to the Bush administration or to our own lives.)

After all, *Matinee* is set during the Cuban missile crisis—it's about war fever in 1962. Moreover it's extremely funny, charming, and entertaining, the way movies are supposed to be but seldom are nowadays. To assume that anything that's so much fun is also telling us something about how we behave both as film spectators and as warmongers, not only three decades ago but right this minute, is to grant a seriousness to our amusement obviously greater than the culture can bear.

But consider how the dark side of spectatorship and the ideology of popular entertainment—the way movies turn us into gremlins—has been central to all of Dante's best work, even at its most nostalgic, film-buffy, and apparently frivolous. His 1984 *Gremlins* gave us adorable little beasties that turned into monsters very much like us—especially in their bratty behavior when they watched a beloved Disney cartoon feature in a movie theater. The Dante segment in *Twilight Zone—The Movie* amplified this idea by establishing a vindictive, Sadean universe created in the mind of a little boy who's watched too many cartoons, while the nightmarish finale of *Explorers* gave us the world of American TV strained through the consciousness, physicality, and technology of extraterrestrials.

Dante's 1989 *The 'Burbs*, which conjured up an old-fashioned horror movie, brought the critique of spectatorship even closer to home by ridiculing the xenophobia of a suburban man (Tom Hanks) spying on his next-door neighbors and satirizing the uninvolved voyeurism of teenagers watching and enjoying this snoop as if they were plunked down in front of their TVs. The earlier *Innerspace* brought new meanings to notions of voyeurism and coexistence by following what happened when a miniaturized Navy pilot (Dennis Quaid) got injected into the body of a hypochondriac (Martin Short), creating intercut parallel narratives that were like movies within movies. Even *Gremlins 2: The New Batch*, though it's the least ambitious conceptually of Dante's recent efforts, brought back the beasties as grubby little versions of ourselves at our most consumerist.

A horror-movie schlockmeister is the central character in *Matinee*—a jovial showman named Lawrence Woolsey (John Goodman) who's clearly modeled on William Castle, master of the horror-exploitation gimmick (and under-rated director of some earlier noirish B-films like *When Strangers Marry* and *The Whistler*), Woolsey's relation to the Cuban missile crisis is clarified when he takes on the role of surrogate father to fifteen-year-old Gene Loomis (Simon Fenton), who has recently moved to Key West with his family. Gene's father, who's in the Navy, has been "sent out" to parts unknown on the day the story opens, shortly before a special bulletin interrupts Art Linkletter's TV show *People Are Funny* to bring on President Kennedy demanding the withdrawal of offensive missile sites recently spotted in Cuba.

In fact, Gene's father never puts in a single appearance in *Matinee*—unless one counts some brief glimpses of him in a home movie his wife (Lucinda Jenney) tearfully watches—so one might say that, mythically and emotionally, Kennedy in his sole TV appearance is the father's replacement. But Woolsey—"America's number-one frightmaster," as he calls himself—is present in the opening scene, in a trailer for his latest horror production, which Gene watches; shortly thereafter we learn that Woolsey will be appearing in person at the theater, on Saturday, to present a special matinee preview of his film. In fact, as soon as Woolsey appears in the flesh, not long after Kennedy's speech, he becomes the movie's most important patriarch, supplanting Kennedy, Adlai Stevenson (who appears briefly at UN hearings on TV), and Gene's missing father—a more ideal version of all of them.

Soon after Woolsey arrives for his show—which involves an elaborate setup with buzzers under the seats and apparitions in the aisles, neatly summarizing some of Castle's most celebrated gimmicks—the panicky theater manager (Robert Picardo) objects that the country is "on red alert." "Exactly," says Woolsey. "What better time to open a horror movie?" And as we discover, Woolsey's arsenal of scare tactics is every bit as effective as Kennedy's. Just as the fear of nuclear holocaust creates a hoarding panic among shoppers at the supermarket, Woolsey's own show reduces his audience to hysterical popcorn fights even before the movie starts. Similarly, the two scaremasters prove equally successful at inspiring hasty retreats; shortly after Woolsey averts disaster by conjuring up a fake nuclear holocaust to drive the audience out of the theater, it's reported in the news that the implied threat of nuclear holocaust has attained comparable results with the Soviets: Khrushchev has promised that the missiles in Cuba will be dismantled.

I don't mean to imply, however, that *Matinee* is didactic, devoted to simple one-to-one correspondences, preachy meanings, or pretentious undertones. And for those who might object to my claims about the movie's contemporary relevance—those who consider the Cuban missile crisis "serious" and the war drums being beaten in Saddam Hussein's ears not, as well as those who think the reverse—my point is merely that the movie traces the kind of unthinking giddiness and/or blood lust that fear produces in an anxious audience.

Whether the sources of anxiety are Castle's *Homicidal* and Nikita Khrushchev or *The Silence of the Lambs* and Saddam Hussein, our taste for horror-movie monsters who provoke bloody reprisals has persisted for most of this century—a taste that becomes especially pronounced whenever our trigger fingers get itchy. (Less persistent are our memory and awareness of the human cost of scratching those itches—most recently, even currently, our slaughter of innocent ethnics unlucky enough to live under the thumb of Saddam Hussein and therefore ideally suited as cannon fodder, for our grand humanitarian schemes as well as his.)

The glory of Dante's comedy in this movie and others—as aided and abetted by his usual production team, producer Michael Finnell, cinematographer John Hora, and screenwriter Charlie Haas—is that it suggests poetic parallels without insisting on them. Just as a backstage bomb shelter—a chamber in which Gene and his radical girlfriend (Lisa Jakub) become briefly and romantically trapped—bears an interesting resemblance to a bank vault, the kind of war fever *Matinee* examines has more than one point of contact with the emotions elicited by bad low-budget horror films: *Matinee* satirically cross-references early-'60s fears of nuclear holocaust with Woolsey's ludicrous new picture, *Mant*, about a man transformed by radiation into a giant ant. ("Young lady," one character intones, "human-insect mutation is far from an exact science.")

Inhabiting a corner of junk heaven in all his pictures, Dante clearly regards each project as a fresh opportunity to show off his appreciation of pop culture. And his pleasure in using familiar bit players such as Jesse White (here the owner of a theater chain) and Dick Miller and John Sayles (members of Citizens for Decent Entertainment) is palpable. As a TV illiterate, I can't comment on the way TV shows past and present have affected casting decisions and the dialogue, though when it comes to movies Dante has obviously taken full advantage of his resources. It doesn't seem accidental, for instance, that Cathy Moriarty—Woolsey's somewhat resigned girlfriend, leading lady, and all-around assistant—reminds us through her accent of her debut role in *Raging Bull*.

We glimpse a profusion of 1962 "one-sheet" movie posters in the lobby of the film's theater, the Key West Strand—a pantheon including *The Man Who Shot Liberty Valance, Hatari!, What Ever Happened to Baby Jane, Lonely Are the Brave,* and *Confessions of an Opium Eater*. It seems Dante is ticking off his favorites, even if this means working in many more posters than one could imagine such a theater displaying at once. He's also created many "excerpts" from movies showing in the theater—including a *Mant* trailer, *Mant* itself (both in black and white), and something called *The Shookup Shopping Cart*, a color feature that suggests both Frank Tashlin and live-action Disney. At the same time that Dante has a field day brutally satirizing our desire to scare ourselves and others, he also re-creates early-'60s clichés with a relish and a feeling for detail that come very close to love.

Sign and Cinema [*In the Land of the Deaf*]

From the Chicago Reader *(August 5, 1994); this was reprinted with the DVD of this film released in the U.K. by Second Run Features.*

Nicolas Philibert's beautiful, illuminating, and energizing documentary, *Le pays des sourds* (*In the Land of the Deaf*) implicitly reflects on three different kinds of language: (1) the different languages spoken in movies, (2) the so-called language of cinema, and (3) sign language, specifically the language of the deaf.

(1) Language in film. I never attended a film school, but during the five years I lived in Paris, from 1969 to 1974, I was unofficially attending something very close to one several days a week—the Cinémathèque Française, which was then operated by its eccentric, visionary main founder, Henri Langlois (1914-1977). The Cinémathèque had two screening facilities that showed together seven or eight films daily, each for a nominal price; if you had a student card, each was less than a dollar. These were films from all over the world, and Langlois was a purist: silent films were almost never shown with musical accompaniment, and little effort was made to show silent or sound films with subtitles that the audience could understand. For Langlois, the essence of cinema was the image, and he saw the Cinémathèque as a kind of utopian Tower of Babel where images carried the essential messages. As if to prove his point, he frequently programmed the only feature ever made in Esperanto—produced, I believe, during the '50s—which virtually no one in the audience could understand.

The obvious drawback of the Cinémathèque was that one often saw movies without fully understanding the dialogue or plot; the equally obvious advantage was that one saw more world cinema than one could have seen anywhere else in the world, and one learned, often by necessity, to glean meanings not contained in the dialogue or intertitles.

(2) "Language" of film. What's usually meant by "the language of cinema" is the set of visual and aural conventions involving editing, framing, *mise en scène*, sound recording, and sound mixing to which all moviegoers respond, though few apart from some academics have bothered to spell them out. Whether these conventions and the messages they send constitute a language is debatable, though there was an entire cottage industry of film theory during the '70s predicated on that assumption. The intricate rules of conventional editing are a good example of what I'm talking about: very few viewers are capable of defining them but nearly everyone responds to them, just as native speakers of a language follow the rules of grammar even if they don't consciously know what they are. This makes editing at least resemble language.

(3) Sign language (or Sign). It seems that the usual response of someone who hears a foreign language is to assume, often unconsciously, that it's a failed attempt at the language one already knows—an assumption subtitling helps to encourage by supposedly providing the "real" meaning. Similarly, unconventional kinds of film editing informed by sophisticated avant-garde strategies might be misread as failed attempts to follow conventions rather than as successful efforts to pursue other ends.

Similarly, when most of us first encounter Sign—of which there's a great deal in *In the Land of the Deaf*, along with English subtitles "translating" it—our likely first response is to "read" it as if it were a form of pantomime. But according to Oliver Sacks in his recent book *Seeing Voices*, this reflects a misconception: "We see . . . in Sign, at every level—lexical, grammatical, syntactic—a linguistic use of space: a use that is amazingly complex, for much of what occurs linearly, sequentially, temporally in speech, becomes simultaneous, concurrent, multileveled in Sign. The 'surface' of Sign may appear simple to the eye, like that of gesture or mime, but one soon finds that this is an illusion, and what looks so simple is extraordinarily complex and consists of innumerable spatial patterns nested, three-dimensionally, in each other."

This observation can be adapted to the so-called language of cinema: young viewers often maintain that silent films are unwatchable today, that they're crude, primitive approximations of what sound movies do much better. But this rejection is of course partially a learned response rather than an innate reaction: the same audience never seems to mind the visual corruptions and limitations of TV and video. One might come closer to the truth by reversing the paradigm: isolating certain silent masterpieces and assuming that current popular sound movies are crude attempts to approximate their expressiveness. Compare Tom Hanks in *Forrest Gump* or Zbigniew Zamachowski in *White* with any of the silent slapstick stars these sad sacks are directly or indirectly patterned after—Chaplin, Keaton, Laurel, Langdon, Lloyd—and the difference is like that between an able conservatory pupil playing an exercise and a virtuoso musician performing in concert.

Better yet, compare the expressiveness of Arnold Schwarzenegger in *True Lies* with that of any of the people speaking Sign in Philibert's documentary, children or adults, male or female, and the differences become astronomical. Despite the benefit of spoken language, Schwarzenegger's palette is so limited that the only "emotions" he registers are actually parodies of emotions, which is why he usually seems miscast as anything but a robot. By contrast the people signing in Philibert's film—and these are almost the only people we see—use their faces and bodies like agile paintbrushes, speaking to us and to each other with all the colors imaginable, vibrantly and directly. (As Jean Gremion writes in *The Planet of the Deaf,* "In sign language, the smallest bat of an eyelash can become an element of syntax.")

Even more remarkable, the fact that most of us in the audience understand English but not Sign plays a secondary role. English subtitles translate for us, but one discovers early on that, like subtitles translating spoken languages, the translation is only a partial, reductive version of what's being expressed. Even if one ignores the subtitles, the range of emotions—from grief to joy, from anger to affection, from enthusiasm to indifference—is so great, and the power behind each of them so immediate, that we often feel blown away by the sheer force of the subjects' personalities. The particulars conveyed in the subtitles are helpful and important, but as the film progresses they begin to seem more and more like footnotes to large-scale texts that only Sign can convey.

To quote Sacks again, "One has only to watch two people signing to see that signing has a playful quality, a style, quite different from that of speech. Signers tend to improvise, to play with signs, to bring all their humor, their imaginativeness, their personality, into their signing, so that signing is not just the manipulation of symbols according to grammatical rules, but, irreducibly, the voice of the signer—a voice given special force, because it utters itself, so immediately, with the body. One can have or imagine disembodied speech, but one cannot have disembodied Sign. The body and soul of the signer, his unique human identity, are continually expressed in the act of signing."

One might also regard the subtitles in Philibert's film the way one regards librettos, as texts without the benefit of either music or performance, which is what the deaf people are supplying. One suspects that Philibert has this analogy in mind, because he begins the film with the camera pulling back from two women and two men performing Sign together to sheet music on music stands, and the musical effect of their individual and collective gestures—their passages in unison and their interactive duets—is immediately obvious.

The relationships between Sign and cinema are obviously deep and complex; significantly, the film's first Sign monologue reveals a mute subject's lifelong fascination with movies. But this doesn't mean that Sign and cinema are automatically interchangeable. The aim and achievement of Philibert's film is to plunge us as completely as possible into the world of communication between deaf people, and in order to do this he's had to rethink, to some extent, the language of cinema—the conventions of framing, editing, and even sound recording. In a fascinating article for the French film magazine *Trafic*, Philibert has described in detail how conventional documentary filming methods proved inadequate for capturing the subtle interactions between deaf people. (For example, "Although sound operates in 360 degrees, in the realm of the deaf the voice-off does not exist: out of sight, communication is not possible; outside the frame, not even a hello.") In the same article he explains why making a purely silent film would not have accurately represented the world of the deaf—which, "contrary to what is believed, is not pure silence. Confused, faraway murmurs, diffuse noises: even for the so-called "stone' deaf, it is not nothingness." Philibert manipulates his own soundtrack at times in order to suggest some of that subjective experience, most noticeably at the very end of the film, and some of the Sign monologues deal with certain aspects of the experience as well. (A mute born into a nearly all deaf family describes the initial experience of using a hearing aid as extremely unpleasant: "The sound of chairs—it was awful.")

But the principal bounty of this film is the relatively unmediated and magnificent spectacle of Sign itself, performed by numerous individuals for whom "acting" and "being" appear to be indissoluble and indistinguishable. These extraordinary people include some of the best child "performers" I've seen since the films of Truffaut, as well as a wondrous, comical Sign teacher whose everyday utterances automatically place him in the pantheon of character actors occupied by such figures as Walter Brennan, Michel Simon, and William Demarest. I'm tempted to say that I haven't seen such emotional, multifaceted physical expressiveness in so many people since the golden age of silent movies; but alas, among contemporary moviegoers that no longer serves as a recommendation. So let me put it differently: if you want to see and hear people who will make you feel more alive, the likes of whom you won't come close to finding in any commercial release now playing, make your way to the Film Center and check this movie out.

Mamma Roma

From the Chicago Reader *(May 19, 1995). I no longer think that Pasolini is "less important" than Antonioni, Fellini, Rossellini, and Visconti.*

Who can predict the changes in intellectual fashion over twenty years? In 1975, when the controversial Italian writer and filmmaker Pier Paolo Pasolini was brutally murdered by a seventeen-year-old boy in a Roman suburb, he was no more in vogue than he had been throughout his stormy career. If any openly gay writer-director was an international star in the mid-'70s, it was Rainer Werner Fassbinder, who at that point was spinning out as many as three or four features a year; he died in 1982 after an orgy of cocaine abuse.

Pasolini and Fassbinder were both maverick leftists who often alienated other leftists as well as everyone on the right, and both had a taste for rough trade, but in terms of their generations (Pasolini was born in 1922, Fassbinder in 1946) and cultural reference points they were radically different. The only reason to compare them now is to note how much their reputations and visibility have changed here over the last two decades. In 1995 Fassbinder is much less a household name in the United States than either Jean-Luc Godard or Andy Warhol, the two artists he was most often compared to when he was alive, whereas Pasolini has much more currency. For one thing, nearly all of Pasolini's features are available on video, and nearly all in their original screen formats—a fact that separates him from Antonioni, Fellini, Rossellini, and Visconti. (All that's missing of his filmography in this country are most of the shorts, many of them major efforts.)

It's unlikely that Pasolini is as important as these four other Italian filmmakers, though as a writer his reputation is well established. (Only a few years ago Alberto Moravia called him "the greatest Italian poet of the second half of the twntieth century.") But he remains a key figure to many major filmmakers. One of the crucial episodes in Nanni Moretti's recent *Caro diario* is Moretti's visit to the site of Pasolini's murder, and when I once asked the late Armenian master Sergei Paradjanov (*Shadows of Our Forgotten Ancestors*, *Sayat Nova*) what filmmakers were important to him, he reflected for about half an hour on why such directors as Luis Buñuel and even his friend Andrei Tarkovsky were too middle-class, then settled on Pasolini as the only contemporary he respected without qualification. Orson Welles, who appeared in a Pasolini short made immediately after *Mamma Roma*, was surprisingly respectful: "Terribly bright and gifted. Crazy mixed-up kid, maybe—but on a very superior level. I mean Pasolini the poet, spoiled Christian, and Marxist ideologue. There's nothing mixed-up about him on a movie set."

As a poet and novelist and in particular as a newspaper writer, Pasolini enjoyed an influence on Italian culture that would be unthinkable for an American intellectual, but scandal followed him there as it followed him everywhere else, and its impact was international. I'll never forget the strident, hysterical hooting of professional critics at a late-'60s New York press screening of Pasolini's remarkable *Teorema*, a deadly serious parable about a contemporary Christ figure (Terence Stamp) seducing every member of an Italian household—father, mother, sister, brother, maid—then disappearing, thereby traumatizing everyone in a different fashion. This movie floored me at the time with its brute eloquence as well as its simple audacity, but it brought irate responses from some of my friends. "The trouble with Pasolini is he wants to be fucked by Jesus and Marx at the same time," one of them said [Annette Michelson], and she certainly had a point; it's hard to think of another artist for whom Marxism, Catholicism, and homosexuality were at once so urgent, so alive, and so outrageously interdependent.

Mamma Roma was Pasolini's second feature, made five years before *Teorema*. It's a good deal less provocative, but it remains one of his better features—and until Martin Scorsese decided to release it, it was the only one that hadn't been distributed in the United States. The movie originally came about because the great actress Anna Magnani saw Pasolini's *Accattone* in 1962 and decided she wanted to make a feature with him. Pasolini spent three weeks writing a vehicle for her, then began shooting almost immediately. What emerged from their encounter was not entirely satisfactory to either of them, but it remains a landmark in both their careers. A *grande dame* and something of a prima donna, Magnani is best known today for her films with Rossellini (*Open*

City, *The Miracle*), Visconti (*Bellissima*), and Renoir (*The Golden Coach*), as well as for her '50s forays into Hollywood opposite Marlon Brando (*The Fugitive Kind*), Burt Lancaster (*The Rose Tattoo*), and Anthony Quinn (*Wild Is the Wind*). She was arguably as much an auteur as Pasolini, and the results of their collaboration are a good deal more memorable than his subsequent teaming with Maria Callas on the 1970 *Medea*.

"In Pasolini's first films, upward mobility is a descent into hell," writes critic P. Adams Sitney in his recent book *Vital Crises in Italian Cinema*. And because upward mobility is all that the title heroine of *Mamma Roma* really aspires to—trying to find a "better" life for her son than she's managed for herself, edging him into the lower middle class—this would be a tragic story even if she succeeded. A former prostitute, she joyously attends the rural wedding of her pimp Carmine (Franco Citti) and a respectable country woman in the film's opening scene: the event signals not only the official end of her servitude but the opportunity to collect her teenage son Ettore (Ettore Garofolo)—who knows nothing about her work—from the countryside and bring him to an apartment she's found for them in the public housing of a Roman suburb. She eventually finds work selling fruits and vegetables in an open market and, with the help of a prostitute friend, begins stage-managing Ettore's sex life—steering him away from a promiscuous older woman and single mother—and conniving to get him the right sort of job, as a restaurant waiter, through an elaborate blackmail scheme. But by this time Carmine, who's left his wife, turns up at her flat demanding that she give him money even if she has to return to prostitution to get it—and threatening to tell Ettore about her past if she refuses.

Pasolini began his filmmaking career as a post-neorealist: Citti and Garofolo, like most of the other actors in the film except Magnani, were working-class nonprofessionals whom he more or less pulled off the street. In fact Citti, whom Pasolini had also cast in in *Accattone*, was arrested and put in prison during the shooting of *Mamma Roma*; Pasolini refused to replace him, holding up the production until Citti was released. When he discovered Garofolo, Pasolini wrote: "It was beautiful, like finding the last verse, the most important, of a poem, like finding a perfect rhyme." But Magnani came from the *petite bourgeoisie*, and the fact that her character—"Mamma Ro," as most of her friends in the film call her—aspires to that class when the actress was actually of it was apparently the source of most of the problems between her and Pasolini.

In *Open City* (1946)—the film that made her famous, and a favorite of Pasolini's—Magnani plays a courageous partisan during World War II who's killed by the Nazis while carrying an unborn child. It's been noted that if she and her child had both lived, they might well have become Mamma Roma and Ettore; certainly they're the right ages. But Pasolini's film communicates an acute pessimism about Italy that makes it as much a critique of *Open City* as a sequel to it. That pessimism continued to the end of his life and career: ultimately he rejected contemporary settings entirely. For him consumer culture and the obliteration of the Italian peasantry were two sides of the same ugly coin; he set his last picture, *Salò* during the final days of Italian fascism and gave his pessimism apocalyptic overtones.

For all its direct emotional power, *Mamma Roma* is choppy and often somewhat disjointed as storytelling. The viewer is frequently confused about how much time has passed between sequences, and the dramatic confrontations that the story seems to demand and promise—such as a scene between mother and son after he discovers her prostitution—are often left out.

Yet *Mamma Roma* remains a delicate and at times beautiful work. For all Magnani's volcanic eruptions in an exuberant bravura performance, this tragedy often seems to have been perceived from a certain distance; the music we hear is mainly Vivaldi (*Concerto in D Minor* and *Concerto in C Major*), and Pasolini's sources for the look of the film came from art history rather than other movies. "That which I carry in my head as vision, as a visual field," he recorded in a diary during the shooting of *Mamma Roma*, "are the frescoes of Masaccio and of Giotto—the painters I love most along with certain mannerists (for example, Pontormo)." It's a tribute to Pasolini's conception that these classical references seem more natural outgrowths of the story than contrivances imposed on it. When Ettore toward the end is linked to images of the crucified Christ, it's only after an extended initiation into the brutality of his surroundings has been presented as a calvary. And it seems appropriate that Pasolini's final image of blighted urban wasteland, a vacant lot surrounded by grimy buildings and a church, should reverberate like an El Greco.

Fresh Clues to an Old Mystery [*The Big Sleep*]

From the Chicago Reader, *June 20, 1997.*

For all its reputation as a classic, and despite the greatness of Howard Hawks as a filmmaker, *The Big Sleep* has never quite belonged in the front rank of his work—at least not to the same degree as *Scarface, Twentieth Century, Only Angels Have Wings, To Have and Have Not, Red River, The Big Sky, Monkey Business, Gentlemen Prefer Blondes*, and *Rio Bravo*, to cite my own list of favorites. Unlike *To Have and Have Not* (1944)—Hawks's previous collaboration with Humphrey Bogart and Lauren Bacall, writers Jules Furthman and William Faulkner, cinematographer Sid Hickox, and composer Max Steiner—it qualifies as neither a personal manifesto on social and sexual behavior nor an abstract meditation on jivey style and braggadocio set within a confined space, though it periodically reminds one that exercises of this kind are what Hawks did best. Most of the time, the film's energy and aplomb are devoted to getting through its labyrinthine gumshoe plot without stumbling—a notable feat in itself, but more a triumph of accommodation than of unbridled self-expression.

Ever since Hawks was discovered as an auteur by a couple of eccentric critics in the '50s—Manny Farber in the United States and Jacques Rivette in France—critical approaches to his work have been hamstrung by his own notion of himself as nothing more than a gentleman jock and journeyman hipster. His main idea of self-expression was figuring out who to hire, how to mold and coddle his employees, and how to have a certain amount of fun with them while holding his own with studio management. Resembling a bandleader-pianist like Basie or Ellington, he understood how to show his personnel to best advantage. Sometimes this was a matter of setting one player off against another, and sometimes it was simply knowing when to lay out, when to solo, and when to feed chords to another player. As Todd McCarthy confirms in his new 756-page biography *Howard Hawks: The Grey Fox of Hollywood*, Hawks didn't even bother to direct the musical numbers in *Gentlemen Prefer Blondes*. But that no more diminishes his stature (or the movie's) than the recent revelation that Billy Strayhorn actually wrote a lot of Ellington's best tunes reduces the composer's greatness (or that of "Take the 'A' Train"). Ellington's best music and Hawks's best movies are both supremely about the joy of people living and working together, and our knowledge of the trade-offs—even in some cases rip-offs—involved in these subtle transactions only enhances our sense of the artist's style and taste. As Farber once put it, Hawks's "whole moviemaking system seems a secret preoccupation with linking, a connections business involving people, plots, and eight-inch hat brims," and it stands to reason that plenty of these connections took place offscreen as well as on.

To demonstrate this idea, take a good look at the two versions of *The Big Sleep* that history has left us with—the first released to U.S. troops overseas in August 1945, and the other, much better known one shown domestically a year later. The recently restored first version—playing this week at Facets Multimedia, along with a fascinating documentary postscript in which film archivist Robert Gitt shows why and how most of the changes were made—reveals not how a terrific movie got better or worse but how, for commercial reasons, it got transformed into another kind of terrific movie. It also helps show us how the second movie has been read or misread in terms of the self-expression of various artists: Hawks, Bogart, Bacall, Faulkner, Furthman, and Brackett.

For years it was widely assumed that the celebrated delicious dialogue of *double entendres* about racehorses between Bogart and Bacall in a plush bar—a scene found only in the second version—was written by Faulkner, although a few commentators opted for Furthman. Now we know it was written by the relatively unsung (and completely uncredited) Philip Epstein, who coscripted *Casablanca*. Long after the other three writers had left the project, Jack Warner hired Epstein to beef up the interplay between Bogart and Bacall and thereby improve Bacall's image, which had been tarnished by her miscast appearance in the poorly received *Confidential Agent*, which appeared before *The Big Sleep* and after *To Have and Have Not*. Her highly influential agent, Charles Feldman, urged Warner to revise *The Big Sleep* in order to repair the damage, and most of the reshooting and reediting—and, in at least one instance, redubbing—was carried out in strict accordance with his suggestions.

Complicating and occasionally enhancing these revisions was the fluctuating relationship between Bacall and Bogart, who'd fallen in love while shooting *To Have and Have Not*. During the initial shoot on *The Big Sleep*, Bogart was still married to someone else and fitfully trying to make that marriage work, and Hawks, who may have had designs of his own on Bacall, was mainly interested in keeping his two stars apart when they weren't working together. By the time the three of them regrouped to shoot the new scenes for the second version, Bogart and Bacall had become inseparable, and as a consequence Hawks's relationship with both had cooled.

Though many of the changes in the movie, like the racehorse dialogue, were clear improvements, much of the plot exposition was excised in the process, leading to a good deal of speculation over the next half-century about who actually killed the chauffeur, Owen Taylor. Out of this grew the tall tale, spread by Hawks, that no one working on the picture knew the answer and that when Hawks wired Chandler to ask him, Chandler replied that he didn't know either. But in fact Faulkner and Brackett's script fully answered this question in the prerelease version, and when their explanation was removed, an already intricate mystery plot became impossible to follow in a few particulars.

Biographer McCarthy builds an interesting thesis out of a comparison of the two versions, which he says "reveals *The Big Sleep* as the indisputable turning point in its director's career. The first cut represents the culmination of Hawks's dedication to narrative, to classical storytelling principles, to the kind of logic that depends upon the intricate interweaving of dramatic threads. The revised, less linear cut sees him abandoning these long-held virtues for the sake of 'scenes,' scenes of often electrifying individual effect, but scenes that were weighted heavily in favor of character over plot and dramatic complexity. When Hawks saw that he could get away with this, it emboldened him to proceed further down this path for the remainder of his career, with results that were variable in terms of the intent and quality of his work."

McCarthy's hypothesis—arrived at after seeing Gitt's restoration of the prerelease version and during the final stages of writing his book, when the impulse to cry "Eureka!" must have been irresistible—is seductive but far from indisputable. After all, Hawks's next picture after *The Big Sleep* was the linear (if somewhat episodic) *Red River*, and a lot more classical storytelling was to come in pictures like *I Was a Male War Bride*, *The Thing From Another World*, *The Big Sky*, and *Land of the Pharaohs*. Eventually he arrived at a looser, less linear kind of moviemaking in pictures like *Rio Bravo* and *Hatari*—unless one concludes that he was already concentrating on "scenes" rather than story line in a comedy like the 1934 *Twentieth Century,* or that the relatively abrupt ending of *Red River* conforms to Hawks's second manner. But McCarthy certainly has a point in singling out the two versions of *The Big Sleep* as emblems of dialectical strands in Hawks's artistic personality—warring impulses that inform most of his career.

During the '60s, when Hawks's personality as well as his artistic credentials were still a matter of dispute, a lot of ink was wasted on the relative merits of his version of Chandler's *The Big Sleep* and John Huston's version of Dashiell Hammett's *The Maltese Falcon*—surely a case of apples and oranges. Back then I was inclined to come down on Hawks's side, but today, when the battle lines are drawn differently, I find too many supplementary factors at play to necessarily draw such a conclusion. Obviously Hammett's writing is superior to both Chandler's and Huston's script based on Hammett—not to mention a good deal of "classic" Hemingway. It's less obvious but still defensible that Hawks's *The Big Sleep* is superior to Chandler's novel (at least if one prefers adolescent stoicism to adolescent self-pity and overlooks Chandler's more extensive grasp of corruption). And clearly Huston is more faithful to his source than Hawks and his writers are to theirs. But I have to admit that I find the macho fatalism of both directors lacking in terms of a comprehensive moral vision. Huston's Sam Spade may be more of a misogynist than Hammett's, and Hawks's Philip Marlowe may be more of a moral elitist than Chandler's, but in each case the change marks a trait in the director that's the flip side of what makes him shine.

In *The Big Sleep*, one has to weigh Bogart's sexual gallantry and attractiveness to Lauren Bacall's character and the various flirty ingenues he encounters on his rounds—most notably Dorothy Malone's bookseller and Joy Barlowe's taxi driver—against the contempt he and the movie express toward Vivian's sister Carmen (Martha Vickers) and a schemer named Agnes (Sonia Darrin), both dismissed as irredeemable, inhuman rodents packed with sex appeal. The cozy clubhouse atmosphere Hawks conjures up with such allure and panache is always predicated on such nonnegotiable exclusions.

If these exclusions seem more problematic here than they do in *To Have and Have Not* and *Rio Bravo*, it's largely because *The Big Sleep* has less affection and compassion overall (apart from a certain tenderness toward the aforementioned ladies and a few stranded patsies, mainly General Sternwood and Elisha Cook Jr.'s unforgettable Harry Jones) and very little of the same *esprit de corps*, apart from Bacall's song at a casino. For me, this is the major limitation of both versions of *The Big Sleep*—the impulse to turn some people into objects and expel them from the human race, which seems more a failure of imagination than an enlightened moral position. (A similar but far uglier position dominates Hawks's last film, *Rio Lobo*, and related forms of callousness in *Bringing Up Baby* and *His Girl Friday* prevent me from including them in my list of Hawks favorites.)

I never met Hawks exactly, but twenty-five summers ago, when the San Sebastian Film Festival, where he was serving as president of the jury, offered its guests a day trip to Pamplona to attend a bullfight, I spent portions of an afternoon as part of his entourage. (It was during the Franco period, when perks of this kind were common.) Like others in the group, I asked Hawks a couple of standard film-buff questions ("Is it true that Andy Williams dubbed part of Bacall's singing voice in *To Have and Have Not?*") and got the standard answers ("Yes, he did, and so did Hoagy Carmichael and several others, but it was Bacall's own voice in *The Big Sleep*"—a half-truth at best, because Bacall's own voice was eventually used in the final cut of *To Have and Have Not* as well.) The main impression I had of him was that he was what my older brother in Alabama would have called a good ol' boy—the sort of cocky, amiable jock who hung around locker rooms and spent his time recounting anecdotes of one-up-manship in which he was always right and everyone else was always wrong.

The threads of desperation laced through such a pose are of course endemic to such a personality. McCarthy reports in his introduction that Hawks "felt so insecure as a director on his first few pictures that he regularly had to pull his car over on his way to work in order to vomit." Yet if it weren't for such desperation, I doubt he'd be remembered as the great director he was: it's the darker, more nihilistic side of his cockiness—his perception of the void—that gives his best work its metaphysical weight. (Is there any filmmaker who conveys a sharper sense of naked fear?) We know from various sources that Hawks was contemptuous of people who committed suicide—Andrew Sarris has some very suggestive things to say on this subject in *The American Cinema*—but surely this was the kind of self-protective cover assumed by someone for whom suicide was at times a genuine temptation.

Indeed, both versions of *The Big Sleep*—a noir whose almost pervasive black-ness and coldness is broken fitfully by little warm nests of camaraderie and friendly lust—conjure up an unstable universe where playfulness and profound uncertainty are kissing cousins. The release version makes better sport of the playfulness and some of the nests even cozier. And the earlier version more lucidly pursues a deductive train of thought through this uncertain world—not only when it comes to explaining the chauffeur's death, but also when Marlowe snoops around a cottage where a murder has just taken place (a wordless piece of pure moviemaking, lamentably trimmed in the release version, that's good enough to recall the opening of *Rio Bravo*). In fact, the prerelease version offers a much better example of Hollywood enchantment than any current release you're likely to find.

High Infidelity [*Other Voices, Other Rooms*]

From the February 13, 1998 Chicago Reader. *I hope that my harshness towards the film I'm reviewing is counterbalanced by my appreciation of Capote's early writing.*

I cannot tell a lie: my first exposures to two great tragic novels, Nathanael West's *Miss Lonelyhearts* (1933) and William Faulkner's *The Sound and the Fury* (1929) were the dreadful Hollywood adaptations released during my teens, both of which had happy endings. As silly as these movies were—Vincent J. Donehue's *Lonelyhearts* (1958) and Martin Ritt's *The Sound and the Fury* (1959)—they piqued my interest in the original novels, and I then discovered, among many other things, the blatant inadequacy of the movie versions.

The same thing could happen to a teenager attending the dreadful film adaptation of Truman Capote's first published novel, *Other Voices, Other Rooms* (1948)—not a novel of the same caliber as West's and Faulkner's, though still a work of real distinction, from his best period—but the odds are slim. For one thing, David Rocksavage's 1994 movie isn't a Hollywood adaptation, with a tradition of glamour exemplified by egregious slick adaptations such as the recent *Great Expectations* or *The Wings of the Dove*—the only sort of "literary" movie contemporary teenagers are likely to see. *Other Voices, Other Rooms* belongs to the tradition of the low-budget, independent art-movie adaptations such as *The Music of Chance* and *Mother Night* (to cite two relatively respectable examples), which typically offer pious earnestness in place of glamour. But I dare say even adventurous teenagers who decide to defy fashion and go to Facets Multimedia could learn much more about Capote's achievement by seeing Alexander Sokurov's exquisite forty-five-minute video *Oriental Elegy* (also playing at Facets this weekend), a virtually plotless reverie about returning to a misty village on a remote Japanese island; most of it is in black and white, with a visual texture so dense you can taste it and a romantic sense of ruins and longing fixated on the past.

This is appropriate, because Capote's strength in *Other Voices, Other Rooms* is above all stylistic and atmospheric—a capacity to evoke a fever dream in exploring a fanciful and allegorical version of his own past. A third-person southern gothic narrative about a thirteen-year-old boy, Joel, sent from New Orleans after the death of his mother to a crumbling, isolated plantation house to live with his father, whom he's never met, the novel was described by Capote as "a poetic explosion in highly suppressed emotion." Its full autobiographical significance dawned on him only after he was more than twice as old as he was when he wrote it. A dark and highly ambivalent account of Capote's turn toward homosexuality, it was sufficiently cloaked in phantasmagoric trappings that it provoked only a fraction of the homophobic response that greeted Gore Vidal's more overt *The City and the Pillar* around the same time (one probable source of the lifelong feud between these writers). Yet it's a politically incorrect treatment of homosexuality by contemporary standards and could hardly be adapted faithfully today without ruffling some feathers. Needless to say, the filmmakers haven't even attempted to honor this aspect of the book, and the pivotal ending gets reversed as a consequence.

The failure of the recent adaptation of Vladimir Nabokov's *Lolita*—directed by Adrian Lyne and scripted by Stephen Schiff—to find an American distributor has been attributed to its politically incorrect erotic agenda and to American puritanism, though there's reason to believe that the studio's asking price has played a more significant role in this "suppression." (The gauging of American morals has proved difficult, despite the absolute confidence of many journalists expounding on the subject; witness the surety with which they warned of Bill Clinton's imminent impeachment.) Having seen *Lolita* three weeks ago in Paris, I can report that in spite of Lyne's clodhopper direction—which predictably runs the gamut from soft-core porn in the manner of David Hamilton to hectoring rhetorical uses of close-ups and wide-angle lenses—this is a genuinely disturbing (if far from literary) adaptation of the novel. And it shines in the area where Stanley Kubrick's 1962 adaptation is deficient: the actress playing Lolita looks like she's fourteen, making this much more a story about corrupted innocence, and it unfolds in American locations in the late '40s. In every other respect, however, Kubrick's version is superior and will clearly endure as the better movie.

I bring all this up in order to stress that fidelity to a literary source is important only when the movie has no higher or at least equally interesting agenda. Kubrick's *Lolita* isn't the novel, but it does use Nabokov to create some worthy configurations of its own; and as a corrective to Kubrick, the highly uneven remake still has a certain legitimacy. Likewise, if ignoring the style and atmosphere of Capote's novel, altering its ambivalent attitude toward homosexuality, and reversing the meaning of its ending had permitted a new story of genuine value to take shape, then Rocksavage (formerly a director of documentaries for British TV) and his cowriter (Sara Flanigan) had every right to play havoc with the original. But this movie offers itself as an act of piety toward the novel and the meaning it supposedly had for Capote, and as such it fails abysmally.

§

Reading George Plimpton's *Truman Capote* and Deborah Solomon's recent biography of Joseph Cornell over the Christmas holidays, I was fascinated to discover the parallels and differences in the lives of these two artists. (The most striking parallel is that late in his life Capote began producing Cornell-like boxes with fetishistic emblems from his own childhood.) Both men were doomed by their troubled family backgrounds—neglect in Capote's case, suffocating involvement and duty in Cornell's. Yet Capote's life during his final decades got steadily worse, while Cornell's in many respects got steadily better, especially after his mother and invalid brother died. One apparent reason for this difference is that Cornell was able to sustain most of whatever peace of mind he had through his work, while Capote, to all appearances, never found the work enough; the career, social life, and public status that came with it counted for more. Loneliness and alienation are fundamental to the work of both artists—a fact that may seem less obvious if one considers only the more crowded and populated aspects of their work—and in *Other Voices, Other Rooms* the sense of isolation is conveyed more starkly and painfully than it is in any of Capote's subsequent works.

One of the many fatal errors of the movie version is to assume the book's autobiographical significance from the beginning by having the story narrated offscreen in first person by an actor (Bob Kingdom) imitating Capote's pip-squeak, Elmer Fudd adult voice. This means that the author is no longer the intuitive young writer who wrote the book, but the sadder and wiser middle-aged queen who re-evaluated it.

Capote's backward glance at the book—"A Voice From a Cloud" (1969), included in his collection *The Dog Barks*—contends that *Other Voices, Other Rooms* was "an attempt to exorcise demons: an unconscious, altogether intuitive attempt, for I was not aware, except for a few incidents and descriptions, of its being in any serious degree autobiographical. Rereading it now, I find such self-deception unpardonable." Eager to grant pardon, the movie adaptation aims at ersatz "conscious" autobiography—a different thing entirely, and all the more dubious when it implicitly cancels out the impulses that made the original book possible. As Capote's best biographer, Gerald Clarke, has pointed out, "In its lack of realism and its reliance on symbolism, *Other Voices* is less a novel than a romance. A novel is, or should be, inhabited by realistic characters with a past and a future, as well as a present; a romance, by contrast, contains unrealistic, stylized figures who stand as psychological archetypes. 'That is why the romance so often radiates a glow of subjective intensity that the novel lacks,' explains the critic Northrop Frye, 'and why a suggestion of allegory is constantly creeping in around the fringes.'" (Elsewhere in "A Voice From a Cloud," Capote plausibly speculates that Poe exerted a strong influence on the novel.)

A glow of subjective intensity and a creeping suggestion of allegory are beautifully and triumphantly apparent in every frame of Sokurov's *Oriental Elegy*, a visionary video that offers by sheer chance plenty of atmospheric moments that closely resemble the weblike textures of Capote's style. Here's a characteristic description by Capote in *Other Voices, Other Rooms* of the Cloud Hotel, the ruins of a former resort hidden in a swamp and inhabited by a black hermit named Little Sunshine: "Swan stairs soft with mildewed carpet curved upward from the hotel's lobby; the diabolic tongue of a cuckoo bird, protruding out of a wall-clock, mutely proclaimed an hour forty years before, and on the room clerk's splintery desk stood dehydrated specimens of potted palm." By contrast, the decaying hotel in Rocksavage's movie has no magic at all, because his own style aspires to realism—an aspiration doomed at the outset because the details of the novel have little to do with realism. That's why Joel's literal as well as allegorical search for his father at the plantation house takes an eternity in the novel; it's resolved much sooner in the movie, which satisfies commonsensical narrative expectations at the cost of much of the psychological and emotional significance of that search. Paradoxically, probably the most realistic patch of narrative in the novel—the flashbacks explaining how the father became a paralytic who can barely speak, a story involving Joel's stepmother, her cousin Randolph, and a Mexican boxer with whom Randolph became infatuated—is the only block of material the filmmakers chose to treat nonrealistically, in a kitschy camp manner that vaguely suggests Raúl Ruiz without any wit or irony. (I'm not counting the unreality of the muddled southern accents and stilted performances, including Anna Thomson's dim memories of Vivien Leigh's Blanche Dubois.)

Literally reversing Capote's stylistic priorities, the filmmakers can only come up with a '90s equivalent to a standard Hollywood absurdity like *Hemingway's Adventures of a Young Man*, minus most of the glitz—not even "a fairy *Huckleberry Finn*," which is what George Davis, one of Capote's mentors, called *Other Voices, Other Rooms*. It would seem that for the filmmakers the novel's only worth is in its foreshadowing of the great writer that the boy and the young novelist later became. But the gifted Capote who wrote the book—the only one who can bring it meaning—is nowhere in sight.

Let the Music Do the Talking [on *Jazz '34*]

This defense of what I consider Robert Altman's most neglected major work appeared in the May 8, 1998 issue of the Chicago Reader. *I continue to dislike the glibness of its "parent" film,* Kansas City.

For more on Charlie Parker, see "Bird Watching," my reviews of Bird *and* Celebrating Bird, *in* Placing Movies, *my first collection, and on my web-site jonathanrosenbaum.net. And for more tenor sax solos that really swing, check out Chu Berry.*

The best Robert Altman feature in more years than I care to remember isn't playing at a theater anywhere. A shortened version aired on PBS's "Great Performances" series last year, but the movie only recently came to my attention when a video copy distributed by Rhapsody Films arrived in the mail. A fascinating adjunct to Altman's much more ambitious *Kansas City* (1996), *Jazz '34: Remembrances of Kansas City Swing* is one of the best jazz films I've ever enjoyed. It's what its parent film promised but failed to deliver—all the more interesting because it's neither a documentary nor a narrative but an eccentric hybrid.

Part of what makes *Kansas City* so difficult is its ugly story, another piece of dime-store fatalism and knee-jerk crosscutting by a TV veteran who perversely falls back on that combo whenever he's trying to be most "personal": a long fall from sustained intuitive dreams like *McCabe & Mrs. Miller, The Long Goodbye*, and *California Split*, if firmly in the class of his formulaic roasts of capitalist greed and media foolishness. Part was how incidental the music turned out to be. And part was that the intermittently dreamy atmosphere was never allowed to build into anything (Altman's poetry is mainly a matter of instinctive, improvisational meanderings that his bitter philosophy tends to interrupt or contradict.) By contrast, the 75-minute *Jazz '34* alternately drifts and surges, without narrative interruptions. Better yet, it demonstrates that atmosphere, music, and narrative can interact so naturally that it's impossible to separate them.

Kansas City was simply the latest in a long line of features that uses jazz the way *Hamlet* uses Rosencrantz and Guildenstern—as interruptions designed to be interrupted. Formally, *Jazz '34* might be said to relate to *Kansas City* the same way that Stoppard's *Rosencrantz and Guildenstern Are Dead* relates to *Hamlet*, but with important differences. Stoppard's focus on background elements in a tragic melodrama is alienated and absurdist; Altman's absorption in their equivalents—musicians jamming in a nightclub at various times of day and night—is neither alienated nor absurdist and is far from melodramatic, a rare departure for Altman.

Properly speaking, Altman's model is not Dudley Murphy and Duke Ellington's *Black and Tan*, which has a fairly nuanced tragic tale to tell between and through its music interludes. Nor is it any of the straight jazz documentaries—a less problematic tradition represented at its most distinguished by *The Last of the Blue Devils* (1979), a ninety-minute account of a reunion of key Kansas City musicians filmed by Bruce Ricker, who later went on to found Rhapsody Films, the premier jazz-on-film video label. Ricker told me that Altman's conscious cinematic model for *Jazz '34* was *Jammin' the Blues*, a short directed by *Life* photographer Gjon Mili in 1944—a documentary of a real jam session set inside a fictional space. It opens with one of its many arty effects: a dim abstract form resembling a bull's-eye wreathed in cigarette smoke tilts to become the top of Lester Young's porkpie hat, as he improvises a slow, relaxed blues over a soft rhythm section. A narrator informs us, "This is a jam session. Quite often these great artists gather and play—ad lib—hot music. It could be called a midnight symphony." Throughout this number and two succeeding ones an assembly of first-rate musicians plays within a highly abstract and mutable space, usually against backdrops that are either all white or all black, posed in various combinations with a stiff jitterbugging couple to create striking configurations in chiaroscuro, silhouette, and multiple exposure. As pretentious as some of it looks, it sounds fabulous, and a few of the images—such as Young's tenor sax cradled in his lap and arms like a swan—are unforgettable.

Jazz '34 opens with a slow track across the street from a re-created block of '30s Kansas City storefronts spotted with period extras. The camera then approaches and enters the Hey Hey Club, while an offscreen Harry Belafonte informs us that 1934 was "when Kansas City defined the word 'swing.' Jazz that was sophisticated, but with a rough-and-tumble spirit Kansas City thrived on. Count Basie, Mary Lou Williams, Hot Lips Page, Ben Webster—greats of jazz gravitated to Kansas City in the '30s, when the scene was wide open and jazz was happening round the clock. Cats came to play. They were really outplaying each other in legendary cutting contests. Like the time Coleman Hawkins and Lester Young locked horns in a battle of the tenors" (which inadvertently evokes a famous scene from *Bambi*).

"Robert Altman grew up in Kansas City and remembers the music of joints like the Hey Hey Club," Belafonte continues. "He's re-created a classic jam session with some of the best musicians of today playing in the spirit of the pin-striped suits—the jazz legends of yesterday. Like those cats in the 1930s, these cats of today came to swing—in Kansas City." By this time a loose cluster of layabouts in period clothes in the general vicinity of the bar are ready to start playing. They launch into "Tickle Toe," a Lester Young tune, and the film is firmly under way.

Even if parts of the preceding narration sound more strained than the verbal introduction to *Jammin'*—is "cats" really the best way, historically, to describe 1934 musicians? The creation of a fictional space for the music is more confident and less pretentious. Ornamental women dance and beat out the time as self-consciously as Mili's jitterbugging couple, and subsequently contribute the same sort of blather about the music (plus a few facts and some atmosphere). But none of this matters much, because the playing is often mesmerizing and it always swings.

To what extent are these musicians "playing" themselves, and to what extent are they playing fictional '30s counterparts? Many of the players clearly suggest '30s figures: Geri Allen, the pianist on "Tickle Toe" and several other numbers, is meant to evoke Mary Lou Williams, and when Cyrus Chestnut turns up on the keyboard he's an evident stand-in for Count Basie—at least until he plays a solo with a few Fats Waller embellishments on "Queer Notions," a Coleman Hawkins tune. Kevin Mahogany as a singing bartender is designed to conjure up memories of Joe Turner, and two figures evoke Charlie Parker—a thirteen- or fourteen-year-old seated in the balcony with his alto sax (who appears as Parker in *Kansas City*) and a sax player with the same build as the adult Parker, who solos on several numbers, sounding most like Parker (during his early stint with Jay McShann) on "Moten Swing". And when the jam session culminates in a climactic "cutting" session between tenor sax players Craig Handy and Joshua Redman, the obvious reference point is the legendary match between Hawkins and Young, already signaled by a poster on the club's front door.

But Ricker told me that Redman wasn't told until after the number was over that he was supposed to be Young, so any distinction between acting and being—or between impersonation and self-expression—can't be precisely drawn.

(Redman's first solo incorporates a few Young-like licks, but given the number and the instrument he's playing, this is unsurprising.) The function of all of these reference points is to provide a few loose guidelines for how we relate to the music, even if some tunes (e.g. Ellington's "Solitude") and individual phrases aren't germane to Kansas City swing. Is it likely or even possible that the tenor sax player who quotes from "Exactly Like You" in his "Moten Swing" solo would have made such an allusion in 1934? As a child of the bebop era who hasn't even read Ross Russell's *Jazz Style in Kansas City and the Southwest*, I can't say. But my point is that one can't always expect the musicians' sense of musical history and their freedom as improvisers to be a perfect fit.

What's more important—at least for those of us born well after 1934—is to feel our way into the period, intuitively, along with the musicians. Making a film that's more interested in launching this project than in monitoring it closely is an awesome existential endeavor, and it's central to what makes *Jazz '34* such a thrilling experience. Any improvisation implies a balance between memory (remembered riffs and phrases, conventions and chord changes) and creativity. The same thing could be said of the live performances of actors in most narrative fictions, which frequently depend on re-creating a text according to the unforeseeable vicissitudes of a given moment. Though they're dressed in '30s garb and playing '30s swing inside a Kansas City location dressed like a '30s set, the musicians are also '90s figures performing in the '90s; the degree to which they're acting or reacting, inventing or remembering, discovering themselves in the past or in the present is never fixed. They're not alone; we too must continually reassess how much we're watching a period re-creation or a contemporary jam session.

This same idea was touched on in Altman's 1991 taping of *Black and Blue*, a brassy all-black, '20s-style dance and musical revue on Broadway (a video aired on PBS in 1993), but this earlier foray has none of the excitement of *Jazz '34*. Altman taped those proceedings with a live audience and took the novel approach of following the performers in their '20s costumes on- and offstage during the show. His restless camera work and editing keep changing our vantage points, so we're never entirely with the audience or with the performers but in some intermediate zone. The characteristics of the live audience—including the number of its members that are black or white—are never allowed to register, and we scarcely learn any more about the backstage identity of the performers, though the mobility of Altman's cameras teases us with the notion that we're getting an insider's view. (The program ends with a seemingly impromptu backstage continuation of the dancing after the curtain calls, ostensibly performed by the cast for their own amusement.)

I suspect that *Black and Blue* is truer to '20s music than *Kansas City* and *Jazz '34* are to '30s music, but I can't say I enjoyed it any more as a consequence; in fact, I liked it much less. The problem is the material as it's packaged for Broadway rather than the talents of the performers: *Black and Blue* is jazzy and bluesy without ever qualifying as jazz or blues, whereas *Jazz '34* offers the genuine article in spite of its postmodern trimmings.

A more apt reference for *Jazz '34* might be Freddie Redd's jazz quartet playing drug addicts performing hard-bop numbers in the Living Theater's 1959 production of Jack Gelber's *The Connection*. To increase the audacity of this move, Redd, Jackie McLean, and the bassist and drummer kept their own names in the play's dialogue, so the degree to which they were simply expressing themselves when they improvised and the degree to which they were fleshing out Gelber's fiction was something no one could determine, including the musicians. (The same ambiguity persists with the same musicians in Shirley Clarke's 1961 film of this production, though the effect of addressing a live audience is missing.)

The crucial difference, in other words, is the improvising. Scoring of music and gesture can be found in both *Black and Blue* and *Jazz '34*, but improvisation is negligible in the former (apart from the mise en scène) and central in the latter. The fidelity of *Black and Blue* to '20s music doesn't allow me to enter an imaginary '20s space, because the elements that go into producing a '90s Broadway show overwhelm any inclination one might have to fantasize about the period.

Jazz '34 does have a loose, episodic narrative—moving from early morning to night to dawn to what appears to be late afternoon—and even a certain moral development, though this needs to be explicated because the commentary contradicts it. Insofar as *Kansas City* represents the repressed, "buried" text in *Jazz '34*—much as the latter represents the "buried" text in *Kansas City*—it's worth considering what this text signifies. The ruthlessness of capitalism is central to that meaning, and the competitive aspect of the "battle of the tenors" gives it a precise musical form; the female narrator we hear immediately after this battle underlines the connection: "They had cuttin' contests like they was gunfighters. Kansas City was the only place where the musicians battled it out with all guns blazin'."

If the climactic musical "duel" actually matched her description, the scene might have unfolded like the famous pissing contest between Charlie Parker and Dizzy Gillespie on their brilliant if often unpleasant *Jazz at Massey Hall* album (1953). But everything I know about Hawkins and Young suggests that they were more supportive than competitive. Young, for instance, was nicknamed "Prez," but said many times that Hawkins better deserved that label, and Hawkins showed comparable generosity. What we see and hear in the final number of *Jazz '34* is something that begins as a standoff—with the two tenors standing several yards apart, like those *Bambi* bucks preparing to charge—and ends with the two of them approaching each other and falling into a friendly duet, shaking hands as soon as the number's over.

The rhetoric of capitalist culture often makes the best jazz sound more aggressive and competitive than it actually is, describing every love match as if it were a duel to the death. Altman does this himself whenever he turns away from the discoveries of his improvs to spout his alleged wisdom. Here that denial is apparent only in the narration (in *Kansas City*, it was apparent in just about everything). If you listen to the exchanges and duets of such fuzzy, warm giants as Warne Marsh and Lee Konitz you hear accommodation, interaction, and mutual discovery, not any sort of one-upmanship. If you listen, for that matter, to most of the music in this movie—not only Allen and Chestnut's duet on "Piano Boogie," but virtually every number—you hear the same thing. As if to clinch this point, Altman concludes his film with another duet, this one noticeably tender, between bassists Ron Carter and Christian McBride, ironically playing "Solitude." It's a very different message from the one delivered in *Kansas City*, and Altman, allowing it to sing and going with the flow for a change, makes it look and sound a lot more believable.

Tsai Ming-liang's *The River*

A different edit of this appeared in the Chicago Reader *(April 14, 2000).*

1. I wouldn't know how to plunge headlong into a single approach towards a film as strange and as shocking as Tsai Ming-liang's third feature, playing this week at Facets Multimedia—so a series of alternative perspectives seems desirable. The problem is, even starting off by labeling this movie a masterpiece reminds me how such an assertion in some cases amounts to a gamble more than a certainty, however much one may prefer to pretend otherwise.

What's my alibi for this lack of confidence? First of all, a sense that when one encounters something as downright peculiar as *The River*, the first impulse is not to assert anything at all but to ask, "What the hell is this?" And to pretend to answer such a question, one ultimately has to fall back on one's experience before even attempting an analysis.

In my case, I've experienced *The River* twice, both times in less than ideal circumstances: with German subtitles at the Vienna Film Festival two and a half years ago, and, just before writing this, a copy of an English commercial video, with English subtitles, that a friend was kind enough to make for me when I discovered that there wasn't any other way I could see this film again before reviewing it. Paradoxically, it was the latter experience that was more problematic—if only because the image in all of Tsai's features is immensely more important than the dialogue, which is minimal, and because the size and clarity of the image are both essential to what Tsai is doing. Critic Kent Jones, the friend who made me the dub, aptly wrote about the film's formidable "monumentality" in the French magazine *Trafic* a couple of years ago, and the only reason why I know he's right is my memory of seeing the film in 35-millimeter in Vienna. Seeing it on video less than an hour ago, while it reminds me of all sorts of other details, can only confuse and dilute that first impression.

The fact that I regard *The River* as a probable masterpiece doesn't mean that I consider it fun or pleasant; terrifying and beautiful would be more appropriate adjectives. It's been a subject of dispute ever since it won the Special Jury Prize in Berlin in 1997, and I can't exactly quarrel with those who complain that it's sick and/or boring since these are both possible and perhaps legitimate responses that I don't happen to share. But that it's also the achieved work of a master I have little doubt.

§

2. Tsai—a Taiwanese director born in Malaysia in 1957 who started out in TV dramas (1989-91), and has made one TV documentary, about AIDS (*My New Friends*, 1995), has made four features to date—*Rebels of the Neon God* (1992), *Vive l'amour* (1994), *The River* (1996), and *The Hole* (1998). All of these features are set in Tapei and deal with loneliness and isolation; the latter, a postmodernist musical of sorts, has also been seen on U.S. cable and elsewhere in a shorter version called *Last Dance*. *The River*, in some ways the most powerful and accomplished of the last three features (I still haven't seen the first), is the one that has been seen the least, probably everywhere, because people don't quite know what to make of it.

§

3. The plot—what there is of it—begins with a young woman (Chen Shiang-chyi) who's working on a film crew and runs into an old friend, Hsiao-kang (Lee Kang-sheng), whom she hasn't seen in a couple of years, going in the opposite direction on an escalator in a mall. She invites him to join her, and they ride on his motorbike to the film shoot, where Hong Kong director Ann Hui, playing herself, is trying to get a fake corpse to float convincingly on the polluted Tanshui River. Complaining that the dummy's feet look fake, Hui asks Hsiao-kang during a lunch break if he'd like to play the corpse, and after some hesitation he agrees. Later his friend takes him to a small hotel to clean up, and they have sex; this is the last we see of her in the film. We also start following the separate daily activities of Hsiao-kang's parents, who live with him, though they're almost never seen together. His mother (Lu Hsiao-ling), an elevator operator, is pursuing a fairly apathetic affair with a man who sells

pornographic videos, and his father (Miao Tien), apparently retired, cruises gay saunas in search of anonymous sex. Around the same time that the son starts complaining of a chronic and debilitating pain in his neck, clearly brought on by an infection he got from the river, his father starts noticing a water leak in his bedroom that's gradually becoming more serious; rather than deal with this problem directly, he uses plastic sheeting to form a canopy over his bed and divert the water toward a drain. Meanwhile the father and mother alternately try to find cures for the son's infection, taking him to different doctors who try out various therapies, none of which appears to work. The leak in the father's bedroom begins to flood the apartment, prompting the mother to climb through a downpour to the empty apartment above to turn off the kitchen faucet. Meanwhile the son is masturbated in one of the dark saunas by an older man, who turns out to be his father. As soon as the father recognizes his son, he slaps him. Father and son sleep in the same bed in a hotel room in a Taipei suburb. In the morning the father, pretending nothing has happened, phones a religious leader, who advises him to return to Taipei with his son and see a doctor, saying they no longer have to visit his temple. The father goes downstairs for breakfast, and Hsiao-kang, before joining him, steps out onto the sunny balcony.

4. Stylistically, Tsai favors filming most action in medium shot or long shot, in extended takes, with the camera typically planted in the center of a room—a fairly cool and detached way of dealing with the sadness and isolation of his characters, whether they're alone or not. (No one ever seems to get much enjoyment out of sex or any other kind of social interaction in a Tsai Ming-Liang movie.) Most of the settings occupied by these characters are new and relatively anonymous; when the father gets cruised by a young gay hustler in an extraordinarily and beautifully developed long take early in the film, before they proceed to a sauna, it's at a McDonald's.

Ever since I first encountered Tsai's work in *Vive l'amour*, I've tended to regard it as a kind of update on the urban melancholia Michelangelo Antonioni used to specialize in, especially during the '50s and '60s—a reference point that can only take one so far, as it does with another Taiwanese modernist, Edward Yang. One of the main differences may be that Antonioni is a master of alienated moods, but atmosphere tends to be more a given than a creation in Tsai's movies, which conjure up more mysteries in relation to what the characters tend to be inarticulate and confused about—sexuality most of all.

§

5. An obsessive filmmaker, Tsai uses the same lead actor playing virtually the same character in all four of his features to date, and the same actors playing his mother and father in *Rebels of the Neon God* and *The River*; he also uses Chen Chao-jung in central roles in *Rebels of the Neon God* and *Vive l'amour* and in a more minor role (as the gay hustler at McDonald's) in *The River*, and Yang Kwei-mei as the female leads in *Vive l'amour* and *The Hole* and in a bit part in *The River*. If one adds to this an ongoing obsession with water as a symbol for sexual desire—which crops up no less centrally in *The Hole*—one might say that Tsai has every bit as fixed and narrow a cosmology as Leos Carax. The parallels between the father's sexual desire and the leak in his bedroom, developed concurrently, are as much a part of this system as the fact that water, seen as a life-force, is also the cause of the hero's nearly constant pain—which persists even in the final shot, and is one of the factors that makes the film so unsettling to watch. Furthermore, the urban alienation that seeps into virtually every shot also affects this film's narrative structure, so that at least half an hour passes before it's clear that the son and his two parents are even related, either to him or to each other. (The same principle makes it seem both logical and inevitable when the friend on the film crew whom Hsiao Kang has sex with simply drops out of the film after that.) Furthermore, as Bérénice Reynaud notes in her excellent recent book *Nouvelles Chines Nouveaux cinémas*, the first time that the son crashes on his motorbike offscreen due to his neck injury and the father, standing nearby, goes to help him, Tsai ambiguously shows the two characters on the street as if they were absolute strangers—making their accidental sexual encounter much later seem a lot more plausible. Tsai's poker-faced distance from his characters may make one think of Buster Keaton or Jacques Tati, as Kent Jones suggests, but it's worth adding that the occasional comic inflections may not always be intentional. In one interview, Tsai mentions that when the father rides behind his son on the motorbike en route to the hospital, holding his head in his hands, this is based on a personal experience Tsai had when Li hurt his neck during the shooting of *Rebels of the Neon God*: "I thought the image had a lot of pathos," he adds, "but to my surprise everyone seems to find it funny." Squaring Tsai's acute grasp of the contemporary with a particular intentionality may ultimately be besides the point, especially for work that is coded and inflected in so personal a manner. Like a certain form of geometry—or would it be physics, tied to engineering?—the characters and their repressions and longings are so palpably realized that all sorts of improbabilities can intervene without causing a dent. Sex and plumbing, seduction and infection, a spray of steam and a torrent of rain are all factored into the same inexorable flow.

The Universe in a Cellar (*The Wind Will Carry Us*)

This appeared in the December 8, 2000 issue of the Chicago Reader. *For further discussion of this film, see my joint audio commentary with Mehrnaz Saeed-Vafa on the Cohen Film DVD and Blu-Ray and our coauthored book,* Abbas Kiarostami *(University of Illinois Press, expanded 2nd ed., 2018).*

Paradoxically, Americans still tend to demonize Iranians at a time when Iranian cinema is becoming almost universally recognized as the most ethical in the world. It's another sign of how limited our understanding of life outside our borders is—which only makes the varied and comprehensive images of Iranian cinema more precious.

It's true that censorship has helped shape Iranian cinema, but that censorship has had interesting consequences. Women film characters are required to wear chadors, but ordinary Iranian women don't wear them indoors—which has led to a good many films being set mainly or exclusively in exteriors and focused on public life and social appearances, including all of Abbas Kiarostami's features since his 1990 *Close-Up*. The pivotal title sequence of *The Wind Will Carry Us* (1999) is set in a dark cellar—and that has a lot to do with what makes this scene metaphysical, momentous, and poetically charged, even though practically nothing of consequence happens there.

This film—one of Kiarostami's greatest and in many ways his richest—has reportedly not yet passed the Iranian censors, though it was screened last year in Tehran at the Fajr Film Festival. I've heard a rumor that the title sequence is the main source of contention. If so, understanding what's at issue might help us reconfigure our skewed and fragmented image of contemporary Iran.

The popular impression of Iran is still colored by images of terrorists dating from the Carter years, even though it's a country of almost sixty-five million individuals—more people than in France or the United Kingdom, and a population whose melting-pot diversity might be said to resemble our own. Moreover, sixty-five percent of Iranians are under the age of twenty-five, and a good many of them are reformist, even radical.

Responsibility for some misimpressions clearly lies within Iran. It's notoriously difficult, for instance, to track specific decisions by Iranian film censors and the reasons for them, which often aren't made public. So I haven't been able to confirm or disprove the rumor that *The Wind Will Carry Us* has been held back from domestic release because of its title sequence—though I'm fascinated that when I've asked Iranians about the possibility they find it perfectly plausible. It also seems possible that Kiarostami's reputation in Iran as a star in the West—even though he's also had enormous influence on other Iranian filmmakers—might play a role in such a decision.

The hero of *The Wind Will Carry Us* is a man from Tehran named Behzad (Behzad Dourani) who drives with a camera crew of three to a remote Kurdish village clinging to the sides of two mountains. There they secretly wait for an ailing 100-year-old woman named Mrs. Malek to die, apparently planning to record the exotic traditional funeral ceremony they expect to take place afterward, as part of which some women mourners scratch and scar their faces. Behzad spends most of the movie biding his time in the village, circulating a false story involving buried treasure about the reason for his presence and chatting with a few locals—mainly a boy named Farzad (Farzad Sohrabi), the old woman's grandson, who serves as his and our main source of information about the village.

Whenever Behzad's mobile phone rings he has to drive to the cemetery on top of a hill overlooking the village to pick up his caller's signal. (The first call he receives is from his family in Tehran, and we discover that by waiting for the old woman's funeral, he'll miss a funeral in his own family. All subsequent calls are from his producer in Tehran—a woman, like the producer in Kiarostami's *Through the Olive Trees*.) At the same location he periodically chats with Youssef, a young man digging a deep hole for unstated "telecommunications" purposes (most likely an antenna tower). Behzad tells Youssef more than once how lucky he is not to be working under any boss, and after glimpsing the retreating figure of the digger's sixteen-year-old fiancee, Zeynab, who brings him tea from time to time, Behzad endeavors to meet her in the village by asking to buy some fresh milk from her family.

In the seven-minute title sequence, occurring roughly halfway through the film, Behzad is directed to a cellar lit only by a hurricane lamp, where Zeynab obligingly milks a cow for him. Over the course of a long take from a stationary camera, Behzad remains offscreen while Zeynab is filmed mainly from behind, though we can see her hands milking the cow. He idly flirts with her and casually remarks, "I'm one of Youssef's friends—in fact, I'm his boss." He also speaks to her somewhat condescendingly about Forough Farrokhzad (1935-67)—a writer of erotic feminist poetry, widely regarded as Persian literature's finest woman poet and Iran's greatest twentieth-century poet. In between his comments and questions, to which she makes minimal responses, he recites one of Farrokhzad's poems in full (translation here by David Martin, which differs from that in the film):

in my small night,
what mounting regret!
wind has a rendezvous
with the trees' leaves
in my small night,
there is terror of desolation
listen! do you hear
the wind of darkness howling?
I watch breathless
-ly and wondrously this alien happiness
I am addicted to my own hopelessness
listen! listen well!
can you hear the darkness
howling?—the dark hell
-wind scything
its way towards us?
in the night now, there is something
passing
the moon is red restless and uneasy
and on this roof—which fears
any moment
—it may cave in—
clouds like crowds of mourners
await to break in rain
ruin
a moment
and then after that, nothing.
behind this window, night shivers

and the earth stands still
behind this window an unknown
something fears for me and you
you who are green from head to toe!
put your hands
—like a burning
memory into my loving hands—
lover's hands!
entrust your lips—your lips
like a warm sense of being!—
entrust!—your lips to the caresses of my
—loving lips—lover's lips!
the wind will carry us with it
the wind will carry us with it

It's important to stress that this poem has never been censored in Iran, and even though Farrokhzad remains a controversial figure—in part because of scandals involving her volatile love life—she's so adored that there would surely be a public outcry if any of her poetry were suppressed. (Most Iranians refer to her affectionately as "Forough.") Another scene in the film briefly and incidentally shows us a pair of fornicating cows, yet no Iranian I've spoken to has suggested that this detail might be worrying the censors. In other words, it appears that they consider the viewer's imagination more dangerous than anything that's seen, and for this reason they find the erotic atmosphere in the cellar unacceptably provocative. It's a scene with echoes in Behzad's encounters with an older woman who runs a local café and some local women he photographs, all of whom seem to see him as an invader and his car and camera as weapons.

My guess is that the cellar scene is provocative mostly because it taps into the sort of emotions and sensations that are stirred by poetry. According to Elaine Sciolino's recent book *Persian Mirrors: The Elusive Face of Iran*, "Simply put, poetry for Iranians is religion, a religion as powerful as Islam." It's hardly exceptional that Kiarostami, who published a collection of his beautiful land-scape photographs in Europe last year, shortly afterward published a collection of his poems in Iran—many of them haikulike images, like sketches for moments in his films.

Literary prose seems to create the same sort of passionate response. I've heard that as many as ten William Faulkner novels are available in Persian translation, but an American who wants to read the works of a comparable twentieth-century Iranian, Sadegh Hedayat (1903-51), will have to be content with a single novella, "The Blind Owl." (Trying to find out what's available from most Persian authors isn't easy because of the variant spellings of names.) "The Blind Owl" is a lush, decadent, necrophiliac fantasy that makes both Poe and Baudelaire seem tame; it's the last thing one might expect from a revered work of Iranian fiction, and it suggests that art assumes an ethical and spiritual magnitude in that culture that effectively confounds most of our received notions about Iranian tastes—they're hardly as prudish as we assume. Ultimately, art is sometimes considered dangerous—dangerous enough to be censored—because it's valued so highly. (Hedayat was, incidentally, a disciple of Jean-Paul Sartre and one of the first Iranians to translate Franz Kafka.)

In the title sequence of *The Wind Will Carry Us*, absences define presences in numerous ways. In fact, many major characters in the film—including Mrs. Malek, Youssef, and all three members of Behzad's crew—are never seen. Most of the sequence unfolds in semidarkness, and it isn't until the very end, after Behzad leaves, that we get to see Zeynab's face in broad daylight, and then only from a distance. (Her refusal to show him her face, even when he asks her to, is obviously a way of resisting his aggressive behavior.) Kiarostami's reasons for leaving things out probably have little to do with censorship and a great deal to do with the viewer's imagination—not to mention an understanding of what human presence consists of in film, particularly when microphones play at least as important a role as cameras in the overall design. (Kiarostami spent months working on this film's soundtrack, which is every bit as creatively selective—and therefore composed—as the images; he told me he studied Robert Bresson's films for guidance.)

Furthermore, Kiarostami's insistence on throwing us back on our own resources—refusing to take us into the village houses, for instance, except for the scene in the cellar, where we can barely see anything—means that we have to become navigators of his elliptical spaces along with Behzad. (In one exterior scene, viewed from a balcony, Behzad accidentally drops a green apple to Farzad, who's on a lower level; it rolls this way and that on a magically unpredictable course—a zigzagging pattern repeated throughout the film, effectively charting the opening shot as well as the last. The recurrence of such patterns in Kiarostami's work—from the path in *Where is the Friend's House?* to the kicked spray can in *Close-Up*—amounts to a directorial signature.)

The TV antennas that dot the village help us realize that these people are no more beyond the reach of media than the media people are beyond the reach of the village. The key point is that they speak different body languages, occupy different time frames, and utilize power quite differently. For instance, the villagers often deferentially refer to Behzad as "the engineer," and in some ways Kiarostami seems as amused by their automatic respect for him as he is by Behzad's equally automatic indifference to most of their concerns.

I began by describing contemporary Iranian cinema as the most ethical in the world. The particular ethics of *The Wind Will Carry Us* consist largely of Kiarostami reflecting on his own practice as a "media person" exploiting poor people: Behzad may be the closest thing in Kiarostami's work to a critical self-portrait, at least since the hero in his highly uncharacteristic 1977 feature *Report*. The most obvious marker of this autocritique is Behzad's cruelty when, during a moment of angry frustration, he kicks a turtle onto its back and leaves it stranded, though the turtle manages to right itself as Behzad drives back down the hill.

A far more telling, if subtle, moment occurs just before the title sequence, when Behzad asks Farzad to fetch him a bowl to carry the milk he's about to get from Zeynab, though the boy keeps insisting he's too busy and wants to get back to his work in the fields. The full ethical resonance of this scene is likely to pass unnoticed by viewers unfamiliar with Kiarostami's shooting methods—he often works without scripted dialogue, directly interviews his nonprofessional actors himself, and then incorporates their responses into dialogue between his fictional characters. (The line between documentary and fiction in his work is always ambiguous.) The following exchange takes place as the camera cuts between the two characters:

Behzad: "Can you answer me frankly?"
Farzad: "Yes."
Behzad: "Do you think I'm bad?"
Farzad: (smiling): "No."
Behzad: "Are you sure?"
Farzad: (assertively): "Yes."
Behzad: "How can you be sure?"
Farzad: (blushing): "I know...you're good."
Behzad: (smiling broadly): "Well, since I'm good, can you get me a bowl to carry the milk?"

When I asked Kiarostami if he was the one asking Farzad these questions, he confirmed my suspicion, adding that he felt he had to ask them because he knew Farzad disliked him—and liked Behzad Dourani, the actor playing Behzad. "So that's why he wasn't very convincing when he called me a good man," Kiarostami said with a laugh. No less telling is Zeynab's circumspection and reticence about responding to Behzad's teasing and bullying. (A more trivial self-reflexive theme in the film is Behzad's frequent difficulty locating his invisible crew; Kiarostami has complained in many interviews about the late rising and frequent unavailability of his cinematographer, Mahmoud Kalari, during shooting.)

My point is that Kiarostami is critiquing the whole premise of his filmmaking, ethically and otherwise. (He also gives an ethical reason for wanting to shoot his next feature on digital video—because it will interfere less with the lives of the people he shoots; he's already used that format to shoot a feature-length documentary about AIDS in Uganda.) Broadly speaking, he's implying that there's no ethical difference between a TV director making a documentary about an old woman's funeral and a celebrated filmmaker-artist like himself entering a village to make a feature. It's worth adding that all his features since 1990—starting with the documentary *Homework* and continuing with the semidocumentary *Close-Up* and the semifictional *Life and Nothing More*, *Through the Olive Trees*, *Taste of Cherry*, and *The Wind Will Carry Us*—deal with interactions between relatively empowered figures such as himself (as filmmaker and potential employer) and relatively disempowered working-class people (his potential employees).

Yet Kiarostami doesn't present Behzad simply as a villain. After a subsequent scene in which Behzad berates Farzad in a particularly demeaning way, he goes out of his way to apologize. In contrast to his gratuitous cruelty toward the turtle, he later watches the Herculean efforts of a dung beetle pushing its load on the same hilltop with genuine admiration. He refuses to get dirty by attempting to dig out Youssef when he's buried by a cave-in and nearly suffocates; but he does drive around frantically enlisting other villagers to do it, and he obviously cares about Youssef's fate. Perhaps the most important thing about Behzad isn't whether he's simply good or bad—the focus of his ambiguous conversation with Farzad—but the contrast between the ways he and the locals relate to the world around them.

Part of this movie's vitality is that it feels as up-to-date as the postelection fracas in Florida—Behzad and his crew waiting for the old woman to die recalls the spin doctors impatiently awaiting recounts and judges' decisions while telling us what they presume we're thinking. (Speak to any stranger about what's going on and you're likely to find yourself in sympathetic accord, regardless of how each of you voted; but turn on the TV and you'll see angry partisan squabbling and name-calling and endless accounts of our alleged impatience.) The faulty technology of the city slicker—Behzad's recalcitrant mobile phone—also calls to mind our flawed balloting machinery. Both induce a frenetic, contorted, slapstick dance in us as we try to overcome our helplessness in the face of the machines that rule our lives.

By concentrating on the death of a century-old woman in the year 1999, Kiarostami also seems to be making some sort of millennial statement—something that means less inside Iran, which has a different calendar. By comically divvying up his world into media "experts" with mobiles and peasants, he's clearly raising the issue of who owns this world and who deserves to.

Is there any more relevant global issue at the moment? This is the film's major theme, though I hasten to add it isn't the only one. One of the major themes of *Taste of Cherry*, Kiarostami's previous feature—mortality in general and the process of being buried in particular—returns here as a secondary theme. (A human thighbone, found in Youssef's hole and carried around for a spell by Behzad, functions as a highly suggestive prop.) And uniting all its themes is poetry—lines from Rumi and *The Rubaiyat of Omar Khayyam* as well as Forough Farrokhzad—which sometimes appears to be the only thing the characters have in common.

With the possible exception of a doctor on a motorbike—who exudes warm and familiar folk wisdom with a little more facility than I would have liked and reminds me too much of the Turkish taxidermist in *Taste of Cherry*—Kiarostami's reading of what separates the media savants from the farming people generally avoids sentimentality and cant. One reason for this that I've already suggested is that Behzad remains a troublingly equivocal figure, a hero we can neither accept nor reject wholeheartedly. The very fact that we're watching a film places us in some respects on his side and against the villagers, whether we want to be there or not, so Kiarostami works overtime attempting to rectify that balance and show us things Behzad is unlikely to notice.

Perhaps the most impressive of these things is the village itself, with all its intricate interweavings, ambiguities, and declivities—it's an architectural marvel both as a subject and a backdrop. *The Wind Will Carry Us* offers an intricately constructed spatial world that's as breathtakingly beautiful, as various, and as cosmically evocative as a Brueghel landscape—a world teeming with diverse kinds of life and activity—and it teases us whenever we want to get to know this world better, seducing and evading us at the same time.

Music For the Eyes [on Oskar Fischinger]

From the Chicago Reader, *April 20, 2001; minor adjustments and trims in 2010 and 2022. For more information, go to http://www.centerforvisualmusic.org/*

While I was living in Paris in my late twenties I used to dream of making a film—if someone were to hand me an outsize check and give me carte blanche, which of course I knew would never happen. I had a particular dream project in mind. I wanted to film all of my best friends dancing as uninhibitedly and joyfully as possible alongside the Seine, and then I wanted to devote the next several years of my life to synchronizing their movements to an up-tempo number by Ahmad Jamal's piano trio. Jamal was unfashionable among many jazz critics—even though Miles Davis delighted in his music—and that only made the project more seductive.

The notion of combining music I loved and people I loved was the key to this idle fantasy. Furthermore, Jamal's music made me want to dance and conjured up moving images, and I wanted to synthesize these sensations. Last week I saw him play with his current trio, and though he was seated, his orchestrated body movements and occasional grunts of pleasure while making characteristically melodramatic shifts in dynamics or telegraphing instructions to his bassist and drummer added up to a kind of ecstatic dance that reminded me of my old pipe dream.

A desire to find visual correspondences with music is no doubt quite common, yet to devote an entire career to fulfilling and justifying such a desire might seem a narrow aspiration. It's certainly possible for art—and not only Hollywood movies—to be extremely beautiful and pleasurable yet not especially interesting to think about. All of the abstract animation of Oskar Fischinger (1900-1967) I've seen brushes against that possibility, so my love for his work has always been qualified by doubt—the kind of doubt that may help explain why Fischinger's position within the avant-garde has never been firmly settled.

He started doing silent work in the 1920s that was a purely visual music, before moving logically toward music and image duets in the 1930s; he then, just as logically, turned again toward silent visual music. His oeuvre—which is contained in almost 200 cans of nitrate and safety film and includes various experiments and fragments as well as advertising films—can be seen as single-minded and varied, rich and monotonous, programmatic and technically innovative.

Fischinger worked for luminaries such as Fritz Lang in Germany and—after 1936, when he moved to the U.S., where he remained until his death—Walt Disney and Orson Welles in Hollywood. He also left behind 700 oil and pastel paintings—most of them unrelated to his animation—though he regarded these canvases as secondary to his filmmaking.

The son of shopkeepers and brewers in Gelnhausen, Germany, Fischinger worked in his teens as an apprentice organ builder, as an architect's draftsman, and, after moving to Frankfurt, as a tool designer. He reportedly discovered his vocation through the newspaper articles of an art critic named Bernhard Diebold, who welcomed a new approach to cinema that involved abstraction and blended painting, sculpture, dance, and music in a bold new synthesis. After making Diebold's acquaintance, Fischinger gave a lecture for a literary club around 1921 that used graphic charts to display the aesthetic "dynamics" of two plays, Shakespeare's *Twelfth Night* and Fritz von Unruh's expressionistic antiwar drama *Ein Geschlecht*. According to Fischinger biographer William Moritz, who wrote a book-length essay on him for *Film Culture* in 1974, "These scroll-like charts do not try to show just the literal movements and gestures of the actors, but rather by abstract designs try to convey the changing moods, the flow of emotion, the intensity, style, and flourish of the ideas and the experiences created by the process of the action." The abstract films that grew out of these charts were contemporaneous with those of Walter Ruttmann, Viking Eggeling, and Hans Richter. The first and perhaps most gifted of these figures, Ruttmann—who worked for Fritz Lang many years before Fischinger, contributing an animated dream sequence to *Die Nibelungen*—premiered the first abstract film in 1921, showing it with a live synchronous musical score.

Fischinger's remaining fifteen years in Germany yielded many of his best films, including a seven-minute triptych using multiple projectors in 1927 (the first and third panels mirroring each other), accompanied by a kind of industrial music; advertising films from the 30s for cigarettes (which dance in chorus lines) and an ad agency named Tolirag (the 1933 *Kreise*, or *Circles*, works from the slogan "Tolirag reaches all circles," creating an arresting blue, red, and green op art of approaching, receding, drifting, and gamboling circles, all to the strains of Wagner and Grieg); the one-and-a-half-minute, black-and-white *Liebesspiel* (1931), "a song without music"; and the magisterial four-minute *Composition in Blue* (1935). There are also many numbered "studies" made between 1929 and 1934 and nonanimated "scrapbooks" of walking trips, including the three-minute, single-frame compilation *Walking from Munich to Berlin* (1927) and the thirteen-minute *Swiss Trip* (1934), which combines single frames and longer takes, all synchronized to Bach's *Third Brandenburg Concerto*. The same period in Germany yielded what was probably Fischinger's most satisfying early work for a film studio—his special-effects work on Fritz Lang's *Woman on the Moon* (1929), which included model rockets, simulated spaceflights, skywriting, flotation in zero gravity, and hallucinations involving gold.

By contrast, most of his early forays into Hollywood studio work were disasters, exacerbated by his inability to speak English and dependence on studio interpreters. After many protracted misunderstandings, nothing of his work wound up in a Paramount B musical called *Big Broadcast of 1937*. A couple of years later he had some hope of becoming a "supervisor of visuals" on Walt Disney's *Fantasia*, but his ambitious ideas for abstract accompaniments to Bach's *Toccata and Fugue in D minor* were so vulgarized he removed his name from the picture's credits and eliminated the film's title from his resumé. (Not that his ideas weren't populist or playful: one that Disney rejected was to have Leopold Stokowski's hands fly away and turn into the piece's opening bars of musical notes before metamorphosing into abstract colors and shapes.) In between came what was perhaps Fischinger's most successful studio contract, with MGM— acquired through the help of his friend, director William Dieterle—which allowed him to take an animation technique using paper cutouts suspended on sticks and wires that he'd introduced in *Composition in Blue* and develop it in *An Optical Poem* (1937), scored to Liszt's *Second Hungarian Rhapsody*. This film survives today only because Fischinger preserved his own copy; MGM, after showing it across the country, allowed the original negative to decompose.

Fischinger's yearlong stint (1941-42) with Orson Welles on the never completed *It's All True*—an episodic potpourri that went through many different incarnations—never yielded a contribution to the movie. But his work with Welles nurtured and may have virtually subsidized his extraordinary silent, four-minute *Radio Dynamics* (1942), which Moritz regards, probably justly, as Fischinger's masterpiece. It also gave him plenty of time to develop his talent for cel animation. Welles—who kept Fischinger as his personal employee at the Mercury unit despite the wartime injunction against hiring "enemy aliens"—first put him to work planning abstract animation to accompany jazz in a biography of Louis Armstrong to be scored by Duke Ellington; when the "story of jazz" mutated into the "story of samba," after Nelson Rockefeller persuaded Welles to make a film in Brazil, Fischinger apparently adapted his designs to live carnival music recorded by Welles in Rio. Fischinger also prepared a credits sequence for *Jane Eyre*, produced by Welles, and designed a dream sequence for Lang's *Secret Beyond the Door*, neither of which was used. A more successful commercial venture was his great one-minute, black-and-white 1952 singing commercial for Muntz TV sets—an endlessly inventive and blossoming explosion of curves, stripes, tonalities, and letters.

I suspect that one thing keeping Fischinger unfashionable in some avant-garde circles is the lack of meaningful correlation between his best work and his most independent work, or between his worst work and his most commercial assignments (leaving aside the work he understandably disowned, such as the Bach segment in *Fantasia*). There's also no meaningful correlation that I can find between the value of individual works and how abstract or representational they are. The perpetually mutating and slithering silhouetted human figures and furniture of *Spiritual Constructions*—a black-and-white film from 1927 that Moritz describes as a "meditation on violence" encapsulating everything Fischinger hated about the drunkenness and aggressive behavior he found in German beer halls—is no less aesthetically pleasing than the pristine ballet of geometrical figures in the color *Composition in Blue*. And whatever the jazz- or samba-related sources of *Radio Dynamics*, what finally emerged, beginning with the pointed title, "No music please—an experiment in color-rhythm," is a luscious and pulsating visual music that's simply too rich to be encapsulated as a Klee or a Kandinsky in a constant state of becoming, even if it fleetingly suggests such a conceit. Instead it's a visual music so generous, plentiful, joyful, and alive it finally makes musical accompaniment superfluous—and makes one want to dance as much as an unfashionable up-tempo Ahmad Jamal solo does.

Jazz on a Summer's Day

Excerpted from "Listening Party," Chicago Reader, August 3, 2001.

The series opens with a classic, perhaps the best of all jazz documentaries when it comes to showing people listening. *Jazz on a Summer's Day* (1960) is still photographer Bert Stern's only film, shot in luscious color. It takes in several groups at the 1958 Newport Jazz Festival, but Stern has more fun with the responses of the audience—how people move (or don't) with the beat and other forms of engagement or disengagement—which are an important part of our pleasure, sometimes even a part of the music. But on other occasions he simply gets bored with the musicians and listeners alike and cuts away to a boat show or another local event, real or contrived, often while the music continues offscreen.

Stern has admitted that he's never been a jazz fan. The choice of what groups to film was made by Columbia Records' George Avakian (more, it seems, for business than aesthetic reasons), though Stern says that if he'd made the decisions he wouldn't have included Miles Davis either, because "he's too far out for me." Stern seems incapable of distinguishing between good, bad, and mediocre jazz, so it isn't surprising that some of the top musicians here—such as Thelonious Monk, Gerry Mulligan, and George Shearing—aren't seen in top form. In much better fettle, especially as camera subjects, are Jimmy Giuffre, Anita O'Day, Louis Armstrong, and Mahalia Jackson.

Feeling the Unthinkable (*25th Hour*)

From the January 17, 2003 issue of the Chicago Reader. *For those who care about such things, there are spoilers ahead....Two other exceptional Lee films worthy of mention:* Four Little Girls *(1997) and* When the Levees Broke: A Requiem in Four Acts *(2006).*

I've complained a lot about Spike Lee as a filmmaker, before he made his remarkable *Do the Right Thing* (1989) and after. But the only time I've been tempted to accuse him of falling back on the tried and true was when he made *Malcolm X* and attempted to adapt his subject's autobiography as if he were Cecil B. De Mille or David O. Selznick. I don't mean that Lee hasn't stubbornly stuck to the same stylistic tropes and mannerisms throughout most of his career—leaving them behind only when the occasion demanded it, as in his expert filming of Roger Guenveur Smith's powerful performance piece *The Huey P. Newton Story*—but the stylistic consistency is his own. Moreover, taking on dissimilar projects he has always moved in exploratory directions, showing a lot of courage and initiative in his creative choices—even when they're half-baked (as some are in *Get on the Bus*) or overblown (as in *Bamboozled*).

25th Hour is Lee's best feature since *Do the Right Thing*, and part of what's so impressive about it is the way it gets us to think as well as feel—about things we're almost never asked to consider, such as what it means to send drug dealers to prison. I suspect one reason this country has more than two million people in prison—we have the second-highest incarceration rate in the world, after Russia—is that the sort of people who wind up there, what they do, and what happens to them inside, are all things we don't really want to think about. The focus of *25th Hour*, adapted by David Benioff from his novel, is how a Manhattan drug dealer named Monty Brogan (Edward Norton) spends his last twenty-four hours before going to prison for seven years. The film also concerns the four people who are most important to him—his girlfriend Naturelle (Rosario Dawson), his father James (Brian Cox), and his two best friends since he was a kid, a prep school teacher named Jake (Philip Seymour Hoffman) and a Wall Street trader named Frank (Barry Pepper). I've heard some people object to a film asking us to think—and therefore care—about what happens to a drug dealer in prison. But would they also object to being asked to care about the people who do care about him? And if we do care about Naturelle, James, Jake, and Frank, how can we not care about Monty?

I hasten to add that there's nothing moralistic or preachy about *25th Hour*—or intellectual either. Lee's movie shows no interest in making any case about whether drug dealers should go to prison. In fact, it might be said that this movie isn't even about drug dealers; it's about Monty, a former drug dealer going to prison, and the people he knows. Yet Lee and his cast are so adept at getting us acquainted with Monty and these other people that we wind up feeling like we've known them for years, and this familiarity affects how we feel about what happens to them.

When Nikolai—the drug baron Monty's been working for, who's spent a considerable portion of his own life in prison—advises Monty to find the weakest, most helpless person there as soon as he arrives and beat him until his eyes bleed, the most horrifying thing about this suggestion is that it sounds more practical than hyperbolic. We believe it in the same way and to the same degree that we believe in Monty and his circle.

Not having read Benioff's novel, I don't know whether it was his decision or Lee's not to show Monty selling drugs in any of the flashbacks. (The closest he comes is a very early scene that shows Monty brushing off a junkie, explaining that he's been busted.) Without quite wanting to accuse the film of cheating, I find this a regrettable omission, though I know its inclusion might have made it harder to persuade us to see Monty sympathetically. In the film's press book Lee is quoted as saying, "I don't choose which films to direct based on how sympathetic the characters are. Monty Brogan is a drug dealer—and people will find that unsympathetic. But a lot of times, unsympathetic characters make the best movies, have the best stories." Yet whether Lee truly shows Monty as unsympathetic is somewhat ambiguous. I don't object to this ambiguity, because it's one of the things in the movie that obliges us to think. And the relatively unsympathetic treatment of the cops who arrest and question Monty—most of whom are black, and most of whom are shown taking a sadistic pleasure in his predicament—only adds to the ambiguity. When Monty's offered an opportunity to lighten his sentence by ratting on others, we're implicitly asked to reflect on what we might do in the same situation.

The classic Lee tropes and mannerisms that appear in *25th Hour* include jump cuts, alternate takes of the same action (Monty and Naturelle rushing toward each other into an embrace) repeated in rapid succession, arias of ethnic abuse, dreamy camera movements that make the characters appear to float or glide in midair, and wall-to-wall music. One such aria starts when Monty encounters the phrase "fuck you" on a bathroom mirror and improvises a somewhat literary and self-conscious monologue that begins "Fuck the whole city" and goes on to list all the local groups and types he hates. Lee illustrates the catalog with a string of slightly bleached-out images of people in each category: Wall Street brokers, "Upper East Side wives," downtown homosexuals, "brothers" playing basketball, cops, priests who abuse boys, the people who protect them, Osama bin Laden, al Qaeda, his friends Jake and Frank, Naturelle (who he believes may have betrayed him to the cops), his father—even himself for getting caught ("You had it all, and you threw it away").

This passage recalls the litany of racial insults in *Do the Right Thing*, though I've read that a version of Monty's monologue figures in Benioff's novel and that Benioff excluded it from his original script and then restored it, over Disney's objections, at Lee's insistence. (This scene includes the lines "Send those Enron bastards to jail for life. Do you think Cheney didn't know about them? Give me a fucking break"; it's one of the moments in the film when a sense of currency enhances the overall emotional thrust—as the haunting images of Ground Zero in lower Manhattan do.) Later, Lee brings back some of these groups and has them wave good-bye to Monty when he leaves the city, treating them as emblems he's sorry to leave behind.

The gliding camera movements accompany the erotic reveries of two characters visiting the same club: that of Mary (Anna Paquin, who played the daughter in *The Piano* a decade ago), a flirtatious high school student who's been coming on to Jake, her teacher, and is drifting to the music, and that of Jake after he kisses her. The relationship between these two is the film's only subplot, and it's a useful one insofar as it shows us the kind of innocence all the other characters have lost.

At one point Frank says to Jake, "You're a rich Jewish kid from the Upper West Side who's ashamed of his wealth." This isn't the only thing Jake feels guilty about; he castigates himself for being attracted to Mary long before he kisses her. But Frank, who shares Monty's working-class Irish roots, is an even more complex character when it comes to guilt; he feels guilty about Monty's predicament and perhaps, more subtly, about some of his activities on Wall Street.

I've tended to think of the wall-to-wall music in Lee's movies as a flaw, because it doesn't give the viewer enough breathing space. But here the music (composed by Lee regular Terence Blanchard) is more functional: it's generally less noticeable, which is to say better integrated. And maybe because Lee relies on and works with the viewer's imagination and initiative in so many other areas, it's less harmful. Sometimes he even sculpts it around the action: when the sound of a tugboat figures briefly in one scene, the music stops long enough to let us hear it.

The very first thing we encounter in the film, at the same time that Disney's Touchstone logo appears, is the sound of a dog being beaten. We don't know who's doing the beating or why, and we never find out—which means we have to think about it. Yet there's nothing gratuitous about this detail, because before the credits come on we see two guys getting out of a car on a New York highway, Monty and a rotund Ukrainian colleague named Kostya (Tony Siragusa)—Monty has seen the dog and insists on stopping. A comic scene ensues as Monty, who wants to adopt the dog even though its hip may be broken, tries to maneuver it into the car's trunk, while the dog keeps growling and snapping at him. Kostya, whose English isn't great, keeps calling the dog a "bullpit" and objecting to the delay; we later figure out they must have been en route to a drug deal. Attempting to invoke Murphy's Law, Kostya comes up with "Doyle's Law," and the next time we see Monty he's walking the fully recovered dog, now named Doyle.

The last thing we see in the film is a close-up of Monty, his face battered and bruised, while his father drives him to prison—a shot that gets us to think much as the sound of Doyle being beaten does. This isn't because we don't know who gave Monty the bruises or why, though he's lied about it to his father. In a previous scene Monty—a handsome guy, named by his late mother after Montgomery Clift—first demands that Frank beat him to a pulp, then goads him, against his will, into it. This is because he knows he's less likely to get raped in prison if he looks a mess when he arrives. Mercifully Lee dispenses with music during this stretch and eliminates most other sounds as well; the scene would clearly be less wrenching with them. As we stare at the close-up of Monty's face we can't help wondering what awaits him during the next seven years.

But what if his father were to go on driving, not to the prison but across the United States, dropping Monty in some inconspicuous desert town with the understanding that they'll never see each other again, that Monty will adopt a new identity, start a new life? This is a possibility the film also gets us to think about at length, though in a different way. Just before that final close-up of Monty in the car, the movie illustrates this plan, his father going through every step in detail, all the way up to Monty's happy and contented old age after having lived an alternate life. We're asked to think about not just how such a plan might be carried out but whether this is the ending to the movie that we want. Is this what actually happens to Monty? And if we prefer the alternate ending, does that mean that we don't think drug dealers should go to prison?

Thinking about a dog being beaten, about a drug dealer going to prison, about a drug dealer not going to prison, doesn't require us to solve a puzzle, to come up with some bright solution. It just means thinking about what happens in our world and theirs—which are really the same world. And as Lee shows us, feeling our way into that world is another way of thinking about it.

Oporto Of My Childhood

From the Chicago Reader *(March 21, 2003). For more on Oliveira, see my essay in* Cinematic Encounters: Portraits and Polemics *and my celebration of* Doomed Love *in* Placing Movies.

Manoel de Oliveira's 2001 masterpiece explores the Portuguese city where he's lived for more than ninety years, though it concentrates on the first thirty or so, suggesting that his childhood must have lasted a very long time. It's a remarkable film for its effortless freedom and grace in passing between past and present, fiction and nonfiction, staged performance and archival footage (including clips from two of his earliest films, *Hard Work on the River Douro* and *Aniki-Bobo*) while integrating and sometimes even synthesizing these modes. He's mainly interested in key images, music, and locations from the Eden of his privileged youth, and some of the film's songs are performed by him or his wife—though we also get a fully orchestrated version of Emmanuel Nunes's *Nachtmusik 1.* In Portuguese with subtitles. 61 minutes.

Too Big For the Screen: On Charles Mingus

From the Chicago Reader, *June 20, 2003.*

The sheer impossibility of encompassing jazz bassist, composer, and band-leader Charles Mingus (1922-1979) in a single film limits Don McGlynn's ambitious 1997 documentary *Charles Mingus: Triumph of the Underdog* from the outset. Which doesn't mean you shouldn't see it. But if you don't already know something about the man's music, this may not be the ideal place to start: I'd recommend instead one of his early albums, like *The Clown, Tijuana Moods, East Coasting, Mingus Dynasty, Charles Mingus Presents Charles Mingus* (the best one with Eric Dolphy), or *Mingus at Monterey* (especially for Bud Powell's five-minute solo on "I'll Remember April").

No single book has succeeded in doing full justice to Mingus either. Maybe it's because he had a genius for straddling musical categories such as traditional, modern, avant-garde, jazz, and classical (as Gunther Schuller points out in one of this film's interviews, Mingus studied Arnold Schoenberg's music in his teens, during the '30s, when few people here were familiar with it). Maybe it's because he straddled existential categories such as art, politics, and life, and emotion and thought. In other words, his personality spills over the edges of the kinds of definitions most books and films rely on for portraiture. Even the ethnic mix of his background—black, Chinese, Swedish—confounds the usual descriptive labels, much as his seamless fusions of gospel, Dixieland, swing, bebop, R&B, and classical confound the generic formulas.

The emotional and thematic continuities between some of Mingus's earliest and last compositions are fully apparent in *Triumph of the Underdog*. In all his best pieces the sound of passionate and unbridled weeping, sobbing, and sometimes wailing that's so apparent in the solo voices of musicians such as Bessie Smith or Charlie Parker is expanded into rich and complex ensembles without any emotional loss. And it's apparent in even fleeting snatches of his music. Yet the task of capturing the dimensions of such a man in a single descriptive work remains formidable.

Let's start with the books. Mingus's eccentric autobiography, *Beneath the Underdog* (1971)—reportedly a pale shadow of the original manuscript—has lots of texture but comes across mainly as a collection of pungent fragments. Brian Priestley's *Mingus: A Critical Biography* (1983) does much more with the music than the life. Janet Coleman and Al Young's slim *Mingus/Mingus: Two Memoirs* (1989) contains the best prose but the fewest details. Gene Santoro's exasperating *Myself When I Am Real: The Life and Music of Charles Mingus* (2001) has the most details and the least sense of what to do with them; it often seems more concerned with precisely how much money the man made and spent than with the shape or feel of his music. *Tonight at Noon: A Love Story* (2002), by Sue Graham Mingus, his fourth and last wife, is invaluable for its glimpses of his last fifteen years, especially his harrowing struggle with Lou Gehrig's disease; understandably it has less to say about the forty-two preceding years, apart from a wonderful catalog of the souvenirs collected in one of their flats.

The best brief description of Mingus may be the first paragraph of Coleman's 67-page portion of *Mingus/Mingus*, if only because of the way it compresses Mingus's mutability into the prose equivalent of a theme park or shopping mall: "I knew Charles Mingus almost twenty years, in various cities, at various weights, in canny and uncanny moments, and through various psychic and aesthetic incarnations. I bore witness to his Shotgun, Bicycle, Camera, Witchcraft, Cuban Cigar and Juice Bar periods, and was familiar with his Afro, Egyptian, English banker, Abercrombie and Fitch, Sanford and Son, and ski bunny costumes. I ate his chicken and dumplings, kidneys and brandy, popcorn and garlic, pigs, rabbits, godknows mice." Even if I bump over that "godknows," which breaks the rhythm, the abrupt swerves in logic and the spicing up of a stew that's already boiling over catch the quintessential Mingus.

Most jazz lives are so compartmentalized by club dates and recording sessions that the wider world is often held at bay. But Mingus insisted on bringing that world into his music every way he could—with lyrics and agitprop recitatives, song titles ("All the Things You Could Be by Now if Sigmund Freud's Wife Was Your Mother," "Meditations on Integration," "Remember Rockefeller at

Attica," "Oh Lord, Don't Let Them Drop That Atom Bomb on Me," "Fables of Faubus"), his whistles and foghorns, his solos, and his "dialogues" with other musicians in musical lines approximating speech. One of my favorite comic outbursts, heard in this documentary, is a chant from Mingus that goes, "Who said Mama's little baby loves shortnin' bread? /That's some lie some American white man said. /Mama's little baby don't like no shortnin' bread, /Mama's little baby likes truffles...caviar... African gold mines...African diamond mines."

It's hard to think of another major jazz figure who crossed over more into the other arts. Duke Ellington, Mingus's principal influence, had plenty of his own encounters with film, theater, and dance, but I can't imagine him writing poetry or taking photographs with the same abandon as Mingus. And even though in the early '40s Ellington mapped out a film project with Orson Welles as director and narrator, Mingus gave hints about what such a collaboration might have entailed when he said of Welles, "I dug his voice. It reminded me of Coleman Hawkins. You could hear it a mile away."

It's both an advantage and a disadvantage that this film tries to deal with the richness of Mingus by cramming in as much material as possible. It starts off with a distracting flurry of sound bites and later even includes several portions of an earlier documentary, Thomas Reichman's hour-long *Mingus* (1968)—a piece of cinéma vérité about Mingus getting evicted from his loft that also gives us long stretches of uninterrupted music.

By contrast, McGlynn's seventy-eight-minute documentary rushes from one brilliant or telling fragment to another, yielding a meal that's almost all hors d'oeuvres, with little of Mingus's feeling for and mastery of larger forms. I had to wait nearly an hour to hear my favorite Mingus tune, "Peggy's Blue Skylight," played all the way through (in a rare up-tempo version, including its exquisite B theme). *Mingus* offers it only in successive bits intercut with the artist speaking to the camera in his loft or getting evicted. A better documentary might show us how the song's opening phrase derives from bars 13 through 15 of Mingus's lovely "Reincarnation of a Lovebird," a demonstration of how key musical themes in his work can go through as many guises and settings as key characters in the novels of Balzac or Faulkner.

The superiority of Reichman's documentary to McGlynn's can be explained in part by their different agendas. *Mingus* is a rough-hewn but homogeneous portrait filmed on the run. *Triumph*, coproduced by Sue Mingus and McGlynn, boldly attempts a multifaceted summation, which is much harder to bring off. Even the title, with its reference to *Beneath the Underdog*, shows the strain of the effort. The "triumph" of course is posthumous and belongs strictly to Mingus's supporters and audience. Inadequate preparation made his only attempt to perform his magnum opus—a work over two hours long that he eventually called *Epitaph*—at a 1962 Town Hall concert a nearly complete shamble; Sue Mingus calls it "the great disaster of his life." So its successful performance conducted by Gunther Schuller at Lincoln Center in 1989 [2022: now available on CD, DVD, and streaming] qualifies as a kind of ahistorical, postmodernist rewrite.

Still, *Triumph* is sufficiently generous to give us some priceless moments, such as when two of Mingus's former wives, Celia and Sue—who inspired two of his loveliest tunes, "Celia" and "Sue's Changes"—gleefully swap personal anecdotes. We also get vivid accounts of how Mingus managed to get fired from Duke Ellington's band and how Charlie Parker managed to hire him by persuading him to quit his job at the post office. Regrettably, we don't get any clips from John Cassavetes' *Shadows* (1960), which fully matches the emotional tenor of its Mingus score. But the accumulation of other bits and pieces does convey what former Mingus sideman John Handy aptly calls his gusto. For the spread and reach of that gusto, search out the albums.

How to Read a Movie [*Stone Reader*]

From the Chicago Reader *(July 18, 2003); tweaked and amplified in October 2022.*

Cinema has traditionally been regarded as the art that encompasses all the other arts. But start considering how successfully cinema encompasses any particular art form and the premise falls apart.

Filmed theater, opera, ballet, and musical performance omit the existential and communal links between performer and audience that their live equivalents rely on. Paintings can be filmed, but films that allow us even some of the freedom viewers have in galleries, museums, and other public and private spaces are rare enough to seem like aberrations. Jean-Marie Straub and Danièle Huillet's *Paul Cézanne im Gespräch mit Joachim Gasquet* (1989) and *Une visite au Louvre* (2004), both of which have the nerve to give us extended views of canvases from fixed camera positions—have never been screened publicly in this country because the filmmakers refused to let it be subtitled, knowing that subtitles would impede our view of the paintings. The more common procedures of cutting between details or panning and tracking across a picture impose itineraries that wouldn't necessarily be our own.

The same problem is apparent in films of sculpture and architecture. In the case of literature, which clearly provides cinema with more material than any of the other arts, the incompatibility is even more acute. Poetry poses the greatest number of obstacles, and one reason I cherish Forough Farrokhzad's twenty-one-minute Iranian documentary *The House Is Black* (1962) is that it manages to merge poetry and cinema without compromising or diluting either. Short stories and novels are more adaptable, yet the experiences of reading a work of fiction and of seeing a film remain radically different and on some level irreconcilable.

These reflections were prompted by *Stone Reader*, a fascinating and compulsively watchable personal documentary by Mark Moskowitz that runs a little over two hours. This is the first feature of a man who's made his living mainly by shooting commercials for political candidates. He's also been a voracious reader since childhood. Three decades ago, when Moskowitz was in his teens, he read an enthusiastic review of a first novel, *The Stones of Summer* by Dow Mossman, in the *New York Times Book Review*. He bought a copy but got bogged down after about twenty pages. A quarter of a century later he finally read the book through and was blown away. He went looking for other titles by Mossman on the Internet but couldn't find any. For that matter, *The Stones of Summer* had practically vanished, though Moskowitz managed to get a few more copies from used-book dealers. And he had trouble finding anyone who'd heard of it or knew anything about Mossman.

Intrigued by one-book authors in general and Mossman's disappearance in particular, Moskowitz embarked on a two-year quest that he chronicles on film, following up clues, interviewing Mossman's friends and acquaintances, ruminating about the meaning of it all. He eventually tracks down Mossman—the story winds up in the vicinity of the University of Iowa, where Mossman once attended the celebrated Writers' Workshop—but the film is in many ways more about Moskowitz, as Mossman himself suggests. While Moskowitz ruminates on the soundtrack, we often see him doing work around his house in rural Pennsylvania, and though the eventual encounter with Mossman is by no means anticlimactic, Moskowitz's personality dominates. The film is also about a good many ancillary topics: success and failure (especially in an American context), what it means to write an ambitious first novel, the ravages of time and memory loss, the unpredictability of fate and fame, and above all, the love of books.

It's important to add that the love of books is distinct from the experience of reading, and *Stone Reader* has much more to say about the former, perhaps because tangible entities such as books and authors can be filmed and the experience of reading can't. The film conveys a lot about what it's like to collect books, cherish them, hunt them down on the Internet, receive them in the mail, and arrange them on shelves. It's especially poignant in exploring the difference between haunting library stacks or bookstores and cruising the Internet—a distinction that's become far more significant now that global networks of used-book dealers have made it much easier to track down rare volumes.

Even after 128 minutes we wind up with very little sense of what Mossman's novel is like, stylistically or in terms of plot—the little that's quoted from it barely registers. And the gleanings we get about Moskowitz's literary taste are so minimal we can't evaluate it and can't be sure we'd agree with his assessment of *The Stones of Summer*. François Truffaut grappled with related issues when he adapted Ray Bradbury's science fiction novella *Fahrenheit 451* in the '60s (which also prompted his liveliest spate of late writing—a diary of its shooting, appearing serially in both *Cahiers du Cinéma* and its English edition, but regrettably never reprinted): books as holy objects and photogenic camera subjects (especially when they're being devoured by flames) versus books as the source of the more elusive experiences that come from reading their contents, which usually can be discussed only in generalities and banalities.

As if to underline the paradox of this, Moskowitz films himself discussing with a critic how powerful the novel's opening paragraph is, then momentarily cuts to the paragraph itself—yet without framing it in such a way that we can read it. He may treasure the experience of reading *The Stones of Summer*, but his film can honor the book only as a material object. (The success of this film has prompted Barnes & Noble to reprint the book, so people will have an opportunity to judge Moskowitz's claims for themselves.)

One reason Moskowitz overtakes Mossman as the subject of interest at certain points is that the specter of failed writer seems to shadow him as well. This is alluded to directly only once in the film, early on, when Moskowitz proudly shows off the fiction on his shelves and explains the books' arrangement by the authors' nationality. Lingering briefly over a Czech novel called *The Engineer of Human Souls*, he notes that its narrator "jumps between his childhood and the present," then adds, "I tried to copy [that] in a novel I once wrote, but I just didn't have any good stories to tell. So after that I stopped writing for a long time." He doesn't clarify when he resumed writing, but a clue is thereby planted that *Stone Reader*—which periodically jumps between Moskowitz's childhood and the present and which, when it moves into emotional high gear toward the end of the film, leaps about with even greater freedom in relation to time and space — is the good story he finally found to tell, an evident substitute for the Great American Novel he couldn't write.

Like some novels, the film is split into titled sections, each prefaced by one or more literary quotes, and certain books—*The Recognitions, Invisible Man, Catch-22*—figure in the ongoing discourse as if they were secondary characters. (The film privileges novels as mythical objects over shorter works of fiction, which seems particularly unfair in the case of J.D. Salinger, whom it labels a one-book author even though "Raise High the Roof Beam, Carpenter", a novella, is to my taste a greater achievement than *The Catcher in the Rye*.) In a curious yet effective example of how Moskowitz adds visual counterpoint to his offscreen narration, his reveries about *Catch-22* are accompanied by footage of a carnival in the daytime and then at night; he also isn't afraid to use mood music as a catalyst. As this film progresses, his focus is increasingly on time, including the discrepancies between tenses that crop up between lived time and film time. Shortly after he receives the 16-millimeter footage of one of his interviews from the lab he says to the audience, "You've probably already seen it, because it's in the film, but I haven't."

Making commercials for political candidates has undoubtedly taught Moskowitz a thing or two about con artistry. Like a magician, he knows when and how to divert our attention from his trickery—sometimes by suggesting that he might be exposing another form of trickery. After driving to Maine to interview John Seelye, the man whose review of *The Stones of Summer* sparked his initial interest, he steps out of the car and sees a rainbow, then remarks to the film audience with a chuckle, "Nice rainbow. It cost us thousands to paint that in." This throwaway joke undercuts our suspicion that just before this he's offered us fakery—a posthumous NPR interview with Mario Puzo that happens to be playing on his car radio as he pulls into town, which seems likely to have been dubbed in later. Similar bits of probable skulduggery turn up elsewhere—as when we get a crystal-clear sound recording of a cellphone conversation—but his gifts as a storyteller encourage us to excuse or overlook these tweaks.

Moskowitz's credibility as a literary sleuth is bolstered by some of the people who agreed to be interviewed by him. Among them are the late Leslie Fiedler, who speaks about his own successful championing of Henry Roth's *Call It Sleep* and pointedly wonders which is potentially more damaging to a novelist, success or failure; Robert Gottlieb, identified as the editor of *Catch-22* and *The Chosen* (but not as the onetime editor of the *New Yorker*); several graduates of and teachers associated with the Iowa writing program, including Frank Conroy; Mossman's former agent; and Mossman himself, who's especially eloquent when he holds forth on Shakespeare as if he knew him personally. All of them have things to say about the psychic cost of serious writing, but as the title suggests, the film's ultimate pact is with readers, not writers.

Metaphysical [on Robert Frank's *One Hour*]

From Frank Films: The Film and Video Work of Robert Frank, *edited by Brigitta Burger-Utzer and Stefan Grissemann, Scalo Zurich—Berlin—New York, 2003; slightly revised and updated.*

"I've seen *La chouette aveugle* [*The Blind Owl*] seven times," Luc Moullet once wrote of Raúl Ruiz's intractable masterpiece, "and I know a little less about the film with each viewing." Apart from being both intractable and a masterpiece, I can't say Robert Frank's *One Hour* has anything in common with the Ruiz film, yet what makes it a masterpiece and intractable is the same paradox: the closer I come to understanding it, the more mysterious it gets.

My first look at this single-take account of Frank and actor Kevin O'Connor either walking or riding in the back of a mini-van through a few blocks of Manhattan's Lower East Side—shot between 3:45 and 4:45 pm on July 26, 1990—led me to interpret it as a spatial event capturing the somewhat uncanny coziness and intimacy of New York street life, the curious experience of eaves-dropping involuntarily on strangers that seems an essential part of being in Manhattan, an island where so many people are crammed together that the existential challenge of everyday coexistence between them seems central to the city's energy and excitement. (The previous sentence—an attempt to approximate the phenomenology of discontinuity within an overall delirium of continuity, like any walk through a busy New York street in summertime—can offer only a pale echo of what Frank's camera does.)

But this was just a first impression. A second look highlighted the degree to which Frank's rambling itinerary seems to recapitulate a tradition of North American experimental cinema harping on the perpetual motion of protagonist and/or camera, encompassing such varied works as Maya Deren's *At Land*, Stan Brakhage's *Dog Star Man*, and Michael Snow's camera movement trilogy, in which narrative becomes a kind of stream of consciousness as well as a sort of journey, even if the journey (as in Snow) proceeds mechanically and in successive jerky zooms or pendulum-like arcs or circles, retracing the same patterns and/or spaces.

Then I encountered the closest thing *One Hour* has to a skeleton key—a tiny book issued first by Hanuman Books in 1992, then in a somewhat larger (yet still small) format by Steidl in 2007—comprising mainly a transcription of the dialogue heard (over 74 pages), but also two pages of credits: half a dozen production or crew workers and 27 actors. Plus an acknowledgment that the film has a script (by Frank and his assistant, Michael Rovier), that a conversation heard in a diner is written by Mika Moses, and that the lines of Peter Orlovsky (intercepted by Frank roughly halfway through the hour, in front of the Angelika Cinema on Houston Street)—who gradually wrests the film's apparent center away from O'Connor—are "total improvisation".

And here's where the mysteries truly begin. How much of Frank's apparently random drift is precisely plotted, how many seeming chance encounters are staged and intricately coordinated, and how much of what we see and hear is extemporaneous? The volatile, unstable mixtures of chance and control can never be entirely sorted out. (What about that guy with a briefcase standing across the street from the Noho Star? He seems to be waiting for someone, but when we find him still there half an hour later, we start to wonder if he's a planted extra.) In short, how much this is a tossed-off home movie about Frank's neighborhood and how much it's a contrived board game spread out over several city blocks ultimately becomes a metaphysical question. So maybe Frank isn't so far away from Ruiz after all.

Bullet Ballet [*Pistol Opera*]

This appeared in the August 22, 2003 Chicago Reader, *and has more recently been reprinted in the online, Eastern European* Camera Lucida. *On the afternoon of September 17, 2014, in Sarajevo at the Film.Factory, I screened this film for the MA students and assigned them to create five-minute remakes. We screened most of the results nine days later at a party, and they were really dazzling—and all quite different from one another. I acted in one of them.*

Can I call a film a masterpiece without being sure that I understand it? I think so, since understanding is always relative and less than clear-cut. Look long enough at the apparent meaning of any conventional work—past the illusion of narrative continuity that persuades us to overlook anomalies, breaks, fissures, and other distractions we can't process—and it usually becomes elusive. Yet it's also true that we have different ways of comprehending meaning.

I first saw Seijun Suzuki's *Pistol Opera* (2001) in early 2002, and half a year later I served on a jury at a film festival in Brisbane that awarded the movie its top prize, calling it "a highly personal blend of traditional and experimental cinema." I can't think of another film I've seen since that has afforded me more unbridled sensual pleasure. Which may explain how I could dip into an unsubtitled DVD any number of times and never worry about not understanding it. (I should note, however, that this film, starting with the eye-popping graphics of the opening credits, needs the big screen to achieve its optimal impact.)

I couldn't give a fully coherent synopsis of *Pistol Opera* if my life depended on it, but it's still the most fun new movie I've seen since *Mulholland Drive* and and *Waking Life* (both also 2001). Yet I have to admit it must not be everybody's idea of a good time: the Music Box is showing it only this weekend and only at midnight and 11:30 AM, and even in Japan it seems to be strictly a cult item and head-scratcher.

Having recently seen the movie again with subtitles and read a few rundowns of the plot, I'm only more confused about its meaning. The gist of the narrative is that a beautiful young hit woman known as Stray Cat (Makiko Esumi)—"No. 3" in the pecking order of the Guild, the unfathomable, invisible organization she works for—aspires to be No. 1 and proceeds to bump off most of her male colleagues.

They include Hundred Eyes, aka Dark Horse, a young dandy with chronic sinus problems who's currently No. 1; Goro Hanada (a character revived from Suzuki's 1967 *Branded to Kill*), who's middle-aged and walks with a crutch, answers to the name of "The Champ," and used to be No. 1; the Teacher, No. 4, who's middle-aged and gets around in a wheelchair; Dr. Painless (Jan Woudstra), No. 5, a Westerner who's built like a Viking and periodically speaks English; and, apparently, Lazy Man, No. 2, who's referred to many times and cited in the credits but whom I seem to have missed. To complicate matters further, many of these men are killed by No. 3 not once but repeatedly, springing back to life like Wile E. Coyote in a Road Runner cartoon—and some of them kill Stray Cat repeatedly as well.

In between these deadly encounters Stray Cat has scenes with females from at least four generations, including a grandmotherly rustic woman who takes care of her; the former No. 11, who sells her a Springfield rifle; a middle-aged agent with a bright purple scarf mask who sends her on missions and period-ically flirts with her; and a little girl named Sayoko who speaks more English than Dr. Painless (reading or reciting, among other things, "Humpty Dumpty" and Wordsworth's "Daffodils") and clearly wants to grow up to be a hit woman herself.

The scenes with the rustic woman and Sayoko tend to register like relaxed family get-togethers. The other meetings with men and women often start as Guild assignments and wind up, at least symbolically, as sexual assignations, full of taunts, teases, and gestures that drip with innuendo. They also come across like children's games: the blade of Dr. Painless's knife is collapsible, all the guns are bandied about like phallic toys or fetish objects, and any pain is clearly make-believe. (As Godard once said of his *Pierrot le fou*, the operative word is "red," not "blood.")

Static poses are often struck; the story unravels more like a ballet than an opera (the movements of actors and camera as well as the cuts are synchronized to pop music, much of it performed on trumpet by a Miles Davis clone); and the action shifts between industrial, rural, or urban locations that are used theatrically and studio sets that often take the form of theatrical stages used for Kabuki, butoh, and Greek or Roman drama (we see columns suggesting a Mediterranean amphitheater). Other scenes appear to be set in some lava-lamp version of an afterlife, with an otherworldly lime-colored dock and a shimmering gold river over which ghostlike figures in white hover.

I don't subscribe to notions of "pure cinema" or "pure style," because even abstraction has content—color, shape, movement. But this free-form and deeply personal movie suggests purity more than any other recent film that comes to mind. It's often as abstract and as stringently codified as Cuban cartoonist Antonio Prohias's *Spy vs Spy* comic strip in *Mad*, though the colors of most of the kimonos are too gorgeously lush to evoke Prohias's minimalism. And the feeling of sacred passion conveyed by many of the compositions—the sense that many of the characters, costumes, props, and settings are the objects of Suzuki's unreasoning worship, as carefully placed and juxtaposed as totems in a Joseph Cornell box—imbues the whole film with some of the aura of ecstatic religious art, even if it's cast in the profanely riotous pop colors of a Frank Tashlin.

Suzuki, who turned eighty last May, directed at least forty quickie features at the Nikkatsu studio between 1956 and 1967—practically all of them B films in the original sense of that term, meaning features designed to accompany A pictures. I've seen half a dozen of these, ranging from the forty-minute *Love Letter* (1959), a black-and-white 'Scope film with a ski-lodge setting, to the ninety-one-minute *Branded to Kill*, a baroque hit-man thriller (also in black-and-white 'Scope) that remains his best-known work—and was, along with Jean-Pierre Melville's *Le samourai*, the major inspiration for Jim Jarmusch's *Ghost Dog*.

Branded to Kill so enraged the president of Nikkatsu that he fired Suzuki for making "incomprehensible" films. A Suzuki support group was duly formed, and Suzuki sued the studio, as he later put it, "to protect my dignity." A full decade would pass before he directed another theatrical feature, and he never returned to Nikkatsu. His output became sporadic, much of it consisting of TV commissions, and eight years of silence preceded *Pistol Opera*.

Before *Pistol Opera* I wasn't one of Suzuki's most ardent fans. Frankly, I didn't know what to make of him, even as a cult figure. According to my favorite Japanese film critic, Shigehiko Hasumi, "Suzuki is appreciated in the West, but essentially he's a traditional Japanese man who regards Western people as barbarians, in the traditional Japanese meaning of that term." This implies that one can't adequately (or accurately) rationalize his craziness by calling him a Japanese Sam Fuller, and one can't palm him off as an old pro churning out entertainments, though that's how he represents himself, at least in part.

In a 1997 interview in Los Angeles included on the DVD of *Branded to Kill*, Suzuki, after insisting that he just wants to make films that are "fun and entertaining," goes on to argue that there's no "grammar" for cinema—at least for his kind of cinema—because he doesn't mind defying the usual rules respecting the cinematic coordinates of time and space: "In my films, spaces and places change [and] time is cheated in the editing. I guess that's the strength of entertainment movies: you can do anything you want, as long as these elements make the movie interesting. That's my theory of the grammar of cinema."

This may sound like a recipe for formalism—especially given that the film's subtitle is *Killing With Style*—but there's far too much content in *Pistol Opera* to make its dream patterns feel arbitrary or reducible to a simple theme-and-variations format. Indeed, one of the reasons I find the film so exhausting is that it doesn't take time out for anything. Whatever it's after, it always feels on-target.

Suzuki's protracted hiatus from filmmaking may be partly responsible for the sense of manic overdrive. Orson Welles once speculated that the hyperbolic style of his *Touch of Evil* was the consequence of feeling bottled up creatively for much too long, and considering all the striking and even stunning locations used in *Pistol Opera*, I'd like to imagine that Suzuki spent years discovering them, saving them for whenever he'd be able to show them off in a film.

Obviously the movie has a lot to do with gender. There's the dominance and aggression of the women (not counting the country grandmother, who seems to belong to a different era), combined with Stray Cat's phallic preoccupations ("I think it's OK to lead my life as a pistol," she says at one point; elsewhere she addresses her gun as "my man") and the pronounced disability of the men (not counting Dr. Painless, who appears to signify "America")—all of which seems like a precise inversion of the structure of Japanese society. The other themes are no less Japanese. There's the obsession with hierarchy, competition, and professional identity. There's the surrealist view of death as lyrical expression: according to the Champ, "Killing blooms into an artwork," and a steam shovel turns up at the door of a rural cottage with rose petals dropping from its jaws. More subtle and profound is the memory of military defeat, made explicit in one of the masked agent's late soliloquies and in a vision of a mushroom cloud that suddenly appears on a rotating stage. Most of these themes seem to come together in the former No. 11's climactic speech about a dream she had in which a headless Yukio Mishima appears and she tries without success to sew his head back on, using all sorts of string and wire.

In fact, *Pistol Opera* registers as so prototypically Japanese in both style and content that the preponderance of English dialogue is notable mainly for the sense of foreignness it conveys. My favorite howler in the dialogue—"I didn't mean to kill each other, really"—sounds like the way adult Americans talk, only funnier. It also perfectly conveys the Japanese language's conflation of singular and plural and all the ambiguous crossovers between self and society that seem to derive from this.

The absence—or rather sublimation—of sex is equally operative. "I don't really like sex," Suzuki declared in a 1969 interview. "It's such a hassle." He then responded to the question "In which period would you have liked to be born?" with the equally defeatist "Well, not as a human, in any case." At first it may be difficult to reconcile this negativity with the film's sense of joyful discovery, but the dream logic whereby opposite attitudes produce each other seems central to *Pistol Opera*—an ambivalence that's conveyed even by its title.

How to Capture an Artist
[*Sylvia* & *In The Mirror of Maya Deren*]

From the Chicago Reader *(October 31, 2003).*

Greasing the bodies of adulterers
Like Hiroshima ash and eating in.
The sin. The sin.
— Sylvia Plath, "Fever 103"

In film, I can make the world dance.
— Maya Deren

In college it always seemed like the guys who were poets got more girls than the prose writers. The assumption was that poets had all the romance and sensuality associated with their medium working for them. Poetry, after all, isn't just a block of printed material; it's an activity, and one that can turn people on sexually as well as spiritually.

In cultures such as those of Russia and Iran sexual and spiritual qualities tend to run neck and neck: the great Persian poet Forough Farrokhzad (1935-67), a fan of Sylvia Plath, retains a mythic allure that combines the auras of Joan of Arc, Billie Holiday, and Marilyn Monroe. And an erotic charge is one of the first things that *Sylvia*, a biopic about Sylvia Plath (1932-63), gets right. It pervades the initial encounters between the title heroine and Ted Hughes in Cambridge, England, in 1956. The film arrives at these meetings with exemplary dispatch, after opening with Plath's excruciating declaration in "Lady Lazarus": "Dying /Is an art, like everything else, /I do it exceptionally well."

The brisk action that follows and the lack of fuss over exposition gave me some assurance that director Christine Jeffs and screenwriter John Brownlow knew what they were up to.

Todd McCarthy writes in *Variety*, "There's a big piece missing from the picture's center: The all-encompassing connection that brought the couple together in the first place is never made palpable." I disagree. The couple's shared passion for poetry, depicted mainly in small but telling details, is certainly an all-encompassing connection, though I can't swear those details are made palpable for everyone.

I object more strenuously to McCarthy's opening gambit—"As grim as much of Sylvia Plath's life may have been, it wasn't as relentlessly bleak as the movie *Sylvia*"—which I'd probably find presumptuous even if it came from one of her friends. Of course presumed knowledge about her life has been a central aspect of the Plath myth ever since her suicide at thirty, which helped to bring that myth into being—especially for those who've fetishized her as a prefeminist martyr. I find nothing bleaker about the life of Plath and Hughes than something this movie pointedly, if understandably, omits: Assia Gutmann Wevill (played in the film by Amira Casar)—with whom Hughes lived after he separated from Plath and with whom he had a daughter, Shura—killed herself and Shura six years after Plath's suicide, when she was thirty-four and Shura two. She turned on the gas in her kitchen stove, just as Plath did. It's worth adding that Wevill was a poet, and that, according to Paul Alexander's biography *Rough Magic*, the "burden of living in the shadow of Plath" played a significant role in motivating her act.

The terrible thing about Plath "dying exceptionally well" is that her suicide appeared to clinch her fame—as if the poetry she wrote wasn't quite enough. I remember how angry I was when one of my professors argued that her suicide "proved" many of the assertions of her poems, giving them a legitimacy they wouldn't have had otherwise. Whether one buys this theory or not, it points to the factor that dooms most literary biopics, including serious ones—the all but obligatory tendency to privilege the life over the work. In this case the filmmakers had legal restrictions on how much they could quote from Plath, guaranteeing that the space for her poetry would be small. (As partial compensation, we get a fair sampling of other people's poetry, including Chaucer's.)

Considering the myth-making that has surrounded Plath's reputation from the outset, a dispassionate view of her life has never been easy, and the film's most admirable achievement is its refusal to take sides in the dispute between her and her late husband, viewing both with sympathy and compassion. One of the best aspects of Gwyneth Paltrow's finely tuned performance is her capacity to convey Plath's chronic depression without making us recoil from it, and Daniel Craig takes on the task of representing Hughes's womanizing with a comparable feeling for complexity and nuance. Making this couple's relationship more important than their poetry surely wasn't the movie's intention, but it becomes the central program nonetheless. And this locks the movie into an imposture, because without their poetry we wouldn't know or care about their relationship.

One reason why it's an imposture is that cinema and poetry aren't merely disparate art forms but largely incompatible ones. (Farrokhzad's only film, *The House Is Black*, is the only successful fusion that comes to mind.) Poetry has to be read slowly—one of the things that makes it sexy—and even though some great films move slowly, commercially minded biopics do so at their peril. Consider the three short lines from Plath's "Fever 103°" quoted above or any five-line stanza from "Daddy," another desperate late poem, written a week before "Fever": the poetry must be allowed to reverberate—to drift and spread, line by line and word by word. And how many movies that star Paltrow have the time for that? Indeed, as I've suggested, one of the nicest things about *Sylvia*, at least in the beginning, is its unusual speed. Yet speed is ultimately relevant only to storytelling; it has almost nothing to do with composing or reading poetry, except when it's recited as quickly as possible for laughs, as happens in one early scene here.

The problem is, people's lives aren't stories. They have to be turned into stories to become fodder for biopics, and the interpretations that shape them are likely to be determined by the needs of dramaturgy. I'm no expert on Plath's life, but even a superficial skimming of *Rough Magic* reveals that her mother played a much larger role in her life than the film's mother (Blythe Danner, the real-life mother of Paltrow). The film uses her character mainly to offer exposition about Plath's past during her sole appearance, when Sylvia brings Hughes home to meet her; once that task is gracefully accomplished by Danner, she's not allowed to interfere with the story again.

I can't imagine what a biopic about Maya Deren (1917-'61)—the person who did the most to create American experimental film as we know it—would be like, and I hope I never have to find out. One of the best things about *In the Mirror of Maya Deren*—a feature-length documentary in English by Austrian director Martina Kudlacek, playing at the Gene Siskel Film Center a dozen times this week—is that it does such a terrific job of showing us what Deren was like that it makes even the notion of a biopic about her seem unnecessary, if not ridiculous.

For one thing, Deren so assiduously chronicled and recorded her filmmaking activities and lectures that Kudlacek had a lot to work with. She makes wonderful use of the material, though lamentably a private recording of Deren singing the standard "Mean to Me" has been cut since I first saw the film in early 2002. Deren's version doesn't threaten Sarah Vaughan's, but it's a collector's item to cherish. I suspect it had to go because the cost of paying the song's copyright holders was too high. The song is still mentioned in the final credits; maybe it was too expensive to redo them. Fortunately the film has a wonderful original score by John Zorn, which makes dramatic use of suspended chords, as well as other samples of Deren singing and several pieces of music she recorded during her four trips to Haiti between 1947 and 1955.

Money was always something of a problem for Deren, at least as an adult, though she was the first filmmaker to ever win a Guggenheim Fellowship grant. She died of a brain hemorrhage at forty-four, and one of her friends suggests that malnutrition may have been a contributing factor—along with amphetamine shots and a legal dispute involving the inheritance of her twenty-six year-old Japanese lover that evidently exercised her fiery temper. Born Eleanora Derenkovskaya in Kiev the year of the Russian Revolution, she had a privileged upbringing as the daughter of Russian Jews, a psychiatrist father and a mother who studied music. When she was still a child the family moved to Syracuse, New York, and in her early teens she attended a Swiss boarding school. But by the time she finished her formal education, in 1939, she was a bohemian poet and working as a secretary. "I was a very poor poet," we hear her say in the film, "because I thought in terms of images...[and] poetry is an effort to put [visual experience] into verbal terms. When I got a camera in my hands, it was like coming home."

Perhaps her most consequential secretarial job was for dancer and anthropologist Katherine Dunham, one of the many fascinating talking heads here; it took her to Los Angeles, where she met the Czech experimental filmmaker Alexander Hammid (another talking head). Collaborating with Hammid, she made her first film, the groundbreaking *Meshes of the Afternoon* (1943)—a series of metaphorical and metaphysical self-portraits as rich in Freudian content as any of Plath's late poems, though made mostly in celebration and without any of Plath's self-loathing.

Deren saw female self-portraiture as a process of perpetual metamorphosis—an explicitly feminist undertaking that's in some ways the opposite of Plath's petrified notions of identity. Clearly the world wasn't quite ready for that sensibility; neither of the best American film reviewers at the time, James Agee and Manny Farber, was any sort of fan, though the larger art community she was part of—including dancers, choreographers, musicians, composers, and other filmmakers—encouraged and supported her.

This milieu is brought to life so vividly in the documentary one can almost smell the kitty litter in Deren's Greenwich Village flat. Better yet, the film performs the nearly miraculous feat of allowing us to know her as a person as well as understand her as an artist, and it does this better than any of the excellent books about her, including the two volumes to date of *The Legend of Maya Deren*—a massive, collectively authored biography and compilation that's been in the works since the '80s—and the recent collection *Maya Deren and the American Avant-Garde*.

A high-strung narcissist and sensualist who anticipated hippie dress codes as well as New Age babble, Deren might seem to gather all the clichés of bohemian Manhattan in the '40s and '50s in one Jungian jumble. Yet the robust power of her charisma is conveyed so affectionately by her friends, even when they recall her with exasperation, that something all her own arises out of the overlapping archetypes she adopted.

If Plath's myth is the creation of her writing—magnified by her suicide and the depths of depression her writing explored—Deren's myth is the product of a steady rush of evolving self-definitions. Those definitions can't be restricted to her films, though the films provide the ideal settings for them. The late Stan Brakhage, who knew her well and provides the most sensitive and provocative appreciation of her films in the documentary, offers a startling view of her as a kind of demiurge when he describes watching her lift and hurl a full-size refrigerator across a kitchen in a moment of rage.

Even if we balk at believing him, we may conclude that the force of her personality was such that it could inspire this sort of belief. In *Maya Deren and the American Avant-Garde*, Jane Brakhage Wodening, who recounts the same story, suggests as much when she writes about Deren, the words spilling out as if she were in a trance: "In Haiti, she was fulfilled. She learned about voodoo, a religion of shamanic power, and this religion was based on dance. And when she danced in Haiti, she was possessed of the voodoo gods and she had power over men. And so she became a priestess and her red hair stuck out all over her head like sparks and she wore her hair that way the rest of her life." This may sound like it belongs in a Cecil B. De Mille opus or in Fritz Lang's *Metropolis*, but it does suggest the effect Deren had on others. It's sad that Plath could exert that kind of power only posthumously, which puts it beyond the reach of any biopic.

The Stuff of Dreams [on *Sunrise*]

From The Guardian, *January 31, 2004.*

Some film industry bigwigs dream of owning a Rembrandt. In the 1920s, William Fox, head of Hollywood's Fox studio, wanted a Murnau. A prestigious German director in his late thirties, F.W. Murnau already had 17 German features to his credit (only nine of which survive today). But this was an unprecedented case of a well-stocked studio giving carte blanche to a foreign director simply for the sake of prestige. Murnau took advantage of this opportunity by creating a universal fable that, as an opening intertitle puts it, could take place anywhere and at any time: his 1927 masterpiece, *Sunrise*.

The standard line about the film is that it lost piles of money for Fox. Maybe it did. But film history often consists of writers dutifully copying the mistakes of their predecessors, and I'm afraid I have to plead guilty to having perpetuated this particular story myself. According to film curator David Pierce, "*Sunrise* was Fox's third-highest-grossing film for 1928, surpassed only by Frank Borzage's *Seventh Heaven* and John Ford's *Four Sons*"—both films that were visibly influenced by Murnau. (The first, for starters, employed Janet Gaynor, the second, some of *Sunrise*'s sets.) Of course, it's theoretically possible that the grosses didn't make back the film's cost, but I'd rather think that Fox's investment paid off in one way or another. After all, it won no fewer than three Oscars—and we're still looking at the film.

Like *Citizen Kane*, *Sunrise* is one of those movies that introduces viewers to the notion of film as art. It was Dorothy B. Jones's sensitive essay about *Sunrise* in a 1960 collection called *Introduction to the Art of Movies* that drove me to see it in the first place. Aside from her article and a couple of short reviews, the most enthusiastic writing I could find about the movie was in French, most of it in the pages of the magazine *Cahiers du Cinéma*. According to a poll of its critics in 1958, Murnau was the greatest of all film directors and *Sunrise* was his greatest film.

Part of what continues to make it great is its creation in a particular utopian moment in film history: the end of the silent era, when movies reached a certain pinnacle of visual expressiveness that was tied to a dream of universality, a belief that cinema could speak an international tongue. Properly speaking, *Sunrise* is less a silent picture than a pre-talkie, existing in a strange netherworld between sound and silence. It has a very beautiful and adroitly stylized soundtrack of music and sound effects, composed by Hugo Reisenfeld, that is an essential part of its magic.

The aesthetics of *Sunrise* have a lot to do with painting, music and literature, brought together in a remarkably interactive way that suggests another utopian dream: a definition of cinema as the meeting point for all the other arts. Subtitled *A Song of Two Humans*, the film has three movements, beginning and ending with slow tempos in a rural setting that are separated by an urban scherzo. Apart from the happy ending, which functions like a coda, the movements might be described as melodramatic, comic, and tragic, in that order—accompanied by a painterly control of light passing from night to day in the first movement, from day to night in the second and again from night to day in the third.

The characters don't have names but generalized labels. The Man (George O'Brien), a simple farmer, is having a torrid affair with a vacationing City Woman (Margaret Livingston, one of the central characters in Peter Bogdanovich's recent film about 1920s Hollywood, *The Cat's Meow*). She signals to him, by whistling, to meet her for a night of lovemaking in the marshes. Wanting him to move with her to the city, she proposes that he drown his Wife (Janet Gaynor) in the nearby lake; but when he tries to carry out this plan the next day, en route to the city, he recoils in horror from the prospect and succeeds only in terrifying his victim. Over a day and an evening in the city, the married couple gradually become reconciled and fall in love all over again. But when a storm breaks out on their way back across the lake, the Wife apparently drowns.

With a story this elemental, inflections are everything, and Murnau's richly imaginative and nuanced direction synthesizes performances, sets, camera movements and special effects (including many different kinds of superimposition) to spell them out. Early on, when the Man walks across the meadow to meet the City Woman in the marshes, the camera, in a startling effect, eerily takes on an independent intelligence: first following the Man, then moving alongside him and finally rushing ahead of him to arrive at the City Woman by a separate route, before he does. And her evocations of the city once they meet are sexually charged expressionist visions rendered through double exposures and camera gyrations, while the overlaps and distortions of the music convey the same cacophony. Even the intertitles are integrated graphically in the visual design: the City Woman's line "Couldn't she get drowned?" sinks and wavers like a body receding below a lake surface covered by mist—an effect complemented at the very end of the movie, when the watery, wavering title "Finis" stiffens from the heat of the rising sun.

"They say that I have a passion for 'camera angles'," Murnau wrote in 1928. "To me the camera represents the eye of a person, through whose mind one is watching the events on the screen. It must follow characters at times into difficult places, as it crashed through the reeds and pools in *Sunrise* at the heels of the Boy, rushing to keep his tryst with the Woman of the City. It must whirl and peep and move from place to place as swiftly as thought itself."

Some actions are deliberately and musically protracted to create an ominous mood; when the Man slowly advances towards his Wife in the boat to throw her overboard, Murnau had twenty pounds of lead placed in O'Brien's shoes to keep his movements sufficiently heavy and slurred. In the justly celebrated trolley ride taken by the couple into the city, the orchestration of O'Brien's and Gaynor's exquisite acting (depicting her fear and his remorse) with the shifting landscapes behind them suggests both a fusion of melody with harmony and a powerful modulation, passing from the minor key of the film's first movement to the major key of its second.

The city itself—a gargantuan set built on Fox's backlot, teeming with choreographed activity—is made to conform to a frightened rural couple's perception of its size, noise, confusion and scale, and the Luna Park they visit in the evening is an even more delirious expressionist construction. Also striking is the embodiment of the couple's enraptured state as they sail home across the lake, when a passing raft with silhouetted figures dancing around a bonfire captures their wild and exalted bliss, with the Wife ecstatically rocking her head back and forth in time to the music.

For all the dated and melodramatic aspects of Murnau's eccentric stylization, the erotic charge of the Man's two relationships—a sexual object for the City Woman, a dominating figure to his Wife—remains startling today in its directness. In more ways than one, *Sunrise* triumphs as a masterwork of thought and emotion rendered in terms of visual music, where light and darkness sing in relation to countless polarities: day and night, fire and water, sky and earth, city and country, man and woman, thought and deed, good and evil, nature and culture.

Silent Ozu

Adapted from an article in the Chicago Reader *(January 14, 2005). For more about Ozu's musicality throughout his career, see "Is Ozu Slow?", included in my collection* Essential Cinema *and at jonathanrosenbaum.net.*

It's no longer controversial to assert that Yasujiro Ozu (1903-63) is one of the greatest filmmakers—certainly one of the top dozen and perhaps the greatest who focused on family life. But getting a fix on his work remains far from easy. Only thirty-four of his fifty-odd films appear to have survived, and two features exist only in fragments.

Tokyo Story (1953)—the first Ozu film seen widely in the West, and still the most highly regarded—is a good starting point for viewers unfamiliar with his work. So are *Late Spring* and *Good Morning.* But these and other masterpieces have led many critics to make incorrect generalizations about Ozu's style and content, claiming that his films are slow and conservative, his technique minimalist.

But such labels don't apply even remotely to his best surviving silent films. In the Ozu retrospective at Chicago's absurdly named Gene Siskel Film Center that originally gave rise to this article, each of the nine silent films was screened only once, but each of the sixteen sound features was shown twice. This is understandable given the bias against silent pictures and the cost of hiring a pianist (though the accompaniments of David Drazin alone were worth the price of admission). But it reinforced a skewed perception of Ozu. His first thirty-five films were silent, and his last twenty were talkies. Many of the silents are now lost, but the ones we still have display a stylistic range and freedom mostly absent from the talkies. The silents were often assignments, yet Ozu made them his own. The "James Maki" credited with many of the stories (and those of Ozu's first two sound features) is Ozu writing under a pen name, and many of the actors and crew members were ones he would use throughout his career. Made over just nine years, these thirty-five works display a remarkable diversity and authority; the only comparable stretch in a great director's career that comes to mind is Jean-Luc Godard's work in the '60s.

On my first trip to Japan in 1999 I appeared on a panel discussing Ozu and learned that all his silent films were available there on video. He'd just come back into fashion in Japan, yet none of the many young film buffs and Ozu fans I spoke with in Tokyo had seen even one of his silents. Many critics seem to have concluded that Ozu spent his first nine years looking for a style and a subject and that the essence of his greatness lies in his later refinement of such techniques as low camera angles and a motionless camera. But to understand his work one needs to consider some of the skills he discarded, apparent in such exciting if eccentric American-style thrillers as *That Night's Wife* and *Dragnet Girl* and in the overt social criticism of such early features as *Tokyo Chorus*, *I Was Born, But…*(my favorite Ozu film), *Passing Fancy*, and *An Inn in Tokyo*.

Ozu's films tend to be physical and physically expressive, and I would argue that in this respect his silent pictures are superior to his talkies. It's one reason he kept directing silents through 1935. Japanese films were late in shifting to sound because the benshis, the live commentators whose creative embroideries were sometimes more popular than the stars' acting, exerted enough power to keep them silent. Ozu was even more reluctant than his colleagues to shift to sound, though his first talkie, *The Only Son* (1936), was another masterpiece. (Charlie Chaplin finally gave his tramp a voice the same year, in *Modern Times*.) Ozu is commonly called "the most Japanese of Japanese directors"—the usual reason given for why his films were slower to reach the West than those of Akira Kurosawa and Kenji Mizoguchi. (When I saw some Ozu films in Paris in 1972, no Ozu film had ever been distributed in France or written about in *Cahiers du Cinéma* or *Positif*, the two leading film monthlies.) Yet Shigehiko Hasumi provocatively maintains that calling Ozu "very Japanese" is "a huge mistake…based on a lack of understanding of his works." (I know his book on Ozu only through its French translation, but its final chapter, which includes this argument, is available in English in a collection edited by David Desser, Ozu's *Tokyo Story*.)

Ozu has been misperceived in many ways. Even a film lover as sophisticated as the late Susan Sontag—who had a passion for Japanese cinema and once compared Ozu to Jane Austen—could write in 1995 that "the great Japanese directors (Ozu, Mizoguchi, Kurosawa, Naruse, Oshima, Imamura) have tended not to be cinephiles." This is grossly wrong in Ozu's case. According to David Bordwell's 1988 *Ozu and the Poetics of Cinema*, by far the most comprehensive book about Ozu in English (and an invaluable resource whose major limitation is its failure to engage with or even mention Hasumi), he "was almost certainly the most cinephiliac major director before the New Wave." Ozu's journals—which I also know only in French, an 800-page monolith titled *Carnets 1933-1963*, published the year after Sontag's essay—contain a record of the numerous films he saw on a regular basis, many of them Hollywood classics. (*Citizen Kane* was his all-time favorite.) His silent films often show traces of his favorite directors, typically signaled by movie posters, e.g. Fritz Lang (*That Night's Wife*), Ernst Lubitsch (*Woman of Tokyo*), Josef von Sternberg (*That Night's Wife, Dragnet Girl*), and King Vidor (*Tokyo Chorus, Passing Fancy*).

Another potential obstacle to grasping Ozu's work is the relevance of Zen Buddhism , a question raised mainly by the only thing written on his gravestone: the Japanese character "mu," which means "nothing." Ozu disparaged the tendency of foreign critics to overemphasize such matters when he said, "They don't understand—that's why they say it is Zen or something like that." I wouldn't want to claim that his religious beliefs are irrelevant to his work. But critics have often concentrated on what's absent or implied in Ozu's films instead of what's visible and audible, then produced a fair amount of mumbo jumbo about what they find exotic—as they have with Robert Bresson, Carl Dreyer, and even a certifiable mystic such as Andrei Tarkovsky. As Hasumi points out, despite the seasonal references in the confusingly similar titles of many of Ozu's later films—*Late Spring, Early Summer, Early Spring, Equinox Flower, Late Autumn, The End of Summer, An Autumn Afternoon*—the films themselves ignore seasonal changes and lack seasonal contexts. Hasumi writes, in what may be the most important sentence in his book, "Ozu's talent lies in choosing an image that can function poetically at a particular moment by being assimilated into the film, not by affixing to the film the image of an object that is considered poetic in a domain outside the film."

This can be readily seen in key moments of *Tokyo Chorus*. The story concerns a young family man who loses his job at an insurance company when he protests the unfair firing of an older employee, has to sell most of his wife's clothes to pay for the care of their sick infant, and ultimately winds up working for a former teacher who runs a cheap restaurant. (Like *Passing Fancy* and *An Inn in Tokyo*, it's very much a Depression film, conveying more of the flavor of what Americans were going through at the time than anything in *The Aviator*.) On his way back from job hunting, the father finds his son fishing, and the son, after borrowing his father's hat to land a fish, tells him his youngest child is ill. They both rush home, and for a few seconds Ozu focuses on the forgotten fish flopping helplessly on the ground—a startling image that depends entirely on its context for its poetry. A similarly uncanny moment occurs much later when the father remarks to his wife, "I feel I'm getting old. I've lost my energy," and his words are sandwiched between two shots of his kids' clothes hanging on a line outside.

Many similar visual asides in *That Night's Wife* (1930) involve expressive hands, especially the hero's. One close-up of him nervously drumming two fingers on the glass pane of a phone booth is especially memorable. Most of this thriller transpires over one night in a small, cluttered apartment, where the hero, who's just robbed his office to get money for his ailing child, and his wife hold a gun on a policeman until they fall asleep and he turns a gun on them. Ozu's focus on their hands clearly serves the plot and the suspense, but he also uses it as a poetic motif.

The power of such images is partly rhythmic, enhanced by the cutting. When the policeman in *That Night's Wife* turns up at the door of the hero's apartment and starts knocking, a sublime frisson is created by a cut from a rapid track up to the door from inside to a rapid track away from the back of the policeman outside. *Dragnet Girl* (1933) opens with a dazzling montage that introduces us indirectly to the title heroine, a typist and gangster's moll (played by the great Kinuyo Tanaka—an Ozu regular who became Kenji Mizoguchi's lead actress in most of his '40s and '50s masterpieces and the first Japanese woman to direct films). The first eleven shots are an overhead view of city pedestrians; the blinds on an open window; two adjacent grandfather clocks that say 3:40 on an office wall alongside the slots for workers' cards; the same workers' cards alongside hats hung on pegs; an electric clock on another wall that says 3:32; the hats, one of which suddenly falls of its own accord and lands on the floor in a separate shot; a tracking shot past the backs of four women typing at adjacent desks; a long track past many more hats on pegs; a track past the same four women that stops at a typewriter on a desk, after which a fifth typist (Tanaka) enters the frame, seen first from the back then, after a cut, from the front as she stands and reads a letter.

Ozu is characteristically playful with the formal beauty of this theme and variations and relatively indifferent to conventional narrative continuity—implied in the cuts between the second and third shots and blatant in the movement from 3:40 PM in the third shot to 3:32 PM in the fifth. Also typical is his fascination with repeating patterns and sameness—clocks, hats, typewriters, tracking shots—which suggest the conformity and predictability of Japanese society. In *I Was Born, But...* (1932) the camera tracks to the right past boys at school marching in military formation, then cuts to a track in the same direction past adult workers at a row of desks, each yawning as the camera passes. When one worker fails to yawn, the camera stops and tracks back to him, waiting for his yawn before resuming its path.

Repetitions are played for laughs on other occasions as well. The prelude to the hero getting fired in *Tokyo Chorus* is a hilariously staged grudge match between him and his boss in which they use identical aggressive gestures. Shortly before that, the hero and his coworkers are seen collecting their bonus checks, and a wonderful extended gag shows each of them retreating to the men's room or the hallway so the others can't see what they got or how they react to the amount.

Even more physical is the inspired slapstick that opens *Passing Fancy* (1933), set at a public music and storytelling performance, where a stray purse is surreptitiously picked up, investigated, and discarded by a succession of audience members, who toss it around like a beanbag—a string of repetitions that overlaps with a series of frenetic dances performed by many of the same people when they're bitten by fleas.

The most obvious source for this film is King Vidor's *The Champ* (1931). As great as that film and its beautifully inflected father-son relationship are, Wallace Beery as the slow-witted but lovable lead doesn't achieve the complex characterization Takeshi Sakamoto does in the equivalent role of a day laborer, and Jackie Cooper as Beery's son isn't any more expressive than Tokkan Kozo is as Sakamoto's son. Sakamoto and Kozo are among the many regulars who turn up so often in Ozu's work they register as fixtures, like Ward Bond and Victor McLaglen in John Ford's films. They are two of the many colors on the master's palette, made fresh by new contexts and combinations. (Kozo's mugging and defiant gestures are even more memorable when he plays the younger of the two brothers in *I Was Born, But...*)

Ozu's films comprise one of the most densely populated oeuvres in cinema, and some of the formal and stylistic features noted above would have much less resonance without the expressive talents of his actors and their continuing presences in the films. Even Chishu Ryu, the male lead in *Tokyo Story*—perhaps the closest equivalent to Ford's John Wayne in terms of his prominence—appears in Ozu's earliest surviving films as well as his last. This is one indication that

Ozu, for all of his experimentation, had created a universe of his own before he even started making what most people now know as "Ozu films". *[2024 update: Ryan Cook's English translation of Hasumi's remarkable book,* Directed by Yasujiro Ozu, *which I've previously known and discussed only through its French translation, has just been published.]*

When it Rains

From the Chicago Reader *(May 7, 2007), added to in October 2022.*

One of my all-time favorite films, this beautiful twelve-minute short by Charles Burnett (*Killer of Sheep, The Glass Shield, To Sleep with Anger*), made for French TV in 1995, is a jazz parable about locating common roots and celebrating community in contemporary Watts and one of those rare movies in which jazz forms directly influence and even propel film narrative. The slender plot involves a Good Samaritan and local griot (Ayuko Babu), who serves as poetic narrator, trying to raise money from his neighbors in the ghetto for a young mother who's about to be evicted, and each person he goes to see registers like a separate solo in a twelve-bar blues. (Eventually a John Handy album recorded in Monterey, a countercultural emblem of the '60s, becomes a crucial barter item.) This neglected gem may well be the most spiritually and socially joyful of Burnett's works in its playful yet exacting improvisations. One early, ecstatic pan past a series of outdoor drummers and dancers defines a form of celebration that recurs throughout.

Three Entries from
"Eleven Treasures of Jazz Performance on DVD"

The full article was commissioned and posted by DVD Beaver in 2007.

Nat "King" Cole: Soundies & Transcriptions. Cole is mainly known today as a singer, but he started out as a highly influential and virtuoso jazz pianist who also sang, mostly with a guitarist and bassist who rounded out his trio, on countless novelty numbers with titles like, "Got a Penny, Benny?" Curiously, he rarely looks at the keyboard while he plays his dazzling solos, typically sitting in a position turned away from the piano and towards the camera (and sometimes microphone), as if he were already schizophrenically split between being a jazz musician and being a pop vocalist. Sometimes bad dancers and other distractions (including other vocalists) turn up, but usually it's just Cole with his trio, occasionally augmented by bongos and/or unseen strings. (When it's strings—as on the mushy final track "Always You," the only one in color—the guitar and bass still appear briefly in cutaways, but they're completely extraneous, because no one's playing jazz anymore.) And in point of fact, some of the numbers here are neither soundies nor transcriptions but clips from low-budget features such as *Breakfast in Hollywood* (1946) and *Killer Diller* (1947) that were made for segregated black movie theaters.

My favorite tune here comes from the former—the jivey "Solid Potato Salad," only about a minute long—which begins with a driving piano solo that might take your breath away. By contrast, on "Breezy and the Bass," a rare instrumental, which comes from the latter feature, Cole's occasional comps to bassist Johnny Miller are delightful, affectionate little pokes.

The Small Black Groups. Both of these aforementioned Cole tracks and seven others are included on this fascinating collection of twenty-two novelty numbers from the 1940s, taken from soundies as well as black features. (Check out the insane zoot suits worn by two acrobatic dancers in Louis Jordan's 1944 "Jordan Jive," with the musicians appearing in soldiers' uniforms.) The strangest by far are half a dozen live performances by guitarist/pianist/vocalist Slim Galliard, the legendary composer of "Flat Foot Floogie"—celebrated in Part Two, Chapter 11 of Jack Kerouac's *On the Road* as the essence of jive, and seen performing here at Billy Berg's club in 1946 with his eccentric trio consisting of bassist and fellow vocalist "Tiny Bam" Brown (often gesticulating and hugging his instrument at the same time) and drummer "Scat Man" Crothers (best known today for his part as the chef in Stanley Kubrick's *The Shining*, and offering plenty of showy stickwork here).

Galliard was a hipster who liked to attach "o'rooney" to the ends of words—an influential tic, judging by Cole's "Oh, Kickeroony" (also in *The Small Black Groups*)—and to chant the names of different kinds of Jewish food as if they were mantras (as on "Dunkin' Bagels," also included); he also turned up for cameos in *Hellzapoppin'* (as part of the duo Slim and Slam) and *Too Late Blues* (scat-singing at a party). The clips here come from an obscure mid-'40s musical called *O'Voutie O'Rooney*, sometimes spelled *O'Voutee O'Rooney*, that I'd love to see unearthed some day, if only to satisfy my curiosity.

'Rahsaan' Roland Kirk in Europe 1962-1967. Out of all the great jazz musicians I've been lucky to see and hear live, one of the few whose dynamic presence has almost never come through adequately on LPs or CDs is Roland Kirk—a commanding blind giant and demonic powerhouse whose New York debut at the Five Spot in the early '60s was a kind of miracle. "He makes Charlie Parker look like shit," a friend hyperbolically said to me at the time, and while I couldn't come close to agreeing—neither of us had in fact ever seen Bird live—the fact that he said "look" instead of "sound" helps to account for at least some of the hyperbole. Wearing shades, Kirk typically lumbered up to the microphone with three separate large saxophones hanging from his neck (two of them virtually extinct instruments that he'd revived, the manzello and the stritch), like the carcasses of felled animals, which he could play all at once, in unison or in harmony, as well as a siren that he liked to blow into curtly at the end of some choruses, which made them function like giddy musical pivots—not to mention one or more flutes stuffed into the bell of one of his saxophones. And once he started to play, it was like being run over by a friendly locomotive.

Maybe it all sounds like it was a circus act, but Kirk used everything at his disposal to make music, and the same applied when he was simultaneously playing his flute and scat singing, with periodic interjections from his nose flute—to mention only one of his other favorite orchestrations. All this is finally visible on this DVD of two European concerts, both routinely shot in black and white for TV. In Kirk's *20 minutes in Milan* (1962), the fact that he's playing with a relatively mechanical musician, Catalonian pianist Tete Montoliu (who's also blind), is offset by the two superlative beboppers rounding off the rhythm section, Tommy Potter (bass) and Kenny Clarke (drums). And in *Prague* (1967), where he's backed by his own rhythm section and plays for 50 minutes, he's every bit as spirited.

Keith Jarrett, Cross-Referencer

From Stop Smiling no. 34, *a special jazz issue, dated February 2008.*

Jazz musicians who like to cross-reference the history of their art rather than simply steal licks from their role models are probably even more plentiful than film directors who do "homages" to favorite sequences and directors. The musicians also generally do a better job of mixing their own style with that of their models than Hollywood directors do when they strive to reproduce particular shots. Closer to Jean-Luc Godard or Alain Resnais than to, say, Peter Bogdanovich or Brian De Palma, they invariably bring something of their own to the table, transforming our sense of the original in the process. Every time Dave Brubeck chooses to shift to stride piano, he's saying something sweet about his predecessors, and whenever Charles Mingus gave us patches of Jelly Roll Morton, Duke Ellington, Lester Young, or Charlie Parker in one of his multifaceted compositions, he was doing a more elaborate version of the same thing.

Some jazz pianists—including a few of the most distinctive ones, like McCoy Tyner and Keith Jarrett—even go so far as to put together entire albums composed of "tributes" to some of their colleagues. The less interesting way of doing this is simply to pick tunes identified with the colleagues, and Jarrett on his two-disc *Tribute* (1989), recorded live in Köln, appears to adopt this habit as much as anyone—playing "All of You" as a nod to Miles, "Solar" as a gesture of respect for Bill Evans, "It's Easy to Remember" as an appreciation of Coltrane, and "I Hear a Rhapsody" to show us how he digs Jim Hall. But when he performs "Just in Time" as a tribute to Charlie Parker, he's offering something stranger and more challenging. This Comden-Green-Styne tune comes from *Bells Are Ringing*, a Broadway musical that didn't even open until the year after Bird died (1956), and although critic Ben Ratliff questions how Parkeresque this up-tempo performance actually is, he does concede the "the piece is festooned with fleet bebop phrases". But in fact, if you use your imagination to substitute Parker's alto sax for Jarrett's piano, you might notice that the way the latter strings his phrases together and pauses briefly between his ideas is distinctly Parkeresque. The fact that "Just in Time" premiered after Parker died is strictly incidental; one can still readily extrapolate the sort of workout he might have given the tune.

Jarrett actually borrows from and/or alludes to other jazz figureheads in a variety of ways, whether he officially signals it or not. When he plays "Poinciana" at a 1999 Paris concert heard on *Whisper Not*, he's not only duplicating Ahmad Jamal's arrangement, tempo, and predilection for upper-register piano keys; he's also pursuing related riffs (while perhaps playing a few more notes than Jamal would have) and contrasts in dynamics, and getting his expert accompanists Gary Peacock (bass) and Jack DeJohnette (drums) to propel a similar kind of swing. In other words, this is a personal kind of flattery/imitation, and one whose most striking divergence from Jamal would probably be the grunts and sighs expressing Jarrett's emotional involvement in his solo. But when he plays "Conception" at the same concert, this isn't exactly a tribute to its composer, George Shearing; for that, he'd probably have to approximate an ecstatic climax in Shearing's locked-hands style.

Or take Jarrett's version of "All the Things You Are" on *Tribute*, dedicated to Sonny Rollins. Rollins is a master of cadenzas, fully capable of spinning out cascading, unaccompanied inventions for protracted periods of uncertain lengths—most often at the very beginning or somewhere towards the end of certain numbers. And one of Rollins' best ways of generating suspense is to suddenly "get stuck" inside the same couple of bars, improvising to the same chord changes endlessly repeated, inviting us to wonder how long he can keep this up before returning to the standard chord sequence. (These should be considered vamps sustained by the rhythm section—something like the intro to Jamal's and Jarrett's version of "Poinciana"—rather than a cappella cadenzas.)

Both of these routines are employed by Jarrett on a regular basis. So what's so special about his "official" Rollins tribute? This begins with a wonderful and very Rollins-like cadenza before succumbing to the melody; and the eventual arrival of the tune is greeted by applause—a sign of surprised recognition which also frequently happens after one of the free-form intros of Rollins (or

Erroll Garner, for that matter). But the previous "Just in Time" ends with an equally Rollins-like vamp section. Could the tribute in this case possibly have something to do with the physicality of Jarrett's performance, which isn't visible on a CD? I'm thinking of the kind of trance-like dance of his upper torso that we can intuit and imagine from other Jarrett performances, which corresponds somewhat to Rollins' occasional practice of walking or pacing around a stage as a kind of visual countermelody to his solos.

Jarrett notes in the liner notes of his recent *Live at Montreaux*, recorded in 2001, "the audience was not really ours until we played, for the first and only time ever in concert, three ragtime versions of standard tunes." For the record, the first two are Fats Waller songs, "Ain't Misbehavin'" and "Honeysuckle Rose," followed by the Rodgers and Hart "You Took Advantage of Me," and a distinctly Walleresque cheerfulness pervades this entire stretch. "It is a perfect demonstration of our commitment to jazz," Jarrett adds, "that these do not come off as mimicry or some kind of joke," and this becomes a key point about his cross-referencing. To mix metaphors and body parts, seeing the world through Waller's eyes is a particular way of rearticulating and re-energizing the Jarrett touch.

Ahmad Jamal

A blog post, May 22, 2008.

Ahmad Jamal Complete Live at the Spotlite Club 1958 (2-CD set, Gambit Records 69265).

You may have to be an Ahmad Jamal completist like myself to take notice of this 2007 expanded edition, which adds three 1958 Chicago studio cuts, totaling about eight minutes, to the twenty-five live ones that have already been available. The latter tracks appeared on two well-known Jamal LPs, *Ahmad Jamal* and the two-disc *Portfolio of Ahmad Jamal,* both recorded at Washington, D.C.'s Spotline Club on September 5 and 6, 1958.

If memory serves, the first of these was the first Jamal record I ever bought, when I was fifteen or sixteen, and it's never gone stale for me—despite the scorn heaped on Jamal by sophisticated jazz critics such as Martin Williams in *Downbeat.* There's always been a curious split between the Jamal idolatry of Miles Davis—who joined forces with Gil Evans on their first joint album to virtually steal (rather than simply play homage to) two tracks from Jamal's 1955 *Chamber Music of the New Jazz,* "New Rumba" and "I Don't Wanna Be Kissed," and based his Quintet's arrangement of "All of You" in *Round Midnight* on Jamal's on the same LP—and the disdain of most jazz critics, who seemed to regard Jamal's popularity with seething resentment, much as they resented Dave Brubeck during the same period. I've always thought that Miles had better taste than those critics when it came to both Jamal and Brubeck (whose lovely compositions "In Your Own Sweet Way" and "The Duke" were both played by

Davis—along with "Someday My Prince Will Come," which I believe Brubeck was the first to adopt as a jazz standard).

Of course, both Brubeck and Jamal have been unapologetic eclectics throughout their careers; the uninhibited pounding attack of Brubeck and the light upper-register tinkle of Jamal have always helped to define the singularity of each of them as musicians. And what delights me the most about the third new track of Jamal on the new Gambit set, "Taking a Chance on Love," less than two minutes long, is the joy he manages to squeeze out of that unfashionable Vernon Duke tune itself, even when he moves further and further away from its contours in his solo before splashing back into its embrace in his final chorus —still allowing Israel Crosby's bass to take over the conclusion of each phrase and even the entire bridge before the abrupt sign-off, after the final eight bars.

Later Reflections (December 2022): Jamal, Davis, Monk: The Art of Paraphrase

Jamal's trio's fifteen-minute masterpiece version of the aptly titled *I Didn't Know What Time It Was*, recorded in the mid-1960s, equitably divvies up solos from all three players, each of whom, every once in a while, abruptly switches tempi or adds counter-rhythms in mid-stream.

(Jamal, of course, specializes in this kind of self-interruption that can change musical syntax in the middle of a phrase, suggesting an odd parallel with some of William S., Burroughs' cutups that redivert utterances in mid-sentence. It's thus a performance that might be said to divvy up solo time as well as solo space, allowing each player to slice up and restructure time differently.

It's like verse that changes its own rules during its periodic breaks, thrashing around its readers as well as its writer in the process. As in Jamal's 1963 version of "Johnny One Note," built on similar principles of slowly but surely tickling one's way out of the monotony of continuous mantralike vamps, its stark juxtapositions of time signatures are part of the way it swings.

Negotiating the Pleasure Principle:
The Recent Work of Adam Curtis

From Film Quarterly, *Fall 2008, commissioned by Rob White, the same editor who previously invited me to write a short book about Jarmusch's* Dead Man. *This essay breaks my rule of including only appreciations in this book, but my demurrals here about jazz aesthetics made it obligatory. I've tweaked and trimmed it here.*

There's been a steady improvement over the course of the three most recent BBC miniseries of Adam Curtis—*The Century of the Self* (2002, four hour-long episodes), *The Power of Nightmares: The Rise of the Politics of Fear* (2004, three hour-long episodes), and *The Trap: What Happened to Our Dream of Freedom* (2007, three hour-long episodes)—both in terms of their intellectual cogency and persuasiveness and in terms of the interest of Curtis's developing, innovative style of filmmaking. One might even contend that each remarkable series has been twice as good as its predecessor. Even so, a closer look at Curtis's style starts to raise a few questions about both the arguments themselves and the way that he propounds them. (Regarding Curtis's earlier TV series—such as the 1992 *Pandora's Box* and the 1999 *The Mayfair Set*, which I've only sampled, and won't be discussing here—one can already see some of the thematic and stylistic seeds of his more recent work there.)

I'm certainly not the first one to address these issues arising out of Curtis's work. Among my predecessors, I've been especially impressed by the arguments of Paul Myerscough ("The Flow," *London Review of Books*, 5 April 2007) and those of the late Paul Arthur ("Adam Curtis's Nightmare Factory: A British Documentarian Declares War on the `War on Terror,'" *Cineaste*, Winter 2007). Starting off with a discussion of televisual "flow" as described by Raymond Williams in 1973, Myerscough voices some misgivings about sensual overkill as well as intellectual shortcuts and simplifications, concluding at one point that "I find myself more worried by his documentaries when I go along with them than when I don't." Arthur expresses comparable doubts while interrogating some of Curtis's intellectual arguments in greater detail, and also explores the possible relevance of the neo-Marxism of Curtis's former schoolmates Jon King and Andy Gill, founders of the postpunk band Gang of Four.

The theses of all three of Curtis's series are clearly interconnected. *The Century of the Self* sketches the appropriation of Freud's theory of the unconscious as a consumerist model for manipulating people economically and politically through their unconscious desires—initially by Freud's American nephew Edward L. Bernays, the inventor of "public relations," and subsequently by Gallup polls, Anna Freud's gospel of social conformity, the "Human Potential" movement that tried to overthrow Anna Freud's principles of social conditioning, and the eventual development of focus groups in both the U.S. and the U.K. to sell products, including such political candidates as Reagan, Clinton, Thatcher, and Blair.

The Power of Nightmares offers a parallel history of militant Islamism as spearheaded by Sayyid Qutb and neo-conservatism as spearheaded by Leo Strauss to trace the development of a political trend in which fear of manufactured and largely imaginary threats have gradually replaced utopian promises of happiness. This culminates in Curtis's most controversial claim in any of these three miniseries—that the existence of the terrorist network Al Qaeda is primarily a fiction that was invented in 2001 as a means of gaining and consolidating power.

The Trap to some extent subsumes and extends both of the arguments in the preceding series by maintaining that the Western idea of freedom has been reformulated over the past half-century or so from political freedom to economic freedom (viewed as spending power), again with disastrous results. Basic to this overarching ideological shift is the conviction—promulgated largely by game theorists as a way of explaining the dynamics of the Cold War, and eventually taken up by economists and politicians—that human beings are fundamentally selfish, suspicious, and isolated from one another; that notions of collective will can't even be theorized according to the new, market-driven models; and that success and happiness are ultimately measurable in numbers rather than in terms of the quality of whatever is being quantified. Here the major villains often seem to be not George W. Bush—even though he does get a characteristically inane sound bite ("I believe that the future of mankind is freedom") in the prologue to the first two parts—but Bill Clinton and Tony Blair, for being elected on liberal/labor platforms and then immediately giving away their hard-won power to the banks and markets, meanwhile increasing class inequality in relation to everything from career opportunities to life expectancies in both the U.S. and the U.K. But more generally, what gets vigorously castigated here are irresponsible forms and applications of social science, especially psychiatry, spurred by various forms of capitalism and the numbers game.

A withering examples of the latter, offered in part two of *The Trap*, "The Lonely Robot," is the way in which normal human reactions such as fear, loneliness, and sadness were redefined as medical disorders in order to sell newly developed drugs such as Prozac and create new forms of social management. My own tragicomic favorite is one of the many grotesque consequences of the performance targets that followed Blair's election in 1997: when the government's aim was to reduce the number of hospital patients who had to wait in corridors on trolleys before receiving care, some hospitals would remove wheels from their trolleys and reclassify them as beds, meanwhile reclassifying some corridors as wards.

In all three of these miniseries, one can trace a certain Hegelian convergence of disciplines and theories that becomes all the more ambiguous, exhilarating, and unsettling once one starts to realize that this convergence is part of Curtis's own methodology as well as his ostensible subject. In other words, I'm continually being won over by grand explanations for most of our contemporary problems, all of which entail other and presumably lesser minds having been similarly seduced; what might more generally be termed the Eureka mentality is thus posited as both the disease and the diagnosis.

I'm reminded of the most stimulating university courses I ever took—a seminar taught by Heinrich Blücher, "Metaphysical Concepts of History and Their Manifestations in Political Reality." Blücher, a former German Communist who never published a word, is lamentably overlooked by many people who didn't know him personally, yet his impact on friends and students as well as on his wife, Hannah Arendt (who dedicated her *Origins of Totalitarianism* to him) is irrefutable. The dialectical subject as well as the dialectical methodology of his seminar, which focused on such figures as Hegel, Nietzsche, Spengler, Marx, and Freud, grew out of the various seductions and dangers of all-purpose explanations. Virtually every lecture Blücher gave in the seminar described an arc that climbed towards fervent belief before descending towards skepticism. For better and for worse, Curtis's audiovisual arguments tend to move in the reverse direction; they all start very promisingly by tearing down some of the ruling myths of our era, and then arguably conclude in far too satisfying a fashion by implying that once we can shatter those myths, we're almost as wised up as we need to be.

Nevertheless, the value of all three works isn't just the strength of their arguments but the overall freshness and pertinence of part of the information they impart. Speaking for myself, I was less excited by *The Century of the Self* because I'd already read Larry Tye's *The Father of Spin: Edward L Bernays & The Birth of Public Relations* (New York: Crown Publishers, 1998)—a book whose revelations for me started in its preface, which explains how the "public relations triumph" that was the "selling of America on the Persian Gulf War…was crafted by one of America's biggest public relations firms, Hill and Knowlton, in a campaign bought and paid for by rich Kuwaitis who were Saddam's archenemies."

If memory serves, this tidbit is missing from *The Century of the Self* (although Tye is one of the people interviewed), but the material imparted about Bernays and his legacy—starting with his own coinage of the term "public relations" as a euphemism for propaganda—is pointed and instructive. (One particular gem in Part 2, "The Engineering of Consent," is the story of how housewives were coerced into buying Betty Crocker cake mix once their egos were stroked by the gratuitous instruction that they add one egg to the mix.) And some of it overlaps neatly with material discussed in Naomi Klein's magisterial *The Shock Doctrine: The Rise of Disaster Capitalism* (New York: Alfred A. Knopf, 2007), a book whose own clarifying synthesis of information seems comparable and complementary to some of Curtis's best insights.

I'm thinking in particular of the terrifying exploits of Dr. Ewan Cameron, whose CIA-funded employments of LSD, PCP, and electroshock to hapless patients begin Klein's narrative and are pointedly referenced by Curtis. One might also note that her postulation of Milton Friedman as a guru from hell essentially "rhymes" with Curtis's uses of Bernays in *The Century of the Self*, Strauss in *The Power of Nightmares*, and even Isaiah Berlin and his concept of "negative liberty" in part three of *The Trap*, "We Will Force You To be Free." Indeed, in the closing stretches of the latter, when Curtis is critiquing the disastrously misguided and theoretically driven employments of "shock therapy" in postcommunist Russia and, more recently, in Iraq, his arguments seem to coincide fairly precisely with those of Klein. (Another film with certain conceptual parallels to Curtis's three series is Mark Achbar, Jennifer Abbott, and Joel Bakan's excellent 2003 documentary *The Corporation*.)

§

The developing style of Curtis's essayistic documentaries is to alternate talking-head interviews with diverse kinds of found footage, the latter sometimes overlaid by music drawn from Hollywood films. Some of the scores borrowed in *The Power of Nightmares* come from John Carpenter's *Halloween* and *Prince of Darkness*, *The Ipcress File*, *Voyage to the Bottom of the Sea*, two Morricone-scored Italian pictures, and *Neptune's Daughter*—he last of these being the source for Johnny Mercer's "Baby, It's Cold Outside," which dominates the first episode. And especially memorable in *The Trap* are Bernard Herrmann themes from films by Welles and Hitchcock—a ploy that periodically becomes distracting, perhaps even more so if one is conscious of where they're coming from. I'm not sure how helpful it is, for instance, for the sprightly chase music from *North by Northwest* to accompany Curtis's aforementioned discussion of performance targets in Blair's version of New Labour and—more briefly later on—his discussion of Franz Fanon and Jean-Paul Sartre's espousals of violence in third-world revolutions. Whatever postmodern ironies Curtis might have in mind with these juxtapositions, they really don't add much to the discussion.

The fact that Curtis hasn't acquired rights to either the clips or the music is largely what accounts for them not being better known outside the U.K., although all three series are readily accessible via the Internet for those who go looking for them.

There seem to be at least three major issues worth addressing about these miniseries. The first is the validity of the intellectual arguments they propound. The second is the validity of the anti-intellectual methodologies they sometimes employ in terms of sound and image, in which the clips and music serve not so much to illustrate the arguments as to weave fanciful and seductive arabesques around them. (These are far more evident in the latter two series, although *The Century of the Self* already suggests this practice when it suddenly intercuts details from 1929 with tracking shots through opulent, apparently Viennese settings that suggest color versions of shots from *Last Year at Marienbad*.) And the third is the seeming incompatibility of these intellectual and anti-intellectual elements, complicated by the fact that the anti-intellectual elements at times seem to resemble the advertising techniques that are being critically addressed throughout the series, which appeal to unconscious desires more than to conscious and rational formulations.

Given how much the polemical agendas of these three series are bound up with the way that apparently rational intellectual positions can eventually lead to irrational and delusional conclusions, there's a great deal at stake in determining how much intellectual honesty Curtis should be credited with as a filmmaker and not simply as a thinker delivering a voiceover. To all appearances, his voiceovers remains serious while his filmmaking periodically oscillates between a serious (that is, rational and readily explicable) illustration of his arguments and fanciful, free-form riffs sailing over the arguments, a bit like jazz improvisations. (There are also some images that might be described as both serious and playful, e.g., the recurring image of red paint being poured over a globe of the world in "The Phantom Victory," part two of *The Power of Nightmares*—a Cold War metaphor with a certain amount of mockery in its literalism, but nonetheless a relatively coherent kind of representation.) And just as jazz solos are typically predicated on following the chords of pre-existing melodies, Curtis's riffs loosely follow the contours of his voiceover arguments that are being heard simultaneously, without being answerable to a comparable linear logic of continuity except by implication.

The issue isn't whether or not the playful improvs are acceptable in their own right. I believe they are, or at least they can be, and on my website I recently wrote a brief defense of a lively DVD extra—Jean-Pierre Gorin's "A '*Pierrot*' Primer" on the Criterion release of Godard's *Pierrot le fou*—that has comparable strengths and limitations. My point there is that once criticism is viewed as a performative act occurring over a fixed period of time, our means of judging such acts can't and shouldn't be precisely the same as the way we regard criticism in print.

Admittedly, even this distinction becomes somewhat problematical as soon as we consider that there are certain instances of print criticism that might be said to function according to performative models. The sole example of the latter that I cited on my website was Manny Farber, although I could have also mentioned the critical prose of several other reviewers, ranging from Godard to Pauline Kael to Manohla Dargis. The only way of resolving this seeming contradiction, I would argue, is that we know and acknowledge what kind of critical discourse we're responding to. And this becomes harder to do when we're confronted with two kinds at once, as we often are in Curtis's televisual discourse.

§

I'm not trying to propound the Marshall McLuhan argument here that the medium is necessarily the message. The point of contention here is journalistic shorthand, which exists both in print and in broadcast media and often entails some difference in meaning and content as well as style. Theoretically speaking, insofar as montages are extensions of the Kuleshov Experiment in which the viewer unconsciously connects certain shots by furnishing them with imagined fictional links, the very act of editing these shots together becomes a form of lying. Thus the juxtaposition of found materials, including the use of Hollywood scores on the soundtracks of Curtis documentaries, might be said to function as vehicles of persuasion—ploys for helping us to accept the voiceovers but not really legitimate parts of the ongoing argument. Whether we identify these ploys as placebos or as less deceptive vehicles of pleasure is the main issue at stake. Quite apart from Curtis's use of such rhetorical tricks in his narration as unjustifiably describing his own arguments as if they were conclusive demonstrations (as pointed out by both Arthur and Myerscough), there's the broader and somewhat less obvious tactic of making them pleasurable to watch—fun and therefore easy to swallow—as if they were TV commercials.

Most of the footage in *The Power of Nightmares* conventionally illustrates Curtis's voiceovers. Yet all three episodes begin with a free-form montage accompanying his narration that's so open-ended it becomes impossible to identify what one's watching, while additional sounds (a howling wind and periodic stabs of percussive music) increase the overall dreamlike effect. All proportions guarded, it's a bit like the difference in exposition between the enigmatic prologue of *Citizen Kane* and the "News on the March" that follows it, with the crucial difference that Curtis uses a voiceover in both segments.

Consider just the first four sentences and the accompanying images: Initially we see what appear to be blinking bright lights on an airstrip over the sound of the wind. Then, as Curtis says, "In the past, politicians promised to create a better world. [Music starts.]. They had different ways of achieving this, but their power and authority came from the optimistic visions they offered their people," we're treated to rapid, disorienting, continuous camera movements in a dark and ambiguous space where people are fleetingly glimpsed in the background that eventually becomes, behind the BBC logo, an empty and overlit TV studio anchor space with a shifting backdrop that's gripped from behind by visible fingers. Then, while Curtis continues, "Those dreams failed and today people have lost faith in ideologies. Increasingly, politicians are seen simply as managers of public life, but now they have discovered a new role that restores their power and authority," we get a burst of TV static, another camera movement traversing an indecipherable flash of orange and yellow, a static shot of an ornate chandelier with fading lights (or is it a fadeout in a shot of a chandelier that remains lit?), and then high-contrast black and white footage of a nighttime, flag-strewn political rally that could conceivably be a clip from Eisenstein or Pudovkin. In short, you might say that Curtis is restoring power and authority to his own voice while tossing us into an intractable labyrinth.

§

If I can be permitted a couple of extended, autobiographical illustrations of comparably pleasurable media tricks, I can say that, like many others, I've benefited as well as suffered from the kinds of routine distortions practiced by these methods. In the mid-'70s, in London, I was interviewed on BBC radio about Robert Altman's innovative employments of sound in conjunction with an Altman retrospective I had just helped to organize. It seemed appropriate to offer an analysis of a particular extract from the soundtrack of *California Split*, so I was mortified to discover when I heard the broadcast that the producer had chosen a different and much simpler extract to illustrate the point I was trying to make—with the result that my analysis sounded both inane and inaccurate. But when I phoned her to complain, she argued that editing fixes of this kind were standard and that I was naïve to raise any fuss about them.

By way of contrast, the way I'm used to deliver the climactic thesis of the feature-length documentary *Hollywoodism: Jews, Movies, and the American Dream* (Simcha Jacobovici, 1997)—that the American Dream as articulated by Hollywood was fundamentally a Jewish invention—is no less sinister, at least in its implications, even though this time I was seemingly boosted rather than undermined by the misrepresentation. Indeed, my talking head is positioned so that the entire thrust of the film's preceding argument—actually the argument of Neal Gabler's first-rate and provocative book *An Empire of Their Own: How the Jews Invented Hollywood*, which this film is adapting—appears to be emanating spontaneously from my lips, when I say, "There was a Hollywoodism then, there is a Hollywoodism today. I would go further and say it is what is the ruling ideology of our culture. Hollywood culture is the dominant culture; it is the fantasy structure that we're living inside." None of which I exactly disbelieve. But the ugly and awkward coinage "Hollywoodism," used as a derivation of "Americanism"—which doesn't even figure in Gabler's book—would never have passed my own lips if the interviewer hadn't planted it there. If memory serves, all I was doing at that point was agreeing with some rough paraphrase of Gabler's thesis that the unheard and unseen interviewer had offered, meanwhile hoping that the modest personal contribution I'd made to the discussion—about the ways my grandfather, a small-town movie exhibitor, shared many of the values of the studio moguls discussed by Gabler—would be used in the film. (It wasn't.) Nevertheless, an old friend of mine, a professional writer of TV documentaries himself, told me that he concluded at the end of *Hollywoodism* that its overall message, including the coinage of its title, was somehow my own invention.

Such are the everyday, routine spinoffs of the Kuleshov effect in most documentaries employing taking heads and clips. In the same documentary, the same sort of leveling effect allows archival footage of European shtetls to casually rub shoulders with a musical number from *Fiddler on the Roof*, and virtually equates the veracity of black and white newsreel footage of HUAC hearings with the authenticity of color extracts from a representation of those hearings in Irwin Winkler's idiotic and reprehensible *Guilty by Suspicion*.

In an interview with Robert Koehler in *Cinema Scope no. 23* (Summer 2005), Curtis defends the practice of his own playful montages as follows: "I don't see why you can't play with pictures when you're being serious. That's my main aim. Because then you get a sense of someone enjoying themselves, and when you get that, then people listen to what you're doing." And I suppose a related argument could be made about some of the more ambiguous procedures in Craig Baldwin's experimental documentaries—*Tribulation 99: Alien Anomalies Under America* (1991), *¡O No Coronado!* (1992), *Sonic Outlaws* (1995), and *Spectres of the Spectrum* (1999)—which simultaneously mock and indulge in paranoid rants while dovetailing as many technological conspiracy theories as possible.

There's something appealing about leaving the overall degree of seriousness behind the arguments up to the viewer, but there's also a calculated risk. Even though Curtis's arguments register much more seriously than Baldwin's, both filmmakers seem to be operating at times with built-in escape clauses. But how many people who watch television are thinking much about the play or, for that matter, the personality of the filmmakers as reflected in such creative decisions?

It's worth adding that Curtis himself speaks the voiceovers in these series, but never uses the word "I"—even though the arguments are always clearly his own, and when we hear the offscreen questions being asked in various onscreen interviews, it's invariably his voice that's asking them. His overall stance is neither that of the traditional voice-of-God narrator nor that of an essayistic filmmaker like Chris Marker who, in *Sans Soleil* (1982), feels that his speaking voice has to be filtered through one or more fictional intermediaries in order to achieve the kind of guarded intimacy that he wants. But Curtis sounds closer to the voice-of-God narrator insofar as he's banking on the appearance if not the fact of conventional television. And it's finally this appearance that makes his work so debatable as well as innovative. Whether or not this is part of his intention (and I suspect it isn't), Curtis is foregrounding some of the double standards that many of us bring to criticism in separate media simply by banking on them.

Dracula Yesterday and Today:
The Poetics and Politics of *Cuadecuc, Vampir*

Commissioned by the Jeonju International Film Festival for a Pere Portabella retrospective catalog in March 2009. More of my fascination with Portabella over the past half-cenutury—furthered by correspondence and warm encounters with him and his family in New York, Chicago, Cambridge, and London—can be tracked on my website.

Thanks to an old appointment book, I can pinpoint that my initial encounter with the cinema of Pere Portabella took place at 7 PM on May 17, 1971 during the Cannes Film Festival, when I first saw *Cuadecuc, Vampir.* It was showing in the Quinzaine des Réalisateurs (Directors Fortnight) at a now-defunct cinema called Le Français. It's worth adding that the name of the filmmaker and the title of his film were both slightly different from the way we know them today, for reasons that are historically significant. The name of this Barcelona-based filmmaker was listed as Pedro Portabella and his film was called simply *Vampir.* Why? Because he was Catalan, a language forbidden in Franco's Spain, making both the name "Pere" and the word "Cuadacuc" (which I'm told is an obscure Catalan term meaning both a worm's tail and the end of a reel of unexposed film stock) equally impermissible. Furthermore, Portabella wasn't present at the screening because, as I later discovered, he was one of the two Spanish producers of Luis Buñuel's *Viridiana* one decade earlier, and the Franco government was punishing him for having helped to engineer this subterfuge by confiscating his passport, making it impossible for him to travel outside Spain. And for those like myself who wondered how a film as unorthodox as this could play in Franco Spain at all, it eventually became clear that it survived, like the Catalan language itself (not to mention *Dracula*), clandestinely, via secret nourishment.

Vampir was my favorite of all the films I saw at Cannes that year. I returned to it several times, and described it afterwards in the *Village Voice* as "at once the most original movie at the festival and the most sophisticated in its audacious modernism". A silent black and white "documentary" about the shooting of *Count Dracula*, a color feature, by Jesus Franco with Christopher Lee, Herbert Lom, and others, it had a remarkable nonsynchronous soundtrack composed by Carles Santos consisting of such varied materials as a barking dog, a jet plane, a pneumatic drill, an operatic aria, a recurring and sumptuous piece of Muzak, and various sinister-sounding electronic drones. (The only use of synch sound occurs in the final sequence, when Lee himself in his dressing room, over two separate takes, eloquently describes the death of Dracula in Bram Stoker's novel.)

Thanks to both Santos' witty aural accompaniments and many of the film's camera movements—which pass back and forth between the story of Dracula and various details exposing the artifice of the Franco film being shot—the film creates a ravishing netherworld that seems to exist in neither the 19th century nor the 20th but in a unique zone oscillating between these eras, just as it seems to occupy a realm of its own that is neither fiction nor non-fiction. The high-contrast cinematography, moreover, suggests some of the meditative beauty of Murnau's *Nosferatu* and Dreyer's *Vampyr* as well as the dissolution and decay experienced when we see these films today in fading prints.

There are other ways of perceiving the special poetics—and politics—of *Vampir, Cuadecuc*. Some have alluded to the subtle ways in which Lee's Count Dracula suggests Generalissimo Franco by offering a ruling narrative that Portabella's lyricism periodically escapes and floats free from, just as Jesus Franco also suggests his near-namesake. But above all is an all-embracing sensual pleasure and humor overriding centuries, generic categories, and conventions.

High and Low: Eisenstein's *Ivan the Terrible*

Written for Criterion's Current (a website), April 21, 2009, and slightly revised for this volume. I continue to find Eisenstein's Ivan *the most intoxicating mix of high and low art in all of cinema.*

I recently had occasion to show *Ivan the Terrible* in a course on forties world cinema I'm teaching at Chicago's School of the Art Institute, and found it more mind-boggling than ever. This has always been the Eisenstein work that's given me the most pleasure—the greatest *Flash Gordon* serial ever made as well as a showcase for the Russian master's boldest graphics. But ever since I first saw it in the 1960s, this is a pleasure I've often had to apologize for, thanks to the vagaries and confusions of Cold War thinking. Such thinking maintained that Eisenstein caved into Stalinist pressures, denounced the montage aesthetic that was central to his best work, and turned out an archaic made-to-order glorification of a dictator.

Part of the problem has been reconciling the film's multiple paradoxes—how much it functions as Eisenstein's autocritique and apologia as well as an attack and glorification of Stalin, meanwhile combining elements of both high and low art at virtually every instant with its tortured angles and extreme melodrama. (Though portions of Part II could be termed inferior to Part I, the moment the film switches to color, using Agfa stock seized from the Germans during World War II, it moves into dizzying high gear, reminding us that Walt Disney was one of Eisenstein's favorite filmmakers.) Some critics did take a slightly more nuanced view of Part II, but even a few of these writers, such as Dwight Macdonald, wound up adding homophobic invective to their charges, maintaining that Eisenstein's homosexuality distorted his view of history—a dubious complaint that, as I later discovered, tended to oversimplify Eisenstein's (bi)sexuality as well as the historical record. At least Orson Welles's two mixed reviews of Part I—written in 1946, when he was a newspaper columnist and saw the film without subtitles at a special United Nations screening—placed proper emphasis on what might be called Eisenstein's visual rhetoric, which tends to drown out most other considerations.

Thanks to the remarkably detailed scholarship of Joan Neuberger and Yuri Tsivian, who have both written invaluable monographs about the film and contributed fascinating audiovisual essays to the Criterion DVD editions, we now know that *Ivan*, far from being any sort of ideological collapse, was in fact Eisenstein's most courageous gesture, above all in its highly ambivalent and often critical treatment of Stalin. Part I, which was milder overall, garnered the Stalin prize, but Part II, whose sexual and stylistic delirium went much further, was banned for a dozen years, following a now legendary February 1947 Kremlin meeting of Eisenstein and his lead actor, Nikolai Cherkasov, with Stalin, Molotov, and Zhdanov. It appears that Eisenstein agreed to make some cosmetic changes but then edited the film to suit himself, and died just afterward—having already vowed in his diary to work himself to death, after apparently being more appalled than pleased by Stalin's initial endorsement of his project (according to Russian film scholar Leonid Kozlov).

Even if he never got around to shooting more than a few fragments of Part III (now lost, apart from a test), what Eisenstein left behind in the preceding two parts is surely one of the most complexly nuanced works in cinema history, simultaneously celebrating, critiquing, and analyzing Ivan, Stalin, and himself. What struck me most of all watching it this time was its shameless embrace of excess on all these fronts, registering both as a giddy kind of pop art and as a morbid exercise in medieval history. Despite its discarding of Eisenstein's earlier montage aesthetic, I don't think he ever made anything else in his career that was more personal or more expressive.

Introduction to the Chinese Edition of *More Than Night*

The following essay was commissioned and written in June 2009. My thanks to the Chinese translator Zhanxiong Xu for giving me permission to publish the original English version.

I'm also pleased that a Chinese translation of one of my own books, Movie Wars: How Hollywood and the Media Limit What Films We Can See, *was published around the same time. I suspect that the subsequent influx of Chinese visitors to my website might have had something to do with its publication.*

Some of the biographical details given here are out of date over a decade later, e.g., Naremore and his wife no longer have a condo in Chicago, but I've updated the bibliographical details.

I

"The Chinese don't accord much importance to things of the past," Maggie Cheung maintained in an interview with a French magazine roughly a decade ago[1], "whether it's films, heritage, or even clothes or furniture. In Asia nothing is preserved, turning towards the past is regarded as stupid, aberrant."

Interestingly, this statement helps to explain why so many of the most important Chinese films, at least for me, are concerned with the discovery of history, and represent various attempts to reclaim a lost past. I'll restrict myself to a short list of a dozen favorite Chinese features, all of which exhibit these traits: Fei Mu's *Xiao cheng zhi chun* (*Spring in a Small Town*, 1948); Hou Hsiao-hsien's *Bei qing cheng shi* (*City of Sadness*, 1989) and *Xi meng ren sheng* (*The Puppetmaster*, 1993); Wong Kar-wai's *A Fei zheng chuan* (*Days of Being Wild*, 1990) and *Fa yeung nin wa* (*In the Mood for Love*, 2000); Edward Yang's *Gu ling jie shao nian sha ren shi jian* (*A Brighter Summer Day*, 1991); Stanley Kwan's *Ruan Lingyu* (*Actress* AKA *Center Stage*, 1992); Tian Zhuangzhuang's *Lan feng zheng* (*The Blue Kite*, 1993); Li Shaohong's *Hong fen* (*Blush*, 1994); and Jia Zhangke's *Zhantai* (*Platform*, 2000), *Sanxia Haoren* (*Still Life*, 2006), and *Er shi si cheng ji* (*24 City*, 2008). As I once described *Ruan Lingyu* in the title of a 2001 essay, this is a bit like "Building History in Quicksand." And even many of my other favorite Chinese films that are stuck in the present, and view this present in all its modernity, such as Hou's *Nan guo zai jan, nan guo* (*Goodbye South, Goodbye*, 1996), Peter Chen's

Tian mi mi (*Comrades: Almost a Love Story*, 1996), and Jia's *Shijie* (*The World*, 2004), might be described as ambitious efforts to view the present historically.

Cheung's statement also describes the biases of many Americans, although it's somewhat less true of the portion of the United States where James Naremore and I both grew up, the South. Ever since losing the Civil War (1861-1865)—the most traumatic cultural crisis our country has suffered to date (in part because it put an end to slavery), depicted in two of the most famous American films, *The Birth of a Nation* (1915) and *Gone With the Wind* (1939)—Southerners have often had a somewhat wistful nostalgia about a mythical Golden Age that supposedly existed before that war. But one could also argue that cherishing an imaginary past is yet another way of devaluing history. It's also a valuable capitalist tool that allows certain products to be sold and resold, especially in a present that both yearns for history and deeply mistrusts it.

Film noir has a complicated and ambiguous relation to the past reflecting this ambivalence, and Naremore is, to the best of my knowledge, the critic and historian who has done by far the best job in describing this phenomenon and helping us to understand it. In a way, he starts from the paradox that virtually anyone who enters a video store in the United States today knows what "film noir" is, yet the original American audiences for the Hollywood classics in this branch of filmmaking, all made during the 1940s and '50s, wouldn't have heard or known this term. Consequently, one could argue that, in certain respects, a taste for film noir today respects a kind of nostalgia for a past that never existed—or at least one that didn't exist in the terms by which we currently know that past.

II

Jim Naremore has been a good friend for over two decades, and I suspect that one thing that has made our tastes and interests so compatible is a tendency to view film at least partially as a branch of literature—a reflection of our academic backgrounds and our reading habits. I consider this background relevant to what makes *More Than Night* the best book about film noir, because, as Naremore himself shows in some detail in his first chapter, even the term "noir" has literary connotations: It was a term partly inspired as well as paralleled by the French publisher Gallimard's *Série noire*—a series of black-jacketed paperback crime novels inaugurated in 1945 by an editor with a background in surrealism, Marcel Duhamel (and, according to the French edition of the online encyclopedia Wikipedia, a series named by an even more celebrated French Surrealist, writer Jacques Prévert—who scripted the famous film

Les enfants du paradis the same year). Even though French writers in the late 1930s had already employed the term "film noir" in reference to such atmospheric French films as *Pépé le Moko* (1936), *Hôtel du Nord* (1938), and *Le jour se lève* (1939), it entered common usage thanks to a book series that specialized in French translations of such American authors as Raymond Chandler, David Goodis, Dashiell Hammett, Ed McBain, Horace McCoy, and Jim Thompson, many of whose works had been (or later would be) adapted into films. (To complicate this lineage, according to Wikipedia, Duhamel also started another book series at Gallimard in 1949 called *Série blême*—literally, "pale series," with green instead of black jackets—devoted to suspense novels; their first title was a French translation of *I Married a Dead Man*, by William Irish, a pseudonym for Cornell Woolrich, the same writer who wrote the original stories for many famous noir films, such as *The Leopard Man, Phantom Lady*, and *The Window*, as well as the Alfred Hitchcock thriller *Rear Window*.)

It's important to add that the association of film with literature, as in the case of noir, is largely a French tradition that came to fruition with the Nouvelle Vague—most obviously in such films as Jean-Luc Godard's *À Bout de Souffle* (1960) and *Alphaville* (1965, where film noir gets cross-bred with science fiction) and François Truffaut's *Tirez sur le Pianiste* (1960, based on a novel by David Goodis) and *La mariée était en noir* (1968, based on a novel by William Irish). Over three decades later, Godard and Anne-Marie Miéville's *2 X 50 ans du cinéma français* (1995) ends with a moving tribute to French film criticism—using that term broadly enough to include precursors as well as poets, art critics, and filmmaker-theorists—by offering a honor roll of fifteen individuals, from Denis Diderot (1713-1784) to Serge Daney (1944-1992), each of whom is accorded a portrait, a page of text, and an offscreen recitation of a brief passage read aloud by either Miéville or Godard. And the same orientation is evident in the film magazine that Daney founded shortly before his death, *Trafic*, which Jim and I have both contributed to. (Jim's contribution, appropriately, was about the classic noir *Double Indemnity*, also discussed in depth in *More Than Night*.)

Naremore's background in literature plays more than an incidental role in his writing. His very first book, *The World Without a Self: Virginia Woolf and the Novel* (New Haven/London: Yale University Press, 1973), is about one of the key figures in early 20th century English modernist fiction. And among the special virtues of his subsequent book *The Magic World of Orson Welles* (3rd edition, Berkeley/Los Angeles/London, University of California Press, 2015)—making it, for me, the best critical study of Welles in any language—is its unusual sensitivity to literary as well as political issues in Welles' career, both of which have tended to receive superficial treatment in most of the other books about him. A similar case could be made on behalf of Naremore's most recent book, *On Kubrick* (London: British Film Institute, 2007), which I similarly regard as the best critical study of Stanley Kubrick, although in this case the mastery that Naremore brings to his subject isn't just a matter of literature (evident in his comprehensive treatments of Kubrick's literary sources) but also a matter of art history (in both his precise account of Kubrick's early career as a photojournalist and his broader treatment of "grotesque" aesthetics, which actually combines visual and literary analysis).

More generally, one of the unusual strengths Naremore has as a critic and historian—no less evident in his groundbreaking *Acting in the Cinema* (Berkeley/Los Angeles: University of California Press, 1988), his short book *The Films of Vincente Minnelli* (Cambridge University Press, 1993), and the study guides he has written or edited devoted to *Psycho, North by Northwest, The Treasure of the Sierra Madre, Citizen Kane*, and film adaptation (not to mention a good many superb essays that have not yet been collected [but were subsequently collected in *An Invention Without a Future*, published by University of California Press in 2014})—is the literary distinction and grace of his prose, which makes him stand apart from his more jargon-ridden academic colleagues.

III

French appreciation of American culture, including literature and film, has had a decisive effect on the appreciation of Americans—including Naremore and myself—for their own culture. This is certainly true in my case, because a major part of my film education was conducted between 1968 and 1974, when I was living in Paris, and had direct access to many of the greatest American films of the past, westerns and noirs in particular, that were less readily available in the United States, especially in commercial cinemas. (Jim has lived in Europe as well, albeit in Germany rather than France.) It's significant that writers as important as Edgar Allen Poe and William Faulkner were taken seriously in France long before they were in their own country, and the same is largely true of such American-based directors as Samuel Fuller, Howard Hawks, Alfred Hitchcock, Nicholas Ray, Douglas Sirk, Frank Tashlin, and Orson Welles, all of whom have been associated with noir at one time or another.

Just as the present-day American taste for noir tends to combine a nostalgic view of the past with a reluctance to view that past historically, there is a similar ambivalence regarding the relation of film noir to political and social criticism. One of the most valuable aspects of Naremore's criticism is the degree to which it's inflected by a leftist critique of American culture. This means, on the one hand, that he's unusually attentive to films that criticize American culture from a political perspective, such as *Try and Get Me* (1950) and *The Glass Shield* (1995), and, on the other hand, he's uncharacteristically critical from a leftist perspective of some of the most popular neo-noir films, including *Chinatown* (1974) and *L.A. Confidential* (1997), in contrast to most other American critics, who tend to accept their defeatist politics without challenge.

Naremore also takes the unusual step of considering experimental films that utilize the imagery and themes of film noir, such as Mark Rappaport's 36-minute *Exterior Night* (1994)—one of the many titles analyzed in detail here that isn't available commercially *[2023: It's available now.]* It's an unfortunate habit of many American film critics, in academia and journalism alike, to reflect passively the whims and omissions of mainstream distributors by either consciously or unconsciously canonizing the few films lucky enough to receive millions of dollars in publicity while frequently ignoring most or all of the others. Like all of the best film critics, Naremore has a view of both culture in general and cinema in particular that's much wider than the marketplace. For the past two years, he has been writing lengthy articles for the magazine *Film Quarterly* devoted to his ten favorite films of the previous year—an unusual step to take for an academic film writer who lives in a small town, even a retired one who spends part of every year in Chicago. (For the remainder of every year, he lives in Bloomington, Indiana, where he used to teach.) But nowadays, with the wide circulation of DVDs, it's no longer necessary to live in New York or Paris or Tokyo or Beijing in order to keep up with the major currents of film history from an artistic as well as commercial standpoint. And it's worth adding that his favorite film in 2008 was *24 City*.

Endnote

1.   *Les inrockuptibles*, December 1, 1999.

On Richard Wright's *Native Son*

Extracted from a February 9, 2010 blog post.

Political incorrectness has a lot to do with what still gives this novel much of its shocking power: the fact that Richard Wright refuses to make Bigger Thomas sympathetic or his crimes in any way excusable, even though he understands perfectly and very cogently how and why this character can murder as readily as he does—not only a white philanthropist's daughter, whom he accidentally smothers, but also Bigger's own girlfriend, whom he kills with a brick quite deliberately, almost immediately after they have sex. Recently reading this 1940 Chicago novel for the second time, I was reminded of both Dostoevsky and Camus (even though, as a novelist, Wright is miles ahead of *L'Étranger*). There's something schizophrenic as well as dialectical about the way Wright can grasp the thought processes of his primitive young hero and then can offer a lengthy intellectual discourse about those processes. Eventually the Communist discourse and arguments in the book's second half drown out Bigger's identity, but the way Bigger himself is allowed to dominate the discourse in the first half is the book's unambiguous and terrifying triumph.

Jerry Lewis by Chris Fujiwara

From Cineaste *(Spring 2010).*

Jerry Lewis
by Chris Fujiwara.
Urbana/Chicago: University of Illinois Press, 162 pp., illus.

I hope I can be forgiven for repeating an anecdote I recounted in these pages in 2004, while writing about Charlie Chaplin's films on DVD. In a Swiss documentary about Chaplin in Switzerland, *Charlie Chaplin: The Forgotten Years*, his daughter Geraldine noted that when he discovered that his invitation to accept an honorary Oscar in the U.S. in 1972 came with a visa that allowed him to remain in the country for only two weeks, he was more delighted than indignant: "They're still afraid of me!" he said with pride—or words to that effect.

The curious process by which unreasoning love for Chaplin in the U.S. was transformed into unreasoning hatred is clearly matched by a comparable metamorphosis in the American psyche regarding Jerry Lewis. For me, the enduring mystery about Lewis isn't any alleged love of "the French" for him—a factoid whose former (and always limited) relevance has by now been out of date for many decades, ever since Woody Allen became far more revered in France than Lewis—but American denial about its own former Lewis infatuation, which was much larger than any French craze for the man could ever have been, and is even what made his French profile possible. (Just for starters, Martin and Lewis's 1954 *Living It Up* made more money than *Singin' in the Rain*, *On the Waterfront*, or *The African Queen*, and three years earlier, their third feature and biggest hit, *Sailor Beware*, was seen by an estimated eighty million people.) So Americans' refusal to deal with Lewis having once been even bigger here than Elvis is the phenomenon that cries out for sociological inquiry, not the understandable respect and affection he continues to receive anywhere else in the world.

An interesting study could be written about why and how certain kinds of physical comedy can unleash such fear and loathing as well as infatuation, but this isn't the sort of project Chris Fujiwara has in mind. Nevertheless, it's hardly an exaggeration to say that his book, the twenty-first title to be published in James Naremore's *Contemporary Film Directors*, is the first extended critical treatment of Lewis in English that Lewis deserves—including a thoughtful, sympathetic, and lucid (yet in no way sycophantic) thirty-two-page interview that is conceivably the best one anyone has ever had with him. And considering that Lewis himself has already ordered a hundred copies of the book, it seems safe to assume that he probably agrees with me.

Why it's taken so long for a filmmaker of Lewis' stature to receive such treatment is a matter of some interest. But it's arguably one of the virtues of Fujiwara's compact study, rightly concluding that the important analytical work can begin only after the pseudo-controversy about Lewis' importance is "settled," to waste little of his space and time addressing this issue with any defensive polemics. Focusing on Lewis mainly as a director while retaining, as he puts it in his opening paragraph, "a sense of continuity in Lewis's work in all its stages," he never stoops to any form of defensiveness or special pleading while describing the unity and coherence of Lewis's vision with the same confidence and scholarly thoroughness that he brought to Jacques Tourneur in his first book a little over a decade ago.

His pithy handling of what might be termed The Opposition occurs early on, after he notes in passing that Lewis's films (as director and actor) in the early '60s "were reviewed more or less indistinguishably by American film critics (except that since [the 1965] *Boeing Boeing*, the only insignificant film among them, is a straight farce rather than slapstick comedy, Lewis, cast in a supporting role behind Tony Curtis, received praise for his restraint)." Fujiwara then briefly notes the more respectful French criticism published during the same period (his other comments in this book suggest that he has been especially attentive to Robert Benayoun), before adding, "The enthusiasm of French intellectuals (shared by the general public) for Lewis has given rise, in the United States, to countless lazy and patronizing jokes at his expense and at that of France from unthinking, conformist pundits—gibes whose ideological nature has become unmistakable and more obnoxious than ever in a period of U.S. history that has witnessed the rebranding of `Freedom Fries.'"

Afterwards, apart from a measured response to Andrew Sarris's charge of sanctimonious moralizing and sentimentality in Lewis's films, Fujiwara chooses to make his reply to Lewis's critical detractors implicit in his overall argument. And what emerges most forcefully from this argument is the conviction that almost all of Lewis's previous critics have erred by simplifying the work—trying to make it conform to diverse industrial norms relating to narrative, humor, and continuity that it meets only superficially and cursorily. Thus, "In discarding the surface logic of narrative and verisimilitude, Lewis's cinema foregrounds its own structural logic. The viewer of a Lewis film follows the unfolding and application of the rules of construction that belong to the film—rules that are independent of the demands of narrative. This is Lewis's formalist, materialist side." This is an especially useful tip in approaching *The Bellboy* (1960) and *The Ladies Man* (1961), Lewis's first two features, although curiously enough, it's his fifth, *The Patsy* (1964), that Fujiwara identifies as "the most fully achieved of Lewis's films".

Halfway through his essay, while taking up the matter of "generic discontinuity," which he sees as "a constant feature of Lewis's work," Fujiwara registers his conviction that several portions of this oeuvre aren't especially funny (e.g., "the first half of *Which Way to the Front?*" [personally, I find the hysterical gibberish in the early scenes flat-out hilarious], "fairly long stretches of *The Family Jewels* and *Hardly Working*, and, perhaps, nearly all of *One More Time*"), adding that "One of my premises is that Lewis's work creates an impure, shifting context within which such a lack need not be accounted a flaw." This is a provocative assertion that warrants some elaboration, and I wish Fujiwara had gone further enough with it to reconcile this claim with my own feeling that some of the funniest moments in Lewis's cinema—such as his character's inability to cross the floor of his psychiatrist's office without falling, in the early stretches of *Cracking Up*—are central rather than incidental to his overall achievement. (I suspect Fujiwara would agree with me on this score, but even so, I would have preferred it if he had spelled out this portion of his argument a bit more fully.)

If the above quotations suggest that Fujiwara's case for Lewis is basically a formalist one, other portions of his essay (which is suggestively titled "An American Dream") move his analysis in a quite different direction, with very fruitful results: "`Home' does not exist in Lewis's world. His biography offers an explanation for this absence: his parents, vaudeville performers, were constantly on the road." (Although Fujiwara doesn't mention this, the fact that Lewis's parents failed to attend his bar mitzvah, as recounted in his 1982 book with Herb Gluck, *Jerry Lewis in Person*, is surely telling.)

And a page later: "Show business constitutes, for Lewis, an alternate psycho-analysis, a therapeutic sphere in which he acts out his obsessions in public and transcends them (see the confession scene in the prom in *The Nutty Professor*). In several films, Lewis depicts show business as an alternate family." As Fujiwara notes, Lewis seems to be fully aware of this factor himself; in D*ean and Me (A Love Story)*—his 2005 memoir written with James Kaplan, which Fujiwara rightly terms as the best account of his early career—he says of Dean Martin and himself, in their meteoric rise to success, "What we really were, in a Freudian age of self-realization, was the explosion of the show-business id." So it's hardly surprising that the same comic who would later build elaborate gag sequences in *Cracking Up* (1983) derived from his near-brush with a suicide attempt and his open-heart surgery would in fact base most of his features on some of his most personal conflicts and issues.

It's my own conviction that Lewis's naked vulnerability as well as his cour-age in brandishing it partially accounts not only for his improvisational genius on live television at the onset of his career but also for the aforemen-tioned fear and loathing in portions of his American audience more recently. Several years ago, during a period when he was appearing onstage as the Devil in *Damn Yankees* during its Chicago run, he graciously agreed to appear at an extended public Q&A at Columbia College—a session that lasted, if memory serves, for at least three hours. The sense of risk and danger in the auditorium that afternoon was palpable, and it came, I think, from the fact that Lewis stayed so close to the edge of his emotions, seemingly as a matter of both policy and temperament. The possibilities of being hurt, and of hurt being transformed into anger and rage, were never entirely absent, even though he managed to keep his cool on the few occasions when one of the questions betrayed some hostility—hostility that may have derived in part from some of the tension generated.

For those commentators who wrongly maintain that Buddy Love in *The Nutty Professor* (1963) derives from Dean Martin and not from Lewis himself, the giddy megalomania of the man who spread his remarkable boarding-house set over two of Paramount's soundstages in *The Ladies Man* (1961) and then filled them with nubile actresses has never been reconciled with the fumbling and bumbling idiot as well as the sexual panic of Lewis' own persona within that space. Fujiwara has made a bracing start at mapping out the relationship between those two seemingly antithetical individuals, and better yet, has a pretty good idea of what these people might have to say to one another.

One of My Favorite Things [On McCoy Tyner]

A blog post (November 22, 2010).

On volume 2 of a superb two-disc set (*One Down, One Up: Live at the Half Note*), recorded on Alan Grant's "Portraits in Jazz" radio show on May 7, 1965, is a spectacular thirteen-minute piano solo by McCoy Tyner on "My Favorite Things" that covers well over half of the number's almost twenty-three minutes. This solo is incidentally bracketed by some of Coltrane's loveliest soprano-sax glisssandos on disc, but what amazes me about Tyner's cascading tour de force is not only how he keeps it going in unforeseeable directions, but also how many different directions this consists of—tonal and atonal, rhythmic and melodic, calm and frenzied—and how steadily it builds to Coltrane's second solo.

What follows is the final draft of a treatment for a documentary about Tyner that I coauthored via email with cinematographer John Bailey in late 2001 and early 2002, at the behest of producer Rick Schmidlin, with and for whom I'd worked as a consultant on the 1998 re-edit of Orson Welles's *Touch of Evil*. This treatment went precisely nowhere, but it did lead to a very lengthy conversation with Tyner about various ideas for the film when he was in Chicago on a gig, after which I mailed him a video of Charles Burnett's *When it Rains*, a particular favorite of mine, as a model for a film that was attuned to jazz aesthetics. As I recalled to Tyner at our meeting, I had attended many sessions of him playing with Coltrane, Jimmy Garrison, and Elvin Jones at the Half Note in the mid-'60s, and part of what remained with me was how concentratedly these musicians listened to one another, as if in a trance. Musicians listening to and watching other musicians is for me the great and usually neglected cornerstone of what jazz documentaries should be; my two main examples of this are Charlie Parker listening to Coleman Hawkins and Buddy Rich in a never-completed Gjon Mili documentary, and Billie Holiday watching and listening to Lester Young in *The Sound of Jazz*.

The Real McCoy: A Proposal

In a dramatically lit closeup, McCoy Tyner recounts how as a teenager in Philadelphia he would often see Bud Powell, the greatest of the bebop pianists, in his own neighborhood—and how Bud would even come over from time to time to play McCoy's piano, not having one of his own. McCoy's voice continues offscreen over an overhead shot of the piano keys as he plays one of Bud's up-tempo tunes, such as "Cleopatra's Dream" or "Parisian Thoroughfare," with his trio in a studio setting. For the first few seconds, without hearing anything, we see only his powerful hands on the keys, moving in slow motion so that we can follow their precise movements and articulations. Then, as the film whips up to normal speed, his fingers become a fast blur, at the same time that the music's sound volume is raised so that we can finally hear the playing—a driving, pounding, up-tempo scorcher with accompaniment by bass and drums (which we see, along with a fuller view of Tyner, as the camera moves back and we cut to many different angles).

At this point Danny Glover, a good friend of Tyner, introduces himself as offscreen narrator and begins to tell us what Tyner's teenage years were like—meeting John Coltrane for the first time, and getting his first serious gig with Art Farmer and Benny Golson's legendary Jazztet—while John Bailey's camera roams freely over period photographs, down city streets, into long-forgotten clubs, recording studios, and haunts.

These three opening segments sum up the overall direction that *The Real*

McCoy is to take in terms of both style and content: a singular survivor in the jazz world, framed in a timeless space of memory and reflection, recalls how he entered, developed, and made it there; in the highly theatrical space of a studio, club, or concert hall we hear him play, and watch him and his fellow musicians play and listen to one another, without the distraction of voiceovers; then Glover's voice leads us into the engrossing details of McCoy Tyner's odyssey—his long stint as John Coltrane's irreplaceable pianist, and his subsequent development as a leader of his own groups, a composer, and an arranger.

The film will be broken into seven parts, each one beginning with a segment featuring interviews and vintage footage to tell another chapter (narrative or thematic) in McCoy's story, followed by a complete performance. The chapter headings will include such topics as "Beginnings," "Coltrane," "McCoy Tyner Plays Duke Ellington," "Monk, Powell, and Tatum," "Passion Dance," "McCoy and the Latin All-Stars," and "Jazz Roots." Each of the musical segments will feature a different lineup with many of the greatest jazz musicians alive. (Tyner's prestige is such that he'll clearly have the pick of the crop.) Each will be shot in a different location: the club in Philadelphia where McCoy first met Coltrane (still active and available); Rudy Van Gelder's legendary studio in Englewood, New Jersey where McCoy, Coltrane, Garrison, and Jones recorded their classic quartet sessions. Other possibilities include the Village Vanguard, the Blue Note, the Monterey Jazz Festival, and perhaps even a concert in Havana, where Chucho Valdez has invited Tyner to perform.

Throughout this documentary, the music will comprise the "action" and story while the biography of Tyner will introduce elements of reflection and context to set these numbers up. And any film that's about listening, as this one will be, will also be about looking—predicated on the philosophy that the way one looks at musicians already helps to determine the way one listens to them.

Lines and Circles [*PlayTime & 2001: A Space Odyssey*]

Posted online in Moving Image Source, December 3, 2010, and tweaked about a dozen years later.

Jacques Tati's *PlayTime*, a contemporary comedy chronicling a day spent by American tourists and various locals in a studio-built Paris, premiered in 65 mm in Paris on December 16, 1967; at the time it was 152 minutes long, and over the next two months—under pressure from exhibitors, and to avoid an intermission—Tati reduced the length by fifteen minutes.

Stanley Kubrick's *2001: A Space Odyssey*, a science fiction adventure that stretches roughly from East Africa in the year 4 billion B.C. to the outskirts of Jupiter around 2002, first opened in Cinerama in Washington, D.C., on April 2, 1968, and then, in the same format, in New York the following day and in Los Angeles on April 4, during which time it was 158 minutes long; over the following week, based on his own responses to audience reactions, Kubrick in New York reduced its length by nineteen minutes, making it only two minutes longer than the shortened *PlayTime*.

Large-format restorations of both these films, along with David Lean's 1962 *Lawrence of Arabia*, are coming this month to the TIFF Bell Lightbox in Toronto for extended runs. The fact that Tati's and Kubrick's masterworks, both handcrafted and intricately choreographed epics, originally opened less than four months apart is stimulating some reflection as well as recollection about the impacts these two films had when they opened—their mixed critical receptions as well as the degree to which they implicitly represented alternative paths for big-screen cinema.

I first saw *2001* in New York the week it opened, before it was recut, at the Capitol (where, interestingly enough, F.W. Murnau's *Faust* also had premiered, on December 5, 1926) when I was twenty-four, along with two of my three brothers, David (26) and Alvin (22). Afterwards we proceeded to the Playboy Club in midtown Manhattan, where David was a member, and we spent most of the evening doggedly trying to figure out the plot over dinner, without very much success or confidence. We were all impressed and stirred by the movie but more than a little puzzled by what we'd seen, and by the time I went back for a second look a week or two later, some portions of the plot—including the role played by the mysterious monolith in the opening sequence, "The Dawn of Man"—had become easier to follow. (The insert of another shot of the monolith before one of the ape-men discovered the use of weapons was especially helpful.) And as subsequently became clear when the drug-taking counterculture embraced the film as a "trip," understanding the film as a narrative was less important in many respects than appreciating it as a spectacle—a factor seemingly lost on a good many of the film's original reviewers.

I didn't catch up with *PlayTime* until the following summer, in Paris, June 1968, by which time it was playing in second or third run, in 35 mm, with a running time that was closer to two hours. One major sequence was missing from the film at the time—Hulot's visit to an apartment house with an old friend ("Schneller, from the army," as one of Criterion's chapter headings puts it) that he runs into by chance. All of this tour de force sequence, most of it wordless, is viewed from the sidewalk, where one can view through huge glass windows the interiors of four apartments on two separate floors, including Schneller's on the ground floor on the left, and on its right, the flat of Monsieur Giffard, who has just spent most of the day fruitlessly looking for Hulot—and whose nose is bandaged as a result of having earlier mistaken Hulot's reflection for Hulot himself and run smack into a glass door.

Transparent glass doors, walls, and windows are indeed a central metaphor in the film, as well as a concrete illustration of how modern architecture divides people, so that the accidental shattering of the glass door leading into the Royal Garden Restaurant ultimately becomes the key gag and social event in the plot, leading to many arcane developments (such as the shards of shattered glass ultimately being emptied into a champagne ice bucket).

Lamentably, the crucial sequence of Hulot visiting Schneller's apartment and family—the only part of the film that shows any of the characters inside domestic spaces—continued to be missing from the film until it was restored shortly before Tati's death, in late 1982; I first saw it the following spring, when

I was teaching at Berkeley. But even without the benefit of this sequence, the most challenging in the film (which is undoubtedly why it was cut), *PlayTime* bemused me almost as much as *2001*, though not in the same way. I was intrigued by the welter and jumble of onscreen details, which distracted and confused me as much as what I took to be the minimalist absence of onscreen narrative detail in much of *2001*.

The seeming overload that Tati had imposed on his vast canvas, especially in the film's breathtaking and extended restaurant sequence, was actually an invitation to carve out one's own individual itineraries in the action, playfully and creatively establishing one's personal priorities in relation to the varying degrees of emphasis in one's attention span. But even though I probably had made at least one return trip to *2001* by then, *PlayTime* provoked me into reseeing it a good many more times in Paris over the course of the summer. And by the time I first met Tati in late November 1972, when I took a bus to the suburb La Garenne-Colombes to interview him in his office (I had then been living in Paris for a little over three years), it had become my favorite film because it had taught me how to deal with the sensory overload imposed by city life. I even told him this at the beginning of our meeting. At that point, *PlayTime* still hadn't opened in the U.S. (not counting a very brief and unheralded opening in a New York suburb that had been engineered as some sort of tax write-off); the putative occasion of our interview was the anticipated U.S. release of his subsequent feature, Trafic, the following month.

Indeed, by the time *PlayTime* finally opened in New York, in late June 1973, I had become friends with Tati's assistant, Marie-France Siegler, written an English voiceover for a 16 mm short of hers, and, thanks to her perception that my meeting with her boss, now bankrupted by the expenses of *PlayTime*, had cheered him up and made him feel like working again, had gotten myself hired as a "script consultant" (actually his audience and sounding board) for a week or so in January. Sadly enough, the American critical establishment was every bit as resistant to the challenges of *PlayTime* as it had been to those of *2001*. (At this point, Tati had lost control over his film due to his bankruptcy and had little if any input about the prints that were being shown.) A few critics remarked that it was reasonably funny, but not a patch on *Trafic* (a film that Tati himself had regarded as a compromised work because of the commercially dictated prominence of his Hulot character); one reviewer even went so far as to label it "inhuman" in his capsule, which was the same sort of epithet that many had accorded to Kubrick's epic.

Tati himself, who admired Kubrick immensely for his craft, was a big fan of *2001*, but I have no idea what Kubrick thought of *PlayTime*. By then many of my friends were squaring off by regarding either *2001* or *PlayTime* as the great film of the modern era. Prominent among the partisans of the former position were Annette Michelson and the novelist and critic Stephen Koch, and I recall that when Annette, a huge fan of *Mr. Hulot's Holiday*, finally caught up with *PlayTime*, her principal demurral was how ugly and formless she found the gadget exposition sequence in the first half of the film, adding that if she went to see the film a second time, she would probably go out into the lobby when that sequence came on. By contrast, her friend Noël Burch had written in *Cahiers du cinéma* when the film opened in Paris that it was one of the few films in the history of cinema that not only had to be seen several times but also had to be seen from several different positions in the auditorium—a comment that has subsequently (and more than once) been falsely attributed to me.

One of the few intellectual acquaintances I knew at the time who found both of these films "jaw-dropping" was Susan Sontag. Most of the others, at least by implication, found these two masterpieces incompatible as touchstones of the modern era. This may be an even more unavoidable conclusion if one compares the films historically as anticipations of the future—according to which *2001* may be the more dated of the two, especially if one factors in the Cold War context dominating the film's second part along with some of the brand names (e.g., Howard Johnson) planted inside a commercial space station that was operational by 2001. Sadly, Kubrick didn't live long enough to see the year 2001, having died unexpectedly in March 1999. (By contrast, it's worth pointing out that Tati placed parking meters in his studio-built city before France actually had them, correctly predicting that they would eventually be installed.)

But a few formal parallels between the two films remain fascinating—above all, the contrast in each between straight lines and circles, as well as between various stiff human interactions and the more playful and dancelike movements of both people and objects (including vehicles). In *2001*, the principal straight lines are those associated with earthbound gravity and the mysterious rectangular monolith that both guides and provokes humanity over the course of several millennia, while the famous "dance" of a rotating satellite to Johann Strauss's *Blue Danube Waltz* and the circular pathway of the main cabin traced by a jogging astronaut in a spacecraft bound for Jupiter make up two of the principal circles. (The breathtaking transition from the film's first sequence, the only one set on Earth, to the *Blue Danube* is traced by the vertical drop of a bone-as-weapon that has been tossed into the air by a triumphant ape-man followed by a match cut to the descent of a satellite in its rotating orbit—

a literal transition from straight line to circle.) The point in the *Blue Danube* sequence at which the trajectory of a spacecraft stewardess wearing magnetized footwear in free-fall moves from horizontal to circular describes part of the film's overall view of the physical liberation arising from the loss of gravity (which inspired Michelson to title her essay on *2001*, published in the February 1969 issue of *Artforum*, "Bodies in Space: Film as Carnal Knowledge"). HAL, the computer on a spacecraft bound for Jupiter that eventually goes "mad," is made up of a circular eye and rectangular circuits. The film's hallucinatory "trip" after HAL is dismantled by astronaut David Bowman (Keir Dullea) mainly juxtaposes the human eye with various straight lines. And after Bowman undergoes a kind of death in an allegorical hotel room ruled by straight lines (including the monolith), he's reborn, in the film's closing shot, as a Star Child inside a spherical bubble confronting the Earth.

Complicating *2001*'s recurring notion of physical liberation is Kubrick and his co-writer Arthur C. Clarke's pessimistic and deterministic view of mankind's destiny being both shaped and circumscribed by a superior race of beings represented by the mysterious monolith. In contrast to the more populist, left-wing orientation of Olaf Stapledon—the English science fiction visionary who was clearly one of Clarke and Kubrick's main inspirations (as he was on Clarke's best novel, *Childhood's End*), above all for his essayistic novels *Last and First Men* (1930, a "history" of mankind over the next two billion years and eighteen successive human species) and *Star Maker* (1937, described on Wikipedia as "an outline history of the Universe")—*2001* arguably posits mankind in far needier terms.

No such determinism can be found in Tati's more democratic and exclusively earthbound perspective, according to which various spontaneous and anarchic circles and dancelike movements triumph over the various inhibitions imposed by architectural rigidity and social engineering—culminating in a merry-go-round of bumper-to-bumper traffic in the film's climactic and euphoric morning sequence, which might be said to exalt Tati's own directorial engineering over the engineering of the social planners he is implicitly criticizing. But the first significant curve in the film that undermines all the straight lines and right angles dictated by the architecture and echoed by all the human movements is the momentary and accidental slip of Monsieur Hulot. Waiting in a sterile antechamber for his appointment with Giffard, attempting to anchor himself on the slippery floor with the tip of his closed umbrella, he slides in a short curve as a result of this misplaced confidence. And the key site of the film's overarching transition between straight lines and circles is not merely the glass door to the Royal Garden that eventually shatters, liberating the two-way traffic into and out of the restaurant, but also the neon sign directly above this door and the empty portal that replaces it—a sign tracing a straight line that curves into an arrow as it points toward the establishment's interior.

The artisanal, almost handmade aspects of both epics and their recurring geometrical forms can't hide the fact that their approaches to big-screen spectacle are hardly the same, either physically or philosophically. But insofar as both masterpieces are concerned with practical ways that viewers can deal with sensory overload—often through playfully and musically organized choreography—they both ultimately qualify as ethereal yet also profoundly engaged with the contemporary world.

O'Neill's Penultimate Masterpiece: *The Iceman Cometh*

Published by the website Fandor on January 4, 2011.

It's widely and justly believed that the two greatest plays of Eugene O'Neill (1888-1953) were both written near the tail end of his career— *The Iceman Cometh*, completed in 1939 and first staged in 1946, and *Long Day's Journey into Night*, completed in 1941 and produced only posthumously in 1956. What's less widely known is that the action of both plays unfolds during the same summer, 1912, when O'Neill was twenty-four, after having attempted to commit suicide the previous spring. As his biographers Arthur and Barbara Gelb note in their 2000 *O'Neill: Life with Monte Cristo* (New York: Applause), "the plays follow almost literally the chronology of O'Neill's youthful years, with *Iceman* (written first) set in 'summer 1912' and *Long Day's Journey* (which can be regarded as its sequel) set on 'a day in August, 1912'."

Both late masterpieces are obsessive distillations of a lifetime of brooding, with the three-hour 1962 film version of *Long Day's Journey into Night* directed by Sidney Lumet and the four-hour 1973 film version of *The Iceman Cometh* directed by John Frankenheimer having served, for many filmgoers, as the versions of reference. (The latter film, incidentally, has no connection of any kind with the enjoyable 1989 Maggie Cheung comedy thriller from Hong Kong, *Ji dong ji xiz*, which happens to use the same English title.) If one adds to this the various TV versions of both plays that are available—the Sidney Lumet version of *Iceman* (1960), which I remember with much fondness, and two I haven't seen, the Peter Wood version of *Long Day's Journey* starring

Laurence Olivier (1973) and the Jonathan Miller version of the latter starring Jack Lemmon (1987)—one isn't obliged to view either film version as definitive.

For me, the 1973 Frankenheimer production of *Iceman*, despite an almost fatal bit of miscasting (Lee Marvin superb as an action hero, but impossible in the pivotal role of Hickey), survives powerfully, thanks above all to Robert Ryan (as Larry Slade) and Fredric March (as Harry Hope), each offering his very last recorded performance—and in Ryan's case, quite possibly his best. It isn't really a movie, even though it went out originally on film, but one could argue that, apart from *The Manchurian Candidate*, Frankenheimer's true métier was live television with its own special tensions and challenges, and this film shares some of the spontaneous performative virtues found in his best TV work (such as *The Comedian* in 1957).

When I was in high school, I must have read about a dozen O'Neill plays within a short period of time, ranging from Greek pastiches like *Desire Under the Elms* and *Mourning Becomes Electra* to contorted mannerist-modernist experiments such as *The Emperor Jones, Lazarus Laughed* (my own favorite as well as O'Neill's—a mad, unproduceable Nietzschean rant), and *Dynamo* (the most ridiculous of them all). What seemed apparent in all of them was a compulsion to try anything and everything that scored only when it was grounded in obsessive personal material, leading eventually to his two late masterpieces. What gives them much of their conviction is a process of purification that boils away all the self-conscious, contemporary cultural sheen while internalizing the sense of structure he learned from the Greeks. In *Long Day's Journey* he reproduced his own family while simplifying his own character by depriving himself of a marriage, child, and divorce, all of which O'Neill had been through before he wound up in a New York flophouse in 1912. In *Iceman*, he split himself between the despair and political defeatism of Larry Slade, a former anarchist like himself, and the confused optimism and snappy salesmanship of Hickey, both ultimately defeated by his murderous misogyny (his own failed marriage clearly resembled O'Neill's own), meanwhile assigning his suicide attempt (in *Iceman*, a successful act in the play's closing moments) to a much younger misogynist and former anarchist, Don Parritt, (played by Jeff Bridges in the Frankenheimer film), who is explicitly regarded as combined younger versions of both Slade and Hickman. For all the bathos and inertia of O'Neill's sedentary characters, who are uniformly soused except for Hickey, the play's dramatic architecture in terms of both the characters and their interactions remains rock-solid.

This ultimately yields in *Iceman* an instinctive anticipation of the Theater of the Absurd. Several terminal alcoholics in a Manhattan flophouse (much like the one where O'Neill resided in early 1912), including Slade and the proprietor, Harry Hope, wait endlessly for the redemptive arrival of a rowdy traveling hardware salesman and drinking buddy, Theodore Hickman, who's nicknamed Hickey. When Hickey finally does turn up—unlike Beckett's Godot, who never materializes, and somewhat more like *The Connection*'s Cowboy, who delivers a long-awaited fix to several junkies—he winds up exploding their fragile pipe dreams instead of cheering them up, self-righteously proclaiming and pretending to cure their ailments in the process as he effectively destroys each of them in turn.

Roughly speaking, O'Neill remained something of a primitive who brought to the American theater some of the same primal energy, dogged persistence, and stylistic clumsiness that Theodore Dreiser brought to the novel, albeit with a much greater sense of formal experimentation and adventure. So it's intriguing to discover from the Gelbs that an English professor, Brenda Murphy, has recently and plausibly hypothesized that Dreiser himself, whom O'Neill had recently met, provided the playwright with one of his key models for Hickey, in background, appearance, temperament, and even first name. Even the incantatory repetitions of "pipe dream" in the dramaturgy comes to resemble some of Dreiser's own obsessions in his dogged thematic pursuits in *An American Tragedy*. And it goes without saying that *The Iceman Cometh* and *Long Day's Journey into Night*, whatever else they might be, are not only tragedies but profoundly American, above all in their sense of fantasy under the constant threat of defeat.

Sunny Satire: *Will Success Spoil Rock Hunter?*

Written in March 2011 for Madman Entertainment, an Australian DVD label for which I've done a lot of congenial work.

One couldn't say that there's any firm consensus that Frank Tashlin's dazzling 1957 satire about advertising and television is his greatest film. Some Tashlin fans would opt for either of the two late Dean Martin and Jerry Lewis vehicles that he directed for Paramount, *Artists and Models* (1955) or *Hollywood or Bust* (1956), or else would select his earlier CinemaScope vehicle for Jayne Mansfield at Twentieth Century-Fox, *The Girl Can't Help It* (1956). But there's certainly no doubt that *Will Success Spoil Rock Hunter?* stands apart from the rest of his work, as the freest and the most deconstructive of all his comedies—and it's worth adding that Tashlin himself cited it to Peter Bogdanovich (who interviewed him in 1962, during the shooting of *It's Only Money*) as the film he was "most satisfied with". (In another interview, he suggested that *The Girl Can't Help It* was his other personal favorite; it appears that the role played by executive producer Buddy Adler in granting Tashlin an unusual amount of freedom and leeway on both pictures had a lot to do with these judgments.) In keeping with George S. Kaufman's maxim that "satire is what closes on Saturday night," *Rock Hunter* flopped at the box office and was disastrous for Tashlin's career. But to paraphrase Roberto Rossellini, both it and Charlie Chaplin's *A King in New York*, released the same year, are the films of free men.

Speaking personally, I regard it as his masterpiece. When I first encountered *Will Success Spoil Rock Hunter?* in my early teens, it was the first movie I ever voluntarily sat through two times in a row, without leaving my seat. As a devotee of *Mad* when it was still a highly transgressive comic book in the early 1950s, before it became a magazine, as well as other parodic and satirical forms of cultural assault from that period, I was certainly primed for its brand of reckless and irreverent humor.

But I was confused at the time about who deserved the credit for all its brilliance. Even though the credited producer, director, and writer was Tashlin, another title card clearly read, "Based on the Play written by George Axelrod and Produced by Jule Styne". And the Axelrod play—which opened at the Belasco Theatre in New York on October 13, 1955 and ran for 444 performances—was staged by Axelrod himself, who had also cast Jayne Mansfield as his female lead, Rita Marlowe, playing (more or less) the same character that she plays in the film. "As a matter of fact," Axelrod said to Patrick McGilligan in an interview (*Backstory 3: Interviews with Screenwriters of the 1960s*, Berkeley: University of California Press, 1997), "I directed [Jayne Mansfield's] first screen test, and sold her contract to 20th [Century-Fox]." But in the same interview, he also maintained, "I never knew Frank Tashlin. I never worked with him. I had nothing to do with the film of *Will Success Spoil Rock Hunter?* I never saw the movie. Not to this day....They didn't use my story, my play, or my script [which implies that Axelrod wrote a never-used screenplay of his own]....I know what they did. I made it about the movies—they made it about television.... Why do I want to torture myself by seeing it?"

Despite—or maybe because of—Axelrod's tenuous and contentious connection with the film, it's worth comparing his vision to that of Tashlin in some detail. Both are quintessential, era-defining figures of the 1950s, and both were satirists of the period's pop culture and its crazed notions of hyperbolic sexuality who were widely criticized for being implicated in the targets of their satire. Both men, one might add, specialized in personal in-jokes as well as wimpy heroes whose masculinity is often challenged by the cultures they live in.

Yet in other respects, one could argue that these two men were diametrically opposed to one another in their views of humanity in general and American culture in particular. The world of Tashlin is essentially one without malice or evil or villains—a striking trait that he shares with director Joe Dante, his artistic heir in many respects—in which the culture they inhabit is skewered from top to bottom but not the people who live within that culture or even those who subscribe to its more ridiculous notions. One might therefore describe Tashlin as a social critic and a humanist but not as a misanthrope or a cynic. But Axelrod, far more metaphysical and unambiguously cynical and misanthropic, more typically depicts a godless universe that is literally ruled by the Devil.

His play *Will Success Spoil Rock Hunter?* is in fact a variation on *Faust*, which accounts for the "Marlowe" in Rita Marlowe, but some of the same metaphysical traits crop up in Axelrod's three novels (*Beggar's Choice*, 1947; *Blackmailer*, 1952; *Where Am I Now—When I Need Me?*, 1971), his other Broadway plays (*The Seven Year Itch*, 1952; *Goodbye Charlie*, 1959), and, arguably, even many of his adapted screenplays (*Bus Stop*, 1956; *Breakfast at Tiffany's*, 1961; *The Manchurian Candidate*, 1962; and *Lord Love a Duck*, 1966, which he also directed—the latter another variation on the Faust theme). A writer who specialized in the Walter Mittyish erotic fantasies of (wimpy) heroes, most of whom suffer from various rude challenges to their sense of their own masculinity (a characteristic that even carries over to the brainwashed mama's boy played by Laurence Harvey in *The Manchurian Candidate*), he also played at times with literal gender switches: in his novel *Beggar's Choice*, the writer hero gets hired out as a family cook while his wife becomes the family chauffeur, and his in play *Goodbye Charlie*, a Hollywood ladies man dies and gets reincarnated as a woman. The combination of these elements often recalls the earlier work of comic novelist Thorne Smith, whose source novels provided the basis for such films as *Topper*, *Turnabout* (a Hal Roach comedy about a gender shift between man and wife), and *I Married a Witch*.

It also seems pertinent that the bowdlerizing of and other changes in Axelrod's first successful play, *The Seven Year Itch*, in the 1955 film adaptation that he wrote with director Billy Wilder, apparently soured Axelrod on movies in general and Hollywood in particular, which fed directly into the satire of his *Rock Hunter*. ("In addition to having a horrible Breen Office problem," he told McGilligan—in reference to the Production Code dictating that the (wimpy) hero of the play, a married man, couldn't have sex with his upstairs neighbor—"the play just didn't adapt. The claustrophobic element of the play is what makes it work—a guy trapped in the little apartment, his imagination soaring out of the apartment. When you open the play up, it loses its tension.")

There was a clear carryover from *The Seven Year Itch* (the play) to *Rock Hunter* (the play), and one that related to more than Jayne Mansfield offering a very broad parody of Marilyn Monroe, who had starred in the Wilder film. In Axelrod's *Rock Hunter*, selling your soul to the Devil and moving from New York to Hollywood are viewed as mutually reinforcing propositions. Tom Ewell, who played the male lead in both the play of *The Seven Year Itch* and the film, wound up as the male lead in Tashlin's *The Girl Can't Help It*, and was originally set to play in the film of *Rock Hunter*, but a commitment to appear in a new play forced him to bow out at the last minute, and Tony Randall stepped into the part only two weeks before shooting started. (Another last-minute casting change involved the film's surprise "guest" star—which was originally supposed to be Jerry Lewis, until Hal Wallis refused to release him from his contract at Paramount, at which point Lewis was replaced by Groucho Marx.) And other sea-changes in the project undoubtedly confirmed Axelrod's demonizing of Hollywood from his own vantage point. Fox was clearly more interested in acquiring Jayne Mansfield (which caused her to drop out of the play in order to costar in *The Girl Can't Help It*) than in acquiring Axelrod's material, as Tashlin's comprehensive rewrite demonstrated.

In Axelrod, one might also say that shifts in gender ultimately lead to shifts in genre—something that also could be said of Tashlin if one regards cartoon animation and live-action as separate "genres", because he started out working in Hollywood animation and eventually shifted many of its principles over to live-action slapstick gags. He uses this background in the molding of *Rock Hunter*'s stars—Tony Randall and Jayne Mansfield, both giving their best performances—into cartoons. Randall's a nerdy Madison Avenue executive with rolling eyeballs, Mansfield's a tall, squeaking, Betty Boop-ish movie star with cleavage. (In tribute to Randall, Tashlin said to Bogdanovich, "Oh, he's great. Like a comic machine. You feel like [violin virtuoso Jascha] Heifetz when you work with him.")

One way of distinguishing the confusing shifts between genres in *The Manchurian Candidate* (which Axelrod produced as well as scripted), including the dizzying oscillations between melodrama and comedy, from those in such contemporary French New Wave features as *Breathless*, *Shoot the Piano Player*, and *Last Year at Marienbad*, is that the French films were grounded in cinephilia, as were Tashlin's comedies, while Axelrod's contemporaneous film, for better and for worse, is grounded in cynical and Pavlovian button-pushing. (It's worth recalling that Tashlin had a huge stylistic impact on the New Wave. *Will Success Spoil Rock Hunter?*—which Jean-Luc Godard cited as his third favorite film of 1957, after *Bitter Victory* and *The Wrong Ma*n, and immediately before *Hollywood or Bust*—can be regarded as the template for Godard 's bold use of primary colors and 'Scope in such '60s films as *A Woman is a Woman* and *Pierrot le Fou*, and *Artists and Models*, about the '50s craze for comic books—starring four more Tashlin cartoons, Dean Martin, Jerry Lewis, Dorothy Malone, and Shirley MacLaine—was the acknowledged inspiration for Jacques Rivette's 1974 *Celine and Julie Go Boating*.)

Hatred for the mass market—best sellers, Hollywood, advertising—is something close to a constant in Axelrod's work. Given that Axelrod was himself entirely a creature of the mass-market, this invariably led to diverse forms of self-hatred, despite (or, again, perhaps because) of the fact that so many of his heroes were writers.

The world-view of Tashlin, by contrast, is decidedly sunnier. Finding American culture ridiculous isn't necessarily or invariably equivalent to hating it; in Tashlin's case, on the contrary, it becomes a means for appreciating it. The published version of Axelrod's play of *Will Success Spoil Rock Hunter?*—which was reportedly called Will Success Spoil Rock Hudson? before Hudson's agent threatened a lawsuit—is prefaced by the words, "Ten percent of this play is dedicated to Irving Lazar," and in fact the plot, which opens in Manhattan before shifting to Hollywood for the next two acts, describes the sale of the soul of the faux-hero George MacCauley (Orson Bean), a fan magazine writer with only one published article to his credit, to a Hollywood agent, Irving LaSalle (Martin Gabel), for successive ten percent increments, in exchange for fame, fortune, and the love of Rita Marlowe. (The "real" hero in the play, however, is a "real" writer—Michael Freeman, played on the stage by Walter Matthau— who resolves everything at the play's end by getting George to accompany him back to "real" Manhattan, just in time for an earthy snowstorm, carrying along only his treasured typewriter as a prized possession.)

The one fan-magazine article written by George is in fact titled "Will Success Spoil Rock Hunter?", but no visible character in the play goes by that name. In his almost completely rewritten script, Tashlin essentially combines Michael and George into a Manhattan-based writer of TV commercials, Rockwell P. Hunter (Randall), who lives with his teenage niece April (Lili Hunter) and is engaged to marry his secretary Jenny Wells (Betsy Drake). Rockwell, like George, once worked for a movie fan magazine, and his own sole published article was entitled, "Will Success Spoil Bobo Brannigansky?" (It's a surname that seems to come straight out of Preston Sturges, whose 1944 *The Miracle of Morgan's Creek* Tashlin would loosely adapt a year later, in *Rock-a-Bye Baby*.) And the only remnant of the Faust theme is that Rockwell does acquire fame, fortune, and the affection (if not the love) of Rita Marlowe, the girlfriend of Bobo Brannigansky (played by Mickey Hargitay, the real-life husband of Jayne Mansfield), but then unexpectedly gives up all three for the pleasures of rural chicken farming. And the fame and fortune come to him as an adman, not as a Hollywood screenwriter—someone who acquires the endorsement of Rita Marlowe for Stay-Put Lipstick in exchange for making Bobo Brannigansky jealous, and at the cost of almost permanently alienating his girlfriend Jenny. Thanks to this endorsement, he becomes first vice-president and then finally president of the La Salle Jr., Raskin, Pooley & Crocket Advertising Agency— replacing Irving La Salle, Jr. (John Williams), who has meanwhile fulfilled his own longtime dream by leaving the firm to become a horticulturist who grows and develops roses. (When Rock pays his former boss a visit in the latter's greenhouse, Junior applauds the hero's ascension to the top with a chilling line that becomes virtually the film's motto: "Success will fit you like a shroud." And sure enough, it proves to be a hollow victory because Rockwell can't keep his pipe lit. As a psychiatrist reportedly told him some time ago, half of him wants to succeed and half of him wants to fail, with the result that he doesn't know whether to inhale or to exhale. Similarly, "got it made" is a phrase that this movie keeps repeating so many times, in so many different ways, like a desperate mantra, that it begins to sound increasingly sinister.

The movie's climax, aptly filmed in CinemaScope, spells this out in glitzy neon. After Hunter, who has just been appointed president of his company, says goodnight to the office cleaning ladies, the scene segues into a solipsistic musical number played out to an unseen celestial chorus chanting "You've got it made" as he literally sees his name in lights, dancing deliriously through the empty executive board room under various shifting forms of expressionistic lighting. Drawing on his background, Tashlin makes it all look like a crazed cartoon, with delirious fadeouts to yellow, red, green, and blue, a vision of Rita Marlowe clothed exclusively in gold coins and dollar bills, and surrounded by singing or signifying typewriters and switchboards celebrating his ascension to power and status. In a way, it's a reprise to Rockwell's earlier victory-plateau, when his colleague Henry Rufus (Henry Jones) presents him with the key to the "executive powder room," cuing in a previous chorus by the same celestial choir. (As Bogdanovich wrote in 1962, "The scene in which Tony Randall is moved to joyous tears when given the key to the executive washroom is exaggerated so little that it becomes almost terrifying in its basic truth. This was a large part of Tashlin's particular genius: he was honest, exaggerating only slightly to make a point.") This was another facet, one might add, that distinguished him from Axelrod.

But by the sequence's end, Hunter also discovers that he can't keep his pipe lit. In the movie's Freudian shorthand, this means that he doesn't really feel successful after all, at least until he discovers that, as he explains it to Jenny, it is his average-guy mediocrity that makes him a success, not his anxiety-ridden elevator to power and status.

The fact that *Will Success Spoil Rock Hunter?* was Tashlin's most avant-garde and political film undoubtedly also made it one of his most misunderstood—rivaled, perhaps, only by Charlie Chaplin's *A King in New York*, also released in 1957, and paralleling Tashlin's vision of America in many particulars (although it goes further in highlighting many of the hysterical '50s excesses, such as the McCarthyite witchhunts, that were systematically left out of Hollywood pictures). Both directors, anticipating Jean-Luc Godard's journalistic directive that one can—and must—place "everything" in a film, create dystopian versions of New York in which TV and advertising (rightly perceived as synonymous) completely obliterate the divisions between public and private. Both jeremiads correctly and prophetically perceive that advertising not only competes with contemporary American culture; it *is* contemporary American culture. A corollary perception, which both pictures spell out in numerous ways, is that television, far from facilitating communication and social interaction, effectively replaces them. Significantly, when Rock Hunter wants to know what has happened to his niece or even, at the onset of his celebrity, what Rita Marlowe is saying downstairs and immediately outside his apartment, on the street, he logically turns on his TV set. And as his Madison Avenue colleague points out, he doesn't have to worry about locating the right channel, because the media's Marlowe coverage extends to all the channels (an eerie prophecy of such relatively recent news events as the deaths of Ronald Reagan, Frank Sinatra, and Michael Jackson).

It's worth considering that one of the main charges hurled against both *A King in New York* and *Will Success Spoil Rock Hunter?* was vulgarity, predicated on the assumption that it was Chaplin's treatment of (say) plastic surgery and Tashlin's treatment of male Americans' fixation on large female breasts that were tasteless, presumably not cosmetic surgery and breast fixation themselves. Andrew Sarris expressed this position against Tashlin as follows: "One can approve vulgarity in theory as a comment on vulgarity, but in practice all vulgarity is inseparable. To ridicule Jayne Mansfield's enormous bust in *Will Success Spoil Rock Hunter?* may be construed as satire, but to ridicule Betsy Drake's small bust in the same film is simply unabashed vulgarity." To which one could reply that neither bust is ridiculed; it's the breast worship engulfing and oppressing both women that Tashlin is mocking—more obviously in the case of Betsy Drake's character when she winds up passing out from her breast-expanding exercises, before taking a doctor's advice and purchasing falsies. But by broaching this subject at all, Tashlin's most daring forms of irreverence could also be mistaken for exploitation. As Diane Johnson, the screenwriter of *The Shining*, once noted, "In the 1950s there were fewer words for oppression."

To complicate matters, discussions of class tend to remain sufficiently taboo within American culture to make charges of vulgarity a partial displacement and relocation of certain class biases that are unacknowledged as such. (In a similar fashion, many of the ill-conceived descriptions of writer-director Samuel

Fuller as a "primitive" might be considered a displacement of the reluctance to confront his working-class origins.) If English critic Raymond Durgnat in 1969 could spot the same "mixture of despair and acquiescence" in both Tashlin and Andy Warhol, most of his Anglo-American contemporaries were too busy segregating the two into the mutually exclusive categories of entertainment and art to ponder the salient parallels. Thus the "coldness", distanciation, and ironic playfulness that critics cited in defense of Warhol's sophistication as a dandy and artist were all regarded as negative factors in relation to Tashlin—proof even of his alleged corruption as an entertainer. While Warhol was declared an acute social analyst who perfectly understood the art market (i.e. the class to which he catered), Tashlin was branded as a man with a breast fixation who was too implicated in what he was satirizing to qualify as a serious artist. Different strokes for different folks—and of course most of the people whom Tashlin addressed didn't read auteurist criticism.

Tashlin once defined his turf as "the nonsense of what we call civilization," which he thought deserved both exuberant celebration and ridicule—a combination that was not dissimilar to Warhol's own ironic ambivalence, expressed in a radically different social milieu.

A few of the jokey period references in *Rock Hunter* may require glosses. I count ten allusions to other mid-'50s Fox releases or stars then under contract to Fox, the most significant of these being Marilyn Monroe. She's never mentioned, but Mansfield is obviously being used as a broad parody of her, as she was in *The Girl can't Help It*, and there's even a veiled allusion to *The Brothers Karamazov* (a treasured Monroe project) and a bit about Rock and Rita getting hitched in Connecticut (where Monroe married Arthur Miller).

Were these references product placements? Tashlin's admission of complicity with the culture he was lampooning? Probably some of both, which also applies to the celebrations and ridicule of rock music in *The Girl Can't Help It*. *Rock Hunter* seems revolted by American notions of success, but when all of the major characters finally renounce these ideas to follow their unglamorous dreams, including even the mating of Rock and Rita's two major sidekicks, the movie seems to mock them. We can't quite believe that Randall's ad executive becomes a chicken farmer, and neither can Tashlin or Randall. Maybe that's why the characters turn up in front of a stage curtain at the end, becoming abstract Brechtian commentators on their own dilemmas.

Still, when Tashlin acknowledges being implicated in what he's satirizing, he's good-natured and relaxed about it—making his populism and optimism seem genuine rather than forced. He has a charming way of being devastatingly critical, affectionate, and hopeful at the same time.

Raúl Ruiz's Interactive Testament: *Mysteries of Lisbon*

Written in October 2011 for the Blu-Ray released by Music Box Films. My earlier discussion of Manoel de Oliveira's Doomed Love *(for me, his greatest film) as a literary adaptation can be found in my first collection,* Placing Movies, *which also includes my* "Mapping the Territory of Raúl Ruiz".

It was disconcerting to see a passage from a 1997 article of mine about Raúl Ruiz (1941-2011) quoted in some of his mainstream obituaries: "Ruiz is the least neurotic of filmmakers; he doesn't even seem to care whether what he's doing is good or not." Not because this was false when I wrote it but because it related to my earliest encounters with his work and its seeming challenges to film commerce, not to his better known big-budget efforts such as Marcel Proust's *Time Regained* (1999) and *Klimt* (2006).

This is why some of these latter films disappointed me, pointing towards what Ruiz himself frankly described to me in a 2002 interview as a "capitulation". But *Mysteries of Lisbon* shows that he may have gained as much from these bigger budgets as he lost, and I'm not speaking about pocket change. What he actually broadened was his film vocabulary, especially his employments of long takes and camera movements. Over the course of well over 100 films, in English, French, Italian, Portuguese and/or Spanish, shot on separate continents over four decades, runs the continuing question of how we position ourselves in relation to a story being told. Whether Ruiz's working model happens to be Orson Welles or Richard Thorpe, Robert Louis Stevenson or Jorge Luis Borges, the usual strategy is to keep us shifting and guessing.

The challenge of adapting Proust may have clouded this issue, especially when it seemed to convert his novel into a theme park. But Ruiz's "capitulation" also enriched his aesthetics while complicating some of his earlier indifference towards success or failure. Despite his soft-spoken, laid-back manner, he remained a radical both as an intellectual and as a director, and, as with Godard, could be as creative in interviews and written texts as in his films, meanwhile remaining a devout believer in both popular cinema and the avant-garde. His ongoing quarrel with what he called the "central conflict theory" behind American-style dramaturgy—which once led him in his early twenties to quit the University of Iowa's writers workshop program, following the suggestion of his advisor, Kurt Vonnegut, Jr.—eventually became the basis of the first chapter in his *Poetics of Cinema* (1995), and one of his avowed motives for working with serials like *Mysteries of Lisbon* was their avoidance of "central" conflicts.

The literary figure behind *Mysteries* is Camilio Castelo Branco (1825-1890), who authored over 260 books—and, according to James Naremore, "was the first Portuguese writer to live entirely by his pen". Castelo Branco had an illegitimate birth and became an orphan soon afterwards, granting him from the outset some confusion about his identity that seems echoed in Pedro de Silva, the young hero of *Mysteries of Lisbon* (1854), one of his earliest books. This three-volume novel seems quite different in structure, tone, and orientation from the same writer's much slimmer *Doomed Love* (1862)—the source of Manoel De Oliveira's eponymous 1979 masterwork, which immediately preceded Oliveira's long association with the great Paulo Branco, producer of most of the great films of both Ruiz and Oliveira (not to mention key features by Chantal Akerman, Pedro Costa, and Wim Wenders). This makes it all the more pertinent that Castelo Branco's near-namesake launched this particular literary adaptation, and hired Carlos Saboga to write it, before Ruiz stepped in to direct it. (In fact, before Ruiz died, he and Paulo Branco, who made over twenty films together, discussed adapting another Castelo Branco novel that follows one of the major characters in *Mysteries*, Father Dinis, as a soldier in Napoleon's army.)

For all the apparent differences between their source novels, Oliveira's *Amor de perdicao* and the theatrical version of *Os Misterios de Lisboa* both run for about 260 minutes (the TV miniseries version of *Misterios* is about 100 minutes longer). But the former might be described as a modernist and exhaustive representation of a novel. Ruiz's masterpiece is a masterful and selective retelling of one, bridging the popular and arcane strands in his oeuvre with fluidity and assurance.

The long takes and camera movements that bigger budgets made more viable became an important part of his style. (In an interview, Ruiz also remarked that the digital Panavision Genesis camera used on *Misterios* "completely alters the meaning of direction," practically eliminating the need for close-ups and representing a return of cinema to more theatrical techniques.) The challenge of his work as a whole while crossing so many boundaries is the way it obliges us to keep repositioning ourselves, and this is precisely, in fact, what his camera movements do.

As I once wrote of Ruiz's Proust film, "not only camera movements but the gliding displacements of objects and characters [re-create] some of the complex, winding journeys of Proust's sentences. At a climactic concert at a party, rows of listeners can be seen gliding off in separate directions as if on separate mind journeys, and in a much earlier surreal sequence featuring newsreel war footage in a cafe, the narrator, reading a letter, can be seen rising with his chair like a film director seated on a crane, all the way to the top of the room, where he encounters his own childhood self running a projector..." In a comparable way, it's Pedro on his deathbed—after over four hours of picaresque adventures and labyrinthine plot twists, either encountering or imagining himself as a child—that bookends *Mysteries of Lisbon*. Ruiz himself was explicit in his interviews about it being an ending that offers the viewer several choices, none of them exclusive.

Many of the camera movements in *Misterios* are mysteries themselves, plotted in and around the mutable aristocratic characters, and sometimes implicitly suggesting the inquisitive and/or critical viewpoints of servants. This in effect deepens as well as sharpens Ruiz's inquisitive skepticism about narrative itself—as well as which class it can sometimes belong to. And where we choose to position ourselves in relation to all this mystery becomes, of course, part of the experience.

Chantal Akerman: The Integrity of Exile and the Everyday

I still haven't fully recovered from the rude shock of hearing about the suicide of Chantal Akerman on October 6, 2015. The following was originally published in Retrospektive Chantal Akerman, *a publication of the Viennale/Austrian Filmmuseum, 2011, and the second issue of the online* Lola *(lolajournal.com), 2012. It grew out of several reviews written for the* Chicago Reader. *I've slightly abridged and tweaked it here.*

Does one's integrity ever lie in what he is not able to do? I think that usually it does, for free will does not mean one will, but many wills conflicting in one man [sic].

— Flannery O'Connor

If I have a reputation for being difficult, it's because I love the everyday and want to present it. In general people go to the movies precisely to escape the everyday.

— Chantal Akerman

A yearning for the ordinary as well as the everyday runs through Akerman's work like a recurring, plaintive refrain. It is a longing that takes many forms: part of it is simply her ambition to make a commercially successful movie; another part is the desire of a self-destructive, somewhat regressive neurotic—Akerman herself in *Saute ma ville* (1968), *La chambre* (1972), *Je, tu, il, elle* (1974), and *L'homme à la valise* (1983); Delphine Seyrig in *Jeanne Dielman, 23 Quai de Commerce, 1080 Bruxelles* (1975); Aurore Clement in *Les rendez-vous d'Anna* (1978); Circé Lethem in *Portrait d'une jeune fille de la fin des années 60 à Bruxelles* (1993)—to go legit and be like "normal" people. *Je, tu, il, elle* and *Les rendez-vous d'Anna* both feature a bisexual heroine who wants to either resolve an unhappy relationship with another woman or to go straight; in *Saute ma ville*, *Je*, *tu*, *il*, *elle*, *Jeanne Dielma*n, and *L'homme à la valise*, the desire to be "normal" is largely reflected in the efforts of the heroine simply to inhabit a domestic space. (This can occasionally develop certain farcical aspects, such as Akerman covering her ankles as well as her shoes with shoe polish in *Saute ma ville*, or in practically all of her 1984 *J'ai faim, j'ai froid*, the opening sketch of *Paris vus par...20s ans après*—an entire coming-of-age film compressed into a dozen frenetic, hilarious, and ultimately touching minutes.)

This desire for normalcy accounts for much of the difficulty of assimilating Akerman's work to any political program, feminist or otherwise. As an account of domestic oppression and repression, *Jeanne Dielman* largely escapes these strictures, and Akerman herself has admitted that this film can be regarded as feminist. But she also once refused to allow *Je*, *tu*, *il*, *elle* to be shown in a gay and lesbian film festival, and more generally has often denied that she considers herself a feminist filmmaker, despite the efforts of certain feminist film critics to claim her as one.

On one hand, her films are extremely varied. Some are in 16-millimeter and some are in 35; some are narrative and some are nonnarrative; the running times range from about 11 minutes to 201 and the genres range from autobiography to personal psychodrama to domestic drama to romantic comedy to musical to documentary—a span that still fails to include a silent, not-exactly-documentary study of a run-down New York hotel (*Hotel Monterey*, 1972), a vast collection of miniplots covering a single night in a city (*Toute une nuit*, 1982), and a feature-length string of Jewish jokes recited by immigrants in a vacant lot in Brooklyn at night (*Food, Family and Philosophy* aka *Histoires d'Amérique*, 1989), among other oddities.

On the other hand, paradoxically, there are few important contemporary filmmakers whose range is as ruthlessly narrow as Akerman's, formally and emotionally. Most of her films, regardless of genre, come across as melancholy, narcissistic meditations charged with feelings of loneliness and anxiety; and nearly all of them have the same hard-edged painterly presence and monumentality, the same precise sense of framing, locations, and empty space.

More generally, if I had to try to summarize the cinema of Chantal Akerman, thematically and formally, in a single phrase, "the discomfort of bodies in rooms" would probably be my first choice. And "the discomfort of bodies inside shots" might be the second.

It's treacherous, of course, to attempt to squeeze an oeuvre as complex and as varied as Akerman's into anything as formulaic as either of those phrases, and one would have to regard some of their applications rather freely. In the case of *D'est* (1993), for example, which is most likely her greatest documentary, "rooms" would have to include such wide-open spaces as a crowded railroad station where sleeping bodies are crowded together like so many dropped handkerchiefs and a no less populated and urban bus stop in Moscow where a blanket of snow is falling, Similarly "open" public spaces dominate her equally melancholic, New-York-based *News from Home* (1977) and *Histoires d'Amérique*. *Toute une nuit*, an insomniac's movie about insomniacs, ends with a sequence in which a couple's lovemaking is gradually smothered, and all but obliterated from our consciousness, by the hectoring sounds of early-morning traffic outside—a kind of dialectical war between interior and exterior. The tortured aggressiveness of such a moment is part of what Akerman's filmmaking is about—cold, elegantly symmetrical compositions and brutal sounds being hammered into our skulls with an obstinate will to power that sometimes makes Sylvester Stallone, Arnold Schwarzenegger, Sam Peckinpah, and Clint Eastwood seem like frolicking pussycats in comparison.

Yet it's hard to be too conclusive about this impression of aggressiveness. By way of contrast, *Nuit et jour* (1991) reverses the mood of *Toute une nuit* and initially presents insomnia as a kind of precondition for the utopian romance of Julie and Jack, an infatuated young couple from the provinces who've recently come to Paris and live in a small flat near Boulevard Sebastopol—a sentiment expressed at the very outset of the film as they lie together in bed: "Are you sleeping?" "No. Are you?" "No." "You and I never sleep." "Never when we are together." "We like movement better." "Yes, it's true." "When I sleep, I don't live." "Neither do I." "Right now, I prefer living." "So do I." A little later their dialogue resumes: "Maybe we should meet people." "Next year." "And get a telephone?" "Next year." And finally, after they make love, this closing exchange: "You must sleep, Jack. You'll have an accident." "Next year." (Later on, when the plot devolves into a variation on *Jules et Jim*—with a female offscreen narrator to replace Truffaut's male one—the romantic tone becomes more complicated.)

And in the case of *Jeanne Dielman*, which is almost certainly Akerman's greatest fiction film, one would have to admit that the discomfort of the title heroine (Delphine Seyrig) in the rooms of her own flat only begins in earnest during the latter portion of this 201-minute feature, when her routinized life slowly starts to become unraveled. Prior to that, however, one could argue that *Jeanne Dielman*'s "comfort" is strictly a matter of her keeping an encroaching sense of panic at bay through her compulsive routines—a feeling of panic that eventually overtakes and engulfs her.

There are of course many other exceptions or variations to my formula that could be found in Akerman's work: "Rooms" may not adequately cover the shopping-mall setting of her musical *Golden Eighties* (1986), and, for that matter, "discomfort" may be imprecise regarding *Les années 80* (1985), its documentary prequel. The shopping mall in *Golden Eighties*, for instance, sets up an interesting ambiguity about whether one is inside or outside—until the shock of the ending, when the film finally moves out into the open air. The frightening entrapments of *La captive* (2000), loosely derived from Proust's *La prisonnière* and *Albertine disparue* (as well as evoking, more indirectly, Bresson's *Les dames du Bois de Boulogne* through its contemporary setting that evokes the past, and Hitchcock's *Vertigo* through its hypnotic, obsessional intensity), may have more to do with brains and feelings than with rooms.

It's also possible that some of the discomforts found in *Nuit et jour*, *A Couch in New York* (1996), and *Demain on déménage* (2004) may be more a matter of real estate than of rooms per se. Toward the end of *Nuit et jour*, Julie (Guilaine Londez) and Jack (Thomas Langmann) decide to knock out a wall in their flat, largely as a means of rejuvenating their own relationship, and the physical change in their apartment leads them to decide to throw a party and join a larger world. *A Couch in New York* develops its initial premises by crosscutting between dissimilar flats in Manhattan and Paris that are exchanged by a psychotherapist (William Hurt) and a dancer (Juliette Binoche), with many farcical results. And *Demain on déménage*—another comedy, set almost entirely in a Paris flat—focuses on a young porn author (Sylvie Testud) whose recently widowed mother (Aurore Clement), a piano teacher, moves into the flat, then tries to sell it.

More generally, any close consideration of Akerman's early films over the first decade of her career—*Saute ma ville* in Brussels, *La chambre* and *Hotel Monterey* in New York, and then, back in Europe, *Je, tu, il, elle, Les rendez-vous d'Anna*, and *News from Home* (which combines images from New York with letters sent from Brussels)—has to acknowledge that the discomfort of bodies in rooms, including Akerman's own body in the first, second, and fourth (and, more implicitly, in the sixth) of these, is a virtual constant. "I want people to lose themselves in the frame and at the same time to be truly confronting the space," Akerman once said of *Hotel Monterey* (as recalled by Michael Koresky, on the DVD of that film released on Criterion's Eclipse label), which implies that the discomfort of spectators—by which I refer to both their placements and their displacements—is as pertinent as the discomfort of the on-screen bodies.

Like Akerman, whose middle name is Anne, Anna Silver in *Les rendez-vous d'Anna* is a Belgian Jewish filmmaker; and like Akerman when she made the film, she's in her late twenties and currently lives in Paris. The film covers a three-day trip she takes by train back to Paris from Cologne, where she introduces a film (an event that we don't see) and picks up Heinrich (Helmut Griem), a schoolteacher whom she later kicks out of her hotel bed.

On her arrival at the Cologne station, she's met by Ida (Magali Noël)—the mother of a former fiancé whom she has twice changed her mind about marrying. They converse until evening, when Anna boards the Paris train where she talks to a young German who's moving to Paris (Hanns Zischler). She gets off the train in Brussels, her hometown, where she's met by her mother (Léa Massari). Instead of going home, where Anna's ailing father is already asleep, they check into a hotel where Anna, lying naked beside her mother in bed, describes a lesbian affair she has recently become involved in and feels good about.

The next night, arriving in Paris, she's picked up by her regular boyfriend (Jean-Pierre Cassel), who takes her to still another hotel. Finding him feverish, she takes a cab to a late-night *pharmacie* to buy him some medicine. Finally returning home—it's still dark—Anna plays back the recorded phone messages that have come during her absence.

As a plot, this is obviously quite minimal. Each of the "encounters" described above consists mostly of a monologue—by Heinrich, Ida, the German on the train, Anna herself (to her mother), her French lover, Anna again (when she sings him a song), and the voices on her recording machine (one of which, incidentally, is Akerman's). In keeping with Akerman's usual respect for real time, large chunks of this mainly unacted material are simply set down like slabs in front of the viewer without the usual punctuation of camera movements, fades, or dissolves. In a manner recalling Bresson, Antonioni and Straub-Huillet, the locations where these monologues are placed seem featured, lingered over—persisting before, during, after, and even in between the words that are spoken there, constantly threatening to swallow them up.

René Magritte's painting *Man With Newspaper* (1927-'28) tells me something about the customary disquiet of Akerman's world. In it, four panels, two on top and two on the bottom, show the same corner of a sitting room, with one difference: in the first panel a man is seated at the table by the window reading a newspaper, and in the other three panels, neither the man nor the newspaper is in evidence. A narrative is implied between the first and second panel—the disappearance of the man and newspaper—without being confirmed, and we're left with the eerie fact of three identical "empty" rooms. Similarly, many of Akerman's settings suggest absence even more than presence.

§

Akerman has described her first film, *Saute ma ville*, made when she was only 18, as her attempt to do something Chaplinesque. I suspect she was thinking about Chaplin's fourth comedy short made at Mutual, his justly celebrated *One A.M.* (1916), where, apart from a cab driver glimpsed briefly at the very beginning, Chaplin is the only actor in sight, his character arriving at his own home and proceeding to interact catastrophically with the various props he encounters as he tries to get upstairs and go to bed

Chaplin's narrative pretext for all the comic chaos engendered is his character's extreme drunkenness. Akerman—whom we hear manically and wordlessly singing offscreen from the very outset, and is also the only character we see, arriving home and in her case restricting her activities there to a kitchen—provides no narrative context of any kind beyond a certain punklike rebellion against the various domestic rituals that she performs or pretends to perform. These are the same sort of rituals, such as cooking, eating, cleaning up, and polishing shoes that, seven years later, Jeanne Dielman will compulsively embrace, although in this case Akerman's own frenzied and parodic enactments eventually culminate in a series of offscreen explosions from a gas stove that fulfill the film's apocalyptic title. (The "cleaning up" that she performs earlier is in such a destructive manner that it recalls the final sequence in Vera Chytilova's *Daisies*, released two years earlier, when the two teenage heroines pretend to "clean up" after their protracted and extravagant food orgy inside a banquet room.)

The two major films of Akerman that follow, both silent—the sixty-five minute *Hotel Monterey* and the eleven-minute *La Chambre*, both shot by Babette Mangolte, who introduced her to the North American avant-garde cinema of that period (a major influence), and would subsequently shoot *Jeanne Dielman*—are also "studies" of solitude, but in this case ones where a minimalist aesthetic and a particular sense of rooms and shots as almost interchangeable predominate.

Akerman appears in almost a third of the films excerpted in her *Chantal Akerman par Chantal Akerman* (1997)—more if one adds a couple in which we hear her offscreen voice—and one of the fascinations of this critical and selective tour is watching her own gestures being reproduced in other films by some of her actresses. (Aurore Clement nibbling food off a stray hotel tray on a hallway floor in *Les rendez-vous d'Anna* comes just after we see Akerman compulsively devouring sugar in *Je, tu, il, elle*.) But Akerman's disarming tactic of using herself as a star—which she criticizes in her introduction as a dubious form of bravado—and some of her stars as versions of herself has to be weighed against her determination to film anonymous, everyday people as if they were just as important and her determination to integrate and intermingle stars and nobodies in films such as *Les années 80* and *Histoires d'Amérique*. Indeed, it's part of the dialectical power of *Jeanne Dielman* to simultaneously present us with both a star performance (by Delphine Seyrig) and a sense of the mundane, giving the everyday and the unexceptional a monumental, epic style. The sorrow and beauty throughout Akerman's work, with its shining nocturnal moods and glowering compulsive activities, has a lot to do with exalting the unexceptional, the neglected corners of the world around us.

By the same token, one could argue that, paraphrasing Flannery O'Connor, Akerman's integrity is partially a matter of what she isn't able to do—which is in part a recurring desire and a relative failure to make lighthearted, commercial genre films, such as a musical à la Jacques Demy and/or a romantic comedy à la Woody Allen. The second of these aspirations, admittedly, crops up only intermittently in *A Couch in New York*—in some of the extended dialogues between friends as they walk through Manhattan, in various gags about New York neurotics speaking to their psychotherapists, and in the use of Cole Porter's "Night and Day" over the final credits. But even though Akerman shows some adeptness in directing both Juliette Binoche and the dog that usually accompanies her, which helps to compensate for her lack of a light touch elsewhere, her style of filmmaking remains almost dialectically opposed to Allen's dialogue-driven comedy, treating the texts of her characters' speeches almost as if they were found objects rather than the patter found in standup routines.

By contrast, it could be argued that the urge to create a Demy-like musical has already yielded at least four separate Akerman features—not only *Les années 80* (forty minutes of videotaped auditions and rehearsals, followed by three completed musical numbers) and *Golden Eighties* (the finished musical, with a somewhat different cast), but also *Toute une nuit* (which often suggests a depressive musical, a musical without music) and the opening stretches of *Nuit et jour*, which arguably represent her most successful effort to date in this direction, perhaps because the "musical" elements here are more integrated and used more lightly, when Julie starts to sing wordlessly along with the lush strings on the sound track—sometimes in unison, sometimes augmenting or complementing the musical backdrop. After she and Jack walk downstairs to go their separate ways—he to his taxi, she on her nightly tour of the city—she begins to sing out loud to the same tune, this time without accompaniment, a kind of celebration of her life as we've come to understand it. "During the day, he tells me about his night, and at night I wander across Paris. . . . We don't have a child; it isn't really the right time. . . . I always get home before him. I wait for the day and erase the night. It's summer in Paris, the time for abandonment, when days are the longest. . . . We don't have a phone, but we don't know anyone anyway." Sometimes we see her singing while she walks and sometimes we merely hear her offscreen, but the movement of her walk and the movement of the melodic line both proceed continuously and fluidly.

One of the more touching aspects of *Les années 80* and *Golden Eighties* is that Akerman's own exuberant conducting of a robust waltz sung by an actress in a sound studio in the former film is far more animated, physical, emotional, and moving than the "finished" version performed by the actress is in the second film. More generally, Akerman's documentaries might be said to run the gamut from the relatively routine (*Un jour Pina a demandé* [1983] to the extremely powerful (*D'est* and *De l'autre côté* [2002]), with *Les années 80* and *Chantal Akerman par Chantal Akerman* somewhere in between these extremes.

Perhaps the two most extreme expressions of neurotic regression in Akerman's work after *Saute ma ville* are the first third of *Je, tu, il, elle* and the last half of *L'homme à la valise*, both mocking self-portraits of a sort as well as speculative fictions which show Akerman alone in a room, her character steadily growing crazier and more obsessive over several days. In the far more comic *L'homme à la valise*, in which she is sharing an apartment with a young American man she hardly knows, she barricades herself in a single room and sets up a TV camera by the window to monitor his various comings and goings.

In *Je, tu, il, elle*, Akerman's first feature (and the only one to date in black and white), she compulsively repositions the mattress in her one-room, ground floor flat as well as the voluminous pages of the letter, apparently to an unnamed friend or lover, that she keeps writing and rewriting (rearranging the various drafts in various rows like playing cards in a game of solitaire), and the clothes (black sweater and trousers) that she keeps taking off and then either putting them back on or draping over her body like bed sheets, meanwhile, no less compulsively, eating spoons full of sugar from a paper bag. Later in this sequence, even the various mounds of sugar get repositioned as well—transferred via her spoon back from the tops of the pages of the letter to the paper bag, for instance. All of these manic activities might be said to resemble the various creative options of an artist working within a minimalist context and strictly for herself (an audience of one), yet completely uncertain about her various decisions—namely, a je who has not yet found a tu, an il, or an elle. And all of this activity is periodically described by her in offscreen narration, recounting her various actions dryly and factually, adding occasional updates on the people or the snow that she sees outside through her window.

Cut to a freeway under a drizzling rain, where we see her picked up as a hitchhiker by a young truck driver, inaugurating the film's second part. It's part of the film's evolution as indicated in its title that she continues to narrate offscreen, but more sparingly, until her offscreen voice disappears in the third sequence. Most of this second sequence unfolds like a road movie without dialogue, much of it punctuated by the silent meals of the two characters (the first and longest of which is accompanied by them watching an offscreen television set in a diner). In one sequence she masturbates him while he's driving; the only words we hear are his various instructions to her and his commentary on his family as well as what's currently happening. Basically, according to what we see and hear, one might almost say that she's "servicing" him like a vehicle; after existing only for herself in the first sequence she appears to exist mainly for this stranger in the second. And only in the third sequence, where she visits a young woman she already knows—a sequence that culminates in their nude lovemaking on a fully made-up bed—does she appear to achieve a relationship with some measure of equality (although even here, one might say that she's initially "serviced" by her friend, who dutifully feeds her when she announces first "I'm hungry" and then, somewhat later, "More").

In *Chantal Akerman par Chantal Akerman*, Akerman speaks about the important influence exerted on her career by having learned that her maternal grandmother painted large canvases, none of which seem to have survived, which showed women who appeared to be looking out at the viewer. She also cites in the same documentary the Second Commandment and Jewish taboos against visual representation, especially art produced by and about women, all of which suggests that both the monumentality of Akerman's own work and its periodic sense of transgression can both be described in part as a form of feminist rebellion.

There are at least two potential obstacles to appreciating Akerman's films that have a lot to do with the terminology routinely employed by film criticism.

The first has to do with the role of a director and how it's perceived. It's widely believed, with some justice, that film criticism and appreciation in general made a significant step forward when the French term *mise en scène* started becoming more widespread during the 1960s. Becoming aware of the director, or metteur en scène, meant becoming aware of a director's style and vision. Mise en scène literally means "place on the stage," making us aware that it is the director who places the actors, the décor, and the camera in relation to one another. It is the stage of filmmaking that takes place after the writing of the script, during the shooting, and before the editing, and because the commercial Hollywood cinema tends to break up these three activities according to a strict division of labor, the importance of mise en scène as a creative concept is that it is distinct from both of the other processes.

But there is another French term, in some ways an even more important one, that hasn't entered common usage: découpage. In terms of its popular French usage, it has three separate but interlocking meanings: the final form of a script, the breakdown of a film into separate shots and sequences prior to filming, and the basic structure of a finished film. (The verb découper means "to cut out" or "to cut up.") The term découpage implies that there is a continuity between script and editing—a continuity imposed not by a writer, director, or editor, but by a filmmaker who carries the project through from beginning to end—and that mise en scène becomes a means toward an end in this continuity rather than an end in itself.

If the term mise en scène implies an industrial model of cinema, the term découpage implies an artistic or artisanal model. The latter term makes sense in France, where a filmmaker's right to final cut is a part of actual law; it makes less sense in countries where even the writer-directors who have an unusual amount of creative freedom—Woody Allen, for instance—do not produce a découpage in the sense that Robert Bresson does. (As we know from Ralph Rosenblum and Robert Karen's book *When the Shooting Stops . . . the Cutting Begins*, practically all of Allen's features are [or were] restructured and re-created in the cutting room, and the original scripts are quite different from the finished products.)

In this context it is misleading to talk merely about Akerman's mise en scène in spite of her close attention to framing, because from that vantage point, many of her movies look rather anemic. It's her découpage that matters—that is, not only what happens in her shots but what happens between them, among them, across them, and through them. (The same thing applies to practically all of the most important filmmakers in the history of movies: Robert Bresson,

Carl Dreyer, Sergei Eisenstein, Alfred Hitchcock, Kenji Mizoguchi, Yasujiro Ozu, Jean Renoir, Andrei Tarkovsky, and Orson Welles may be known to us as master directors, but their art is ultimately the art of découpage rather than simply mise en scène.) Consequently, comparing Akerman to someone like Woody Allen, Paul Mazursky, or Steven Soderbergh on the level of "mise en scène" is about as meaningless as comparing a microscope to a microwave, or a minimalist artist to an entertainer.

"Carl Dreyer's basic problem as an artist," wrote the late Robert Warshow in 1948, reflecting on Dreyer's *Day of Wrath*, "is one that seems almost inevitably to confront the self-conscious creator of 'art' films: the conflict between a love for the purely visual and the tendencies of a medium that is not only visual but also dramatic." This is a problem addressed in one way or another by each of Akerman's features to date.

Her many efforts to combine and somehow reconcile the visual with the dramatic start with *Jeanne Dielman*. *News From Home* is essentially a nonnarrative study of Manhattan exteriors accompanied by Akerman's voice as she reads letters she received from her mother while she was in New York, material that inevitably introduces narrative elements. A similar mix is operative in *Histoires d'Amérique*, although here the setting is a single park and the narrative elements come from the various jokes being told. *Les rendez-vous d'Anna*, *L'homme à la valise*, and *Golden Eighties* are all unabashed story films, but the first two make use of some of the claustrophobic painterly elements in *Hotel Monterey*, while the third defines narrative as an interlocking series of mini-plots. *Toute une nuit* is also made up of mini-plots, but other than occurring over a single night most of them don't interlock, and the overall effect is more painterly than narrative. *Les années 80*, about Akerman auditioning and rehearsing actresses for *Golden Eighties*, regards these actresses in part as painterly subjects or models and incorporates narrative only in the sense that it charts the development of certain songs and performances.

In broad terms, the polarity between painting and narrative is one between persistence and development. A painting exists in space, a narrative in time; persisting is what a painting does in time, and developing is what a narrative does in space. Consequently, insofar as Akerman's films resemble paintings, character and plot development is always something of a problem, and insofar as they impose narratives, the persistence of people and places without any development is also something of a problem.

The second obstacle to appreciating Akerman's films has to do with Akerman being a Belgian Jew—even though she has spent extended periods of her adult life and shot several of her films in both France and the U.S. Most of her films are in French, and it has been all too easy for many critics to discuss her work as if it were essentially part of the French cinema; but this is an impulse that should be resisted. The cultural dominance of France and the U.S. in relation to such countries as Belgium, Switzerland, and Canada has led to a streak of cultural imperialism that confuses our understanding of filmmakers as important as Michael Snow (Canadian) and Jean-Luc Godard (Swiss)—two of Akerman's major influences—as well as Akerman herself.

The main point to be stressed is that because she is both Belgian and Jewish, Akerman has a stance that is essentially that of an outsider in an international context. If one combines this stance with her preoccupation with normality and the everyday, one is reminded of what the English writer and broadcaster George Melly once said about Magritte: "He is a secret agent, his object is to bring into disrepute the whole apparatus of bourgeois reality. Like all saboteurs, he avoids detection by dressing and behaving like everybody else."

While it is possible to link her work to that of a few other, much lesser known Belgian independents—such as Samy Szlingerbaum, with whom she collaborated on one of her earliest films, the hardly ever shown *Le 15/8* (1973)—and to see connections with a few Belgian painters (not only Magritte, but also Paul Delvaux, whose surrealist night scenes bear an eerie resemblance to some of her shots—although she once told me that she thought his lighting was "much better" than hers), it is probably even more pertinent to note the degree to which exile is a recurring theme in her work that climaxes in one of her last films.

De l'autre côté is worth considering in some detail, both for its personal significance and for the way it can be seen as the concluding part of a documentary trilogy preceded by *D'est* and the much inferior 1999 *Sud*. *D'est*, which travels from East Germany to Moscow soon after the collapse of communism, contains no interviews, and might be said to trace some of Akerman's own personal family roots at the very moment when many of the people she's filming are being uprooted, both physically and emotionally. *Sud*, contains several interviews, though it elides her questions; it focuses on the town of Jasper, Texas, shortly after the brutal and racist murder there of James Boyd Jr. Here she's basically a sympathetic tourist bearing mute witness to a hate crime—appalled by what she hears and imagines, but not bringing any fresh insights to her subject.

In *De l'autre côté* we hear Akerman interviewing Mexicans in Spanish and Americans in English. This time it's evident that her interest in her subject goes well beyond sympathetic tourism. The final sequence, shot from the front of a car traveling down a freeway at night, features her own beautiful and moving monologue, spoken in French, in which she speculates about the fate of an interviewee's mother, who disappeared after crossing the border into the U.S. We never see this woman, and she isn't mentioned before this monologue, so we wind up imagining her as we would a character in a short story. Akerman traces some of her jobs and finds oblique references to her in the stray comments of other people, following the woman's elusive trajectory as if she were a ghost fading into the anonymity of the hypnotic superhighway. This character's fugitive and semifictional existence, which flits in and out of our consciousness before vanishing, provides a heartbreaking summation of all the hard facts about her and other Mexican migrants we've been absorbing over the previous ninety minutes. This is sensitive portraiture and investigative journalism, maintaining a respectful, inquisitive distance from its subjects that recalls some of Walker Evans's photographs of Alabama sharecroppers in his book with James Agee, *Let Us Now Praise Famous Men*. In a way, Akerman's powerful monologue serves as a kind of counterpart to Agee's impassioned and empathetic prose.

She begins the film by interviewing a twenty-one-year-old Mexican on the Mexican side of the border about his older brother; he tried to cross to the U.S. with a group, and all of them eventually perished in the desert. Next she focuses on portions of the border itself—a wide, dusty road, a field where three kids play baseball, and another road flanked by a high wall. Then she interviews Delfina, a woman in her late seventies, about her family, including the son and grandson she lost when they tried to cross the border. Her husband less stoically bemoans their loss. Akerman then turns back to the various landscapes along the border. Only much later in the film does she finally get around to people and places on the American side—spending time in a restaurant, then talking to a rancher and his wife, who express fears about Mexicans "taking over and doing a lot of damage" by, for instance, carrying diseases. We hear Akerman ask them if September 11 has changed things. The wife says, "It makes us realize life is short." Her husband responds by saying he considers anyone who comes onto his property a trespasser, and the warning sign doesn't have to be in Spanish either. "This is America," he concludes.

The cumulative impact of the eventless shots of the border wall that appear periodically over the course of the film is striking. In themselves the shots are fairly nondescript and uninteresting, but the more we accept the wall as part of the everyday surroundings, the more disquieting and menacing it becomes. This is especially true after we see lights on it at night and helicopters with searchlights moving along it, giving the settings some of the ambience of a lunar landscape. And we can't shake that impression when we see illegal aliens being tracked from the vantage point of a plane in the daytime. The wall that appeared to be a neutral dividing line at the beginning of the film seems more and more like a scar once we see the kinds of pain and anguish it causes. And as Akerman's title suggests, which side of the border we're viewing it from can make all the difference. Being outside and being displaced remain not only constants in her work, along with an absorption in the everyday; they become defining values.

A Matter of Life and Death: *A.I. Artificial Intelligence*

Written for the 40th anniversary issue of the French quarterly magazine Trafic *(Winter 2011). I subsequently introduced a screening of this film at the Centre Georges Pompidou on January 12, 2012 as part of a film series built around this issue.*

1

Am I weeping for the death of David's mother, for the death of humans, for the death of photography, or for the death of movies?

—James Naremore, *On Kubrick*

The scene in question, the final one in *A.I. Artificial Intelligence*, features a robot boy, David (Haley Joel Osment), and a cloned duplication of a human woman, Monica (Frances O'Connor), who died centuries before and whom David was still earlier programmed by Monica to love as a mother. These characters are shown going to bed together and falling asleep, the robot for the first time and Monica for the last time, after spending a happy day together. This is an experience of orgasmic closure and extinction afforded to David by sympathetic extraterrestials visiting Earth who have found him frozen in ice long after mankind has perished, and have searched his memory for cinematic images of his life that they share among themselves and then reproduce in actuality. The day itself that they create for David is a fiction made up of these shared images—an Oedipal birthday party for David, who never had a birthday because he was never born, enjoyed without the presence of a father or brother, where David draws "storyboards" of his adventures 2000 years earlier to show to a receptive if uncomprehending Monica.

David—the first in a line of robots designed to love humans—was purchased by Monica's husband Henry after their real-life son Martin entered a long-term coma from which he might never recover. In other words, David was invented in order to fill a gap, and we also discover that David's unscrupulous inventor, Allen Hobby (William Hurt), made him a precise replica of his own lost son. So he can never be anything more than an approximate substitute, just as the clone of Monica, created from a lock of the real Monica's hair preserved for 2000 years by David's teddy bear (a fellow super-toy named Teddy), can also never be anything else.

In David's case, however, the differences between a real and ersatz Monica are crucial because only the latter can love him. Two millennia earlier, some time after she programmed David to love her, the original Monica discarded and abandoned him. He became unacceptable once her own son recovered from his coma and returned home, even though initially David was treated like a second child. But after a series of taunts and challenges by Martin towards his sibling rival, the boy robot started to malfunction—attempted to eat spinach at one family meal, which necessitated mechanical surgery, and at a birthday party for Martin, after some of Martin's friends threatened to cut David with a knife, David seized Martin, asking for his protection, and fell with him to the bottom of a swimming pool.

David has always been a simulacra, and in the film's final scene the resurrected Monica is one as well; both are as reproducible as the separate prints of a film. Viewers who criticize their final scene together—also an improved simulacrum, in this case of much earlier scenes between them—as sentimental usually overlook that it is occurring long after humanity has died out. This means that the death Naremore refers to has to be the death of an emotion or idea—even if, as the film's offscreen narration implies, it is also the birth of a dream, a robot's dream. Perhaps it could be regarded as an artificial and A.I.-manufactured footnote to the human race, a sort of ghostly echo. Something, in short, that is very much like a film.

Like Naremore, I weep during the final scene of *A.I.* and I don't know who or what I'm weeping for—even though, like him, I can recall the line cited in the film by Yeats (a poet who also once wrote, "In dreams begin responsibilities"): "The world's more full of weeping/ than you can understand." Like him, I suspect that my tears must have something to do with both the loss of my own mother and my experience of cinema—what it means to be born and then to be abandoned, and also what it means to bask in the familial warmth and shelter of a film and a film theater before being ejected from both. Prior to this scene, what has dominated this tragic film has involved a feeling of chill and abandonment, from the ocean waves in the first shot through various images of boys in frozen coffins that recall the "sleeping" astronauts in suspended animation in Kubrick's *2001: A Space Odyssey* (1968) to an image of David, bereft and alone, at the bottom of the swimming pool. (Similarly, David's frozen underwater prison in the ruins of Coney Island is created by a detached ferris wheel, an image drawn from Spielberg's 1979 film *1941*.)

In the pessimistic cosmology shared by Kubrick and Spielberg, cinema and death appear to be the only enduring realities, each one dominated by fixation on a maternal figure. The Blue Fairy, a deity from *Pinocchio*, is described by Hobby as "part of the great human flaw—to wish for things that don't exist"; David seeks her out to make him a "real" boy and thus gain Monica's love. And the Monica who loves David and appears only in the film's final scene is a deity derived from life, but no less a fiction. For Hobby, a version of both Mephistopheles and Frankenstein, human flaws, including his own, can be "great" and therefore cherished, but for David, condemned to love someone who won't love him back, they can only be lamented. Both characters, in effect, are incurable cinephiles. And the film brings us closer to David than to Hobby, so that we ultimately love a film that refuses to love us back.

A.I. is a film about having been programmed emotionally—something that the cinema does to us all, and a subject that my first book, (1980), *Moving Places: A Life at the Movies*, attempted to explore. This is one reason why, as a profound meditation on the difference between the human and the mechanical, *A.I.* constitutes one of the best allegories about cinema that I know. And to recount this allegory in terms of a mother's love makes it even more devastating.

2

Perhaps the most overrated virtue in science fiction is an aptitude for prophecy. This virtue has almost nothing to do with why Olaf Stapledon's *Star Maker* (1937), which recounts the life and breadth of the cosmos, is for me the greatest of all science fiction novels. "Stapledon doesn't shore up inventions to distract or stupefy the reader," Jorge Luis Borges in his 1965 Preface to the novel; "with an honest rigor, he pursues and retraces the complex and obscure vicissitudes of his coherent dream." And the true basis of this coherent dream was Stapledon's grasp of 1937 England, not so much his very beautiful and persuasive vision of the birth, death, and breadth of the cosmos that derived from this concrete experience.

Stanley Kubrick died in the same country sixty-two years later, only two years prior to 2001 (ironically, the same year that *A.I.* was released), and among the many plausible reasons for considering *2001* a masterpiece, prophecy about the persistence of the Cold War into the second millennium, with the planet neatly divided between the U.S. and Russia, clearly isn't one of them. By contrast, the initial vision of the future in *A.I.* seems frighteningly plausible from the vantage point of 1999 or 2001 or 2011 (when this essay is being written). Just as *2001* extends portions of the Cold War premises of *Doctor Strangelove*, *A.I.* develops the premise of artificial intelligence as represented by HAL in *2001*. Yet what seems most prophetically plausible is the prediction of what happens to Earth and humanity prior to this development—the destruction of the Earth as we know it that makes the displacement of humans by robots inevitable. "They made us too smart, too quick, and too many," Gigolo Joe (Jude Law) says to David. "We're suffering for the mistakes they made because when the end comes, all that will be left is us. That's why they hate us." And, by the same token, this is why we prefer the robots in this story to the humans.

Over the image and sound of crashing ocean waves, an offscreen male narrator says, "Those were the years after the ice caps had melted because of the greenhouse gases, and the oceans had risen to drown so many cities along all the shorelines of the world. Amsterdam, Venice, New York, forever lost. Millions of people were displaced, climate became chaotic. Hundreds of millions of people starved in poorer countries. Elsewhere a high degree of prosperity survived when most governments in the developed world introduced legal sanctions to strictly license pregnancies. Which is why robots, who were never hungry and did not consume resources beyond that of their first manufacture, were so essential an economic link in the chain mail of society."

This prelude morphs into a lecture by Professor Allan Hobby (William Hurt) at Cybertronics, a company in a New Jersey facility, about robots, during which he stabs a woman robot in the hand and casually asks her to start undressing as portions of his demonstration. He proposes building a robot who can love humans, creating "a love that will never end," and the moral issue raised by a woman in the audience, which Hobby refuses to address, remains at the film's center. I've argued elsewhere that Kubrick was more of a moralist than Arthur Schnitzler and *Eyes Wide Shut*, unlike *Traumnovelle*, has a villain (Sydney Pollack's Victor Ziegler), so it's important to emphasize that the villains of *A.I.* (Hobby first of all; secondarily Martin, the natural child of Monica and Henry; and more incidentally, the working-class mob of the Flesh Fair) are exclusively human, and that the recurring *détournement* performed by the narrative is to shift our identification from humans to androids. Repeatedly the film turns from making us uncomfortable about the otherness of robots to make us even more uncomfortable about the thoughtlessness and cruelty of humans—and by ending the first sequence with Hobby's female robot applying makeup just before beginning the second sequence with the human Monica applying makeup, the film is already asking us to make comparisons. Ostensibly the film is about the programming of a robot by his adoptive human mother to love her, but the self-programming of Monica—first to accept David as a human and then to reject him—is no less crucial.

Yet one thing that limits *A.I.* both as prophecy and as vision throughout is a venerable Hollywood staple, the reduction of the world to "America." After the fleeting reference to Amsterdam and Venice in the opening narration (a concession that already limits humanity to the West, thereby consigning most of Earth's population to oblivion), the rest of the world ceases to exist for the remainder of the narrative, which restricts all its action over two millennia to New York and environs. Ironically, Disney's *Pinocchio* (1940) was worldlier in its placement of its own American hero and American Blue Fairy within a European setting populated by various Italian and English characters. Yet curiously and inexplicably, the only English as opposed to American accent that we hear in *A.I.* is that of the offscreen narrator. So the conception of a 21st century in *A.I.* that is generically and exclusively American already dates the film as a 20th century conception. (Ironically, Stapledon's own first book, in 1930, *Last and First Men*, purporting to recount the remaining two billion years of human history, founders at least partially as prophecy on a similarly shortsighted premise of an "Americanized" planet.)

3

Unlike many of my colleagues, I can't simply accept *A.I.* as either "a film by Steven Spielberg" or "a film by Stanley Kubrick." I can only read it as a film deriving from the will and consciousness of both of them—one alive and one dead, and encompassing all the dialectical contradictions that this strange collaboration entails. In a way these contradictions become those of cinema itself, what Gilberto Perez has called the material ghost, which confound us about what is living or dead, animate or inanimate, human or robotic—or, in the terms of *A.I.*, "orga" or "mecha."

When he was alive, Kubrick proposed that Spielberg—a friend who first read a treatment for *A.I.* in 1984—direct the film. He gave two reasons: because Spielberg could direct a boy actor more quickly than he could, before the boy had time to visibly age, and because he believed Spielberg would be more adept in handling the story's emotions. Perhaps he was also correctly thinking of Spielberg as the only true successor of Walt Disney, whose major emotional theme is the traumatic loss or absence of parents—especially in *Pinocchio, Dumbo, Bambi*, and *Song of the South*. But it's worth adding that Kubrick arrived at the notion of Spielberg directing *A.I.* only after he explored and then rejected the possibility of a robot playing the robot hero. To my mind, Haley Joel Osment's performance as David is one of the greatest child performances in the history of cinema, but for Kubrick, it seems that any human performance in the role would necessarily qualify as a compromise and concession. So it isn't surprising that the film makes us care chiefly about the robot characters, not about the human ones.

After Kubrick died, his widow and brother-in-law again proposed that Spielberg make the film, because otherwise it would never exist, and Spielberg, after agreeing, wrote his own script derived from the materials generated or supervised by Kubrick—a forty-page treatment by Ian Watson, inspired both by a 1969 Brian Aldiss story ("Super-Toys Last All Summer Long") and by Carlo Collodi's 1883 novel *Pinocchio*, and over a thousand detailed drawings by Chris Baker.

I suspect that Spielberg brought far more faithfulness and seriousness to this project, at least within his own limitations, than he brought to Thomas Keneally's novel of *Schindler's List* or, for that matter, to the subject of the Holocaust. But this is only a suspicion on my part, based mainly on Spielberg's various statements. (He has published many of Baker's drawings, both as DVD extras and in a large-format book about *A.I.* edited by Kubrick's brother-in-law Jan Harlan and Jane M. Struthers [New York: Thames & Hudson, 2009]; but virtually none of Watson's treatment apart from a few stray pages reproduced in the latter has become available.)

I must confess that, even though Spielberg may have made the film's beginning and ending more emotionally powerful than Kubrick could have, his less focused handling of the film's middle section as a succession of fairground attractions (Flesh Fair, Rouge City, a drowned Manhattan and Coney Island) where the sense of spectacle periodically threatens to overwhelm the narrative is somewhat less convincing. Arguably, the only sequence in this section that recovers the purity of the film's beginning and end is David's visit to the factory where he discovers with horror not only his doppelgänger but an endless, assembly-line procession of Davids. Yet even here, the film falters by misplacing Hobby—the principal villain whom neither the film nor David himself ever quite succeeds in morally confronting. By this time, the narrative has become so disgruntled with humanity that it can only turn away from Hobby and his coworkers to concentrate on David and Gigolo Joe and their separate forms of existential doom. (Only Teddy, the film's Jiminy Cricket, seems exempt from the wretchedness of their immortality). Even Joe, who lacks David's capacity for love, becomes morally superior to Hobby, whose morbid love for his dead son led to the blighted creation of David.

Even though Joe, unlike Monica and Hobby, can't experience death, there is no extinction in the film that feels more tragic than his as he's being reeled away like a captured fish, when he says to David, "I am—I was," a four-word summary of his existential dilemma. Cinema lives; but is this a blessing or a malediction?

Discovering *Margaret*

Written for FIPRESCI's website (fipresci.org) on November 7, 2012.

The potential everyday glibness of journalism is surely one of the key factors that distinguishes film reviewing from film criticism. This was painfully brought home to me shortly after reseeing at the Viennale the 150-minute version of Kenneth Lonergan's remarkable *Margaret*, the winner of my jury's FIPRESCI prize, almost a year after first encountering the film at the Gene Siskel Film Center in Chicago. In between these two viewings, I saw Lonergan's 186-minute cut of the same film on a Blu-Ray containing both versions of the film, prompting me to write the following paragraph in my latest column for the Canadian quarterly *Cinema Scope*:

> I'm grateful to Kenneth Lonergan for clarifying in interviews that the 150-minute *Margaret*, which I saw in December 2011 and the 186-minute cut, which I saw in July, are both 'director's cuts,' and now that Fox has released both in one Blu-Ray package, it's hard to say which version I prefer. Both are brilliant messes and finely distilled renderings of the New York Jewish upper-middle-class zeitgeist circa 2003, regardless of whether one regards Anna Paquin's teenage heroine as someone to identify with (apparently the writer-director's position), or as monstrous, or as both (my position). Being able to accommodate all three attitudes, with just as much ambivalence about most of the other major characters, has a lot to do with what keeps this film so vital and worrying. (Jeannie Berlin is a particular standout, but this

movie also contains the only Jean Reno performance I've seen so far that I find likeable.)

Rereading this paragraph shortly after reseeing *Margaret* in Vienna, I was embarrassed by what I'd written, however much I still agree with most of it, because it's now clear to me that the film is anything but a mess. The latter in fact is anything but sprawling or rambling in its storytelling, but is in fact both economical and carefully structured. Whenever Lonergan cuts away to shots of Manhattan cityscapes or to some of the classroom discussions at the private school attended by Lisa (Anna Paquin), the seventeen-year old protagonist—two forms of narrative suspension in relation to the overall plot—the effect is always musical while remaining thematically relevant to the film's larger concerns. As I wrote for the Viennale while trying to encapsulate some of the motivations of my jury in giving *Margaret* our prize, "Evoking some of the massive novels of the late 19th and early 20th century by writers such as Zola and Dreiser, Kenneth Lonergan's masterpiece captures the zeitgeist of Manhattan circa 2003 [that is, in the recent aftermath of the decimation of the World Trade Center and roughly 3,000 people on September 11, 2001] with precision and insight, using its broad cast of flawed characters as microscopes as well as telescopes trained on our conflicted as well as troubled sensibilities."

Among these characters are Lisa, her actress mother (J. Smith-Cameron, Lonergan's real-life spouse) and estranged father (Lonergan himself), the latter's current partner, a stranger named Monica whose grisly death in a traffic accident near the beginning of the film is caused by Lisa's flirtation with a negligent bus driver (Mark Ruffalo), the stranger's best friend (Jeannie Berlin), a Latin American businessman (Jean Reno) dating Lisa's mother, and some of Lisa's teachers and classmates. The fact that *Margaret* boasts over a dozen such figures, all of them unusually well observed and compellingly acted, is part of the film's uncommon achievement. (Arguably the only one who seems unnecessarily skimped and overlooked is Lisa's younger brother.) But beyond this, the film's intricate charting of the seeming impossibility of Lisa finding justice or closure in relation to her traumatic involvement in a stranger's death is especially masterful: the dozen or so characters listed above don't even include the film's remarkable gallery of cops and lawyers, all of them adroitly profiled as well as performed.

This is what finally makes the description of *Margaret* as novelistic ultimately seem insufficient—and not only because the film's title derives from a poem by Gerard Manley Hopkins, but also because Lonergan's skill with actors clearly matches his storytelling gifts.

Diminuendo and Crescendo in Film Criticism: A Conversation with Ehsan Khoshbakht (excerpted)

This piece for Fandor's Keyframe *originally appeared on the day before my seventieth birthday (February 26, 2013). I've expanded and revised a few of my comments.*

In 2015, Ehsan and I put together a sidebar for Il Cinema Ritrovato *in Bologna, Italy, "Jazz Goes to the Movies," and then a reconfigured version a few months later at the Festival on Wheels in Ankara, Turkey, which led both of us to revisit many of these titles and releases.*

I've deleted Ehsan's flattering introduction to our dialogue, which recalls my confession of having briefly fantasized becoming a jazz pianist when I was a teenager, "but then ruled out the possibility after deciding that the life lived by jazz musicians was too difficult and too grim."

Keyframe: You once wrote, "I used to dream of making a film—if someone were to hand me an outsize check and give me carte blanche, which of course I knew would never happen. I wanted to film all of my best friends dancing as uninhibitedly and joyfully as possible alongside the Seine, and then I wanted to devote the next several years of my life to synchronizing their movements to an up-tempo number by Ahmad Jamal's piano trio." Why Ahmad Jamal?

Jonathan Rosenbaum: Maybe because there's so much delight as well as delicacy in his playing, as well as an awesome dynamic range. Plus the fact that he swings so much, and plays with such marvelous economy.

Keyframe: How did you discover jazz and how did your jazz life grow out of that moment?

JR: One of my New York cousins while I was growing up, David Lelyveld, was a big fan of bebop and the Lennie Tristano school (especially Warne Marsh), and he introduced me to those figures. But on my own I had already discovered many others, including Brubeck, Jamal, Miles (specifically, his *'Round Midnight LP*), the MJQ and Stan Kenton. And as mentioned in my autobiographical *Moving Places* (1980), on February 22, 1957, shortly before my fourteenth birthday, I went with my girlfriend at the time, Jean McIntosh, to hear a Louis Armstrong concert at the Sheffield Community Center, in northwestern Alabama. (Because of the Jim Crow laws, we went to the 7 pm show for whites only, not the 9:30 show for "colored" only, although it's worth adding that Satchmo played with his white drummer, Barrett Deems, at both concerts—someone whom I wouldn't see perform live again for almost another forty years, when I caught him one New Year's Eve in Chicago, shortly before his death.) I should add that my mother, who was deeply involved with classical music when she was younger, and played the piano for many years, also had a minor interest in jazz, and she once went to the trouble of getting me a few lessons from a local piano teacher who knew a little bit about jazz, taught me a few chords, and even gave me a couple of his old albums that he no longer listened to—Billy Taylor with Candido and the Oscar Peterson Trio. I also played clarinet in my high school band, and participated in a few local jam sessions. (The usual drummer at those was Donnie Fritts, who years later became a professional pianist for Kris Kristofferson and a composer.)

Later, after I started college at New York University, I got to see a lot of stuff live—most notably (and this list is far from complete, and doesn't include concerts), Mingus, Bud Powell, and Chico Hamilton at Birdland, Miles at the Jazz Gallery (I can recall one stupendous weekday evening—when I got in for only one dollar, a student discount price—he was playing with Coltrane, Cannonball, J.J. Johnson, Bill Evans, Paul Chambers and Philly Joe; and, believe it or not, the Teddy Wilson Trio was playing alternate sets), Miles and Mingus and Bill Evans with Scott LaFaro (among many others) at the Village Vanguard, Roland Kirk and Monk and Ornette Coleman at the Five Spot, and Coltrane's classic quartet as well as Tristano with Marsh and Konitz at the Half Note, Kenny Dorham as well as Roland Kirk at Slug's, and Archie Shepp at some long-gone hangout only a block from NYU. I also saw Martial Solal and Billy Taylor at the Hickory House, but this was probably some years later. Actually, I went to see Mingus at many clubs, with many separate groups, and one of my fondest memories from that period was going up to him at many of those dates and requesting that he play "Peggy's Blue Skylight," which he always did.

After three semesters at NYU, I transferred to Bard College, a two-hour train ride up the Hudson River, where I learned some more piano chords from a few classmates, played in a few jam sessions (at which Chevy Chase played drums—and I once also accompanied Blythe Danner when she sang "Round Midnight" at a club on campus), and heard more live jazz in New York during some weekends. I also produced one concert there myself (hiring Herbie Hancock, Ron Carter, and Tony Williams) and helped to promote another one that was produced by Chevy and Blythe, for the Bill Evans Trio....Incidentally, during my five years in Paris, I was friendly for a brief period with the avant-garde alto sax player Noah Howard, and did an interview with him that I sent off to *Downbeat*. They didn't accept it, but the editor, Don Morgenstern, wrote me back, encouraging me to submit more pieces, which I never did.

Keyframe: How did you incorporate various elements of jazz (mainly improvisation) into your film criticism or your writing in general?

JR: Liberating one's imagination is obviously part of this, and the rhythm of one's prose is another part. In *Moving Places*, the fact that I did a lot of factual research before I did most of the writing was for me a lot like establishing the chords or changes before inventing a solo to ride over them.

Keyframe: "A Jam Session on Non-Narrative" was the intriguing subtitle of a 1978 article of yours. What is the significance of jazz improvisation to you, especially when it comes to film literature?

JR: In this case, the notion of group improvisation was obviously important—complicated by the fact that the two other participants in "Obscure Objects of Desire," Raymond Durgnat and David Ehrenstein, only met for the first time several years after the piece was done. Of course, one of the best things that can happen in a jam session is one idea sparking or giving rise to another; and sometimes one idea can even synthesize one or two other ideas from one or two other individuals preceding it.

Keyframe: Although it is improvisation which is usually associated with jazz as the most prominent and influential factor in that music, for many jazz musicians another term is just as relevant: "swing". We may both agree that it is utterly indefinable, while its connection to a specific rhythmic pulse (which causes joy) is unquestionable, and, to borrow from Richard Cook, it always conveys a sense of forward momentum. Improvisation has been used in cinema and other arts, but is there any possibility that we can employ "swing," too? Personally, I think this feature—which more or less is related to use of language—can be traced in the writings of two essentially American critics, Whitney Balliett (in jazz) and Manny Farber (in cinema). Do you see any practicality in borrowing the term from jazz for our use in film literature?

JR: I wouldn't know how to answer this, except to agree with you that Farber and Balliett both swing (unlike, say, Agee or Ferguson or Martin Williams or even Hodeir as a critic, whatever their other virtues). And, as I believe I've already indicated to you in the past, I think Rafi Zabor's descriptions of jazz solos in his novel *The Bear Comes Home* swing like crazy.

Keyframe: Speaking of André Hodeir, you were his colleague in *Cinema: A Critical Dictionary*, and of course he was a great jazz historian and jazz critic who also wrote about cinema. Have you met him in person?

JR: No, never, alas. But I met and befriended his major English-language translator, Noël Burch, who was also a teaching colleague of his (as well as one of mine much later). For me, Hodeir is something of a role model, especially in what he's taught me about form, and in some ways more as an artist than as a critic—especially his masterpiece *Anna Livia Plurabelle*, which has probably afforded me more listening pleasure than any other jazz work—although I also love it when, as a critic, he compared Gil Evans' work transforming the compositions of others on *Miles Ahead* with the work of Jorge Luis Borges. More generally, I think he's had more to say (and do) regarding the interface between jazz and literature than anyone else has, apart from Rafi Zabor.

I'm fascinated by the fact that, even when Hodeir arguably has his singers on *Anna Livia Plurabelle* mispronounce some of Joyce's puns, there always seems to be a musical reason for doing this. And the fact that this long work undergoes continual transformations is part of its attraction, even though not a single note in it is improvised. I do think it swings, however.

In fact, *Anna Livia Plurabelle* is only the high point in Hodeir's overall transition from music to literature—preceded by *The Worlds of Jazz*, a book of jazz criticism written in diverse literary forms, and followed by *Bitter Ending* (a less notable musical work deriving from another passage in *Finnegans Wake*), and then a series of novels and stories adapting musical forms that occupied him for the remainder of his life and career.

Keyframe: Generally speaking, I don't remember any outstanding reference to jazz among the *Cahiers* circle, and more interestingly, not even in their films, while they had the benefit of hosting many American jazz expatriates in Paris of the late 1950s. For instance, in the four-volume English translation of selected *Cahiers* articles, the word 'jazz' has been used only once. Since you know the cultural environment of France in the 1960s, how do you explain the absence of jazz in *Cahiers*' criticism?

JR: A good question, but I don't know the answer, except to say that Godard, Truffaut, Rivette, Rohmer and Straub-Huillet could basically be described as classicists rather than modernists when it comes to music (with a few notable exceptions, such as the Stockhausen percussion piece effectively used in *La Chinoise* and the free jazz performed in *Merry-Go-Round*). It seems evident now that Solal's excellent score for *Breathless* came about mainly because of the producer and Jean-Pierre Melville rather than Godard's own taste. And of course Louis Malle's use of Miles Davis on his first feature should be mentioned.

Keyframe: Speaking of representation of jazz in movies, it seems not much has changed since you wrote "three errors in four words," when De Niro in *New York, New York* was depicted as "a gifted avant-gardist playing bebop." How would you "update" your comments on the matter of representations?

JR: All I'd like to emphasize here is my conviction that the main missing element in most depictions of jazz on film is musicians listening to one another. (As I said to McCoy Tyner when I met him, one of the most memorable things about the Coltrane Quartet at the Half Note was the intense way they listened to one another—and I also have a powerful memory of sitting next to Lennie Tristano late one night at the Half Note's bar, after his last set, while he was playing back a tape of his own group with Marsh and Konitz, and reacting very audibly as well as visibly to what he liked or didn't like in each of the solos, including his own....Recently watching the beginning of Ingmar Bergman's film of *The Magic Flute*, I was especially struck by the way he focused on listeners in the audience during the Overture. And the way he cut and moved his camera in relation to the music was also impressive, and could probably be studied with profit by the makers of jazz documentaries.

Keyframe: It comes as a surprise that one of the best examples of employing jazz in cinema is accomplished by Iranian film director, Abbas Kiarostami and his *Taste of Cherry* that truly exploits the emotional depth and integrity of "St. James Infirmary," played by Louis Armstrong. It clearly stands in contrast to, let's say Woody Allen, who knows jazz and plays jazz, but his use of this music is limited to nostalgic functions and not necessarily a very clever one. What do you think is the key to Kiarostami's unique achievement in there—a man who is not specifically a jazz fan.

JR: I think I can answer this in one word: soul. But, for whatever it's worth, I also loved the use he made of "Autumn Leaves" when I once got to see *ABC Africa* on an editing table in work print form. He later told me that he decided to use a different kind of music there precisely because "Autumn Leaves" was noticed and recognized by me and others, which wasn't the kind of response he wanted at that point. This makes perfect sense to me, although I still wish he'd kept it in.

Keyframe: Do you see any relation between your favorite jazz musicians and favorite film directors?

JR: I've always thought that Mingus had a lot in common with Godard, especially in the way he incorporated both cultural history and the history of his own art, obliterating many of the distinctions we often make between modern and classical or at least making most of them seem secondary. Frank Zappa also had some of that expansive sweep. I think these artists are political, polemical, and stylistically eclectic in many comparable ways. They have a genius for bringing together styles, forms, and even topics that are generally believed to be incompatible. Otherwise, there might be some similarities in the playful rhythmic games played by Thelonious Monk and Jacques Tati.

Keyframe: As someone who has shown strong ties, as well as intellectual commitment to both art forms—jazz and cinema—how do you think it has widened your scope?

JR: A loose observation I can make linking jazz and film and writing for me, or what I like about all three: I'm preoccupied in a lot of my work with the coexistence of being alone and being part of a group, and discovering expressiveness that way. For me, much of the best jazz, film, and writing grows out of a dialectic between these two kinds of expressiveness, as well as two kinds of response to that expressiveness.

This article was cross-published with *Film Monthly* (Farsi/Persian) and *Dilema Veche* (Romanian). For more on Rosenbaum's jazz writing, see Ehsan Khoshbakht's blog at https://ehsankhoshbakht.blogspot.com/2013/02/JRindex. html, where he's created a jazz-article index for Rosenbaum.

Chunhyang: Im Kwon-taek's Shotgun Marriage

Written for the Busan International Film Festival's Korean Film retrospective catalogue, Fly High, Run Far: The Making of Korean Master Im Kwon-taek, *Fall 2013.*

Preface

I can't pretend to be familiar with Korean history in general and traditional Korean music in particular. But rather than attempt to disguise my ignorance with a handful of facts gleaned from superficial research, I prefer to approach *Chunhyang* (2000, 136 min.) in broader, more generalized, and less historical terms as a film confronting issues of representation relating to live performance as well as cinema, and the survival of relatively ancient forms of music and performance in the present. These are the issues that have drawn me to *Chunhyang* in the first place, despite an overall ignorance about Korean culture that extends to most of its cinema—including even most of the oeuvre of its most celebrated auteur, Im Kwon-taek.

I hope that this admission of my lack of knowledge and innocence can be regarded as a form of clarification and honesty rather than as an expression of arrogance. My theoretical assumption is that the most common form of journalistic bluff regarding such matters—conveying an unearned and unwarranted stance of authority, typically justified through a series of lazy intellectual shortcuts and/or appropriations (such as, for example, describing *pansori* as some Korean variant of the American blues)—is ultimately more imperialistic in effect than any honest admission of cultural ignorance.

At the same time. because I fully believe that the most important innovations in art, especially those with some relation to the avant-garde, generally come about through a drive to express formerly unexpressed and otherwise inexpressible content, motivated most often by a sense of personal necessity, I fully acknowledge the likelihood that some of the motivations underlying Im Kwon-taek's *Chunhyang* are deeply personal—a notion which is spelled out in some detail by Chung Sung-ill in his book about the filmmaker:

> [Among]...the four representative *pansori* musicals in Korea, *Chunhyang-jeon* is the most famous one. Behind the artful verse, humor, and satire in *pansori* are Korean tears and laughter. However, we must not overlook one point. This story is staged in the southwestern part of Korea, in Namwon. In other words, no matter how many different versions there are, the background of the story, Namwon in Jeolla Province, doesn't change. For Im, shooting *Chunhyang* meant shooting the sounds of his own hometown, proudly showing off his hometown in his return. (Just like Lee Mong-ryong who comes back as a king's undercover agent and saves Chunhyang from prison.) ...By stating that *Chunhyang* is concentrating on formalities, this actually means Im is desperately looking for the way to his hometown.
>
> According to his words, *Chunhyang* is his answer to *Sopyonje*. While he was making *Sopyonje*, he listened to the complete version of Chunhyang-jeon, then decided that his ultimate goal was to put the deep emotions of the *pansori* musical itself into a movie. If the artistic features of *pansori* can be illustrated through the system and form, movement structure, and the graph of sensibility of a movie, then the products of the modern West and Korean cultural heritage can finally be reconciled harmoniously. This is to embrace and overlap two very different forms of art with two different histories without any common denominators. Could these two make one world by co-existing with the peculiarity of each other's powers? Im questions over and over again in *Chunhyang* how he can bend the movie into *pansori* structure (reconstruction of mise en scène), straighten curves (editing that follows the sound), then bend it again (very brave omission), and produce it on one stage (story and the musical).[1]

All this suggests that the issues of representation that crop up repeatedly in the film, the focus of my following remarks (which are restricted mostly to examples drawn from the film's first half), are not merely academic concerns but pressing existential questions and practical strategies resulting from them. They seem to point to a fundamental anxiety about translating from one art form to another as well as to an onrush of creative strategies for attempting both to assuage and to benefit from that anxiety. The frequency of the camera movements, which are nearly always expressive rather than simply expositional, is emblematic of this restlessness and uncertainty, and the expressiveness, though mostly tied to the viewpoint of Lee Mong-ryong (and including subjective camera angles), occasionally encompasses other viewpoints as well—including Chunhyang's, when the offscreen *pansori* performance privileges her feelings, but also, much later and more implicitly, the viewpoint of her mother, when Lee Mong-ryong, dressed as a beggar, arrives at their home.

1

Chunhyang begins, in long shot, with a *pansori* performance in a dark, abstract space that appears to be an auditorium or concert stage, judging from the looks and gestures of the singer and main performer (which seem to be aimed alternately at the drummer and in the same general direction as the camera), but without any visible or audible sign of any audience.

We cut to an overhead descending crane shot over a contemporary urban street alongside a street sign pointing with an arrow towards Chŏngdong Theater. Several teenagers are seen stepping out of a blue car in front of this theater, where a boy and girl in the group who linger behind the others have the following exchange:

Boy: "Traditional music is good and all, but how are we going to stand it for five hours?"

Girl: "I think there is a reason why we were told to watch it."

Boy: "What reason? It's the same old tale of *Chunhyang*."

Already, two important parameters are being established: (a) Practically anyone who has started watching the film will already know that it runs for 136 minutes, not for five hours (or 300 minutes), meaning that an important distinction between a *pansori* performance of *Chunhyang* and this film entitled *Chunhyang* is already being made. (b) The primary audience being addressed by the film is Korean, i.e. an audience that will be able to identify and recognize what "the same old tale of *Chunhyang*" means.

As I've already suggested, these parameters both attest to a certain anxiety about translating an ancient art and practice into the norms of contemporary commercial cinema, highlighting a discrepancy that is equally apparent in the synopsis accorded to the film in Chung Sung-ill's book.[2] Apart from a short footnote, this synopsis seems to equate the film with the traditional tale that serves as the basis for a corresponding *pansori* performance—one that is referenced and excerpted but not actually reproduced in any comprehensive fashion. And the footnote mentions the *pansori* performer Cho Sang-hyun—credited with furnishing the film's "original idea," but not as an actor or performer—beginning and ending the film with a performance of "Sa-rang-ga, a love song," with his voice taking "the role of narration" in between, but it makes no allusion to the teenage spectators that function initially as our surrogates. Thus, paradoxically, what I would identify as the major creative and analytical contribution of the film, which involves the cinematic "translation" of the tale and takes many shifting forms, is virtually elided from the synopsis.

It's worth adding that the performance of "Sa-rang-ga" will return a little over half an hour later, offscreen, to accompany a scene of lovemaking and erotic cavorting between Lee Mong-ryong and Chunhyang. Here, again, the visual strategies of representation are restlessly kaleidoscopic; the shifting etiquette of exposure and concealment as the characters move on and offscreen, periodically moving behind walls and screens, is adroitly echoed and counterpointed by the revealing or masking movements of the camera, so that soon after their nudity is discreetly shown on the right side of the frame, the camera moves briefly away from them to the left, as if out of modesty. (A little later, during a second sequence of this kind, we see their bodies retreat into darkness.)

When the film's prologue follows the group of teenagers into the theater lobby and then into the auditorium to take their seats, we learn further that their attendance at this event is required, apparently by a school assignment ("Hey, isn't anyone going to buy the pamphlet? We're going to need it for the report") and that many of them are expecting to be bored; they even make jokes about taking turns at falling asleep. One boy even starts to leave, hoping to crib whatever information he needs for the report from the Internet, until a girl gets him to sit back down and "Hang in there."

A long shot in reverse angle shows the two *pansori* performers arrive on the stage to applause. This leads us to question the precise place and time of the preceding *pansori* performance that we saw at the film's opening, which seems to have had the same two performers, but with a different backdrop and (apparently) occurring on a different, unspecified occasion. It's almost as if the first performance we see qualifies generically as *"pansori"* while the second qualifies as a particular and specific instance of it—and the second is prefaced by the main performer's announcement that it will run for five hours, already distinguishing it once again from the film that we're watching. He also mentions that there will be two intermissions, makes a joke about the trips to the bathroom that this will permit, and asks for the audience's "encouragement" of his live performance—three more factors separating this performance from the film we're watching and pointing towards an assumption that the film's spectators, like the teenagers in the auditorium, wouldn't welcome a classic five-hour *pansori* performance, meaning that an abridgement as well as a cinematic translation has to be fashioned as some sort of evocation and substitute for that experience.

Finally, continuing in his speaking voice, Cho introduces the scene, period, and hero (Lee Mong-ryong) of the story while the camera is seen approaching the latter in separate stages and shots. A dialogue between Mong-ryong and his servant, Bang-ja, follows, establishing that he wants to go for a ride after being cooped up for months; there's a cut to him climbing onto his horse, at which point Cho's sung narration begins.

2

Much of the film's dynamism can be felt in the almost constantly shifting relation between word and image in the brief passage that immediately follows, which I have tried to annotate in a rudimentary fashion (with a few slight adjustments to the English subtitles to make them more grammatically consistent with one another):

"He mounts the horse" (close-up of Mong-ryong's foot entering his horse's stirrup) "and Bang-ja leads the way" (medium shot of Mong-ryong on his horse in profile being led by Bang-ja—a reverse angle of the previous shot). "As he leaves the South Gate, [with] a fan shaped like a crane's yellow wing" (an extreme long shot of Mong-ryong, framed more frontally on his horse as he moves towards the camera, surrounded on all sides by other figures), "he flips it open to block the sun" (a close-up of Mong-ryong in profile opening his fan to block the sunlight) "as he travels down the South Road. The breezy dust from each trot" (a long shot following Mong-ryong from behind, again surrounded by other figures; the fan, barely visible from this angle, is no longer shielding his face or parallel with it, but held somewhat lower; and no dust or breeze is visible) "flutters in the air with the scent of peach flowers…" (a long shot in motion of Mong-ryong riding on his horse in profile, moving from right to left).

Although the two close-ups approach a simple equivalence between narration and what's being shown (Mong-ryong mounting his horse or flipping open his fan), the medium shots and long shots show an increasing disparity, not only in what they neglect to show or reveal ("the breezy dust," "the scent of peach flowers"), but also in the wealth of visual details that are included relating to the setting, landscape, and multiple surrounding figures but are missing from the narration. Many of these details continually threaten to overwhelm the narrative thread—and, indeed, would probably overwhelm this thread if they didn't have the clarifying contexts of the narration and the two close-ups. Thus they might be said to highlight the overall disparity between the linear thrust and forward movement of the words and music on the one hand and the nonlinear, nonnarrative, and painterly dispersal of the visual details on the other. In short, the shotgun marriage being staged by Im between *pansori* and cinema shifts from moments of apparent fusion to other moments when they seem to be miles apart, and the choreography of their interaction becomes central to the film's dynamic poetry.

3

Chung notes that Im spent four months concentrating on "the scene where Bang-ja is ordered by Mong-ryong to go to Chunhyang to inform her of Mong-ryong's feelings. He shot it over and over again," and "didn't just edit to fit the sounds, but...cut the shots to fit the rhythm and then [filmed each] shot with [a different lense]," with corresponding changes in focus and/or forward and reverse zooms designed to match Bang-ja's movements.[3] This section reaches a sort of climax when Chunhyang delivers a proverb as a message to Mong-ryong that appears onscreen as a Korean subtitle: "The wild geese desire the sea, the crabs desire their holes, and a butterfly desires a flower." Later on, during the second sequence that celebrates the couple's erotic discovery of one another, a single Korean word, apparently meaning "one," will also appear onscreen, and in both cases, it would seem that the prestige of literary poetry briefly trumps the prestige of *pansori* performance.

4

I'd like to conclude with what may be Chunhyang's most complicated stretch in terms of narration, point-of-view, and mise en scène, all of which become interactive and at times almost interchangeable, approximately ninety minutes into the film. It begins with the on-screen singing narration of Bang-la, carrying Chunhyang's letter to Lee; after he recognizes Lee in his beggar clothes and gives him the letter, the narration is taken over by Chunhyang's voice offscreen, reciting her letter to offscreen musical accompaniment. Then the *pansori* singer takes over: "When the sun is about to set..." (over a shot of the sunset) "he arrives in front of Chunhyang's home..." (a long shot of the house at night, with a slow zoom forward) "In the back of the garden is a silent cry." (The same forward zoom continues.) "He's drawn to the sound" (in another shot, the camera moves from right to left across the side of the house) "to take a closer look" (the same camera movement continues).

Complicating the above sequence, apart from the anomaly of Lee "hearing" a "silent cry," is the fact that the shots of the house appear to be partially drawn and partially photographed, and the additional fact that the camera movements along the side of the house suggest without actually replicating Lee's point of view as he moves in that direction. Then we hear that Lee sees Chunhyang's mother "at a small altar in the backyard... with lit candles...and a bowl of clean water" at almost precisely the same moment that we see these details, but a much closer shot of the mother in the foreground that moves forward and past her to the bowl and candles suggests a switch to her viewpoint, complicated by a cut to an overhead shot of her praying that slowly pans down while the *pansori* singer then begins to speak for the mother: "I pray...to the gods of heaven and earth...Please come and help me." This becomes in turn a prayer that Lee come to her assistance, at which point we cut to a shot in which the camera approaches Lee himself, speaking to her. Over the space of a few moments, the characters and the story, objectivity and subjectivity, and *pansori* and cinema finally speak with the same collective voice.

End Notes

1. Translated into English by Han-Na-ra, Seoul: Korean Film Council, 2006, 49-50.

2. *Ibid.*, 142-14

3. *Ibid.*, 50.

Peanuts, Yesterday, Today and Tomorrow

Fantagraphics Books' Gary Groth commissioned this Introduction to the first volume of Charles Schulz's Sunday color strips of Peanuts, *covering the early 1950s, which was published in November 2013.*

"...I've made a lot of mistakes down through the years doing things I never should have done. But fortunately, in a comic strip, yesterday doesn't mean anything. The only thing that matters is today and tomorrow."

—Charles Schultz to Gary Groth "At 3 o'clock in the Morning," *Comics Journal #200*, December 1997

It was one thing to read Sunday color *Peanuts* comic strips from 1952 to 1955 at the rate of one per week, when they came out—and not only because they would have wound up in the trash like the rest of the Sunday paper, long before my brothers and I went to sleep that night. And it's quite another thing to read them all today, piled together in the present volume, one after the other, seven or eight panels at a time, as if they're the successive chapters of an ongoing serial—or maybe just the latest portions of an endless white picket fence that stretches towards some version of infinity or eternity (or at least roughly half a century of dependable continuity, in any case).

It's likely that I saw a good many of these strips between the ages of eight and thirteen. If the Birmingham paper my family had delivered each morning had carried the preceding weekday black and white *Peanuts* strips that started fifteen months earlier, shortly after I entered the first grade, my curiosity as an early reader might have brought me to a few of them, even though I'm fairly sure I wouldn't have understood any of the jokes—if jokes, indeed, are what those enigmatic exchanges and incidents consisted of. I'm confident, in any case, that whenever I first encountered *Peanuts*, the full extent of my curiosity never went beyond the issue of what these kids with beach-ball heads were saying, thinking, and/or doing that particular week. And, at least in the world of *Peanuts* as I understood it even then, saying and thinking was at least as important as doing, and maybe even indistinguishable from the latter.

The near-equivalence between thinking, saying, and doing is surely an important part of what made *Peanuts* different from the strips surrounding it. But it might be equally instructive to inquire what some of the common traits were between *Peanuts* and some of its Sunday morning siblings. The notion of a world ruled largely by an authoritative, sometimes bossy female was arguably a common trait in *Blondie*, *Bringing Up Father* (more popularly known as Jiggs and Maggie), *The Katzenjammer Kids*, *Li'l Abner* (as ruled by Mammy Yokum), and *Mary Worth*—in contrast, say, to *Barney Google* and *Snuffy Smith*, *Dick Tracy*, *Gasoline Alley*, *Little Orphan Annie*, and *Mutt and Jeff*. It's worth adding, however, that the dominance of Lucy over Charlie Brown wasn't as apparent at the beginning, while she was still just a tyke, as it would become later—even though an older girl, a redhead named Patty, would already anticipate some of her traits (in contrast to the usually more sweet-tempered Violet), and Lucy herself would grow up so quickly that she would soon put her youthful subservience behind her.

In 1975, her creator, Charles Schultz, pointed out, "As the strip progressed from the fall of the year 1950, the characters began to change. Charlie Brown was a flippant little guy, who soon turned into the loser he is known as today. This was the first of the formulas to develop. Formulas are truly the backbone of the comic strip. In fact, they are probably the backbone of any continuing entertainment." He added that, among the other characters, Lucy had already developed at least part of her fussbudget personality during the first year of the strip, inspired by some of the traits of his oldest daughter, Meredith. Furthermore, "Snoopy was the slowest to develop, and it was his eventually walking around on two feet that turned him into a lead character. It has certainly been difficult to keep him from taking over the feature."

In the early appearances of Snoopy, it often isn't clear if Schultz is postulating a dog who thinks he's human, a human who thinks he's a dog, or some perpetual, seesawing arrangement between these two peculiar mismatches. Eventually, one might postulate that he evolves into some version of all three; Schultz acknowledged in 1975 that his "appearance and personality have changed probably more than those of any of the other characters." But for the Italian semiologist Umberto Eco, he is simply a dog who can't accept being a dog—an animal who "carries to the last metaphysical frontier the neurotic failure to adjust."

On Halloween, 1952, we see him sporting a fright mask to accompany two boys under bed sheets, and proving to be just as ineffectual as they are when it comes to scaring Lucy. The previous week, we saw him dancing some sort of hornpipe to the classical strains of Schroeder's toy piano, then brooding and sulking afterwards about Charlie, Schroeder, and Patty leaving him alone rather than inviting him over to spend the night—and then defiantly entering his humble doghouse to watch TV in order to "prove" he doesn't need their company anyway. Or does he?

In mid-February 1953, he thinks he outsmarts Lucy when he devours two of her cookies while she goes away to answer the doorbell, then winds up baffled when she figures it out afterwards, despite her eccentric and seemingly chaotic method of counting. And five weeks later, Schultz combines two of Snoopy's specialties, dance and consuming human food—dancing his hornpipe to Schroeder's rendition of Modest Moussorgsky's "Hopak," then becoming miffed when he gets banished to the kitchen at lunchtime, only to discover, after Lucy brings him 'three kinds of sandwiches" and "a salad, cake, ice cream and hot chocolate"—so much human food, in fact, that two separate dialogue bubbles are required to accommodate Lucy's list. This leads him to conclude (but to himself only), "Pride is a foolish thing!"

Consider the multiple forms of fantasy conceit that Schultz manages to shoehorn into the latter strip: Schroeder performing "Hopak" (and on a toy piano, no less); Snoopy performing his dance (again, at the request of Charlie Brown); five kids including Linus clapping their encouragement without any signs of amazement about either feat (four of them barking out, "Hey!" for rhythmic emphasis); Lucy explaining to Snoopy why he has to go to the kitchen and then, as he sulkily starts to head for home instead, delivering a veritable banquet to him (neither act impossible, but both highly unlikely in most of the worlds we're familiar with); Snoopy undergoing querulous resentment about not being treated like a human before being startled and then placated by a bounty of human food, which leads to some philosophical self-deprecation. And Snoopy's taste for human food—not only cookies, sandwiches, salad, cake, ice cream, and hot chocolate, but also candy three weeks later, and bread the following week—clearly functions as an obsessive theme, perhaps in part because, like TV and choreography, it implies a kind of membership in the human race, although his desire to become a member gets expressed only privately, to himself. (Presumably and peculiarly, his talent for both dancing and playing Trick-or-Treat are viewed by the kids as more proper canine attributes; and if Snoopy ever expresses his feelings of maladjustment to other animals, we don't hear about it.)

In short, more than a few impossibilities coupled with several highly unlikely human and nonhuman responses are in full operation here, yet we can accept all of them as naturally and as effortlessly as if we were watching a string of quite ordinary events. In a similar fashion, we don't really care about the fact that Snoopy's doghouse carries a TV antenna while the unseen TV set inside apparently functions without an electric cord, even though the pool of luminosity spilling out of the doghouse interior is every bit as bright as the crescent moon in the sky. And we're not even encouraged to ask whether Snoopy's Halloween mask was suggested and/or provided by Charlie Brown or whether he managed to acquire it and/or put it on following his own initiative.

Later, in September 1953, we see him self-consciously and mischievously smile, grin, turn his head, flip upside down, and frown in front of Charlie Brown's camera, then laugh at his photographer's exasperation. But then, a week later, we see him failing in his effort to imitate Lucy in gracefully going down a playground slide. And a week after that, we see him trying to behave like an ordinary dog by growling at a bird, then chasing after it and barking until he's eventually gasping with exhaustion—at which point the bird yawns and Snoopy sighs at all this wasted effort. Yet apart from his recurring hornpipes and a few other passing fancies—such as his skipping rope with Lucy in separate strips in May and July 1955—we don't yet see Snoopy walking around on two feet very often in this early phase of *Peanuts*, and when he does (as in one of the black and white dailies in November 1955, when he's trotting that way behind Lucy), Charlie Brown warns him that he's asking for trouble. Once he fully enters a world of his own, however, his trouble will become more metaphysical or philosophical than social—as it sometimes does for Charlie Brown, in spite of his own everyday humiliations.

How does Schultz do it? The testimony of one fantasy-driven filmmaker about another—independent writer-director Sara Driver speaking to me in an interview a few years ago—suggests one important clue: "You know, I'm such a lover of Jacques Tourneur's films, and I remember reading about him and how if you anchor things in a sense of reality, you can go anywhere from there." This becomes especially true when a sense of reality is grounded in a solid grasp of character, so that the reality of, say, a frigid, newlywed Serbian fashion artist

(Simone Simon) in *Cat People* (1942) and quite a few non-zombies in *I Walked with a Zombie* (1943), Tourneur's first two pictures for Val Lewton—like that of Driver's schizophrenic heroine in *You Are Not I* (1981) and a schleppy and lazy jazz musician in *When Pigs Fly* (1993)—enables us to accept many kinds of outlandishness in those films (such as a heroine who switches bodies with her sane sister, or a dog belonging to the jazz musician who has jazz dreams of his own, featuring other musical dogs). And the reality of Charlie Brown, Lucy, Schroeder, Linus, Patty, and yes, even Snoopy—and, most of all, the shifting and volatile emotions of these characters, human or canine—allows Schultz to get us to accept any number of absurdities, anomalies, inconsistencies, and strategic absences (starting with the nonappearance of adults) involving what they say, think, and do, even (and maybe even especially) when all three of these activities get collapsed into one.

§

A lifelong movie fan, Schultz occasionally referred to the "camera angles" in his strips, despite the absence of any camera, to describe his habitually adopted eye-level angle of vision. His main filmic reference points were obviously American—William Wellman's *Beau Geste* (1939), Orson Welles's *Citizen Kane* (1941), Norman Foster's *Davy Crockett: King of the Wild Frontier* (after the 1955 release of this this live-action Walt Disney adventure set off a national craze in coonskin hats, occasioning one of Schultz's infrequent excursions into the topical), along with Laurel and Hardy and many Saturday matinee serials. But if any cinematic cross-references are helpful in getting at Schultz's style and vision, one could argue that, in at least a few respects, the late films of Yasujiro Ozu come closer to the mark—without forgetting that Ozu himself was such a fanatical devotee of Hollywood (as evidenced even by the movie posters glimpsed on the domestic walls of his characters) that his sharpest critic, Shigehiko Hasumi, has pointed out that even the weather in Ozu's movies is closer to that of Southern California than to the more drizzly weather of Japan. Obviously, Ozu's characters encompassed more than small fry, but the minimalistic canvas of their everyday domestic events and rituals, the repeated use over decades of the same actors (as a rough equivalent to Schultz's reliance on the same characters) and the same low and eye-level "camera angles", and the quiet and deadly slow burns and petty frustrations of family and neighborhood entanglements all suggest some of the same habits and preoccupations.

Where Ozu and Schultz decisively part company is in how they cope with fantasy—not at all in the case of Ozu, who adheres strictly to the familiar and the feasible, and so frequently and integrally in the case of Schultz that it sometimes becomes hard to separate the fantasy conceits from the everyday emblems and rituals. The minimalistic canvas tends to equalize all the elements in Schultz's universe, including all the elemental traits, so that inexpressiveness and expressiveness are less than an inch apart, and fullness and emptiness can sometimes be no less difficult to separate. Even while objecting to some of the cuteness and debilitating "good taste" of *Peanuts* in a 1959 essay, critic Donald Phelps conceded that "Charles Schultz may be the most accomplished master of blankness in contemporary art since Mark Rothko drifted onto the scene with his filets of Grand Canyon. He can fluff out an almost gagless strip with dogs and children doing tumble-weed dances. (This has produced some of his funniest panels: those featuring his best character, Charlie Brown's dog, Snoopy.) He posts his characters against great swatches and bandaids of empty space and a little stubby grass, so that the vapid doodling of figures takes on the deadpan suggestiveness which perked up Buster Keaton's fascination for so many years". As Eco reminds us, Charlie Brown is an epic hero who is invariably referred to by his whole name, even by his unseen mother, so the coexistence of small events against those great swatches and bandaids is part of what makes his world seem so real to us—that is, tiny from a cosmic vantage point yet vast from the close quarters of our childish perspective. It's this sense of relativity that remained with Schultz at the same time that his characters and their predilections were still being shaped, and this amused and evenly balanced distance remains fundamental to his wit.

Shoah & Ten-Best Documentary List

Written for Sight and Sound*'s documentary film poll in their September 2014 issue; posted online with partial corrections and new errors. Two unfortunate differences between my list and the ones published are the reduction of Peter Thompson's* Universal Hotel/ Universal Citizen *to a single title and my specification that I was referring only to the French version of Rossellini's* India—*a version I vastly prefer to the Italian version, though more as fiction than for any "documentary" reasons (which applies to most or all of my other choices). This gives an added truth to James Benning's own bold contribution to the same poll, worth quoting in full: "*Titanic *(Cameron). This is my only vote: an amazing document of bad acting. And, I might add, all films are fictions."*

Shoah. There are documentary filmmakers who plant their stakes within existing traditions and those for whom cinema has to be reinvented. Claude Lanzmann clearly belongs in the latter category. Of course cinema already had to exist in order to allow Lanzmann to make *Shoah* (1985)—named after the Hebrew word for annihilation—but he also had to rethink what cinema could be. His 550-minute examination of the Jewish Holocaust falls within the documentary tradition of investigative journalism, but what he does with that form is so confrontational and relentless that it demands to be described in philosophical/spiritual terms rather than simply cinematically. Determined to make us imagine the unimaginable, Lanzmann literalizes a quote from philosopher Emil Fackenheim: "The European Jews massacred are not just of the past, they are the presence of an absence."

One could even describe *Shoah* as a kind of cruel but determined shotgun marriage between Judaism and existentialism—a match between Lanzmann's sense of his tribal roots (having been born in 1925 to a French and Jewish family of Eastern European immigrants, and having joined the French Resistance at the age of eighteen) and his adopted intellectual roots (having become during his twenties both the editor of Jean-Paul Sartre's journal *Les Temps Modernes* and the lover of Simone de Beauvoir).

How does one negotiate between a religion founded on the dictates of the past and a philosophy founded on the needs and challenges of the present? First of all, in the case of *Shoah*, by refusing any historical or archival footage or narration, depending exclusively on interviews and footage shot in the present, either at certain key places where the Holocaust occurred (on the trains carrying Jews to the death camps, or at what remains of the camps themselves in Chelmno, Sobibor, Treblinka, Ausschwitz) or in other relevant locations in Wlodawa, Kolo, Berlin, Belzec, Warsaw—even, most memorably, in an Israeli barbershop. Secondly, by recording Lanzmann and others in their own languages (including German, Hebrew, Polish, and Yiddish) and including the translations into French, which are then subtitled in English in Anglo-American prints of the film. And thirdly, as de Beauvoir noted in her preface to the film's published text, by editing the sequences not according to any chronological order, but poetically. "To write poetry after Auschwitz is barbaric," Theodor Adorno once wrote, and Lanzmann's singular achievement is to both challenge and corroborate that statement.

Ten Best Documentaries

1. *Shoah* (Claude Lanzmann, 1985)

2. *Les Statues Meurent Aussi* (Alain Resnais/Chris Marker, 1952)

3. *The House is Black* (Forough Farrokhzad, 1962)

4. *Une Histoire de Vent* (Joris Ivens & Marceline Loridan, 1988)

5. *India Matri Buhmi* (French version) (Roberto Rossellini, 1958)

6. *Operai, Contadini* (Jean-Marie Straub & Danièle Huillet, 2001)

7. *Sans Soleil* (Chris Marker, 1983)

8. *Mix-Up* (Françoise Romand, 1985)

9. *Universal Hotel/Universal Citizen* (Peter Thompson, 1987)

10. *RR* (James Benning, 2007)

Final thoughts:

I regret the absence of any silent films (the first of which might be Dziga-Vertov's *The Man with the Movie Camera*), but I also lament having to exclude, among others, Michael Snow's *La Région Centrale* (1971), Abbas Kiarostami's *Orderly or Disorderly* (1981), Edgardo Cozarinsky's *Le Guerre d'un seul homme* (1982), Robb Moss's *The Same River Twice* (2003), and Adam Curtis's *The Trap: What Happened to Our Dream of Freedom* (2007).

Interactivity as Art and Vice Versa: *A Bread Factory*

Published on Artforum'*s website on April 18, 2019, under the title "Leaven Learn".*

"The justification for [a] pretense to disengagement," writes Dave Hickey in *Air Guitar*, "derives from our Victorian habit of marginalizing the experience of art, of treating it as if it were somehow 'special'—and, lately, as if it were somehow curable. This is a preposterous assumption to make in a culture that is irrevocably saturated with pictures and music, in which every elevator serves as a combination picture gallery and concert hall . . . All we do by ignoring the live effects of art is suppress the fact that these experiences, in one way or another, inform our every waking hour."

To some extent, Patrick Wang's dazzling two-part, four-hour comedy *A Bread Factory* (2018)—shot over twenty-four days in Hudson, New York, after ten days of rehearsal with well over sixty professional or semiprofessional actors—is an epic anthology of performance art, filmed both inside and outside a Hudson art center housed in a former bread factory. What makes it special are the peculiar dots connecting "inside" and "outside." Inside the eponymous, fictionalized forty-year-old Bread Factory we find theater, film, music, sculpture, and poetry, and inside a trendy, new rival art center with corporate financing is a pseudo-Chinese couple called May Ray doing minimalist, rebus-like performance pieces with prerecorded laughter and applause. Outside is everyday life in Checkford (the thinly veiled Hudson): city council meetings, sessions at the local newsroom, conversations in living rooms, bedrooms, and kitchens, and diverse exchanges at a local café-bar-restaurant. These interactivities, or collisions, between inside and outside, art and mundane events, aren't simply illustrations of theater as "poor people's therapy" (as one character puts it) or as vehicles for self-expression. They also serve as modes or models of perception, interpretation, organization, political activism, or simply as reasons for getting together (or not getting together, as sometimes happens).

Part one, subtitled "For the Sake of Gold," sees continuities and harmonies between inside and outside that fulfill Hickey's notion of the aesthetics of everyday life, rendered mainly in realistic terms about the competitive struggles of Bread Factory and May Ray for a city council grant, and with a happy ending. Part two, subtitled "Walk with Me a While"—which starts with a swiftly mimed recap of part one on stage right while a string quartet plays on stage left and concludes with an unhappy or bittersweet ending, when the city council decision gets reversed—is more concerned with discordances, with singing tourists on the street and tapdancing tech workers in the café. But it also culminates in an abbreviated rendition of the Bread Factory's production of Euripides's *Hecuba* seen being blocked and rehearsed throughout part one, performed now to a disappointingly if foreseeably small audience. As a theater director himself, Wang has focused often on Greek tragedy, and his charting of the various stages (in both senses) of *Hecuba* moving toward realization, with the fictional director's partner cast in a leading role, is what has led many critics to compare *A Bread Factory*, which premiered last autumn, to Jacques Rivette's *L'amour fou* (1969) and *Out 1* (1971). Perhaps the biggest differences are that Wang has written everything apart from *Hecuba*, including even the verse in a poetry reading—the only improvised material is gestural, not verbal—and that his Rivettean sense of process is wholly American.

At latest count, thirty-seven rave reviews of *A Bread Factory* in the US and Europe, many from mainstream outlets, are on the film's website. Yet it's a work, however striking and original, that continues to exist below the radar on both continents and in all the disunited states where it periodically continues to surface, media profile be damned. It's worth adding, however, that Wang, after self-distributing his three features for the past decade and not releasing them on DVD or Blu-Ray (which has contributed to their scarcity), has recently acquired a distributor, Grasshopper Films, which has already offered us digital editions of such irreplaceable items as *Chronicle of Anna Magdalena Bach*, *Vampir-Cuadecuc*, *Casa de Lava*, and *Did You Wonder Who Fired the Gun?* So it may still be invisible in mainstream terms, but it isn't going away.

Existing below the radar is largely what *A Bread Factory* is about, so it's unsurprising that Wang often chooses to focus on characters who are very old or very young, such as the elderly lesbian couple Dorothea and Greta (beautifully played by Tyne Daly and Elisabeth Henry) who run the center and the little boy Simon (Keaton Nigel Cooke) who serves for a time as its projectionist. It also seems relevant that Wang lives in Manhattan but has chosen to shoot all his features to date in what Manhattan regards as the sticks. ("I have a connection to smaller towns. I once lived in a small town in Argentina as an exchange student, and that was a very formative experience. In dramatic literature, a small town is often the setting because you can show everything going on in that town," as in Ibsen and Brecht.) Furthermore, to explore the omnipresence and multifunctional purposes of art in a country that fundamentally and passionately hates art—and, as Wang reminded me, has felt this way at least as far back as de Tocqueville—necessarily entails working below the radar, which arguably turns out to be the best place to function.

This is a film of appreciation and celebration of both art and everyday life far more than one of complaint. The huge cast challenges us to keep up with the characters, to chart their multiple interconnections, inviting and rewarding return visits to tease out every thread. Even the film's satirical targets—starting with the hilarious May Ray and their links to big cities and celebrity culture and extending to mobile phones and selfies employed as shields—are approached with head-scratching amusement and bemusement more than bile. And the implicit dialectical conversation between parts one and two about what constitutes realism—such as a local newspaper staffed exclusively by little boys after the editor, Jan (Glynnis O'Connor), mysteriously disappears, leaving behind her teenage protégé Max (Zachary Sayle) to replace her—is an important part of the fun and games.

As Wang put it during a Q&A I recently conducted at the Gene Siskel Film Center (a recording of which is included on the film's DVD), what matters most to him about May Ray isn't just their strident silliness (my terms) but the way "they're turbocharged by capital"—reminding me now, while transcribing that phrase, how my late Chicago colleague Siskel was himself turbocharged by capital far more than he was by cinema. "To communicate between segments of society and to express systems of power, money comes up," is how Wang puts it. (At M.I.T., he started as a physics major before shifting to economics, and minored in "music and theater arts".) And regarding the isolations and blocked connections that proliferate in part two, he views the singing and dancing as other forms of communication "that don't allow for [any] conversation." Max—who gets a superb lesson in journalistic ethics from Jan after copying phrases from a press release in his review of a May Ray performance—later delivers a harsh autocritique to Sir Walter (the late Brian Murray) in his office after another review causes Ray to get fired (to be replaced by another Ray).

But we already know that Sir Walter, an actor himself, still refuses to speak to another local reviewer who gave him a bad notice half a century ago, though he defends Max's review to Max, in part because he doesn't regard Ray #1 as an actor at all.

Max is dating Julie (Erica Durham), a cast member of *Hecuba*. When she runs off with a movie star who turns up to support May Ray getting a grant from the city council and supplanting the Bread Factory, he's so distraught that he goes to Dorothea for comfort. Dorothea coaxes him into reading the lines of the grief-stricken ghost of Polydorus in *Hecuba*, not because she necessarily needs him for the part but because she suspects it's the only way to distance Max from his pain, for him to vent, via another imagination, some of his feelings. It seems to work.

Another performance at the Bread Factory, by Elaine Bromka, is a Chekhov spoof written by Wang years ago that he told me is a parody of what he regards as "Chekhov performance style," and still another, delivered in the newsroom by Sir Walter, is a more "earnest" pastiche of a Chekhov protégé, Ivan Bunin, linked to literature rather than theater. How do we connect these two monologues to each other, and to everything else? Even if we can't, or don't, Yang's sense of play and his freedom to take risks and the pleasures to be found in what the actors are doing provide ample continuity with everything else, as do all the shifts in acting techniques. What occasionally registers as a hit-or-miss jumble of methodologies and proficiencies, a sort of perpetual tryout, laid back yet ever hopeful, bears more than a passing resemblance to life as it's routinely lived.

A Brighter Summer Day

Written for Asia's 100 Films, *a volume edited for the 20th Busan International Film Festival (held during the 1st through the 10th of October, 2015).*

I'm happy to report that I attended the world premiere of the full 237-minute version of this film in Taipei, at the Golden Horse Film Festival, during my first visit to Asia. (I also visited the school where much of the action was shot, right across from the Royal Palace Museum.) This was after having seen the inferior, shorter cut that Edward Yang was forced to make at a couple of other festivals. As I concluded in my capsule review for the *Chicago Reader*, "This is a film about alienated identities in a country undergoing a profound existential crisis—a *Rebel Without a Cause* with much of the same nocturnal lyricism and cosmic despair. Notwithstanding the masterpieces of Hou Hsiao-hsien, the Taiwanese new wave starts here."

A Brighter Summer Day was inspired by a true incident, a touchstone from Yang's youth: the killing of a fourteen-year-old girl by a male high school student in Taipei on June 15, 1961. Yang frames the film with recitations over the radio of the names of students graduating from the same school in 1960 and '61. The title comes from the lyrics of the Elvis Presley song "Are You Lonesome Tonight?", phonetically transcribed by the hero's sister so that a younger friend, Cat, can learn to sing them.

This song is only one of many cherished artifacts belonging to the film's characters that come from somewhere else. A samurai sword found by the hero, Si'r, in his family's Japanese house becomes the murder weapon, and a tape recorder left by the American army in the '50s records Cat's version of the

Elvis song. An old radio that for most of the picture doesn't work eventually broadcasts the list of graduating students. And a flashlight Si'r steals in the first extended scene from a film studio next to the school, where he periodically hides in the rafters to watch movies being shot, makes a fascinating progress through the film.

A charismatic gang leader in hiding who becomes a role model for Si'r describes spending most of his cloistered time reading "swordsmen" novels; he cites *War and Peace* as his favorite in that genre. A Russian novel being seen as part of a Japanese tradition only begins to describe the cultural alienation and isolation of a country occupied by the Japanese and Kuomintang, not to mention the American army.

The social landscape of *A Brighter Summer Day* is haunted by the absence of strong father figures and a sense of perpetual exile: Si'r's father, a civil servant who came to Taipei from Shanghai (as did Yang's father), is so weakened by the repression of the secret police and Taiwan's militarized culture that he blames himself for his son's failures at school. (The father and son's two memorable walks home from school with their bikes, each time after Si'r has gotten into serious trouble, touchingly recognize their shared vulnerability.) Ming—the sensitive, flirtatious, unstable teenager Si'r falls for—is growing up without any father at all and is saddled with a mother as vulnerable as Si'r's father. Refusing to judge any of his characters, Yang accords them all a compassionate respect and understanding that compel us to share their dilemmas.

Poetry

Written for Asia's 100 Films, *a volume edited for the 20th Busan International Film Festival (held during the 1st through the 10th of October, 2015 1-10 October).*

To explain why Lee Chang-dong's extraordinary *Poetry* (2010) is my favorite Korean film, I first need to confess to a feeling of alienation from a good many other South Korean films and what I regard as their excessive reliance on rape and serial killers as subjects. Admittedly, these themes are by no means restricted to South Korean cinema or even more generally to Asian cinema, but they also help to account to my resistance to such highly praised European touchstones involving rape as Ingmar Bergman's *The Virgin Spring* and Luchino Visconti's *Rocco and His Brothers* (both 1960), and such American films regarding serial killers as Jonathan Demme's *The Silence of the Lambs* (1991) and Ethan and Joel Coen's *No Country for Old Men* (2007). The tendency of all these films to exploit and/or sentimentalize these subjects (such as making serial killers into holy figures) is scrupulously avoided by Lee and handled throughout with tact, delicacy, and a finely nuanced sense of development in its heroine's ethical and aesthetic consciousness. Consequently, *Poetry* offers a profound social critique by addressing the theme of rape and its role in Korean society quite directly.

The film centers on the suicide by drowning of a suburban, small-town schoolgirl who had been raped by several of her teenage classmates. Yang Mi-ja (played by Yoon Jeong-hee—a major star of Korean cinema in the '60s and '70s who had not appeared in a film since 1994, and had to be lured out of retirement by Lee), the grandmother of one of the rapists, subsists on welfare and on working as a part-time caregiver for a wealthy and elderly man who has had a stroke while she lives with her self-absorbed grandson, whose divorced mother lives in Busan. Diagnosed with Alzheimer's disease, Mi-ja responds to her encroaching forgetfulness by enrolling in a poetry class at a local community center, where she's encouraged to write one poem about what she sees in everyday life. Meanwhile, she is summoned to a meeting by the fathers of several of the boys who raped the girl who drowned herself, proposing a bribe of 30 million won to the girl's mother.

I suspect that Lee's former experiences as both a novelist and, in 2003-2004, as South Korea's Minister of Culture and Tourism, served him well in his conception of and preparations for *Poetry*, which deservedly won the Best Screenplay Award at the Cannes Film Festival and many separate awards elsewhere for Yoon's singular and powerful performance.

Lost in Auschwitz: *Son of Saul*

From the Chicago Reader *(January 28, 2016).*

The sense of being lost is what we wanted to convey. That is what was missing before [in most earlier movies about the Holocaust]: one individual being lost.

—László Nemes to Andrea Gronvall, *Movie City News*

László Nemes' first feature, opening this week at the Music Box, is easily the most exciting new film I've seen over the past year, and a casual look at the prizes and accolades it's received over the past eight months, starting with the Grand Prix and FIPRESCI prize at Cannes, shows that I'm far from alone in feeling this way. Even my colleagues who dislike or dismiss the films concede that it's a stunning technical achievement. But the moment one starts to describe what the film does, or even what it's about, a certain amount of troubling dissension sets in.

Nemes and his lead actor Géza Röhrig have consistently described their intentions as wanting viewers to experience viscerally and as accurately as possible what Sonderkommando members went through in Auschwitz in October 1944. These were the Jewish prisoners obliged to lead other Jews into the gas chambers, search their clothes for valuables before, during, and after they were being gassed, and then dispose of their bodies—carting them off, burning them, and then shoveling away their ashes, receiving in return slightly better food and quarters before eventually being exterminated themselves. The only direct records we have of their experience were written and buried by a few members—we may be witnessing one such burial, out of focus, in the film's opening shot—to be read by future generations, and Nemes made his film to honor these accounts, adding that he's left interpretations of this experience quite open.

But complicating this is the narrative thread Nemes has chosen—a Hungarian member named Saul Ausländer (Röhrig) present at the seeming miracle of a Jewish boy briefly surviving the gas chamber (before being smothered to death by a Nazi soldier) and then becoming obsessed with the notion of giving his corpse a proper Jewish funeral with a rabbi, improbably declaring to other prisoners that the boy is his son. Futhermore, Nemes compels us to witness the horrors of the Holocaust only peripherally, the way that Saul sees them while being forced to do his work. I assume this is what led the *New York Times'* Manohla Dargis to describe the film as "radically dehistoricized" and "intellectually repellent"—attributes that I'd be more inclined to assign to the period bloodbaths of Quintin Tarantino, including the latest one, also showing at the Music Box. But Tarantino's pop credentials seem to grant him a certain leeway denied to art movies. Dargis's *Times* colleague A.O. Scott concluded his mainly respectful review by writing that Nemes' "skill is undeniable, but also troubling. The movie offers less insight than sensation, an emotional experience that sits too comfortably within the norms of entertainment." In some respects, this dimly recalls Theodor Adorno's famous 1949 statement—"To write poetry after Auschwitz is barbaric"—albeit presumably revised to allow for the playfully impudent entertainments of a Tarantino, if not for the visceral art strategies of a Nemes, where the stakes are higher.

The film begins and ends with images that exist independently of Saul's perceptions, and most of the shots in between, while not literally subjective, are restricted to what remains visible within his field of vision, often in close-up. In many ways, Nemes remains old-fashioned in his visual strategies, using a narrow screen ratio and shooting in 35-millimeter: the reason why *Son of Saul* is showing in Chicago at the Music Box rather than elsewhere is that he wants it to be seen on film rather than digitally. This is undoubtedly the way surviving members of the Sonderkommando would imagine it being shown. And the dialogue by Nemes and his cowriter, novelist Clara Royer—in German, Yiddish, Hugarian, and Polish--is equally constrained, consisting of terse and telegraphic whispered exchanges that are all the prisoners can manage while being hustled or hurtled from one job to the next.

Given Saul's own circumstances, including his stated conviction to another prisoner that "we're already dead", his obsession with granting the boy a

Jewish funeral is completely irrational—though as filmmaker Mehrnaz Saeed-Vafa has pointed out to me, no more irrational than the obsession of Mr. Badii in Abbas Kiarostami's *Taste of Cherry* to find someone who will agree to bury him after he commits suicide in an open grave. This is a given we're obliged to accept in order to follow the narrative in either film, and once we accept it, we find ourselves at the center of an ambiguous parable about life as well as death. This is arguably where the real dissension begins. Formulating my own interpretation, I've concluded that Saul's behavior and mission are actually a practical way of holding onto his sanity in the midst of facilitating the genocide of his own people, even while he fails to help implement a planned escape from the Auschwitz camp and even unwittingly causes the death of at least one other member of his crew. I still think this is true, but J. Hoberman claims that *Son of Saul* is "a movie set in Auschwitz that concerns a member of the Sonderkommando who goes mad," and I suppose this makes an equal amount of sense, given his own interpretation.

As a former assistant to Béla Tarr, another Hungarian, Nemes is no less concerned with implicating the viewer in the movements and perceptions of his characters and in their moral and humanist consequences, without ever explicitly judging who they are or what they do—the style of a rigorous existential taskmaster. But Tarr's rhythms are slow while Nemes' are frenetic, giving us, like Saul, less time to think or reflect and more compulsion to act or react spontaneously. Seeing the film as a Jew who knew about the Sonderkommando (and who regarded their job and fate as the very worst of all the Nazis' crimes) but who'd never been forced to identify with them, I find myself sharing Saul's panic, and that response becomes part of the meaning and significance of the parable.

The hero's full name becomes another part—not only "Ausländer", German for "foreigner", but also "Saul", which suggests both the king of the Hebrew Bible and the Saul who became Paul on the road to Damascus—leading me to conclude that the parable may finally relate to something broader and more transcendental than tribal Judaism, decreed in Auschwitz by Nazis and Saul alike as an ultimate curse or blessing—has been broken and something more transcendental, fleeting, and even faintly hopeful emerges, in the film's closing moments.

Selected Moments: Some Recollections of Movie Time

Commissioned by and written for a collection entitled Time, *published in February 2016 by Punto de Vista, Festival Internacional de Cine Documental de Navarra in Pamplona, Spain. In some respects, this can be regarded as a kind of crash course in some of the major concerns of my film and literary criticism. (For more on* Light in August *and* Sátántangó, *see my essay in my previous collection,* Cinematic Encounters: Portraits and Polemics.*)*

1. My first sixteen years (1943-1959)—growing up in northwestern Alabama as the grandson and son of Jewish movie theater exhibitors—ensured that time and cinema were alternately parallel and crisscrossing rivers that coursed through my childhood, along with the Tennessee River that separated Florence from Sheffield. Florence, where I lived, had three of the Rosenbaum theaters, at least until 1951, all within a three-block radius, while Sheffield, which I could see across the river from my backyard, had two more theaters, one around the corner from the other. For Southerners like myself, the past was always present, a kind of double vision that movies taught me as well—a camera's recording of the past becoming the present of both a screen and an audience, which then in retrospective memory becomes the past as well. And for Jews like myself, the past was also identity—meaning one's past, present, and future. This explains why Lanzmann's *Shoah* represents a shotgun marriage between the present tense of existentialism and the past tense of Judaism.

During my childhood, movies were a way of measuring time and time was a way of measuring movies, even if my easy access into most of the local theaters meant that my own time could easily and often did supersede the movie's time. As was common for everyone during most of that period, I could go to the movies without specific schedules or timetables, sometimes entering in the middle of a feature and then staying to roughly the same point in the following screening of the same feature, or leaving temporarily in the middle of a film to buy a comic book down the street before returning. An additional privilege that

I had, if I wanted to use it, was glancing inside the ticket-taker's booth in the lobby—an "insider's" look—to read the precise menu of feature(s) and shorts to be found later in the auditorium, complete with titles and running times. In a manner of speaking, you might say I was able to be inside and outside the film experience at the same time, a privilege afforded today by digital home viewing. Back then, in a certain fashion, it made me a film critic long before I even knew what the term meant, and I even had a choice of entrances at a couple of theaters denied to ordinary patrons—staff entrances that led directly from my father and grandfather's upstairs offices into the balcony at the largest Florence theater, the Shoals, which opened in 1948, or from their previous ground-floor offices towards the downstairs seats at the Princess.

Walking from either the street or the offices into the Princess or Shoals meant stepping from Alabama time into movie time, where Alabama time was suddenly suspended. And movie time wasn't necessarily or invariably different from literary time: only a few counties away, in Oxford, Mississippi—a dozen years before I was born, a year before he went to work for Howard Hawks in Hollywood—William Faulkner was writing my favorite novel, *Light in August*, which begins in and periodically reverts to the present tense, the immediacy of movie time: "Sitting beside the road, watching the wagon mount the hill towards her, Lena thinks, 'I have come from Alabama: a fur piece.'" All the way from Alabama a-walking. A fur piece.' Faulkner clearly learned as much from movies as he did from Joseph Conrad (another cinematic writer).

This sense of cinematic literary time is no less evident in the beginning of the novel's sixth chapter, plunging us into the consciousness and memory of the other major character, Joe Christmas, as metaphysical/expressionistic and as cluttered with debris as Lena Grove's is physical/realistic and economically tidy: "Memory believes before knowing remembers. Believes longer than recollects, longer than knowing even wonders. Knows remembers believes a corridor in a big long garbled cold echoing building of dark red brick sootbleakened by more chimneys than its own, set in a grassless cinderstrewnpacked compound surrounded by smoking factory purlieus and enclosed by a ten foot steel-and-wire fence like a penitentiary or a zoo, where in random erratic surges, with sparrowlike childtrembling, orphans in identical and uniform blue denim in and out of remembering but in knowing constant as the bleak walls, the bleak windows where in rain soot from the yearly adjacenting chimneys streaked like black tears." Cinematically speaking, Lena's mind is like *Rio Bravo* and Joe's is like *Eraserhead*. Or, in the literary terms of Erich Auerbach's great essay ("Odysseus' Scar"), Lena's mind is Homeric and continuous (or, in Faulkner's terms, "like something moving forever and without progress across an urn"), whereas Joe's is as riddled with narrative gaps, unexplained motivations, and sudden leaps forward as the Old Testament.

Today, of course, digital home viewing has altered all these temporal options, so that my time now supersedes movie time. I can stop the movie and start it up again or reverse or fast-forward or freeze the flow, meanwhile altering the shape and size of the image, and Chicago time has relatively little to do with either my time or movie time—which is why I'm fond of saying that I live on the Internet, which has a time and flow of its own, and relatively speaking, only sleep and eat in Chicago.

How, then, can I explain or examine the rift between today's home-digital movie time and my childhood's theater-analog movie time, except to say that literary time has more to do with the latter than with the former? Today I can bookmark, scan, retrace, and even quote from my movies, as I've just quoted from *Light in August*, and furthermore feel far more qualified to call them mine because I can handle them like books—turning to favorite passages, skipping certain parts, or freezing their flow whenever I want to.

And in tracing the steps between Alabama and Illinois, between "Now and Then" (the title of my first published work in prose, significantly a tale about time travel), all that I can hope to do here is to list a few temporal way-stations within that yawning rift, a selection of diverse moments, places, and occasions involving movie time—or my own writing or reading at various times about movie time. *(Note: all of my own texts quoted from here and some additional texts about all the works cited can be found in their entirety at jonathanrosenbaum.net.)*

One effort of mine to navigate this background is my memoir *Moving Places*, the longest chapter of which, "On Moonlight Bay as Time Machine," runs through that Doris Day musical in order to access myself respectively at age eight, seeing the film for the first time at the Shoals in October 1951; myself at ten, reseeing it at a Jewish boys' camp in Maine in July 1953; and myself at age 34, in December 1977, reseeing the film on a rented color TV in southern California while smoking a joint and taping the soundtrack on a cassette recorder, then playing the cassette back and writing about the film at diverse times over the following year. (The joint is worth mentioning because it subjectively slows time down.)

2. It was during my two years at a boarding school in Putney, Vermont (1959-61) that I first saw *Citizen Kane*, and during my year and a half at New York University (1961-62), before moving up the Hudson River to Bard College,

that I first saw *L'Année Dernière à Marienbad* (again and again, over a single week)—two seminal and formative spatiotemporal encounters that fractured and scrambled conventional narrative time frames and spatial parameters, leapfrogging between and within shots, places, and mental spaces.

3. During most of my years at Bard (1962-66), running the Friday night film series, I booked and showed such films as *Greed, Variety, Freaks, Trouble in Paradise, The Magnificent Ambersons, Ivan the Terrible, Ikiru, The Phenix City Story, Sawdust and Tinsel, This Sporting Life, Jules et Jim,* and *Zazie dans le métro*—essentially conducting my own film history seminar long before such a course could or would have been offered academically at Bard, and meanwhile picking up what I could from these films about other periods and countries.

The only film I wound up screening twice at Bard was my favorite at the time, Murnau's *Sunrise*, and one of its emotional high points for me was George O'Brien's walk across the marshes at night towards his secret erotic rendezvous with Margaret Livingstone, accompanied by a camera movement that begins as purely physical and then suddenly rushes ahead of him through the thicket to become metaphysical, arriving at the appointed spot before he does. The lesson of this voluptuous transition was in part grammatical—the realization that just as a single sentence could move from the physical to the metaphysical, so could a camera movement within a single shot or take.

But it's worth adding that a shot and a take aren't precisely or necessarily the same thing, especially in relation to time and narrative as they're perceived. Much of my schooling in the difference between the two came from the Nouvelle Vague of Godard, Rivette, and Truffaut and the critical dimension that informed their filmmaking, leading to an overall sense that they and not their characters were the true heroes of their films. And part of their heroism came from their metaphysical appreciations of American physicality, which influenced an entire generation of subsequent American critics (myself undoubtedly included).

Andrew Sarris once argued (in 1966) that the slow lap dissolves in Josef von Sternberg's *The Docks of New York* "serve the same function as Godard's jump cuts in *Breathless*, and that is to indicate the meaninglessness of the time intervals between moral decisions." This is existentialism with a vengeance, ignoring the musical as well as physical differences between slow dissolves and fast cuts for the sake of moral and metaphysical blueprints, and I think it could be argued that this type of reasoning is profoundly American in its implicit privileging of transcendental and symbolic meanings over material realities. (The same sort of impulse has made it impossible for American mainstream discourse to cope with the notion of a Barack Obama—or a Joe Christmas— who is half white and half black, existentially limiting their identities to black by default in both cases. And of course the very terms "white" and "black" to describe these people are more symbolic than physically descriptive.)

4. First encountering Jacques Tati's *PlayTime* as an American tourist in Paris in 1968, before moving more permanently to that city from New York the following year, I was struck by how successfully the film managed to encapsulate the events of an entire day in only two hours without any obvious ellipses. Like a magician's sleight of hand, this becomes a trick of implied temporal continuity that is gently imposed over the multiple spatial discontinuities created by architectural uniformity and the diverse confusions of glass reflections and competing focal points. One way in which this film gradually teaches me how to live in cities is its lesson in how to look creatively, carving one's own spatial symmetries and counter-balances out of the chaos of sensory overload that assaults us whenever we're walking down a city street. The film gradually evolves in terms of gazes and other human movements from regimented straight lines and right angles into playful and spontaneous curves and circles, with the film's populace developing in the same fashion, much as the music that we hear gradually evolves from tunes in 4/4 time to waltzes. In fact, the gift of music is what makes this liberation possible by turning one's own exploratory glances into impromptu dance movements.

5. In the first of my "Paris Journals" written for *Film Comment* (Fall 1971), published almost halfway through my five years in that city (1969-74), the two films that excited me most, both of which I was belatedly catching up with at the time, were two tales about encroaching madness, Jean-Daniel Pollet's 37-minute *Le Horla* (1966) and Jacques Rivette's 252-minute *L'amour fou* (1968), each of which excelled in a different way through its treatment of time.

Regarding the first, "Pollet has indicated in an interview that his interest in the project was not so much De Maupassant's horror story itself but the problem of integrating the text into a cinematic structure. Part of his solution is to maintain a fluid continuity in the spoken first-person narration while locating this discourse through montage in three alternating 'relative' tenses: past (the plot unfolding beneath the narration), present (the narrator recounting the action into a tape recorder), and future (the tape recorder playing his voice in an abandoned rowboat). Thus while the story's chronology and continuity are respected, the montage enables the film to achieve a semi-autonomous achronological structure of its own, and the tensions between these coexisting forms produces some extraordinary effects—effects, moreover, which serve the original story admirably, enclosing its intimations of possession and madness in a rigid continuum of haunting finality. Equally striking is a bold thematic use of color, with the richest blues this side of *Pierrot le fou*." Even more, the solitary hero's crazed intimations of an invisible *doppelgänger* lurking nearby and waiting to replace him, even reading the same texts over his shoulders, are neatly replicated by the camera's own positions and activities, and the hero's fear of being supplanted by the monster seems borne out by the way that the tape recorder replaces Laurent Terzieff in the otherwise empty rowboat.

Bulle Ogier's monologues into a tape recorder in *L'amour fou* are no less unsettling, but in this case the main temporal issue is duration rather than tense—the consequences of living with the principal characters for over four hours—and the main source of visual contrast is the oscillation between 16-millimeter and 35-millimeter during the theater rehearsals. In both of these seminal film experiments, the shifts between recording mechanisms disrupt the transparency of what's being recorded, so that our grasp of any firm distinction between storytelling and subject becomes as unhinged as our grasp of the differences between sanity and madness. (In *Light in August*, a comparable form of madness known as racism arises from the inability of determining whether Joe Christmas is "white" or "black", an abstraction in either case—which forces us to acknowledge that "sanity," "insanity," "white," and "black" are ultimately social definitions, not material attributes.)

6. From "Gertrud as Nonnarrative: The Desire for the Image" (*Sight and Sound*, Winter 1985-86): "There are narrative and nonnarrative ways of summing up a life or conjuring a work of art, but when it comes to analyzing life or art in dramatic terms, it is usually the narrative method that wins hands down. Our news, fiction, and daily conversations all tend to take a story form, and our reflexes define that form as consecutive and causal—a chain of events moving in the direction of an inquiry, the solution of a riddle. Faced with a succession of film frames, our desire to impose a narrative is usually so strong that only the most ruthless and delicate of strategies can allow us to perceive anything else.

"Carl Dreyer allows us to perceive something else, but never without a battle. The nonnarrative specter that haunts the narrative of *Gertrud* (1964), contained in the figure of Gertrud herself, is threatened at every turn by dogs snapping at her heels—a narrative world of men with pasts and futures who stake a claim on her. But Gertrud, who lives only in a continuous present, persistent and changeless, eludes them all. And if she eludes us as well, this may be because our narrative equipment can read her only as a monotone—an arrested moment (as in painting) or a suspended moment (as in music) that can lead to no higher logic. Yet from the vantage point of her refusal to inquire, she has a lot to say to the men."

7. Another film that superimposes past over present within the same shots is Françoise Romand's highly unorthodox TV documentary *Mix-up* (1985), tracing the extended repercussions on two extended families of an accidental mix-up of babies in an English hospital in the 1930s and the confirmation of this error only three decades later. Because various stages in this long narrative are made to coexist in the present, the plot and characters eventually register with the "density of a 500-page novel. And the subject is treated so exhaustively that the film's sixty-three minutes register like a much longer film. Interviewing virtually all the members of both families, including the daughters who grew up with the wrong parents, Romand also restages some key scenes in the midst of these interviews, conducting a sort of collective psychoanalysis, so that when one brother "crouches as an adult under a table to describe a conversation he overheard under the same table at age thirteen, the moment is uncanny." (*Sight and Sound*, October 2010).

8. "It's obvious that most of us watch films while we're seated. But just because it's obvious doesn't mean that it isn't worthy of some reflection—and reflection, after all, is something else that's often best done while we're sitting. Yet the artificial sensation of speed that characterizes so much of contemporary commercial cinema, American cinema in particular—the speed of fast cars and explosions and what we call 'action', not to mention the speed of much TV editing, all of which tends to make Ozu seem 'conservative' and 'old-fashioned' by comparison—tends to deny this fact, to operate as if we were literally watching films on the run, without any opportunities for reflection.

"Ozu's acknowledgment that we watch films while sitting seems to me a fundamental aspect of his style, and a great deal that is considered difficult or problematical or simply 'slow' in his style derives from this essential fact. As a rule, characters in Ozu films are seated when they eat and when they converse. *In I Was Born, But...*, the two little boys who are the central characters are mainly seen on their feet, but early in the film they are seated when they have breakfast, when they put on their shoes before leaving their house, and then when they decide to skip school and have their lunch in a field. They are also seated when they attend school the following day, when they watch home movies at the home of the father's boss, and later, after their fight with their father, when they refuse to eat. All of these occasions might be described as times of relative reflection.

"But this is a film in which social behavior and social conditioning are at least as important as reflection, and the issue of speed is relevant to all three activities. Early in the film, after the boys skip school out of fear of getting beaten up and have their lunch in the field, one of the brothers reminds the other, 'We're supposed to get an A in writing today.' Soon afterwards they both stand up to finish their lunch on their feet, an action which implies, as much else in the film does, that getting ahead in the world requires alertness and motion, both of which are usually more obtainable from a standing position." (From "Is Ozu Slow?", a lecture delivered at a symposium, "Yasujiro Ozu in the World," in Tokyo, December 11, 1998.)

9. "*The Clock* is certainly dumb: a 24-hour movie made entirely from other movies in which the depicted screen time corresponds precisely to the actual time of the screening with plenty of clock inserts and shots in which clocks appear, sometimes incidentally. I'm sure I'm not the first to ask, why didn't I think of that? But is *The Clock* dumb enough?" (Thom Andersen, "Random Notes on a Projection of *The Clock* by Christian Marclay at the Los Angeles County Museum of Art, 4:32 pm, July 28, 2011-5:02 pm, July 29, 2011" (*Cinema Scope*, Fall 2011).

10. A few other things I could have discussed: films involving real time and long takes (e.g., Robert Frank's 1990 *One Hour*, Béla Tarr's 1994 *Sátántangó*, László Nemes' *Son of Saul*—all three masterpieces); Resnais' *Hiroshima, Marienbad*, and *Providence*, not to mention *Je t'aime, je t'aime* and *Mélo*; evocations of cosmic time in *2001: A Space Odyssey* (1968), *A.I. Artificial Intelligence* (2001), Olaf Stapledon's *Star Maker* (1937), and the TV series *Big History* (2014); and implications of psychoanalytical time in the first four films of Peter Thompson (1982 and 1986).

Johnny Guitar: The First Existential Western?

Written for the Olive Films Blu-Ray in 2016.

François Truffaut called it the *Beauty and the Beast* of Westerns, without saying who was the beauty and who was the beast. (One could find many candidates for either role). And Jean-Luc Godard, in his second feature, *Le petit soldat*, offered a spin on the movie's most celebrated dialogue exchange, before offering explicit references to *Johnny Guitar* in several other films he made in the '60s:

> **Johnny (Sterling Hayden):** Tell me something nice.
> **Vienna (Joan Crawford):** Sure. What would you like to hear?
> **Johnny:** Lie to me, tell me that all these years you've waited, tell me.
> **Vienna:** All these years I've waited.
> **Johnny:** Tell me you'd have died if I hadn't come back.
> **Vienna:** I would have died if you hadn't come back.
> **Johnny:** Tell me you still love me like I love you.
> **Vienna:** I still love you like you love me.
> **Johnny:** (softly and sarcastically, about to down another shot of whisky) Thanks.
> **Bruno (Michel Subor):** Lie to me . . . Say you aren't sad that I'm leaving.
> **Véronica (Anna Karina):** I'm not sad that you're leaving. I'm not in love with you. I won't join you in Brazil. I don't kiss you tenderly.

Back in 1954, at age eleven, I was lucky enough to see *Johnny Guitar* on a big screen, during its first run, and it was already clear to me that this movie was something special. When a wounded teenage gunslinger named Turkey (Ben Cooper) was forced by an angry mob to betray his only friend, Vienna, with a lie in order to save his life but then was lynched anyway, I couldn't yet read this outrage as a conscious reference to the contemporaneous horrors of the Hollywood witch hunt. But the scene, as shocking as it was, nevertheless felt real and authentic in its awful immediacy, and that was only one of the many shocks that the film had to offer. This is a film, after all, that literally opens with an explosion, and one where even the rolling of a shot glass across a bar counter is made to seem almost cataclysmic. So even if, as I would learn much later, Joan Crawford, Sterling Hayden, and the movie's director, Nicholas Ray, all initially regarded *Johnny Guitar* with distaste and disdain, for reasons that I'll get to shortly, this certainly wasn't the way that I and thousands of other filmgoers thought and felt about this movie at the time; it was even a hit. Many of the original reviewers were dismissive—especially in the trade press, where the giddy style of it all made them regard it as something like a bad joke—but this only goes to show how unreliable such reviews can be.

Later on, *Johnny Guitar* became known as one of the first "adult" Westerns, along with such equally Freudian productions as *Pursued* (1947) and *The Furies* (1950), which seems just in some respects. Nicholas Ray was one of the first Hollywood directors of the period who could somehow convey to audiences that his romantic couples actually had sex together—Dixon Steele (Humphrey Bogart) and Laurel Gray (Gloria Graham) in *In a Lonely Place* (1950), Johnny Logan aka Johnny Guitar and Vienna (not to mention The Dancing Kid [Scott Brady] and Vienna)—even though their relationships remain troubled and unstable. The sexual reunion of Vienna and Johnny is even highlighted by the ironic reprise of Johnny's line that all a man needs is a cup of coffee and a cigarette by Old Tom (John Carradine).

Yet it's indeed the troubled relation these characters have to their assigned gender roles, the sense that these are constantly on the verge of slipping out of gear, that makes Johnny, The Dancing Kid, Turkey, Vienna, and even the latter's major adversary, Emma (Mercedes McCambridge), seem so contemporary in their common neuroses. "Westerns may be an essentially masculine genre," critic Imogen Sara Smith has aptly pointed out, "but Ray's androgynous, operatic film reveals the flamboyance and feverish anxiety ingrained in that anxiety." Even the supposedly peaceable and affable Johnny Guitar turns out to be "gun crazy" or trigger-happy when Turkey starts shooting up the saloon, as volatile as Dixon Steele was.

All these characters operate according to the existential postulate that you are what you do and vice versa—and that what you do is most of all what other people see you doing. ("What's going on with you two?" The Dancing Kid asks Vienna and Johnny, and the latter responds, "Just what you see, friend.") Thus Johnny proves his identity by strumming his guitar, and The Dancing Kid establishes his credentials by taking Emma for an impromptu turn across the floor of Vienna's saloon, while the masculine credentials of both men, and Turkey and Bart (Ernest Borgnine) to boot, have to be further tested with various dares, taunts, and acts of bravado. Even more confusingly, Vienna's shifting status as boss, lover, mother, desperado, or peacemaker has to be continually proven and reproven, sometimes with costume changes to match the various shifts. She first appears in trousers, but when she later comes back downstairs to engage in the dialogue with Johnny quoted above, supposedly because she can't sleep, she's improbably wearing an evening dress, as if to contradict her claim that her sexual and romantic interest in Johnny Logan has turned into ashes. At another point, Vienna claims that Emma's undying hatred for her stems from her inability to accept that she's sexually attracted to The Dancing Kid, but more than one commentator has surmised that some other form of puritanical repression and transference—maybe even a denial of her lust for Vienna—might be involved. (Indeed, one could argue that the only evidence of visible and unbridled sexual excitement in the entire film is Emma's look of ecstatic triumph as Vienna's saloon is going up in flames.) No one—except, perhaps, for an old-school meanie and self-absorbed villain like Bart—is entirely whom he or she seems to be, despite the apparent necessity to proclaim who and what s(he) is at every turn, which only begins to account for some of the existential conflicts involved. And in keeping with some of Ray's other films, even though the romantic relationships in *Johnny Guitar* are peppered with rivalries, resentments, and bitter regrets, many surrogate families abound: Vienna and her employees, her maternal bond with Turkey, The Dancing Kid and his gang, and even the members of a funeral party that quickly mutates into a lynch mob.

All these characters have troubled and anguished backstories that are only partially spelled out, and the actors' and director's backstories play some part in these fragmented legacies. One might even postulate that the fact that all four of the actors playing The Dancing Kid's gang—Scott Brady, Ernest Borgnine, Ben Cooper, and Royal Dano—were New Yorkers contributed to the contemporary hipster atmosphere that Ray already brought to his more personal projects, in this case lending a touch of city smarts to the pastoral and frontier settings. And even though Nicholas Ray is commonly regarded nowadays as the sole auteur of *Johnny Guitar*, there's plenty of evidence to support Joan Crawford as a full partner in some of the creative decisions, for better and for worse, starting with the fact that she was the film's producer. Her famous feud with Mercedes McCambridge during the film's production, which led to her shredding Emma's costumes and scattering them on the street after McCambridge was applauded by the crew for her performance, and was followed by her bringing in Philip Yordan to write "five new scenes," was clearly stoked by her former romantic and sexual entanglements with both McCambridge's current husband (the Canadian producer, director, and actor Fletcher Markle, best known for his work in radio and television) and, more recently, with Ray himself. It was undoubtedly exacerbated by Ray's friendship with McCambridge, by most of the crew and other actors taking sides with McCambridge in the feud, and by the fact that the local and eventually the national press (including Los Angeles newspapers and *Confidential*) had a field day with the battling female egos, which may have helped to secure the film's commercial success. Hayden, who was still traumatized by his recent testimony as a "friendly witness" before the House Committee on Un-American Activities, and who didn't know how to play a guitar, ride a horse, or fire a gun, was sufficiently alienated from the emotional crossfire and tensions on the set to consider the film a dud, and later declared, "There is not enough money in Hollywood to lure me into making another picture with Joan Crawford. Her treatment of Mercedes was a shameful thing."

The film's original script was written by a friend of Crawford's, Roy Chanselor, adapting his own novel, which was likely written with Crawford in mind, and one of her reasons for summoning Philip Yordan—a celebrated script doctor (as well as a blacklist front)—to the Sedona, Arizona location to write new scenes was to make her part more that of a male lead. As Yordan recounted her instructions to Ray's first biographer, Bernard Eisenschitz (in *Nicholas Ray: An American Journey* [London/Boston: Faber and Faber, 1993]), "She said that she wanted to play the man's role. She said, 'I'm Clark Gable, it's Vienna that's gotta be the leading part.'" And according to Ray's second biographer, Patrick McGilligan (in *Nicholas Ray: The Glorious Failure of an American Director* [New York: HarperCollins, 2011]), Crawford complained to Yordan, " I have no part. I just stand around with boots on and have a few stupid scenes. I want to play the man. I want to shoot it out at the end with Mercedes McCambridge and instead of me playing with myself in a corner. Let Sterling play with himself in the corner...."

It's also clear that Ray collaborated with Yordan on writing the new scenes, although the extent of their collaboration has never been fully clarified, so that one can't establish beyond a shadow of a doubt that it was Ray who wrote the famous dialogue between Vienna and Johnny quoted above, much as Ray's champions have always wanted to attribute it to him. (According to Yordan again, Ray "collaborated with me less on the dramatic than on the architectural level, creating settings like the saloon, working on the geometrical relationships between places.")

Ray embarked on this film with expectations of it being his first effort as an independent producer (as well as director), but once Crawford took over enough of the production to crowd out his producer's credit, his personal stamp, while still visible, wasn't as comprehensive as what he'd hoped for. Where it flourishes most clearly is in the décor and costumes, the vibrant color-coding and the intensity of the actors' performances. Having virtually begun his career as a student of Frank Lloyd Wright, a member of Wright's Taliesin Fellowship (a stint that proved short-lived, perhaps due in part to Ray's bisexuality and Wright's homophobia), Ray shows that influence most strikingly in the interior design of Vienna's saloon—the integral use of red rock and the shape of the rafters. As for the color-coding, what he does with red, yellow, and black becomes as integral to the dramaturgy as it would be the following year in *Rebel Without a Cause*, with such items as Vienna's and Turkey's shirts and Emma's mourning veil playing central roles.

Yet for all its modernity, what still makes *Johnny Guitar* fit Truffaut's description as the "Beauty and the Beast" of Westerns is its poetry, its feeling of timeless myth—its ordering of all four elements (red rock, air, fire, waterfall) into the shape of a fairy tale or a folk ballad. Given Ray's experience during the Depression of collecting and recording folk music with Alan Lomax, his brilliant uses of Victor Young's evocative title tune, which sounds both traditional and contemporary, encapsulate the film's double-dealing strategy of seeming both historical and up-to-the-minute.

Orson Welles's *Macbeth*s

Written for the Olive Films Blu-Ray in 2016.

[Orson Welles's] desire to transcend the barriers separating the classics, the avant-garde, and popular culture remains, I believe, his most enduring legacy.

— Michael Andregg, Orson Welles, *Shakespeare and Popular Culture* (1999)

It seems probable that no American film director ever rattled the American mainstream more than Orson Welles, and none of his features rattled that mainstream more than his two versions of *Macbeth*, made successively out of the same material he shot in 1947, released successively in the U.S. in 1948 and 1950. Welles's fifth completed feature was the first of many that would come out in more than one version, and the first that decisively shifted his public status, against his own wishes, from that of commercial studio director to that of arthouse auteur—a profile that would be deviated from only by *Touch of Evil* a decade later, the only other studio feature he would ever make.

Welles's approach to the material is wildly neo-primitive and so expressionistic that one can never be entirely sure whether the action is taking place in interiors or exteriors; the same ambiguity persists in the spoken text, where off-screen internal monologue and on-screen external speech often seem only a breath apart. The witches' foaming, bubbling cauldron and Macbeth's equally unstable consciousness are the closest we can get to any continuous sense of location, and the unabashed B-movie artificiality of the sets confirms that Welles wanted to draft something closer to a charcoal sketch than a finished canvas. This skyless world of cave dwellers and fog is split obscurely between pagan Druid artifacts that resemble pitchforks and the no less barbaric crosses of early Christianity (the latter signaled by Alan Napier's Holy Father, a character invented by Welles, whose lines are drawn from those of other characters)—a polarity that only intensifies the atmosphere of moral confusion. As in Welles's never-realized first Hollywood project, *Heart of Darkness*, bestiality and tyranny are seen as opposite sides of the same coin.

An aristocrat and a populist whose taste was both highbrow and lowbrow—and thus opposed to the middle-brow, middle-class taste that ruled American culture at mid-century, especially when it came to William Shakespeare—Welles, born in 1915, was as much a child of the nineteenth century as he was a prophet of the twentieth, which meant that his view of Shakespeare harked back to the time when Shakespeare was a staple of American popular "low" culture, not a prized exhibit in elitist and effete "high" culture. As Lawrence W. Levine demonstrates in *Highbrow/Lowbrow: The Emergence of Culture Hierarchy in America* (Harvard University Press, 1988), this was a version of Shakespeare subject to massive cuts and anachronistic interpolations, teeming with melodrama, that spoke directly to all walks of life: "Shakespeare was performed not merely alongside popular entertainment as an elite supplement to it; Shakespeare was performed as an integral part of it. Shakespeare was popular entertainment in nineteenth-century America. The theater in the first half of the nineteenth century played the role that movies played in the first half of the twentieth: it was a kaleidoscopic, democratic institution presenting a widely varying bill of fare to all classes and socioeconomic groups." As early as the 1830s, when he was touring the U.S., Alexis de Tocqueville found that "There is hardly a pioneer's hut that does not contain a few odd volumes of Shakespeare. I remember that I read the feudal drama of *Henry V* for the first time in a log cabin."

This lost tradition evokes Welles's intentions for his film of *Macbeth*, but not, alas, the film's negative reception in the U.S. (It was greeted much more favorably in France, where its champions included Robert Bresson, Marcel Carné, and Jean Cocteau.) Yet it seems that Welles came much closer to succeeding on his own ambitious terms when he performed the play twice on the stage—first in Harlem in 1936, with an all-black cast and the setting switched to Haiti (his famous "voodoo" *Macbeth*), then in Salt Lake City in 1947 with the original Scottish setting, in preparation for the film, with the same principal actors he would use and elements of the same design. And in between those productions he did two audio versions, in 1937 on CBS radio (with Irving Reis directing) and then in 1940 for 78-rpm records (a full-scale performance by his Mercury players, with music by Bernard Herrmann, only three months before he began to shoot *Citizen Kane*—a recording that is still available today).

According to Welles biographer Simon Callow, the Salt Lake City production "was the sort of thing—less considered, less detailed, but equally electric in its impact—that Max Reinhardt had done in Salzburg: a kind of sophisticated folk theatre, attended by the whole town (or as near as dammit). It was, said Governor Herbert Maw, 'the greatest thing that ever happened in Utah,' which certainly puts Brigham Young in his place." It opened with the audience plunged into total darkness (even the exit signs were illegally masked) and listening to the sounds of six bagpipes slowly crossing the auditorium from the rear and then exiting, followed by an explosion in the orchestra pit that unleashed the three witches. Although the show ran for only four days (with two matinees added for schoolchildren), it received favorable reviews in both *Variety* and the *New York Times*. Yet when American reviewers encountered the film carved out of this production, it was almost universally scorned. *Life* magazine devoted a three-page spread to ridiculing it, headlined, "MURDER! Orson Welles doth foully slaughter Shakespeare in dialect version of his Tragedy of Macbeth," and remarked of one still, "The scene opposite is not, as you might think, from a musical comedy skit in an alcoholics' ward..."

What happened? Obviously the differences between stage and screen are profound, but no one knew this better than Welles himself. Despite his plan to use the stage production as a sort of trial run for the film, he clearly wasn't interested in simply filming that production but in making something different out of the same raw materials that was equally theatrical in its own way. Just for starters, he had a musical overture that lasted for almost eight minutes before the picture even started—utilizing not bagpipes but a sinister orchestral score by French composer Jacques Ibert that was recorded in Europe. (His original plan for Herrmann to write the score lamentably fell through because Herrmann arrived in Hollywood before a rough cut was available, and he refused to work without one.) Combined with three-and-a-half additional minutes of creepy exit music, this was a horror-show package designed to oppress the viewer on all sides.

The fact that his film abounds in close-ups, which are impossible to achieve on the stage (and which Welles employed only sparingly, at a few key moments, in almost all of his other films), already proves that he was after something quite different from what he had done in Salt Lake City, and closer to his unfulfilled late project to film *King Lear*. More importantly, all his versions of *Macbeth* were part of a much larger effort on behalf of Shakespeare that included a book series called *Everybody's Shakespeare*, coedited with Welles's mentor Roger Hill in the 1930s, an accompanying series of audio recordings of four Shakespeare plays (the *Mercury Text Records*, the last of which was the aforementioned *Macbeth*), and various other forays ranging from a 1938 article about "the teaching of Shakespeare" to hosting and narrating a 1973 educational documentary about *Macbeth*.

The timing of *Macbeth*'s 1948 premiere, in Boston—only a week after Laurence Olivier's much slicker, highly revered, and distinctly middle-brow *Hamlet* (which had already garnered a celebratory eleven-page spread in *Life*) opened in the same city—couldn't have been worse. By this time, Welles had already been persuaded to withdraw *Macbeth* from competition at the Venice Film Festival with the fear of Olivier's *Hamlet* stealing its thunder there. And the U.S. reception was so poor that Republic, in panic mode, obliged Welles to cut half an hour from the film (including the ten minutes of overture and exit music), add an opening voiceover to paper over some of the gaps, and redub what was left without the Scottish accents—although, to his credit, studio boss Herbert J. Yates allowed Welles to carry out this work himself.

Welles had by this time relocated to Italy to star in *Black Magic* and start shooting *Othello* (his first independent production), and had to do the re-editing of *Macbeth* there, with associate producer Richard Wilson serving as stateside intermediary and Welles returning briefly to Republic only to supervise the redubbing.

The curious fact that *Macbeth* resembles at times both a Western and a musical is actually intrinsic to how it was made. (It's worth noting that in 1941, Welles, cinematographer Gregg Toland, and art director Perry Ferguson were scouting locations for a *Life of Christ* conceived as "a kind of primitive Western" set in turn-of-the-century America.) Welles shot it in only three weeks at Republic, a studio specializing in low-budget Westerns (and a few more costly ones, such as the subsequent *Johnny Guitar*), and the experimental method he employed was to prerecord most of the dialogue and then have the actors lip-sync it to playback, the same technique used for songs in musicals. This was a technique Welles had already tried out, and eventually rejected, on his second feature, *The Magnificent Ambersons*, but he had several reasons for reviving it here. Because he had to shoot everything in a hurry, often having two separate crews filming separate scenes at the same time, he figured that not having to worry about the dialogue being properly spoken and recorded at the same time would make it easier for both the actors and the crews. As a longtime veteran of radio, he thought a lot about sound, and he decided that thinking about the sound before and after the shooting would also give him more creative leeway. Regrettably, the actors were also deprived of much of their potential spontaneity, and eventually the prerecording had to be tossed out for the redubbing. Another major loss in the second version was a ten-minute take recording all the events before, during, and immediately after the off-screen murder of Duncan, a year before Alfred Hitchcock made *Rope* (which consists largely of ten-minute takes).

The film's most poetic defense comes from Cocteau, who caught the film in Venice: "Orson Welles's *Macbeth* has a kind of crude, irreverent power. Clad in animal skins like motorists at the turn of the century, horns and cardboard crowns on their heads, his actors haunt the corridors of some dreamlike subway, an abandoned coal mine, and ruined cellars oozing with water. Not a single shot is left to chance. The camera is always placed just where destiny itself would observe its victims. Sometimes we wonder in what period this nightmare is unfolding, and when, for the first time, we see Lady Macbeth, before the camera moves back to situate her, it is almost a woman in modern dress that we are seeing, reclining on a fur-covered divan beside the telephone."

Callow notes that this description makes it all sound like a Cocteau film, which he finds "misleading". But one could also argue that the comparison is apt: both directors are "amateurs" in the best sense (the term derives from the Latin word for "lovers") who playfully juxtapose ancient with contemporary, and both display a knack for making theater cinematic and cinema theatrical—which helps to explain, as Cocteau recounts in the same essay, Welles's own enthusiasm when he saw Cocteau's *Les Parents Terribles* at the same Venice festival. We also know that while Welles was scrupulous about making most of the costumes and sets in *Macbeth* historically accurate, he was no less explicit about making his Lady Macbeth anachronistic—a rather jaundiced version of the contemporary glamour-puss housewife. In other words, Welles's experimental hodgepodge, second-guessing us all while playing for the rafters, is as challenging now as it was in 1948.

Self-Indexing and Shifting Spectators in Varda's *Vagabond*

Adapted from a lecture given at the Filmmuseum Pottsdam, July 6, 2016.

It's unfortunate that Agnès Varda only began to assume the status of a major filmmaker after her husband died and she became known as the custodian of Jacques Demy's precious legacy. Prior to that, she was mainly known, affectionately but somewhat condescendingly, as a sort of mascot of the French New Wave whose public profile remained almost as superficial as that of her eponymous heroine in *Cleo from 5 to 7* (1962). And the troubling, ironic sting at the end of *La Bonheur* (1965) tended to be either misunderstood or ignored. Thanks to the diversity of her films, stylistic and otherwise, she was easy to overlook due to her reluctance to brand herself, unlike her male colleagues.

One fascinating trait that Varda shared with her late husband, however, was the compulsion to become a tireless indexer and cross-referencer of her own work. But instead of bringing back her fictional characters in subsequent films, as Demy did, she more often brought back her locations and her interview subjects. And she went far beyond Demy in becoming her own explicator and analyst, in effect telling her audience what to look for and even how to find it. Two years after she made *The Gleaners and I* (2000), she filmed a series of updates that became a DVD extra. Whenever a particular gleaner appeared in *Two Years Later* (2002), one could hit a flashing potato icon in the upper right corner of the frame with one's remote control that carried one back to the same gleaner in the original film, engaging in a kind of instantaneous time travel.

A twelve-minute extra on the Criterion edition of *Vagabond* about the film's deployments of both music and "dolly" shots (also known as "tracking shots" or, in French, "travelings") serves as a kind of critical cheat-sheet by Varda that allows us to understand significant aspects of the film's form and meaning. She explains that she wanted a woman composer to furnish the music for the film's twelve dolly shots moving from right to left—the camera accompanying Mona (Sandrine Bonnaire), her homeless, teenage heroine, as she walks alone down a road but often not following the same trajectory as her, deviating into separate paths at different angles and sometimes moving past her. Moreover, around ten minutes pass between any two of these consecutive shots, yet Varda forges an implied continuity between them by beginning each shot and camera movement with the same object (e.g., a street sign, phone booth, piece of farm machinery, tree branch) with which the previous shot ended. Thus these dozen shots can be said to "support" the narrative like twelve evenly spaced tent poles even while they continually alter our viewpoints in relation to Mona, moving into and away from identification with her and her own vantage points. This perpetual drift comprises a kind of visual music, so it seems natural that Varda would want musical accompaniments for these dozen shots.

She explains that after discovering Joanna Bruzdowicz and her first string quartet, she got Bruzdowicz to adapt a dozen of her thematic variations in that work for each of the dolly shots. So while the shifting relationships of the camera towards Mona replicates our own shifting relationships with her in terms of our sympathy with and understanding of her character, this becomes reflected in the unresolved harmonies of the plaintive music.

This armature is also complicated by the various "witnesses" of Mona— the people she encounters during her seemingly aimless wanderings, who are interviewed or shown conversing about their final impressions of her, as in a documentary—people who are absent from these dolly shots and from this DVD extra. In certain ways, these "witnesses" are like the people interviewed by the semi-invisible news reporter in *Citizen Kane*; in other respects, they sometimes evoke the gossiping townsfolk in *The Magnificent Ambersons*, with Varda's narration at the beginning being gradually overtaken by various members of a theatrical chorus. Sometimes we agree with these voices and sometimes we don't. Either way, they basically function as our surrogates and stand-ins, representing possible attitudes that we might take towards Mona, whom Varda refuses to "explain" or sentimentalize, apart from the mythological notations offered at the beginning and end of the picture. (Mona is respectively introduced as if emerging from the sea and later stained by wine resembling blood at a wine festival shortly before her death.)

This woman of mystery reminds me of John Cassavetes' *A Woman of Mystery*, his last fully achieved work—a play he wrote and directed, starring Gena Rowlands as a "bag lady," that I was lucky enough to see at the Court Theater in West Hollywood in May 1987, during its two-week run.

As in *A Woman of Mystery*, Varda's *Sans toit ni loi* (meaning "without shelter, without law"—a play on the French expression *sans foi ni loi*, which means "godless, lawless"), this is a work about us as well as a work about the homeless—a work about how we both relate and/or fail to relate to homeless people. The tragic premise of Cassavetes' play is that the lack of definition—meaning the lack of social definition—assumed by homeless people alienates both them from us and us from them, which is quite close to Varda's concept. Rowland's character, a lady wandering the streets with a shopping cart, remains every bit as ambiguous as a Samuel Beckett character; as with Mona, we remain clueless about both where she's from and where she's going.

The way we usually view film syntax is to regard a shot as something roughly equivalent to a declarative sentence, but Varda at her best is always at least partially an investigative journalist who regards a shot as a question looking for (but not necessarily finding) an answer. This gives her an unexpected kinship with filmmakers as otherwise disparate as Roberto Rossellini, Michelangelo Antonioni, Otto Preminger, Abbas Kiarostami, and, indeed, Cassavetes.

So many of her basic strategies in *Vagabond* are involved with shifting our perspectives, making our emotional and intellectual roles as spectators as restless and as unstable as Mona herself. She clearly took pains to avoid making the character too sympathetic or too unsympathetic.

Each time I resee *Vagabond*, I'm reminded almost incongruously of Robert Bresson due to the aspects of rural France present in the worlds that Mona passes through—worlds that remind me of *Au Hasard Balthazar* and *Mouchette* (with Mona functioning like the donkey Balathazar or the girl Mouchette as a catalyst for revealing French society) and even portions of *L'argent*. In many of his greatest works, Bresson is also concerned with solitary women and the way they're judged and treated (usually misjudged and mistreated) by their communities.

Vagabond isn't really a survey of homeless people in the same way that *Les Glaneurs et la Glaneuse* is a survey of gleaners. But it's important to note that Varda did extensive research on the homeless before making this film. She based Mona on a homeless teenager she met during her research, who plays a bit part in the film, and other people she encountered during her travels, homeless and otherwise, make appearances as themselves (such as the philosophical shepherd who puts Mona up for a spell and the older man who recounts some of his past as a homeless orphan).

By mixing "real" people with her actors, Varda joins the forefront of what might be regarded as a progressive and provocative strain in cinema, blurring the assumed boundaries between fiction and non-fiction, that can be traced all the way from Robert Flaherty to the present. (Although this isn't widely known, Nanook's "wife" in *Nanook of the North* was actually "played" by Flaherty's girlfriend at the time. And it's worth noting that Cassavetes hired real homeless people to perform for his audience during the intermission in *A Woman of Mystery*.) It's another source of the film's narrative instability—to which we should add various digressions, such as the material about dead trees, and the professor (Macha Méril) whom Mona meets and who almost dies of electric shock, which may or may not be intended as metaphorical commentaries on or cross-references to Mona's death but doesn't clearly function as such.

Significantly, *Vagabond* is dedicated to Nathalie Sarraute (1900-1999), a literary writer known especially for her shifting perspectives and points of view and the indeterminacy in much of her fiction. (Her discussion about the film with Varda comprises another DVD extra.) This evokes the French view of cinema as literature by another means that can be traced back to the 1920s and perhaps even earlier—a tradition reflected, for instance, in the quarterly magazine *Trafic* (1991-2021) launched by Serge Daney that I've often written for, a literary magazine about cinema containing no illustrations apart from a single photo on the cover of each issue. (Godard concludes his video *2 X 50 Years of French Cinema* with a compact summary and celebration of that tradition, entitled "From Diderot to Daney" and quoting a sliver of text from each.) Moreover, the contrapuntal form of Varda's first feature, *La Pointe Courte* (1955), was inspired by Faulkner's *The Wild Palms*. So if one considers the degree to which Faulkner was clearly influenced by film—from the present-tense opening of *Light in August* to the reference to Eisenstein in *The Wild Palms*—Varda was only returning the compliment. And in *Vagabond*, she's freely borrowing from the novelistic tradition known as the picaresque.

How Do We Judge Actors?

Written in August 2016 for my November 2016 "En movimiento" column in Caimán Cuadernos de Cine.

Do we value actors for their visible and audible skills, or for their capacity to make us forget that they're actors? Over the past month, both at the Melbourne International Film Festival and back in Chicago, at cinemas or watching home videos, I've been asking myself this question in relation to such new films as Jim Jarmusch's *Paterson*, Albert Serra's *La Mort de Louis XIV*, Maren Ade's *Toni Erdmann*, Paul Verhoeven's *Elle*, David Mackenzie's *Hell or High Water*, and Stephen Frears' *Florence Foster Jenkins*, and such older films as Anthony Mann's *Winchester '73*, Tony Richardson's *A Taste of Honey*, and Jerry Lewis's *Smorgasbord*. And, needless to say, my answers to this question differ enormously, mainly according to how familiar I am with the actors involved—which doesn't necessarily mean how many times I've seen them before. For instance, prior to *Paterson*, I'd already seen Adam Driver in *J. Edgar*, *Frances Ha*, *Lincoln*, *Inside Llewyn Davis*, and *Midnight Special*, but I only know this now because I just looked up his credits. On the other hand, my familiarity with Jeff Bridges and my unfamiliarity with Chris Pine and Ben Foster, his costars in *Hell or High Water*, had a lot to do with my admiration for Bridges' departure from his usual persona in his portrait of a crochety Texas Ranger nearing retirement, unlike some of my younger colleagues who were more impressed by Pine and/or Foster. And in *Toni Erdmann*, my former unfamiliarity with Sandra Huller and Peter Simonischek, the two leads, obviously helped to enhance my sense of their characters as original creations.

Prior to seeing Jean-Pierre Léaud play Louis XIV in Serra's film, I considered this casting perverse, only to discover that it seemed like perfect casting once I could see how Serra's minimalist direction of Léaud's maximalist acting operated dialectically by making the performance appear life-size. On the other hand, the pre-existing life-size personas of Isabelle Huppert (in *Elle*), James Stewart (in *Winchester '73*), and Hugh Grant (in *Florence Foster Jenkins*) helped to shape and determine the impact of their characters in these films, just as the more grandiloquent and cartoonish traits of Meryl Streep in *Florence Foster Jenkins*, Rita Tushingham in *A Taste of Honey*, and Jerry Lewis in *Smorgasbord/Cracking Up* periodically undercut or challenge the documentary (i.e., biographical or autobiographical) authenticity of their material because in all three cases we're apt to respond more to the mugging than to the character.

Manny Farber once devoted a rather brutal column to what he perceived as Tushingham's overacting, which he associated with Jeanne Moreau, the Nouvelle Vague, widescreen framing, TV, and the decline of the bit actor as orchestrated by Preston Sturges. Missing from this analysis was any recognition of how much it was gendered: Sturges' wonderful comedy with both bit players and his male leads revolved around different varieties of thwarted masculinity, while the triumphs of Tushingham, Huppert, and Streep's characters all suggest lessons in how to survive different varieties of female adversity in men-driven worlds.

Of course, when we watch Jerry Lewis or James Stewart (or John Wayne or Marilyn Monroe), we're usually more concerned with star personas and their auras than with whatever characters they happen to be playing. This makes it more striking when Anthony Mann and Alfred Hitchcock periodically explore the neurotic and obsessive aspects of Stewart's persona to play against his all-American innocence and earnestness, or when Lewis persists in playing adolescent misfits after he's gone well past middle-age, thereby suggesting, inadvertently or otherwise, how many of his spectators retain their teenage insecurities after supposedly outgrowing them.

I was disturbed to find Travis Bickle dolls on sale at a Melbourne museum promoting its traveling Martin Scorsese exhibition, along with "You talkin' to me?" T-shirts. But I was also relieved to see that the dolls bore no resemblance to *Taxi Driver*'s Bickle, and to read Robert De Niro himself deriding Donald Trump (whose body language owes much to De Niro's Bickle) and his promotion by the media as another version of Bickle's fame. Are the people who buy these dolls honoring De Niro, mass murder, or entertainment? And are they bothering to distinguish between them?

Letter to Shigehiko Hasumi (December 2016)

Written for the Japanese literary magazine Eureka's *special issue devoted to Shigehiko Hasumi in early 2017.*

14 December 2016

Dear Shigehiko,

I'm indebted to you for a good many things, including my very first visit to Japan. This was eighteen years ago, in December 1998, to participate in a panel about Ozu that you organized for Shochiko in Tokyo, significantly titled "Yasujiro Ozu in the World," along with Jean Douchet, Hou Hsiao-hsien, Thierry Jousse, and Tien-wen Chu. Undoubtedly the most luminous moment of that event for me was being approached in the lobby immediately afterwards by an elderly gentleman who spoke in Japanese to Hou and myself, shook our hands, and then walked away—a puzzling encounter that immediately (and appropriately) became explained to me via mime, as soon as Hou imitated for me the signature comic gesture of Tomio "Tokkankozo" Aoki, the younger son in *I Was Born, But...*—thus identifying the child actor discovered by Ozu who went on to enjoy a screen career that would eventually last seventy-five years, encompassing even Suzuki's *Pistol Opera*. All of which made up for the disturbing fact that apparently none of the film students I spoke with at Tokyo University had seen any of Ozu's silent films, even though all of the surviving ones were available on VHS.

My second and so far only other visit to Japan—one year later, thanks to receiving a Japan Foundation grant, during which I recorded an extended conversation between us about Howard Hawks and Yasuzo Masumura for a collection entitled *Movie Mutations*—grew directly out of the first. (As I recall, these were your second and third years as Tokyo University's president.) I still treasure the beautiful Japanese book by and about Masumura that you gave me on that visit.

I've often wondered how you came to invite me to be on that Ozu panel and, to my further delight, subsequently included a link to my contribution, "Is Ozu Slow?", on your own website. Prior to my first visit to Japan, I wrote about Ozu twice—once in my "Paris Journal" for *Film Comment* (Summer 1972), which included a report of the first Ozu retrospective ever held at the Cinémathèque Française, and then in a lengthy article in *Sight and Sound* three years later entitled "Richie's Ozu: Our Prehistoric Present"—a violent attack on the first book-length study of Ozu in English that I currently regret enough to exclude from my own fairly comprehensive website. *[2020 note: over two years later, I belatedly posted this article, in spite of some continuing misgivings about it.]*

When I wrote this text, I hadn't yet met Donald Richie (1924-2013), who became a friend when I returned to Japan in December 1999, after he graciously accepted my apology for having written this article. Although my objections to his critical approach to Ozu remained—and remain to this day—there is also an unbridgeable difference between Richie's role as an American intermediary and guide to Japanese culture and your own role as a Francophile Japanese critic whose book on Ozu I mainly know from its 1998 French translation. And indeed, there's an irreconcilable difference between Richie's assertion that Ozu is the "most Japanese" of all Japanese filmmakers and your own suggestion, based on Ozu's reverence for Hollywood cinema, that he may in fact be the "least Japanese". Yet it's precisely in this difference that I find your book on Ozu so illuminating: the exemplary aim to liberate Ozu from the aura of exoticism brought by Western viewers, many of whom appear to want to use his cinema as a tool for discovering the otherness of Japanese culture. More generally, the challenges you offer to such Western aficionados of Ozu as Richie, Paul Schrader, David Bordwell, and Kristin Thompson, all of whom seem to value his work for its deviations from Hollywood studio practices, remind us that Ozu was in fact interested in emulating many of those practices, at least as he understood them. In much the same fashion, William Faulkner was acutely conscious of stealing John Keats' image of the Grecian urn on the opening pages of his great novel *Light in August* and apparently not so interested in his emulation of cinema in his use of the present tense on those same pages. Dizzy Gillespie, by his own account, developed his own style by trying and failing to imitate Roy Eldridge, somewhat as Jean-Luc Godard in

A bout de souffle presumably forged his own version of modernism by trying and failing to imitate Hawks's *Scarface.*

In retrospect, I suspect that what led me to attack Richie's book on Ozu so vehemently was what I took to be a position promoting a sense of cleavage between the formal beauty of his films and their thematic and emotional meanings—a cleavage that your own book on Ozu fails to recognize or honor, even while you clarify some of the cleavages that can exist between what Western viewers identify as a shot of a vase in *Late Spring* and what Japanese viewers perceive as a cluster of visual details. Had I been able to read your own book on Ozu in the mid-1970s instead of in 1998, when it appeared in French translation (after having been published in Japanese in 1983), my attack on Richie's book would have been unnecessary. (Incidentally, it's worth noting that it included, as a positive counter-example to Richie's approach, an extract on Ozu from Noël Burch's then-still-unpublished *To the Distant Observer* that would subsequently be deleted from his manuscript, and which consequently survives only in my article.)

I alluded indirectly to my objection to Richie's position towards Ozu in my presentation on your Ozu panel, as follows, in my discussion of *I Was Born, But...*:"During the home movie projection which marks the critical turning point in the film from comedy to tragedy, and shortly before the clowning of the father in front of his boss appears in one of the home movies, the father's two little boys start having a debate about the zebra they see on the screen—does it have black stripes on white, or white stripes on black?—creating a disturbance that momentarily halts the screening. In comparable fashion, a spurious, distracting, and no less innocent debate has been persisting about Ozu for years: is he a realist or a formalist? What seems lamentable about this debate is that it fails to perceive that cinematic forms and social forms are not alternatives in the world of Ozu but opposite sides of the same coin, so that it should be impossible to speak about one without speaking about the other. I regard this fact as the linchpin of my argument, and I hope that the remainder of my discussion will bear this out."

For me, the most important sentence in your book, at least from my Western perspective, reads as follows: "Ozu's talent lies in choosing an image that can function poetically at a particular moment by being assimilated into the film, not by affixing to the film the image of an object that is considered poetic in a domain outside the film." This is quite consistent with your critical approaches towards Costa, Erice, Ford, Hawks, Naruse, and Suzuki—to cite only those in English or French that I have been able to read, which I also find both illuminating and original. But it is the commonsensical lucidity of your arguments about Ozu that have taught me the most—not only about film poetics but also about cultural differences, and, above all, how we perceive (and sometimes fail to perceive) those poetics and differences.

All my best and warmest wishes,

Jonathan

Sexual Repression and Rebellion in the Early 1950s:
Philip Roth's *Indignation*

Written for Library of America's website The Moviegoer. *The version published there on May 3, 2017 differs from the original version posted here, especially the ending.*

No less than seven features to date have been based on works by Philip Roth, and three of these have been directed by first-timers, all of whom previously made their cinematic mark in other professional capacities. Ernest Lehman (1915-2005) had a long and distinguished screenwriting career before directing his own stridently unwatchable adaptation of *Portnoy's Complaint* in 1972, and Ewan McGregor acted in over four dozen features before directing *American Pastoral* forty-four years later. James Schamus, a film professor at Columbia University, had over fifty producing credits—plus writing and producing credits on all but three of Ang Lee's features—before he added direction to his producing and writing on *Indignation*. This has yielded what Stephen Holden in the *New York Times* has called "easily the best film made of a Roth novel, which is saying a lot."

Schamus's dexterity in navigating both commercial film production and academia has served him well on this project, enabling him to honor his source while rendering it both accessible and personal. Even though the film's action unfolds during the Korean war (1950-52) and Schamus wasn't born until 1959, his handling of period is as nimble and evocative as his grasp of Jewish-American speech patterns, and he combines this sensitivity with certain elements and inflections that make the film seem contemporary as well. Part of what gave the book currency when it came out in 2008 was the Pentagon's ban on photographing the homecomings and burials of dead American soldiers shipped back from Iraq and Afghanistan. What makes Schamus's 2016 version of the story seem contemporary is more subtle (spoilers ahead), and much of it has to do with the handling of the story's young heroine, Olivia Hutton (Sarah Gadon).

The thread that connects *Indignation* with Schamus's collaborations with Ang Lee is sexual repression—a major concern in *The Ice Storm*, *Brokeback Mountain*, and the appropriately titled *Lust, Caution*. Significantly, the story's main setting is a rural college in Ohio known as Winesburg—an allusion to Sherwood Anderson's 1919 story collection *Winesburg, Ohio*, where sexual repression is a major preoccupation. Roth's short novel belongs to a doom-ridden quartet of novels concerned with death and the fragility of the human body (potently centered here in the figure of a vulnerable college sophomore), entitled *Nemeses* and consisting of *Everyman* (2006), *Indignation* (2008), *The Humbling* (2009—itself the source of a 2014 feature), and *Nemesis* (2010), published together in a single volume by the Library of America.

Marcus Messner (Logan Lerman), the only child of a kosher butcher in Newark, a virginal straight-A student who sometimes works as his father's assistant, transfers to Winesburg during his sophomore year in order to escape the neurotic worries and excessive attentions of his father—a move that corresponds closely to Roth's own transfer to Bucknell University in Pennsylvania from Rutgers in 1951. Acutely aware of both the sacrifices made by his parents (neither of whom went to college) for his education and the loss of many cousins during World War II and some friends in Korea, Marcus wants at all costs to evade the draft. One aspect of the novel strikingly conveyed in the film is the shocking relation between Marcus's experiences in a butcher shop and the fatal butchery he perceives and ultimately suffers in Korea: "I envisioned my father's knives and cleavers whenever I read about the bayonet combat against the Chinese in Korea. I knew how murderously sharp sharp could be. And I knew what blood looked like, encrusted around the necks of chickens where they had been ritually slaughtered, dripping out of the beef onto my hands when I was cutting a rib steak along the bone, seeping through the brown paper bags despite the wax paper wrappings within, settling into the grooves crosshatched into the chopping block by the force of the cleaver crashing down."

After Marcus falls in love with Olivia, another transfer student and a troubled non-Jew, the fact that she once attempted suicide by slitting one wrist becomes another cross-reference to his background in butchery: "Had she been successful," he reflects, somewhat callowly, in the novel, "had she expertly completed the job with a single perfect slice of the blade, she would have rendered herself kosher in accordance with rabbinical law."

It's one limitation of the novel's first-person narration that our sense of the other characters, Olivia in particular, is restricted to Marcus's naïve and immature perceptions of them. Significantly, even Roth's sympathetic biographer and friend Claudia Roth Pierpont regards Marcus's subjectivity in the novel as a drawback: "[Marcus] is a wholly believable figure and, in his desperately proud and confused youth, rather heartbreaking (without ever being sentimentalized). The characters around him, though, are less credible: their motivations are obscure, and none seem designed to do much more than advance the story." Schamus minimizes this drawback by employing the narration only half a dozen times, and meanwhile complicates its function by adding separate voiceovers of Marcus and Olivia reading their letters to one another (and by illustrating Olivia's voiceover with brief shots that can be read either as objective flashbacks or as Marcus's subjective responses to her letter). As a result, promiscuous Olivia, for example, becomes more aggressive in the movie. In both book and film, she gives Marcus a blow-job on their first date and later masturbates him in the hospital more than once after his appendectomy. Roth's Marcus discreetly prompts her, but Schamus's Olivia makes the first moves. Yet, to borrow Pierpont's phrase, the movie still, like the book, "moves forward like a missile on a carefully plotted trajectory."

Marcus dies a virgin—according to his Newark pals, a fate even worse than simple death—and indeed, as in Ambrose Bierce's grim Civil War story "An Occurrence at Owl Creek Bridge," the entirety of the hero's story as he remembers it turns out to be a feverish deathbed recollection. And even though his narration persuades us to share some of his scorn for both his father's fears and the concerns of Dean Caudwell (Tracy Letts) about his isolation, both Roth and Schamus give these adult viewpoints a certain amount of credence. Marcus's father's supposedly irrational fears for his son turn out to be well-founded, and Marcus meets Caudwell's nosy (if compassionate) concerns about his isolation as well as his narrow-minded dismissals of Bertrand Russell with the rants of a self-righteous prig.

Some of Schamus's changes as an adaptor are expedient simplifications of the material, such as Marcus changing his dorm room once rather than twice after clashes with his roommates (although this makes the Dean's worries in the film about a single room change more excessive), or having him work at the university library rather than as a taproom waiter. But other alterations yield significant if delicate differences in interpretation. Most of the novella is a lengthy chapter called "Under Morphine" narrated by Marcus (and followed by a very brief third-person chapter, "Out from Under"), yet, as previously noted, the movie's use of Marcus's first-person narration is quite sparing.

Schamus does his most incisive and resonant re-imagining with Olivia. In an interview, he has mentioned modeling her on Sylvia Plath. He begins and ends the film in the present, over half a century later, with a glimpse of Olivia in a sanitarium, framed against a wallpaper design of flowers that visually rhymes with the bouquet she brings to Marcus in the hospital. He also names the present-day Olivia "Mrs. Anderson," which informs us that, after her involvement with Marcus, she married someone else.

Schamus completely omits two of the novel's climaxes—Marcus's discovery of the trashing of his dorm room by his former roommate Flusser, and a massive student riot that begins as a snowball fight and panty raid, and ends in several expulsions. Both these events relate to sexual repression (in the case of Flusser, his homosexual attraction to Marcus, which the film only hints at). Even though a conventional reading of the student riot as "cinematic" would appear to have made it obligatory, Schamus' exclusion of this episode implies that he rightly regarded it as both thematically redundant and a distraction to the story he wants to tell (Marcus is not even a participant). Far more important to him are Marcus's conversations with Dean Caudwell, the first of which he allows to run for over seventeen minutes, and this scene, delivered almost intact from the novel, is clearly the film's centerpiece.

Part of what makes this sequence a *tour de force* is the care with which Schamus calibrates its separate stages of rising tension on Marcus's part without ever overloading one's sympathies simply or unequivocally on either side of the discussion. What for Roth and the actors (Lerman and Letts) qualifies as a triumph of dramatic equipoise becomes for Schamus a triumph of mise en scène as the dialogue passes from his change of dorm rooms after a conflict with his roommates to his avoidance of any ethnic identification on his college application (listing his father's profession as "butcher" but not "kosher butcher") to his relationship to his parents to his dating to his resentment of being obliged to attend chapel, his proud atheism, and his reverence for Bertrand Russell's *Why I Am Not a Christian*, and finally to baseball before he collapses from an attack of acute appendicitis.

Although most of this sequence's power clearly comes from Roth, Schamus contrives to make it his own by preparing for it in numerous ways, thematically as well as dramatically. Ten minutes into the film, when we see Marcus reading after a day's work at Messner's Meat & Poultry, it's a pamphlet by Bertrand Russell pointedly called *Stoicism and Mental Health*. He also invents an entire dialogue in the hospital between Marcus, his mother (beautifully played by Linda Emond), and Olivia about her parents, the courses in American history and culture that Marcus is taking, and Olivia's citation of a definition of democracy attributed to Benjamin Franklin: "two wolves and a lamb voting on what to have for lunch." If we emerge from this film less than certain about which characters qualify as wolves and which qualify as lambs, Roth and Schamus seem jointly responsible.

Roth's one-word title derives from a line in the English translation of the Chinese national anthem, which Marcus learns in grade school during World War II, when China was a U.S. ally. It's an anthem he defiantly recites to himself while attending compulsory chapel against his will (not as a Jew, but as an atheist), when China has become the ally of a U.S. enemy in Korea. (None of this anthem figures in the film, undoubtedly because it would have been too cumbersome to explain and illustrate.) If all this sounds somewhat remote to American experience in 2017, I should confess that when I started to watch Schamus's feature again on a Blu-Ray, virtually the first thing to appear on my home screen was the motto, "Piracy is not a victimless crime," followed by a lengthy series of obligatory trailers for other movies (including *American Pastoral*), and this goaded me into muttering to myself, "Capitalism is not a victimless crime." Which is only to suggest that, even though many of us are more enlightened today about freedom of religion and (say) gender equality than we might have been in 1950, we still have our own set of everyday ideological roadblocks to contend with.

Foreword to Dave Kehr's *Movies That Mattered*

Commissioned by the University of Chicago Press and written in September 2016; published in November 2017.

For all the differences between the history of cinema and the history of the Internet, one disturbing point they have in common is the degree to which our canons in both film and film criticism are determined by historical accidents. Thus we've canonized F.W. Murnau's third American film, *City Girl* (1930), ever since a copy was belatedly discovered in the 1970s, but not his second, *The Four Devils* (1928), because no known print of that film survives. Similarly, we canonize Josef von Sternberg's remarkable *The Docks of New York* (1928), but not the lost Sternberg films that preceded and followed it, *The Dragnet* (1928) and *The Case of Lena Smith* (1929). And it's no less a matter of luck that all my long reviews for the *Chicago Reader*, published between 1987 and 2008, are available online, but none of Dave Kehr's long reviews for the same publication, published between 1974 and 1986—a body of work that, together with Kehr's columns for *Chicago* magazine in the 1980s, strikes me as being the most remarkable extended stretch of auteurist criticism in American journalism.

I hasten to add that, unlike the missing films of Murnau and Sternberg, Kehr's writing for the *Reader* and *Chicago* has never been lost. Yet it's one of the crueler aspects of Internet culture that items that aren't online are effectively treated as nonexistent—which is what gives this collection and its predecessor, *When Movies Mattered* (2011), the force of revelation, especially to younger readers encountering Kehr's pieces for the first time. For the range of films and film-makers treated, the analytical tools employed, and the intellectual confidence and lucidity of the arguments, Kehr's prose really has no parallels, which is why so much of it reads as freshly as if it were written yesterday.

The range of films being dealt with is especially impressive: children's films and Westerns, international art films and American blockbusters, porn and horror, literary adaptations and remakes, comedies and melodramas—all get treated with equal amounts of unpatronizing scrutiny. And because Kehr is also a public intellectual as well as a passionate cinephile, his analyses invariably go beyond issues of style, form, and genre, which are examined with rigorous care, to broader social and cultural matters. The epigrammatic brilliance that often shines in Kehr's capsule reviews for the *Reader* is developed into arguments that illuminate entire careers. ("For [Werner] Herzog, plot is mainly a support structure: it holds the images, it doesn't generate or advance them.") And sometimes aesthetic points merge seamlessly into social critique: *Kramer vs. Kramer*'s "chief failing as art—its wavering point of view—becomes its most potent commercial guarantor." Furthermore, in the course of describing what makes *Used Cars* "the first post-OPEC comedy, the first film to perceive how treacherously our symbols have turned on us in the past few recessionary, deflationary years," Kehr carves out an elegant, poetic prose summary of a national zeitgeist:

> The affordable family car once represented the fruit of American life: unchecked personal mobility, the unlimited flow of material goods, the triumph of free enterprise—the chrome-plated proof that every American could live like a king. But when those symbols won't start, when their tanks run dry, they mock us. Rusting in the driveway, they're like the skull—the memento mori—that Renaissance gentlemen kept on their writing desks: they stare back with intimations of mortality. When the dream car loses its patina, its promise of health, wealth, and happiness, every car becomes a used car—a ton of metal twisting in the sun.

Writing about adaptations of Joseph Conrad, F. Scott Fitzgerald, E.M. Forster, Thomas Hardy, Ernest Hemingway, and William Shakespeare, Kehr demonstrates that he's also a first-rate literary critic, but not one who ever loses sight of the cinematic, historical, and cultural issues at stake in these adaptations. And despite his decision to subdivide these essays between appreciations of favorites and "autopsies/minority reports," these examinations rarely qualify as "thumbs up" or "thumbs down" reviews. His exemplary consideration of Bernardo Bertolucci's much-reviled *Luna*—possibly the best critical treatment that film has received anywhere, and one that drove me immediately to take a second look—turns out to be every bit as conflicted as the object of its focus, even though it's grouped with Kehr's favorites:

> The usual line on films as radical as this is that you'll either love 'em or hate 'em. I found myself loving and hating *Luna* indiscriminately, and sometimes simultaneously. I hated its hermeticism, its inconsistency, and its lack of discipline, but I loved its size, its audacity, and its complete unpredictability. The film may turn out to be more valuable for its outrages than for its accomplishments: if it doesn't satisfy, it still gives a damn good shake. Meanwhile, it's worth bearing in mind that one of the more pertinent derivatives of the Latin luna is "loony."

In short, even though Kehr remains one of the most responsible of film critics, he also proves that one reason why he deserves this distinction is that he knows the value of irresponsibility—as his treatment of Russ Meyer's *Supervixens* also demonstrates.

In order to appreciate fully the historical importance of these essays, one should distinguish between the relative homogeneity of academic and journalistic criticism in Continental Europe and the United Kingdom and the relative estrangement between those realms in the United States—an estrangement that becomes especially pertinent during the 1970s and 1980s, the same period when Kehr was publishing these essays.

In his introduction to *When Movies Mattered*, aptly subtitled *Reviews from a Transformative Decade*, Kehr focuses on the parallel developments of the alternative press and auteurist criticism as sparked by Andrew Sarris's seminal *The American Cinema* (1968), inspired in turn by writing about Hollywood that appeared in *Cahiers du Cinéma* during the 1950s and 1960s, before more theoretical and ideological persuasions overtook that magazine for a spell in the 1970s, in response to the uprisings in May 1968. Although Kehr discusses these developments chiefly in order to clarify his distance from them, it's important to acknowledge that while Roland Barthes and Umberto Eco were able to air their positions in mainstream newspapers, and Peter Wollen, writing under the pseudonym of Lee Russell in *New Left Review* in the U.K., was able to combine a certain amount of academic film theory with auteurist journalism, Kehr was operating from a different set of platforms in the pages of the *Reader* and *Chicago*, where no such accommodations would have been tolerated. Yet in spite of these distinctions, the differences between Lee Russell's "structural" analyses of Samuel Fuller, Budd Boetticher, and Anthony Mann and Kehr's treatments of Boetticher, Clint Eastwood, Stanley Donen, and Elaine May is arguably more a matter of terminology and prose than one of critical and analytical substance. Stated differently, Kehr's acquaintance with theory, ideology, and critical methodology often arguably runs deeper than his writing is ready to acknowledge, given the orientation of his audience.

§

When the *Reader* started to post its movie reviews online in March 1996, I had already been their staff critic for nearly a decade, thanks to Kehr having named me as his successor—a gift that afforded me not only the best job in my career but a unique one in terms of space and freedom because of Dave's own initiatives during his stint at that alternative weekly. The posting of the *Reader*'s extended film reviews gradually proceeded backwards, from present to past, eventually encompassing all my long reviews but lamentably stopping short of including any of Dave's. This had the untoward effect of creating an unfortunate cleavage between our online profiles that has persisted ever since, despite the posting of all of Dave's capsule reviews on the *Reader*'s web site and all his *New York Times* writing (including his superb weekly DVD column, which lasted from 1999 through 2013) on their own site, not to mention the excellent film blog open to group discussions ("reports from the lost continent of cinephilia") that he maintained for many years at davekehr.com (no longer active or available).

That Kehr considers cinephilia a "lost" continent and that the titles of his collections are in the past tense are what mainly separate his current position from mine—a position that I'm sure has also been inflected by the urgency of his exciting and vigorous second career as a adjunct curator and archivist at the Film Department of the Museum of Modern Art since late 2013, which is dedicated to resurrecting and preserving treasures that otherwise might be lost. I'm sure his pessimism is well founded (and grounded), even if I can't entirely share it. I also wonder if the banishment of his best prose from the Internet may have played some role in his viewing of cinephilia as largely a thing of the past. Reading this prose now, and coordinating some of my own viewing in relation to it, it feels very much alive to me.

The Mysterious Leo McCarey

Written for Cineaste *(Winter 2018).*

Auteur Theory and My Son John
by James Morrison.
New York: Bloomsbury Academic, 2018. 190 pp.

My admiration for and my demurrals about James Morrison's brilliant mono-graph both begin on the first pages of his introduction. He quotes the title subject of *Mike Nichols: An American Master* (2016) on the "froggy conspiracy" which elevates figures like Howard Hawks and Jerry Lewis at the expense of George Stevens, Billy Wilder, William Wyler, and Fred Zinnemann ("our greatest directors"), a statement that Morrison aptly compares to the vulgar parodies of existential beatniks in Stanley Donen's *Funny Face*. Yet two pages later, when he calls Nichols "countable as one of the 'auteurs' who by common consent ushered in the New Hollywood," Morrison seems to be indulging in aspects of the same parody, especially when one considers that he's decided to suppress the information that *Mike Nichols: An American Master* is the work of a genuine auteur, Elaine May (coincidentally, Donen's current partner), and not only because, unlike Nichols, she functions as a film writer as well as a film director. I presume that Morrison chose to suppress May's involvement in this glib claptrap because it complicates his argument, especially when he goes on to show that Nichols' tirade is seemingly bolstered by May's montage of dumb quotes from Bosley Crowther about *Bonnie and Clyde*, and from Pauline Kael and Renata Adler about *2001*, constituting what Morrison rightly calls "a slam against film criticism as such". Even though being an auteur (however brilliant) and skewering film criticism (however crassly) are very different matters, it suits Morrison's sense of polemical decorum to elevate Nichols as an auteur, even with suitable scare quotes, at the expense of his erstwhile sparring partner. In May's case as well as his own, it all depends on whom you think you're addressing.

Having spent a delightful evening with May in 2010, I can attest that, in spite of her cordiality due to my enthusiasm for her work, her lack of any serious interest in film criticism was unmistakable. And Morrison clearly is addressing his own remarks to academia, not to the mainstream arena where most film-makers like May and Donen live and operate—although it's to his credit that his superb history and analysis of auteurist criticism, which forms the first half of this book, is sufficiently far-ranging to include the now largely forgotten nonacademic *New York Film Bulletin* in the early '60s. Lamentably, it doesn't include the three issues of the more intellectual and literary New York auteurist journal *Moviegoer* from the same period, which featured such writers as Susan Sontag and Paul Goodman as well as Andrew Sarris and Roger Greenspun, not to mention a very thoughtful defense of *My Son John* by Donald Phelps against much of the attack of Robert Warshow. Given Morrison's unfriendly review of Gilberto Perez's *The Material Ghost* in *Screen*, this might suggest a bias against literary auteurists in general, apart from Robin Wood, were it not for the fact that Morrison himself, a fiction writer as well as a critic, writes with some literary distinction. (Example: "The [French] auteurist model was essentially antinarrative, defined by the lyric strophe, the poetic intuition, the soaring crescendo or the dying fall, the rhythmic creation of beauty.")

Where Morrison's analysis of auteurist thinking becomes especially acute and valuable is in the ways he distinguishes between the Surrealism-inflected "Eureka!" reflexes of the French critics looking for poetic explosions and mod-ernist social critiques amidst flaws and compromises and the more conservative and idealistic habits of American critics such as Andrew Sarris looking for over-all unity and coherence, with André Bazin's beliefs in realism and the "genius of the system" implicitly serving as a sort of relay between these positions. No less implicitly, though without ever saying so, Morrison also helps us to understand what distinguishes the modernism of Godard, Rivette, and Truffaut as filmmakers from the premodernism of Bogdanovich and the postmodernism of De Palma and Scorsese, based on their own auteurist groundings.

When it comes to outlining Leo McCarey's characteristics as an auteur he is no less authoritative, especially when it comes to delineating the dynamics of individual performances as offset and propelled by McCarey's mise en scène.

He rightly focuses on Helen Hayes' remarkable performance as Lucille Jefferson in *My Son John* as the film's emotional center, even more than Robert Walker's in the title role, although he seems bemused by a striking moment of her gestural pantomime in an early scene, correctly labeling that moment as a sign of her feisty independence from the family but not appearing to recognize it as a mocking parody of the mental instability she feels her doctor and husband are both assigning to her by urging her to take medication. (As long as I'm cataloguing minor grouses, the only actual error in the book that I spotted is Morrison misidentifying "a murder shown in full blood-and-gore detail" in *Once Upon a Honeymoon* as "the assassination of an American double agent"—an event that occurs offscreen—rather than a Polish general.)

Having first seen *My Son John* when it came out, at the tender age of nine, when I only dimly understood what it was saying and doing, and then having rediscovered it many times—first as a deranged Cold War fantasy, then as a flawed masterpiece about family dysfunction, and eventually as both—I've often felt frustrated about not knowing more about the original script, the sort of changes necessitated by Robert Walker's sudden death in the midst of shooting, and the paranoid conditions underlying both the theme—an all-American couple discovering that their son (Walker) is a Communist spy—and the film's strained completion (including the fact that Walker's death was initially hidden from the public). Morrison's research answers most of my queries, though not how McCarey and/or Paramount managed to conceal the death as long as they did (nor how long that stretch was). At most, I could glean from Serge Daney and Louis Skorecki's interview with McCarey in *Cahiers du Cinéma* that John's death was necessitated by Walker's and that McCarey's decision to dub his dying words himself was motivated by all the secrecy.

My own sense of McCarey's contradictory singularity as an auteur is that he's both an ideological primitive and a highly sophisticated dialectician who makes the comedy of embarrassment and the tragedy of excruciation virtually interchangeable and equally incapable of achieving any resolution. This is apparent not only in the determination to make Dean Jagger's Dan Jefferson, the father in *My Son John*, a bumbling fool even while espousing McCarey's most cherished, simplistic notions about family, democracy, and anticommunism, and it is no less evident in his abortive final feature *Satan Never Sleeps*, where he seeks to derive both comedy and tragedy from the sexual attraction of a priest (a miscast William Holden) for a Chinese girl (Francis Nuyen) who's innocently smitten with him. McCarey ultimately quit this film in disgust after Holden refused to let his character die in a suicidal escape, which presumably would have contradicted McCarey's Catholic faith as decisively as Jagger's idiocy in *John* contradicts the writer-director's patriotism. As Morrison observes, "Dan Jefferson is the most fully sketched father in McCarey's films and the least sympathetic by far, though a conflicted attitude toward him ultimately circumscribes the film's most pressing critical problems." One might add that Gary Cooper's far more sympathetic (if still quite irritating) title character and father in *Good Sam* (1948), another troubled self-portrait—and a film I value much more than Morrison does—offers many of the same fascinating conundrums.

As a master of disbelief as well as belief, McCarey is as much of a dialectician as Carl Dreyer—a claim supported by Morrison's apt if unexpected comparison of *John*'s closing image with the final shot of *Ordet*. Indeed, McCarey manages to make Walker's John in the film's first half so compelling that it becomes impossible to believe that his scripted conversion could have been made plausible even if the actor had lived, in spite of Walker's resourcefulness (which includes even a hint of gayness as a carryover from his performance as Bruno in *Strangers on a Train*, portions of which McCarey recycled in his inept conclusion). The degree to which an FBI agent named Steadman (Van Heflin) assumes the role of father-confessor rather than a bumbling priest (Frank McHugh) was Warshow's most valid objection to the film's muddle-headedness, and this confirms McCarey's impulses to sabotage his own ideological agendas.

Within such a context, Hayes' tremulous Lucille functions as the battleground between the dialectic of Dan's all-American stupidity and John's poker-faced Communism, even if McCarey couldn't really imagine what that Communism might consist of, and thus her separate scenes with Jagger and Walker are central to the film's complex, ambiguous power. Yet Morrison's analysis reaches its own giddy highpoint, in auteurist terms, when it allow us to see John's bottled-up distaste for Dan as an echo of Ruggles'/Charles Laughton's repressed disapproval of his hick employers in *Ruggles of Red Gap*, and, in the following paragraph, persuasively links Dan bopping John on the head with a Bible, causing him to fall over a table—a moment usually seen as noncomic—as a slapstick maneuver traceable back to Laurel and Hardy, a team McCarey invented as well as directed.

Postscript, excerpted from my Fall 2014 DVD column for Cinema Scope:

Leo McCarey's *Good Sam* (1948), on an Olive Films Blu-ray, may be the most neglected masterpiece in the entire McCarey canon, although it's commonly regarded as a failure, even as a disaster. (In fact, it enjoyed a modest commercial success.) In some respects it's McCarey's most serious and profound movie, even though it's ostensibly a comedy: a sustained look by a devout Catholic at the catastrophic consequences that can ensue from someone actually following the Gospels. It's clearly one of McCarey's most personal efforts, made by his own production company, but it's closer to being an investigation of its troubling subject—and reportedly a personal autocritique as well—than the propounding of any conclusive thesis, which is part of why I treasure it as much as I do (and why I suspect some other viewers don't). Gary Cooper plays the eponymous lead to perfection, and Ann Sheridan as his suffering wife Lu is just as good.

In trying to account for this film's poor reputation, I wonder if the characteristic McCarey trait of laughter becoming indistinguishable from tears has been pushed so far in this case that it seriously confuses some of our emotional responses. The film identifies sanity mainly with Lu's "realism" and heroic forbearance while surviving and/or cleaning up the messes left by Sam's goodness (or perhaps only his would-be goodness, which is almost never defined in relation to "realism"), but this balance is unexpectedly and dramatically reversed during the film's closing stretches. It's also significant that in the first of Lu's big scenes with Sam, she's laughing hysterically at the latest of his messes (a wonderful scene); in the second, she's sobbing; and in the film's final scene, set during the Christmas season, we can't even tell whether she's laughing or sobbing.

Most of the time, McCarey adopts and asks us to share Lu's ambivalent viewpoint, but his tragicomic view of things is far from cynical, even though Sam's world is largely inhabited by selfish and sometimes mean-spirited free-loaders, some of whom capitalize on his kindness and some of whom actively resent it—but then again, some of these characters wind up surprising us. Finally, I think this film demands to be read as McCarey's complex response and "reply" to the desperation of Capra's *It's a Wonderful Life*, made two years earlier, and as such, I think it offers a far more persuasive and nuanced view of the human condition in all its ambiguities and complexities than Capra's more Manichean universe.

Intruder in the Dust

Excerpted from my "Global Discoveries on DVD" column in Cinema Scope, *Spring 2019.*

I was spurred into re-seeing Clarence Brown and Ben Maddow's 1949 adaptation of Faulkner's *Intruder in the Dust* by Mark Rappaport's latest video, *America's Grandpa*, which includes a clip from *Intruder* featuring the video's subject, Will Geer. I'm concerned less with the film's fidelity to the novel (not one of my favorite Faulkners, though it's probably one of his better late works) than with its fidelity to the Deep South, which is singular, and with its politics, which are unusually advanced for 1949—and even, in some respects, for 2019. This movie would make a terrific double-bill with Jacques Tourneur's *Stars in My Crown* (1950), another highly uncharacteristic MGM release—not only because of the Southern small-town settings and the memorable central roles played by the magnificent Juano Hernandez in each film, but also because the virtues and wisdom of both of these masterpieces are complementary. *Stars*, for all its greatness, is not notable for any of its Southern particulars or its actorly pirouettes the way that *Intruder* is, whereas *Intruder* is generally less notable for its domestic details (apart from the cabin of Hernandez's character Lucas Beauchamp) and family interactions than *Stars*. *Stars* is metaphysical, *Intruder* more social, but both movies explore both the darker and the brighter sides of small-town communities. In *Intruder*, the way a crowd turns up in carloads, busloads, and wagonloads in a town square with the loud strains of "Runnin' Wild" and "Tiger Rag" piped in on speakers to watch a lynching anticipates the dark, carnivalesque atmosphere of Billy Wilder's *Ace in the Hole* (1951), and it's even possible that Wilder was influenced by it. But Wilder's cynicism is miles away from the Faulknerian postulate that only a teenage boy (Claude Jarman

Jr.'s Chick Mallison) and an old maid (Elizabeth Patterson's Miss Habersham, whose name might have been suggested by *Great Expectations*' Miss Havisham) can be unblinkered enough to trust in the innocence of a black man. And, to consolidate this movie's absence of cynicism, in the film's final scene we hear the same festive music on the speakers to greet an ordinary Saturday afternoon shopping crowd after the lynching is averted.

Where *Intruder* truly excels is in its wealth of seemingly irrelevant yet flavorsome and telling incidental details—multiple responses to the sheriff's awful-tasting coffee, the way Porter Hall's rustic, one-armed patriarch fastidiously unbuttons and rebuttons his shirt before extracting or returning his pistol—because it's more interested in seeing its characters in the round than in passing out indictments or merit badges. Even the teenage semi-hero and his lawyer uncle (David Brian, who took over the part after Joel McCrea turned it down) have their own moments of bigotry and presumption, and the dignified Beauchamp is allowed some arrogance as well. As far as I know, *Intruder* is the only Faulkner film adaptation that won the author's public praise: "I'm not much of a moviegoer," he said in a 1958 interview, "but I did see that one. I thought it was a fine job. That Juano Hernandez is a fine actor—and man, too." (At a Q&A session at the Museum of Modern Art many years ago, I asked Douglas Sirk if he knew what Faulkner thought of *The Tarnished Angels*, his 1957 adaptation of *Pylon*; Sirk replied that he won Faulkner's thanks and approval during a brief parking-lot encounter.) The film's authenticity is usually attributed to director-producer Clarence Brown—who moved to Tennessee from Massachusetts at the age of eleven and later lived in Alabama before he went to work for Jacques Tourneur's dad Maurice in Fort Lee—but Maddow's terrific screenplay (which incorporates much of Faulkner's wit and irony) and the location shooting in and around Oxford, Mississippi, including the use of locals as extras, also play significant parts in the film's distinction. Apart from a few Kazan features and Phil Karlson's *The Phenix City Story* (1955), this is one of the very few Hollywood pictures that shows the Deep South persuasively.

Greed and Other Fantasies:
American Corruptions Viewed by Europeans (two excerpts)

Drawn from a longer piece that also discusses Point Blank, Hammett, *and* The State of Things, *commissioned by Shanay Jhaveri for his collection* America: Films from Elsewhere *(Mumbai: The Shoestring Publisher, 2019).*

America—sheer physical space, no irony, no metaphor, distance no object.

—Chris Petit, *Negative Space* (1999)

"Perhaps an American director would not have seen greed as a vice," wrote the reviewer—presumably the American reviewer—of Erich von Stroheim's *Greed* (1924) in the 25 March 1925 issue of *Picture Play*. What is most stupefying about such a statement, at least in the pre-Donald Trump universe, is the notion that anyone, American or otherwise, could have thought or written it. And the best response to such a speculation was voiced many months earlier, by Stroheim himself, while *Greed* was still in production:

> They said I was crazy to do an American story. It is foolish to say that [Frank Norris's] *McTeague* is American any more than *Nana* is French. They are international....Plot is a pattern, the mechanism by which infantile minds are intrigued. It is a riddle, a puzzle, or the skeleton on which melodrama, comedies, detective stories are hung. But life, raw, immense, swirling, has no plot. Its riddle can never be solved.

We probably have no way of knowing today whether it was Stroheim or someone else at MGM who gave Stroheim's adaptation of Norris's *McTeague* its title. Whoever thought of it, we can question how apt it actually is in describing the deterioration of a marriage between a miser (Zasu Pitts' Trina) and a simpleton (Gibson Gowland's Mac), or the deterioration of a friendship between that same simpleton and a somewhat envious blowhard (Jean Hersholt's Marcus). It's also worth remarking that "greed" is a recurring term in Marxist texts, yet *Greed* has rarely (if ever) been analyzed in Marxist terminology, perhaps because Stroheim's own forms of determinism regarding money and character elude a Marxist framework.

We do know, however, that even if it was an Austrian Jew who was adapting a novel by an American WASP (albeit a Jew who claimed to have non-Jewish, aristocratic origins), it was also someone who knew poverty and hard labor in the U.S. far more intimately than Norris ever could have with his privileged upbringing and his Paris, Berkeley, and Harvard-based education. Stroheim biographer Richard Koszarski notes that although *Greed* was Stroheim's only film with a literary source, "The world of German-speaking immigrants in America, working-class struggles in prewar San Francisco, the corrosive effects of financial problems on a young marriage—all could have been chapters in his own life. Von Stroheim seldom posed for elaborately staged publicity shots in connection with his films, but he did for this one: in one photo, he is dressed up in workman's clothes, swinging a pick and shovel, to illustrate how he had once been a railroad worker in these same parts; another shows him crouched down, shooting craps with a track-laying gang of blacks and Chicanos."

What arguably remains most European about *Greed* is its unabashed demand to be considered a work of art, not a mere attraction or spectacle or exposé or entertainment. This also means, bearing in mind Chris Petit's listing above of American traits, heavy doses of irony and metaphor—particularly in all the symbolic shots of gold (as well as in the shots of a predatory cat and canaries) that punctuate the narrative—and also including uses of "sheer physical space" and "distance" that employ both, most clearly in Death Valley, although here the European influences on Norris also clearly played some role. The fact that Stroheim was determined to shoot this film in real locations but willing to tear down an apartment wall if it interfered with the best camera set-ups is characteristic of his contradictory notions of realism, as was his decision to update Norris's story from the last years of the 19th century to 1908 and afterwards (roughly corresponding to his own first years in America) while permitting the extras in crowd scenes to be dressed in the contemporary styles of 1923.

Stroheim's preferred title for his first feature had been *The Pinnacle*, which also smacks of a symbolic impulse—tied in this case to a literary bent and a taste for abstraction, even though it also alludes to a particular Alpine mountain peak. He was so incensed by Universal's New York sales office changing it to *Blind Husbands* (another abstraction—and a somewhat misleading one, insofar as only one blind husband figures in the story) that he ran a full-page ad in *Motion Picture News* registering his protest. Yet ironically, the film was such a hit that he subsequently had no such objections to titling its far more opulent spinoff, the similarly generic *Foolish Wives*. And whether or not the title of *Greed* was his own idea, his multiple additions to Norris's novel included everything from some of its opening titles ("Dedicated to my mother," "Personally directed by Erich von Stroheim," a quote from Norris about his telling the truth that is clearly also meant to reflect on Stroheim, and a patch of verse about gold) to the events covered in the first 69 pages of his 277-page screenplay, most of them devoted to McTeague's life before becoming a dentist, as well as a good many extra-diegetic literary/symbolic shots of gold interspersed throughout the narrative.

Regarding the opening verse about gold, MGM substituted verse of its own, and a comparison of the two quotations offers a succinct summary of some of the major differences between a European artist and an American studio:

Stroheim's epigraph (from Robert Blair's *The Grave*):

Oh cursed lust of gold! When for thy sake the fool
Throws up his interest in both words. First, starves
In this, then damn'd in that to come.

MGM's epigraph (from Thomas Hood's *Miss Kilmansegg: Her Moral*):

Gold—gold—gold—gold,
Bright and yellow, hard and cold,
Molten, graven, hammered, rolled,
Hard to get and light to hold,
Stolen, borrowed, squandered, doled.

In short, a fatalistic moral statement about gold as an ideology is replaced by a fetish and an incantation, two Hollywood specialties. One could also say that a fateful reflection on human behavior is supplanted mainly by a brute material fact—an illustration of obsession more than a commentary or analysis.

Trying to explain to students why Stroheim remains a major figure for me, I commonly argue that he understands people (keeping the verb in present tense) better than Francis Ford Coppola, Martin Scorsese, or Steven Spielberg, and by "better" I mean more variously, ambiguously, and mysteriously, not necessarily more intellectually or digestibly. All his characters tend to be monsters, yet he loves them simultaneously because of and in spite of their monstrosity. I don't know if there's anything particularly European about this trait, even if one also finds it in (say) Balzac and Flaubert, but given that it's also shared by Ernst Lubitsch, Elaine May, Mel Brooks, and Stanley Kubrick, I wonder if it might be characteristically Jewish in its ironic and bittersweet humor. (Orson Welles once had the wit to describe Stroheim's art as "Jewish baroque" to a French interviewer, before the posthumous public discovery that the "von" was a fantasy projection.) It's an attitude that I suspect bound Stroheim in an uneasy truce with the studio bosses he tangled with, most of them Eastern European Jews with repressed pasts that partly leaked into their accents and body language, with the consequence (according to my conversations with Stroheim scholar Rick Schmidlin, who produced the expanded 239-minute version of *Greed* in 1999) that they knew about Stroheim's actual background even if most of his audience during the silent era didn't. In Hollywood, being a Jew in hiding might resemble in some cases being an artist in hiding, but not for Stroheim, whose artistry was proudly and confidently brandished while his ethnicity stayed expediently buried. Even so, it's doubtful that the blatant grotesquerie of Trina Sieppe's unassimilated German family would have registered so fully if an American director had adapted *McTeague*.

§

Love hit me like an elephant, and I
was thrown into a jungle of dreams.
If Columbus were alive today, I don't think he'd think I was crazy for trying
to make a machine that would fly.
Because history is all dreams. No rules or books, it's just that. Waiting
to be discovered like when Columbus
crossed the Atlantic and found this
whole place. I don't know if he found
the dream he was looking for, but maybe he didn't even have a choice,
because once you're in the middle of a storm, you can't turn back.

—Axel (Johnny Depp) in *Arizona Dream*

The hostility expressed by a few American mainstream reviewers towards Emir Kusturica's *Arizona Dream* (1993) may be due in part to its mainstream American stars (Johnny Depp, Faye Dunaway, Jerry Lewis, Vincent Gallo) and its use of American locations (New York and Arizona), despite the fact that Kusturica made it with several members of his usual (then) Yugoslav production team (cinematographer, editor, production designer, composer). Even with a script co-written by one of the director's screenwriting students at Columbia University, the impression of obscure tomfoolery is plainly spelled out in the "final thoughts" of Jason Bailey and Nick Hartel in their 2010 reviews for *DVD Talk*, posted respectively on March 16 and April 24:

> It took a lot of smart people to make *Arizona Dream*, and I can't imagine any of them thought the film was actually entertaining or enlightening. The best I can put together is that the purposeful intention was to confuse and confound the audience. If that's the case, then the picture is a huge success.

> A notable failure of a movie, *Arizona Dream* is worth seeking out only to give credit to the solid effort. Kusturica's narrative appears far beyond salvation, a surreal mess that may very well have some sort of soulful punch line. Unfortunately, even the most obtuse movie speaks to the viewer on the initial viewing; *Dream* would really like to tell you about love and life, but, like a child learning to speak, doesn't know what it's saying. Unless you're a huge fan of the cast, Skip It.

By contrast, most mainstream American reviews were favorable, and the film won the Silver Bear in Berlin, yet Warner Brothers had so little confidence in its prospects that it delayed a stateside opening for over a year and then released it initially in a version reduced from 142 minutes to 119. Despite a $19 million budget, it made back only $112,547 in the US.

Dedicated to the memory of Kusturica's father—whose death, along with the outbreak of the Bosnian war, occurred during the film's year-long production, occasioning a three-month break in the shooting—*Arizona Dream*, I think it's safe to assume, knows what it's saying and doesn't deliberately set out to confuse anyone. But there's no question that it revels in eccentric, cartoonish characters with hysterical behavior. Objections about the film being "self-indulgent" seem misplaced if one considers the breathtaking fourteen-minute sequence, including a virtuoso ten-minute take covering the hero's eventual wedding to Millie (Paulina Porizkova), his uncle's former fiancée (and the film's only Eastern European character), that Kusturica chose to delete from the film. But *Arizona Dream* does offer a disturbing satirical view of America, very much in keeping with Kusturica's treatment of his native Yugoslavia as a delusionary site—of diverse fantasies and accompanying denials, all of which wind up going haywire. Like *Underworld* (1995), his masterpiece about World War II black marketers, made just afterwards, this film glories in chaotic messes with farcical consequences—Felliniesque circuses where wild animals are always breaking loose and where mordant Eastern European reflections underlie the various celebrations. It's hardly surprising that most (if not all) of the flights in the film, including many flights of fancy, end in crash landings.

The first of these flights and crashes, which precedes the opening credits, involves an Eskimo, dogs, a giant fish, bitter wind, and icy water—and it isn't clear for some time whether this is memory or dream, family history or personal fantasy. In fact, all of the film's characters share the same difficulty in being able to distinguish between the two. By the time we discover that it's a personal fantasy of the hero, Axel (Depp), whose family history is sketched in only later (his father was an Arizona border guard, not an Eskimo), we've already embarked on a form of magical realism that views American dreams as solipsistic by their very nature. Furthermore, any efforts to share them—Axel's uncle Leo Sweetie (Lewis) trying to turn Axel into a Cadillac salesman like himself, or Axel trying to build a flying machine so that the older woman he loves, Elaine Stalker (Dunaway), can realize her dream of flight—invariably produce tragic-comic disasters.

The film as a whole concerns such fantasies, and the characters' doomed efforts to share them with others—or else their inability to recognize that they already share them, such as Leo protesting to Elaine that she's old enough to be Axel's mother, which ignores the fact that he's old enough to be the grandfather of his own fiancée. Moreover, after Axel's plan to murder Grace becomes a shared game of Russian roulette (her second suicide attempt), his more genuine attempt to shoot himself provokes her complaint that he's cheating.

The fact that even the most superficially "normal" of the film's characters, Axel's cousin Paul (Vincent Gallo), is in some ways the most deluded, is made clear once we witness his public "performances" as an aspiring actor where he reproduces the dialogue and/or gestures of movie stars in favorite movies—Robert De Niro and Joe Pesci in *Raging Bull* (Martin Scorsese, 1980), Cary Grant in the crop-dusting sequence of *North by Northwest* (Alfred Hitchcock, 1959), Al Pacino and John Cazale in *The Godfather* (Francis Ford Coppola, 1972). The first happens in a movie theater, with the giant movie playing behind him, in the duplicating manner of *Rocky Horror Picture Show* (Jim Sharman, 1975) cultists—though here the spectacle is shared by a dog who's idly wandered onto the same stage. The second, enacted in a Tucson talent show, is done without the film—although we, unlike the laughing audience, can see relevant portions intercut with Paul's gestures with a few pathetic cornstalks that have been brought onstage as props. In the third, awash with self-pity while watching a scene of familial banishment on TV with another dog as his sole companion, Paul simply recites the dialogue along with the actors, performing for himself.

All three enactments offer an implicit yet devastating critique of American postmodernism—an actorly equivalent to the practice of the "Movie Brats" (Bogdanovich, De Palma, Schrader, Scorsese, and their progeny such as Tarantino) to achieve their notion of greatness by copying shots from their favorite pictures. But for film viewers unaccustomed to such ironic metaphors, it must simply look as demented as the character does while taking a congested club's stage for the sheer space of a Midwestern cornfield. And within the deranged terms of this fantasy of duplication, subsequently reproducing Cary Grant's drop to the ground on the real space of an Arizona field while Elaine flies overhead is no real improvement.

PlayTime

Written in 2013 for a 2019 Taschen publication, Jacques Tati. The Complete Works, *edited by Alison Castle. In the same multivolume monolith I have essays on each of Tati's five other features and a memoir about him, all of which are also available on my website. I tweaked and slightly abbreviated this essay in early 2023.*

1. The Title

First of all, what *is* the title? Like most other critics, I've generally known and written it as *Playtime*, but the final draft of the screenplay in late 1964 called it only *Film Tati No. 4*. Other early and tentative titles included *Récreation (Recess)* and *La grande ville (The Big City)*. In 1979, based on the credits sequence and ad logos, film academic Kristin Thompson wrote that the correct title was *Play Time*. But according to this volume's editor, "Tati himself referred to it in correspondence always in capitals and always (at least from what I've seen) as one word," i.e. as "PLAYTIME". And "Macha Makeieff, as the rights holder to the Tati estate, took an official decision a few years back that the official spelling is now to be '*PlayTime*,' i.e. in one word but with a capital 'T'."

Do such distinctions matter? I think they do. American historian Rick Perlstein has called *Play Time* "a sentence, not a word, and a command," adding that one can even "read it as two verbs, a double command." But what arguably makes "*PlayTime*" better than either "*Playtime*" or "*Play Time*" is its emphasizing the fact that it isn't either a French or an English title. It's a non-word belonging to no existing language except for "franglais"—the perception of English through a French sensibility, which also produced such relatively new terms in France during the same period as "parking, "weekend," and "Drugstore".

"Parking" got adopted somewhat awkwardly because, like other French nouns, it had to be preceded by an article, making it "un parking", while "Drugstore" was actually the chic invention of a Paris publicist—an early and relatively compact version of an enclosed shopping mall, such as the one we see in *PlayTime* just a short distance from the Royal Garden Restaurant. (A London version in Chelsea, immortalized in a Rolling Stones hit, also turns up in Kubrick's *A Clockwork Orange*.) All such terms, dating from the era of *PlayTime*, were indirect acknowledgments of what might be called the Americanization of the planet, which is plainly part of the film's subject, even though, practically speaking, the differences between the theory and actual practice of Americanization (and, more generally, modernization) are crucial. Think of the gradual physical collapse of the Royal Garden—its name another example of both franglais and the theory of how things should look and behave rather than the practice of how they actually function.

In many ways, the ambiguity of Tati's strange title—is *"PlayTime"* a thing or an activity, a dream or an actual, living possibility?—corresponds to what could be described as the lessons of its architecture. By this I mean not only the city-wide set that Tati had constructed on the outskirts of Paris on which to play out his concepts, but also the architecture and structure of the film itself, and what it does to our sense of how we manage our everyday space as well as our everyday time. Looking straight ahead, which is where the regimented architecture leads and takes us, we make a futile effort to discover or pursue a particular story, until, like Monsieur Hulot, we become lost, or else, like Monsjeur Giffard, the gentleman who spends much of the day looking for him, we wind up smashing into a glass door. But once the glass of another door finally shatters—and once our observation starts to superimpose a playful dance of scanning exploration and improvisation across the rigid space of the buildings—we can spend our time as creative citizens in an interactive community.

2. *PlayTime*'s Origins

Tati once told *France-Soir* that the film's first inspiration was a bathroom leak in a sleek but soulless Lisbon hotel where he once stayed, bringing in a steady stream of "experts" that gradually evolved into a crowded party. It's an anecdote recalling the famous stateroom sequence in the Marx Brothers' *A Night at the Opera*, but with a happy moral tacked on at the end. And as pointed out by biographer David Bellos, he was also undoubtedly influenced by his own ambitious and innovative *Jour de fête à l'Olympia*—a live show he was asked to put on (replacing an indisposed Edith Piaf) in the spring of 1964 that incorporated the screening of a retooled version of his first feature, which tried in diverse ways to break down the usual distinctions made between spectacle and life. In this show, he even employed a group of Monsieur Hulot lookalikes designed to confound audience expectations—a teasing trick that would become central to his design for *PlayTime*.

Certain aspects of *PlayTime* can clearly be traced back to Tati's previous features. The notion of vacation-time, and the leisurely pacing that comes with it, was central to both *Jour de fête* and *Mr. Hulot's Holiday*, and a critique of alienating aspects of contemporary architecture was already fully present in *Mon oncle*. More abstractly and formally, Tati's penchant for switching from one center of attention to another in *Mr. Hulot's Holiday*—having a detail in the background of one shot become a prominent foreground element in the next shot—introduced a notion of simultaneous gags and actions that would become central to the overall conception of *PlayTime*, above all in the climactic Royal Garden sequence. Similarly, the alternations between boredom and interest, idleness and activity, emptiness and fullness that defined the rhythmic structure of the first Hulot feature provided part of the basis for the way gags would blossom or develop in Tati's fourth and most ambitious feature, where the notion of a storyline would mainly be limited to the shape of a single day, much as *Mr. Hulot's Holiday* was shaped to the overall pattern of a summer holiday season.

Written like a ballet in a detailed, 447-page script that concentrated far more on physical action than on dialogue, Tati worked with his friend Jacques Lagrange, who had helped him in writing his previous two features, a teacher at the École des Beaux Arts who was especially good at providing sketches.

3. Building Tativille

PlayTime's only real "star" was the gigantic city set Tati had constructed east of Paris, near the Bois de Vincennes and designed by Eugène Roman, after a wasteland there was attacked by bulldozers—requiring over 3500 square yards of timber, 4300 square yards of plastic, 5400 square yards of concrete, and 1300 square yards of glass, built and fitted by a hundred workman working with a dozen technicians over a five-month period. As Tati said to me in an interview, "For my construction, we couldn't go to the Drugstore and Orly and stop work there, it would've been impossible. And I wanted this uniformity: all the chairs, for instance, in the restaurant, in the bank—they're all the same. [In fact, while we were speaking, in his office, I was sitting in one of them.] The floor's the same, the paint's the same. It cost a lot of money, of course, but it's there—and it's not more expensive than Sophia Loren."

Tativille included real streets and traffic lights, some smaller buildings that could be moved around on rails, and even some (though not enough) real advertising to pay for it all, especially after a heavy wind knocked much of the set down, requiring extensive reconstruction, and some rain the next July caused many further delays. Altogether, the shooting took 365 nonconsecutive days.

The best comparisons that spring to mind when it comes to extravagant studio-built cities controlled by single artistic visions—Monte Carlo in Erich von Stroheim's *Foolish Wives*, Fritz Lang's *Metropolis*, the nameless city in F.W. Murnau's *Sunrise*—are all great silent pictures, which seems apt because *PlayTime* was also shot silently, like Tati's other features. An essential part of Tati's design was the sense of placelessness intentionally conveyed by this enormous set. From the opening sequence, part of Tati's point is that we no longer can be sure where we are in the modern world, either nationally or architecturally. Is it a hospital waiting room, an office building, or a terminal of some kind? And in what country? It's roughly akin to a question that Barbara asks Hulot much later—"How do you say 'Drugstore' in French?"—and to the posters we see in a travel agency, showing us identical buildings around the globe.

4. Casting *PlayTime*

Most of the actors chosen were nonprofessionals, and the few professionals and semiprofessionals that Tati employed were sometimes used against the grain of their usual profiles. To consider only the three principal American characters: Barbara, the most prominent of the younger tourists, was played by Barbara Denneke, who wasn't American at all, but Bavarian—an *au-pair* who worked for neighbors of his on Rue Voltaire. John Abbey—playing the stiff and mechanical American businessman whom Hulot observes in a waiting-room and whom we also see with his secretary in an office, and who later turns up at the Royal Garden—also took the title role in William Klein's satirical *Mr. Freedom* (1969) during the same period. And Billy Kearns, who plays Mr. Schulz—the free-spending customer at the Royal Garden who first seems like a stereotypical Ugly American but winds up as the virtual hero of the film's second half, the benign benefactor and ringmaster of the impromptu party that develops—was a busy TV character actor who can also be seen in many other notable French features of the period, such as *Purple Noon*, *The Trial*, *Is Paris Burning?*, and *Bed and Board*. It's a paradoxical fact about Mr. Schulz that, out of all the film's characters, he makes the loudest entrance and the most unobtrusive final exit. (After paying for all his guests' breakfast in a café, he quietly sneaks off and steps into a car in the background of a crowded shot, not waiting to be thanked by anyone.)

5. Shooting *PlayTime*

In contrast to *PlayTime*'s 365 nonconsecutive shooting days, *Metropolis* required a mere 310 days and 60 nights, and the most famous myth about Eric von Stroheim's mania for detail in his own gargantuan sets and costumes—supposedly requiring his extras on one film to wear monogrammed silk underwear, most likely the invention of a studio publicist, because Stroheim's profligacy was paradoxically brandished by his studios as one of his selling points—actually finds a faint echo in the more verifiable fact, cited by biographer David Bellos, that Tati once insisted on reshooting a very complicated three-second shot in the Royal Garden sequence for reasons of continuity because the waiter with torn trousers was wearing white rather than striped undershorts.

This suggests a perfectionist temperament, but it's worth adding that Tati could be relatively lax when it came to satisfying conventional standards of narrative continuity. How, for instance, can Barbara depart on the bus for Orly at the film's end without any sign of her returning to her hotel or packing her suitcase? How viewers looked at the screen clearly mattered a lot more to Tati than how—or maybe even if—they processed a story, and so did how they listened. It's however worth noting the astonishing fact that he knew his 447-page script by heart, at least in terms of the contents of every shot.

6. *PlayTime*'s Soundtrack and Editing

The creation of the film's six-track stereo sound (including various aural cues to aid or confuse us in following or interpreting the images) as well as the editing required nine months more after the shooting, and when it came to fashioning the particular sound of the waiter's trousers ripping, Tati's assistant Marie-France Siegler—who started working for him during the preparations for *PlayTime* (helping to round up U.S. army officer wives in Paris to play most of the American tourists) and can be briefly seen sitting next to Barbara in the bus bound for Orly—once told me that her boss even tried using his own voice.

As was customary for Tati, slightly different soundtracks were prepared for different countries. Even though the dialogue was intended to be overheard rather than heard, making subtitles unnecessary (even though optional English subtitles are offered today on the American and English DVDs and Blu-Rays), there was somewhat more French heard in the French version, somewhat more English in the version prepared for the U.K., and so on. Tati even engaged the American humorist and *Washington Post* columnist Art Buchwald (1925-2007) to write the dialogue of the American tourists, based on his own indications of what he wanted to be conveyed at various junctures (and arranging to have a rough cut screened for Buchwald in early 1967), and wound up assigning him a special screen credit for this work.

Two important aspects of the editing of *PlayTime* are worth noting: (1) This is the first film on which Tati's daughter, Sophie Tatischeff, worked as an editor, starting off in this case as an assistant. (2) Like the camera movements in *PlayTime*, which are invisible by design—that is, intended not to be noticed, so that they often follow the same normal paths that the viewer's gaze would follow—the editing is similarly at the service of the action rather than something to be noticed in its own right. Two especially notable exceptions to this rule—cuts that are meant to produce surprises—show (a) a skyscraper accompanied by a "heavenly choir" on the soundtrack (the film's opening shot, after the credits) and (b) the climactic overhead image of Paris traffic as a merry-go-round. A far more typical edit is the continuity cut, such as the one between the second and third shots, following the progress of two nuns as they walk down a hallway and then across a waiting-room.

7. The "Plot" of *PlayTime*

Any synopsis of *PlayTime* necessarily betrays its experience because it has no heroes or plot in any normal sense, and the number of narrative details that we can see in many shots makes it impossible to take it all in over a single viewing; we have to make choices, making us creative participants in a kind of interactive, life-size board game. Each extra is theoretically and potentially a major character with a separate story and pathway; to follow them all, one essentially has to join them, sharing their disorientation (which makes us all tourists) as well as their eventual enjoyment of one another.

A group of American women tourists arrives at Orly airport. (One should note, incidentally, that *PlayTime* was made prior to the construction of Charles De Gaulle airport, which would replace Orly for international flights.) Over their day in Paris, these tourists see that the skyscrapers of steel and glass resemble not only one another but the ones back home and the ones they've glimpsed in other foreign capitols on their tour. The "old Paris" they'd hoped to see (the Eiffel Tower, Concorde, Sacre-Coeur) appears only fleetingly, as reflections on the glass doors. Periodically crossing their paths is Hulot, who has an appointment in one of these buildings with a M. Giffard; the two briefly meet, then lose sight and track of one another while Hulot and some of the tourists wander through an international gadget fair. There, through a case of mistaken identity, a German executive in charge of an exhibit promoting doors that close (or slam) silently believes that Hulot and not a younger man who resembles him has gone through his desk during his absence, looking for free circulars, and Giffard injures his nose by running into a glass door while chasing after someone else whom he mistakenly believes to be Hulot.

That evening, Hulot and Giffard finally meet up by chance outside the opening of a new restaurant, and Hulot also encounters a couple of old army pals; one briefly invites him home (in another skyscraper—glimpsed by us along with other flats only from outside, through its windows), the other is the doorman at the new restaurant, the Royal Garden, with a glass door of its own that eventually shatters. There Hulot also meets Barbara, one of the younger tourists, as well as the German executive at the gadget exhibition, now in a friendlier mood. Due to the restaurant opening hastily and prematurely, it gradually and accidentally falls to pieces (like its front door) while its diverse clientele, led by a boisterous, free-spending American named Schulz, have a party that lasts all night. After breakfast in a nearby café, Hulot buys Barbara plastic flowers as a farewell gift before she boards her bus, then gets stuck in a line and has to ask a young man who resembles him to deliver it. Opening the parcel on her way to Orly, she sees that the flowers resemble the lampposts flanking the highway.

8. The False Hulots

The young man who delivers Hulot's plastic flowers to Barbara in the final sequence of *PlayTime* is only the last in a long line of "false" Hulots spread across the film's terrain, most of them designed to confound our expectations as well as those of other characters. Three characters resembling Hulot have already turned up very briefly at Orly airport during the opening sequence. More precisely, whether these are separate characters or the same one reappearing twice—or even whether one of them is Hulot/Tati himself (as was indicated in the script)—is ultimately irrelevant. Tati was determined to prove that "the comic effect belongs to everyone" (as he put it to me in our interview), not something to be assigned primarily to any central character.

To make his point even more explicit, Tati brings together two separate Hulot figures—a false Hulot and an irrefutably real Hulot—a little over twelve minutes into the picture, both of them stepping off an old-fashioned Paris bus (which is seen in explicit contrast to the more modern-looking tourist bus that we have just followed into Paris from Orly airport). They come together in a single gag while exiting the bus when their separate umbrellas accidentally become stuck together and the two characters have to dis-entangle them. (Like all the other false Hulots that turn up in the film, this one is visibly younger than Hulot himself, which implicitly becomes Tati's way of acknowledging his age while generously suggesting that he has to make room for diverse comic "replacements.") In fact, this umbrella gag is a near-replay of one of the first explicit gags in *Mr. Hulot's Holiday*, and significantly one in which Hulot doesn't figure at all: two men hurrying to board another tourist bus via separate doors both lose their umbrellas when these accidentally become hooked together and fall to the ground.

9. *PlayTime*'s Original Critical Reception

Back in the '60s and '70s, *PlayTime* was as a rule more easily accepted and understood by ordinary viewers than it was by film critics, but sadly enough, not enough ordinary viewers found their way to the film to make it commercially successful. The film's prestige has grown steadily since 1967-1968, but it was widely misperceived and a source of bewilderment in its own era—especially, it seems, in the U.S. and the U.K., where the film's failure to follow the conventional rules of movie storytelling mainly yielded boredom, emptiness, and apparent formlessness. This was the impression left by both Penelope Houston in *Sight and Sound* (who made a point of insisting that neither Tati's techniques nor his ideas were "ahead of their time") and Brenda Davies in the *Monthly Film Bulletin* in London, in 1968. In New York, where the film wouldn't get a proper launch for another five years (and then only in 35mm, after Tati had lost control over the film), it elicited a rave review in the *New York Times* from Vincent Canby, calling it Tati's "most brilliant film," but terse, alienated dismissals from both Andrew Sarris and Pauline Kael. Speaking for myself, I can't say I was fully aware of the film's greatness the first time I saw it, as a tourist in Paris during the summer of 1968, even though it intrigued me enough to go back for a second look. Yet by the time I moved to Paris from Manhattan a year later, I'd come to discover that the film had taught me how to cope creatively and imaginatively with the sensory overload of city life. More simply, it had shown me how I could live in a modern city without feeling crushed, alienated, and overwhelmed by it.

The first critics to appreciate the importance of the film's innovations in any depth were some of those at *Cahiers du Cinéma*—especially Jean-André Fieschi and Noël Burch, who had a particularly good feel for the film's unusual sense of form. When Fieschi and Jean Narboni published an extensive interview with Tati, their first question, marveling at the film's 447-page script, was how such a complicated construction could ever have been mapped out on paper.

(Fieschi even began his subsequent article about the film by randomly quoting shot #269, at the Royal Garden, which alone required fifteen short paragraphs over a couple of pages.) Maintaining that *PlayTime* was "the precise opposite of a literary film," and that it was written "like a ballet," Tati said, "I know my film by heart, and on the set I was no longer looking at the script."

In his own essay, Burch was fascinated by the original way the film either developed or refused to develop particular gags—a process that in some cases entailed not the execution of the gag but the mere suggestion or possibility that it might occur. Burch saw this strange tendency in formal terms, but it's also relevant to see it as part of Tati's philosophical position: to view the world as a place where funny things might happen is to conjure up a universe of poetic potentiality—a multitude of virtual realities in place of a single reality. For viewers trained to follow stories that lead to narrative payoffs—morals, solutions, dramatic climaxes—one can easily understand how *PlayTime*, if viewed less interactively and creatively, might seem empty and uneventful rather than teeming with lively possibilities. Happily, and triumphantly, it is the possibilities and the poetry that remain today, waiting to be rediscovered, played with, and savored.

10. *PlayTime*'s Lasting Legacy

Many of the greatest filmmakers are individuals who can be said to have reinvented the cinema for their own purposes, and clearly Tati was one of these. This suggests that it's misleading to see him as part of any logical or organic evolution leading from, say, Buster Keaton to Woody Allen (even though Tati was a fan of both these comics), and more fruitful in many ways to regard him as an artist with a particular view of the world who turned to cinema as the best way of expressing that view. In the case of *PlayTime*, this became a philosophical as well as a practical vision, physical as well as metaphysical, which essentially sprang from a conviction that everyone in the world is funny coupled with a regret that everyone hasn't discovered this yet. Becoming a man with a mission, he saw his job as showing some people how they might better appreciate the world they were living in.

One might even describe *PlayTime* as a nightmarish maze of confusion, obstruction, and frustration that becomes a utopia once the people take over their surroundings—a gradual process, as Tati conceived it, of human, dancelike movements, either spontaneous or accidental, triumphing over regimented, rect-angular spaces. This already starts in the film's second and third shots, when a pair of nuns, guided by the architecture, execute one sharp left turn in unison, then two equally sharp right turns, the cornets in their habits audibly flapping like wings; these are soon followed by the equally sharp turns or glances of at least half a dozen other people we see, including a worker pushing a cart, a trash collector, and a nurse. Then, almost another quarter of an hour will pass before we see Hulot momentarily slipping with the tip of his closed umbrella in an equally sterile waiting room, when the possibility of breaking with this regimentation is most clearly introduced. And much later in the film, once we learn with the help of the bands at the Royal Garden restaurant how to navigate the space with our eyes as if we were dancing, the delighted discovery of the people around us and what's funny about them becomes a kind of liberation.

Utopia and Apocalypse: Pynchon's Populist/Fatalist Cinema

Commissioned by Patrice Rollet for Trafic *and published in their Spring 2020 issue. For the record, I've reviewed every Pynchon novel apart from the first and the most recent one; all six reviews can be found at my website.*

The rhythmic clapping resonates inside these walls, which are hard and glossy as coal: Come-on! Start-the-show! Come-on! Start-the-show! The screen is a dim page spread before us, white and silent. The film has broken, or a projector bulb has burned out. It was difficult even for us, old fans who've always been at the movies (haven't we?), to tell which before the darkness swept in.

—from the last page of *Gravity's Rainbow*

To begin with a personal anecdote: Writing my first book (to be published) in the late 1970s, an experimental autobiography titled *Moving Places: A Life at the Movies* (Harper & Row, 1980), I wanted to include four texts by other authors—two short stories ("In Dreams Begin Responsibilities" by Delmore Schwartz, "The Secret Integration" by Thomas Pynchon) and two essays ("The Carole Lombard in Macy's Window" by Charles Eckert, "My Life With Kong" by Elliott Stein)—but was prevented from doing so by my editor, who argued that because the book was mine, texts by other authors didn't belong there. My motives were both pluralistic and populist: a desire both to respect fiction and non-fiction as equal creative partners and to insist that the book was about more than just myself and my own life. Because my book was largely about the creative roles played by the fictions of cinema on the non-fictions of personal lives, the anti-elitist nature of cinema played a crucial part in these transactions.

In the case of Pynchon's 1964 story—which twenty years later, in his collection *Slow Learner*, he would admit was the only early story of his that he still liked—the cinematic relevance to *Moving Places* could be found in a single fleeting but resonant detail: the momentary bonding of a little white boy named Tim Santora with a black, homeless, alcoholic jazz musician named Carl McAfee in a hotel room when they discover that they've both seen *Blood Alley* (1955), an anticommunist action-adventure with John Wayne and Lauren Bacall, directed by William Wellman. Pynchon mentions only the film's title, but the complex synergy of this passing moment of mutual recognition between two of its dissimilar viewers represented for me an epiphany, in part because of the irony of such casual camaraderie occurring in relation to a routine example of Manichean Cold War mythology. Moreover, as a right-wing cinematic touchstone, *Blood Alley* is dialectically complemented in the same story by Tim and his friends categorizing their rebellious schoolboy pranks as Operation Spartacus, inspired by the left-wing *Spartacus* (1960) of Kirk Douglas, Dalton Trumbo, and Stanley Kubrick.

For better and for worse, all of Pynchon's fiction partakes of this populism by customarily defining cinema as the cultural air that everyone breathes, or at least the river in which everyone swims and bathes. This is equally apparent in the only Pynchon novel that qualifies as hackwork, *Inherent Vice* (2009), and the fact that Paul Thomas Anderson's adaptation of it is also his worst film to date—a hippie remake of *Chinatown* in the same way that the novel is a hippie remake of Raymond Chandler and Ross Macdonald—seems logical insofar as it seems to have been written with an eye towards selling the screen rights. As Geoffrey O'Brien observed (while defending this indefensible book and film) in the *New York Review of Books* (January 3, 2015), "Perhaps the novel really was crying out for such a cinematic transformation, for in its pages people watch movies, remember them, compare events in the 'real world' to their plots, re-experience their soundtracks as auditory hallucinations, even work their technical components (the lighting style of cinematographer James Wong Howe, for instance) into aspects of complex conspiratorial schemes." (Despite a few glancing virtues, such as Josh Brolin's Nixonesque performance as "Bigfoot" Bjornsen, Anderson's film seems just as cynical as its source and infused with the same sort of misplaced would-be nostalgia for the counterculture of the late '60s and early '70s, pitched to a generation that didn't experience it, as Bertolucci's *Innocents: The Dreamers*.)

From *The Crying of Lot 49*'s evocation of an orgasm in cinematic terms ("She awoke at last to find herself getting laid; she'd come in on a sexual crescendo in progress, like a cut to a scene where the camera's already moving") to the magical-surreal guest star appearance of Mickey Rooney in wartime Europe in *Gravity's Rainbow*, cinema is invariably a form of lingua franca in Pynchon's fiction, an expedient form of shorthand, calling up common experiences that seem light years away from the sectarianism of the politique des auteurs. This explains why his novels set in mid-20th century, such as the two just cited, when cinema was still a common currency cutting across classes, age groups, and diverse levels of education, tend to have the greatest number of movie references. In *Gravity's Rainbow*—set mostly in war-torn Europe, with a few flashbacks to the east coast U.S. and flash-forwards to the contemporary west coast—this even includes such anachronistic pop ephemera as the 1949 serial *King of the Rocket Men* and the 1955 Western *The Return of Jack Slade* (which a character named Waxwing Blodgett is said to have seen at U.S. Army bases during World War II no less than twenty-seven times), along with various comic books.

Significantly, "The Secret Integration", a title evoking both conspiracy and countercultural utopia, is set in the same cozy suburban neighborhood in the Berkshires from which Tyrone Slothrop, the wartime hero or antihero of *Gravity's Rainbow* (1973), aka "Rocketman," springs, with his kid brother and father among the story's characters. It's also the same region where Pynchon himself grew up. And *Gravity's Rainbow*, Pynchon's magnum opus and richest work, is by all measures the most film-drenched of his novels in its design as well as its details—so much so that even its blocks of text are separated typographically by what resemble sprocket holes. Unlike, say, *Vineland* (1990), where cinema figures mostly in terms of imaginary TV reruns (e.g., Woody Allen in *Young Kissinger*) and diverse cultural appropriations (e.g., a Noir Center shopping mall), or the post-cinematic adventures in cyberspace found in the noirish (and far superior) east-coast companion volume to *Inherent Vice*, *Bleeding Edge* (2013), cinema in *Gravity's Rainbow* is basically a theatrical event with a social impact, where Fritz Lang's invention of the rocket countdown as a suspense device (in the 1929 *Frau im mond*) and the separate "frames" of a rocket's trajectory are equally relevant and operative factors. There are also passing references to Lang's *Der müde Tod*, *Die Nibelungen*, *Dr. Mabuse, der Spieler*, and *Metropolis*—not to mention De Mille's *Cleopatra*, *Dumbo*, *Freaks*, *Son of Frankenstein*, *White Zombie*, at least two Fred Astaire and Ginger Rogers musicals, Pabst, and Lubitsch—and the epigraphs introducing the novel's second and third sections ("You will have the tallest, darkest leading man in Hollywood. —Merian C. Cooper to Fay Wray" and "Toto, I have a feeling we're not in Kansas any more....—Dorothy, arriving in Oz") are equally steeped in familiar movie mythology.

These are all populist allusions, yet the bane of populism as a rightwing curse is another near-constant in Pynchon's work. The same ambivalence can be felt in the novel's last two words, "Now everybody—", at once frightening and comforting in its immediacy and universality. With the possible exception of *Mason & Dixon* (1997), every Pynchon novel over the past three decades—*Vineland, Against the Day* (2006), *Inherent Vice,* and *Bleeding Edge*—has an attractive, prominent, and sympathetic female character betraying or at least acting against her leftist roots and/or principles by being first drawn erotically towards and then being seduced by a fascistic male. In *Bleeding Edge,* this even happens to the novel's earthy protagonist, the middle-aged detective Maxine Tarnow. Given the teasing amount of autobiographical concealment and revelation Pynchon carries on with his public while rigorously avoiding the press, it is tempting to see this recurring theme as a personal obsession grounded in some private psychic wound, and one that points to sadder-but-wiser challenges brought by Pynchon to his own populism, eventually reflecting a certain cynicism about human behavior. It also calls to mind some of the reflections of Luc Moullet (in "Sainte Janet," *Cahiers du cinéma no. 86,* août 1958) aroused by Howard Hughes' and Josef von Sternberg's *Jet Pilot* and (more incidentally) by Ayn Rand's and King Vidor's *The Fountainhead* whereby "erotic verve" is tied to a contempt for collectivity—implicitly suggesting that rightwing art may be sexier than leftwing art, especially if the sexual delirium in question has some of the adolescent energy found in, for example, Hughes, Sternberg, Rand, Vidor, Kubrick, Tashlin, Jerry Lewis, and, yes, Pynchon.

One of the most impressive things about Pynchon's fiction is the way in which it often represents the narrative shapes of individual novels in explicit visual terms. *V,* his first novel, has two heroes and narrative lines that converge at the bottom point of a *V; Gravity's Rainbow,* his third—a *V2* in more ways than one—unfolds across an epic skyscape like a rocket's (linear) ascent and its (scattered) descent; *Vineland* offers a narrative tangle of lives to rhyme with its crisscrossing vines, and the curving ampersand in the middle of *Mason & Dixon* suggests another form of digressive tangle between its two male leads; *Against the Day,* which opens with a balloon flight, seems to follow the curving shape and rotation of the planet.

This compulsive patterning suggests that the sprocket-hole design in *Gravity's Rainbow's* section breaks is more than just a decorative detail. The recurrence of sprockets and film frames carries metaphorical resonance in the novel's action, so that Franz Pökler, a German rocket engineer allowed by his superiors to see his long-lost daughter (whom he calls his "movie child" because she was conceived the night he and her mother saw a porn film) only once a year, at a children's village called Zwölfkinder, and can't even be sure if it's the same girl each time:

> So it has gone for the six years since. A daughter a year, each one about a year older, each time taking up nearly from scratch. The only continuity has been her name, and Zwölfkinder, and Pökler's love—love something like the persistence of vision, for They have used it to create for him the moving image of a daughter, flashing him only these summertime frames of her, leaving it to him to build the illusion of a single child—what would the time scale matter, a 24th of a second or a year (no more, the engineer thought, than in a wind tunnel, or an oscillograph whose turning drum you can speed or slow at will...)?

§

Cinema, in short, is both delightful and sinister—a utopian dream and an apocalyptic nightmare, a stark juxtaposition reflected in the abrupt shift in the earlier Pynchon passage quoted at the beginning of this essay from present tense to past tense, and from third person to first person. Much the same could be said about the various displacements experienced while moving from the positive to the negative consequences of populism.

Pynchon's allegiance to the irreverent vulgarity of kazoos sounding like farts and concomitant Spike Jones parodies seems wholly in keeping with his disdain for David Raksin and Johnny Mercer's popular song "Laura" and what he perceives as the snobbish elitism of the Preminger film it derives from, as expressed in his passionate liner notes to the CD compilation *Spiked!: The Music of Spike Jones* a half-century later:

> The song had been featured in the 1945 movie of the same name, supposed to evoke the hotsy-totsy social life where all these sophisticated New York City folks had time for faces in the misty light and so forth, not to mention expensive outfits, fancy interiors, witty repartee—a world of pseudos as inviting to...class hostility as fish in a barrel, including a presumed audience fatally unhip enough to still believe in the old prewar fantasies, though surely it was already too late for that, Tin Pan Alley wisdom about life had not stood a chance under the realities of global war, too many people by then knew better.

Consequently, neither art cinema nor auteur cinema figures much in Pynchon's otherwise hefty lexicon of film culture, aside from a jokey mention of a Bengt Ekerot/Maria Casares Film Festival (actors playing Death in *The Seventh Seal* and *Orphée*) held in Los Angeles—and significantly, even the "underground", 16-millimeter radical political filmmaking in northern California charted in *Vineland* becomes emblematic of the perceived failure of the '60s counterculture as a whole. This also helps to account for why the paranoia and solipsism found in Jacques Rivette's *Paris nous appartient* and *Out 1*, perhaps the closest equivalents to Pynchon's own notions of mass conspiracy juxtaposed with solitary despair, are never mentioned in his writing, and the films that are referenced belong almost exclusively to the commercial mainstream, unlike the examples of painting, music, and literature, such as the surrealist painting of Remedios Varo described in detail at the beginning of *The Crying of Lot 49*, the importance of Ornette Coleman in *V* and Anton Webern in *Gravity's Rainbow*, or the visible impact of both Jorge Luis Borges and William S. Burroughs on the latter novel.[1] And much of the novel's supply of movie folklore—e.g., the fatal ambushing of John Dillinger while leaving Chicago's Biograph theater—is mainstream as well.

Nevertheless, one can find a fairly precise philosophical and metaphysical description of these aforementioned Rivette films in *Gravity's Rainbow*: "If there is something comforting—religious, if you want—about paranoia, there is still also anti-paranoia, where nothing is connected to anything, a condition not many of us can bear for long." And the white, empty movie screen that appears apocalyptically on the novel's final page—as white and as blank as the fusion of all the colors in a rainbow—also appears in Rivette's first feature when a 16-millimeter print of Lang's *Metropolis* breaks during the projection of the Tower of Babel sequence.

Is such a physically and metaphysically similar affective climax of a halted film projection foretelling an apocalypse a mere coincidence? It's impossible to know whether Pynchon might have seen *Paris nous appartient* during its brief New York appearances in the early '60s. But even if he hadn't (or still hasn't), a bitter sense of betrayed utopian possibilities in that film, in *Out 1*, and in most of his fiction is hard to overlook. Old fans who've always been at the movies (haven't we?) don't like to be woken from their dreams.

End Note

1.   For this reason, among others, I'm skeptical about accepting the hypothesis of the otherwise reliable Pynchon critic Richard Poirier that *Gravity's*

Rainbow's enigmatic references to "the Kenosha Kid" might allude to Orson Welles, who was born in Kenosha, Wisconsin. Steven C. Weisenburger, in *A Gravity's Rainbow Companion* (Athens/London: The University of Georgia Press, 2006), reports more plausibly that "the Kenosha Kid" was a pulp magazine character created by Forbes Parkhill in Western stories published from the 1920s through the 1940s. Once again, Pynchon's populism trumps—i.e. exceeds—his cinephilia.

Alexander Dovzhenko, Hillbilly Avant-Gardist

Written for MUBI Notebook *in April 2020 and shortened here to delete a factual blunder.*

It's disconcerting that the collected writings in English of one of the world's greatest filmmakers currently sells for $852 on Amazon—or a whopping $980, if you opt for the paperback—while the only American book about him downgrades his work's artistic value in its very title (Vance Kepley's 1985 *In the Service of the State: The Cinema of Alexander Dovzhenko*). Look him up on Wikipedia, and you find that his name is shared by a poker player and a psychiatrist—hardly fit company for the epic, poetic Alexander Dovzhenko (1894-1956), a pagan mystic whose masterful films look as wildly experimental, as dreamlike, as hysterically funny, as fiercely tragic, and as beautiful today as they did a century ago.

A Cold War casualty, often defined in the West as a Russian Communist and in Russia as a turncoat, this Ukrainian nationalist lived under KGB surveillance for most of his life—which may help to explain why his devoted second wife Julia Solntseva, who filmed many of his unrealized scripts after his death, had joined the KGB herself, possibly in order to protect her husband. And as one of his better Western explicators, Ray Uzwyshyn, has pointed out, "With regard to the non-Russian republics (i.e. Georgia, Armenia, Moldavia, Azerbaijan, et al.), the larger cinematic histories of these republics, like Ukrainian cinema, largely remains a blank slate for the West..."

To suggest just how blank it can be, consider film critic James Agee, one of Dovzhenko's most passionate American supporters, writing to his *Time* editors circa 1947, proposing a cover story on Sergei Eisenstein, and maintaining that "another Russian [sic] director of very great ability, Alexander Dovzhenko, has not, thus far, gotten into any trouble." Yet trouble was his middle name from the get-go, even before he ran afoul of Stalinist censors and functionaries blocking his projects, by virtue of his lifelong commitments to Ukrainian culture and independence. It was a commitment that ultimately led to a bureaucratic stifling of his art after the 1930s, and eventually it killed him.

The seventh child of illiterate farmers who had fourteen offspring, only one other of whom was still alive when he turned eleven, Dovzhenko was persuaded by a semiliterate grandfather to attend school, and became a teacher in his late teens. After serving in the Red Army and working as a diplomatic assistant in both Warsaw and Berlin (where he also studied art with George Grosz), he worked as a graphic artist and cartoonist back in the U.S.S.R., and finally turned to filmmaking around the time he was pushing thirty.

"Whenever I think of my childhood and of my home," he once wrote, "in my mind I see crying and funerals"—and death figures as a near-constant in his work, especially in *Zvenigora* (1928), *Arsenal* (1929), and *Earth* (1930), his last three silent films (and, many would say, his greatest). In the first two, deaths are violent and connected to warfare. *Earth*, mainly concerned with collectivized farming, begins with the peaceful death of an old man (modelled on Dovzhenko's grandfather), viewed as an event occurring in harmony with nature.

To understand Dovzheko's visionary talent, one has to factor in his ecstatic love of nature and all the other arts that fed into his cinema: not just painting but also sculpture, literature (according to Uzwyshyn, "Dovzhenko's literary output is considered seminal in Ukrainian literary history"), theater (especially in *Zvenigora* and *Aerograd* [1935]), music (both classical and folk, and complete with singing horses in *Arsenal*), and dance—perhaps even landscaping if one considers his lyrical ways of capturing and harnessing (or unleashing) sunflowers, fields, rivers, and forests.

These diverse arts and crafts—also including such varied cinematic tools as slapstick, slow motion, fast montage, equally epic closeups and long shots, audiovisual counterpoint, superimposition, and changes in focus—are employed not as references but as ways of expressing Dovzhenko's boundless exuberance. This is why his art is justly regarded more as poetry than as prose, and why it comes across in leaps, swerves, and bends. His structures often seem closer to music than to dramatic narrative—or, rather, closer to music as drama and narrative, as in opera and ballet. *Arsenal* is staccato, *Earth* legato. And contrary to our clichéd notions of Soviet propaganda in praise of tractors and dams, his peculiar brands of agitprop in the '20s and '30s, when his art could still flourish, are neither ecologically nor politically correct. In *Earth*, a stalled tractor gets fueled with workers' urine and a beautiful woman savagely mourns her boyfriend's death by tearing off all her clothes (two sequences cut by Stalin's censors but eventually restored). A crusty old slacker in Dovzhenko's next film, *Ivan* (his first talkie, 1932), is comically celebrated for proudly refusing to do a lick of work in building a mighty dam.

I would argue that Dovzhenko's undeserved marginality derives in part from the marginal way we tend to regard country folk, especially when they display the unbridled freedom of avant-garde artists. (Two other major examples: William Faulkner in literature, Jia Zhangke in cinema.) Many of us unconsciously adopt the city-bred bias that innovative art belongs to urban audiences and depends on some form of city smartness, reluctant to believe it can also come from hillbillies. That these artists seem to reinvent their own art forms may lead us to think that they somehow arrived at their discoveries by brute instinct rather than by study or intellect, but this means overlooking the fact that Faulkner read James Joyce and Dovzhenko was exposed to modern art in Warsaw, Berlin, and Odessa. At the same time, his view of urban decadence could be scathing. Near the end of *Zvenigora*, a reactionary Cossack, to finance a Ukrainian treasure hunt, pretends to shoot himself onstage as part of an avant-garde "happening", and the predatory city audience that cheers him on is depicted with the sort of cartoonist's savagery that we associate with a Kubrick. But one reason why he could direct rustic nonprofessionals seamlessly is that one never feels that they're being regarded snobbishly from a big-city perspective, which would filter our unimpeded view of them. This doesn't mean that Dovzhenko was any sort of primitive, yet our cultural baggage suggests otherwise.

"Oh, a mother had three sons," reads the first intertitle of *Arsenal*, as if beginning a folk ballad about war, just after we see that mother brooding in her shack, and shortly before we see the three sons cramped together in the open car of a moving train. Only a moment later, she no longer has three sons.

Postwar Consequences: Tonino Guerra's *Equilibrium*

Commissioned by MUBI in July 2020.

Chances are, if you've seen many of the late films of Theodoros Angelopoulos, Michelangelo Antonioni (everything since *L'avventura*), Marco Bellocchio, Vittorio De Sica (*Sunflower, A Place for Lovers, Marriage Italian Style*), Federico Fellini (almost everything since *Amarcord*), Mario Monicelli, Elio Petri, Francesco Rosi, Andrei Tarkovsky (*Nostalghia*), the Taviani brothers, and/or Luchino Visconti, and paid much attention to their script credits, you know who Tonino Guerra (1920–2012) is—a ubiquitous presence in modernist European cinema, especially its Italian branches. Petri was his first cinematic employer, after Guerra started out as a schoolteacher and poet whose parents were illiterate; later on, he became a visual artist as well as a screenwriter with over a hundred credits.

Even after one acknowledges the exceptionally collaborative role played by multiple writers on Italian films, it seems that no one else was considered quite as essential by so many important directors. In Nicola Tranquillino's documentary about Tonino (visible on YouTube), Tonino himself suggests that what he brought to their films was a certain poetry. Yet what that poetry consisted of has been less than obvious to me. Even though he won an Oscar for his work on *Amarcord*, how can we tease out his contributions to a movie based on Fellini's childhood memories?

Maybe if I knew Italian and could read his actual poetry I'd have a better idea. But now that an English translation of his 1967 novella *Equilibrium* is being reprinted by Moist, a small press in the U.K., and becoming available again for the first time in over half a century, it's clear that he was a lot more than a helpful collaborator—and a close and treasured friend of Antonioni and Tarkovsky, both of whom attended his wedding to a Russian woman in Russia. Jazz pianist Marcus Roberts generally disappoints me on his own albums, but when he's a sideman for Wynton Marsalis, he's likelier to become an exciting, inventive improviser. By contrast, Guerra as a solo artist turns out to be every bit as talented, original, and challenging as the directors he worked with.

His story is a disturbing and gripping mind-boggler, at once hilarious and nightmarish. Inspired both by Guerra's traumatic internment at a Nazi camp and by his reflexes as an artist in shaping material, his novel creates a kind of ongoing surrealist dialogue between these irreconcilable parts of his brain that gradually collapse and merge into one another.

Michael Bracewell, in his new introduction, cross-references *Equilibrium* with Fellini's *City of Women*, Kathy Acker, Thomas Pynchon, and two Russian novels, *Moscow Circles* (also known as *Moscow To the End of the Line*). I would also cite Tarkovsky's *Nostalghia*, László Nemes' *Son of Saul*, and *Foreign Bodies* (Richard Howard's translation of *Les corps étrangers*, 1959, a novel by Jean Cayrol, the screenwriter of Alain Resnais' *Night* and *Fog* and *Muriel*).

The strange compulsions of the exiled Russian hero of *Nostalghia* and the Hungarian member of the Sonderkommando in *Son of Saul*—respectively, to carry a lit candle across a mineral pool and to give a proper Jewish burial to a murdered boy—are irrational, allegorical missions, at once religious and therapeutic, to cope with unbearable and untenable situations, and the virtuosity required of both these heroes in fulfilling these tasks matches that of Guerra's nameless hero-narrator in simply surviving, especially within the mounting uncertainties of his troubled consciousness. (Similarly, one could say that Guerra's own virtuosity as a writer matches that of Tarkovsky and Nemes as filmmakers.) The narrator-hero of Cayrol's novel is both a compulsive liar and a former Nazi collaborator, so the periodic deconstruction of the narrative that occurs whenever he exposes his own lies to the reader might be said to correspond to the moral and spiritual deterioration of many French citizens during the Occupation.

The narrator of *Equilibrium*, an Italian antifascist partisan during World War II and a graphic designer based in Milan two decades later, is neither a Nazi nor a collaborator, yet his harrowing and often absurdist war experiences make it impossible for him to be sure of anything—even to be able to separate the world between "good guys" and "bad guys".

Even worse, Guerra's protagonist often can't distinguish between good and bad decisions, between his professional impulses for designing ads (and for working his materials into pleasing shapes) and his personal compulsiveness in organizing his life and activities, or even between his past and his present. Meanwhile, he has more and more trouble making sense of the behavior of others, dehumanizing both them and himself in the process. As his confusion escalates, he finds that he can't distinguish his wife from his mistress with any certainty. (The fact that they resemble one another and live in almost identical postwar flats and apartment houses adds to his disorientation.)

When he arrives at the camp, the teenage commander asks the prisoners for the return of a stolen watch, and when no one steps forward, he proceeds to fire three random bullets into the prisoners' dark quarters every night until his watch is returned. It never is—although the narrator eventually discovers, many pointless deaths later, after the Americans have arrived and the commander has hanged himself, that he's wearing a cheap watch that doesn't even work.

I'm not sufficiently conversant with 1960s Italian fiction to know whether Guerra's novella can be linked to other examples from this period. But one thing I find impressive about it is how much it has to say about postwar European society (including its standardized architecture and its mass-market ads) as well as its wartime confusions, and how much the former grew reactively out of the latter—an implicit theme that is never spelled out directly because Guerra trusts readers to identify it on their own terms.

Equally impressive are the diverse ways that Guerra represents his narrator's divided consciousness stylistically, as in the poetic fragments that serve as his chapter titles, which point to Guerra's literary origins as a poet.

Here are the third and fifth of these ten chapter headings:

"When you fall in love, for instance, you fall in love with yourself, but when you commit suicide you kill someone else"

"Whenever I tie up a parcel, for instance, I end up by finding myself tied up inside it"

Distinguishing one's self from the world that one lives in, including other people, is the common theme in these and the eight other chapter titles, and the fact that all of them contain the phrase "for instance," suggesting a series of other examples, points to the opposite theme of seeing one's self as part of a collective entity that we call mankind, as well as seeing both one's self and ourselves living in relation to various patterns and repetitions. As we live through a pandemic and election season that we vainly but persistently insist on calling "historic", trying to discover what's distinctive as well as indistinct about both ourselves and others, *Equilibrium* laughs at our nightmares and cordially invites us to think about them.

Crossing Kelly Reichardt's Wilderness

Commissioned by the Viennale in August 2020 for a late October publication called Textur #2 *and devoted to Kelly Reichardt.*

"More nameless things around here than you can shake an eel at."

—King-Lu in *First Cow*

I suspect that the first important step in learning how to process Kelly Reichardt's films is discovering how not to watch them. A few unfortunate viewing habits have already clustered around her seven features to date, fed by buzz-words ranging from "neorealism" (applied ahistorically) to "slow cinema" (an ahistorical term to begin with)—especially inappropriate with a filmmaker so acutely attuned to history, including a capacity to view the present historically—and, in keeping with much auteurist criticism, confusing the personal with the autobiographical.

Interviewed by Katherine Fusco and Nicole Seymour, the coauthors of a monograph about her, Reichardt rightly resists fully accepting any of these categories,[1] however useful they might appear as journalistic shortcuts. (e.g., J. Hoberman on *Wendy and Lucy* in the *Village Voice*: "Reichardt has choreographed one of the most stripped-down existential quests since Vittorio De Sica sent his unemployed worker wandering through the streets of Rome searching for his purloined bicycle, and as heartbreaking a dog story as De Sica's *Umberto D.*")[2]

Admittedly, her atypical first feature, *River of Grass* (1994), might foster some false impressions by having been shot in Florida, where Reichardt grew up, and by making its heroine's father, like her own, a crime scene detective. But if this film's title anticipates her subsequent oeuvre by focusing on a wild landscape, most of its images tell a different story—a wry comedy of absence played in counterpoint to the second-hand media images imbibed by the inept protagonists, doggedly viewing themselves as a generic "couple on the run" when they can't even begin to match that movie cliché. When, at the film's end, Cozy Ryder (Lisa Bowman), a bored ex-housewife and negligent mother, actually shoots her would-be partner in crime (Larry Fessenden)—the film's only real violence, occurring offscreen, without her even looking at him—her main motivation seems to be more boredom, along with rage at having been conned into regarding the two of them as some version of Bonnie and Clyde.

Furthermore, the film's punchy style, with its Godardian chapter headings and its editing synched to offscreen jazz drumming by the heroine's father, seems to introduce Reichardt as a montage-oriented filmmaker—another false clue, like the film's title, because it was Fessenden, not Reichardt, who edited the footage. One suspects that if Reichardt shared anything at all with her hapless heroine, it was a burning desire to escape from Florida.

Once she left, understandings of what came next vary. Most accounts, defining her career in relation to commerce and theatrical features, posit a twelve-year gap in her work between *River of Grass* (1994) and *Old Joy* (2006) that is made to seem almost Biblical: twelve years spent in the wilderness. And for about five of those years, she was crashing on various friends' sofas in New York, giving her a certain kinship with Kurt (Will Oldham), the troubled drifter in *Old Joy* (another rare autobiographical element in her work she has admitted to—"Stuff sneaks in," she told Fusco and Seymour—to which one might add the itinerant Wendy in *Wendy and Lucy*, a film co-starring her own dog). But insofar as all her features are largely set in some kind of wilderness, physical and/or spiritual, most often in the Pacific Northwest and usually among off-the-chart characters, a closer look at what's being defined as a gap and as wilderness becomes essential.

Three items in Reichardt's filmography, commonly omitted—*Ode* (1999, 46 minutes), a super-8 mm narrative made mostly with a two-person cast and a two-person crew (including Reichardt as cinematographer), adapted by Reichardt from a novel by Herman Raucher, and two non-narrative shorts, *Then a Year* (2001, 14 minutes) and *Travis* (2004, 12 minutes)—fill this gap, as does the beginning of Reichardt's teaching career; she would later join the faculty at Bard College, in a film department oriented towards experimental non-narrative work. (*First Cow* is dedicated to the memory of one of her cherished colleagues there, the late Peter Hutton.) It's worth adding that *Ode* is the last Reichardt film not to be edited by her and that she began as a solo editor on her two shorts. She has expressed some ambivalence about these three films—none has turned up as an extra on any of the DVDs or Blu-Rays of her features—without in any way rejecting their status as independent or experimental efforts. "It's alright; it's good they are lost," she assured interviewer Orla Smith in a Canadian anthology devoted to her work, suggestively called *Roads to Nowhere*.[3] "They were just learning tools."

Yet if we also use them as learning tools in relation to Reichardt's subsequent work, they offer many intriguing lessons. All three films place an emphasis on music and/or using words musically as a formal device that is also present in *River of Grass* but relatively attenuated in Reichardt's subsequent work, apart from the importance of the sound editing. *Ode* is based on the pop song "Ode to Billy Joe," about a rural teenage suicide, and the radical and minimalist *Travis* uses "guitar noises" and a few `looped words spoken by a bereaved mother about her son killed in Afghanistan, taken from a Portland radio broadcast and endlessly repeated, accompanied by unidentifiable out-of-focus images of various colors. The exclusion of the source and meaning of the woman's voice, obliquely referenced only in the film's title, makes this a purely formalist work in contrast to *Then a Year*, whose verbal fragments and suburban landscapes point towards both a love story and a crime scene—the two unfulfilled fantasies hovering over *River of Grass*.

One could argue, in fact, that unfulfilled fantasies belonging to viewers and characters alike are present in all of Reichardt's features—namely, the failure of life and the world (nature, humans, society, even sometimes animals) to conform to the expectations molded by culture, genres, and many other conditioned reflexes. It's a condition akin to artistic frustration, but one applied to life more than art. (Birds play an important role in Reinhardt's universe, and a rare moment of clear communication in *Certain Women* ironically comments on how more adept quails usually are in communicating with one another.)

More generally, the significance of *Ode*, *Then a Year*, and *Travis* on Kelly Reichardt's career is that they represent early efforts to reinvent herself—and they're by no means the last. Indeed, these films are so dissimilar from her features that they seem like the work of different filmmakers. (*Ode*—despite being shot in super-8, which Reichardt has described as a liberating experience—seems aimed at a mainstream audience, this can hardly be said of either *Then a Year* or *Travis*. Moreover, in her writing and interviews, Reichardt's cinematic reference points are all over the map, encompassing *Shampoo* (1975) and (in her written appreciation of critic Manny Farber) Robert Altman as well as Anthony Mann, Kenji Mizoguchi, Satyajit Ray, and her experimental colleagues at Bard. Her relocation to Oregon and collaborations with writer Jonathan Raymond and (on her last four features) cinematographer Christopher Blauvelt count as other such reinventions, as does her move to Montana (and her decision to take a break from collaborating with Raymond to work from short stories by Maile Meloy) on *Certain Women*.

Reading the two short stories adapted by Reichardt—"Old Joy" and "Train Choir", the first and last stories in Raymond's collection *Livability*[4]—into *Old Joy* and *Wendy and Lucy*, I find the films' overall faithfulness (especially to the dialogue, apart from trimming) and departures from the originals equally striking. "Old Joy" is recounted in the first person by Mark, which allows for many more back stories, but doesn't allow for the film's epilogue showing Kurt alone on the street, after Mark drops him off. Most conspicuously missing are the film's two females, Mark's pregnant wife and his dog Lucy. (The terse and somewhat testy dialogue between Mark and his wife when he asks for her permission—or, as she says, pretends to ask her permission—to drive to the hot springs with Kurt already hints that their marriage is less than ideal.) It's worth adding that Kurt does the driving in the story and Mark supplies the marijuana (more of which is smoked)—and that Mark as a focused homebody and Kurt as a restless wanderer are to some extent first drafts of the more loving and interactive duo of "Cookie" and King-Lu in *First Cow*.

The dogs in both "Train Choir" and *Wendy and Lucy* have the same name, Lucy, raising the strong possibility that Reichardt named her own dog—belonging to a different kind of mixed breed—after the dog in the story. (*Certain Women*, one should add, is dedicated to Lucy.) Raymond's narrative is in the third person but from the viewpoint of his heroine, Verna, which again allows for more back stories—about Verna's overall car journey from Indiana as well as her expectations about her arrival in Alaska. The significance of trains in the original story isn't abandoned, even though the title is: Reichardt's opening shot is of a train yard, and she uses passing trains throughout as poetic punctuations to evoke distance, danger, fear (the threat of senseless male violence, which also crops up in the first story of *Certain Women* and throughout *First Cow*) or other kinds of uncertainty, as well as a certain calming continuity in spite of everything else.

§

Apart from their shared counter-cultural politics, one trait Reichardt seems to share with minimalist independent Jim Jarmusch, whose *Dead Man* (1995) suggests some parallels with *Meek's Cutoff* and *First Cow*—and whose *Coffee and Cigarettes* (2003) has some looser parallels with *Certain Women*—is that her minimalism sometimes serves as a practical consideration and is not only a matter of aesthetics. One instance of this is the decision in *Meek's Cutoff* to have Joseph Meek's lost wagon train in 1845 consist of eight people and three wagons rather than the estimated 1500 people on that epic trek cited by historians And Reichardt has often pointed out that her artistic control, including final cut, is virtually guaranteed by her films' modest budgets.

Other minimalist strategies in *Meek's Cutoff* include filming at night and in long shot and using dialogue sparsely, all of which Reichardt does in her other features. The avoidance of a widescreen aspect ratio can be justified both by the film's privileging of the viewpoints of the women, framed by their spacious bonnets, and by the present-tense aspects of the journey that makes many events unforeseeable. The decision not to subtitle the Indian character's dialogue is predicated on Reinhardt's desire for viewers to share the ignorance of her other characters, whereas Jarmusch's expressed motivation for his own refusal to subtitle the Native American dialogue was to offer a special 'gift' to the film's Native American viewers—not an option available to Reichardt, because the Cayuse language spoken in her film is nearly extinct.

Reinhardt's minimalist procedures are already well established in *Old Joy*, which also recruits at least two of her major future collaborators, writer Jonathan Raymond (who will write or co-write all but one of her subsequent features to date) and her dog Lucy (the eponymous costar of her next feature, *Wendy and Lucy*), along with Michelle Williams, another major collaborator who, like Lucy, will wind up appearing in three Reichardt features, albeit playing a very different character each time.

It seems important to credit Lucy's collaboration, not only because Reichardt also used to bring her along to her Bard classes (as is indicated in *Old Joy*, her dog doesn't like to be excluded from human activities) but also because, like many other animals featured in Reichardt's work, she contributes a documentary dimension by virtue of being not entirely predictable or controllable, which affects all the crew members and actors in turn—keeping all of them on their toes and even keeping them honest, so to speak.

The economy that *Wendy and Lucy* is concerned with is not only a matter of dwindling money, time, and resources ("You can't get a job without a job, you can't get an address without an address," says a kindly security guard); it's also a question of narrative economy considering how little we know about Wendy apart from her immediate concerns (car, dog, money). And immediate concerns within short time frames are basic to all Reichardt features.

I'm puzzled why Reichardt's next feature, *Night Moves* (2013), borrows its title from one of Arthur Penn's better features, a 1975 political thriller that also features a boat called Night Moves. Even though it's impeccably realized (shot, acted, directed), this is my least favorite Reinhardt feature, largely because it's the most conventional and predictable—even more so in some respects than *Ode*. Rightly or wrongly, I tend to see this film about not very bright eco-ter- rorists—a cooperative farm worker (Jesse Eisenberg), a rich employee at a spa (Dakota Fanning), and a former Marine (Peter Sarsgaard) blowing up a hydroelectric dam in Oregon—as an effort to do something commercial with popular young stars (Eisenberg and Fanning) going through all-too-familiar genre exercises. To her credit, Reichardt doesn't compromise her meditative style while doing this, and she even includes a thoughtful dialogue scene explaining why the plot to bomb the dam was misguided. But even if her plot is "character driven," as she has said, the characters who drive the narrative don't strike me as being very interesting or substantial. I hasten to add that if I ever find any critical defenses of *Night Moves* that don't bore me as well, I'd be more than happy to change my mind.

The changes made by Reichardt to Meloy's "Native Sandstone" for the second story in *Certain Women* are mostly related to gender—though less so than the re-gendering applied to "Travis, B.," the first story in Meloy's second collection, *Both Ways is the Only Way I Want It,*[5] which turns its central character, a ranch hand, from male to female. (The original hero is alluded to only briefly in the film, as the ranch hand's brother.) The sandstone story is restricted to the visit of a couple, Susan and Clay, to Albert, an elderly local who has a pile of sandstone blocks in his front yard, the remains of an ancient demolished schoolhouse, that Susan wants for the summer house that Clay is planning to build. The story, told in the third person, is anchored in Susan's reactions, largely self-critical. In the film—whose action begins earlier, with the wife jogging alone—the couple, renamed Gina (Michelle Williams) and Ryan (James Le Gros), have a sullen teenage daughter named Guthrie (Sara Rodier), who resents both her mother and being along on the trip, choosing to remain in the car with her earphones while her parents visit Albert (René Auberjonois). After Albert tentatively agrees to part with his sandstone blocks and Gina goes out to look at them, Albert remarks to Ryan, "Your wife works for you," to which Ryan replies, "That's funny. No—she's the boss, actually."

This exchange isn't in the story, and the wife's bossy character registers differently here because we aren't privy to so many self-doubts, making her chiding of her husband and daughter seem more self-centered.

This is my subjective reaction, and it's a delicate matter because all three of Meloy's stories and Reichardt's film are concerned with the ethics of everyday human interactions, according to which the wife's behavior even in Meloy's story seems less principled than the behavior of a patient lawyer (Laura Dern) handling an emotionally unstable former client (Jared Harris) in "Tome" and the film's opening story. The closest thing to an epiphany in "Native Sandstone" is the wife's sad admission in the final paragraph that she doesn't even know what to do with those blocks once she has them. Yet the fact that Albert mostly ignores her and Ryan fails to ask him about the sandstone, as she requested, adds more ambiguous layers to the scene. Other subjective responses are indeed possible, and a vital part of Reichardt's storytelling strategies are to make them possible—even when they risk producing boredom, as they do for me in *Night Moves*. In the prologue added to the sandstone story, Gina's seeming rapport with nature and the film's focus on landscape might lead some viewers to arrive at more sympathetic feelings about the character, and in the added epilogue, Gina busily cooking for friends and family, then sneaking a cigarette while gazing at the pile of blocks, might do that as well.

Story collections that are structured with interactive parts are rare: James Joyce's *Dubliners* is one example, and Meloy herself has suggested that J.D. Salinger's *Nine Stories* is another. Reinhardt's own collection, composed of three Meloy stories, innovates with this form by following her third story with epilogues to all three (which in the first story is Meloy's own conclusion). The thematic constants throughout include obsessional behavior, social awkwardness, and loneliness. There are lawyers in the first and third stories (with Lily Gladstone's shy stable hand becoming helplessly smitten with Kristen Stewart's lawyer teacher) and building/construction figures in the first and second (carpentry is the former job of Laura Dern's aggrieved client, causing his disability). Making them all contribute to telling the same story is Reichardt's special talent, and even more special is her refusal to give her characters tribal identities. The ranch hand in "Travis, B."—a title referring to the lawyer-teacher, Beth Travis, not to him— is named Chet Moran and he has a mother who's "three-quarters Cheyenne" and an Irish father. His female replacement in the film is nameless and we're told nothing about her ethnic background (although Lily Gladstone, who plays her, is Native American) or her sexual orientation, obliging us to understand her without such cliché-ridden standbys as "indigenous" or "lesbian", which, like "neorealism" and "slow cinema," often confuse as much as they clarify.

The same approach couldn't work for *First Cow* (2019), mostly set in 1820s Oregon, an almost prehistorical period where tribal definitions gain even greater primacy than in *Meek's Cutoff*. The film unfolds in a multiracial, multiethnic wilderness full of both immigrants and "Indians" and dominated by the beaver trade—a world whose creation is perhaps the film's most impressive accomplishment, along with its voluptuous capturing of nature. "You speak good English—for an Indian," says Otis "Cookie" Figowitz (John Magaro), one of the two protagonists, who cooks for fur trappers, just after meeting the other in the wilderness, who is on the run from a band of Russians after killing a man. "Uh, I'm not Indian. I'm Chinese," replies King-Lu (Orion Lee). At the same time, the film begins with one of William Blake's *Proverbs of Hell*—"The bird a nest, the spider a web, man friendship"—before showing us a woman and her dog discovering two skeletons buried side by side in the woods. The forging of human kinship in a savage wilderness where the multicultural injustices and inequalities of the present day are already clearly in evidence is the film's implicit theme, at once simple and complex, with its specters of early capitalism in a settlement that hasn't yet been defined as Oregon. (One might add that smaller examples of succeeding or failing in human interactions—what Reichardt describes as an interest in "small politics"—are also the focus of *Certain Women*.)

I haven't read Raymond's first novel, *The Half-Life*,[6] which he and Reinhardt adapted for the screenplay. I'm told it spans four decades but is also partly set in Portland in the 1990s, includes a trip to China, and King-Lu combines two of its characters. Yet its plot doesn't include a cow, so apparently its compression is comparable to that done by *Meek's Cutoff* in relation to the historical record. It seems to reflect as well as anticipate the present in an uncanny number of ways, introducing us to a strange world of primitive unrest seeking order both peacefully and violently, via sharing or grabbing. As Reichardt's wilderness steadily grows wider, richer, and more mysterious, it also becomes more recognizable as we cross its unpredictable contours.

End Notes

1.   Katherine Fusco and Nicole Seymour, *Kelly Reichardt* (Urbana/ Chicago/ Springfield: University of Illinois Press, 2017).

2.   J. Hoberman, "Wendy and Lucy," in *Village Voice* (New York), 10.12.08, available online at https://www.villagevoice.com/2008/12/10/wendy-and-lucy/.

3.   Orla Smith, "An Interview with Kelly Reichardt," in Alex Heeney and Orla Smith, eds., *Roads to Nowhere* (Toronto: Seventh Row, 2020), pp. 16-25.

4.   Jonathan Raymond, *Livability* (New York/London/Berlin: Bloomsbury, 2009).

5.   Maile Meloy, *Both Ways is the Only Way I Want It* (New York: Riverhead Books, 2009)

6.   Jonathan Raymond, *The Half Life* (New York: Bloomsbury, 2004).

Ideas and Afterthoughts, Passion and Repression, Freedom and Predestination: Fei Mu's *Spring in a Small Town*

Written for the 120th and final issue of Trafic, *Fall 2021, where it appears in Jean-Luc Megus' French translation. Contributors to this special issue were invited to write about something they treasured, bearing in mind the quote from Ezra Pound that's cited.*

"I never know how I should end my solos," John Coltrane reportedly once said to Miles Davis, to which his boss gruffly replied: "Try taking your horn out of your mouth."

Coltrane's conceptual orientation versus Davis's blunt practicality can be felt in the former's symmetrical, multi-note flurries and rude honks up and down scales, furiously covering almost every available silence with his "sheets of sound", and the latter's jagged, elliptical smears and little-boy cries separated by sudden pauses that often register like either interruptions or abrupt afterthoughts, second-guessing himself.

An almost sexual alternation of giving and withholding in a jazz solo becomes a tug of war between conflicting formal as well as sexual impulses—Davis's version of coitus interruptus versus Coltrane's giddy flirtations and unresolved foreplay. It persists throughout director Fei Mu's and screenwriter Li Tianji's extraordinary *Spring in a Small Town* (1948), a troubled and troubling piece of cinematic chamber music that seems all the more passionate yet intensely bottled up during the romantic and sexual frustrations of the Coronavirus pandemic. This torrential yet quiet film is full of both poise and chaos, control and abandon, starting with an overload of determinations regarding time, place, character, and latent passions and ending unexpectedly with an almost arbitrary sense of abstraction about the future. In the final shot, the heroine, outdoors with her husband, is happily pointing to some distant vista that remains conveniently unseen and unidentified—as if she's dreaming of a postwar (or post-pandemic) utopia where sexual and romantic fulfillments finally become possible again, at least with her husband if not with her lover. It's an attempt to end the film with "mature," adult desires, yet it's the adolescent ones that dominate, painfully, in what precedes them.

For many years, one of the persistent mysteries surrounding this masterpiece is why Chinese cinephiles commonly consider it the greatest of all Chinese films while Westerners typically consider it not so much beneath their consideration as outside it—seldom seen or discussed, and, until recently, not often available with subtitles in decent prints. Could its own withheld emotions be too Asian for Western tastes? And if so, why does it speak to me so directly during the protracted loneliness and stifled social interactions of the pandemic? Could my desire to write a mimetic appreciation of its strangled feelings have succeeded too well with its first reader, who felt it lacked emotion? Did I simply take the horn out of my mouth too soon? Or was I unconsciously trying to become Asian myself by hiding my feelings about it?

Shot quickly as a B-film, sandwiched uneasily between the Sino-Chinese War and the Communist Chinese Revolution, *Spring in a Small Town* isn't even mentioned in Jay Leyda's 1972 *Dianying: an account of films and the film audience in China* (although Fei Mu gets profiled in the same book), probably because the political incorrectness of Fei Mu's last feature led to its suppression during that period. This undoubtedly makes it more resonant for Chinese people discovering it after new prints were struck in the early 1980s, and perhaps more perplexing for Westerners such as myself who have only a dim understanding of its historical context. But it's worth stressing that in 2005, the Hong Kong Film Awards Association named it the greatest of all Chinese films, and the relevance of this film to Jia Zhangke's oeuvre (to cite only one example of its influence among many) immediately becomes apparent through the title of an essay that I haven't read—Jie Li's "Home and Nation Amid the Rubble, Fei Mu's *Spring in a Small Town* and Jia Zhangke's *Still Life*"[1]—and a wonderful interview with the film's lead actress, Wei Wei, about the film, its director, and her costar, Wei Li, in *I Wish I Knew*, conducted inside a barber shop in 2009. In any case, it isn't surprising that I owe my first acquaintance with this film to a Chinese film critic, Stephen Teo, who in the early 1990s sent me an English subtitled VHS copy taken from SBS, the multicultural, state-run Australian television channel.

Traditionally, history in China is something that belongs to the Emperor—or to his latter-day equivalents, starting with Mao—and perhaps the same can be said about traditional and classical Chinese art. So it isn't surprising that a perpetual yearning for a lost past can be felt in much of Chinese art cinema, whether it comes from Taipei (Hou Hsiao-hsien's *City of Sadness*, Edward Yang's *A Brighter Summer Day*, Tsai Ming-liang's *Goodbye, Dragon Inn*), Shanghai (Stanley Kwan's *Ruan Lingyu* aka *Center Stage* aka *Actress*, where Fei Mu figures as a character), Hong Kong (Wong Kar-Wai's *Days of Being Wild* and *In the Mood for Love*), Fenyang (Jia Zhangke's *Platform*), Pingyao (Zhang Yimou's *Raise the Red Lantern*), or Beijing (Li Shaohong's *Blush*, Chen Kaige's *Farewell My Concubine*, Tian Zhuangzhuang's *The Blue Kite*)— to sketch a list of masterpieces that is by no means exhaustive. Indeed, given the sheer breadth of both Chinese art and history as displayed in Taipei's National Palace Museum—whose ground floor, devoted to world history, with many spacious rooms to traverse before Western history even starts—the degree to which they accompany one another in both cinema and film history seems only logical. And one can't overlook that the most salient Chinese art films set in the present—another set of major works encompassing most features of Jia Zhangke and Tsai Ming-liang, Peter Chen's *Comrades, Almost a Love Story*, Wong Kar-wai's *Happy Together*, and, indeed, Fei Mu's *Spring in a Small Town*—are above all efforts to historicize the present. For this reason, the conventional nostalgia expressed in Wong's *In the Mood for Love* seems to owe a lot to Wong's nostalgia for Fei Mu's masterpiece and its own "nostalgia for the present", which then becomes the more conventional nostalgia of the film's Chinese viewers many years later.

To start with the film's puzzling, contradictory narrative viewpoint, it opens with the voiceover of its heroine, Yuwen (Wei Wei), a young wife whom we see walking along a broken wall, away from a nearby small town that we will never see, despite the film's deceptive title, which like much of the film seems to offer an unfulfilled promise, a sexual tease. "Please bear in mind the following words," this actress recalls Fei Mu saying to her in *I Wish I Knew*. "The most passionate emotions are those most held in check"—a statement that could serve as the film's motto, with consequences that are both voluptuous and torturous, beautiful and feverish. Wei Wei also says that the director encouraged her to entice her romantically inexperienced costar Li Wei to fall in love with her, a task she says she carried out all too well when he followed her back to Shanghai after the shooting.

Yuwen's narration is both personal (she explains she likes to walk after her shopping, and is carrying vegetables and medicine in her basket) and uncannily omniscient (she goes on to describe—and the images corroborate—exactly what the three other members of her household are doing in her absence): the aged male servant Huang (Cui Chaoming), whose daily chores we follow, beginning with him emptying his master's medicine dregs outside the back gate, until he finally locates him, Liyan (Yu Shi), and then Liyan's teenage sister Xiu (Zhang Hongmei).

This is after eight years of war with Japan—the largest Asian war of the 20th century, said to have had as many as twenty million Chinese civilian casualties—and we see the house is in scattered ruins. Each character is viewed alone in a different part of this disarray, as if associated with a separate wound that echoes their emotional state. And the various camera movements introducing us to these characters often seem to blend subjectivity and omniscience, like Yuwen's offscreen voice, albeit expressing some moods and longings more directly than she can allow herself to do. (Her teenage sister-in-law has an easier time venting her emotions, maybe in part because this is expected of adolescents, but of course Yuwen was an adolescent herself when her romantic feelings were first aroused.)

After Huang knocks on Liyan's door and discovers he isn't there, Yuwen interjects, "Liyan doesn't see me more than twice a day...I leave in the morning to buy groceries. He goes into the garden, where no one can find him. He says he has tuberculosis, but I think it's neurosis." A sudden rightward pan across a broken wall that suggests a Miles Davis flourish discovers Huang again, who in turn discovers Liyan through a gap in the wall as she says in voiceover, "I'm afraid to die, but he seems afraid to live." (As we will learn, their marriage has already lasted eight years, like the war, producing its own sense of ruins.) Then the camera, instead of following Huang as he hands his master a scarf, reaches Liyan by moving through a separate gap in the wall. This recalls the camera's impulsive, impatient detour in *Sunrise* away from the hero and through a dense thicket towards the City Woman he's meeting by the lake, thus arriving at his destination before he does. And after Liyan asks if his kid sister has left for school yet, there is a cut to the camera approaching her window just in time for her to open and then appear in it, imposing another form of predestination fueled by desire. Yuwen proceeds to tell us over her sister-in-law's animated movements that she's nothing like her brother.

The oddly layered effect of this contradictory mix of subjectivity and omniscience is intensified by the names of the actors playing these characters, each name appearing onscreen shortly after each character is introduced, and the musical precision with which these intertitles appear alerts us to the film's immaculate découpage. Like Yuen's offscreen voice, it tells us that everything we see and hear can be made to signify at least two things at once. This is arguably also the principle of the mise en scène, including the camera's exploratory dances, playful or distraught, around each of the characters, which are more like Coltrane's cascading scales than Davis' broken fragments. Even so, this is very much a film of absences: a massive unseen war, a buried past, passions held perpetually in check (and thus teetering on the edges of madness and violence).

For me, the fatal flaw of Tian Zhuangzhuang's 2002 remake is its exclusion of Yuwen's voiceover. Treating this element as inessential is as serious a mistake as treating the characters Lockwood and his housekeeper Nelly Dean in *Wuthering Heights* as unnecessary narrative filters in conveying the story and the explosive passions of Heathcliff and Cathy, a mistake lamentably made by Wyler, Buñuel, and Rivette in their separate adaptations. Yet in the case of Emily Bronte's novel, this is for the opposite reason. It's an error to eliminate the incomprehension of the aptly named Lockwood and his maid because we are called upon to imagine and thus furnish the missing outbursts and rages these two characters plainly lack. But it's also a mistake to leave out an all-knowing narrative voice that perceives action both globally and personally, as Yuwen's voice does, because her bifocal vision allows us to view a stifled love story as part of a wider world—that is to say, historically—which ultimately means inside China as a complex and abstract sociopolitical entity. Indeed, it's the interaction between these two vantage points, at once "impossible" yet "necessary," that traces and determines much of the tightly unwinding poetry of the mise en scène. And the "message" of this poetry is Ezra Pound's:

sky's clear
        night's sea
        green of the mountain pool
        shone from the unmasked eyes in half-mask's space.
What thou lovest well remains,

                                    the rest is dross
What thou lov'st well shall not be reft from thee
What thou lov'st well is thy true heritage
Whose world, or mine or theirs

                                    or is it of none?

§

Beginning with a suite of leftward pans behind the opening credits, punctuated by an upward tilt, Fei Mu's camera offers a loving commentary even more than Yuwen's offscreen voice—settling appreciatively, for instance, on a blooming plant as if to illustrate the "spring" of the title, if not the town. And to confound our sense of a linear narrative, he inserts at the end of this prologue, over the director's credit, a shot of three indistinct figures instead of Yuwen walking down the same path—a shot that we later discover is a radical flash-forward, recurring shortly before the film's end and including the pivotal fifth and final character, Zhang (Li Wei)—a doctor from Shanghai who arrives to visit his old friend Liyan, not realizing that he is now married to his former lover Yuwen—accompanied here by Yuwen's young sister-in-law and the family servant.

Significantly, even before this doctor has been introduced, we see him leaving—another form of predestation that ends the story before it can begin. Questioning, in effect, who or what this story finally belongs to—"Whose world, or mine or theirs/or is it of none?"—is another way of asking if the characters' ethical decisions are free or predetermined, whether they are, as adults, "free" to gratify their aching adolescent desires. And does the future belong to them, or to an abstraction known as China? Paradoxically, it seems to belong to both—like the absent small town that seems to be absent throughout this film, even though one is made to feel that it determines everything.

Before the doctor's unexpected arrival, there is a guarded dialogue between Yuwen and Liyan, after he throws away the medicine she's bought for him and she retrieves it. Enraged by his sense of failures as a husband and that she instead of their servant fetches his medicine, he wonders whether they should separate. She walks off to her room, refusing a discussion while meanwhile resuming her voiceover as she carries her needlework to her sister-in-law's room. (Is this avoidance of a confrontation grown-up, or childish? The film doesn't say.) Over a shot of the doctor approaching the camera on a road with his luggage, she reflects, "Who could have known that someone would come?"—another moment of omniscience, because this clearly isn't a point-of-view shot. She continues, "He came from the train station. He walked through the city gate," just as we (but not she) see that he's about to do so. "I had no idea that he would come. How does he know that I live here?" Then, after a printed title identifies the character, his narrative function, and the actor playing him ("Zhang Zhichen 'The Guest'—Li Wei") as we see him approach the property's back gate, her omniscience becomes even more blatant: "He recognizes the back gate to the house. He stops. He steps through the medicine dregs. That's right, he studied medicine….He knocks on the door but no one hears him. " (Zhang is the film's only character who sports Western dress, including a noirish trench coat in this scene, marking him as a seductive outsider and, perhaps more implicitly, a social activist.)

After a cut from Zhang to Liyan sitting on a hill amidst rubble, "He knows his way around Liyan's house so well, he goes around the lane and into the back garden.,,,He even calls out Liyan's name. I didn't know that he was Liyan's friend as well. He climbs through the wall of the flower garden." This is a very literary form of omniscience, and assigning it to a physically absent Yuwen creates an eerie effect—a feminized Voice of God attached to a very human and vulnerable character. And perhaps the uncanniest effect of all is the ease with which we can accept this anomaly.

Having led us to this warm reunion of old friends—subsequently joined by the old servant, who also remembers Zhang from prewar days—Yuwen resumes her narration in order to chart her dawning realization that the visitor, a former classmate of her husband, is in fact her former lover, which she last saw at age sixteen. Once she recognizes this fact, the major issue becomes what she and Zhang will or won't do. In this case, "historizing" the present means coming to terms in some fashion with the past. All we know at first is that she regards it as a vexing problem rather than an opportunity; only later does Zhang become the focus of her present desires. Zhang at once recognizes her and explains to Liyen that they used to be neighbors; their status as former "lovers" (who presumably never had sex) is kept a secret, but Liyan gradually intuits it, as does his sister, and it continues to serve as a vital subtext to all the scenes that follow. The very fact that he's authoritative about his medical advice also seems to qualify him as a kind of savior to everyone else, potentially freeing them all from their various personal traps.

The camera focusing initially on Yuwen's feet as she brings Zhang water in his guest room may evoke Bresson, just as the lack of eye contact between them (apart from a couple of quick, furtive glances) evokes *Gertrud*, but these resemblances belong to the future of cinema; this film's mastery of indirection is entirely its own. Yuwen insists on treating Zhang as an honored guest and solicits his candor only about her husband's health. (She learns that he'll recover from his tuberculosis, but that he also has a weak heart.) Two cutaway shots of Liyan asleep in his own room only further spells out their unspoken tension, which culminates in her silent tears.

The remainder of the doctor's visit is mostly uneventful yet rich with piercing erotic inflections. It is further complicated by Xiu's exuberance and her growing infatuation with Zhang, which tells us as much about Yuwen's feelings for him at the same age as any flashback would. This leads Liyan to ask Yuwen to become a matchmaker between them (projecting a possible marriage once she turns eighteen), and also by Liyan's rekindled sexual feelings for his wife and his awareness of Yuwen's happiness caused by Zhang's visit, which eventually leads to his suicide attempt. Thus the "spring" of the film's title alludes to the erotic stirrings of all four characters, at once implicit and omnipresent.

The morning after the doctor's arrival, he and the three family members go for a walk; when Yuwen joins the others after walking behind them, Zhang briefly takes and squeezes her hand, a glancing detail that has a Bressonian impact. Later, on what she calls "the third morning," he proposes that they walk together to the "old wall" after breakfast to "talk things over" (something she will do in turn several days later). Their dialogue and gestures continue through awkward indirections and indecisions—issues of whether she's changed since the war, whether he'll ask her to leave with him, whether he means to ask her, whether they touch one another or not as they walk. Everything becomes conditional, and comparable questions, gestures, disavowals, and retreats recur whenever they're alone together, always generating suspense.

Zhang announces his departure on the ninth day of his visit, but like everything else, this winds up being postponed. And the film's second half chronicles more indecision, culminating in Xiu's raucous and drunken sixteenth birthday party and Liyan's suicide attempt the next morning—a jagged and protracted Miles Davis solo full of broken riffs, with Yuwen and Zhang each becoming aggressive and violent in turn. She storms into his room against his wishes; he lifts her up, changes his mind and sets her down, locks her inside as he leaves; she drives her fist through the door's glass pane; he rushes back inside, dresses her wound, and passionately kisses her hand; she says "Thank you" and leaves, returning to her own room. All these "explosions" and retreats and those that follow occur late at night, in darkness, after the town's electricity has been shut off, sporadically illuminated by flickering candlelight that provides as much of a dance macabre as the camera movements following, embracing, and abandoning the characters in turn. Then Yuwen becomes omniscient again: over shots of Zhang, alone, taking a pill, intercut with her alone in her own room, she says, "He needs to take a sleeping pill. He's thinking to himself that maybe I will commit suicide. All I have is regret. I want to die. I can no longer face the world. He remembers that Liyan has some sleeping pills." Each in turn winds up in Liyan's room, where Zhang says he'll leave in the morning, despite Liyan's protests, and Yuwen lies to him about how she injured her hand. In the morning, it isn't until Huang fails to rouse Liyan that everyone becomes aware of his suicide attempt, and Zhang and Yuwen revive him.

I'm embarrassed by some of the emotions that this film stirs in me, and one reason why may be that I'm an American. Manny Farber once admitted to me that he never really "survived" the Depression, and like many, perhaps even most Americans, I'm not sure if I ever really "survived" my adolescence, because many of its wounds have never healed, including those that Pound might even ironically call my "true heritage"—what I lov'st well and lost. *Spring in a Small Town* was made when I was still a toddler, yet even at age 78 many of its emotions still make me want to run and hide, as its haunted and frustrated characters often do, trying to behave properly yet clearly traumatized.

Yuwen is last seen walking by the ruined wall with Liyan, hoping to rebuild her marriage. Unlike Xiu, she hasn't accompanied Zhang to the train station. But Zhang says he will return next spring, and Xiu says she hopes he'll be back by the summer—which implies that the conditional tense in which both women live could be extended indefinitely—unsatisfied longings reaching out into infinity, like unresolved chords. There are other musical refrains or rhyme effects—not just two meetings of the former lovers at the city wall, but Yuwen's infatuation for Zhang at age sixteen before the war anticipating Xiu's infatuation now. Zhang, like Coltrane, may have temporarily removed the horn from his mouth, but the music, the desire, the ongoing dance of the mise en scène will continue to blaze in his mind and spirit, as it does in ours, in mine, seventy-three years later.

Footnote

1.   *Modern Chinese Literature and Culture*, Vol. 21, No. 2 (Fall 2009), 86-125

The Intellectual and Sociopolitical Exploitations
of Yasuzô Masumura

Commissioned by New York's Metrograph *and posted by them on December 2, 2021. For more on Masumura, see "Two Auteurs" (coauthored by Shigehiko Hasumi) in* Movie Mutations *(a collection coedited by Adrian Martin, London: BFI, 2003), diverse items on my website, and my audiovisual essays on the Arrow releases of* Black Test Car *and* Red Angel.

What do we mean when we talk about exploitation films? Most often, we're alluding to sensation-driven movies that are politically incorrect, like those of Quentin Tarantino. And what are we saying when we complain that we can't identify with any of a film's characters? Some of us tend to resist movies that make us think both inside and outside their stories rather than swallow them whole, and identifying with characters is arguably one way of limiting our thought processes.

What's singular about many of the films of Yasuzô Masumura (1924–1986) is that they're intellectual forms of exploitation—politically incorrect experiences that are consciously sociopolitical critiques, unlike the roller-coaster rides of Tarantino. You might even say that they shock us into thinking. But it's hard to make too many generalizations about someone who made fifty-eight films, mostly assignments at Daiei before that studio closed in 1971. A fair number of Masumura's films are routine time-wasters, but the best of them, which for me include at least three of the five Metrograph is showing—*Giants and Toys* (1958), *Black Test Car* (1962), and *Irezumi* (1966)—are quite remarkable. The other two are *The Black Report* (1963), a fair to middling noir, and *Blind Beast* (1969), a cruder exploitation item that has its passionate defenders.

After receiving an undergraduate law degree at Tokyo University, Masumura became a part-time philosophy student there while starting to work at Daiei, where he would eventually become assistant director to both Kenji Mizoguchi and Kon Ichikawa. Before that would happen, he won a scholarship to study film at the Centro Sperimentale di Cinematografia in Rome, where one of his mentors was reportedly Antonioni (who later became both an influence and one of Masumura's most faithful fans). Back in Japan, after returning to Tokyo University, where he wrote a dissertation on Kierkegaard, he started his filmmaking career with *Kisses* (1957)—a romance about alienated youth whose title was already a provocation (kisses had been forbidden by Japanese film censors before the war, and were still relatively sparse on Japanese screens outside of foreign releases). The film helped to win the enthusiastic support of Nagisa Ōshima, who soon afterward would embark on his own edgy first feature.

Giants and Toys, a grotesque satirical comedy that evokes Frank Tashlin, and the noirish *Black Test Car* are both industrial spy thrillers, a subgenre that was one of Masumura's specialties. *Irezumi* is a period drama about tattooing, notable on at least three counts: it is one of three strong films he adapted from the great writer Junichiro Tanizaki; it stars the extraordinarily gifted and sensuous Ayako Wakao, a powerful actress Masumura discovered while working on Mizoguchi's *Street of Shame* (1956) and who would subsequently star in at least twenty of his films and most of his masterpieces, including *A False Student* (1960), *A Wife Confesses* (1961), and *Red Angel* (1966); and it was shot in color by cinematographer Kazuo Miyagawa (who also shot 1950's *Rashomon*, 1953's *Ugetsu*, and 1954's *Sansho the Bailiff*). Masumura was said to have objected to *Irezumi*'s striking and gorgeous diptych compositions because he felt they distracted viewers from the story. "Some believe more in the image, others believe in the story," he avowed in one interview. "Personally I believe in the story. Because images aren't absolute, one can't express everything with them."

What Masumura was primarily interested in was a defiance of certain fundamental traits of Japanese culture, creating a cinema of crazy people, aspects of which can be found particularly in *Giants and Toys* and *Black Test Car* (where capitalism is depicted as a form of insanity) and *Blind Beast* (where a mad sculptor uses female bodies as his raw material). A film critic as well as a filmmaker, Masumura responded in a 1958 article to those who accused him of making bleak and tasteless cinema that lacked sentiment and featured comically exaggerated and unbelievable characters without any depiction of environment or atmosphere. Boasting that he was guilty as charged on all counts, Masumura replied as follows:

> "I dislike sentiment. This is because sentiment in Japanese cinema consists of self-regulation, harmony, resignation, sorrow, defeat, and flight. The Japanese don't think of dynamic vitality, conflicts, and

death struggles or pleasure, victory, and pursuit as sentiment. ... I dare to defend honest, coarse, and egotistic expression because the Japanese are so prone to restrain and suppress their desires and lose sight of their true emotions. ... There is no such thing as an absolutely free expression of desire. Someone who exposed their raw desire could only be seen as insane. ... But I am not interested in portraying a stable character who takes the measure of reality and adjusts the expression of his or her desires accordingly. I am not interested in depicting a human being with 'human' traits. I want to show an insane person who expresses his or her passion without shame, regardless of what people think."[1]

One way of seeing how this was played out in his work would be to consider his war films. According to scholar Earl Jackson Jr., Masumura designed his war films to subvert those that were deemed acceptable at the time in Japan: anti-war films that addressed viewers' consciences, comedies, and spectacles. In his *Hoodlum Soldier* (1965), for instance, a Manchuria-set World War II comedy, all the slapping and bone-crunching shown and heard comes from Japanese soldiers brawling with other Japanese soldiers, and none of it involves the Chinese they're fighting against. (Desertion, meanwhile, is treated as a sane and responsible activity.) Within the first few minutes of *Red Angel*, a Japanese nurse (Wakao) is raped by a Japanese soldier in the Sino-Japanese war. Much later, she offers to have sex with a morphine-addicted surgeon for a pint of blood that might save the life of the rapist—not because she forgives him but because she doesn't want him to die thinking that she's taking revenge. In *Nakano Spy School* (1966), everyone winds up betraying everyone else (as in the industrial thrillers) because the system itself is intrinsically rotten and promotes fanaticism. The narrator-hero graduates from officer training school in 1937 and tells his fiancée to wait a couple of years until his discharge. He never sees her again until he hears that she's spying for the British, and is ordered to kill her. Needless to say, he makes love to her first—a seeming staple of this form of exploitation.

End Note

1.   Yasuzô Masumura, "Aru benmei: Jocho to shinjitsu to fun'iki ni se o mukete" (*A Defense: Turning my Back on Sentiment, Authenticity, and Atmosphere*), translation by Chika Kinoshita and Michael Raine.

Discovering Muratova on the Internet:
A Personal Case Study, a Few Baby Steps

Written for Another Gaze, *an English feminist journal (December 2021).*

Even before the Coronavirus pandemic set in and many of us suddenly had more time to explore new modes of online viewing and even canon-building, I've been trying to develop and expand my limited acquaintance with the films of Kira Miratova (1934-2018), initially sparked by my 1996 encounter with her masterpiece *The Asthenic Syndrome*—reportedly the first post-glasnost film in Russia to be banned, at least temporarily. Since then, I've gradually arrived at the conclusion that any public engagement with Muratova in the West is likelier to come via personal initiatives with the assistance of YouTube and various pirate sites than through capitalist distribution and exhibition or such institutional gatekeepers as the New York Film Festival. (As a one-time member of the latter's selection committee in 1994-1997, shortly after it rejected *The Asthenic Syndrome*, I tried and failed to get any of her other films accepted.)

It's worth considering both why Muratova's cinema is apparently considered beyond the pale by mainstream American arthouse taste and also why I've been drawn to it—and why her Russian audience was sufficiently large during the last three decades of her life to keep her working productively. Indeed, if one compares the ten features she managed to complete and release during this period to the three completed by Carl Dreyer and the six by Orson Welles during the last three decades of their own lives, this was a remarkable achievement, especially if one considers both the international reputations of the latter two filmmakers and the supposedly indigestible aspects of Muratova's work.

An important part of what makes them "difficult" is the unusually aggressive kind of dialogue delivery she favours, which her English language biographer Nancy Condee traces back to her most influential teacher in film school, Sergei Gerasimov, a former actor with the radically "neoexpressionist" F.E.K.S. (Factory of the Eccentric Actors) in 1920s Leningrad.

Yet it's clear from Vladimir Nepevny's excellent forty-eight-minute documentary *Kira* (2003)—available on the same Ruscico DVD as *Chekhovian Motifs*—that many Russians not only tolerate Muratova but adore her.

And the fact that she habitually works with a team of favorite actors and crew members, like Ingmar Bergman or John Ford, only adds to her appeal and her legendary status. However, the same Ruscico DVD, even though it's equipped with English, French, German, Italian, Portuguese, and Spanish subtitles, has only Russian writing on its box, which may scare away some non-Russian customers. If we recall that one reason why the West was able to discover Yasujiro Ozu only after being introduced much earlier to Akira Kurosawa and Kenji Mizoguchi was that he was felt to be "too Japanese" for foreign consumption, it appears that Muratova is considered 'too Russian' for Western viewers.

Part of the Western resistance to her films can undoubtedly be traced back to a Cold War ideology that also helped to block appreciation and understanding of such radical Soviet-bloc filmmakers as Věra Chytilová, Miklós Jancsó, and Dušan Makavejev. As I've argued elsewhere on several occasions, such films as Chytilová's *Something Different* (1963) and *Daisies* (1966), Jancsó's *Red Psalm* (1971), and Makavejev's *WR: Mysteries of the Organism* (1971) can be regarded as far more radical politically as well as formally than, say, Lindsay Anderson's *If...* (1968), Bernardo Bertolucci's *Before the Revolution* (1964), and Jean-Luc Godard's *La Chinoise* (1967), yet it was the latter Western European arthouse films that captured the imaginations and interest of Western progressives during the 1960s and 1970s far more than those from Eastern Europe. Apart from the linguistic barriers pertaining to Czech, Hungarian, and Serbo-Croat, a relative lack of familiarity with those societies and cultures clearly led to the reduced legibility of their films to Western viewers that is clearly shared by Russian films.

The lack of any clear understanding of what we even mean by "Russian" (as opposed to "Soviet") is especially pertinent when it comes to Muratova. Much as the no less neglected Belgian filmmaker André Delvaux owes part of his neglect to his separate French and Flemish roots and characteristics, Muratova's Jewish Romanian mother and Russian father—combined with her having been born Kira Korotkova in 1934 in a part of Romania that is now Moldova, having attended both Romanian and Russian schools as a child (often hiding her Russian identity at the former and her Romanian identity at the latter), before attending film school in Moscow in her twenties, and having then lived and worked in the Ukrainian city of Odessa for most of her career (even though I believe that all her films are in Russian)—conjures up a multicultural salad that is bound to be confusing to Western outsiders. I hasten to add that comparable confusions attend the reception of films by Nico Papatakis, whereby the semi-falsehood that Papatakis was Greek, an identification clearly arrived at through a kind of media shorthand, elides the fact that his mother was a "black" Ethiopian and his father a "white" Greek stationed in Ethiopia. Like the endlessly regurgitated half-truth that Barack Obama is "black", which also elides his own mother's racial identity, this is an excellent example of the strangulated and deceitful discourse of American political speech (which has already created a false dialectic by calling pinkish Caucasians "white" and many brown people "black")—according to which the military occupation of Iraq becomes the "Iraq war" and Donald Trump's "Make America Great Again" becomes a "politically correct" version of "Make America White Again". Likewise, the means by which Jean-Luc Godard and Chantal Akerman both often get misidentified as French—and some Canadian filmmakers get mislabeled by some French people as "Americans" but not as "North Americans"—testify to other imperial traces (to borrow a phrase from Nancy Condee) and their confusions.

Finally, one apparent obstacle to any compatibility between Muratova's art and Anglo-American culture is the former's perception that cinema is literature by another means—a perception shared by the film cultures of France and Eastern Europe as well as by Russia and Iran (especially regarding the prestige of poetry in the latter two countries) but not by most other societies.

One obvious advantage to following one's own desires and predilections rather than a conventional academic syllabus, whether the focus is on Muratova or any other film-related interest, is that one is obliged to become an active (and not merely reactive) critic and canon-builder in the course of ferreting out and defining one's chosen subject and predilections rather than the passive recipient of others' critical positions and programs.

It's worth recalling that when Penelope Houston and Peter Wollen jointly launched the Cinema One book series at the British Film Institute in the 1960s—an influential line of volumes that would include Richard Roud's early monographs on Jean-Luc Godard and Jean-Marie Straub (the latter then defined as a solo artist, before his partner Danièle Huillet was credited as an equally important participant in the filmmaking), Wollen's own *Signs and Meaning in the Cinema*, and separate studies of, among others, John Ford, Howard Hawks, Rouben Mamoulian, Luchino Visconti, and Orson Welles, by Andrew Sarris, Robin Wood, Tom Milne, Geoffrey Nowell-Smith, and Joseph McBride, respectively, one striking difference between the books commissioned and edited by Houston and those overseen by Wollen was that the former routinely and conventionally dealt with films in chronological order whereas the latter expressly forbade this method of organization, requiring the author to come up with a different structure and different rationale for that configuration.

Bearing this difference in mind, one distinct disadvantage for me in attempting to tackle Muratova's films chronologically is the fact that her first films are either unavailable to me (her codirected features with her first husband, Aleksandr Muratov, *By the Steep Ravine* [1961] and *Our Honest Bread* [1964], and her codirected documentary with Theodore Holcomb, *Russia* [1972]) or are of lesser interest to me. Her first two solo features, *Brief Encounters* (1967) and *Long Farewells* (1971), both in black and white, which she has ironically labeled "provincial melodramas", seemingly have few of the transgressive qualities that have attracted me to her other films, even though the first of these had only marginal exposure prior to glasnost and the latter, for reasons that are far from immediately apparent, was originally banned altogether. Consequently, the main source of interest for me about these films is my curiosity about what was once perceived to be transgressive about them, and this curiosity may be better satisfied by Nancy Condee's chapter on Muratova in her *The Imperial Trace: Recent Russian Cinema* (New York: Oxford University Press, 2009)—specifically, by what Condee calls the "fragmented characters" in Muratova's work, which for me reflects her separate Romanian, Jewish, Russian, and Ukrainian identities—than by wrestling with these films. Frankly and truthfully, I regard Condee's notion of character fragmentation as a sort of place holder for future encounters with *Brief Encounters* and *Long Farewells* rather than as a currently workable skeleton key. And I would defend this attitude practically more than intellectually, admitting that the intellectual shortcuts and potential misunderstandings that it entails are the inevitable side-product of the exploratory bricolage that I'm employing and espousing here.

Rather than adopt either Houston's or Wollen's principal of organization, chronological or structural, exclusively, I propose to combine portions of these approaches by tracing the structuring use of repetition through a few of Muratova's features, some (but not all) of which are considered in chronological order. More generally, I will offer these samplings of my own haphazard discoveries and notations not as models for others to follow but as examples of the sort of viewing and analysis available to individuals using the resources of the Internet (as well as other materials) to match their own inclinations. And for those who object to online viewing as an asocial activity that undermines the communal aspect of filmgoing, I would counter that(1) online viewing reconfigures the social aspects of cinema without necessarily eliminating them (so that blogging and articles such as this one become part of the reconfiguration) and(2) the social and communal aspects of public filmgoing have already been thoroughly undermined—by the film industry via targeting and other ways of subdividing audiences and by the asocial aspects of mobile phones and the oxymoronic characteristics of "social media" when they overtake public spaces.

§

Starting my discussion with Muratova's third solo feature, *Getting to Know the Big Wide World* (1978), her first in color, my main textual reference points are Jane Taubman's six pages in her 2005 monograph on Muratova (London/New York: I.B. Taurus, 2005), Veronika Ferdman's 2013 essay (http://www.lolajournal.com/4/world.html), and my 2005 capsule review for the *Chicago Reader*, written when I initially saw the film at a Muratova retrospective: "Kira Muratova's flaky 1978 feature, said to be her favorite, also goes by the title *Understanding Life*, but as often happens with her movies, appreciation ultimately triumphs over understanding. A loosely plotted comedy about a romantic triangle, set in and around a rural wasteland, it alternates between silence and sound, stopping and starting, with the cheekiness of '60s Godard. The relative chaos of the construction-site location, like the ones in Alexander Dovzhenko's *Ivan and Aerograd*, is what Muratova seems to like most about this. As usual with her movies, the actors—including regulars Nina Ruslanova and Sergei Popov—are wonderful."

The multiple pleasures—indeed, the joys—of *Getting to Know the Big Wide World* are largely a matter of sensual repetitions and echoes involving noise and quiet (intervals of silence on the soundtrack become as visceral as abrasive mechanical sounds or patches of solo piano), motion and stasis, melody and speech, rhymes of color and visual patterning, interplays of sight and sound, action and reaction, montage and performance art in which a splash becomes a giggle, a screaming argument morphs into an automotive rumble or a song. As in Boris Barnet's *By the Bluest of Seas*, one feels at times that the erotic-romantic triangle becomes musical, the diverse voicings and blendings of three human instruments. Appreciation becomes a mode of understanding—appreciating life—as one poetic speech about the value of love gets reiterated twice: first heard as a disembodied, anonymous woman's voice resonating against silence, then as an amplified, celebratory announcement by Lyuba at a wedding, and finally recalled in a conversation she has with Misha. A camera movement that follows someone walking gets reprised and continued by the forward drive of a truck. Even the liquid names of the three leads—Lyuba, Misha, Kolya—become parts of the film's musical refrains, along with their separate emotional timbres (yearning, gentle, macho-aggressive), and both the twin girls in the building crew and the strategic employments of mirrors in the mise en scène suggest other forms of repetition. But if all this adds up to the standard Soviet social-ist-realist charge of formalism, it's arguably formalism with socialist-realist as well as hedonistic aims and consequences—and why do these separate values habitually have to be seen as being in conflict? (Muratova's parents, one should note in passing, were both highly ranked Communist Party members.)

Sometimes the sound carries the image and sometimes these priorities are reversed. Either way, the exuberance becomes shared, collectivized. And almost all of it takes place in a muddy field.

It's impossible for me to be authoritative about Muratova's filmography when some titles (e.g., *Sentimental Policeman* [1992]) haven't yet been sub-titled in English, but it appears that her 'discovery' of verbal repetition in *Getting To Know the Big Wide World* had major repercussions on the remain-der of her career—perhaps most consequentially on her final feature, *Eternal Redemption: The Casting* (2012). Much as Elaine May, to all appearances, chose in her mid-eighties to play an elderly woman losing her memory in her 2018 Broadway stage performance in Kenneth Lonergan's *The Waverly Gallery*, presumably in order to stare down her own personal fears about senility by illustrating and embodying them in a black comedy, Muratova's last film mostly consists of the same scene endlessly repeated with different actors, settings, and mises en scène before we belatedly discover that the film's (fictional) director died in the midst of shooting and that its producers and editors are still trying to decide what to do with this intractable footage. It seems both significant and logical that Muratova's final black-comedy premise would concern the difficulties the 'normal' world might continue to have with her transgressive cinema, this film included.

More generally, one overall effect of repeating various speeches (or sentences or phrases) in films by both Muratova and Godard is to abstract language from its usual naturalistic placements in cinema and to "bare the device," as the Russian formalists put it. Another effect, less obvious, is to exploit language's resemblance to music.

I've decided to skip over Muratova's next feature, *Among the Gray Stones* (1983)—even though I enjoyed most of it after downloading it without subtitles from YouTube and then finding English subtitles for it elsewhere on the Internet—because she disowned it and even took her name off it after she lost control over its editing, crediting the film pseudonymously to "Ivan Sidorov". But it should be noted that her following feature, *Change of Fortune* (1987), also sometimes known as *Change of Fate* or *Change of Destiny*—Muratova's idiosyncratic adaptation of W. Somerset Maugham's story "The Letter," about a British wife in Singapore who shoots her lover (which served as the basis for Maugham's 1927 play and William Wyler's 1940 film, neither of which Muratova was familiar with)—begins with a scene and dialogue between the adulterous couple inside a huge greenhouse full of trees and other vegetation, a scene that is immediately repeated aurally and with the same actors, but not cinematographically. We eventually learn that this repetition corresponds on some level to the woman revising and rehearsing her prepared testimony at her murder trial. Her original claim that the murder was in self-defense after an attempted rape (seen in the first version) has to be altered after a passionate letter she sent to her lover emerges as part of the trial evidence. To complicate matters further, both versions of this dialogue (accompanied by the mournful, distant howling of a dog or wolf), with its shifting moods and emotions, move between the asynchronous offscreen voices and the synchronous onscreen voices of the couple, who are viewed in what appears to be scrambled, achronological fragments of the same scene. Then a third, partially whispered version of this dialogue is heard over another set of images moving into a mainly cavelike setting, followed by a scene with the woman washing herself with the help of a male servant inside her prison cell and then we return to the adulterous couple repeating portions of their dialogue yet again, apparently inside the greenhouse once more, but this time in amorous close-up.

Finally, a warden enters the heroine's cell to deliver a racist monologue about the superiority of "white" people, who need to "stick together," and to introduce her to three people who will provide her with some "light entertainment".

Without harping too much on the naturalistic pretexts for repeating the opening dialogue several times, I suspect Muratova's taste for repetition has more to do with her own activity as a filmmaker, including rehearsals, than it does with her heroine's deliberations. From Taubman's account of this film, we learn that the trio providing "light entertainment" (one makes faces, a second performs sleight-of-hand magic, a third chews glass) are introduced simply because Muratova liked them and because they had previously been cut out of *Among the Gray Stones*—a capricious form of impulsiveness, seemingly like the racist speech, that suggests another parallel with 1960s Godard, the determination that one can insert anything and everything into a film. Condee notes that Muratova's "most beloved eccentrics are those who, as she does, produce their own private art—most characteristically, bad art with no value other than its psychotropic effect," which gives her work a certain kinship with early John Waters as well.

At this point, I've described—and in fact seen—only the first seventeen minutes of *Change of Fortune*, omitting from my account the heroine's periodic crochet work because I couldn't find a way of incorporating it. Rather than watch or attempt to synopsize any more of the film now, I'd rather save the eighty-odd remaining minutes for some rainy day when I could use some "light entertainment" and good/bad/psychotropic art of my own rather than when I need to think about finishing this article. And inspired by Muratova's transgressive example in shirking my "commercial" duties (and exercising an irresponsible and perhaps irritating option that would be unthinkable if I were attending a theatrical Muratova retrospective), I'd like to leapfrog over her 1989 masterpiece *The Asthenic Syndrome* (which I've written about elsewhere), the aforementioned *Sentimental Policeman*, her relatively popular 1994 *Passions* (apparently her only film that's currently available on an American DVD), her *Three Stories* (the feature of hers that I tried and failed to get into the New York Film Festival in 1997), and her *Second Class Citizens* (2001), which I recently had the pleasure of discovering on YouTube, to conclude my abbreviated survey with what must be the craziest of all her black-and-white features, *Chekhov's Motives* (2002, also known a *Chekhovian Motifs*), where her affinity for both children and animals is even more evident than it is in *Among Gray Stones*, and where her incantatory uses of repetition are especially evident.

My *Chicago Reader* capsule: "Members of a farming family incessantly repeat the same lines of dialogue while a student prepares to leave home for school; guests at an interminable wedding cackle maniacally while the ghost of the groom's lover interferes with the ceremony. Born in 1934, the great Russian filmmaker Kira Muratova (*The Asthenic Syndrome*) seems to get wilder and more transgressive with every passing year. This updated merging of two early Anton Chekhov texts (the short play *Tatiana Repina* and the story "Difficult People") veers closer to the mad lucidity of Gogol than to the wry realism of *The Cherry Orchard*. I found the extreme stylization mesmerizing, hilarious, and ultimately closer to hyperrealism than to absurdism, though if you enter this without any warning you might wind up fleeing in terror."

The aforementioned "merging" has the student eventually hitching a ride with someone driving to a rural wedding rather than to his school in Moscow. Shorn of its repetitions, "Difficult People" (1886), readily available in a Constance Garnett translation (www.onlineliterature.com/anton_chekhov/1185/), has basically the same settings, plot, and characters as Muratova's adaptation, at least until the son leaves home, but its mood and style are drastically different. (In Chekhov's story, the son returns home to berate his father for his selfishness before leaving again—something he does in this film as well, but only after he attends the wedding.)

At the protracted family meal that dominates the first sequence, multiple repeated phrases seem to function as weapons, as assertions of identity, as tantrums, and as other forms of delirium, whether these are the student's request for money from his father, the father's list of his expenses, the mother's request to the father to buy the student a sweater (or her affectionate addresses to a kitten), or two of the youngest boys' assertions, begun in an earlier sequence, that a barn and not a pet food shop—or a pet food shop and not a barn—is being built in the muddy farmyard (to cite only five examples of repeated phrases). And because the fictional worlds of Chekhov are full of commonplace statements, Muratova's insistence on turning them into manic mantras (that is, mantras that are anything but meditative, and delivered passionately rather than mechanically) seems at least partially a function of considering how strange they might sound or become—and how they might reduce, elevate, or at least level out a family meal by being treated as a strident form of music, a roundelay of refrains—a relation that is even acknowledged in this film's title. (We even see an infant nodding rhythmically and sleepily to one of the father's tirades, as if being "conducted" by it.)

This description hardly does justice to the complex construction of this sequence—including the calming effect that a film of a ballerina, seen on television when a teenage daughter turns it on and composed of lap dissolves, has on the mother, which literalizes the musical aspects of the preceding quarrels by substituting another kind of music and motion.

Needless to say, this segment is entirely Muratova's invention and has no counterpart in Chekhov. But the following shots of carpentry, pigs, geese, and chickens accompanied by an offscreen lieder being sung by a male voice (in fact, a song previously composed for and heard in *Getting to Know the Big Wide World*), then shots of a turkey rooster and horses accompanied by the sound of sawing, differs from the Chekhov story only in the addition of the lieder, which carries over some of the lyrical and meditative feeling of the ballet.

I haven't been able to read *Tatiana Repina* (1889)—a one-act play written by Chekhov in one sitting as a private joke for his friend Alexy Suvorin, conceived as a sequel to Suvorin's four-act comedy of the same title, and intended neither for publication nor for performance. Yet Muratova's version of it, running for seventy-odd minutes, seems to be every bit as faithful or as unfaithful as her forty-odd-minute rendition of "Difficult People;" at least in terms of its more obvious details of character, action, and setting rather than its language, which I can't comment on directly. (I can, however, note with amusement that Taubman reports that Muratova retained most of Chekhov's dialogue "word for word" while Condee insists that "the original texts are barely discernible in Muratova's renditions"—a perfect illustration of how much subjectivity Muratova can provoke in her commentators, myself included.)

As indicated in my capsule, most of the film's second section consists of a complete and interminable church wedding, and the maniacal cackling or giggling of various attending guests periodically calls to mind Eugene O'Neill's virtually unproduced and unproducible 1925 *Lazarus Laughed: A Play for Imaginative Theatre*, which requires over a hundred masked actors and the almost continuous laughter of its title character. Otherwise, the degree to which repetitions are already an integral part of Russian Orthodox wedding services means that Muratova doesn't need to add any, as she does to speeches in "Difficult People"; as in certain films of Luis Buñuel, one is made to feel at times that Christianity might be regarded as the ultimate surrealism. I suspect that the recurring laughter and gossip from wedding guests is at least partially Muratova's contribution, even though the play was written as a joke, but the many musical refrains apparently derive from the wedding ceremony and therefore from Chekhov's text.

Once the ceremony is over, the groom tells a friend three times in a row that now is the time for them to go to the cemetery, presumably in order to make sure that his suicided mistress, whose ghost he saw at the wedding, is dead and buried there. Then, to the strains of an offscreen piano, while striding out with his friend and bride into the sunlight, he bellows out the same lieder that we heard in the farmyard. Then we and the farmer's son listen to idle chitchat from the priests, and the hooded ghost reappears, only she proves to be not a ghost at all but the daughter of one of the priests who wanted to disrupt his wedding service. (In Chekhov's play, Taubman informs us, she was a friend of the dead mistress.)

Back at the farm, after the son's berating of his father devolves into a scream-ing match in front of his mother, we see him contemplating a human skull in his bedroom like Hamlet, collapsing on his bed, and cradling the family's kitten. After the clock strikes five, he saddles a horse and says goodbye to his family, including his father.

In interviews, Muratova maintained that the reason why she made *Chekhov's Motives* was to support love and family values—and, unlikely as it sounds, there is reason to believe she was being sincere about this. The film ends conventionally, in spite of all its preceding violations of conventions, and bearing in mind that *The Asthenic Syndrome* begins at least allegorically with the grief, rage, and despair (rather than any sense of liberation) aroused by the death of Stalin, one could indeed argue that conservative and reactionary sentiments are every bit as operative and as relevant in Muratova's oeuvre as radical and rebellious impulses. One might even conclude that the conflicts between these feelings and reflexes are what keep her works alive and challenging, so that reaching back towards the Communist dreams of building a future in *Getting to Know the Big Wide World* or towards the humanist values of Chekhov in *Chekhov's Motives* ultimately means testing them against the horrible uncertainties of the present, and letting the chips fall and scatter where they may. Such, in any case, is my current presumption in an investigation that is still in progress

Jean-Luc Godard as Airplane

From the online New Lines, *September 15, 2022. This was written two days earlier, on the same day Godard's death (by legally assisted suicide) was announced, because the magazine asked for my text "as soon as possible". So it was drafted by instinct, almost like automatic writing, with little time for reflection, and it ran with few alterations apart from the elimination of my title. Only afterwards, I recalled an amusing anecdote I might have included: I had asked Godard in Toronto in 1996 if he could write a preface to my forthcoming collection* Movies as Politics, *and he had agreed; later I arranged to have the book's galleys sent to him in Rolle. But when no text had emerged by the deadline and I asked him about it, he replied he was too busy rereading* The Brothers Karamazov *to write anything. Finally, I asked him if we could just use his praise of me at his Toronto press conference as a jacket blurb, and he said yes.*

"He wasn't sick. He was simply exhausted," someone close to him said to *Libération*. But not so exhausted that he couldn't confound his public, including his fans, one last time, by deciding to end his life by assisted suicide—that is to say, to end it nobly, willfully, and seriously, even existentially, rather than fatefully and inadvertently.

The fact that he was hated as much as Orson Welles was by the commodifiers who couldn't find any way of commodifying his art, thus predicting and thereby marketing his next moves the way they could with a Woody Allen or an Ingmar Bergman or a Federico Fellini, meant that he could fool us all one last time, by following his own path rather than ours. Was his way of dying a selfish act? Yes and no. Insofar as it tells us who he was (and still is), it yielded an honest and considered end rather than an involuntary and haphazard one.

I first encountered his work when I was 17 and saw *A bout de souffle* (*Breathless*, 1960) in New York. But I didn't meet him in person until 1972, when I tried to interview him and Jean-Pierre Gorin in Paris about *Tout va bien*. When I met them both at the Cinémathèque at Palais de Chaillot, he politely canceled the interview because he was still on the mend from his auto accident (which I later learned sexually wounded him, at the same time it led to his meeting with his final partner and eventual next-door neighbor in his native Switzerland, Anne-Marie Melville). Eight more years would pass before I finally interviewed him for *Soho News* about *Sauve qui peut (la vie)* (*Every Man for Himself*, 1980), during a limo ride that took us from midtown Manhattan to LaGuardia airport, where he was flying to the Toronto International Film Festival, which enabled us to have our first conversation. Our second, third, and fourth conversations—more precisely, all the remaining ones we would ever have—had to wait until we met at that same festival sixteen years later.

In between those dates, I first learned about his liking of my work from a colleague, Serge Daney, in 1982 (after Godard had read my reflections on Welles in *Trafic*, the new French quarterly that Serge had just launched) and then from Tom Luddy in 1988 (who phoned me at Godard's request to thank me for my review of his *King Lear*, which Luddy had produced). Then, in 1995, Godard had invited me to be on a panel at the Locarno International Film Festival about his still-in-progress video series *Histoire(s) du cinéma*. I was serving at the time on the New York Film Festival's selection committee, and was permitted to shirk my duties there for a weekend—long enough to be on the panel (which Godard didn't attend), but not long enough to travel to Rolle, Switzerland beforehand to preview with Godard chapters 3a and 3b devoted to Italian Neorealism and the French New Wave.

Slightly over a year later, Godard brought those chapters and a more recent one—4a, on Alfred Hitchcock—to Toronto in order to show them to me in his hotel suite, which led to me interviewing him a second time. The suggestion of doing this was mine, but it could have just as easily been his, because his showing me the three chapters implied as much.

There's no question that Godard's maternal grandfather, a banker and close associate of Paul Valéry, was a rabid antisemite, but grandsons don't always take after their grandfathers, and Godard's thievery during his youth—often practiced against family members and subsequently echoed in his habit of stealing various quotations in his own texts and films from other writers— sounds more like rebellion than emulation. And it's worth adding that some of Godard's more selfless gifts—such as his anonymous financial assistance to Jean-Marie Straub and Danièle Huillet (on *Chronicle of Anna Magdalena Bach*) and Jean Eustache (on *Santa Claus Has Blue Eyes*), and his producing (again without credit) Rob Tregenza's *Inside/Out*—were as important as his thefts; they might even be described as thefts against himself, picking his own pockets. (Faxes from Godard pertaining to his work with Tregenza can be accessed in *Jean-Luc Godard: Documents*, a huge compendium published by the Centre Pompidou in 2006.)

At the same festival in Toronto in 1996—where Godard was publicly showing

For Ever Mozart, for me the absolute worst of his late features, which I had successfully argued against the New York Film Festival showing, although we (thankfully) didn't discuss this film in our interview—Godard praised me extravagantly during his press conference, comparing me to both James Agee and André Bazin. We met immediately afterwards, for our last interview session, and when I remarked, "That was really nice what you said about me," he replied, "I hope it helps you more than it hurts you, considering whom it's coming from."

I managed to spend several hours with him in Toronto that year on a more casual basis, and one thing I discovered about him was how often he liked to keep people at a certain distance, during which time he often seemed to be lost in his own thoughts but was actually being quite observant of what was happening around him. I suspect that this had something to do with a certain resistance towards being an all-purpose guru at every moment, even though he played that role to the hilt at other moments. At one juncture, during a meeting he had with ECM CEO Manfred Eicher, I recall him idly pouring catsup into a glass of water, stirring it with a spoon, and then drinking the results, as if to emphasize his total independence from whatever was happening around him. It was similar to the comic persona that he liked to play, or play with, in some of his features, notably *Prénom: Carmen* (1983), *Soigne ta droite* (*Keep Your Right Up*, 1987) and *King Lear* (1988).

Our mutual friend Rob Tregenza (whose third feature he was producing at the time) was present at many of those casual moments, and when I spoke to Rob at one point about how the films of Robert Bresson didn't function well on video because video foregrounded sound over image while film did the reverse, Rob argued that a good sound system might change this. Godard seemed to be away on the moon during this discussion, but a day later, when Godard and I were chatting alone, he suddenly and unexpectedly brought up this previous discussion, siding with me rather than with Rob.

On some matters he was inflexible. My efforts to convince him to see François Truffaut's *La chambre verte* (*The Green Room*, 1978) and Michelangelo Antonioni's *Al di là delle nuvolen* (*Beyond The Clouds*, 1995) were as fruitless as my insistence that the plot of Alfred Hitchcock's *The Wrong Man* doesn't include a real-life miracle but one that Hitchcock and his screenwriters invented; in all three matters his critical positions regarding Truffaut, Antonioni, and Hitchcock were firmly settled, not subject to any second thoughts or corrections—a stubbornness I associated with the Germanic, Goethe-like side of his personality (which also comes to the fore in his video *JLG/JLG—autoportrait de décembre*,

1995) and the funereal pronouncements it gave rise to, not the more slippery French side that seemed subject to constant and playful revisions.

My last physical encounter with Godard was at his press conference at Cannes in 1997 for his recently completed *Histoire(s) du cinéma*. I was seated in the audience, near the front, after presenting Godard with a copy of my new collection *Movies as Politics* and having received a bilingual pamphlet pairing my "Trailer for *Histoire(s) du cinéma*" with Hollis Frampton's "For a metahistory of film" (which had also appeared in *Trafic*). Godard deferred to me a couple of times during the press conference (e.g., asking me to furnish the title *A Place in the Sun* when his memory failed him), and this was truly the last of our exchanges—apart from my friend Nicole Brenez, his recently acquired picture consultant, bringing one of my more recent books to him in 2019. But in 2015, in Zagreb, at Tanja Vrvilo's ninth annual "Movie Mutations" event (named after an anthology I coedited with Australian film critic Adrian Martin), I was able to hang out with Fabrice Aragno, Godard's cinematographer and all-around technical assistant since 2004. One of the first things he said to me was that he didn't consider himself a "Godard fan"—his own aesthetic preferences were closer to Antonioni and Kiarostami—but that he loved "working with Jean-Luc." I also learned from him that after Godard booked two passages on the cruise ship Costa Concordia for both himself and Aragno for *Film Socialisme*, he decided not to go himself on the second passage, and instructed Aragno to go alone and either shoot his own material or shoot nothing, depending on his own preferences, but refused to give him any instructions about what he might shoot. And Aragno wound up shooting a good deal of material that Godard used in the film. For *Adieu au langage* (2014), he devised the 3-D system that was used with Godard's input and shot a test reel of 3-D visuals and sound separations (a fascinating document that he screened in Zagreb), and the little boy and girl viewed periodically in the film are his own children.

Even though mainstream media has branded Godard as a grouch and an obscurantist as often as it chided Welles for his weight (which even alleged friends such as Gore Vidal tended to harp on), the real mainstream crime of these artists, apart from being unapologetic intellectuals, was their unpredictability, which, as I've suggested above, made them relatively unmarketable, at least when they were alive. For all the love lavished by Quentin Tarantino and others on *Bande à part* (*Band of Outsiders*, 1964), it's important to recall that this movie failed abysmally at the box office, both in France and the U.S., when it was first released—for the same reason, I would maintain, that Truffaut's *Tirez sur la pianiste* (*Shoot the Piano Player*, 1960) flopped: for its switching back and forth relentlessly between tragedy and farce, confusing genre and marketplace identities and signals as well as our emotions and his own in the process. *Breathless* also did this mixing of moods and modes, but in a less affectively challenging fashion by remaining always a thriller—or at least seeming to follow this consistency. (As Godard once argued, when great films succeed commercially, this is often because of a misunderstanding, and *Breathless* may have shared this trait.)

After Godard became politically radicalized in 1968, he took drastic steps to alienate his cinephile fans while forging less pleasurable forms of ranting and theorizing. This was embraced by some academics and who found the results "teachable" in an armchair leftist fashion, but for Godard it was chiefly a way of shedding his skin and restarting his career. In contrast to the more humanist aims of his strongest political films—*Ici et ailleurs* (*Here and Elsewhere*, 1976) and *Numéro deux* (*Number Two*, 1975), and two series also made with Anne-Marie Miéville for French TV in Grenoble (both broadcast in ways that undermined many of their objectives) were the nonhumanist *Vent d'est* (*Wind from the East*, 1975) and *Vladimir et Rosa*, 1976), which the academics tended to prefer, perhaps because they were easier to diagram on a blackboard. Yet it seems significant that Godard avoids referencing these films in his *Histoire(s)*. By the time he returned to making masterpieces, albeit difficult ones, such as *Passion* (1982) and *Nouvelle Vague* (1990), he had lost his mainstream champions ("The party's over," concluded the *New York Times*' Vincent Canby of the latter film), many of whom tended to link his commercial failures with supposed character flaws.

What made Godard's international influence from the 1960s onwards as huge as Welles's from the 1940s onwards was a function of both his framing and his editing—added to which was his activity as a film critic, especially when this overlapped or coincided with his activity as a filmmaker. Truthfully, Godard and his critical colleagues comprised the first generation of cinephiles who treated film history as part of cultural history—an obvious approach today, yet one of the things that made Susan Sontag so controversial in the 1960s was the fact that she was the only visible New York intellectual to take this approach. And indeed, this critical position, even when it was misunderstood and/or vulgarized, may have changed the face of modern cinema as much as the use of jump cuts in *Breathless* or Godard's capacity throughout most of the 1960s to make his films resemble global newspapers.

To function as a film critic through one's filmmaking was a talent shared by Jacques Rivette and, to a lesser extent, Luc Moullet, but not by other critics at *Cahiers du Cinéma* such as Truffaut, Claude Chabrol, Eric Rohmer, André Téchiné, and Olivier Assayas. Nor was it practiced by the Hollywood "brats" influenced in diverse ways by Godard's example: Woody Allen, Peter Bogdanovich, Francis Ford Coppola, Brian De Palma, Paul Schrader, and Martin Scorsese, all of whom substituted homages for critiques—rubber stamps of imitation and approval that did nothing to inform our appreciations of what they were duplicating. (Curiously, Alain Resnais had the same sort of critical intelligence as a filmmaker as Godard, even though he never wrote any criticism; his particular slants on 1940s melodramas and 1950s MGM musicals in his own films are always personal commentaries, not mere copycat references.)

Back in Toronto, Godard admitted to me that much of his on-screen criticism was done unconsciously—that apart from a few obvious references that resembled the homages of the movie brats, his overall critiques of German Expressionist cinema in *Alphaville*, which I'd written about in my first article for *Sight and Sound*, only became apparent to him afterwards—something he also acknowledges in chapter 3b of *Histoire(s)*, when he superimposes shots from Fritz *Lang's Destiny* (1921) over shots from *Alphaville*...or is it vice versa?

In striking contrast to the sweet and sour reflections that we read or hear from American journalists about Godard's death, grumbling almost as much as they say Godard did, *Libération* brought out a celebratory 28-page special issue in color devoted exclusively to Godard only a day later, including contributions from such Americans as Jim Jarmusch and Daniel Mendelsohn. The fact that the box office "performance" of Godard's late features was reportedly even worse in France than it was in the U.S. only proves that marketplace value has little or nothing to do with the love of art, and that there's no way of gauging the latter via the former, especially insofar as the intensity of the love and the qualities of the audience experiencing and expressing it aren't even remotely quantifiable.

I suspect that the future final look at Godard that many of us will have and remember is Mitra Farahani's startling *À vendredi, Robinson* (*See You Friday, Robinson*), which is opening in Paris this weekend, and which I was lucky enough to see last summer at Il Cinema Ritrovato in Bologna. A staged internet encounter between two nonagenarian New Wave pioneers—Jean-Luc Godard of the French New Wave and Ebrahim Golestan of the First Iranian New Wave—who meet one another only digitally, thanks to the filmmaker, an Iranian woman based in Europe, this abrasive, Godardian feature, whatever its intentions, has a lot to say about the class that Farahani, Godard, and Golestan all belong to, the high bourgeoisie. The dialectically contrasting self-portraits that emerge from the weekly exchanges (which all take place on Fridays—thus occasioning the title, derived from one of Godard's sign-off statements) are rather brutal in terms of their differences in both décor and styles of self-presentation: Golestan, director of *Brick and Mirror* (1964) and *The Iranian Crown Jewels* (1965), both masterpieces that brilliantly skewer the greed and pretensions of the ruling class, presents himself like a sultan in palatial surroundings, clearly enunciating all his arguments; Godard presents himself simply and modestly, as if he were a peasant, even though what he has to say about his distrust of language sometimes borders on the incomprehensible.

I suspect that the wisest thing Godard ever said to me came in our first interview, in 1980. "People like to think of themselves as stations or terminals," he said, "not as trains or planes between airports. I like to think of myself as an airplane, not an airport."

I asked him, "So that people should use you to get certain places and then get off?

"Yes. I'll work much more on that in my next film."

As with many of Godard's pronouncements, I'm not entirely sure I know what he meant by this. But what I can *use* is perfectly clear. It's the fact that texts and movies are vehicles that take us places, and the destinations of those that make them don't have to be the same as the destinations of those who climb into those vehicles. I'm a maker of some of those vehicles, which others use to take them where they (not I) want to go, and I'm someone who takes the vehicles of others (Godard's, for instance), which take me where I want to go. I think that's more or less what poetry does.

Straub as Rural Sensualist

Commissioned by New Left Review's *online Sidecar, and published there on December 6, 2022.*

To say that I knew Jean-Marie Straub (1933-2022) and Jean-Luc Godard (1930-2022) equally well is another way of saying I knew them equally poorly. Yet I know that they wound up dying sixty-odd days apart in the same Swiss village (Rolle), close to where Godard spent much of his childhood and later shot some of his best (*Nouvelle Vague, King Lear*) as well as his worst (*For Ever Mozart*) work—an area I've never visited. Straub was born in Metz, which I don't know either—a small city that belonged to Germany before World War I and then for a spell during World War II before reverting to France, giving him a sort of divided nationality like Godard—who, although born in Paris, was French/Swiss, straddling another kind of division.

From 1963 to 2006, Straub was half of a two-headed, four-handed filmmaking team—based in Paris, Munich, and close to Rome—with Danièle Huillet, his French wife, the more practical-minded member of the couple, who only gained full credit as coauthor about a decade after they started, which she then retained until her untimely death in 2006. Circa 2011, Barbara Ulrich, who is Swiss, became Straub's producer, partner, occasional actress, and business manager, most likely occasioning their move to Rolle.

One thing that tended to make both Godard and Straub indigestible to Anglo-Americans was their having grown up in a French culture where avant-garde art and mainstream entertainment weren't mutually exclusive, as the careers of René Clair, Jean Cocteau, and Marcel L'Herbier amply demonstrated.

Moreover, the fact that both of these chain smokers belonged to the *Cahiers du Cinéma* crowd (with Straub qualifying as a junior member, like Luc Moullet), which embraced Hollywood populism but shied away from avant-garde elitism, meant that their own avant-garde practices, including a reluctance or inability to tell stories, were couched in mainstream terms even as they confounded mainstream editing protocols.

Godard had anonymously helped in the financing of Straub's first full-length feature, *Chronik der Anna Magdelena Bach* (1968), and politically as well as esthetically, they remained comrades-in-arms for well over half a century, effectively serving as the two most imposing pillars of cinematic modernism in Western Europe, particularly as this applied to their grappling with texts, their love of direct sound, their preoccupations with history, and their sharp critical reflexes.

I knew each of them only fleetingly. I interviewed Godard in 1980 and 1996 and curated the first Jean-Marie Straub and Danièle Huillet retrospective (supplemented by about a dozen films by others that they considered exemplary) held in the U.S. in 1982, with an accompanying catalogue that benefitted from their input. At the Viennale in 2004, where they were presenting a John Ford retrospective, I had a dinner with both the two of them and (quite awkwardly) a colleague I wasn't speaking to, a critic who unlike me was fluent in Italian; the fact that they showed no awareness of the incompatibility and discomfort of their two guests was characteristic of both their single-mindedness and their social clumsiness. (An English friend once described the problems she faced upon presenting them with a gift, which they didn't know how to receive.)

Another thing Godard and Straub-Huillet had and have in common is that no one quite knows what to do with their work. In the case of Straub-Huillet's reception in the U.K., *Screen Magazine* appeared to be far more comfortable printing their screenplays than explaining why it was deemed important to do so. As for their reception in the U.S., the silence and/or incomprehension prior to 1982 was such that I was moved to turn the catalogue into an angry polemic. Jean-Marie himself was livid that the *New York Times'* Vincent Canby had reviewed their *Moses and Aaron* as *Aaron and Moses*, and he seemed equally irritated when another reviewer added a 'the' before *Chronicle of Anna Magdelena Bach* (an error shared by Wikipedia and many others), implying that they had adapted an existing document rather than compiled one of their own invention. (The *New York Times'* recent Straub obituary is no less befuddled, maintaining that the lengthy subtitle of their *Othon* [*Les Yeux ne veulent pas en tout temps se fermer, ou Peut-être qu'un jour Rome se permettra de choisir à son tour*] was given in English and that Straub-Huillet didn't even care if people walked out of their films.) As for Godard, even in this magazine, Fredric Jameson recently found himself asking "what we were to do with the final works of the 'humanist' period, where they came from, and whether they meant a falling off or a genuine renewal."

The most significant difference between these figures, at least for me, is that Godard was a city slicker and Straub was a rube, a hillbilly—by which I mean existentially if not literally. In both cases, this was for the better as well as for the worse. It applied to both their respective social skills and (especially in Straub's case) their lack of same, which paradoxically seemed just as evident. Both of them were snobs as well as populists, gadflies as well as traditionalists. Each reinvented the cinema for his own purposes, as did Alexander Dovzhenko, Federico Fellini, and Jia Zhangke (three other inspired hick directors of innovative epics), and William Faulkner (who reinvented the novel in comparably epic and innovative ways).

Straub's undeserved marginality derives in part from the way we tend to regard country folk, especially when they display the unbridled freedom of avant-garde artists. Many of us unconsciously adopt the city-bred bias that innovative art belongs to urban audiences and depends on some form of city smartness, reluctant to believe it can also come from hillbillies. That these artists seem to reinvent their own art forms may lead us to think that they somehow arrived at their discoveries by brute instinct rather than by study or intellect, but this means overlooking that Faulkner read James Joyce and Dovzhenko was exposed to modern art in Warsaw, Berlin, and Odessa. Straub and Huillet studied both the subjects of their films (music by Bach and Schoenberg, texts by Böll, Brecht, Corneille, Duras, Hölderlin, Kafka, Mallarmé, Montagne, Pavese, and Vittorini, and paintings by Cézanne, among many others) and the films of Bresson, Buñuel, Chaplin, Dreyer, Ford, Hawks, Lubitsch, Renoir, and Tati, their masters. The ways that they accommodated their subjects to their masters are fairly easy to detect, especially in the traces of Bresson and Dreyer in the performance styles of Straub-Huillet films (especially the early ones) but are less easily found in their Hollywood and French commercial models (Ford, Hawks, Lubitsch, Renoir) and their comic-independent ones (Chaplin and Tati). But the stamps of these and other populist heroes remained none the less present in Straub's critical vocabulary and his grasp of his own art. In Pedro Costa's extraordinary *Where Does Your Hidden Smile Lie?* (2001), aptly described as a romantic comedy about Straub-Huillet—which shows Huillet physically and meticulously editing one of the multiple versions of their 1999 *Sicilia!* while Straub advises, kibbitzes, paces, smokes, and pontificates—Straub identifies Chaplin, of all people, as the greatest of all film editors (an argument he often made elsewhere) because Chaplin knew precisely when a gesture began and ended. In an earlier documentary by Harun Farocki, we see Straub suggest to a German actor he's directing in *Class Relations* (1984) that he deliver a line by Franz Kafka the way that Ricky Nelson says a line in Hawks' *Rio Bravo*. (Defying the notion that works of art need to be singular, Straub-Huillet sometimes edited several different versions of their films using different takes of shots so that, for instance, the sound of an offscreen rooster crowing might be heard in the German subtitled version but not in the English subtitled one.)

The seeming incongruity of matching a radical vision with a mainstream product also proposes cinema as a grappling or juggling with a text (written, composed, painted, or filmed) in order to approach history, a trait Straub shared with Godard. This in turn redefines both political will and reality as things that Chaplin, Dreyer, Ford, Griffith, Hawks, Lubitsch, Mizoguchi, Renoir, Stroheim and Tati can teach us important lessons about. This became especially apparent when I conducted a Q&A with Jean-Marie and Danièle in New York and attended their lengthy debate session with some art students about why John Ford was more dialectically correct than Sergei Eisenstein, which left many of the kids stunned and speechless. Straub's often inflammatory rhetoric tended to be leftist and/or anarchist, but the underlying feelings were often related to conservative peons to preserving the status quo such as *Rio Bravo*, ably put together by storytellers with often-bittersweet conclusions about upholding the law and bowing to homespun convention. Indeed, Straub's intense love for the material world arguably suggests a kind of conservativism complicating if not undermining his Marxism.

By the time Straub-Huillet became landscape artists in the '70s and '80s—arguably starting with *Moses und Aron* (1975) and *Fortini/Cani* (1976) and climaxing in such masterpieces as *Trop tôt/trop tard* (1982) and *Operai, contadini* (2001)—the sensuality of places and people, of animals, insects, and vegetation, became more central to their art, even as their chosen texts continued to help generate it. (Despite the intermittent power of its visuals, it's the sound of German being spoken that comprises most of the beauty of *The Death of Empedocles*.) Pedro Costa told me that they once spent their spare time translating some of Shakespeare's plays into Italian, not because they wanted to film the results but simply because they found the existing translations "shit." This passion for exactitude while struggling with texts, meanwhile valuing their resistance to texts as well as their predilections, also led them to insert patches of black leader to represent textual cuts in their *Introduction to Arnold Schoenberg's Accompaniment to a Cinematic Scene* (1973). But regarding what they did with landscapes, Huillet, in a letter to *Artificial Eye's* Andi Engel about *Too Early, Too Late*, may have done a better job of describing their art than any of their more discerning critics, such as Gilberto Perez and Barton Byg: "What is recounted: struggles, revolts, defeats, delays and anticipations, statistics; what is represented: history, topography, geography, geology, light, lights, wind and clouds, land (worked and transformed by men), traces—erased or still visible—and sky (lots of sky); we tried finding the right perspective (the only one), the right height, the right proportions between the earth and the sky, to be able to pan without having to change the horizon line, even at 360-degrees."

Unlike Godard, who had social skills even when it came to informing his public that he wanted to be left alone, Straub tended to create unnecessary scandals and misunderstandings wherever he went and even when he stayed behind. For all its sincerity, the angry bluster of his political rhetoric—which inspired him to announce in absentia at Venice in 2006 (where he was receiving a lifetime achievement award), quoting Franco Fortini without acknowledgment, that as long as there was American imperialist capitalism, there could never be enough terrorists in the world—seemed motored by nervousness and clumsy shyness, which apparently led him to overlook the terrorism of American imperialist capitalism. It was the same provincialism that reportedly led him to reject a Canadian retrospective because "you can't trust Americans with prints" and prompted him and Huillet to title their early video *Europa 2005 - 27 octobre*, as if they assumed that everyone in their audience already knew about the electrocuted French teenagers. But it was also a tender provincialism whose innocence produced the splendors and wonders of workers and peasants in a vibrant, humming forest explaining how to make risotto. If this sounds like hyperbole, Straub made the very practice of spouting and spreading such hyperbole contagious, and, as with Godard, we will continue to celebrate him not only for what he produced but also for what he inspired in some of his disciples and commentators.

Snowfall: Michael Snow (1928-2023)

Written for Sight and Sound, *January 2023, and published in their March 2023 issue.*

Manny Farber, one of his earliest critical defenders, described Michael Snow to me as "a prince," and there's no question that he was a proud bohemian who carried his own sense of royalty within the art world with grace and style. European fans such as Jacques Rivette who mistook him for an "American" (he was born and died in Toronto) may not have understood that the state funding that allowed Snow to flourish in Canada wouldn't have been as feasible in the U.S. It's even been speculated that if Snow hadn't filmed his 1967 *Wavelength* in a Manhattan loft during his extended New York sojourn, many of us might never have heard of him. It was basically the enthusiasm of New York critics—Farber, Jonas Mekas, Annette Michelson, and, perhaps most of all, P. Adams Sitney and his term "structural film"—that placed Snow on the map, even while such reference sources as Ephraim Katz's *A Film Encyclopedia* and David Thomson's *A Biographical Dictionary of the Cinema* failed to acknowledge his existence.

Starting out as a self-taught jazz pianist who evolved from Dixieland to bebop (and later, to free jazz), Snow turned next to painting, sculpture, instillations, photography, film (starting in animation), video, holography, audio, and conceptually shaped books such as *Cover to Cover* (1975) and *High School* (1979). As J. Hoberman recalled in his thoughtful *New York Times* obituary, Snow announced in 1967, "I am not a professional. My paintings are done by a filmmaker, sculpture by a musician, films by a painter, music by a filmmaker, paintings by a sculptor, sculpture by a filmmaker, films by a musician, music by a sculptor… sometimes they all work together […]"

Like Godard, he produced a veritable avalanche of works, robust, playful, loaded with puns and measured afterthoughts, and often self-referential or cross-referential. (The "walking woman" in many of his early paintings, for instance, reappears either figuratively or literally in some of the films. And his magisterial 1979 *Flight Stop*, a photographic sculpture of sixty fiberglass landing geese in a huge Toronto mall, is quintessentially cinematic, or at least precinematic.)

And when he took up film, he characteristically wound up reinventing the medium on his own terms—exploring camera movement in his famous trilogy of *Wavelength*, ‹------› (*Back and Forth*, 1969), and *La région centrale* (1971), sound and image juxtapositions in *"Rameau's Nephew" by Diderot (Thanx to Dennis Young) by Wilma Schoen* (1974), and digital shape-shifting in **Corpus Callosum* (2002), to cite only five of his major works.

It's remarkable that Snow should die at age ninety-four only a few weeks after the deaths of Godard and Straub—not because these innovative giants all inhabited the same universe but because they were all frequently greeted, rejected, or ignored with a great deal of confusion. (I wouldn't be surprised to learn that most people reading this obituary "know" *Wavelength*, if at all, only through Martin Scorsese's brief homage to it in *Taxi Driver*, as cited by Manny Farber and Patricia Patterson in *Film Comment*.) Considering Godard French rather than Swiss and not knowing that Straub came from a city that was alternately French and German suggests an easy parallel with Rivette's confusion about Snow.

Independent American filmmaker Jon Jost has praised the concepts behind *Wavelength* and *La région centrale* but faulted the executions of those films as lazy and slipshod (while adding that hallucinogenic drugs helped to make their alleged failings more tolerable), but the late Argentinian writer-director Eduardo de Gregorio told me that what impressed him the most about Snow's work was its technical precision. One reason why it's impossible to reconcile these seemingly antithetical responses is that Snow's experimental cinema, unlike the radical art cinemas of Godard and Straub, refuses any relationship to mainstream cinema, either positive or negative. Whereas Godard and Straub situated themselves in relation to film history, Snow, whose interest in film history was minimal, placed himself in the history of art. Consequently, the received ideas we have about mainstream cinema, derived from such sources as Oscars and other forms of industry propaganda (including the assumption that the only films worth mentioning are industrial products) can't be applied in any meaningful way to Snow's work, which has scant interest in either storytelling or narrative verisimilitude. The closest it gets to mainstream cinema are occasional forms of mockery or defiance, such as placing the credits in the middle of a film.

Another thing that clearly distinguished Snow from Godard and Straub, at least in my encounters with them, was his relative serenity. After I was commissioned to interview him in Toronto about his *Presents* in 1981, we became friends, so that I spent enjoyable evenings smoking grass with him at his Toronto home and then going to Chinatown for dinner (and once attending one of his weekly free-jazz jam sessions). Our friendship led to a second interview about his minimalist film *So is This* (1982), and it ended only after I published a book in 1983 that criticized two of his New York champions. But even when he expressed his disapproval—which might have been exacerbated by my probing of his political incorrectness involving women in *Presents* (as with Kubrick, his sense of humor sometimes resembles that of a teenage boy)—he remained a gentleman about it.

In *Wavelength*, we lurch across a room in a series of zooms overlaid by numerous shifts in color and texture: in *Back and Forth*, we're shuttled back and forth in a series of horizontal and vertical pans in a classroom; in the three-hour *La région centrale*, set in a mountain wilderness, we rotate in 360-degree loops every which way. Like Godard and Kubrick (filmmakers for whom he showed some interest), Snow regarded film as a vehicle for thought and exploration, which should situate him within our grasp of film history, if not necessarily within his. The sensuality of thought was part of what intrigued him, making the camera movements of his trilogy both challenging and rewarding, like demonic fairground rides that constantly oblige us to readjust. Associating a flow of ideas (mainly philosophical) with a sensorial experience refutes the very notion of intellectual activity as an alternative to "life," as a Puritan mindset might have it, and Snow's almost carnal form of engagement actually gives us plenty to think about.

His notion of camera movement as aggression receives two comic postscripts that could serve in a way as alternate versions of *Wavelength* and *Back and Forth*, respectively: *Breakfast* AKA *Table-Top Dolly* (1976), a short in which a transparent sheet in front of a camera lens crushes a lot of groceries, comically equating camera movement with mastication and/or digestion, and the opening sequence of *Presents*, in which a stage set with actors is no less messily demolished by forklifts shaking it, with the forklifts becoming a surrogate for the camera as it wreaks its destruction.

For me, *Corpus Callosum* remains Snow's greatest film, not only because it manages to encapsulate so much of his previous oeuvre (even concluding with a bit of animation from his earliest film work), but also because it manages to combine, seemingly for the first time in his career, an acute sense of social history with its formal, technical, and comic hijinks. Exploring the progression (and/or regression) from analog to digital, the film oscillates between (a) a workstation in a skyscraper with wall-sized windows and employees seated in front of computers and (b) a windowless bunker with a family seated on a sofa in front of a TV, emblematic of half a century earlier. The various rhymes and clashes between these sites, as well as the digitally generated distortions of bodies and spaces within both, are endlessly suggestive.

Satchmo's Politics, and Ours

Written for the first paper issue of New Lines Magazine, *January 15, 2023, and published there in a different form, with fewer political reflections.*

For me, the two best talking heads in Sacha Jenkins' recent documentary, *Louis Armstrong's Black & Blues*, are those of Orson Welles and Ossie Davis, both of whom significantly started out as performers and theater people. Welles—whom we hear as the film begins, warmly introducing Armstrong as a friend on a TV talk show, explaining that he once planned to make a film that would recount the history of jazz through Armstrong's life—insists on his preeminence as a performer "not on the principle of escapism but on the principle of affirmation." Given that the entire career of Armstrong as a blazing maestro of the cornet and trumpet can be summed up by the word "affirmation," Welles's introduction couldn't have been more apt.

Ossie Davis, who once had a character in his play *Purlie Victorious* say to someone, "You're a disgrace to the Negro profession," recalls that he and his friends used to laugh derisively at Satchmo's performing antics and clowning as a creepy form of Uncle Tomism until the two of them worked together on a movie, *A Man Called Adam* (1966)—significantly, a film that deals directly with the issue of black rage. Sitting with Armstrong in a dressing room, Davis was struck by how sad the man looked during a reflective "off" moment until he was called back to work and snapped back into his signature toothy grin, suddenly alerting Davis to the sort of behavior his own black parents and grandparents had had to display in order to survive. Thereafter, he admits, he never laughed at Satchmo again.

Clearly, dealing with Louis Armstrong today necessitates dealing with a complicated historical past, sometimes even personally if you're a white Southerner such as myself. A few days before my fourteenth birthday, in 1957, I attended a Louis Armstrong concert in Sheffield, Alabama—the 7 o'clock show for "whites," not the 9:30 one for "coloreds," according to the Jim Crow laws and protocols of the time—although I don't know if the colored tickets were cheaper than those for the whites, as they were at the segregated movie theaters in town. But I do recall that Armstrong played in Sheffield with Barrett Deems, the white drummer in his band for many years, and Satchmo was most likely the only jazz musician able at the time to play in a racially "mixed" group in the Deep South (apart from the pitifully few venues held in that period for the Dave Brubeck Quartet, which lost most of its playdates due to its insistence on retaining its black bassist, Eugene Wright). But even Armstrong was taking a risk with Deems. On the same 1957 Southern tour, in Knoxville, Tennessee, a bomb exploded outside an Armstrong All-Stars concert, and Satchmo diplomatically stepped up to the microphone and said, "That's okay, folks—it was jus' my phone ringin'." Recalling Welles' introduction, what could be more affirmative than that?

He grew up at an international crossroads—New Orleans at the dawn of the twentieth century—nurtured in turn by his unmarried prostitute mother who sang in church, a family of Jewish Lithuanian rag merchants who helped him purchase his first cornet, and even a reform-school orphanage just outside the city with military-style discipline that he was sent to after firing his mother's pistol on New Year's Eve. Armstrong later recalled his time at the orphanage fondly and even nostalgically, perhaps because it gave order and purpose to a life that had up until then been mainly chaotic. And even if he hadn't been born on July 4, 1900, as he later claimed (his registered birth was actually on August 4, 1901), the symbolic myth seemed appropriate, especially once he arguably became the most recognizable and appreciated American and artist on the planet—the universal embodiment of both freedom and art that was associated with his origins, perceived more as American than as African. Although it's impossible to quantify the full reach of such a reputation. it appears that Armstrong's world-wide fame reached its peak around the middle of the twentieth century when he started to tour for the U.S. State Department.

As an autodidact who authored his own memoirs without collaborators, he comprised a veritable monument to the American art of self-invention, and insofar as the art of jazz improvisation that he helped to create and popularize is one in which spontaneity equals a form of honesty, his ongoing self-creation was both audible and visible to everyone. This made him especially eligible to become America's good-will ambassador around the world, a role that his status as a jazz pioneer only helped to foster.

This became acknowledged and celebrated in a musical concocted by jazz pianist Dave Brubeck and his wife Iola that premiered at the Monterey Jazz Festival in 1962 and became an ambitious soundtrack album the same year. It featured Armstrong, Brubeck's Quartet, the vocal trio Lambert, Hendricks & Bavan, and Carmen McRae, with music by Brubeck and lyrics by his wife, and dealt with such issues as America's place in the world during the Cold War, the Civil Rights Movement, the image and nature of God, and the music business. Set in a fictional African country, *The Real Ambassadors* on CD features Armstrong as its star and central character, with his shining trumpet and his gravel-mouthed vocals delivering the memorable Brubeck score.

The implication was that Armstrong, like America, was a beacon for the whole world. But if you belong to everyone in the world, this means, in effect, that you've taken or at the very least assumed a particular position in relation to that world. And if you belong to the American mainstream, it could be argued that the easiest way to be political without creating a disturbance is to pretend that you have no politics at all. The European lesson for this very American form of self-deception is that claiming to have no politics ultimately means adopting the sort of bad politics that entails accepting the status quo. This was far from being the message of *The Real Ambassadors*, but for many people even today, it often registers as the Armstrong persona.

To believe, as Ossie Davis once did, that Armstrong's racial politics were set by the mercenary white folks who succeeded the slave owners was to believe that those politics were reactionary, that even Satchmo's duet with Barbra Streisand on "Hello, Dolly!" or his crooning "It's a Wonderful World" was corny and shopworn. And it's worth noting that Armstrong's dislike of bebop—expressed in one interview as his enthusiastic preference for Guy Lombardo, a nonjazz bandleader associated with mainstream schmaltz—probably had as much to do with the lifestyles of beboppers as it did with modernist musical forms. (Moreover, as someone who happily imbibed pot daily, he had no bones about hiring and befriending bebopper Dexter Gordon, a fellow grass smoker.) As recounted by one of his biographers, the late Terry Teachout, a former jazz musician himself, "Except for [Dizzy] Gillespie, whose jokey demeanor on the bandstand was more like Armstrong's than either man cared to admit, the boppers disdained the showmanship that was his trademark. More than a few of them were heroin addicts (that was what he had in mind when he spoke of their 'pipe-dream music') whose habits made it impossible for them to conduct themselves with the professionalism that was his byword. Above all, though, their music was uncompromising in a way that he saw as threatening to the public's acceptance of jazz."

Yet Armstrong's own musical genius could attain a burning and cascading complexity of its own—at least in his early recordings, and more fitfully afterwards. To my untutored ear, his famous cadenza at the start of his *West End Blues*, recorded with his Hot Five in 1928, even anticipates some of the multifaceted virtuoso breaks of Charlie Parker, the supreme bebopper, two decades later, rhythmically as well as melodically. Teachout, for instance, points to "a shift of gears known to contemporary classical composers as a 'metric modulation,' in which he turns a single beat in the second measure…into two-thirds of a beat in the third measure."

Armstrong's ascent from the bottom of society to the top of the music world suggests a certain parallel with the career of another Charlie and another autodidact, namely Chaplin, although the differences are as salient as the similarities. Chaplin's leftist politics were plainly visible, along with his sexual lifestyle and wealth, and these eventually led to him being barred from re-entry into the United States in 1952. Armstrong, by contrast, continued to live by choice in a working-class neighborhood in Queens, and, quite the opposite of Chaplin, left all his business decisions, including the hiring of his sidemen, to his Jewish manager, Joe Glaser, a former associate of Al Capone whose mob connections helped to protect Armstrong from the gangsters who wanted to control his career. One might add that Glaser's handling of the Satchmo trademark continued to protect and shelter his client from the uglier aspects of capitalism. "I never tried in no way to ever be real real filthy rich like some people do," Armstrong wrote, "and after they do they die just the same." Yet by the same token, Glaser, who also became the manager of Brubeck and Billie Holiday, protected Armstrong from the controversy that would have come from expressing his political views more openly. These were privately expressed in many of the tape recordings that Armstrong made for friends and for his own amusement, and *Louis Armstrong's Black & Blues* allows us to hear several lively patches from them.

Yet he also made *When it's Sleepy Time Down South* one of his theme songs, with its reference to "darkies [who] dance till the break of day"—even though he started to substitute "people" for "darkies" during the 1950s. But it was during that same decade, during the racial turmoil over school integration in Little Rock, Arkansas, in 1957, that he broke with precedent by calling the much-beloved Dwight D. Eisenhower a "two-faced" President with "no guts" in an interview with a journalism student. He went on to call Arkansas governor Faubus a "no-good motherfucker," assigned the same epithet to Secretary of State John Foster Dulles, and canceled on the spot his planned tour of the Soviet Union for the State Department, saying, "The way they are treating my people in the South, the government can go to hell."

He refused to retract his statement, but three years later, he unknowingly traveled to the Congo at the behest of the CIA, who, as reported by historian Susan Williams in her recent book *White Malice: The CIA and the Covert Recolonization of Africa*, cynically used Armstrong as a "Trojan Horse" for furthering its interests, which included acquiring uranium and assassinating the Congo's first democratically elected prime minister, Patrice Lumumba. This was the likely low point of the use of Armstrong's good will as an unwitting and innocent tool of Cold War propaganda and skullduggery.

After his 1957 outburst, he mostly restricted his dissenting comments to his tape recorder, preferring to send out his message of love to everyone. I find it difficult to blame him for this. Even when he dressed his love and his celebration in the trappings of tired clichés and outworn stereotypes, I assume he believed that they still meant something—an assumption that carries a particular amount of weight today, in a divided country where everything that its populace shares and commonly reveres tends to be overlooked or else minimized by deafening and fearful battle cries.

The problem is, mainstream politics in the U.S., whether it's leftist or conservative or (most often) scrambled, abounds in linguistic misrepresentations and historical gaps and confusions while being expressed almost exclusively in the form of light entertainment. Satchmo saw himself as an entertainer as much as Donald Trump does, but the messages of the two are hardly the same, and the language we have to express our own views seems even more inadequate than it was in the 1950s. Most American "blacks" are actually brown, alleged "whites" are brownish pink, it's politically incorrect to identify Barack Obama as half "white" (which he is), and the U.S. military occupation of Iraq is usually called "the Iraqi war" or "the war in Iraq" to make it sound more respectable. Even the term "America" imperialistically collapses North America, Central America, and South America into the so-called United States. With a language already full of such deceptive half-truths and deceptions, the banning of a passionately antiracist novel, *Huckleberry Finn*, as racist or "insensitive" by various school boards becomes easier to understand as an ahistorical grasp of language that ignores its changing connotations whereby "Negro" ceases to become an acceptable term and is replaced by the less accurate "black" because it reminds too many people of the N-word, which was once regarded as more commonplace and neutral.

Satchmo's art and gift to us is the happiness of cameraderie, expressed musically, personally, humorously, honestly, and at its best, spontaneously. Its morality is not very different from Huck Finn's code of loyalty to an escaped slave who is also a pal. Coming from a culture that arose out of slavery and social rejection and finding delight in its discovery of freedom, it's something we should all continue to cherish.

Dangerous Sex and Scattered Focus, Fifty Years Apart (*WR: Mysteries of the Organism* and *Bad Luck Banging or Loony Porn*)

Written for the first (and, alas, final) issue of Trafic Almanach, *published in January 2023 in the late Jean-Luc Mengus's French translation.*

> To burglarize Marx, we don't make love under circumstances we choose, we make love under the circumstances we inherit, and even pre-pandemic, the inherited circumstances had been feeling pretty toxic when it came to bodily matters....If love is a matter of attractions and repulsions, of bodies and how they collide, the afflictions of the social body bleed into our individual desires and disgusts too.
>
> —Laura Kipnis, *Love in the Time of Contagion*

The bracing shock delivered by Radu Jude's entertaining *Bad Luck Banging or Loony Porn* (2021) reminds me of the shock carried by another entertaining Eastern European feature dealing with both sex and fear of sex, both contemporary culture and contemporary cultural restrictions, half a century earlier: Dušan Makavejev's *WR: Mysteries of the Organism* (1971).

Of course, 1971 and 2021 are separated from each other by more than just fifty years and two notions of entertainment. The struggle to reconcile Freud with Marx that animated so much of the oeuvre of Bernardo Bertolucci, at least until its simplified resolution at the end of *The Last Emperor* (1987) in favor of Marx ("Is that so terrible?" Jin Yuan replies to Lu Yi in a prison yard. "To be useful?") also clearly preoccupied Makavejev a quarter of a century earlier, when he arguably gave the edge to Freud, even while sadly acknowledging that Freudians, communists, socialists, and capitalists all proved to be equally scornful of Reich, at least in his later developments. But both Bertolucci and Makavejev were steeped in the obligatory either-or options of the Cold War, whereas Radu Jude, regarding Romania as a casualty of both Soviet Communism and Nazism, ruefully sees the choice his own country has faced in the form of two competing newspaper headlines, "Viva Stalin!" and "Viva Hitler!" If his post-Marxist melancholy bears some traces of Freudian pessimism, these seem to be the logical result of his conviction that acknowledging the shameful and repressed history of his country is both morally necessary and, in the current cultural climate, practically impossible. Thus sarcasm becomes his habitual reflex—like "political correctness," both a veiled admission and a frustrated expression of political defeat.

More generally, Jude is living inside a wider but far less focused set of intellectual reference points—a cloud of philosophical and metaphysical chaos that produces the sensation of freefall in outer space, a descent or ascent into a void without gravity and therefore without a clear sense of direction: we're all falling, meanwhile lacking any clear notion of where, how, or even if we might land. And because this is the condition we all share nowadays, his confusions become more instructive than the narrower uncertainties of Bertolucci and Makavejev because they're more up to date. Living through both a pandemic with no foreseeable end and a global warming whose consequences are all too foreseeable, issues of sex and freedom begin to seem less urgent, hence more subject to sarcastic complaints.

The many sources of our disrupted attention spans are diagnosed in Johann Hari's recent book *Stolen Focus: Why You Can't Pay Attention-and How to Think Deeply Again* (New York: Crown, 2022)—the ways that surveillance capitalism weaponized by technology and its training of our reflexes to gratify our deepest (as well as our most momentary) desires tend to infantilize us, turning us into automatic spending machines (with money replacing tears) and passive consumers. These ways include "the increase in speed, switching, and filtering," "the crippling of our flow states," "the collapse of sustained reading," "the disruption of mind-wandering," and many other forms of interruption. This suggests the fragmented and dispersed attention spans that both *WR* and *Bad Luck* address with their diverse entertainments, though only the latter film attacks this problem with formal procedures more discursive and expansive than simple crosscutting.

The English titles of both films seem like awkwardly inexact translations of Serbo-Croat and Romanian. Surely mysteries of the orgasm, not "mysteries of the organism," is what "*WR*" [*Wilhelm Reich*] evokes, and both "*bad luck banging*" and "*loony porn*" sound like unidiomatic approximations of Romanian slang. This is one way of suggesting that both films remain slightly beyond our reach, at least if we're neither Serbian nor Romanian, even within their own historical periods. And indeed, what was once meant by "private" and "public" in 1971 can hardly be the same as what we mean after social media via mobiles, emails, and the Internet have overtaken and redefined them, sometimes to the point of making them sound almost anachronistic. (If *PlayTime*'s restaurant sequence were to be reshot today, its resurrection of public space would have to depend on deactivating mobiles, not architectural collapse.)

A redefinition of "public" and "private"—thanks to a mobile's video recording of a married couple's kinky sex "going viral" on the Internet—helped along by the pandemic's diverse deprivations and uncertainties, is the subject of Jude's film. Combine social media with the pandemic, factoring in multiple forms of fragmentation, regression, repression, and dislocation associated with both, and we arrive at a topic coinciding with our current cultural moment. And yet *WR*, with its own forms of fragmentation, regression, repression, and dislocation, seems just as contemporary. Unlike Jude's film, it was shot on and intercuts between two continents, in two separate languages, in two film gauges (16-millimeter in New York, 35-millimeter in Belgrade). and in two political environments.

Yet the only repressions examined in detail and at length in *WR* are those of Wilhelm Reich's work and his imprisonment in the U.S., and, more implicitly, the repression of Yugoslavia by Soviet Russia, whereas the problems and repressions examined in *Bad Luck* are far more universal, yet shown only locally. By contrast, hippie Tuli Kupferberg can carry a machine gun, wear a battle helmet and army fatigues, and cavort in front of New York's Lincoln Center without interference or even attracting much notice, and transsexual Jackie Curtis can pick up a man on the same Manhattan streets without anyone raising an eyebrow. In *Bad Luck*'s Bucharest, repressions of different kinds are visible in the face masks and in portions of what people say, but Jude remains stubbornly and exclusively within his own country, refusing to step outside apart from his use of literary quotations, which come from a wider geographical spread. (This is a film that, in Godardian fashion, lists twenty-five cited authors in its final credits, including such familiar international standbys as Benjamin, Brecht, Cioran, Malraux, and Woolf.)

Perhaps starting with Jackie Raynal's *Deux fois* in 1968 and Godard's *1+1* in 1969, a good many experimental films of Makavejev's era—among others, Hollis Frampton's *Zorns Lemma* (1970) and *(nostalgia)* (1971), Pere Portabella's

Umbracle (1970), Edgardo Cozarinsky's ... (1971), and Mark Rappaport's *Casual Relations* (1973)—are based on principles of accumulation and/or list-making, of cataloguing separate items that fail to merge, a form of dialectics refusing or at least failing to arrive at any synthesis. *WR: Mysteries of the Organism* clearly belongs in this company, crosscutting between sexual ideas and practices, and between fiction and non-fiction, in both New York and Belgrade (even though the fictional characters in Belgrade carry the same names as the actors playing them). But so in some ways does *Bad Luck*, which in spite of its (unresolved) narrative devotes its second section to a "short dictionary of anecdotes, signs, and wonders" with items that flagrantly refuse to join one another except glancingly, mainly remaining detached from both the main story and from each other—a section that evokes in its bitter sarcasm both Ambrose Bierce's *The Devil's Dictionary* (1906), which it also quotes from, and Flaubert's *Le Dictionnaire des idées reçues* (1911). But the freedom in crossing national borders evidenced by *Deux Fois* (shot in Barcelona), *1+1* (shot in London), and *WR* (New York and Belgrade) isn't shared by *Bad Luck*, in spite of the greater virtual access offered by the Internet. Perhaps this is related to the dictates of global surveillance capitalism: even if the big companies tend to do the same things everywhere, they still depend on a divide-and-conquer strategy through the isolation of national markets from one another. Viewing problems globally might lead to global boycotts, whereas keeping things provincial makes the world more manageable from the standpoint of multicorporations.

§

A certain cinematic cliché about depicted sex infects both *WR* and *Bad Luck*—an association of vitality with speed and frenzied music that rejects tenderness entirely. Recall the sped-up motion and the *William Tell Overture* accompanying Alex (Malcolm McDowell) having sex with two teenyboppers in Kubrick's *A Clockwork Orange* for the reductio ad absurdum/ad nauseum of this attitude—a form of Victorian hysteria masquerading as celebration. But Kubrick's adolescent sense of humor is only a shade worse than the hyperventilation of the "loony porn" in Jude's film and the manic intercourse of Jagoda (Jagoda Kaloper), the randy flatmate of Milena (Milena Dravic), in Makavejev's film, which suggests that sex has to be gulped or guzzled like cheap wine in order to be appreciated rather than slowly sipped and savored. Admittedly, Jagoda's compulsive screwing is intended as a comic rebuke to Milena, who habitually spouts Reichian principles to everyone within earshot without ever getting laid herself (although when she finally does, she gets beheaded by a Russian ice-skating star as a direct result). And the frantic sex of schoolteacher Emilia Colibiu (Katia Pascariu) with her husband, periodically interrupted by the offscreen demands of a babysitter, may not be accompanied by jaunty music, or music of any other kind, unlike the film's final lurid fantasy sequence (Emilia as Wonder Woman performs a massive rape on all her accusers). Yet the association of kinkiness and/or sexiness with speed and force is no less pronounced. This also raises the vexing issue that one can't always distinguish between Jude's denunciation of Romanian vulgarity and his own apparent vulgarity in drawing our attention to it—an issue that hovers over all of this film's depictions of sex (and much fewer of Makavejev's). I'll concede that both *WR* and *Bad Luck* see themselves as being at war with puritanism, which makes fast-motion and bouncy music weapons of cheerful defiance. Even so, it's worth recalling that defiance is only one kind of pleasure, and not necessarily the most pleasurable kind.

For me, the most pleasurable, provocative, and innovative section of *Bad Luck* is neither its "loony porn" prologue (which strikes me as being neither loony nor porn, properly speaking, because it seems far too generic as a pro-saic demonstration of what such private, kinky sex videos are expected to be like) nor the Godardian second section of quotes and clips but the preceding first section, the longest in the film, titled "One-Way Street" in homage to Benjamin and devoted to Emilia's walking across Bucharest as she goes on various errands, en route to a staff meeting at her prestigious school occasioned by the sex tape going online.

What's remarkable about this sequence is the camera's frequent independence from her trajectories as it moves horizontally or vertically away from her or her paths to explore other parts of the landscape, usually architectural or anec-dotal—sometimes human, but most often not—often proceeding inquisitively or tentatively rather than declaratively, as if idly straying briefly from its assigned journey. In contrast to Emilia's sex and her actual errands, which register at times like theorems about which Jude displays little curiosity, her long walks through Bucharest between those errands are pure adventures in exploration.

I've always been somewhat bored by Jeanne Moreau's symbol-laden walk through Milan in Antonioni's *La notte* (1961), which inspired Dwight Macdonald to remark that the Talkies had become the Walkies. In striking contrast to the more mysterious wanderings of Monica Vitti in *L'avventura*, *L'eclisse*, and *Il deserto rosso*, where the absence or uncertainties of meanings are far more provocative than the alleged significance of a broken clock and launched rockets in *La notte*, I find Katia Pascariu's even more protracted walk through Bucharest neither boring nor pretentious, perhaps because Jude's camera style is far more interrogative and exploratory, repeatedly panning away from her to her surroundings to discover how they might relate or else fail to relate to her. Antonioni clearly had a Statement in his mind about Moreau's character and the modern world that he wanted to illustrate, whereas Jude is more open about what he doesn't already know and needs to search for, acknowledging a wider world beyond his grasp.

The only (partial) precedent I know for this kind of narrative digression/distractiom is the style of cinematographer Masaki Tamura in such films as Shinsuke Ogawa's 1973 documentary *Narita: Heta Village* and Nobuhiro Suwa's first fiction feature, *2/Duo* (1996), where the unpredictable drifts of the camera away from the ostensible narrative focus often redefine what the subject of a particular shot might be. Tamura's way of shooting an informal political discussion in *Narita: Heta Village* sometimes involves panning away from the person speaking—displaying an attentiveness to group interaction that finds responses to talk as important as the talk itself. And the placements and displacements of his camera in *2/Duo* are often extraordinary in elucidating the essence of a scene. What initially might seem a perverse choice of camera angle turns out to be a highly original and compelling definition of where documentary and dramatic truth might be found—a definition that rethinks and resculpts conventional priorities regarding how a particular scene should be read, thereby encouraging us to reconceptualize its meaning.

What seems pertinent about this manner of de-centering a narrative path is that it suggests alternate paths for the viewer in engaging with Jude's film as a whole: many possible paths and centers rather than a single linear itinerary—another version of the multiple viewing options offered in the restaurant sequence of Tati's *PlayTime*, but applied over the separate sections of the film rather than within the multiple options of a single crowded shot. For once we start to ponder each section of the film, there are multiple options offered in each case: different kinds of sex offered in the prologue (first a whip, then a bed), different stray details in Emilia's stroll through Bucharest, different quotes and anecdotes of varying relevance to Emilia's story, different responses to the sex tape among her colleagues, and, finally, different outcomes to the debate. Life, in other words, assumes the shape of a multiple-choice question, the answer to which is left to us.

In his constant juggling between sexual options in New York and Belgrade, Makavejev projects a comparable kind of multiplicity (straight versus gay, intercourse versus masturbation, terror versus exaltation or ecstasy, talk or artmaking versus sex), although in his case an either/or pattern limits one's choices: sex for Milena leads to Ivan's madness and the loss of her head, even though her head continues to talk and she even concludes the film by smiling. Tuli Kupferberg's "Kill for Peace" song suggests a similar irrational dialectic.

One might conclude that Makavejev's emotional view of 1971 is tragicomic and dialectical in other respects, whereas Jude's emotional view of 2021 is less fixed and more dependent on the viewer's biases: Here is our chaotic mess, he seems to be saying, and here are a few possible ways we might begin to cope with it. Hence drift and flow are his preferred modes, a series of searchlights that we're invited to join or dismiss. Makavejev's dialectical view ultimately springs from the possibilities as well as the limits of the Cold War; Jude's multilateral view benefits as well as suffers from the confusions of the pandemic. Everyone to some degree is in the same mess, and no one knows exactly what this mess is.

Too nuanced and complex in his thinking to be a simple utopian, Makavejev perceives sex as an unleashing of potentially dangerous energies that threaten not only puritanical and authoritarian systems but also, in some limit cases, sanity (especially if we acknowledge that the latter term is commonly defined socially and legally more than psychologically or medically). So in *WR*, Milena's eventual success in seducing Vladimir Ilyich ultimately leads to her getting beheaded by him with one of his ice skates—exposing certain dark mysteries of orgasms as well as organisms. To cite a suggestive formula proposed by the late Raymond Durgnat in his cogent 1999 book about the film in the BFI Modern Classics, Makavejev's vision is that of a tragic Rabelaisian Marxist—an artist so dialectical in spirit that he can juxtapose his politically incorrect celebration of Nancy Godfrey in New York sculpting a plaster-cast replica of *Screw* editor Jim Buckley's erect penis with a satirical song by Tuli Kupferberg about the destructive links between sex and capitalist ownership: "I'm gonna kill myself over your dead body if you fuck anybody but me."

Makavejev was obviously risking not only censorship (and indeed, *WR* was banned in Yugoslavia for sixteen years, leading eventually to his exile), but also the danger of being misunderstood as some sort of ideologue. That is, in undertaking the same sort of juxtaposition of clashing ideological discourses proposed by Godard in *La Chinoise* (1967) and by Spike Lee in *Do the Right Thing* (1989), he risked being misread as a simplistic anti-Communist liber-tarian—much as Godard could be (and often was) misread as a Maoist, or Lee could be misread as a Malcolm X supporter dismissing the pacifism of Martin Luther King. In fact, Makavejev was attempting something far more difficult and valuable: a critical account of the possibilities and limits of two contradictory societies in relation to sex. Durgnat simplistically but accurately summarizes part of the result as, "The USA has more freedom than socialism, Yugoslavia has more socialism than freedom." But one should stress that the comparison never takes the form of a simple contest in which there can only be one winner—the sort of sports analogy that Americans tend to favor, reducing all ideological issues to a battle between the home team and the enemy team. Even Jude in his landlocked sarcasm occasionally seems to echo this provincialism, at times discussing social problems that are shared around the globe as if they were specifically or even exclusively Romanian.[1]

Durgnat called *WR* "the first, and, along with Wajda's *Danton* (1982) and Kusturica's *Underground* (1995), the boldest exploration of social breakdown in Eastern European Communism." Yet one can surely forgive Makavejev if his prescience in 1971 didn't extend to the ways in which capitalist greed would ultimately overtake America's grasp of entitlements, helped along by the eight years of the Ronald Reagan presidency (1981-89), during which ethics became reconfigured as a branch of public relations. During the war in Vietnam, it was unthinkable that any pundit could say that Lyndon Johnson or Richard Nixon was "bad for America [or the world] but good for television" the same way that many future pundits would remark about Donald Trump, if only because America, "the world," and television weren't considered such neatly separable entities in the '60s and '70s. Moreover, the very notion of using an expression like "good for television" as a euphemism for "good for making billionaires richer" might have been beyond Makavejev's full grasp of the foreseeable future as reflected in language. How could anyone back then have predicted the fatalistic, tribal belief that algorhthms, not human beings, were somehow to blame for making hatred and hysterical panic more profitable for billionaires investing in journalism and shaping "the news" than love, wisdom, or patience? Yet insofar as Makavejev and Jude have news of their own to impart, the degree of their own success has to be evaluated by different standards.

I recall a college classmate of mine in 1964 weeping at the end of Kubrick's *Dr. Strangelove*, refusing to see the end of the world as a fit subject for laughter. People were really worried back then about nuclear bombs falling, whereas no one seems half as worried about this danger today, when the risk of it happening due to nuclear proliferation may well be greater, and when the prospect of polar icecaps melting may lead to consequences just as dire. Why is it that many of us can no longer remember our friends' phone numbers, as we once did, because we supposedly have technology to "take care of" that for us? Whose "progress" is being mandated by this change? Are we better people now because our memories and attention spans have shrunk?

Makavejev and Jude clearly share a taste for anarchic exploration to counter the nefarious whims of our overlords. But the implicit hope implied by the severed head of a Reichian heroine continuing to talk to us and even to smile isn't matched by the vision of a sexually free and intelligent schoolteacher raping her intolerant colleagues, even if that sour vision turns out to be good for both algorthms and box office while all of us glumly await the apocalypse. In fact, Emilia's victory, defeat, and revenge are presented as options in Jude's multiple choice question, which means that they share with her marital sex and her errands the status of theorems—postulates needed to construct Jude's narrative, not actions meant to arouse our curiosity. It is only his detours in her journey across Bucharest and his collection of quotations and anecdotes, providing detours of another kind, that constitute his true adventures, his leaps into the void—and as Godard once argued, writing about Jacques Becker's *Montparnasse 19*, "He who leaps into the void owes no explanations to those who watch."

End Note

1.　From an email sent by James Naremore on February 22, 2022: "...I wonder if you've placed too much emphasis on the 'exclusively Romanian' quality of the film. One of the things the tour of streets establishes is how much global capitalism has infiltrated everything—the Coca-Cola/Pepsi fast-food shops, the Xanax in the pharmacy, the plastic shopping bags, the plastic children's toys, the graffiti, and even the shops in more expensive parts of town. Local or national culture is seen only in ruins or government architecture. The 'trial' scene provokes arguments that could be heard in any American school board meeting and even mentions Fox news. (Notice also the joke about the school-teacher transforming herself and getting revenge by becoming a character in a Hollywood superhero movie.)"

Reading, Hearing, Watching:
Anna Livia Plurabelle, the he and the she of it

Written expressly for this book in 2022-2023.

This is what I was coming to: that the cinematograph can ally itself with the marvelous, as I see it, if it is content to be a vehicle for it and it does not try to produce it.

—Jean Cocteau, *The Difficulty of Being*[1]

[T]here is this sensation of shifting from one world into another: from the world of daylight into the world of night. The work's structure, which, overall, expresses the flow of water…is grounded in the idea of fluid shifts. There is a harmonic shift from dissonance to consonance, from a precise tempo to a blurred one, from nontonality to tonality, from a harsh musical color (the brass) to a pastel color (vibraphone, guitar), etc.

—André Hodeir, "To Hear All about Anna Livia"[2]

But what was the game in her mixed baggyrhatty? Just the tembo in her tumbo or pilipili from her pepperpot? Saas and saas and specis bizaas. And where in thunder did she plunder? Fore the battle or efter the ball? I want to get it frisk from the soorce. I aubette my bearb it's worth while poaching on. Shake it up, do, do! That's a good old son of a ditch! I promise I'll make it worth your while. And I don't mean maybe. Nor yet with a goodfor. Spey me pruth and I'll tale you true.

—James Joyce, *"Anna Livia Plurabelle"*[3]

If it qualifies as some sort of jazz, it's also what its classically trained composer André Hodeir (1921-2011) called a cantata featuring simulated improvisation, using edited and excerpted passages of James Joyce's "Anna Livia Plurabelle" from *Finnegans Wake* as a libretto for an alto and soprano in dialogue and duet, backed by a full orchestra.

And if this qualifies as some sort of cinema, it's only the simplest and most cursory form of it—a recording of a live studio performance presented on France Musique on March 6, 2021, still available on YouTube the last time I looked and listened.

§

My memories of the first version of *Anna Livia Plurabelle* (or *ALP*, for short) rule many of my responses (both positive and negative) to the second and third, and my preference for the mainly sung second half in any version over the mainly spoken first half only becomes amplified when I can see it performed.

As a James Joyce enthusiast, I seem to be in a minority in preferring Joyce's first and last first books of fiction, *Dubliners* and *Finnegans Wake*, to *Portrait of the Artist as a Young Man* and *Ulysses*. I value the latter novel more often as an extraordinary achievement and as a complicated artifact than as an experience. But to complicate matters, I've read *Ulysses* twice, but haven't read *Finnegans Wake* straight through even once. (I can't even say "from beginning to end" because it has neither of these, starting as well as concluding in midsentence.) For me it's a river to bathe and swim in more than a narrative to pursue or be pursued by. Play recordings of it being read aloud and some young children who hear it are apt to giggle, and not because they're enjoying it as a story. It's likelier to be because it sounds just like the way grownups talk, only funnier.

(As Samuel Beckett astutely observed in 1929, "Mr. Joyce has desophisticated language." And a page earlier, in the same essay about *Finnegans Wake*: "His writing is not about something; it is that something itself.")

As an André Hodeir enthusiast, though by no means any sort of Hodeir expert[4], I love some of his late musical compositions even more than his insightful and provocative if often cranky music criticism (the latter of which once inspired Miles Davis to say that he was the only French critic who understood what he was doing). These compositions include his collaborations with Martial Solal improvising on piano to Hodeir's charts for small groups or orchestras (the wittiest of these, *Jazz et Jazz*, has Solal exchanging phrases with patches of electronic music) or Solal conducting other Hodeir works, plus Hodeir's sublime *ALP*. I've heard the latter, which lasts almost an hour, performed on three separate recordings, the most recent of which is audiovisual. For me the best is the original, also the first that I've heard, with Monique Alderbert (soprano) and Nicole Croisille (alto), conducted by Hodeir and released on LP in 1969 (Philips PHS 900-255). The second version is with Valérie Philipin (soprano) and Elisabeth Lagneau (alto), conducted by Patrice Caratini and released on CD in 1993 (Label Bleu LBLC 6563). The televised performance has Ellinoa (soprano) and Chloé Cailleton (alto), and is again conducted by Caratini.

I can't exactly claim to be a fan of Camille Lannier, the credited director and editor of this audiovisual *ALP*, because I'm unfamiliar with any of her other work, although I should note that she has a page of her own on Facebook ("Camille Lannier - Créations audiovisuelles"). But I'm certainly a big fan of her directorial and editorial choices on *ALP*, which enhance and celebrate the contributions of Joyce and Hodeir in what could be described as a feminist manner yet without ever losing sight (or sound) of the text or music—or, for that matter, the male musicians and conductor. Can Joyce's and Hodeir's presumptions in writing/composing female discourse still be presumed acceptable, during a spell when the U.S. is having an agonizingly slow nervous breakdown over identity politics? I hope so. But even if they can't or couldn't be, Lannier does a lot to adjust the balance.

Joyce and Hodeir both anticipate certain aspects of Lannier's directorial and editorial choices (what the French would call her découpage) by privileging the voices of women—a process that seems to begin with the Molly Bloom soliloquy ending *Ulysses* and continue in the mid-60s with Hodeir's *Jazz Cantata* (which features scat-singing by one woman), making room not only for the two washerwomen whose dialogue ends Part I of the *Wake* but also for the two vocalists who speak and sing these women's flighty and yet very physical exchanges, adapted and orchestrated by Hodeir. What Lannier contributes to this discussion is an attentiveness towards the central female presences in the performance, including not only the two singers as well as a drummer and a couple of clarinetists (one of them a soloist) positioned nearby. I hasten to add that this attentiveness can't be separated from an alertness to the music and the text (even though I regret the absence of subtitles for the latter)—an appreciation of *ALP*, in short, that also extends to the expressions and gestures of the singers as well as some musicians when they're listening but not performing, and which shifts our viewpoint as often and as briskly as Hodeir shifts his musical settings and their textures. The kaleidoscopic effect of all this is at once cinematic, literary, and musical, with all three media working towards the same sensual and aesthetic ends.

"Anna was, Livia is, Plurabelle's to be." The two women's voices, alto and soprano, chime together to make pleasing chords with the orchestra, like those in a hymn. When Hodeir dares to propose as the climax of their contrapuntal duet—coming just after most of the passage quoted above, a lengthy stretch of wordless scat singing—it doesn't feel like he's left Joyce's prose so much as applied a kind of pedal-point extension to some of its bustling riffs, if only to watch them shimmer.

Trying to unpack my appreciation of *ALP* as it has grown and developed over more than half a century, I should confess that listening to the original LP while reading Joyce's text (around the same time that I was also discovering Luciano Berio's *Thema* [*Omaggio a Joyce*]) made enough of a lasting impression to make me more tolerant of the subsequent inferior versions, including the difficulties presented by the TV version, in which the mainly spoken first half substitutes a French translation for Joyce's polyglot original and some of the pauses between sections seem awkwardly protracted.

In his "To Hear All about Anna Livia" (an essay in French with an English title), Hodeir describes the work's genesis as follows:

> In the early 1960s, I read Jean Paris's short book devoted to James Joyce. The author compares the prose of *Finnegans Wake* to scat singing, that is to say to the successions of onomatopoeic syllables that nourish the vocal improvisations of a Louis Armstrong or an Ella Fitzgerald. I got hold of a copy of Joyce's masterpiece, and was convinced. Joyce's language, its fluidity, its speed, its syncopated rhythm and its rich alliteration strongly encouraged me to undertake the work on *Anna Livia Plurabelle*. (my translation).[5]

Hodeir's earlier *Osymetrios*, performed in two separate arrangements (with Solal and Kenny Clarke among the soloists), is a sort of musical anagram, with phrases and riffs drawn from Thelonious Monk's *Mysterioso*—a repositioning of notes corresponding to a scrambling of letters, suggesting a parallel and/or alliance between literary and musical impulses that will form the basis of Hodeir's latter career as a fiction writer experimenting with musical forms, each practice in turn regarded as the reverse side of the same currency.[6]

Indeed, I'm fascinated by Hodeir's gradual shift from composing music to writing prose, starting with his weird experimental collection of jazz criticism "composed" in various fictional, pedagogical, and rhetorical forms (*The Worlds of Jazz*, trans. Noel Burch, New York: Grove, 1972) and gradually leading up to stories and novels that contrive to adopt or adapt musical forms, as well as his last two musical pieces, *ALP* (which took him a year to compose) and the far less interesting or memorable *Bitter Ending* (a work commissioned by the Swingle Singers, built around another passage from *Finnegans Wake*). In other words, he used literature to create music and created a form of literature as if it were music.

Hodeir's experiments in prose, starting with *The Worlds of Jazz*, are theoretical and aesthetic arguments about music couched in various literary/rhetorical and/or/institutional/pedagogical forms—a brazen idea that sounds a lot better than it reads (or plays). But once he puts his theories into practice as a composer, the ideas become what is recited, sung, and played—feelings, textures, shadings, plus graceful and ambiguous transitions inspired by those of Gil Evans on the album *Miles Ahead* (weaving diverse tapestries into a continuous unraveling of music with various overarching developments, such as moving gradually over the course of *ALP*'s hour from recitative speech to piercing and lyrical song).

The biggest controversy about Hodeir's relation to jazz remains his defense and practice of "simulated improvisation"—composing solos that sound improvised but aren't. (Some might also object to Hodeir's recording the orchestra and singers separately in the first version; pianist Lennie Tristano's similarly idealist employment of multiple overlapping tracks and other audio manipulations on his first LP was widely criticized on similar grounds, regarded as some sort of existential cheat.) For those who reject such a premise as inauthentic and/or formalist by definition, the best and perhaps only defense is Duke Ellington's axiom, "If it sounds good, it is good." To which I can only suggest an updated version of this statement for *ALP* televised: "If it sounds and looks good, then it must be good, no?"

Presumably not for Adam Shatz, who curtly dismisses Hodeir's entire work as a composer after praising his mastery as a jazz critic:

> His attempt to fuse classical modernism and big band music in what he called 'simulated improvisation' was a French cousin of the American 'Third Stream' of composers, such as Gunther Schuller and George Russell, and the results were even more ersatz and mannered.[7]

I'm willing to concede the possibility of some mannerism in Schuller, but if Russell and Hodeir are ersatz mannerists, I can only consider myself lucky to have been misguided into enjoying and learning a lot from many of their dubious enterprises. But clearly Shatz is speaking only of music, not of its bigamous marriages to literature and/or cinema, and without even clarifying whether he's ever bothered to listen to any version of *ALP*—even though it was largely my love of Joyce that led me to Hodeir and my love of jazz, literature, and cinema that prompted this essay.

Shatz is of course free to prefer Hodeir's exceptional criticism, even when that entails the crankiness alluded to above, exemplified by the ten pages in *Toward Jazz* devoted to explaining why he regards Benny Carter as a third-rate alto saxophonist rather than a second-rate one, buttressed by some questionable gender politics when he compares Carter's tone to Marcel Mule's: "Now that tone, if I may be forgiven the expression, is an effeminate tone. Though it has every imaginable charm, it lacks that essential factor, virility. Too intent upon being pretty, it can never attain real beauty."[8] (By "real," Hodeir appears to mean "macho.")

§

The abrupt yet smooth and nearly constant transitions between various passages of Hodeir's *ALP*—in terms of texture, tone, tempi, mood—are already cinematic to begin with, no doubt reflecting both Hodeir's mostly routine commercial film scores and his earlier and generally more vital collaborations with Michel Fano, Georges Franju, Ado Kyrou, Chris Marker, Alain Resnais, and Agnès Varda, among many others.

Charles Mingus and George Russell were both clearly fascinated by the relationships between music and speech, with speech often used to propel or bracket or even perform some part of the music, which is often inspired by various speech patterns, and sometimes takes them in a quasi-literary direction, as in Jon Hendricks' jazzy, rhyming, thematic verse with musical accompaniment introducing each track on Russell's masterful *New York, N.Y.* (1959)—beginning with Hendricks' speech in duet with Max Roach's propulsive brushes: "Think you can lick it,/Get to the wicket,/Buy you a ticket,/ Go!')

Mingus experimented with words and jazz on many occasions and in many ways, including the Beat practice popularized by Jack Kerouac and others of accompanying poetry with jazz and the denunciations of diverse political leaders in *Fables of Faubus*. On *What Love*, the penultimate track of *Charles Mingus Presents Charles Mingus*, this notion of speechified music even becomes literalized in a wordless quarrel between Mingus' bass and Eric Dolphy's alto sax and bass clarinet, exchanges full of petulance and rejoinders. A more succinct example: Miles Davis titling the first tune on his famous *Kind of Blue* album *"So What"*, thus giving a touch of verbal sarcasm to its two-note riff and refrain. (Sarcastic afterthought: Russell seems to have invented modal improvisation in the late '40s with a chart commissioned by Dizzy Gillespie, but Miles and Coltrane and *Kind of Blue* seem to get about 95% of the credit. Yet I should add that as an amateur jazz pianist, I found that it was *So What* that opened doors for me by broadening my choices and making improvisation easier.)

You might say that each of my above examples creates a fictional drama of sorts, an aural movie of the mind, and it's significant that Russell biographer Duncan Heining describes more than one Russell composition as "filmic" or "cinematic".

Some of the literary experiments in *The Worlds of Jazz* become a bit torturous (i.e. ersatz and mannerist) when one feels that Hodeir is trying to flesh out a theorem rather than actually discover a new synthesis. But when it comes to the three separate performances of *ALP*, we have to move beyond formal conceptions and realize that we're faced with the more unpredictable and less controllable chemistry of many people relating to one another as well as to us and themselves while tangling with a tricky score, a communal and social encounter in which our own responses are necessarily improvised and thus an integral part of the shared jazz experience, even if the musicians' input is interpretation (another potential but less obvious form of improvisation) rather than invention. Joyce and Hodeir stand outside the communities of washerwomen and readers or listeners that they're depicting or addressing, yet the reader and listener should clearly be a joiner and a participating member of that community rather than an observer or a spy. *Anna Livia* was written/ composed by Joyce and Hodeir alike, to be read and heard, that is, experienced, not simply decoded or analyzed. Yet the historical and personal placements of *Finnegans Wake* and Joyce are overlaid by the very different historical and personal placements of Hodeir's cantata—not only the time of its composition but the time of Hodeir as a figure grounded in the 1950s.

I grew up between the ages of six and sixteen during that decade, and I'm sure that some of what drew me to Hodeir, Russell, Mingus, Davis, and Evans (both Bill and Gil) are the auras of the 1950s and 1960s as experienced through jazz, which suggests that my own overlays may be as consequential to my enjoyment as those of Joyce, Hodeir, and many musicians (including the singers). To cite only one example of what I mean, some of the pleasure that I found during the '50s when I listened to June Christy and Chris Connor and their musical accompaniments is rekindled by *ALP*, regardless of the different responses Hodeir might have had to those vocalists' records. And yet for all our differences, Hodeir and I, we've found a compatible way of coexisting, just as I believe Joyce, Hodeir, and cinema have found a compatible coexistence.

As already suggested, some of this may be a matter of the generation I belong to. When I interviewed Jonas Mekas in 1982 for a commissioned book of mine about independent and experimental film[9], he maintained that critics and curators are essentially limited by and to the generations to which they belong: "There's a certain period when one really gets involved for ten or fifteen years. And if that is really done deeply, so much energy goes into it that later it takes another decade or two just to consummate it." In my case, my appreciations of Russell and Hodeir are grounded in both my adolescence in the '50s (when I discovered Russell) and my time in Paris in the early '70s (when I discovered *ALP*). And my appreciation of both Joyce and film as an art form began in the '60s—a more freewheeling decade that helped to expand what I'd learned in the '50s and would learn in the '70s. Members of other generations will approach these artists and their art with different groundings.

To my ear, George Russell's collaborations with Bill Evans (especially on *All about Rosie, Concerto for Billy the Kid*, and all four tracks on *New York, N.Y.*) are as fruitful as Gil Evans' with Miles Davis—maybe even more so insofar as Russell's charts bring out a spikey assertiveness in Bill Evans' playing that's infrequent in his own recordings. And more generally, Russell's fusion of bebop with modern Western classical traditions and his pioneering forays into Afro-Cuban and modal forms of jazz, combined with his theoretical work on the "Lydian mode of tonal organization" (briefly explained by Russell on the TV show *The Subject is Jazz*, also available on YouTube) give him a cultural importance that goes well beyond Hodeir when it also encompasses both folk music and politics. Heining's conscientious *Stratusphunk: The Life and Work of George Russell* clarifies this point in relation to Russell's remarkable *The Day John Brown Was Hanged* (1957):

> It is a highly political work, though not in a "agitprop" sense. It is a quintessentially American work using American forms and subject matter and derived from an American sensibility. It acknowledges division, past and current, on racial matters, in particular in its second section. It notes the ambivalence with which Brown as a historical figure is held, despite his partial appropriation by the political establishment. Russell is perhaps suggesting that so radical a figure cannot

be contained within the status quo implied by the "Battle Hymn [of the Republic]." Its sophistication lies in the fact that Russell does not state his own position but implies those held by others—slaves and emancipated Negroes, southerners, Republicans and the north-eastern liberal political elite. He asks instead that listeners consider their own position in relation to those implied above. In these respects "The Day John Brown Was Hanged" goes far beyond anything before and much since in jazz.[10]

The fact that Russell was born illegitimately to a white father and a black mother arguably played some role in establishing in his sense of musical possibility what could be called a narrative polyphony and a polytonal sense of character that are "cinematic" in their fluidity. By the same token, on the *Subject is Jazz* program cited above, when asked by Gilbert Seldes about the future of jazz, Russell replies that this is inseparable from the future of America.

A personal confession: Although I've been a Russell fan since my teens, it was only after I started work on this essay that I discovered that he wasn't "simply" Caucasian and in fact grew up in what was then known as a Negro neighborhood in Cincinnati. Did this affect the way I listened and listen to his music? Undoubtedly, and even though I believe I intuitively grasped at least some of the political ambiguity of *The Day John Brown Was Hanged* when I was fourteen or fifteen, I'm indebted to Heining for spelling out some of the implications and nuances of my belated discovery of his ethnic origins.

§

The exquisite ending of *ALP* is the soft delicacy and delivery of the word "Night!" by the two singers. In all three performances, it registers more like a natural sound such as a rush of air than as a word or a musical note, yet it also seems to combine the textures of a whisper and a gasp, much as night itself can do. Thanks to cinema, you can pretend that Joycean air is blowing right into your face.

End Notes

1. Translated by Elizabeth Sprigge. New York: Coward, McCann, Inc., 1967, 49.

2. Translated by Jean-Louis Pautrot in his Introduction to *The André Hodeir Jazz Reader* (which he edited), Ann Arbor, The University of Michigan Press,

2006, 10. The original French text appears in *International Jazz Archives Journal, No. 1, Vol. 3*, Fall 1995, where Hodeir's original paragraph concludes with a sensual point: "There is even a stereophonic shift in the original recording: the two washerwomen change places, symbolically crossing the Liffey, as the text suggests: 'Reeve Gootch was right and Reeve Drughad was sinistrous.'" (my translation)

3. *Finnegans Wake*, Hertfordshire, UK: Wordsworth Classics, 2012, 209.

4. The best source of information about Hodeir's life and career is Pierre Fargeton's *André Hodeir: le jazz et son double* (*Lyon: collection Symétrie recherche, série 20-21, 2017*), which is 772 large-format pages long. But even this monolith deals only skimpily with Hodeir's late career as a writer of fiction and children's books, perhaps because Fargeton finds this less engaging.

5. 2nd ed., Framlingham, Suffolk, U.K: Jazz Internationale, 2020, 93. I should add that *The Day John Brown Was Hanged* and the other Russell works cited are available on YouTube.

A striking cinematic parallel to Russell's approach to the issue of slavery through competing viewpoints can be found in Charles Burnett's *Nat Turner: A Troublesome Property* (2003), reviewed in detail on my website.

6. Although I own copies of Hodeir's three novels and two story collections, my grasp of French is too mediocre for me to get very much out of them, much less evaluate them. I'm similarly ill-equipped to deal with the use of a French translation of *Finnegans Wake* in the libretti of the spoken first section of the televised *ALP*—an apparent concession to francophone listeners who can't follow the anglophone puns.

7. "Le Jazz Hot," *The New York Review of Books*, July 9, 2015.

8. Trans. Noel Burch. New York: Grove Press, 1962, 11.

9. "Tenants of the House: A Conversation with Jonas Mekas," *Film: The Front Line* 1983, Denver, CO: Arden Press, 1983, 11-28.

10. *Stratusphunk*, op. cit, 93.

Index

In Dreams Begin Responsibilities by Jonathan Rosenbaum
First North American Edition, 2024

ISBN 978-1-955125-32-1
10 9 8 7 6 5 4 3 2 1

Cover Design by Nola Burger
Book Design by Sabrina Che
Printed by Versa Press in USA

Front cover: *2001: A Space Odyssey* (1968, Metro-Goldwyn-Mayer) directed by Stanley Kubrick;
Play Time (1967, France).

Back cover: Charlie Parker with Coleman Hawkins (from an unfinished film shot in 1950 by
Gjon Mili, produced by Norman Granz); *Ivan the Terrible* (1944, Russia) directed by Sergei
Eisenstein

This book was produced in partnership with Invisible Republic, an arts nonprofit and programming initiative of Future Roots, Inc., a 501c3 organization.

Hat & Beard Press books are published by
Hat & Beard, LLC
713 N La Fayette Park Place
Los Angeles, CA 90026

www.hatandbeard.com
IG: @hatandbeardpress

HAT & BEARD PRESS   INVISIBLE REPUBLIC